TURBULENCE IN
WORLD POLITICS

TURBULENCE IN
WORLD POLITICS

A Theory of Change and Continuity

JAMES N. ROSENAU

(1990)

PRINCETON UNIVERSITY PRESS I PRINCETON, NEW JERSEY

Copyright © 1990 by Princeton University Press
Published by Princeton University Press, 41 William Street,
Princeton, New Jersey 08540

All Rights Reserved

Library of Congress Cataloging-in-Publication Data
Rosenau, James N.
Turbulence in world politics : a theory of change and continuity
James N. Rosenau.
p. cm.
Includes bibliographical references.
ISBN 0-691-07820-3 (alk. paper) — ISBN 0-691-02308-5
(pbk : alk. paper)
1. International relations. I. Title.
JX1391.R585 1990
327.1—dc20   89-24378   CIP

This book has been composed in
Linotron Sabon and Gill Sans Bold

Princeton University Press books are printed on acid-free paper
and meet the guidelines for permanence and durability of the
Committee on Production Guidelines for Book Longevity of the
Council on Library Resources

Printed in the United States of America

10   9   8   7   6   5   4

For Pauline and Harry

CONTENTS

FIGURES

TABLES

PREFACE

ASIDE FROM A TENDENCY to overanalyze, there are at least five good reasons why this is a lengthy book. First, it dares to encompass all of world politics. Second, it seeks to tease coherent meaning out of the chaos and turbulence that underlie the current course of events. Third, it focuses on the ways in which world politics may be undergoing profound and enduring change. Fourth, it attempts to break with habitual modes of analysis and to approach politics and change on a global scale with fresh conceptual equipment that seems especially suitable as the millennium comes to an end. Fifth, it undertakes to support the case for a new theoretical perspective by offering evidence based mainly on a plethora of contemporary examples.

These are not tasks that conduce to brevity. Much as I would have preferred to accomplish them in a short, concise volume, it seemed preferable to ask the reader's indulgence for an extended treatment rather than to truncate the analysis on the basis of some arbitrary notion of what constitutes proper length.

Let me illustrate. In the spring of 1989, the world was mesmerized by a series of events in China, starting with student protests in Beijing's Tiananmen Square and culminating in a violent crackdown by the Chinese army, which revealed the extent to which the global politics of today derive from multiple sources that transcend conventional boundaries. Among the factors involved in the events were the capacities and motives of individuals, the underlying socioeconomic tensions of a huge society in transition, the succession struggles of the Chinese Communist party, the practices and coverage of the world's communications media, and the readiness of many multinational corporations to do business in China, as well as the policies of foreign governments. Such complex relationships are not unique to the events in Tiananmen

Square. They were a manifestation of a new global pattern, which presents a daunting challenge to anyone seeking to comprehend world affairs. It means that the study of global politics requires probing beyond the interaction of states and delving into the wellsprings of national and local politics as well as into the ways in which individual orientations and actions are translated into collective outcomes. Given such a perspective, the book could not be limited to the more conventional foci of interstate diplomacy and international economics.

Nor was it methodologically possible to develop a parsimonious formulation. While physicists can employ mathematical formulas to investigate the dynamics of turbulent winds and rivers, those of us concerned with global politics have yet to devise a set of elegant propositions on which to base the analysis. We are perforce impelled to elaborate in ordinary language the variability of turbulent processes if their underlying patterns are to be uncovered and assessed.

Nor could the task be simplified by merely asserting what is meant by change, turbulence, aggregation, authority, and a host of other concepts that now seem relevant to the course of events. Rather, so as to have a fresh basis for grasping the emergent bases of world politics, it seemed necessary to provide a full explanation and justification of the conceptual equipment on which the analysis is founded. Furthermore, to refine this equipment for application at all levels of global life—from the cognitive processes of individuals to the mobilizing processes of collectivities—a variety of literatures had to be explored and cited.

And then there is the question of evidence. Given a focus on emergent patterns that have yet to leave a rich paper trail in standard historical documents, a wide range of recent developments had to be cited from diverse sources so as to provide readers with a basis for assessing the utility and accuracy of the analysis. The heavy dependence on newspaper reports may seem inappropriate to a scholarly inquiry into the structures of world politics, but there is little choice if any credence is to be given to the argument that the present era differs sharply from the eras that preceded it. I have attempted to suggest the global scope of the theoretical perspective by employing examples of orientations and actions from all regions of the world, although relying primarily on U.S. sources. (As far as possible, citations to the *New York Times* are to its New York edition.)

In short, rather than offer an apology for the extensiveness of the following inquiry, I invite the reader to join me in an inquisitive frame of mind and thereby share with me the joy that comes with discovery. This is the spirit that launched and sustained the project: that special feeling that one is breaking into unexplored realms wherein new and eye-opening understandings lie ahead. There are few places left in the physical world where one can still experience such a spirit, but in the social world there are still endless opportunities to be energized by it, to sense that some of the dynamics of human organization and collective action are so elusive as to justify venturesome exploration.

Although they have been rewritten a number of times, some sections of several chapters were drawn from parts of previously published papers. I am grateful to the following for allowing me to reproduce the indicated materials in revised form: Butterworth & Company, for permission to include in chapters 1, 2, and 10 several paragraphs from my article, "Patterned Chaos in Global Life: Structure and Process in the Two Worlds of World Politics," *International Political Science Review* 9 (October 1988): 357–94; Lexington Books, for permission to include in chapter 4 material from my introduction to E. O. Czempiel and J. N. Rosenau, eds., *Global Changes and Theoretical Challenges: Approaches to World Politics for the 1990s* (Lexington, Mass.: Lexington Books, 1989), pp. 1–20; Sage Publications, for permission to include in chapter 6 excerpts from my article, "The State in an Era of Cascading Politics: Wavering Concept, Widening Competence, Withering Colossus, or Weathering Change?" *Comparative Political Studies* 21 (April 1988): 13–44; Dartmouth Publishing Company Ltd., for permission to include in chapters 8 and 15 material from my chapter in James N. Rosenau and Hylke Tromp, eds., *Interdependence and Conflict in World Politics* (Aldershot, Hants, U.K.: Dartmouth, 1989); Butterworth & Company, for permission to include in chapter 9 a section from my article, "A Pre-Theory Revisited: World Politics in an Era of Cascading Interdependence," *International Studies Quarterly* 28 (September 1984): 245–306; the World Peace Foundation and the Massachusetts Institute of Technology, for permission to include in chapter 9 several paragraphs from my article, "Before Cooperation: Hegemons, Regimes, and Habit-Driven Actors in World Politics," *International Organization* 40 (Autumn 1986): 849–94; and Lexington Books, for permission to include in chapter 12 sections of my contribution to Stephen J. Cimbala, ed., *Artificial Intelligence and National Security* (Lexington, Mass.: Lexington Books, 1987), pp. 1–18.

Gratitude also is extended to the following for permission to reproduce several of the tables:UNESCO, for permission to use tables 13.1, 13.2, 13.3, 13.4, and A.1, and figure 13.2, from the *Statistical Yearbook* (Paris, 1987), pp. 2.32–2.33, 3.7, and 6.19 to 6.22; University of Texas Press, for permission to use table 13.5 from James N. Danziger, "Social Science and the Social Impacts of Computer Technology," *Social Science Quarterly* 66 no. 1 (March 1985): 9; Jossey-Bass Publishers, for permission to use figure 12.1 from Gareth Morgan, *Riding the Waves of Change: Developing Managerial Competencies for a Turbulent World* (San Francisco: Jossey-Bass, 1989), p. 3; Child and Waters, Inc., for permission to use table 13.7 from *Travel Industry World Yearbook* (New York, 1985); Arvind Singhal and Everett M. Rogers, for permission to use figure 13.1 from their paper, "Television Soap Operas for Development in India," presented at the annual meeting of the International Communication Association (Montreal, May 1987); Kluwer Academic Publishers, for permission to reprint table 14.1 from Charles Tilly, "Space for Capital, Space for States," *Theory and Society* 15 (1986): 307; Gunnar P. Nielsson, for permission to use table 14.2 from his paper, "On the Concepts of Ethnicity, National, and State," presented at the Workshop on the Sociology of Nationalism, Second World Basque Conference (Vitoria-Gasteiz, Spain, September 1987); and Frances Pinter Publishers for permission to reproduce Tables 14.3 and 14.4 from Anthony Judge, "International Institutions: Diversity, Borderline Cases, Functional Substitutes, and Possible Alternatives," in P. Taylor and J. Groom, eds., *International Organization: A Conceptual Approach* (London: Frances Pinter, 1978), pp. 81, 83.

In retrospect, it seems clear that my preoccupation with the dynamics of change has been moving toward culmination in a book for a decade or more. As a result, I have benefited enormously from a continuous flow of suggestions, criticisms, and clarifications across the years. It is a measure of the cooperative community in which social scientists work that this flow has accelerated as word of the project spread through presentations of one or another of its aspects at meetings of professional associations and a number of faculty and graduate student colloquia around the country and abroad. Colleagues have sent articles they felt I needed to consider; graduate students in various universities who heard my presentations have written long letters suggesting alternative formulations; and friends have reacted to early drafts of various chapters with many clarifying suggestions and criticisms. It is not possible to list all the members of this invisible college to whom I feel so very grateful, but it is a pleasure to be able to take note of its existence and to express the hope that I will be able to continue to reciprocate through membership in their colleges. Such memberships are an indebtedness we all share, one that derives its imperative from the invisibility of the people and the visibility of the ideas that sustain every college.

But some colleagues have been very visible, with several having provided feedback on the entire manuscript, an act of collegiality that is so valuable as to defy a full expression of appreciation. But one has to try: I am especially grateful to Harry C. Bredemeier, who provided invaluable criticism of each and every chapter of this book. A dear friend for more than forty years who, right from the start, heightened my sensitivities to the ways of social systems, Harry has seen me through the ups and downs of some turbulent times. It is a pleasure to be able to dedicate this book to him. ("Hey, what do you mean by that?" he will ask; I mean a deep sense of gratitude, Harry!)

Michael Brecher and Dina A. Zinnes also took time from their busy schedules to provide detailed reactions to the entire manuscript. In addition, I have received helpful suggestions or materials from Hayward Alker, Richard K. Ashley, David A. Baldwin, James A. Caporaso, Nazli Choucri, James der Derian, S. Nelson Drew, Raymond D. Duvall, Joshua S. Goldstein, Joe D. Hagan, Peter M. Haas, K. J. Holsti, Ole R. Holsti, Michael Intrilligator, Stephen D. Krasner, Vendulka Kubalkova, John P. Lovell, Evan C. McKenzie, Dwain Mefford, Richard L. Merritt, Everett M. Rogers, John Gerard Ruggie, Melvin Seeman, Paul R. Viotti, and Stephen G. Walker. Geoff Martin and David Andrews, at the time graduate students at York University and the Massachusetts Institute of Technology, respectively, suggested important modifications, which I subsequently incorporated into the manuscript. I am also pleased to record my appreciation to the thirteen graduate students in Political Science 512 at the University of Southern California in the summer of 1988, who registered their reactions to every page in ways that greatly clarified the analysis.

I am particularly grateful to the John Simon Guggenheim Memorial Foundation for freeing up the time needed to work through a number of the inquiry's core concepts. Without the opportunity provided by a fellowship from the foundation, the book could not have been written.

The resources of the Institute for Transnational Studies of the University of Southern California were, as always, crucial in a number of ways, perhaps most notably through the dedicated work of its administrative assistant, Martha Decker. The university's Center for International Studies also provided vital support in the form of three able research assistants, Brian Findley, Imre Meszaros, and Mahmood Sariolghalam, who helped immeasurably in going over several drafts of the manuscript and checking out its many citations.

I also want to record a special word of thanks to Robert A. Feldmesser. In working with him to clarify the ideas, strengthen the emphases, remove the contradictions, and otherwise improve the presentation of this book, I learned a great deal about craft, high standards, and persistence. He taught me that any paragraph is susceptible to improvement and that there is no reason to settle for ambiguous formulations.

Finally, my indebtedness to Pauline Rosenau for her substantive reactions and loving support is incalculable. To be able to merge intellectual collegiality and emotional partnership is surely among the most satisfying rewards one can have. Our time together has spanned the life of this manuscript, a long period as far as the research and writing is concerned but all too short in terms of our partnership. It is with lots of respect and love that this book is also dedicated to her.

Needless to say, none of the foregoing is responsible for the final product. For that I alone am accountable—both for the sheer craziness that underlies the attempt to reconceptualize world politics and for the way in which it has been carried out.

NOTE: The final draft of this book was readied for publication in August 1989—just weeks before the upheavals that culminated in the onset of considerable turbulence in the Soviet Union and the rapid-fire collapse of communist regimes in East Germany, Czechoslovakia, Bulgaria, Hungary, Romania, and Yugoslavia. My reading of the page proofs in January 1990 has therefore been a remarkable experience. Unable to incorporate these recent and continuing developments into the argument of the book, and yet highly sensitive to the possibility that one or another aspect of its theory may have been called into question by the flood of events, I experienced every paragraph as a challenge. Taken together, they seemed an endless series of hypotheses that were being prematurely, even unfairly, subjected to the severe test of a startling and ongoing reality. Happily, they all survived. So far as I am concerned, at least, none of the broad foundations of global turbulence set forth in the ensuing pages was negated by the months following the summer of 1989, and more than a few of the specific propositions can fairly be said to have been upheld. Doubtless, readers will reach their own conclusions as to whether the turbulence model presented here enriches their comprehension of the changes that have unfolded, but they should be aware that my original formulation has not been altered in any way. The schedule for the book denied me the benefit of hindsight; on the other hand, it did provide an opportunity for theory testing.

J.N.R.
January 27, 1990

PART ONE

ORGANIZED
OVERVIEW

CHAPTER I

PREVIEWING POSTINTERNATIONAL POLITICS

There can be an awareness of world changes without an awareness of that awareness.
—F. E. Emery and E. L. Trist[1]

Even the sorts of things that haven't changed are different. All sorts of tonalities—emotional, moral, personal—have somehow altered.
—Clifford Geertz[2]

Spread out and examine the pattern of events, and you will find yourself face to face with a new scheme of being, hitherto unimaginable by the human mind.
—H. G. Wells[3]

THESE OBSERVATIONS set the tone for this book. They highlight the extent to which the underlying argument is founded on a dim awareness of transformation, on tonalities, on a broad spreading out of global patterns that has brought the author face to face with political dynamics that appear to be a new scheme for world affairs.

What follows, in other words, consists of theoretical claims rather than empirical proof. As such, it offers readers a choice: they can dismiss the delineation of a postinternational politics as absurd speculation, or they can allow for the possibility that the claims are sufficiently plausible to justify consideration as a basis for interpreting the course of events.

This is not as easy a choice as it may seem. It involves one's overall

---

[1] *Toward a Social Ecology* (New York: Plenum, 1975), p. 32.
[2] Quoted in *New York Times*, May 11, 1988, p. B6.
[3] *The Mind at the End of Its Tether* (London: William Heineman, 1945), p. 4.

3

perspective on the goals, people, and organizations that move history, and on the receptivity of communities to change and their capacity to shape their own destinies. Thus, as a choice derived from one's most basic approach to human affairs, it turns on questions that precede evidence and proof. At issue, indeed, are the conceptual-temperamental contexts within which evidence and proof are assessed. If some "unimaginable scheme" does underlie world politics, how does one imagine it? discern it? ponder it? refine it? Certainly not through evidence alone. One must first allow for its very recognition, by suspending the impulse to demand proof until the outlines of the scheme come into focus. Such is the purpose here: to give pause, not to prove; to trace emerging signs, not to document established patterns; to heighten sensitivities to change, not to claim that its dynamics have been adequately grasped; to cite illustrations and anomalies as bases for insight, not as evidence that the existence of an unimaginable scheme has been scientifically demonstrated.

The extent to which readers, like the author, must proceed on the basis of underlying perspectives is perhaps best exemplified by the choices they make in appraising the nature of history and, in particular, the idea that sharp departures from past practices can occur in the affairs of people and their communities. Unimaginable schemes cannot be envisioned without allowing for historical discontinuities, for major turns in new directions, and for a readiness to view each current development as possibly more than another instance of a long-standing pattern. Consider plane hijackings, AIDS (acquired immune-deficiency syndrome), and the recent wave of challenges to authority in Taiwan, Sri Lanka, Soviet Armenia and Estonia, Algeria, UNESCO (United Nations Educational, Scientific, and Cultural Organization), Mexico, the Catholic church, Ethiopia, Iran, the PLO (Palestine Liberation Organization), Singapore, Argentina, India, Poland, Hungary, Afghanistan, the Philippines, the Israeli-occupied West Bank, Burma, South Africa, the Sudan, Yugoslavia, and East Germany. Readers can choose to interpret these as merely modern cases of the same dynamics whereby terrorism, epidemics, and uprisings marked earlier centuries—or they can pause and wonder whether such developments, coming so fast upon each other, are not the first surfacings of historical departures in which the dynamics of constancy and change are brought into new forms of tension which, in turn, are altering the fundamental structures of world politics.

Moreover, if one senses that exploding technologies and expanding interdependencies are of great moment, then one must suspend normal standards of evidence long enough to consider alternative interpretations of what may be at work on the global scene. World politics is too fluid, too pervaded by signs of deep-seated change, to do otherwise.[4]

A GENERIC CONCEPTION

Of the several themes developed here that call attention to the possibility of an unimaginable scheme, three are especially challenging. One involves the present era as a historical breakpoint. The second concerns a bifurcation of macro global structures into what is called "the two worlds of world politics." The third focuses on the micro level and the hypothesis that the analytic and emotional skills of adults in every country are increasing.

Taken together with the impact of modern technologies and the many other sources that are rendering the world ever more interdependent, the bifurcated structures and the more skillful citizens are conceived to have fostered such a profound transformation in world politics that the lessons of history may no longer be very helpful. Global life may have entered a period of turbulence the likes of which it has not known for three hundred years and the outcomes of which are still far from clear. It is, I suppose, a far-fetched argument if emphasis is placed on the time span; but if prominence is given to the concept of global turbulence, it matters little whether three hundred years is too much or too little. What matters is whether the dynamics conceived to be operating do indeed have the implications claimed for them.

To assert that the lessons of history are becoming obscure is to presume that the changes are so thoroughgoing as to render obsolete the rules and procedures by which politics are conducted, thereby leaving observers without any paradigms or theories that adequately explain the course of events. To be sure, they can always dismiss discrepant events as mere anomalies; but what if, as I think is the case today, the anomalies are more pervasive than the recurrent patterns and the discontinuities are more prominent than the continuities? The answer is that theorizing must begin anew, and present premises and understandings of history's dynamics must be treated as conceptual jails

---

[4] Interestingly, science today is in very much the same position of sensing that new perspectives may be needed to account for previously unrecognized dynamics. As two observers of science have put it, "In the past few decades something very dramatic has been happening in science, something as unexpected as the birth of geometry or the grand vision of the cosmos as expressed in Newton's work. We are becoming more and more conscious of the fact that on all levels, from elementary particles to cosmology . . . our vision of nature is undergoing a radical change toward the multiple, the temporal, and the complex." Ilya Prigogine and Isabelle Stengers, *Order out of Chaos: Man's New Dialogue with Nature* (New York: Bantam Books, 1984), pp. xxviii, 2.

from which an escape can be engineered only by allowing for the possibility that a breakpoint in human affairs is imminent, if not upon us, as the twentieth century comes to an end.

If this is the case, it seems awkward to continue referring to the field in which the changes are occurring as "international politics." The very notion of "international relations" seems obsolete in the face of an apparent trend in which more and more of the interactions that sustain world politics unfold without the direct involvement of nations or states. So a new term is needed, one that denotes the presence of new structures and processes while at the same time allowing for still further structural development. A suitable label would be *postinternational politics*. The social sciences are now pervaded by analyses of postindustrial, postcapitalist, postsocialist, and postideological society, post-Marxism and postmodernism, the post-Christian era, and many other such "posts."[5] Profound changes in world affairs can surely, then, be regarded as constituting postinternational politics.

But use of this label involves more than conforming to fashion. Postinternational politics is an appropriate designation because it clearly suggests the decline of long-standing patterns without at the same time indicating where the changes may be leading. It suggests flux and transition even as it implies the presence and functioning of stable structures. It allows for chaos even as it hints at coherence.[6] It reminds us that "international" matters may no longer be the dominant dimension of global life, or at least that other dimensions have emerged to challenge or offset the interactions of nation-states. And, not least, it permits us to avoid premature judgment as to whether present-day tur-

---

[5] Daniel Bell, *The Coming of Post-Industrial Society: A Venture in Social Forecasting* (New York: Basic Books, 1973).

[6] That postinternational politics may evolve in either chaotic or coherent directions needs to be underlined at the outset. It is not conceived here as the political form of those versions of the postmodernist philosophy that assert, on the basis of unsystematic evidence, that the expiration of the modern industrial age has resulted in a postmodern epoch wherein humankind will be unable to manage its affairs and thus sink into unmitigated disarray, perhaps even extinction. Rather, the perspective of the postinternational politics treats ultimate outcomes as an open question, as a set of issues to be explored empirically. It allows, in other words, for a variety of outcomes, the gloomy one anticipated by the postmodernists no less than the more optimistic one of surviving modernists who believe that somehow—perhaps when the nuclear, resource, and management crises become acute—humankind will successfully cope with the turbulent conditions presently unfolding. For a succinct summary of the several postmodernist versions of what lies ahead for world politics, see John S. Nelson, "Postmodern Meanings of Politics" (paper presented at the annual meeting of the American Political Science Association, Chicago, September 1987), pp. 3–4.

bulence consists of enduring systemic arrangements or is merely a transitional condition.

Accordingly, the term will henceforth be used to designate the historical era that began after World War II and continues to unfold today. It is a shorthand for the changes wrought by global turbulence; for an ever more dynamic interdependence in which labor is increasingly specialized and the number of collective actors thereby proliferates; for the centralizing and decentralizing tendencies that are altering the identity and number of actors on the world stage; for the shifting orientations that are transforming authority relations among the actors; and for the dynamics of structural bifurcation that are fostering new arrangements through which the diverse actors pursue their goals. Postinternational politics is that hitherto unimaginable scheme, a generic conception of how the human links that span the globe have been affected by the complexity and dynamism that are coming into view as the present millennium draws to a close.

TURBULENT CHANGE

Doubtless every era seems chaotic to the people who live through it, and the last decades of the twentieth century are no exception. It is as if Spaceship Earth daily encounters squalls, downdrafts, and wind shears as it careens into changing and unchartered realms of experience. Sometimes the turbulence is furiously evident as thunderclouds of war gather or the lightning of a crisis streaks across the global sky; but often the turbulence is of a clear-air kind, the havoc it wreaks unrecognized until after its challenges have been met or its damage done.

In seeking here to account for this turbulence in world politics and the changes that it both reflects and promotes, the analysis will focus on the underlying and enduring dynamics out of which daily events and current issues flow. Some of the dynamics are located at micro levels, where individuals learn and groups cohere; others originate at macro levels, where new technologies are operative and collectivities conflict; and still others derive from clashes between opposing forces at the two levels—between continuity and change, between the pulls of the past and the lures of the future, between the requirements of interdependence and the demands for independence, between centralizing and decentralizing tendencies within and among nations.

While equating the turbulence of world affairs to stormy weather captures well the current human condition, its use here as a metaphor may divert from my larger purpose. The goal in identifying a hitherto unimaginable scheme is to facilitate empirical explanation rather than to provide poetic expression. What is needed is a conception of turbulence that denotes the tensions and changes that ensue when the structures and processes that normally sustain world politics are unsettled and appear to be undergoing rearrangement. Turbulence is thus more than the commotion that accompanies shifts in major variables. Such fluctuations make up the day-to-day life of any system, be it social or meteorological. Just as shifts from cloudiness to showers to sunshine constitute normal weather patterns, so do electoral shifts from right to center to left or industrial shifts from high to moderate to low productivity form standard political and economic patterns, thereby allowing the analysis of such shifts to proceed by treating the system's boundaries as constant and the range within which the variables fluctuate as a measure of underlying stability. When the system's boundaries no longer contain the fluctuations of the variables, however, anomalies arise and irregularities set in as structures waver, new processes evolve, outcomes become transitory, and the system enters a period of prolonged disequilibrium. These are the hallmarks of turbulence. Meteorologically, it appears in the form of hurricanes, tornadoes, tidal waves, droughts, and other "abnormalities" of nature that transform the terrain across which they sweep. Socially, it is manifested in technological breakthroughs, authority crises, consensus breakdowns, revolutionary upheavals, generational conflicts, and other forces that restructure the human landscape in which they erupt.

It follows that uncertainty is a prime characteristic of turbulent politics. While the fluctuations of variables usually adhere to recognizable patterns, regularities disappear when turbulence sets in. At such times, the structures and processes of world politics enter a realm without prior rules or boundaries. Anything may happen, or so it seems, as demands are intensified, tensions exacerbated, relationships transformed, policymaking paralyzed, or outcomes otherwise rendered less certain and the future more obscure.

Closely related to the uncertainties associated with political turbulence is the pace at which it moves. Unlike conventional diplomatic or organizational situations, which evolve in the context of formal procedures, cautious bargaining, and bureaucratic inertia, those beset by turbulent conditions develop rapidly as the repercussions of the various participants' actions cascade through their networks of interdependence. Sustained by the complexity and dynamism of diverse actors whose goals and activities are inextricably linked to each other, and facilitated by technologies that transmit information almost instantaneously, turbulent situations tend to be marked by quick responses, insistent demands, temporary coalitions, and policy reversals, all of which propel the course of events swiftly if erratically along the fault lines of conflict and cooperation.

Viewed in this context, it is not surprising that, in 1988, protests and uprisings followed quickly upon each other in Soviet Armenia, the West Bank, Poland, Burma, and Yugoslavia, or that the same time span was marked by regimes being shaken up in the Soviet Union, Chile, Haiti, and Lebanon. Likewise, and no less conspicuous, 1988 witnessed cascades of cooperation: within weeks of each other, negotiations to end wars were initiated in Afghanistan, Angola, Central America, Cambodia, the Western Sahara, and the Persian Gulf.[7] The winds of turbulence, in short, can propel postinternational politics in many directions, through the world's diplomatic and legislative chambers, where compromises are reached, no less than through its streets and battlefields, where conflicts are joined.

But how to extend the analysis beyond a suggestive metaphor? How to employ turbulence as a serious and systematic analytic concept that helps to account for the emergence of postinternational politics? This question is taken up in chapter 3, and an answer is found in the field of organizational theory, where the concept of turbulence is well developed and widely used. In particular, reliance is placed on a model of organizations that identifies turbulence as the condition they face when their environments are marked by high degrees of complexity and dynamism. In this formulation, high complexity is not a synonym for events and trends that are difficult to understand. It refers, rather, to such an inordinate number of actors in the environment, and such an extensive degree of interdependence among them, that the environment is dense (rather than thin) with causal layers. This density is conceived to be so great as to enable any event to give rise to a restless commotion, which reverberates in fast-paced and unexpected ways throughout the environment and its diverse systems. When the dynamism of the environment is also high—i.e., when great variability marks the conduct of its actors—the interdependence of its many parts is bound to be greatly affected by the volatility that accompanies large-scale social transformations.

It could be argued that high complexity and high dynamism are not new to world politics, that global wars, revolutions, and depressions reflect such conditions, and accordingly, that change has always been at work in world politics. In order to differentiate the familiar and

---

[7] For an analysis of these developments, see James N. Rosenau, "Interdependence and the Simultaneity Puzzle: Notes on the Outbreak of Peace," in Charles W. Kegley, Jr., ed., *The Long Postwar Peace: The Sources of Great Power Stability* (forthcoming), chapter 15.

commonplace changes from the profound kind of transformations that seem to be occurring today, one other attribute of political turbulence needs to be noted—namely, it involves *parametric* change. Only when the basic parameters of world politics, those boundary constraints that shape and confine the fluctuations of its variables, are engulfed by high complexity and high dynamism is turbulence considered to have set in. Being boundaries, parameters are normally stable. They make possible the continuities of political life, the ability of individual and collective actors to get from one day to the next and from one era to the next. Hence, when the orientations, skills, relationships, and structures that have sustained the parameters of world politics begin to crumble—i.e., when the complexity and dynamism of the parameters reach a point where the existing rules of conduct no longer serve to constrain behavior and outcomes—the course of events is bound to turn turbulent.

Three dimensions of world politics are conceptualized as its main parameters. One of these operates at the micro level of individuals, one functions at the macro level of collectivities, and the third involves a mix of the two levels. The micro parameter consists of the orientations and skills by which citizens of states and members of nonstate organizations link themselves to the macro world of global politics. I refer to this set of boundary constraints as the *orientational* or *skill* parameter. The macro parameter is here designated the *structural* parameter, and it refers to the constraints embedded in the distribution of power among and within the collectivities of the global system. The mixed parameter is called the *relational* one; it focuses on the nature of the authority relations that prevail between individuals at the micro level and their macro collectivities.

All three of these parameters are judged to be undergoing such a thoroughgoing transformation today as to bring about the first turbulence in world politics since comparable shifts culminated in the Treaty of Westphalia in 1648.[8] At first glance, it doubtless seems excessive to argue that the turbulence of the present era is the first in more than three hundred years. Clearly, the history of most countries is marked by periods of turmoil. As already noted, however, the claim being made here pertains to turbulence in the international system and not to the upheavals experienced within national systems, to the transfor-

---

[8] The Treaty of Westphalia is generally recognized as the beginning of the modern system of nation-states. However, this is not a unanimous view. Wight, for example, argues that the start of the French-Spanish struggle over Italy in 1494 marked the origin of the modern system, noting that "at Westphalia the state system does not come into existence; it comes of age." M. Wight, *Systems of States* (Leicester: Leicester University Press, 1977), p. 152.

mation of three specific parametric patterns and not to the commotion that attends the waging of wars or the fluctuation of economies. In the case of the structural parameter, the transformation is marked by a bifurcation in which the state-centric system now coexists with an equally powerful, though more decentralized, multi-centric system. Although these two worlds of world politics have overlapping elements and concerns, their norms, structures, and processes tend to be mutually exclusive, thus giving rise to a set of global arrangements that are new and possibly enduring, as well as extremely complex and dynamic.[9] In the case of the relational parameter, the long-standing pattern whereby compliance with authority tends to be unquestioning and automatic is conceived to have been replaced by a more elaborate set of norms that make the successful exercise of authority much more problematic, thus fostering leadership and followership conflicts within and among state and nonstate collectivities that can fairly be judged as amounting to a series of authority crises which, in both their pervasiveness and their scale, are new and global in scope. Lastly, at the micro level, the analytic skills of individuals have increased to a point where they now play a different and significant role in world politics, a role which has intensified both the processes of structural bifurcation and the breakdown of authority relations.

It is the simultaneity and interaction of these parametric changes that distinguish the present period from the previous three centuries. By virtue of their newly acquired skills, people are more able and ready to question authority, and in turn the new authority relationships have facilitated the development of new, more decentralized global structures. But the causal flows also move from the macro to the micro level as the centralized structures invite the formation of new authority relationships, which then serve to refine further the skills and orientations through which individuals link themselves to their collectivities. Earlier eras have witnessed wars that shifted global structures from multipolar to bipolar foundations and revolutions that undermined the prevailing authority relationships; but not since the seventeenth century have circumstances arisen in which the values of all three of these fundamental parameters underwent reinforcing realignments.

---

[9] For reasons indicated in chapter 10, it seems appropriate to treat the state- and multi-centric systems as separate "worlds," a formulation not to be confused with the generic label "world politics" that is used throughout to designate structures and processes of global scope. The frequent references to the "two worlds of world politics" (or, occasionally, to the "two-world political universe") are intended to serve as a continual reminder that the global system has structure even though it lacks unity, having entered a period of far-reaching (and possibly irreversible) bifurcation.

Between Peace and War

The turbulent conditions of postinternational politics should not be equated to those of violence. While uncertainty may promote the possibility of armed conflict in world politics, there is no one-to-one relationship between them. Turbulence can prevail within communities, markets, organizations, and alliances without their conflicts bringing on a resort to armed force. To study turbulence is to analyze responses to uncertainty, to the changes wrought by technology and an ever-expanding global interdependence, and war is but one of those responses. What follows, therefore, is only incidentally an analysis of violence in world politics. Indeed, as indicated in chapter 8, there are good reasons to anticipate that responses involving force will diminish as world politics becomes more turbulent.

In some important respects, in fact, war is free of the uncertainties that accompany turbulence. When war breaks out, adversarial relationships become clear, the goals of policy making self-evident, and the tasks ahead unmistakable. Viewed in this way, turbulence may be more a prewar or postwar condition than a mark of wartime. And of course it is not a characteristic of peacetime, if by the latter is meant stable circumstances in which parameters remain essentially fixed.

In both peace and war, in other words, the day-to-day fluctuations are familiar. They are within the range of variations that have occurred before, that people know how to cope with and adjust to. Under turbulent conditions, on the other hand, even the slightest fluctuation can seem portentous, with each shift confirming that change is the norm, that patterns are fragile, and that expectations can be frustrated.

The Sources of Change

What are the forces at work toward the end of the twentieth century that drive these parametric transformations? Five seem particularly relevant. One involves the shift from an industrial to a postindustrial order and focuses on the dynamics of technology, particularly on those technologies associated with the microelectronic revolution that have made social, economic, and political distances so much shorter, the movement of ideas, pictures, currencies, and information so much faster, and thus the interdependence of people and events so much greater.[10] A second engine of global change is the emergence of is-

[10] For a thorough exploration of the diverse dimensions of the microelectronic revolution, see Rob van Tulder and Gerd Junne, *European Multinationals in Core Technologies* (Chichester: John Wiley, 1988).

sues—such as atmospheric pollution, terrorism, the drug trade, currency crises, and AIDS—that are the direct products of new technologies or of the world's greater interdependence and are distinguished from traditional political issues by virtue of being transnational rather than national or local in scope. A third dynamic is the reduced capability of states and governments to provide satisfactory solutions to the major issues on their political agendas, partly because the new issues are not wholly within their jurisdiction, partly because the old issues are also increasingly intertwined with significant international components (e.g., agricultural markets and labor productivity), and partly because the compliance of their citizenries can no longer be taken for granted. Fourth, with the weakening of whole systems, subsystems have acquired a correspondingly greater coherence and effectiveness, thereby fostering tendencies toward decentralization (what I call *subgroupism*) at all organizational levels that are in stark contrast to the centralizing tendencies (here regarded as *nation-statism* or *transnationalism*) that marked the early decades of this century and those that preceded it. Finally, there is the feedback of the consequences of all the foregoing for the skills and orientations of the world's adults who comprise the groups, states, and other collectivities that have had to cope with the new issues of interdependence and adjust to the new technologies of the postindustrial order; with their analytic skills enlarged and their orientations toward authority more self-conscious, today's persons-in-the-street are no longer as uninvolved, ignorant, and manipulable with respect to world affairs as were their forebears.

The hypothesized interactions among these five sources of change, and an indication of the historical setting in which they accelerated, are presented diagrammatically in figure 1.1 This causal model involves more than a simple identification of five prime sources of global turbulence and a presumption that they are highly interactive. One of the five dynamics, the shift in micro capabilities and orientations, is deemed to be more powerful than the other four, so much so as to be a requisite to the expansivity and intensity of the other four. That is, although world politics would not be on a new course today if the microelectronic and other technological revolutions had not occurred, if the new interdependence issues had not arisen, if states and governments had not become weaker, and if subgroupism had not mushroomed, none of these dynamics would have produced parametric change if adults in every country and in all walks of life had remained essentially unskilled and detached with respect to global affairs. To be sure, these shifts in skills and orientations have been hastened and refined by the other dynamics, and in this sense the latter can also be

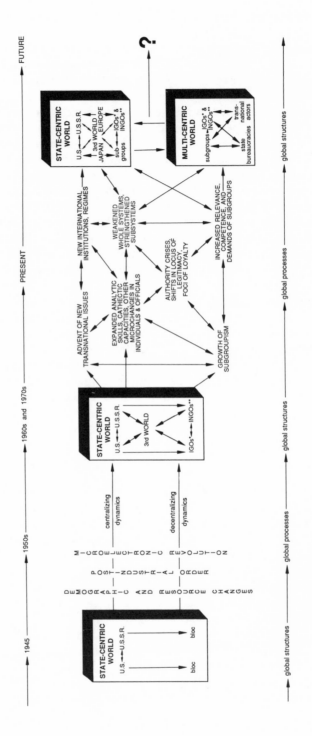

FIGURE 1.1. Evolution of the Two Worlds of World Politics

* IGOs – International Governmental Organizations
** INGOs – International Non-governmental Organizations

viewed as necessary determinants of the turbulence. Without the micro transformations, however, none of the others could have emerged on a worldwide scale, and in this sense the enlargements of the capacities of citizens is the primary prerequisite for global turbulence.

The analysis, then, is not based on a single-cause model. Nor does it presume that the micro changes preceded the others in time. On the contrary, all of them are seen as being initially responses to the technological upheavals that underlay the ever-growing interdependencies of economic, political, and social life. Once the micro level shifts began, however, alterations in the status of states, governments, and subgroups were bound to follow, as people became receptive to the decentralizing consequences inherent in their growing capacity to locate their own interests more clearly in the flow of events. The subtlety of these interactive processes is perhaps most clearly evident in the links between the expansion of citizen skills and the technologies made available by the microelectronic revolution. If one asks what the advent of instantaneous communications and information retrieval—of satellites bringing pictures of ongoing events into homes everywhere and of computers storing, processing, and disseminating information heretofore unknown and ungatherable—may be doing to individuals as actors on the global stage, the answer seems inescapable that the new technologies have had a profound, if not always desirable, impact upon how individuals perceive, comprehend, judge, enter, avoid, or otherwise interact with the world beyond their workplace and home. For example, the new electronic technologies have so greatly collapsed the time in which organizations and movements can be mobilized that the competence of citizens feeds on itself, in the sense that they can virtually "see" their skills and orientations being cumulated into larger aggregates that have consequence for the course of events. No longer does the translation of commitment into action await word brought by stagecoach that like-minded citizens are banding together or that leaders discern an opportunity for effective participation. Today, events and the words about them are, in effect, simultaneous occurrences. Unlike any prior time in history, therefore, citizens are now able to intrude themselves readily into a situation anywhere in the world, because information about its latest twists and turns is immediately at hand.

Indeed, even if the ensuing analysis exaggerates the extent to which the skills and orientations of citizens have enlarged, the ability to mobilize those skills and orientations is so much greater and speedier than in the past that the practical effect is an expanded capacity for identifying and articulating self-interests and participating effectively in collective action. And if, as seems likely, those who head organizations recognize the effects of this capacity on their leadership circumstances, then their sensitivities to the wishes and demands of their followers will intensify and lend further credence to the perception of citizens as undergoing an expansion and redirection of their skills and orientations.

THE TECHNOLOGICAL DYNAMIC

Given the conception of turbulence as a process of parameter realignment, a further question arises as to the sources of turbulence. Except for the dynamics unleashed by technological innovations, those noted so far are embraced by the three parameters of the global political system and are thus endogenous to it. But there may be exogenous sources in addition to those that derive from technological developments. That is, while turbulence partly feeds on itself, as each parametric alteration gives rise to circumstances that exert pressure for further alterations, political systems are also subject to a broad array of changes originating in the economy and society, all of which are also sufficiently dynamic to spur still further changes once they have been absorbed by the polity.

Following the insightful formulation of Choucri and North, three dynamics are conceived to be especially relevant as exogenous sources of global turbulence.[11] As indicated in figure 1.1, one is the pressures created by extensive changes in the structure and size of populations in recent decades. A second involves the shifting availability and distribution of natural resources, especially those related to the generation of energy. The third derives from the previously mentioned consequences of technologies in all fields of human endeavor, from information processing to medicine, biogenetics and agriculture.

Since it has also contributed to the shifts in population and natural resources, technology is perhaps the most powerful of the exogenous dynamics. For it is technological developments, those combinations of human ingenuity and material nature, that have transformed the industrial order and brought into being the age of information, the postindustrial society, the technocratic era, the microelectronic revolution—whatever one may wish to call the emergent arrangements by which people move toward goals, satisfy needs, and otherwise conduct their affairs. Technology has expanded the capacity to generate and manipulate information and knowledge even more than the ability to

[11] Nazli Choucri and Robert C. North, *Nations in Conflict: National Growth and International Violence* (San Francisco: W. H. Freeman, 1975).

produce material goods, leading to a situation in which the service industries have come to replace the manufacturing industries as the cutting edge of societal life. It is technology too, that has so greatly diminished geographic and social distances through the jet-powered airliner, the computer, the orbiting satellite, and the many other innovations that now move people, ideas, and goods more rapidly and surely across space and time than ever before. It is technology that has profoundly altered the scale on which human affairs take place, allowing more people to do more things in less time and with wider repercussions than could have been imagined in earlier eras. It is technology, in short, that has fostered an interdependence of local, national, and international communities that is far greater than any previously experienced.[12]

The impact of these technology-driven exogenous dynamics on societies, economies, and polities has been imaginatively and fully recorded by students of national systems. One needs only read the works of Daniel Bell, Peter Drucker, John Naisbitt, and Daniel Yankelovich—to mention a few of the many observers who have focused on the social consequences of modern technology—to appreciate the extraordinary transformations through which the world is passing.[13] They convincingly demonstrate that families, marriages, acquaintanceships, work, unions, businesses, leisure, agriculture, productivity, housing, travel, electoral politics, and every other aspect of life have recently undergone, and still continue to undergo, changes of great magnitude.

Yet somehow, students of global politics have not begun to take account of the transformations at work within societies. While they do not ignore the domestic sources of international relationships when internal conflicts, consensuses, or stalemates predominate, the dynamics of the postindustrial society tend to be taken for granted. That the world is considerably more interdependent is widely recognized, but the ways in which the sources of expanding interdependence sustain or alter the structures and processes of world politics have not been foci

[12] For a succinct and cogent discussion of the diverse ways in which new electronic technologies have changed the face of politics at all levels, see Walter B. Wriston, "Technology and Sovereignty," *Foreign Affairs* 67 (Winter 1988/89): 63–75.

[13] These authors have each written more than one work on the dynamics of change in the late twentieth century, but their views can be readily grasped in Bell, *Coming of Post-Industrial Society*; Peter Drucker, *Managing in Turbulent Times* (New York: Harper & Row, 1980); John Naisbitt, *Megatrends: Ten New Directions Transforming Our Lives* (New York: Warner Books, 1982); and Daniel Yankelovich, *New Rules: Searching for Self-Fulfillment in A World Turned Upside Down* (New York: Random House, 1981).

of intensive investigation.[14] The prevailing orientation seems, rather, to presume that the basic structures and processes of international politics remain intact even as change swirls through its component parts.

Likewise, students of the postindustrial society have not been especially concerned with the implications of their findings and insights for global politics. While Drucker, for example, does explore these implications for international economics, his analysis is limited to the problems of politically managing the world economy and does not get into the even larger question of management in world politics itself. Similarly, Bell anticipates "that the post-industrial society will involve *more* politics than ever before, for the very reason that choice becomes conscious and the decision-centers more visible,"[15] but his inquiry does not extend beyond the politics of who rules the community and society. The possibility that the global effects of the relatively few postindustrial societies might give rise to worldwide norms and practices that influence the development of preindustrial and industrial societies is not entertained.

AN OVERVIEW

Political turbulence is not so powerful as to sweep away existing institutional arrangements and cultural patterns without resistance. If we are to comprehend the tensions inherent in the clash between the forces that sustain the prevailing order and those that promote transformation, we need to be clear about the concepts of turbulence and change as well as the procedures employed to analyze them. Chapter 2 takes up the latter, setting forth the theoretical and methodological premises on which the inquiry is founded, and the two chapters that follow it address the problem of clarifying the concepts of turbulence and change so that their empirical referents can be traced. Chapter 3 explores the nature of turbulence and how it has been applied in other disciplines, concluding with the derivation of a formulation that facilitates its application to postinternational politics. Chapter 4 deals with the nature of sociopolitical change, the circumstances under which it results in parameter shifts, and the constraints by which the parameters are kept in place. It stresses that unless we are alert to the tensions

---

[14] Exceptions to this generalization can be found in James N. Danziger, "Computing and the Political World," *Computers and the Social Sciences* 2 (1986): 183–200, and Robert Gilpin, "The Computer and World Affairs," in M. L. Dertouzos and J. Moses, eds., *The Computer Age: A Twenty-Year View* (Cambridge, Mass.: MIT Press, 1979), pp. 229–53.

[15] Bell, *Coming of Post-Industrial Society*, p. 263 (italics in original).

between transformation and constancy in human affairs, we run the risk of oversimplifying, of treating the course of events as either a product of immediate stimuli or a recurrence of history's unwavering imperatives. Change and continuity are thus conceived to be opposite sides of the same coin. Inevitably they accompany each other, interact with each other, tug at each other, shape each other. In any action or situation, both are likely to be present, and each will account for a proportion of the outcome.

Equipped with a conception of turbulence as a condition in which the three main parameters of world politics are overwhelmed by increasing complexity and dynamism, chapter 5 undertakes to trace the history of these parameters in terms of their vulnerability to turbulence. Here is presented an elaboration of the notion that only in the 1950s did the three parameters begin to undergo transformation simultaneously, giving rise to the era of postinternational politics.

Inasmuch as one of the central features of postinternational politics is the diminished role played by states relative to the other actors that initiate and sustain sequences of action on the world stage, the analysis pauses in chapter 6 to enumerate and assess the full range of major actors at both the micro and macro levels. Eight generic actors, three at the micro level and five at the macro level, are identified and subjected to close scrutiny.

Since the complexity of societies and the interdependence of the macro actors have heightened the latter's vulnerability to the influence of the micro actors, an understanding of postinternational politics requires tracing how collectivities are shaped by—and shape—the individuals of whom they are comprised. Chapter 7 offers a formulation of these macro-micro interactions and indicates how they both constrain and facilitate the changes that mark global affairs.

The four chapters of Part 3 examine the three major parameters of world politics from several points of view. The central thrust is to assess the essential nature of each parameter, with special emphasis upon its operation prior to the onset of turbulence. Then, in the four chapters of Part 4, the parameters are reexamined in the context of the forces presently at work in global politics that are extending their complexity and dynamism to the point where they can be fairly regarded as engulfed by turbulence.

Part 5 (chapter 16) speculates about the circumstances that may lie beyond turbulence and the structures that may evolve in the future. As is the case throughout, the analysis here is marked by contradictory themes, by reasons to fear that the balance between centralizing and decentralizing dynamics will lead to ever greater incoherence and by equally persuasive bases for hoping that clear skies will follow the turbulence and permit Spaceship Earth to confront its dilemmas more coherently and incisively.

In sum, by exploring turbulence in world politics we are investigating a major analytic gap that needs to be filled. The gap is that nexus wherein politics on a global scale have been transformed by the diverse dynamics that have taken modern life beyond the rules and arrangements that prevailed throughout the industrial era. The need to fill the gap stems from the premise that it is inconceivable that so many great changes could occur within societies without major consequences for the conduct of affairs among them.

CHAPTER 2

JUSTIFYING JAILBREAKS

The Limits of Contemporary Concepts and Methods

One of the hallmarks of human history in the late twentieth century is the increasing internationalization of the world: in production, trade, finance, technology, threats to security, communications, research, education, and culture. One major consequence of this is that the mutual penetration of economic, political, and social forces among the nations of the world is increasingly salient; and it may be the case that the governments of nation-states are progressively losing degrees of direct control over the global forces that affect them. For social scientists, this phenomenon of internationalization poses a kind of conceptual challenge: to re-think the fundamental assumption, long established in our disciplines, that the primary unit of analysis is the nation, the society, or the culture.

—Neil J. Smelser[1]

Indeed, we are on the verge of living in a world . . . which constitutes one single economic system, within which private transnational actors allocate resources with a global calculus; a world which is not quite a competitive market and not quite a politically coordinated one, in which nation-states compete economically in part by opening and closing their frontiers to economic transactions; a world divided by political alliances of economic competitors, a world of weak international institutions, tacit agreements, and informal norms. This is a world in which there is diffusion, externalities, transnational public goods, jointly binding constraints, regimes of weak coordina-

---

[1] "External and Internal Factors in Theories of Social Change" (paper presented at the German-American Conference on Social Change and Modernization, Berkeley, Calif., August 1986), p. 1.

tion, and threats of force. Domestic politics often originate in this world from international sources. . . . As of now we do not know how to study this interdependent world.

—Adam Przeworski[2]

THE MESSAGE SEEMS CLEAR: not only are profound changes under way on a global scale, but two distinguished observers argue that our capacity to analyze their dynamics and consequences lags, thereby posing a severe challenge to social scientists in every discipline. Smelser says we have to rethink fundamental assumptions, and Przeworski says we do not know how to do it. In part, this may be due to the extraordinary pace and complexity of present-day turbulence, with events moving so swiftly that we have not had time to update our analytic equipment. In part, too, it may be that we are ill equipped to study the dynamics of interdependence because of a tendency to cling to old analytic habits. To consider abandoning the nation, the society, and the culture as primary units of analysis, as Smelser suggests, is an awesome thought, one that can be so inhibiting as to make us all the more reluctant to put aside long-standing conceptions and try out fresh approaches.

While sensitivity to this reluctance is a major step toward overcoming it, there remain good reasons to pause and explicate the procedures used to circumvent analytic habits and rethink fundamental assumptions. To break into uncharted domains of the field is not to abdicate responsibility for proceeding in a careful and disciplined fashion. On the contrary, lest the efforts to meet the Smelser-Przeworski challenge appear as no more than wild guesswork, the need to be cautious and systematic is perhaps especially acute. Perhaps one should hunker down in a cellar until atmospheric turbulence blows over, but social turbulence is best met through a straightforward confrontation in which one draws on all the ingenuity and discipline one can command.

The purpose of this chapter is thus to clarify the theoretical and methodological premises on which the book rests. In so doing, it offers a justification for an unremitting effort to break out of the conceptual jails in which the study of world politics is deemed to be incarcerated.

[2] *Methods of Cross-National Research 1970–1983: An Overview* (West Berlin: Wissenschaftzentrum, 1983), p. 23, quoted in Tom R. Burns, Thomas Baumgartner, and Phillip DeVille, *Man, Decision, Society: The Theory of Actor-System Dynamics for Social Scientists* (New York: Gordon & Breach, 1985), p. xi.

A Perspective on Multi-level Theory

Some might question whether useful theory can be fashioned out of all the factors noted in chapter 1. Scientific convention stresses that theory should be parsimonious, that the complexity inherent in the interaction of a large number of variables precludes meaningful theoretical insights, much less the kind of theoretical elegance that makes for deep understanding.

The theory developed here is not intended as a rejection of this line of reasoning. It is surely preferable to derive explanations of world politics from a few organizing principles that underlie the conduct of states and the outcomes of their interactions. One can only be envious of those analysts who are able to account for the course of events by positing all actors as egoistic power maximizers,[3] or who can reduce modern international history to a clash between security and economic interests,[4] or who can ascribe all causation to the structural requirements of the global capitalist economy,[5] or who use the requirements imposed by the state system to cast a wide explanatory net,[6] or who explain the long cycles of war in terms of one or another master variable.[7] These are elegant theoretical perspectives that provide rich and penetrating insights into the nature of global life. However, all of them presume a prevailing order, and thus none is sufficient to account for the parametric changes that underlie the turbulence of our time. The very parsimony that enables them to explain so much also serves to simplify too much. Virtually by definition, parsimonious theories are compelled to ignore the multiple macro and micro levels at which the sources of turbulence stir and gather momentum. For such theories to do otherwise, for them to acknowledge multiple layers of causation, would be to forgo the ability to explain the course of events in terms of one type of actor (the rational interest-maximizer), one form of eco-

---

[3] Kenneth A. Oye, ed., *Cooperation under Anarchy* (Princeton: Princeton University Press, 1986).

[4] See, for instance, Richard Rosecrance, *The Rise of the Trading State: Commerce and Conquest in the Modern World* (New York: Basic Books, 1986).

[5] For example, see Immanuel Wallerstein, *The Modern World-System: Capitalist Agriculture and the Origins of the European World-Economy in the Sixteenth Century* (New York: Academic Press, 1974).

[6] Kenneth Waltz, *Theory of International Politics* (Reading, Mass.: Addison-Wesley, 1979).

[7] For a penetrating analysis of various "long-wave" schools, see Joshua S. Goldstein, *Long Cycles: Prosperity and War in the Modern Age* (New Haven: Yale University Press, 1988).

nomic organization (the capitalist world economy), or one political structure (the state system).

Of course, some simplification is necessary. It would be futile to counter the dilemmas of excessive parsimony by founding a theory on a conception of postinternational politics in which the origins of turbulence were treated as being so diverse as to be located in every actor and unique to every conflict situation. Such a perspective would be too dependent on the particulars of time and place. It would render fruitless any effort to generalize across countries and eras. It would yield only encyclopedic descriptions, with every instance of turbulence being so different from every other that no explanatory theory could ever be fashioned. One would have to start from scratch every time one sought to understand the course of events.

Between the extremes of excessive parsimony and undisciplined encyclopedism lies an approach that allows for the construction of viable theory that is neither oblivious to nor overwhelmed by the complexities of postinternational politics or by the cascading interdependence that sustains it.[8] As indicated in chapter 1, the crux of this approach is to confine theorizing to those parameters that normally are sufficiently constant as to be operative across time and place but that precipitate global repercussions during those periods when they do undergo transformation. Viewed in this way, the sources of turbulence are not unduly numerous but, being parametric in nature, together they serve to initiate and nourish it.

Stated differently, this view of global turbulence is much like the recently adopted approach to the aging process. Students of aging have lately, if reluctantly, abandoned attempts to fashion a unified theory of the process. Instead, they now see it as deriving from several disparate sources. Diet, heredity, culture, and genetic factors are considered prime contributors to aging, with each having its own dynamic even as together they converge and interact to produce the processes and outcomes whereby the young become old.[9] So it is with postinternational politics. It has evolved only as the parameters that underlie the coherence of collectivities at the macro level and those that bound the conduct of individuals at the micro level have interactively undergone change and moved global life onto new foundations.

In short, only multilevel theory seems capable of coping with the puzzles posed by the turbulence presently roiling the actors and struc-

---

[8] The processes of cascading interdependence are elaborated upon in chapter 11.

[9] Erik Eckholm, "Aging: Studies Point toward Ways to Slow It," *New York Times*, June 10, 1986, p. C1.

tures of world politics. It may not be as elegant or parsimonious as one would like,[10] but it is incisive even as it acknowledges the complexities of the current scene.

Despite its reliance on multilevel theory, the analysis that follows is not lacking in a distinctive point of view. As noted, the parameter that governs the micro sources of global life is accorded a preeminent position. Throughout, it is argued that while several dynamics lead to the onset of turbulence, its prolonged duration derives from the changes that are transforming the analytic skills, affective capabilities, and legitimacy sentiments of individuals in all parts of the world. This preeminence is due partly to the disjointed pace at which the micro parameter undergoes change. The enlarged capacity of individuals to recognize and advance their interests tends to feed on itself, thereby prolonging the repercussions of the parametric shift and the uncertainties that attend the process of learning. Much of the turbulence in post-international politics can thus be traced to the conduct of identifiable citizens and officials, and it is the operation of this dynamic that frames the point of view developed in the following chapters.

The intense and prolonged effects that flow from the transformation of the micro parameter is not the only reason why this particular dynamic is singled out for special emphasis. The stress on individuals also stems from a conviction that most theories of world politics tend to underestimate, even ignore, the interplay of macro and micro dynamics and the many ways in which the coherence of national collectivities, the stability of international structures, and the composition of systemic agendas are linked to the activities of officials and citizens. To a very great extent, the prevailing approaches to the subject treat the micro level as a constant, as if the skills and orientations of individuals somehow remain fixed and peripheral relative to the great changes wrought by technology and the requirements of interdependence in a nuclear age. Here the argument is made that the presumption of constancy at the micro level overlooks some of the key dimensions of global politics. As long as individuals continue to enlarge their analytic skills, deepen their affective capabilities, and revise their legitimacy sentiments, it is contended, turbulence in world affairs is likely to continue.

---

[10] Among other reasons, elegance is thwarted by the need for extensive cross-referencing. With the three parameters and the several exogenous dynamics all interactive, one can hardly develop a coherent presentation without noting how the operation of one parameter is shaped by that of another and then asking the reader to look elsewhere for the discussion of the interactive processes. Thus it is, most notably, that the chapters of Parts 3 and 4 are pervaded with cross-references to each other.

Turbulence as Policy Problem and Intellectual Puzzle

One is led to the study of global turbulence because its uncertainties and outcomes involve the future well-being of peoples everywhere. The policy challenges it poses stagger the imagination and raise questions about the ability of leaders and publics to manage their affairs. So it is reasonable to presume that the better the circumstances and dynamics that foster turbulent conditions are understood, the greater the probability that policies designed to cope with its ill effects can be framed and implemented. Whatever good may stem from upheavals of the prevailing order, a prolonged period of global turbulence, if left to unfold without comprehension and management, could result in immense and irreversible setbacks for humankind.

The task of sorting out and clarifying the nature of global turbulence, in other words, is compelling because it has thrown the world's images of political institutions and its conceptions of political processes into flux. Redefinitions of political life are developing and, along with them, respecifications of the norms, habits, and practices that constitute global politics are evolving. Hence, it is time for intellectual leadership, for students of world affairs to offer new understandings of politics that are consistent with the emergent patterns and that may thus enhance the way in which the world's politicians, journalists, and publics perceive the processes in which they participate. In the absence of such leadership, global political institutions may change faster than the world's capacity to comprehend them, and orderly mechanisms for resolving conflict will then surely be more unobtainable than ever.

But it is not only policy problems that provoke inquiry into the nature of postinternational politics. It is also intellectually provocative. It poses a puzzle that triggers curiosity and elicits an urge to probe beyond policy concerns to those deeper levels of experience where only broad-gauged theory can begin to offer meaningful explanations. The puzzle is embodied in the fact that turbulent conditions have developed despite the wishes of all concerned. With few exceptions, no one wants or enjoys prolonged turbulence. Calm and stability are everywhere preferred to commotion and uncertainty, and yet swift-moving cascades have become a prime characteristic of world politics. Why? If governments, publics, and citizens much prefer routinized and predictable politics, how is it that these preferences have so little effect on the prevailing realities?

Easy answers abound. Human greed and aggression might be cited. So could the power drives of ruling elites. Appealing as such explanations might be, however, they are largely erroneous. For the greedy, the aggressive, and the power-hungry are no less anxious to avoid turbulence than anyone else. They are better able to realize their aspirations in a static environment than in a dynamic one. The more commotion disturbs the course of events, the less certain it is that their exploitative goals will be met. Like everyone else, therefore, even the most noxious of actors are unlikely to perceive turbulence as a desirable condition. They may differ as to what constitutes stability, and these differences may lead to conflicts that contribute to turbulence, but their goals are based on a preference for an order that accommodates their conflicts within established parameters.

The turbulence puzzle, then, is a profound one. It consists of complex pieces that do not fit readily together and thus serves as an endless provocation to the intellect, to our capacity to grasp those individual, organizational, and international dynamics in which actions are negations of values and outcomes are discrepant from intentions. Such is the puzzle that energizes the ensuing chapters.

A NOTE ON METHODOLOGY

While it is readily acknowledged that the theory presented here is founded on inferences and interpretations rather than systematic data, on hypotheses that cry out for rigorous assessment as well as vigorous assertion, there is nevertheless throughout an underlying sensitivity to questions of method. To be short on evidence is not to be inattentive to the need for evidence, and the recognition that theoretical propositions must ultimately be subjected to empirical tests serves to constrain and discipline the inquiry.

What follows, in short, is not unfettered interpretation. It does have a methodology, which might be called that of *potential observability*. In this procedure, each step in the construction of a model is taken only after a determination of whether its components are at least theoretically susceptible to being observed, even if some innovation in observational technologies must first be made. If such a susceptibility cannot be specified with respect to any component—if, say, a component is conceived in mystical terms—then the method of potential observability requires that it be reformulated or abandoned. Accordingly, while the model may be abstract and speculative, it is grounded in hypothetical observables that may or may not uphold its propositions.

The choice of such a methodology stems from the convictions that the processes of knowledge building are variable, that they can only be as rigorous as prior understandings of the subject allow, and that the methods one uses must thus be compatible with these substantive limits. Since knowledge of change and turbulence in world affairs is in key respects rudimentary, so must be the procedures used to trace the dynamics that drive global politics. This is not the time to sacrifice perspective for rigor, or at least it is not such a time if the literature does not provide bases for assessing transformations and differentiating them from continuities. Yet neither is it a time for sheer conjecture or unrestrained intuition. Some discipline needs to guide the inquiry, some sense of what can be systematically explored and what is beyond documentation; and to maintain this modicum of discipline, the broad perspective on which the analysis is founded must be cast in terms of that which would be observable if the resources and technologies for observation become available.

The dynamics of atmospheric turbulence provide a good example of how the method of potential observability can yield valuable insights. Until recently, the task of describing how a tornado forms in a fast-moving thunderstorm was one of the most complex and vexing scientific problems, requiring dozens of mathematical equations that could be solved only through the derivation of billions of numbers. With the advent of powerful supercomputers, however, not only can such problems be solved, but, equally important, the supercomputers, by converting the numbers into images that appear as two- or three-dimensional pictures or movies on computer screens, make it possible to observe how a tornado forms. In like manner, three-dimensional simulations of the functioning of transistors, human bodies, and cricket brains are among the many other previously inaccessible processes that have now become visible. In effect, what was once only theoretically observable has become actually observable, a classic case of how the methodology of potential observability allows for cogent theorizing in the absence of presently available empirical materials.[11]

This is not to imply that all the evidence relevant to turbulent political change is murky. Some of it consists of clear-cut socioeconomic indicators that depict the expansion of interdependence on a global scale. Greater interdependence among the world's financial institutions, for example, is readily discernible in data on capital flows, just as the global repercussions of resource shortages and population explosions are readily traced in energy and demographic statistics. On the other hand, the argument pertaining to the transformation of underlying political structures and processes also focuses on emergent sociopsychological patterns that are not nearly so manifest and thus require inferences from a skimpy and inchoate data base. Consider, for

[11] Cf. John Markoff, "Supercomputer Pictures Solve the Once Insoluble," *New York Times*, October 30, 1988, sec. 1, p. 1.

instance, the shifting patterns of legitimacy, loyalty, and authority relations that might be weakening whole systems and strengthening subgroups: one's political antennae can pick up the emergence and spread of such attitudinal dynamics even though systematic empirical materials that demonstrate their operation have yet to be compiled. An anomalous situation, an isolated discrepancy, an unusual development, a transient sequence, an arresting event—these must be, perforce, included among the components of the data base, leaving the analyst who makes the case for the supersession of the state-centric system by a bifurcated global politics vulnerable to charges of engaging more in fantasizing than theorizing.

Yet, while adhering to the rule that allowance must be made for eventual systematic observation, analysts need not shy away from probing unusual and anomalous circumstances. If practiced conscientiously, the method of potential observability enables them to rely on their political antennae while protecting them from the danger of succumbing to impulsive interpretations, wishful thinking, or any other form of unrestrained impressions. The appearance of dramatic and unmistakable changes that cascaded across the world scene in 1988 are illustrative in this regard. Within the space of a few weeks, the Soviet Union, Taiwan, Mexico, and South Korea witnessed sharp reversals of course, turning points in which long-standing patterns, institutions, or policies were abandoned and replaced with others that were unthinkable only a short time earlier. Each of these developments—the Communist party conference convened by General Secretary Mikhail Gorbachev in Moscow, the Taiwan regime's grant of permission for visits to the mainland, the governing party's electoral losses in Mexico, and South Korea's announcement that it would allow trade, family visits, and student exchanges with North Korea—can be explained by particular historical circumstances unique to each country and consistent with the realist presumption that political actors endlessly seek to maximize their power. But, relying on the method of potential observability, one may well detect other signals amid the noise of idiosyncratic events. Why did all these reversals occur within the same brief span of time? The simultaneity of such developments becomes even more impressive when the time span is broadened by a few years, yielding comparable events in Poland, Germany, the Philippines, Sri Lanka, India, Haiti, UNESCO, the Catholic church, the Episcopal church, and the West Bank (to mention but a few of the more conspicuous examples). Is it sheer fantasizing to seek in these events a causal dynamic that is more encompassing than their particular historical antecedents and, in so doing, to discern that in each case stirrings at the micro level were at work? Is it mere wishful thinking to note that in at least three of these instances, the upheavals occurred to the surprise and without the initial support of established leaderships—the workers at Polish steel plants struck without encouragement from the leaders of the Solidarity trade union, the young people in Gaza and the West Bank launched their uprising without the leadership of the PLO, and the students in Seoul rioted without support from the leaders of the opposition parties in South Korea—and to believe that the similarity of these developments suggests the presence of shifting orientations toward authority and legitimacy? Does one avoid searching for patterns in the confluence of these diverse instances of change only because systematic data for probing their juxtaposition are not presently available?

Clearly, negative responses are in order. If one finds simultaneity as well as similarity among such events in so many diverse locales of the global system, and if the method of potential observability provides confidence that such developments are susceptible to systematic analysis, then it is surely reasonable to proceed from the hypothesis that underlying structural changes at the macro level and fundamental skill transformations at the micro level may be causally operative.

Perhaps an even more important advantage of the potential observability methodology is that it enables one to hypothesize about the ways in which minuscule developments at the micro level may culminate in unexpected and seemingly discrepant macro outcomes. Substantial time lags involving changes across generations, for example, can intervene between shifts in the attitudinal dynamics underlying authority relations and the manifestations of these parametric transformations in the structures of whole systems and their subsystems. Yet such systemic outcomes cannot be anticipated if one's methods confine analysis only to those short-run patterns that are immediately subject to observation.

Medical science offers an apt analogy for the analysis of discrepancies between micro events and macro outcomes. Consider the situation that obtains when the human heart undergoes fibrillation, a process that consists of a frenzied heartbeat which results in death unless the fibrillation can be stopped: even as the heart's muscle tissue writhes in a chaotic way that renders it unable to pump blood, the individual muscle cells continue to function normally as each receives its stimulus, contracts, passes the stimulus on, and relaxes to wait for the next stimulus. The result is that "the parts seem to be working, yet the whole goes fatally awry."[12] In the same way, it seems plausible that for a

[12] James Gleick, "Computers Attack Heart Disease," *New York Times*, August 5, 1986, p. C3.

lengthy period individuals and publics act in conventional ways, exhibiting the signs of legitimacy, loyalty, and compliance to authority that are appropriate to a state-centric system, even as their underlying orientations are undergoing redirection toward their most salient subgroups. Then, just as the heart suddenly collapses, so there is a point when it becomes evident that the appearance of continuity in world politics masks the presence of extensive turbulence, when the state-centric system has been superseded by one that is bifurcated.[13]

Further amplification of how one's political antennae may have to rely on an inchoate data base to trace the flow of attitudinal dynamics and the advent of a bifurcated world is offered in chapter 5. It outlines a number of anomalous events that have lately marked the global scene—diverse events that bear no relation to each other but are all anomalies in the sense that none can be satisfactorily explained by any existing theories of world politics. Anomalies may or may not be important indicators of change. Some may prove to be merely random, nonsignificant deviations from a long-term trend: a particular leader with a quirky personality, a radical movement with a fickle following, a natural disaster that ravages an economy. The impact of such anomalies can fade quickly as time passes and the underlying tendencies resume. Yet it is only in retrospect that anomalies can be judged as irrelevant. At the time of their occurrence, there is no way of knowing whether or not they are the first surfacing of shifts in underlying structures. What does the advent of the quirky leader indicate about the coherence and values of the community that facilitated his rise to the top? What does the emergence of the radical movement suggest about that society's potential for change? What does the slow recovery from the natural disaster reveal about the robustness of that country's economy? Such are the questions to which anomalies give rise, and, under conditions of political turbulence, they ought not be lightly dismissed. It is always possible that the anomaly is a forerunner—that the quirky leader reflected public demands in the process of crystallization, that the radical movement gave voice to widespread latent frustrations, that the natural disaster proved disastrous because the economy's infrastructure had been in a long period of unrecognized decay.

So attention to anomalies must accompany any effort to conceptu-

---

[13] As will be seen, apparent turbulence can also mask the reality of an underlying continuity, depending on the time and systemic perspective employed. If events seem capable of disturbing the parameters of a system—as often happens during cabinet crises in Italy—a period of turbulence may seem in the offing. But if the parameters hold firm and the crisis subsides—as normally occurs when new cabinets are formed in Italy—the seeming threat of turbulence is belied by the system's underlying equilibrium.

alize and trace transformations in world affairs. At the very least, they alert one to the possible onset of change. At most, they can lay bare the dynamics that may be transforming global structures and processes even though all the parts seem to be functioning normally. And indeed, as the seizure of the U.S. embassy in Iran in 1979 revealed, today's anomalies do loom as portents of profound transformations in the norms that sustain interstate relations. Strong passions are at work in world politics, burdening one's antennae with overload, with intimations that surface appearances may, like the fibrillating heart, conceal an unstable world going awry.

If inchoate data provoke a dim sense of change, if an intuitive piecing together of diverse, seemingly unrelated occurrences hints at the presence of underlying forces far more powerful and profound than we can begin to imagine, then there is reason to adopt the methodology of potential observability. For, to repeat, it is a methodology that allows for theorizing about dynamics that may not yet have surfaced in the form of clear-cut socioeconomic patterns, even while it insists that developments in global politics be susceptible to empirical analysis.

The presumption that potentially observable patterns underlie anomalies and ambiguous developments poses a difficult measurement problem. By what criteria does the observer dismiss some anomalies and ambiguities as isolated events while regarding others as the basis for hypothesizing about the presence of emergent patterns? This question is necessarily answered with a generalization, but one that takes advantage of a unit of measurement that is sufficiently flexible to be applied to a wide array of turbulent situations. The criteria are those that distinguish anomalies and ambiguities reflective of noticeable and durable changes from those that are inconspicuous and transitory. Much of the warp and woof of daily life consists of minor fluctuations, momentary deviations which soon revert back to established modes. Persistent differences and new patterns are rare occurrences. These differences, even those that may at first be barely noticeable, do not evolve out of peripheral events or minor developments; rather, they derive from systemic changes, else they would not persist as discernable alterations of prior practices. Thus, enduring changes cannot be distinguished from ephemeral ones without a clear conception of how the observed anomalies and ambiguities are linked to underlying processes capable of bringing forth new structures and processes. In the absence of such a conception, the anomalies and ambiguities might well be treated as mere aberrations of little lasting consequence.

The notion of a *just noticeable difference* (JND) will be used here as the basis for exploring the onset and consequences of turbulence. Coupled with the methodology of potential observability, a JND becomes, in effect, a measurement unit for making an initial foray into seemingly new and unfamiliar developments. If it is reasonable to presume that such developments constitute at least one JND and that they are therefore potentially susceptible to being traced, it also seems imperative to investigate their possible sources and consequences.

To propose that a change must amount to at least one JND before it merits our attention is to impose discipline on our analysis. Detecting the presence of a JND requires that we avoid guesswork and instead engage in careful hypothesizing about the implications of unfamiliar occurrences. To be sure, at some point JNDs must be rendered more specific and precisely operationalized in different ways, depending on whether one is analyzing changes in, say, the compliance of citizens, the scope of authority, or the competence of governments. For present purposes, however, they serve well as generic units of measurement designed to spur and clarify thought about possible developments that seem likely to deviate enough from expected patterns to be provocative and worthy of explanation.

A Note on the Observer

A comment is also in order as to where the analyst fits in the method of potential observability. Clearly, he or she is not neutral. The readiness to follow a dim, intuitive sense that change is at work, the reliance on analytic antennae, the recognition of anomalies, and the identification of JNDs all draw upon the values of observers as well as upon their analytic skills. What one analyst looking for change treats as an anomaly, another wedded to continuity interprets as merely one more instance of a recurring pattern. It cannot be otherwise. There may be an objective reality in world politics, but analysts can perceive it only through prisms fashioned by their past experiences and present values as well as by their training and methodological discipline.

Inevitably, therefore, science is not so much a value-free enterprise as a value-explicit one. It requires observers to be clear about their presence in the research, to acknowledge biases and idiosyncratic perspectives that may skew their interpretations. Most of all, it demands that observers alert their readers to the dangers of being taken in by the analysis, and remind them that what they are reading is not so much a detached view of the world as one analyst's perspective, with all the possibilities of distortion that may be involved. In this way, science insures that its findings can be checked and, if need be, revised or rejected.

Here, the presence of the observer has been insured in at least three ways. A point of view that emphasizes the role of micro dynamics has already been noted; in later chapters, the possibility that this viewpoint may be rooted in an idealistic liberalism is also acknowledged (but denied). Second, by adopting an explicit methodology that necessitates concern for observability, the reader is offered a basis for ascertaining whether the observer is living by his own discipline. Lastly, the titles of the first eleven chapters have been deliberately worded for the purpose of indicating that the analyst is ever present. That the remaining chapter titles are not so worded is only to spare readers undue repetition. Hopefully, they will need no reminders of the presence of the author by the time they reach the last sections of the book.[14]

NOTES ON TERMINOLOGY

If the world is changing as much as the ensuing analysis contends, thus confronting us with the monumental challenge of breaking out of our present conceptual jails in order to appreciate the transformations, it seems imperative to make terminological adjustments that allow for a departure from conventional analytic habits and facilitate recognition of emergent structures and processes. Periods of transformation tend to undermine conceptual clarity. Inevitably, there is a lag between changes in public affairs and the terminological adjustments needed to fully grasp the changes. As one observer puts it:

> Clear categories seem to have accompanied imperial world structures. Periods such as the late 19th Century or the 1950s and 1960s, in which we have clear conceptualizations of what the social sciences ought to be doing, have been periods in which the world itself appeared to be much clearer, at least in terms of architectonic world structures. As these structures lose their clarity, so do the categories of social science lose their limpidity and rigor. We are in a period today, both conceptually and structurally, that is characterized by imprecision and amorphousness.[15]

So as to avoid, or at least minimize, the ambiguities that attach to the conventional labels presently used to probe world politics, several new terms have been developed and applied in the ensuing analysis.

[14] This is another way of saying that I do not subscribe to the tenets of postmodern inquiry most succinctly summarized in "The Death of the Author," a chapter of Roland Barthes, *Image, Music, Text* (New York: Hill & Wang, 1977), pp. 143–48.

[15] Frederic E. Wakeman, Jr., "Transnational and Comparative Research," *Items* 42 (December 1988): 87.

One of the ambiguities has already been noted: it would surely be difficult to appreciate fully the bifurcation of global life if we continue to approach it from the perspective of "international politics." Much of the politics here subjected to scrutiny is not international at all. It extends across national boundaries, to be sure, but it is not confined to the interaction of nation-states. Hence, except when there is occasion to refer exclusively to government-to-government relations in the state-centric world, the term "international" has been eschewed in the chapters that follow and, instead, the terms *global, world,* or *postinternational* politics are used to refer to people, goods, and ideas that span the borders of countries in a political context.[16]

At the same time, world politics is not conceived to refer only to those activities with repercussions that reach into every corner of the globe. Some issues, such as nuclear energy or human rights, do encompass macro and micro actors everywhere, but many are only regional, subregional, or dyadic in scope. Nevertheless, these more limited activities are conceived to be aspects of global politics in the sense that the structures and processes of the bifurcated world have brought the entire range of such phenomenon into the same context, making them all potentially subject to the boundary-crossing repercussions precipitated by any of them.

In other words, just as knowledge about the national politics of a country involves comprehension of developments in its southwestern or northeastern subsystems and not just issues involving all or most of its actors, so does a full grasp of global politics require an understanding of the repercussions of events in East Asia or the Caribbean, of an explosion at Chernobyl or an intervention in Vietnam. Similarly, to cite another example of the broad meaning attached to the concept of world politics, just as a specialist in U.S. politics can anticipate the ramifications for the Republican or Democratic parties of a persistent increase in the rate of inflation, so ought a competent student of global politics know enough about the dynamics of its structures to appreciate that the rise of an outspoken and cohesive trade-union movement in Poland or a plan to bury German-American wartime animosities by a presidential visit to Bitburg will precipitate particular kinds of

---

[16] Tooze has applied a similar line of reasoning to the realm of economics: "Given the existence of a world economy of production, service, finance and knowledge structures—which are not territorially bounded—alongside 'traditional' international economy, the term 'world political economy' is more appropriate and captures the complexity of the present configuration in a way that 'international' cannot." Roger Tooze, "The Unwritten Preface: 'International Political Economy' and Epistemology," *Millennium: Journal of International Studies* 17 (Summer 1988): 287.

boundary-crossing repercussions that traverse a path through specific types of collectivities and subgroups.

In order to achieve an analytic parallel among the actors of the state-centric and multi-centric worlds, it also seems appropriate to use terminology that treats the state as merely one type of politically relevant entity. Hence, the terms *collectivity* and *whole system* are employed as generic labels for any organized, multipurpose cluster of people whose coordinated actions or concerns have boundary-crossing consequences.

States are surely central types of actors, and their presence in world politics thus ought not be downgraded or dismissed, but the analysis would be needlessly obscured if its terminology prevented recognition of any decline in their competence relative to other types of collectivities. Accordingly, so as to avoid attaching an unwarranted preeminence to states, the term "nonstate actor" does not appear again in this volume. This term creates a residual category for all collectivities other than states, implying that they occupy subordinate statuses in the ranks of postinternational politics. Such may be the case in the state-centric world, but it does not apply to the structure of the multi-centric world. How, then, to differentiate among collectivities that are states and those that are not? The answer proposed here suggests both the essential difference between the two types of actors and the nonhierarchical structure of the multi-centric world: states are conceived to be *sovereignty-bound* actors, while multinational corporations, ethnic groups, bureaucratic agencies, political parties, subnational governments, transnational societies, international organizations, and a host of other types of collectivities are called *sovereignty-free* actors.

The virtue of this terminology is that it calls attention to the ways in which states are limited by the very considerations that are usually regarded as the source of their strengths. To regard a state as bound by its sovereign responsibilities—the need to monitor the vast array of issues that comprise the global agenda and then to allocate resources among them in order to preserve and enhance its integrity and welfare—is to underscore its vulnerabilities and its inability to concentrate prerogatives and energies upon a few selective goals. The responsibilities of sovereignty-free collectivities, on the other hand, are not so dispersed. They can pursue limited objectives, and they can move forward without diverting their resources to a wide range of other obligations. Thus, the new terminology serves as a continual reminder that the differences between states and other collectivities may not be as one-sided as they are usually assumed to be.

One other terminological innovation needs to be noted. In order to avoid losing touch with the premise that the form and direction of actions in world politics spring from a combination of habits that perpetuate continuity and adaptive learning that fosters change, a new term is coined (see chapter 9) that reflects their synthesis. Those hypothetically located at the two extremes are referred to, respectively, as *rote-like* and *adaptive* actors, while those who stand between extremes are considered to be *habdaptive* actors. This term may seen ungainly and offensive at first, but eventually those disadvantages will be outweighed by its utility as a reminder of the prime components of action.

Breaking Out of Conceptual Jails

The inclusion in this chapter of remarks on the necessity of employing a special form of theorizing, a distinctive methodology, and different terminology suggests that the study of turbulence in world politics is, like turbulence itself, attended by disruptive consequences. And indeed it is. The proposition that the parameters of global politics are undergoing profound and permanent transformation challenges analysts to be open to making corresponding alterations in the conceptual premises with which they organize and interpret the course of events. As stressed earlier, this can mean that long-standing and comfortable analytic impulses may have to be quelled, even abandoned, if the portents of the observed changes are to be adequately assessed; it can necessitate acknowledging that what was once given is now problematic; it can even require accepting that what once seemed conceptually impossible may now be emerging as empirical reality—all startling steps that can disturb even the most dedicated observers and burden them with a sense of being caught up in unfamiliar analytic tasks that can readily slip out of control.

No less than anyone else, students of world politics live and work in conceptual jails: while their frameworks, models, and paradigms serve them well as creative guides to the framing and analysis of problems, the same conceptual equipment may blind them to change that lies outside its scope. Such is the dilemma we face today. Accustomed to presuming a state system predominantly composed of sovereign states authorized to address and cope with change, we are unlikely to inquire whether states have been weakened and their micro components strengthened, whether the nature of force, legitimacy, and authority relations has undergone meaningful redefinition, whether the state system continues to be the prime organizer of global politics, or whether another world has emerged alongside the state system as the basis for world order.

Furthermore, the sturdiness of our conceptual jails derives from cultural premises as well as from analytic needs. One can imagine success at refurbishing or replacing the concepts we employ, but moving beyond the values rooted in our cultural experience can seem impossible. Consider, for example, the problem posed for Western analysts by North-South issues, by the demands emanating from the countries of the Third World. Just as politicians and publics in industrialized countries have often misread the values, motives, and structures that constitute life in the developing countries—the U.S. blunders in Vietnam being but the most obvious of many examples that could be cited—so it may be that many First World students of world politics have inappropriately imposed their Western conceptions of international processes on the interactions that sustain relationships among countries of the Third World and between them and the First and Second Worlds. Analysts in developing countries tend to proceed from the premise that states ordinarily ground their behavior on a mix of legal and rational calculations that, whatever their ultimate effectiveness, involve compliance with certain rules through which comity and a minimal degree of order are maintained. Even resort to violence and war is presumed to be undertaken in the framework of Western precedents and constraints. Whether the same mix of decision rules operates as unfailingly in the Third World, however, has not been adequately conceptualized and is thus open to question.[17]

So how to proceed? Since our paradigms do provide us with a coherent view of the world in which we live and with a basis for rejecting any alternative explanations of why and how that world functions as it does, how can we move outside them? How can we, as first-world analysts, diminish the value biases in our conceptual equipment so that it is equally sensitive to the dynamics of developed and developing countries and enables us to analyze their actions and interactions in a common context? How can we frame explanations of the conditions under which non-Western actors resort to terrorism, resist seemingly superior military force, defy threats of economic sanctions, unilaterally cancel foreign debts, or otherwise engage in practices that violate the underlying values and practices of the Western state system and capitalistic world economy?[18]

[17] Cf. Bahgat Korany, "The Take-Off of Third World Studies? The Case of Foreign Policy," World Politics 35 (April 1983): 465–87, and Bahgat Korany, "Strategic Studies and the Third World," International Social Science Journal 38, no. 4 (1986): 547–62.

[18] This is not to imply that assessments of north-south differences undertaken by a

One line of answers to such questions derives from the convictions that the most efficacious way to break free of conceptual jails is to do it boldly, all at once, cleanly. This means finding, where possible, conceptual equipment that is relatively free of cultural bias, that embraces cultures rather than reflecting only one or another of them. In the case of North-South relations, for example, such a daring break can be accomplished by founding analysis, not on the Western concept of a state system, but on structures and processes that are so universal as to be central in both the First and the Third Worlds. That is, with the globe becoming smaller and more interdependent, with causal flows cascading among and within collectivities in crazy-quilt patterns new to world politics, and with Western perspectives no longer predominant, we can break free by conceiving of humanity, not as a collection of countries or relations among states, but as a congeries of authority relationships, some of which are coterminous with countries and states and others of which are either located within or extend beyond state boundaries. Mapped in this way, the globe more nearly approximates present-day experience than does the conventional portrayal of some 160 territorial units. Such a map highlights the many subnational, supranational, and transnational entities that have acquired salience as the complexity and interdependence of global life have become ever greater. This step also allows us to focus on the full array of North-South interactions without loading the analysis in a "northerly" direction.[19]

While this escape route is used in the ensuing discussion, it is plainly not sufficient for a successful jailbreak if one is seeking to ascertain whether a new form of world order is superseding the state system. For that, an even more innovative method is needed, if we are to free ourselves from the clutches of the prevailing state-centered paradigm. Effective jailbreaks require giant steps, a counterintuitive daring that ignores long-standing givens and starts afresh with new but not unreasonable assumptions. What is needed, in other words, are intel-

---

Western analyst are bound to be erroneous. It is possible that the behavior of actors from the First and Third Worlds differs only in form, that otherwise it stems from similar motives and common sources, so that at least some of the same conceptual equipment can be used in the analysis of both. In the absence of relevant evidence, however, it seems preferable to assume that significant differences do exist. At the very least, such a procedure forces us to assess the adequacy of our conceptual storehouse; at best, it may lead us to new and important insights into the fundamental dynamics of global politics today.

[19] Admittedly, though, reliance on authority relationships as a universal concept may not be as sure a route to a jailbreak as it seems. Quite possibly, such relationships can serve as a universal concept "central in both the North and the South" precisely because, historically, the former has imposed its conceptions of authority on the latter.

lectual leaps that carry one beyond the confines of existing models and enable one to see nation-states as merely embedded in, rather than presiding over, the complexities of a shrinking, ever-more interdependent political universe.

To effect such a jailbreak, the following analysis is founded on five main guidelines, each of which is designed to facilitate delineation of a multi-centric world of postinternational politics while at the same time not precluding the continued functioning of the state-centric world. The former may never supersede the latter, but glimpses of its existence ought at least to be possible through adherence to the five guidelines. These guidelines are set forth below and also serve as a measure of the seriousness with which the need for a thoroughgoing jailbreak is regarded:

1. Suspend a tendency to describe actors' statuses in terms of sovereignty and resources, and instead identify actors by first locating the authority structures out of which their action emanates and then clarifying the ways in which the structures shape the consequences that flow from the exercise of authority.

   1.1. Recognize that what makes actors effective in world politics derives not from the sovereignty they possess or the legal privileges thereby accorded them, but rather lies in relational phenomena, in the authority they can command and the compliance they can thereby elicit.

   1.2. Accept the proposition that the sovereignty of actors may constrain their actions and effectiveness (in the sense that it imposes responsibilities and obligations which must be met in order to preserve their authority and which can thus divert resources and energy from the service of other goals) and that those actors who lack sovereignty may therefore be freer to exercise the full measure of their authority on behalf of goals.

   1.3. Reinforce the foregoing by expanding the terminology used to analyze world politics in such a way as to use labels that do not automatically accord superior status to nation-states. As noted, this can be accomplished by not clustering all other entities under the residual category of "nonstate actors" but instead by designating states as "sovereignty-bound" actors and referring to the others as "sovereignty-free" actors.

   1.4. Allow for the possibility that, when actors are defined in terms of authority structures, global politics emerges as a universe of two interactive worlds, one organized in terms of the state-centric institutions of sovereignty-bound actors and another that operates through the multi-centric processes of sovereignty-bound and sovereignty-free actors.

    1.5. Appreciate that the virtue of referring to the two clusters of collectivities as "worlds" is that they are thus differentiated without any implication that they are themselves actors or that they possess the coherence and authority structures that distinguish collectivities and systems.

2. Having traced actions and reactions to structures of authority, cease attempting to rank these structures in a hierarchical order of importance and, instead, acknowledge that importance attaches to all those who have authority to initiate and sustain actions that may have repercussions beyond the boundaries of countries.

    2.1. Do not retreat if the initiators-of-action perspective leads to the presumption that subnational and supranational actors are just as important as national actors.

    2.2. Strengthen the resistance to a hierarchical conception of relations among actors by recalling that outcomes occur in relationships mainly through bargaining and only seldom through the unrestrained exercise of superior capabilities (that is, except under the most unusual circumstances, superiors have to negotiate with subordinates if they are to achieve the latters' compliance with their directives).

3. Having accepted that subnational and supranational sovereignty-free actors may be as relevant as sovereignty-bound actors, render all of them comparable on the same analytic plane by conceiving of whole systems and subsystems as the cast of characters at the macro level that, along with individuals at the micro level, act out global dramas.

    3.1. Identify whole systems as collectivities or organizations with agendas open to a broad range of issues, whereas subsystems are collectivities or organizations with narrow agendas receptive to only selected types of issues.

    3.2. Treat the boundaries of whole systems and subsystems as those traced by the structures of authority through which their agendas are compiled and considered.

    3.3. Recognize that this mode of identifying systems and subsystems negates the conventional notion of systemic levels, for some whole systems may be embedded in the authority structures of other whole systems even as they encompass their own subsystems.

3.4. Understand, too, that giving up the traditional idea of systemic levels also involves breaking free of the presumption that the domain of "domestic" politics is separate from the domain of "international" politics and, instead, viewing the two as woven together around and through the historical and legal boundaries that allegedly separate them.

4. Avoid defining interdependence in terms of overlapping needs and wants in favor of conceiving of it as existing whenever two or more whole systems and/or subsystems have one or more of the same issues on their agendas.

4.1. Understand that actions relevant to issues on the agendas of two or more whole systems or subsystems in the multicentric world are likely to cascade across and through all systems via diverse routes and with varying intensities, resulting in what might be called a *repercussive* politics, paralleling the *interactive* politics of the state-to-state world.

4.2. Appreciate also that different types of cascades give rise to different forms of interdependence—among whole systems as well as between whole systems and the subsystems of other whole systems.

5. Abandon the preoccupation with the locus of final authority, the existence of sovereignty, and the capacity to enforce decisions, and focus instead on how outcomes are produced and controlled.

5.1. Conceive of outcomes as the product of both symmetrical interactions and asymmetrical cascades, in which each action may either provoke reactions or trigger actions directed at other parties.

5.2. Recognize that increasingly severe limits constrain the threat and use of armed force as a means of controlling outcomes in global politics.

5.3. Be prepared to accept that, with resort to armed force ordinarily not feasible and its infeasibility understood by all actors, most important outcomes are produced by so many diverse whole systems and subsystems as to result in their effective control by none.

Taking such huge steps is, to repeat, far from easy. Among other things, they arouse a deep ambivalence. On the other hand, a heady sense of intellectual freedom and power accompanies breaks from conceptual jails. It leads one to want to demonstrate the superiority of the perspectives achieved through the jailbreak over those left behind—

say, by delineating how a focus on outcomes identifies a number of ways in which some systems and subsystems do, despite numerous assertions to the contrary,[20] rival the most powerful of nation-states; or by contrasting the notion of a transnational cascade with that of an international event and showing how the former may be more reflective of the emergent structures and processes of global politics than the latter; or by stressing how the inclusion of subsystems as sources of action brings out the crucial role of bureaucracies and obviates the necessity of treating the state as a unitary actor.

On the other hand, conceptual jailbreaks also induce apprehension, a fear of wandering aimlessly or of eventually getting caught and being reincarcerated within the confines of the same limited and outmoded perspectives. Most notable, perhaps, is the uneasy sense that to depart so sharply from the conventional is to risk the possibility that one is tailoring reality to fit theory, rather than vice versa, a sobering consideration that exerts pressure to backtrack and introduce a host of qualifications and modifications that, in effect, reduce the intellectual leaps to a token crawl.

But then the ambivalence swings back in a positive direction: once outside the state-centric paradigm, it is important to resist the temptation to defend or modify the steps taken to get there. The opportunities afforded by the jailbreak need to be seized before the enormity of the task paralyzes the will to do so. At least, the idea that global life consists of two coexistent, relatively independent political worlds needs to be explored long enough to see where the five guidelines set forth above lead and whether they facilitate an understanding of the emergent global order better than do the extant approaches. There will be ample inducement to return to the comfort of earlier paradigms if the guidelines prove to be inadequate to the task of clarifying the dynamics presently transforming world politics.

And then still another reversal: Will the guidelines indeed lead to an effective jailbreak? Will they prove responsive to Smelser's call for a rethinking of fundamental assumptions about the primary unit of analysis? Are they a proper answer to Przeworski's assertion that we are ill prepared to study interdependence on a global scale? Are they enough to overcome the inclination to interpret anomalous events as temporary deviations rather than as portents of a new order? Are they sufficient to prevent us from ransacking history for examples that demonstrate that the seemingly new developments are merely old patterns unfolding in a contemporary context? Do they lead us to succumb so

[20] See, for example, Waltz, *Theory of International Politics*, p. 95.

fully to the jailbreaking impulse that it becomes a goal unto itself, a driving aspiration that leads to the overinterpretation of change and the neglect of historical continuities that remain in place?

Readers will, of course, have to develop their own answers to such questions even as they consider mine, which have evolved through the course of adhering to the foregoing guidelines and resisting all temptations to retreat to earlier formulations. Here, the delineation of the need for multilevel theorizing, for the method of potential observability, for the use of new terminology, and for fashioning a jailbreak offers only the beginning of an inner turbulence that leads the analysis into a consideration of counterintuitive perspectives and a disciplined openness both to reaffirming established concepts where appropriate and to replacing them with new formulations where necessary. It is an inner turbulence that befits the time and the task.

PART TWO

ESSENTIAL
ELEMENTS

CHAPTER 3

DELINEATING DISORDER
Chaos, Complexity, and Change

> We like patterns—we like patterns in waves, and we like pat-
> terns in a fire, and we see a flock of birds in the sky and we see
> a pattern in the overall movement. That's the beauty of the
> whole system, but it's also the thing that screws up human in-
> vestigators.
>
> —William M. Hamner[1]

> The habits of the past have been compelling, and even though
> previous experience warns of caution, the sense of social
> change is so vivid and the changes in social structure so dra-
> matic that each sociological theorist of any pretension carries
> a distinctive conceptual map of the social terrain and a set of
> signposts to the society ahead.
>
> —Daniel Bell[2]

TO KEEP ABREAST of the rapid pace of global events and place
them in a larger context that enables one to tease meaning out of their
apparent disorder, it is not enough to sense that deep changes are at
work. Rather, one has to develop an overall perspective on the essential nature of world politics through which to transform the perceptions of a disorderly world into sensitivities for the sources and consequences of the dynamics of change.

There can, of course, be wide disagreements over the adequacy of
particular approaches to world politics. Analysts may differ over the
strength and direction of causal processes, and they may even dispute
whether the resulting changes are especially significant. But the adequacy of a given analytic framework is not the central point here. The

---

[1] As quoted in James Gleick, "New Appreciation of the Complexity in a Flock of
Birds," *New York Times*, November 24, 1987, p. C17. Hamner is a zoologist.

[2] *The Coming of Post-Industrial Society: A Venture in Social Forecasting* (New York:
Basic Books, 1973), p. 50.

point is, rather, that some overall approach is needed if the seeming disorder of global life is to be delineated and understood. The lack of such a perspective allows some developments to be inexplicable and thus forecloses the possibility of ever having a coherent and consistent understanding of the unfolding scene. No less serious, to avoid articulating a perspective is to proceed as if it were possible to treat every issue as unique and thus to abandon any hope of discerning whether deep and recurrent patterns underlie the course of events.

Such a perspective need not be elaborate or sophisticated. It need only be explicit and facilitate taking a position on whether causal or random processes are at work in world politics. Being self-conscious about whether one's perspective posits the turbulence of postinternational politics as founded on utter chaos or on underlying structures is a necessary first step in extending one's grasp beyond the current scene and beneath the daily headlines. Without taking such a step, one is always at risk of falling back on the intuitions of the moment and thus failing to see that one's interpretation of issues could spring from some larger context.

As both the zoologist and the sociologist quoted above imply, however, developing an overall perspective is not a simple matter. The dynamics of change can be operative at many points in the social, economic, and political structures that sustain world politics, and discerning the larger patterns they form can be an unrewarding, if not impossible, task, making it easy to yield to the temptation to dismiss the global scene as chaotic and unpredictable. Much of the daily turbulence does appear to be permeated with chaos and randomness. There is hardly a moment when one cannot point to one or another development as confusing and contradictory. For every generalization one can make about actors or situations, there are contrary circumstances that seem to negate it. Such a negative orientation toward causality, however, is intrinsic not to the nature of global politics, but to us as observers. It lies in our capacity to be so overwhelmed by apparent turbulence that we cling to the view that randomness may be at work.

Of course, it is conceivable that all the chaos does reflect randomness. Such a conclusion, however, should be based on more than impressions. At the very least, it is a conclusion that ought not to be reached without first exploring the possibility that appearances are deceiving, that all the disorder we observe is, in fact, ordered, if not orderly. If mathematicians have demonstrated that even chaos can be approached as an expression of underlying patterns,[3] and if it is the

[3] Arun V. Holden, ed., *Chaos* (Princeton: Princeton University Press, 1986).

case that the study of chaos is "a fast-growing movement that is re-shaping the fabric of the scientific establishment,"[4] surely we can afford to pause before yielding to the temptation to view postinternational politics as beset by random turbulence.

There are two good reasons, moreover, why satisfying results will follow from the adoption of an overall perspective based on the premise that what happens in world politics derives from systematic sources and a fundamental orderliness. One is that the alternative to such a procedure is intellectually unacceptable. For the alternative is to assume that things happen by chance, that randomness governs the course of events. Such an assumption is bound, in effect, to bring inquiry and reflection to an end. It means that explanations are deceptive and interpretations meaningless, since that which is being explained or interpreted may well have occurred for no reason whatever. If things can happen for no reason, capriciously, then there is little point for me to continue writing and the reader to continue reading.

Second, if one has any aspiration to use knowledge, or to support its application for the purpose of improving the human condition, then one has to proceed as if there may be an underlying order. This is not so much a matter of idealism—since one's notion of the underlying order may well rest on a conception of political turbulence as rooted in greed and aggressive predispositions—as of practicality. The view that human intelligence is capable of resolving or at least ameliorating problems leaves little choice but to presume that randomness does not govern the problems to which knowledge is applied.

In arguing for the existence of an underlying order, it must be stressed, there is no implication that the order is the one outlined in these chapters. Much of the ensuing analysis may be unduly speculative, perhaps even a bit exaggerated, lending itself more to empirical exploration than to confident assertion. But the presumption is that some underlying order obtains and that it undergirds the course of world politics. It is not more than that, just an initial premise, an article of faith, that is subject neither to proof nor to negation. Any system of thought, be it mathematical or social scientific, must rest on some initial premises—whether they consist of basic axioms for the mathematician, God's design for the spiritual person, or human proclivities for

---

[4] James Gleick, *Chaos: Making a New Science* (New York: Viking, 1987), p. 4. For an exceedingly insightful analysis along similar lines, see Ilya Prigogine and Isabelle Stengers, *Order out of Chaos: Man's New Dialogue with Nature* (New York: Bantam Books, 1984). A more technical discussion of the issues underlying the transformation of modern science is Pierre Bergé, Yves Pomeau, and Christian Vidal, *Order within Chaos: Towards a Deterministic Approach to Turbulence* (New York: John Wiley, 1984).

the social scientist—else there can be no systematizing of the ideas involved.

It is quite another matter, of course, whether the order depicted in the ensuing chapters comes through to the reader as a compelling account of global life at the outset of a new millennium. Hopefully, the account is at least sufficient to counter any inclinations to presume the absence of an underlying order. Chaotic as things may seem, they need not be viewed as beyond comprehension.

The Order in Disorder

While it may at first seem absurd to search for order beneath the disorder of world affairs, this contradiction is resolved when it is recognized that two different concepts of order are involved. In one case, the concept denotes the presumption of causation, the idea that there is a cause for every effect, that nothing happens at random. The causes may not be presently knowable because the technology, resources, or time necessary to observe them is not available, but the premise of an underlying order springs from theoretical and not empirical possibilities. That is, when causative rather than random factors are presumed to be operative, nothing is theoretically beyond comprehension. In this sense, the world is, by an initial, unprovable (but also irrefutable) assumption, an orderly place even though it may also be baffling and mysterious because the tools of observation are inadequate to the tasks of explanation. So as to avoid confusion, this underlying order that is taken on faith and that organizes inquiry will hereafter be referred to as Order 1.

The second meaning of order is quite different. It focuses on content, on the observed patterns of world politics, on what follows from the systematic stimuli that guide behavior, giving it coherence and rendering it repetitive. Variable as people can be, neither individuals nor groups have a boundless repertoire of behaviors on which they can draw to respond to situations. The number of possible responses is limited by culture, by environmental constraints, by role expectations, by historical memories, and by situational determinants. Put differently, the available responses are shaped by intelligence, habits, goals, and needs, so that what people say and do in global life tends to be patterned even as, of course, deviations from the central tendencies are also present and observable. Few, if any, of the patterns are universal, since what people say and do is conditioned by their cultural, regional, and other circumstances, but taken together, the clusters of motives, attitudes, actions, interactions, and relationships form the fundamental arrangements which order the course of events during any historical period. Indeed, it is indicative that when such arrangements break down or otherwise undergo transformation, we speak of the "old order" giving way to a "new" one. Henceforth, so to avoid confusing these structured arrangements with the order posited by the premise that effects have causes, they will be referred to as Order II.

What makes today's Order II seem so chaotic is that many of the basic patterns presently at work in global politics are marked by intense contradictions and erratic fluctuations. One looks out on the world scene and sees upheaval within countries and tensions between them, abject poverty in the Third World and extensive wealth in the First World; and whatever the geographic context, the scene is marked by shrill demands and counterdemands as various groups assert aspirations to which others refuse to accede. So, being distressed by what we observe, we understandably conceive of the world as a very disorderly place, overlooking that all the turbulence reflects the predominant order of present-day global politics, the arrangements through which people relate to each other and over which governments contest each other. Thus it is that there can be order in disorder, a presumption of underlying order (I) and an observation of profound turbulence (II).

It has not always been so and it may not always be so in the future. In other eras, such as the period of balance of power that prevailed through much of the nineteenth century, the arrangements for processing issues were relatively orderly and the challenges to the existing structures of world politics were sporadic and relatively brief. It is not inconceivable that the requirements of an ever more interdependent world will eventually foster movement out of the present disorder and into structures and processes that represent a new, not previously experienced global order.

It is important to stress that the various patterns formed by the dynamics of Order II are not necessarily coordinated. To discern an overall pattern in seemingly disparate activities is to run the risk of presuming that Order II is purposeful, that it is the product of planning or at least of a minimal degree of coordination that enables the pattern to persist. Such need not be the case. As will be seen in the discussion of how macro wholes are fashioned out of micro parts,[5] oft-times the overall patterns of human affairs result from the separate uncoordinated actions of numerous individuals. The "invisible hand" that Adam Smith long ago noted as a central dynamic of capitalist economies is a classic example of uncoordinated Order II. Or consider the

---

[5] See especially the discussion of unintended aggregations in chapter 7.

more mundane illustration of congested traffic: seen from a helicopter, the traffic on a freeway can appear as a smooth pattern in which all motorists are cooperating, an observation which may not be shared by most of the motorists involved.

But, the reader might ask, suppose one concluded that, given the absence of purposeful coordination, the variability of Order II is today one of sheer randomness. Would not one then have to forgo the postulation of an underlying order? Not necessarily. Order I is not a hypothesis to be tested, but an organizing assumption that one holds as a matter of faith and reason. If one's method of inquiry yields an Order II that seems too chaotic to be the result of causes, then one must employ other observational techniques and keep searching for the underlying threads that weave their way through the disorder.[6] Viewed in this way, a central task of this book is to reaffirm Order I by offering an Order II in world politics that makes sense out of the apparent chaos and thereby suggests a solution to the puzzle of why the human condition is marked by turbulence when everyone prefers tranquility.

FROM SUGGESTIVE METAPHOR TO ANALYTIC CONCEPT

Another reason why Order II seems so disorderly is that the late twentieth century is marked by extensive and profound change in numerous realms of individual and collective life. When habits are weakening and new patterns are emerging, when structures and institutions are changing rapidly, when everything seems unsettled and the future thus more obscure than is the case when constancy is the central pattern,

---

[6] A recent example of how new observational techniques can transform chaos into order is provided by oceanographers, who have developed a method analogous to brain scanning that is providing the first global views of the oceans' complex patterns of circulation of temperature. Called *ocean acoustic tomography*, the method has begun to yield "once-hidden movements in the ocean that are apparently as complex as those in the atmosphere." Walter Sullivan, "Vast Effort Aims to Reveal Oceans' Hidden Patterns," *New York Times*, July 28, 1987, p. C1. Another recent example, in this case using computer simulations, involves the patterned behavior of flocks of birds and schools of fish. They were once presumed to be the product of a high level of coordination that far exceeded the intelligence and abilities of any single fish or bird, but computerized techniques are now revealing that the flocking and schooling stems from "the actions of individual fish following individual rules for fleeing predators and staying clear of their neighbors. Thousands of simulated animals are programmed to fly or swim independently, and flock- and school-like behavior emerges on its own." Gleick, "Complexity in a Flock of Birds," p. C1. For a discussion of how economists have subjected the stock market crash of October 1987 to similar types of analysis based on chaos theory, see James Gleick, "When Chaos Rules the Market," *New York Times*, November 22, 1987, sec. 3, p. 1.

then virtually by definition world affairs seem turbulent, out of control, bordering on sheer chaos. Such an appearance is all the more impressive because in fact not everything is changing. Some continuities are also at work, and the endless tensions between change and continuity add to the sense that disorder is pervasive, that Order II has overwhelmed Order I.

It follows that to develop an overall perspective on global politics, we need to formulate a conception of the basic processes at work on the world scene. Disorder is not in itself a process. It is merely a characterization of the system, an interpretation generated by the processes of turbulence, change, and continuity, and it is these three concepts that need to be developed as precise analytic tools.

As noted in chapter 1, it is possible to use the concept of turbulence as a metaphor. It lends itself well to images of what transpires when human affairs are pervaded by commotion, disarray, and the clash of opposing forces. A picture does get conveyed by depicting the world as "hurtling into the future without a sense of the recalcitrances of people and the constraints of institutions that create turbulences in the winds of change."[7] Similarly, the images do seem meaningful when, in the absence of precise terms, stock markets are often portrayed in business columns as turbulent, and elsewhere adolescence is referred to as a turbulent stage of the life cycle, the problems of long-range planning are viewed as more difficult because of "an induced turbulence created by the capacity of central government to change the rules of the game," the entry and exit of firms in an industry is seen as so turbulent as to foster competition, and interdependence in world politics is described as "turbulent" in the title of an article that does not use the word in the text itself.[8]

Analogies to the commotions of nature, in other words, can seem compelling as descriptions of our own plight. They allow us to acknowledge the presence of powerful forces which may, as in nature, eventually subside. That is, since nature is also marked by moments of

[7] Daniel Bell, "The World and the United States in 2013," *Daedalus* 116 (Summer 1987): 5.

[8] Saul Scheidlinger, "The Adolescent Peer Group Revisited: Turbulence or Adaptation?" *Small Group Behavior* 15 (August 1984): 387-97; J. P. Edwards and D. J. Harris, "Planning in a State of Turbulence," *Long Range Planning* 10 (June 1977): 43; M. E. Beesley and R. T. Hamilton, "Small Firms' Seedbed Role and the Concept of Turbulence," *Journal of Industrial Economics* 33 (December 1984): 217–31; J.G.H. Halstead, "Turbulence of World Scene Underlines Interdependence," *International Perspectives*, September/October 1980, pp. 4–8.

calm and tranquility, there is comfort in analogizing to its times of fury, to seeing ourselves, as one author has put it,

> in the rapids of change. The white waters carry us quickly on; we cannot slow down the changes coming to our culture, our society, ourselves. But we do have a choice: we can learn to enjoy turbulence rather than be overwhelmed by it.[9]

Compelling as metaphoric analogies may be, however, they are more a hindrance than a guide if one seeks to acquire a systematic and enduring grasp of world politics. Such is the case here. Our goal is to probe the human condition in its own terms and not through images of stormy weather or rough seas.

Fortunately, pursuit of this goal is facilitated by the fact that there are several disciplines in which the concept of turbulence has been developed as a serious analytic tool. It is, for example, used in various branches of physics, in chemical engineering, and in organizational theory. Indeed, physicists are inclined to see the processes of turbulence as omnipresent:

> Most flows occurring in nature and in engineering applications are turbulent. The boundary layer in the earth's atmosphere is turbulent (except possibly in very stable condition); jet streams in the upper troposphere are turbulent; cumulus clouds are in turbulent motion. The water currents below the surface of the oceans are turbulent; the Gulf Stream is a turbulent wall-jet kind of flow. The photosphere of the sun and the photospheres of similar stars are in turbulent motion; interstellar gas clouds . . . are turbulent; the wake of the earth in the solar wind is presumably a turbulent wake. Boundary layers growing on aircraft wings are turbulent. Most combustion processes involve turbulence and often even depend on it; the flow of natural gas and oil in pipelines is turbulent. Chemical engineers use turbulence to mix and homogenize fluid mixtures and to accelerate chemical reaction rates in liquids or gases. The flow of water in rivers and canals is turbulent; the wakes of ships, cars, submarines, and aircraft are in turbulent motion. The study of turbulence clearly is an interdisciplinary activity, which has a very wide range of applications . . . [Furthermore,] many turbulent flows can be observed easily; watching

[9] Robert Theobald, *The Rapids of Change: Social Entrepreneurship in Turbulent Times* (Indianapolis: Knowledge Systems, 1987), p. 11.

cumulus clouds or the plume of a smokestack is not time wasted for a student of turbulence.[10]

Given the pervasiveness of such phenomena, it is hardly surprising that a large literature, much of it experimental but some also mathematical and analytic, has been produced in physics around what has come to be called "turbulence theory." It is no surprise, given the commotion and uncertainty that attach to turbulence in nature, that many of the central themes of this literature are relevant to our concerns here. Like students of world politics, physicists are captivated by the sheer complexity of their subject matter: "Turbulence is a complicated and many-faceted phenomenon. Notably, turbulent flows have striking and varied spatial organizations, and the onset of a time-dependent turbulence is frequently preceded by the development of fascinatingly complex stationary spatial patterns."[11]

Similarly, with respect to Order I, physicists are not led by the many-faceted dimensions of turbulence to back off from the article of faith on which Order I rests: "Until recently, the practical definition [of turbulence] has been the appearance of apparent randomness in photographs of flows containing materials which permit visualization of streamlines or other features. However, this approach omits the possibility of complex flow patterns that are nevertheless highly ordered."[12] Indeed, a consensus has recently emerged in physics that turbulence is not random, that it does not possess an infinite number of degrees of freedom, that a turbulent flow is not "a structureless meandering" but has, rather, "a well-defined structure," an "order in the midst of chaotic motion."[13]

In the same way, actions in world politics are unlikely to be totally random because, if they violate the underlying order, counteractions

[10] H. Tennekes and J. L. Lumley, *A First Course in Turbulence* (Cambridge: MIT Press, 1972), p. 1.

[11] O. E. Lanford, "Strange Attractors and Turbulence," in H. L. Swinney and J. P. Gollub, eds., *Hydrodynamic Instabilities and the Transition to Turbulence* (New York: Springer-Verlag, 1981), p. 7.

[12] H. L. Swinney and J. P. Gollub, Introduction to Swinney and Gollub, *Hydrodynamic Instabilities*, p. 1.

[13] Trevor H. Moulden, "An Introduction to Turbulence Phenomena," in Walter Frost and Trevor H. Moulden, eds., *Handbook of Turbulence*, vol. 1, *Fundamentals and Applications* (New York: Plenum, 1977), pp. 25–26; Alexandre Chorin, "Lecture II: Theories of Turbulence," in A. Dold and B. Eckmann, eds., *Lecture Notes in Mathematics: Turbulence Seminar, Berkeley 1976/77* (New York: Springer-Verlag, 1977), p. 41. For a similar conclusion, see Trevor H. Moulden, Walter Frost, and Albert H. Garner, "The Complexity of Turbulent Fluid Motion," in Frost and Moulden, *Handbook of Turbulence* 1:3–4.

will be evoked and systemic structures thereby imposed. Thus have aggressors usually produced resistance rather than acquiescence to their expansionist policies; thus have international currency crises often generated cooperative rather than competitive responses; and thus, too, when terrorist organizations strike, they evoke political and diplomatic reactions that, in effect, narrow the degree of freedom within which they can thereafter be active.[14]

As for Order II, the agreed-upon characteristics of turbulent flows in nature have considerable relevance for the analysis of world politics developed in subsequent chapters. Most notably, just as physicists agree that turbulent flows are marked by diffusivity and dissipation, so does the growing interdependence of world politics highlight the degree to which the effects of events in one part of the world tend to spread widely to other corners of the globe and then, eventually, to peter out as public issues. As has been said about the physical world, so can it be said about the political world: "Turbulence needs a continuous supply of energy. . . . If no energy is applied, turbulence decays rapidly."[15]

It follows that "turbulence is not a feature of fluids but of fluid flows,"[16] a conclusion that is central to the present analysis in serving as a reminder that turbulence in world politics is to be found not in individuals or groups but in their interactions. There is nothing inherent in the people of the Soviet Union, the United States, or Iran that renders global life so turbulent. The turbulence is rooted, rather, in the multiplicity and rapidity of the flows of action that link groups and societies together and that conduce to uncertainty as they diffuse widely across the political landscape.

Moreover, just as the turbulence of air flows in the atmosphere derives from diverse sources and from sharp differences in temperature and pressure and wind velocity, so do the inputs into global life originate in all parts of the world and differ vastly in intensity, direction, and scale. If, for example, some of the dynamics that contribute to turbulence in world politics are listed alongside an enumeration of the number and variety of atmospheric processes which, as they simultaneously strengthen or weaken one another, give rise to turbulent air flows, one is likely to be impressed by how similar are the multiplicity,

[14] For example, see Jeffrey T. Richelson and Desmond Ball, *The Ties That Bind: Intelligence Cooperation between the UKUSA Countries—The United Kingdom, the United States of America, Canada, Australia, and New Zealand* (London: Allen & Unwin, 1985).

[15] Tennekes and Lumley, *First Court in Turbulence*, pp. 2–3.

[16] Tennekes and Lumley, *First Course in Turbulence*, p. 3.

complexity, and power of the forces that foster these two forms of turbulence. Table 3.1 presents such a list, to suggest how nature and politics are both driven by the confluence of diverse forces to become worlds in unceasing motion.

Nor are the parallels between turbulence in nature and politics confined to specific empirical processes. Although more coincidence than deliberate convergence, a remarkable correspondence in some of the concepts and terms used to analyze key dynamics in the two fields can

TABLE 3.1. Some Sources of Atmospheric and Political Turbulence

Atmospheric Turbulence[a]	Global Political Turbulence
The friction of the air flow at the Earth's surface and the formation of a wind-velocity profile with large vertical gradients in the lower part of the atmosphere.	The outward pressure of fundamentalist religions and the reactions of conservative governments.
Unequal heating of different regions of the underlying surface of the Earth and the concomitant development of thermal convection.	A felt obligation on the part of superpowers to be involved in issues in any part of the world.
Cloud-forming processes involving the release of the heat of condensation and crystallization and changes in the nature of the temperature and wind-velocity fields.	Efforts by domestic politicians to divert attention to external problems.
Convergence and interaction of air masses with different characteristics near atmospheric fronts and high-altitude frontal zones, where horizontal differences in temperature and wind velocity are large.	Discrepancies in resources and productivity among nations, giving rise to trade imbalances, indebtedness in the Third World, and overextension of the First World's banking system.
Loss of stability by waves formed in inversion layers, at the tropopause, and near other atmospheric surfaces.	Agitation by ethnic minorities in all regions of the world for statehood or greater autonomy.
Deformation of air flows by mountain barriers that produce wavelike disturbances and rotor motions on their lee side.	New technologies in arms, agriculture, communications, and biogenetics.

[a] This column is derived from N. K. Vinnichenko et al., *Turbulence in the Free Atmosphere*, 2nd ed., trans. Frank L. Sinclair (New York: Consultants Bureau, 1980), p. 2.

be discerned. Just as the transformation of the interstate system is here conceived to foster a bifurcation of world politics that may or may not prove to be stable and permanent, so have physicists come to rely on the mathematics of "bifurcation theory" to analyze turbulent flows and trace what happens when these flows "push a system beyond the threshold of stability."[17] The notion that world politics is undergoing bifurcation was developed by abstracting from a series of substantive anomalies, but the use of the concept in physics to uncover the order intrinsic to the breakdown of established patterns—what is called "the primary bifurcation"—closely approximates the effort to uncover the underlying patterns of the seemingly chaotic multi-centric world that has emerged to rival the state-centric world.[18] Just as it is argued here (see chapter 11) that events of world politics can be treated as "cascades," so students of the physical world are investigating "cascading bifurcations and the transitions to chaos."[19] And just as the present analysis culminates in an effort to assess the several scenarios that might evolve out of the bifurcation of world politics (see chapter 16), so have physicists used the idea of "bifurcation," a word coined at the beginning of the twentieth century by Henri Poincaré in his work on systems of differential equations, "to designate the emergence of several solutions from a given solution."[20]

Epistemologically and methodologically, too, the study of turbulence in physics can serve as a guide to clarifying its presence in world affairs. Physicists recognize that "every flow is different," but they nevertheless "disregard the uniqueness of any particular turbulent flow and concentrate on the discovery and formulation of laws that describe entire classes or families of turbulent flows."[21] In much the same manner, the ensuing analysis allows that many details of every international event are distinguishable from every other event, but at the same time it seeks to delineate the common qualities of turbulence in, say, the flows of capital, public protests, and terrorist activities.

Perhaps it is also instructive that, despite widening areas of agreement as to the nature of turbulent motion, physicists are not pleased

[17] Prigogine and Stengers, *Order out of Chaos*, p. 167.

[18] Wallerstein also takes note of this formulation in physics by positing at one point the capitalist world-economy as a "concrete singular historical system" presently undergoing "bifurcating turbulence." Immanuel Wallerstein, *The Politics of the World-Economy: The States, the Movements, and the Civilizations* (Cambridge: Cambridge University Press, 1984), pp. 37–38.

[19] Prigogine and Stengers, *Order out of Chaos*, p. 167.

[20] Bergé, Pomeau, and Vidal, *Order within Chaos*, p. 271.

[21] N. K. Vinnichenko, et al., *Turbulence in the Free Atmosphere*, 2nd ed., trans. Frank L. Sinclair (New York: Consultants Bureau, 1980), p. 2.

with the pace of their progress. Arguing that "turbulence needs spirited inventors just as badly as dedicated analysts,"[22] they complain that "turbulent flows have been investigated for more than a century, but . . . no general approach to the solution of problems in turbulence exists" and that, despite the ease with which such phenomena can be observed in cumulus clouds or the plumes of smokestacks, "it is very difficult to give a precise definition of turbulence."[23]

TURBULENCE AS COMPLEXITY AND DYNAMISM

It is in a branch of the social sciences, organizational theory, that a precise definition of turbulence can be found which is suggestive of how the concept can be usefully applied to world politics.[24] Organizational theory's interest in turbulence derives from a concern with the challenges that organizations face in coping with the trend toward greater interconnectedness among the actors in their environments and the tendency for these interconnections to fluctuate more frequently and more rapidly—a condition that has been referred to as "the increasing complexity and dynamics of modern society moving from an industrial to a post-industrial stage of development."[25] As the external challenges to an organization become more intense, so do their internal consequences, in that they foster needs to revise strategies, streamline decisional processes, and ameliorate bureaucratic tensions; thus, the organization becomes part of the very interconnectedness in its environment with which it seeks to cope.

The challenges are considered especially acute in what organizational theorists call a *turbulent environment*, one in which the degrees of both complexity and dynamism are high. To be sure, there is no shortage of difficulties in coping with other types of environments, in which complexity and dynamism are both low (the *placid-randomized*

---

[22] Vinnichenko et al., *Turbulence in the Free Atmosphere*, p. 2. For a similar appeal to students of world politics, see James N. Rosenau, "Thinking Theory Thoroughly," in P. R. Viotti and M. V. Kauppi, eds., *International Relations Theory: Realism, Pluralism, Globalism* (New York: Macmillan, 1987), pp. 20–31.

[23] Vinnichenko et al., *Turbulence in the Free Atmosphere*, pp. 4, 1.

[24] In one instance, the definition has even been operationalized; see Kim S. Cameron, Myung U. Kim, and David A. Whetten, "Organizational Effects of Decline and Turbulence," *Administrative Science Quarterly* 32 (June 1987): 231. For an operational definition of uncertainty, a central element in turbulence, see Wendell R. Garner, *Uncertainty and Structure as Psychological Concepts* (New York: John Wiley, 1962), pp. 20–25.

[25] Runo Axelsson and Lennart Rosenberg, "Decision-making and Organizational Turbulence," *Acta Sociologica* 22, no. 1 (1979): 45.

environment) or in which one is high and the other low (the *placid-clustered* and *disturbed reactive* environments), but these difficulties are of a different and much less severe kind than those that arise when the environment is turbulent.[26] It is characteristic of a turbulent environment that, compared with other types, the actors in it are more numerous and interdependent, with the result that it becomes less stable and predictable, thereby altering the conditions to which the actors have to adapt and heightening the probability that increasing numbers of them will fail to adapt, developments which can in turn lead to changes in the environment's structures and processes.

Some analysts posit a fifth type of environment, *hyperturbulence*, which is distinguished by such high degrees of dynamism and complexity as to utterly exceed the adaptive capacities of collectivities. Under this circumstance, the turbulence becomes so great that it is no longer manageable, a condition that may induce the actors to partition the environment and, in effect, relocate themselves back in one or another of the placid environments.[27]

In any case, the notion of fluid environmental structures and processes suggests a central attribute of turbulence in any political system: it is profoundly a product of interactions among micro and macro actors. Turbulence sets in when numerous micro actions culminate in macro outcomes that lie outside the system's normal functioning. An oft-cited illustration of this process is that of a regiment marching in step across a bridge: the rhythm of the marching causes a swaying of the bridge (i.e, a new structural condition) that cannot be attributed either to the bridge or to the action of any single soldier but that nonetheless requires an adaptive adjustment on the part of each soldier.[28] Thus, as will be seen at greater length in chapter 7, political turbulence is rooted neither in individuals nor in their collectivities; rather, it comes into being when the high dynamism of the former interacts with the high complexity of the latter to create new circumstances to which all actors must adapt.

If the global system is conceived as comparable to the environment of a collectivity, the relevance of the foregoing formulation to world pol-

---

[26] These four types of environments were first described and named in the seminal article by F. E. Emery and E. L. Trist, "The Causal Texture of Organizational Environments," *Human Relations* 18 (February 1965): 21–32.

[27] For an elaboration of this perspective, see Joseph E. McCann and John Selsky, "Hyperturbulence and the Emergence of Type 5 Environments," *Academy of Management Review* 9 (July 1984): 460–70.

[28] This insightful analogy was first used in Emery and Trist, "Causal Texture of Organizational Environments," p. 26.

itics begins to take shape. Numerous collectivities in every corner of the earth are becoming increasingly complex and dynamic as they enter the postindustrial era. Some of them, especially those that have not undergone much industrialization and are thus only partially affected by postindustrial conditions, may still be marked by simple and static structures, but enough of them are moving toward greater complexity and dynamism to confront all of them with a turbulent environment. To refer again to the analogy of the soldiers on the bridge, enough collectivities are experiencing internal change and turmoil to produce a global system that is in motion, that fluctuates erratically in ways that are a product of their collective inputs. And as the global system thus becomes increasingly turbulent, this condition adds further to the complexity and dynamism of the collectivities that constitute it and of the individuals that constitute the collectivities. In other words, global turbulence is both a source and a consequence of the changes unfolding at every level of politics.

But what is meant by complexity? Without some clarification of this concept, we can easily slip into using it as merely a label for those aspects of situations that we do not understand. One approach to clarification is to describe the essential components of the concept in only a very broad way. Herbert Simon, for example, defines a "complex system" as "one made up of a large number of parts that interact in a nonsimple way. In such systems, the whole is more than the sum of the parts, not in an ultimate, metaphysical sense, but in the important pragmatic sense that, given the properties of the parts and the laws of their interaction, it is not a trivial matter to infer the properties of the whole."[29] For present purposes, however, such a general formulation is not sufficient. In order to identify the presence of turbulence, we need to differentiate between high and less-than-high degrees of complexity. This means that we need to specify at least a few of the main dimensions along which some of the "nonsimple" interactions constituting complexity occur.

Organizational theorists again provide some useful guidelines.[30] They have identified three dimensions that characterize complexity in social systems (and that, of course, can be said to characterize complexity in environments as well). One is the number of actors. The greater the number, the greater is the likelihood that the interactions

[29] Herbert A. Simon, "The Architecture of Complexity," in *General Systems Yearbook*, vol. 10 (Ann Arbor, Mich.: Society for General Systems Research, 1965), pp. 63–64.

[30] See especially the essays in Todd R. La Porte, ed., *Organized Social Complexity: Challenge to Politics and Policy* (Princeton: Princeton University Press, 1975).

among them will be complicated rather than simple. The second dimension involves the extent of dissimilarity or variety among the actors, with greater variety resulting in more elaborate interactions. The third dimension focuses on the interdependencies among the actors: the higher the degree of interdependence, the more likely it is that an action of one will have consequences for others and thus the greater will be the intricacies of their interactions. Hence, a social system (or an environment) is highly complex when the number, dissimilarity, and interdependence of its actors are all high.[31] If these numerous, diverse, and interdependent actors are also characterized by high dynamism—a high degree of variability across time in their goals and activities—the interactions among them are bound to undergo continuous commotion and render the high complexity ever more challenging.

Such is the problem that an organization faces when its environment takes on the characteristics of turbulence: with the number, differentiation, and interdependencies of the actors, issues, and situations in the environment inordinately high, and with the rapidity of the variations in these actors, issues, and situations also especially great, it is confronted with conditions over which it cannot readily exercise control. It is constantly involved in situations marked by ambiguity and uncertainty, circumstances that are not conducive to reliance on rational action. Among other challenges, a turbulent environment tends to put an organization at odds with itself: high complexity needs to be addressed with intense intellectual effort in the analysis of information and the planning for contingencies, while high dynamism calls for a great deal of sociopolitical energy, for bargaining, compromising, and mobilizing, resulting in two activities so inherently antithetical to each other that one type can be increased only at the expense of the other. Small wonder that organizations begin to mirror the turbulence of their environments.

Although theirs is a minority position, some organization theorists employ microeconomic theory to argue that the condition of high complexity and high dynamism eventually leads not to a turbulent environment but to a placid-randomized environment. Their reasoning stresses the interaction between the organization and its environment.

[31] La Porte has expressed this in the following way: "The degree of complexity of organized social systems (Q) is a function of the *number* of system components (C_i), the relative *differentiation* or variety of these components (D_j), and the degree of *interdependence* among these components (I_k). Then, by definition, the greater C_i, D_j and I_k, the greater the complexity of the organized system (Q)." Todd R. La Porte, "Organized Social Complexity: Explication of a Concept," in La Porte, *Organized Social Complexity*, p. 6.

Organizations are not merely passive responders to their environments. Rather, to move toward their goals, they need to control their environments, and under the high-high condition the need to reduce the complexity and dynamism in their environments will be particularly acute and they will thus be impelled to take steps toward creating oligopolistic and monopolistic environmental conditions, over which they can more effectively exercise control. Accordingly, this reasoning concludes, the high-high condition is likely to become a placid, predictable field dominated by multinational conglomerates, while the organizations in a low-low condition will be small enterprises that cannot control their environment, thereby rendering it one of pure competition and subject to the uncertainties associated with turbulence.[32]

Whatever the validity of this line of reasoning for business organizations, its relevance for global politics in an era of ever-expanding interdependence is dubious. Actors on the global scene today lack the capacity to create the political equivalent of monopolistic and oligopolistic environments. For a host of reasons (discussed in subsequent chapters), the political world is too complex and too dynamic to lend itself to effective control and a meaningful reduction of its interconnectedness and variability. Even the superpowers are often at the mercy of events and trends that they would like to redirect, terminate, or otherwise influence but cannot.

One important modification of organization theory is needed if it is to be usefully applied to the study of postinternational politics. Organization theorists assume that the environments with which organizations must contend consist of organized rather than unorganized complexity. They conceive of organized complexity as the circumstance in which the actors in the environment engage "in relatively self-conscious interaction with each other, recognizing their common relatedness to one another within the system."[33] In unorganized complexity, on the other hand, the actors or variables affecting the outcomes are not so intimately linked to each other, a condition which organization theorists do not see as characteristic of an environment to which organizations must be responsive.[34] This distinction between two types of complexity, however, is not applicable to the environment of postin-

[32] This argument is developed in Michael C. White, Michael D. Crino, and Ben L. Kedia, "Environmental Turbulence: A Reappraisal of Emery and Trist," *Administration and Society* 16 (May 1984): 97–116.

[33] La Porte, "Organized Social Complexity," p. 6.

[34] For a discussion of the distinction between organized and unorganized complexity, see La Porte, "Organized Social Complexity," pp. 5–6.

ternational politics. It embraces both organized and unorganized complexity: while many of its actors are often conscious of their interdependencies, there are also numerous occasions (as will be seen in chapter 11) when the participants in the cascading events that unfold on the world scene are quite unaware of the repercussions of their actions and the ways in which they are linked to each other.

If organization theory is thus modified to allow for both types of complexity, it provides a basis for conceptualizing turbulence in world politics. Only a glance at the right-hand column of table 3.1 is needed to appreciate the degree to which high complexity and high dynamism are presently at work in world politics. The conditions that constrain superpowers conform exactly to the conditions of a high-high environment. Placid or disturbed environments can be said to have prevailed in earlier eras, when the uncertainties and interdependencies of global life were minimal and manageable because the number of actors was smaller and their authority more secure; even as recently as the 1950s, the processes of world politics were more calm than turbulent because the superpowers dominated their respective blocs and prevented the emergence of interconnections and variabilities over which they could not exercise control. But the postindustrial and microelectronic revolutions have ended any resemblance to these conditions. Now subgroupism has greatly multiplied the number of supranational, national, and subnational actors and the commitments and goals that differentiate them, not to mention the interdependent relationships and boundary-spanning activities that link them. Now individuals are more knowledgeable and skillful, more ready to shift their orientations, intensify their demands, and even reverse their course. Now the legitimacy of leaders is much more frequently questioned, and thus their capacity to mobilize resources and get things done is much more precarious and limited. The points at which action originates and variability occurs are much more diffuse, numerous, and interconnected, and they converge ever more forcefully from every corner of the earth to create a dynamism of their own. Now, in short, the Order ii of world politics is that of a turbulent field writ large.[35]

---

[35] For other explorations of the utility of systematically treating key dimensions of world politics as forms of chaos and turbulence, see Miriam Campanella, ed., *Between Rationality and Cognition: Policy-making under Conditions of Uncertainty, Complexity, and Turbulence* (Torino, Italy: Albert Meynier, 1988), and Barbara Jancar, "Chaos As an Explanation of the Role of Environmental Groups in East Europe Politics" (paper presented at the annual meeting of the International Studies Association, London, March 1989).

Turbulence as Cause and Effect

To define political turbulence as extraordinarily high degrees of complexity and dynamism does not make clear whether our concern is with turbulence as a causal agent or as a consequence of postindustrial dynamics. Are we seeking to explain the sources of the inordinate complexity and dynamism? Or is the task to anticipate how such degrees of complexity and dynamism might shape the evolution of world politics and its structures? Or is the goal to account for the interaction among the causes and effects of turbulence as it weaves, tumbles, and careens through the collectivities active on the world stage?

The answer is affirmative to all three questions. In order to construct a viable theory of turbulence, there is a need to treat it as a dependent variable—i.e., to account for the sources of the high complexity, dynamism, and interconnectedness at work in the global system. At the same time, the consequences of these conditions can hardly be ignored, which necessitates analyzing them as independent variables, as forces that may give rise to new circumstances in world politics. But if one treats turbulence as both cause and consequence, it is logical to consider the way in which its consequences feed back on its causes.

In short, turbulence both accounts for the dynamism of actors and is in itself dynamic. It reflects change and it can stir further change. An example of this dual role can be discerned in the sequences that follow from the introduction of new knowledge and technologies in the postindustrial era. They bring about a substantial increase in the components of systems, as the need to use and manage the knowledge and technologies requires greater specialization and diversity. As systems and actors become more specialized, they must rely on others for support in those areas that lie outside their specializations. Hence, they become increasingly interdependent and their relationships become increasingly complex. At the same time, the greater degrees of specialization render the new technologies more effective. As communication and transportation technologies become increasingly refined, geographic and social distances shrink and events are shortened in duration. As events become shorter, more events occur in any given unit of time, thus adding further to the complexity, interdependence, and dynamism of the prevailing circumstances and, in effect, sustaining a process whereby turbulence feeds on itself.[36]

[36] This sequence is drawn from the analysis in George P. Huber, "The Nature and Design of Post-Industrial Organizations," *Management Science* 30 (August 1984): 928–51.

TURBULENCE AND CHANGE

The conception of turbulence in world politics as high complexity and high dynamism needs to be considered in the context of the tensions between change and continuity. The presence of change is not constant across a turbulent environment. Being variable in purpose and structure, actors do not respond to conditions in the same way. Some have a greater capacity for adaptation than others; some may even manage to prosper under conditions of high complexity and dynamism, while others founder and undergo transformation.[37]

Put differently, there can be big changes and little changes, changes that alter the course of history and changes that are merely momentary deviations from central tendencies. Much depends on the vantage point from which they are assessed. A stock market can undergo wide swings in the short term, but these can seem flattened out, gentle slopes rather than steep peaks and valleys, when seen from a longer-term perspective. Similarly, with nearly fifty cabinet collapses in four decades, Italian politics can seem pervaded by commotion when viewed from the perspective of any moment in time but the overall impression of postwar Italy is one of structured crises and not of endemic turbulence.

Not all the changes at work in the world, in other words, are indicative of global turbulence. It is not difficult to conceive of slow evolutions that never erupt into turbulence. It is also possible to conceive of turbulence that does not accompany or foster change, in the sense of a subsystemic turbulence that spreads neither to other subsystems nor to the more encompassing whole system.

Under what circumstances, then, is it appropriate to speak of global turbulence, of complexities and variations that are worldwide in scope and that are transforming the structures and processes of world politics? An answer to this question requires further specification of both the definition of turbulence and the meaning of change in a global context. Such is the task of the next chapter.

---

[37] The variability of adaptive capacity in the face of turbulent conditions is stressed in McCann and Selsky, "Hyperturbulence," pp. 461–64.

CHAPTER 4

CONCEPTUALIZING CHANGE
Fluctuations and Transformations

BETHLEHEM, Israeli-Occupied West Bank—Some diplomats from the U.S. consulate in Jerusalem were having more trouble than usual in pinning down their schedule at a recent weekly planning session. Finally, said one participant, "We realized that the reason we couldn't plan our week was because we didn't have the latest leaflet" issued by the clandestine Unified National Leadership for the Uprising in the Occupied Territories [which lists] the various forms of protest planned for the roughly two-week period ahead.

—News item[1]

In the 1940's the most frequent discipline problems [in California schools] included talking, chewing gum, making noise, running in the halls, getting out of turn in line, wearing improper clothing and not putting paper in wastebaskets. In the 1980's, the problems include drug abuse, alcohol abuse, rape, robbery, assault, burglary, arson, bombings, murder, absenteeism, vandalism, extortion, gang warfare, abortion and venereal disease.

—News item[2]

The trouble with change in human affairs is that it is so hard to pin down. It happens all the time. But while it happens it eludes our grasp, and once we feel able to come to grips with it, it has become past history.

—Ralf Dahrendorf[3]

[1] Dan Fisher, "Arab Uprising Is Now the Routine," *Los Angeles Times*, July 19, 1988, sec. 1, p. 10.

[2] Joseph F. Sullivan, "Jersey Seeking Plans to Aid Students with 80's Problems," *New York Times*, December 5, 1987, p. 29.

[3] "The Europeanization of Europe," in Andrew J. Pierre, ed., *A Widening Atlantic?*

TO RECOGNIZE that turbulence in world politics arises when extensive complexity and dynamism attach to the interconnections of its actors and structures is to take an important intellectual step. It is to treat turbulence as a form of order that can be understood and not as a chaos that is so random, so utterly unpredictable, as to be beyond comprehension.

But what kind of order is the present-day turbulence of world politics? Is it simply a transitory period of intense commotion in the state system through which the Order II that has prevailed for centuries will be reaffirmed? That is, is it a period in which the complexity and dynamism of actors and structures will settle back into the more simple and static patterns of the past? Or is it a period of transition in which the state system is giving way to new global arrangements, to an emergent Order II that has no parallel in history? Will the structures and actors of the newly emergent Order II become less complex and variable as the transition ends and the new arrangements become more habitual? Or will complexity and dynamism remain high, so that turbulence will have become a permanent condition of global life?

Implicit in these questions is the need to formulate a conception of change that allows for a time frame of weeks and months (as exemplified by the first news story quoted above) as well as years and decades (as in the case of the second news story above). To fail to develop a basis for conceptualizing emergent changes and the ways in which they may be linked to both the stable and the turbulent periods of world politics would be to yield to Dahrendorf's lament, also quoted above, that transformations can be recognized only after they have occurred.

Conceptualizing change, however, requires more than a little patience. The case for presuming the emergence of a world transformed by an ever-expanding interdependence is arresting. It encourages one to assert that profound change is under way on a global scale and then to move immediately to the challenge to think afresh without ever having paused to consider what is meant by change. To do so would be a mistake.

THE AMBIGUITIES OF CHANGE

The processes of change are sufficiently ambiguous, elusive, and disparate to compel us to proceed with caution. Change, transformation, turbulence, and the other descriptors of dynamism take on meaning

---

Domestic Change and Foreign Policy (New York: Council on Foreign Relations, 1986), p. 5.

only as they can be clearly differentiated from those that depict the statics of continuity. It is all too easy to speak loosely of "global change"—to call attention to its presence if today's events seem overwhelming or to stress its absence if the same events appear as just more of the conflicts in which people regularly embroil themselves. The past offers an endless supply of events with superficial resemblances to those of the present if one is predisposed to see current affairs as subject to rapid obsolescence and history as essentially repetitive. Contrariwise, the past seems barren of guidance if one is inclined to treat the dynamism of technology as endlessly creating new plateaus from which human affairs evolve.

Moreover, pausing to conceptualize the dynamics of change is a means of disciplining inquiry. The raw premise that change is under way offers no guidelines as to where to look for it and how to appraise it. And, indeed, its identity can be difficult to establish. Without a conception of what constitutes fundamental change, as distinguished from temporary or minor fluctuations, we are likely to be overwhelmed by the welter of activities that make up world affairs. Without a conception of when the complexities and dynamism of world politics are giving rise to enduring changes and when they are merely reinforcing existing continuities, we may too readily presume that nothing remains constant and thus overlook how the tensions between past and present can result in stalemate as well as in transformation.

If nothing else, therefore, clarity about the nature of change can serve as a useful reminder that even the most pronounced changes have antecedents, that the past cannot be ignored, and that there is always a danger of mistaking mere commotion for turbulence and thus exaggerating the depth and breadth of change. Because political turbulence involves swift-moving flows of activity, flows that often gather in strength and surge irregularly in diverse directions, it conveys the impression of constant change, of individuals, officials, collectivities, and institutions being caught up in the course of events and adjusting to them by altering their ways. Yet, as in the case of whirlpools and hurricanes, the activities of turbulent social systems need not always result in enduring change. They can form repetitive patterns that are marked by constancy: both people and societies can be on the move, only to encounter constraints that redirect them back to where they began, a circular process that is distinguished by both short-term changes and long-term continuities.

Pausing to sort out the controversy over present-day transformations also serves as a cogent reminder of the possibility that one's posture toward change may be a matter of temperament. What is new for one person can be more of the same for another, depending in large part on how each feels about the present situation and the prospects for future progress. Perhaps for a variety of reasons, some analysts derive comfort from feeling that the present is but a continuation of the past, while others are uncomfortable with the idea that new departures do not occur in history. Although there may be no way to suspend one's temperament, its relevance to analysis is better recognized than denied. For, obviously, in the absence of the constraints imposed by explication, our temperamental impulses can get out of control, with persons who adhere to one historical perspective rejecting any evidence that change is under way and those inclined toward another dismissing any signs of underlying transformations. Such extreme responses are unfortunate because they blind us to the more likely position that change and continuity are both operative in history, that the tensions between them are the sources of both progress and retrogression.

Finally, even if our temperaments are put aside, our guidelines for discerning change can surely benefit from being made explicit. Wherever there are expectations of what lies ahead, there are also implicit notions of change and of its pace, direction, and problems. In any conception of the human condition, notions of change and continuity, and the tensions between them, are unavoidably a central focus. We ponder problems in a context of time, comparing current conditions with those experienced, cherished, or abhorred in the past and those anticipated, desired, or feared in the future.

The present situation in South Africa is illustrative of the pervasiveness of our assumptions and hypotheses about the nature of change. At first glance, there seems to be considerable logic in the widespread belief that "sooner or later," the confrontation of blacks and whites in that strife-torn society will erupt into large-scale violence and change. But closer inspection reveals that this expectation rests on a set of notions that express a particular philosophical perspective on change and time. One is that under certain conditions change is more likely than continuity; another is that at certain points in the course of history it is beyond the ability of any actors to insure continuity; a third is that time is not neutral, that it engenders pressures for the resolution of confrontations; a fourth is that certain kinds of change cannot simply evolve but instead are bound to culminate in upheaval; a fifth is that knowledge of the first four is not sufficient to insure success on the part of those who have the will to interrupt the dynamics of change.

There are, of course, difficulties in conceptualizing change. While there is utility in a formulation which specifies, say, the nature of the actors, the structures of governance, and the processes of interaction as three types of change that may be under way in the world,[4] such typologies do not go far enough. They tell us where to look for change but not how to recognize it when we come upon it. They say nothing about the kinds of anomalies to probe and the kinds to ignore. Does the establishment of a new state amount to change in the system? Of ten new states? Fifty? Does the imposition of new and stringent requirements on borrowing countries by the International Monetary Fund (IMF) constitute structural change? Does the breakup of an alliance and its replacement by a series of bilateral relationships represent meaningful change in global processes? Would the advent of substantially more analytic and articulate publics—to anticipate a central theme of the ensuing analysis—constitute irrelevant, peripheral, or fundamental change?

Put more abstractly, is turbulence episodic? cyclical? self-sustaining? To the extent change is evolutionary, how much evolution must there be before it can properly be viewed as basic change?

What is required to answer these questions is a broad perspective on global life from which empirical indicators of continuity and change can be derived. As a minimum, such a perspective must specify the time frame, the systems or subsystems, and the relationships within which the presence of change may be detected. In effect, one needs to articulate a philosophical approach that differentiates not only changes from continuities but also abrupt from evolutionary transformations, variables from parameters, erratic fluctuations from turbulent flows, and significant anomalies from transitory exceptions. To anticipate the conception developed here, the recognition of enduring changes, portentous anomalies, and turbulent flows is linked to the transformation of three parameters that constrain world politics, whereas shifts in the values of the variables of world politics are viewed as fluctuations within the ongoing equilibrium rather than as significant changes.

Two Extreme Perspectives

There are as many philosophies of change as there are theories of the human spirit and the capacity of people to shape their own destiny.[5]

---

[4] These distinctions organize the analysis of Robert Gilpin, *War and Change in World Politics* (New York: Cambridge University Press, 1981), pp. 39–49.

[5] For extended and incisive discussions of various philosophical approaches to change and history, see Gertrude Himmelfarb, *The New History and the Old* (Cambridge: Harvard University Press, 1987); Christopher Lloyd, *Explanation in Social History* (Oxford: Basil Blackwell, 1986), esp. Part 3; and Richard E. Neustadt and Ernest R. May,

For present purposes, only three of these perspectives need be noted. Two are at the opposite poles of the balance between continuity and change, while the third falls between the extremes and is the perspective that underlies this book.

One of the two polar philosophies stresses the openness of social systems to redirection and transformation. It tends to equate crises with breaking points, to view tensions in world affairs as perturbations that herald important changes. It emphasizes the suceptibility of systems to shocks of violence and upheaval. At the other pole is a tendency to perceive history as a seamless web in which there are no breaking points. This perspective stresses the power of habit, the pervasiveness of cultural norms, and the constraints of prior experience as predisposing systems toward continuity.[6]

The tendency to exaggerate the dynamics of change during moments of tension and crisis is readily understandable. At such moments, uncertainty is so pervasive that new developments loom as fundamental alterations in the course of events. Without a broad overview on change, we are prone to see unfamiliar dimensions of crises not as minor disturbances in the overall trend line but as sharp breaks with prior patterns. Thus it was, to cite a concrete example, that President Reagan's first reaction to the downing of a Korean airliner by Soviet aircraft in 1983 was to describe it as a "turning point in world affairs because it produced a worldwide 'fundamental and long overdue reappraisal' of the Soviet Union and had virtually isolated it internationally."[7] Thus also was it said, at one point in the maneuvering over arms control, that the Soviet Union was gambling that the protests in West Germany against the deployment of new nuclear missiles signaled a "seismic shift" in the latter country's political dynamics.[8]

Although one can appreciate the propensity to view crises as eventuating in significant change, a broader time perspective allows the recognition that long-established patterns often resume once crisis pertur-

---

Thinking in Time: The Uses of History for Decision Makers (New York: Free Press, 1986).

[6] For a series of incisive essays that explore the susceptibility of international systems to the dynamics of change, see Barry Buzan and R. J. Barry Jones, eds., *Change and the Study of International Relations: The Evaded Dimension* (New York: St. Martin's, 1981). For an elaborate and cogent analysis of the barriers to systemic change, see Harry Eckstein, "A Culturalist Theory of Political Change," *American Political Science Review* 82 (September 1988): 789–804.

[7] Bernard Gwertzman, "U.S. Aides Pessimistic on Soviet Ties," *New York Times*, October 23, 1983, sec. 1, p. 14.

[8] James M. Markham, "German Missile Protests: Mixed Signals for Kohl," *New York Times*, October 24, 1983, p. A3.

bations subside. Collectivities are too deeply embedded in their own cultures, societies, economies, and histories to undergo fundamental change with every crisis. Hence, it is hardly surprising that, not long after President Reagan characterized the airliner incident as a "turning point," the established patterns of interaction with the Soviet Union resumed and its isolation in global politics came to an end. Likewise, the deployment of missiles in West Germany proceeded on schedule and revealed the Soviet gamble on a "seismic shift" to be based on an exaggeration of West Germany's potential for change.

The opposite tendency—to treat history as so continuous as to preclude fundamental change—originates in part from a compelling sense that, given a choice, people will opt for long-established ways of doing things and that therefore social and political patterns repeat themselves endlessly. This perspective may also spring from a predisposition to be nostalgic about history and, accordingly, to resist acknowledging that its continuities can come to an end and its parameters can be reshuffled and reset. Often the nostalgia even takes the form of implying that no self-respective student of world affairs can proceed without acknowledging that Thucydides still remains relevant. Somehow, it would seem, comfort can be derived from viewing human experience as an unbroken chain in which each generation is in part a product of its predecessor. Change is unsettling, and sharp change even more so. It brings values into question and renders the future vague. Hence, to insist that historical counterparts are always available—that one must rely on the lessons of history and avoid being deceived by superficial discrepancies—is to relieve anxiety, because it fosters the belief that current challenges will be surmounted just as systems in prior eras managed to overcome their crises and survive.

Indeed, the need to cling to the relevance of history can lead to an overemphasis on continuity. Gilpin, for example, while acknowledging that technological, economic, and other developments have transformed the world, stresses that the problem of war has yet to be solved and therefore fundamental changes in global structures have yet to occur.[9] The possibility that similar outcomes may result from vastly different structures and processes is neglected; all that counts is that problems persist across generations and millennia. It is like arguing that male-female relations were not fundamentally altered after Freud, the birth-control pill, and the other dynamics of the sexual revolution because women still have babies. Or, more relevantly, it is like saying that election campaigns in the United States were not basically transformed

---

[9] Gilpin, *War and Change in World Politics*, p. 213.

by the advent of television and the subsequent decline of whistle-stops, bumper stickers, and city-hall rallies because voters still vote. Even more relevantly, it is like arguing that, despite an ever-expanding global interdependence, little has changed in world politics because states still conduct foreign policy.

Furthermore, by clinging to the idea that clues to the present can always be found in the past, history offers a convenient scapegoat when things go awry. Equipped with hindsight, both the analyst and the advocate can explain away or condemn any untoward development by locating those links in its causal chain where errors of judgment were made. Used in this way, history becomes a catchall that allows us to justify our perspectives and to offer a seemingly unchallengeable explanation for a past which we have difficulty accepting. As a former U.S. ambassador to the United Nations observed in arguing for policies to prevent future Irans and Nicaraguas, "The neglect of history lies . . . at the root of most of our failures in foreign policy."[10]

In any event, whatever the degree to which tendencies toward nostalgia and scapegoating may be a source of confusion, thinking about change in world politics tends to be marked by ambivalence and imprecision.[11] Perhaps confounded by the variety and complexity of a growing interdependence and yet constrained by a felt need to pay homage to the forces of history, all too many analysts proceed without clearly distinguishing between continuity and change. They observe movement in the structures and processes of the global system, but in the absence of theoretical specification—and driven by a conviction that the hidden hand of history must somehow be at work—they vacillate with respect to the degree to which changes are occurring and continuities are being terminated and superseded. Thus it is, for example, that in a single paragraph Gilpin asserts, first, "that the fundamental nature of international relations has not changed over the millennia," but then, after a sentence about how a reincarnated Thucydides would feel at home in the late twentieth century, reverses

[10] William E. Farrell, "Mrs. Kirkpatrick Criticizes Soviet," *New York Times*, October 5, 1983, p. A15.

[11] For notable exceptions to this generalization, see Buzan and Jones, *Change and the Study of International Relations*; Michael Brecher and Patrick James, *Crisis and Change in World Politics* (Boulder, Colo.: Westview, 1986), pp. 13–25; Charles F. Doran, "Modes, Mechanisms, and Turning Points: Perspectives on Systems Transformation" (paper delivered at the annual meeting of the American Political Science Association, Washington, D.C., August–September 1979); Ole R. Holsti, Randolph M. Siverson, and Alexander L. George, eds., *Change in the International System* (Boulder, Colo.: Westview, 1980); and John A. Vasquez and Richard W. Mansbach, "The Issue Cycle and Global Change," *International Organization*, 37 (Spring 1983): 257–79.

himself and notes, "Yet important changes have taken place," and one sentence later reverses himself once again, saying, "Nevertheless, we contend that the fundamentals have not been altered."[12]

All of this is not to argue that nostalgia should be replaced with myopia. Some part of today's actions and patterns are always a function of yesterday's experience. Stated differently (and in terms further developed in chapter 9), long-standing habits are always in tension with stimuli to new learning. Thus, the lessons of the past, even if erroneously understood, always operate as guides, whether as signposts of paths to take or as warnings of behavior to avoid. And beyond the felt lessons of history lies culture, that deep well of norms, concepts, and inclinations which reach across centuries and serve as filters through which the present is perceived and experienced.

At the same time, a useful purpose is served by pointing out the dangers of a perspective that presumes constancy. That purpose is to focus theoretical attention on breaking points, on the temporality and vulnerability of the parameters of the global system, and on the blockages that may inhibit our recognition of their capacity for transformation. Our theories tend to be biased in the direction of explaining the maintenance of equilibria.[13] As a result, they often downplay the dynamics wherein the seeds of change can develop into major historical breaks. This potential is inherent in all social systems, given the multiplicity of their internal structures and external challenges. There is good reason to be sensitive to the ever-present possibility that fundamental change is about to take place.[14]

Accepting that systems may be on the verge of reconfiguration at any time has the additional merit of highlighting the essential weakness of any dividing line that may be drawn between continuity and change. Only the analyst's sense of tidiness is served by efforts to construct compartments that neatly delineate where continuity ends and change begins. The efforts themselves are bound to fail: given both the rigidities and the flexibilities of culture, continuity and change are not mutually exclusive in complex systems, and the presence of both is bound to render any chronological line arbitrary and misleading: arbitrary in the sense that such a line can never fully distinguish a pattern from its

[12] Gilpin, *War and Change in World Politics*, p. 7.

[13] For an exceptional theoretical formulation that is anything but static, see Nazli Choucri and Robert C. North, *Nations in Conflict: National Growth and International Violence* (San Francisco: W. H. Freeman, 1975).

[14] For an elaboration of this point, see James N. Rosenau, "Before Cooperation: Hegemons, Regimes, and Habit-Driven Actors in World Politics," *International Organization* 40 (Autumn 1986): 884–86.

antecedents, and misleading in the sense that an understanding of the interaction of historic constraints and current dynamics is likely to be blurred by an excessive concern for definitional precision.

BETWEEN THE EXTREMES

In short, if we are going to probe incisively into the turbulence of global life, we need to move beyond nostalgia over the past and myopia with respect to the present. What is needed is a third conception of history, one that falls between the polar extremes and that allows for both change and continuity, simultaneously and sequentially. Given the need to be sensitive to the problem of measuring change, this conception should be cast in probabilistic rather than absolutistic terms, and it should provide logical rather than arbitrary bases for operationalizing the indicators of change.

What is missing from the two polar perspectives on change is any differentiation as to its nature. Both present too broad a conception of where, when, and how change occurs. Neither specifies a time horizon or a systemic perspective from which analysis can proceed. In effect, they are both atheoretical in that they can be applied to any situation at all times and under all conditions, whereas incisive analysis requires that we posit historical circumstances that are neither so static nor so volatile as to preclude a variability in which the dynamics of change sometimes predominate even though often the inertia of continuity prevails.

Several basic assumptions are requisite to such a perspective. Self-evident as it may be, the first of these assumptions serves to bring the problem of conceptualizing global change into focus:

1. The interpretation of continuity and change depends on the systemic and time perspectives from which they are assessed.

Change and continuity, in other words, are not objective phenomena. Their observation acquires form through conceptual formulation, not from empirical "reality." It is not history that dictates whether change has occurred, but rather the interests of observers, the scales of time and space in which they seek to trace changes in the past and to evaluate those that may lie ahead in the future. Consider the difference between a system and any of its subsystems: a sea change for the latter may be merely an instance of a pervasive tendency for the former. The birth of a first child, for example, involves a monumental transformation for a family, but this same event is only a minute bit of data for a demographer. Similarly, the advent of a new government may have enormous consequences for that society, but for the global system this development may be simply another case of periodic change in the personnel of national governments.

Stated more generally, micro changes can cumulate to macro consistencies as well as to macro changes, depending on the perspective from which change is being judged. Happily, an analyst is free to employ any perspective. Unlike the actor, whose time frame is necessarily the immediate moment and whose systemic perspective is that of the current situation, the analyst can look across broad horizons. The perspective here is that of the most encompassing political system of all, for we wish to comprehend the sources and processes through which the global system undergoes enduring and fundamental change.

To conduct our inquiry on this level of abstraction, however, we have to explicate a second basic assumption:

2. The longer the time span and the more encompassing the system, the greater the probability that the statics of continuity will prevail over the dynamics of change.

In focusing on the global system, we recognize that, while a particular country or region, even a continent, can undergo profound and prolonged upheaval and transformation, such developments do not fall within the scope of our concerns unless their repercussions cascade on a global scale. From this perspective, most of the conflicts and crises that are the subjects of daily news reports are only momentary shifts in the normal course of public affairs. They may well bring important change to those involved, but in a global context they are minor fluctuations of the ongoing equilibrium.

This assumption calls for a broad perspective on time as well as on space. The global system is too cumbersome and diverse to undergo enduring changes in days or weeks. Rather, its transformations are likely to extend across months and years, perhaps even decades and centuries.

If the probabilities are thus considerable that continuity will predominate in the global system, when, how, and under what conditions is it likely to undergo enduring and fundamental change? The answer to this crucial question lies in a distinction drawn between the parameters and the variables of the system, with the former being viewed as setting limits within which the latter vary. This distinction is elaborated upon below, but its derivation and implications are evident in three additional assumptions:

3. Political systems have three primary parameters that serve as the boundaries within which their structures and processes operate.

4. Basic changes in a political system take place only at those times when its primary parameters are in flux.
5. For a system to experience enduring change, all three of its primary parameters must be affected.

In other words, the global system will change in a fundamental way only when its primary parameters are engulfed to the point of no longer being fixed and constant—when, in effect, they become variables.

But a further question now arises: How do we know when a parameter has been irrevocably engulfed, rather than merely being bent or stretched? Although the answer requires careful delineation of the three primary parameters, its conceptual foundation is a movement from a relatively simple and clear-cut set of arrangements for conducting the affairs of the system to interconnections that are dense, elaborate, uncertain, and thus in the process of evolving into a previously unfamiliar pattern.

The foregoing assumptions and the analysis of the previous chapter allow for a succinct specification of what is meant by the title of this book: *Global turbulence can be defined as a worldwide state of affairs in which the interconnections that sustain the primary parameters of world politics are marked by extensive complexity and variability.* As will be seen in the next chapter, an application of this perspective to the history of the global system's three primary parameters suggests that the present period may be witnessing the first turbulence to beset world politics since the seventeenth century.

FORMS, BOUNDARIES, PARAMETERS, AND VARIABLES

Of course, much hinges on how parameters are conceptualized. The perspective being set forth here acquires meaning only insofar as the primary parameters are clearly specified and their role in system functioning delineated. In doing so, it will also be helpful to distinguish, as in mathematics, among the functional form, the boundary conditions, the parameters, and the variables of social systems, and to focus on the different ways these interact and change.

Like any system, that of global politics has an overall form that is bounded by nature and that acquires concrete shape from the parameters which serve as the limits within which its variables operate. The *functional form* of the global system is conceived to be that of maintaining interaction among organized collectivities with different cultures, histories, purposes, capabilities, and jurisdictions. The *boundary conditions* are those permanent nonhuman circumstances (such as geography or the weather) that affect the interaction. The *parameters* are those enduring human circumstances of the system's form (such as its hierarchical structure, cultural norms, and authority orientations) that are systemwide in scope and set the context for interaction among its diverse collectivities and individuals.[15] The *variables* consist of both the nonhuman dynamics (such as technology and agricultural resources) and the human structures and processes (such as the composition and objectives of nation-states) through which the collectivities interact.[16] These system components change with different frequencies: the system's functional form and boundary conditions are highly constant, its parameters undergo transformation very rarely, and its variables are (within the limits set by the boundaries and parameters) continuously fluctuating in response to internal and external challenges.

For present purposes, the distinction between parameters and variables is the most important one. It lies at the heart of the tension between constancy and change. As perceived here, the parameters of a system are the wellsprings of continuity—the norms, procedures, and institutions evolved and tested through long experience that represent, as it were, "history's dictates" and that thus exert pressure against any developments that might lead to fundamental transformations. Put differently, parameters are the basic rules and organizing principles of a system that prescribe the goals, means, and resources of the system's role-occupants, including the mechanisms of enforcement. Most activities in most systems conform to the rules most of the time and thereby reinforce the system's parameters. Such activities may involve alterations in the lives of the system's members, but they nevertheless also preserve the system's structures.

[15] There is no universally accepted definition of a parameter. One dictionary notes that the term "is sometimes used in the sense of a 'constant, a given, or a precondition' and sometimes in the sense of a 'limit or boundary' . . . *We must stay within the parameters of public debate. Violence and rebellion are parameters of modern life.* None of these examples is acceptable to a majority of the Usage Panel [of one hundred experts."] *American Heritage Dictionary,* 2nd ed. (Boston: Houghton Mifflin, 1985), p. 901 (italics in original). In the present work, the term is used as both a precondition and a boundary.

[16] Drawing on a diverse literature, Zinnes has identified seven variables that most analysts would agree are central to the operation of any international system: (1) the number of nations; (2) the distribution of power among the nations; (3) the objectives of the nations; (4) the types of governments and decision making in the nations; (5) the rules and customs governing interactions among the nations; (6) the relational patterns among the nations; and (7) the nations' perceptions of each other. Dina A. Zinnes, "Prerequisites for the Study of System Transformation," in Holsti, Siverson, and George, *Change in the International System,* pp. 9–13.

It follows that parameters, being rooted in long-standing habits and historic rationales, are not usually complex or dyanmic. They are, rather, accepted by the members of the system as "the way things are," as the givens that make the course of events meaningful and manageable. In effect, they are the underlying order, those arrangements that are recognized as the constraints and opportunities of what is here called Order II.

Besides being enduring, parameters impose the same conditions on all the system's components and thereby determine the limits within which its variables operate and interact. Different parameters limit different activities in the system (e.g., the forming of alliances and the mobilizing of citizenries), and different systems have different parameters (e.g., religious fundamentalism constrains politics in Iran today while secular norms do the same for the Netherlands), but each parameter of any system similarly limits all the actors within its range.

The variables of a system, on the other hand, are the wellsprings of change. Their values fluctuate as individuals, collectivities, and institutions respond to the course of events. In so doing, they are also ever capable of entering on a collision course with the parameters, pushing the range of their variation against the parametric constraints. For reasons discussed in later chapters, more often than not the inertia inherent in the parameters of the global system prevails over the initiatives and aspirations pushing for greater variability, but the tensions between the two are nonetheless a central and continuing feature of world politics.

However, the parameter-variable distinction can be ambiguous. There are occasions when parameters do change in meaningful ways, and when this happens, the distinction between them and variables may seem misleading and arbitrary. If parameter values are capable of undergoing variation, of becoming variables at least momentarily, is it not deceptive to posit them as constants during other periods? In the end, does not the observer rely on impressionistic rather than theoretical criteria to denote some variables as parameters while holding that others are too subject to change to be classified as parameters? And if arbitrariness is thus inherent in the distinction, is it not pointless to strive for a generalized conception of global change? Why not simply designate as changes those differences between time 1 and time 2 that seem relevant and proceed to analyze them accordingly? Why worry over whether they are parametric shifts or variable fluctuations? Is it not their contents and consequences that count, not how they are labeled?

The argument is compelling in that the differentiation between parameters and variables derives not from reality but from the analyst's perspective on the nature of political systems and their vulnerability to change. Yet this need not be sheer arbitrariness. If the analyst makes a persuasive case for treating some aspects of a system as more central to its functioning than others and as thus setting the conditions for the operation of the less central aspects, a theoretical context can be developed that endows the differences between times *1* and *2* with a larger meaning that transcends whatever particular issues may be at work.

As another way of distinguishing between parameters and variables, Ashby declares that "every system is formed by selecting some variables out of the totality of possible variables" and that variables that are not included in the system, that are external to it, are its parameters. Parameters that have an especially close relation to the system he designates as *effective parameters* (equivalent to what are here referred to as "primary" parameters), and he then proceeds to argue that a change in a variable alters only conditions prevailing within the system, while a change in an effective parameter alters the system itself. In this sense, the distinction between parameters and variables "can hardly be over-estimated," because systems have established procedures for accommodating variable changes, but "a change of parameter-value will in general change a system's stability in some way."[17]

Since parameters constitute the basic rules and arrangements whereby social systems function, they are bound to be the focus of turbulence when the continuities they represent are subjected to severe strain. The system's boundary conditions are not normally subjected to such strain, because they are fixed in nature.[18] Nor are variable changes likely to involve historic junctures, inasmuch as their consequences are usually localized in subsystems rather than extended throughout whole systems. The values of variables may fluctuate wildly and their changes may be extensive, but they will nevertheless be restrained by the continuities of the past, and their effects will be

[17] W. Ross Ashby, *Design for a Brain: The Origin of Adaptive Behavior* (New York: John Wiley, 1960), pp. 71, 73, 77.

[18] Note should be taken, however, of the warning that the global system's "socio-biospheric" problems are mounting and that its boundaries can no longer be taken for granted: Andrew M. Scott, "The Study of Socio-Biospheric Problems" (paper presented at the annual meeting of the International Studies Association, Mexico City, April 1983). The recent forecasts of a "greenhouse effect," in which the earth will get noticeably warmer in the twenty-first century, thereby melting ice sheets at the poles, raising sea levels, disrupting agriculture, and changing fertile lands to deserts, are one indication that under extraordinary circumstances even boundary conditions are susceptible to variation.

differently mediated by the diverse histories and circumstances of the subsystems. By definition, however, parameters are systemwide in scope, and thus the structures and processes they encompass are likely to break away from prior patterns on those rare occasions when they themselves are changing.

Only a few of the many patterns that sustain a system at the micro and macro levels are broad enough in scale and dominant enough in influence to constitute its parameters. Most patterns are limited to subsystems and thus operate only as variables within the system. If profound transformations, as distinguished from transient disturbances, are to overtake and redirect the system, the dynamics driving change must engulf and realign all its parameters in such a way that thereafter they settle into altered patterns. The dynamics can, and often will, induce substantial reactions in the system's external environment (such as a coalition among adversaries or a technological innovation) as well as severe internal variations (such as widespread popular protests or party realignments), but these give rise to turbulence only when they encompass and transform the full complement of parameters that have previously operated as systemic constraints.

Evolutionary and Breakpoint Change

The distinction between changes within and of a system—between changes in its variables and changes in its parameters—can be further clarified by differentiating between an *evolutionary* and a *breakpoint* change in a parameter's values. The former is, of course, a slow change over a long period of time, the latter a more or less abrupt change. This distinction is crucial, because the degree to which a system remains stable depends on the pace at which its parameter values change. If they evolve, the system is likely to retain its stability, inasmuch as it has time to adjust to the new values. But if the shift is abrupt, it is more likely to be followed by instability, as the system's components are suddenly faced with a new Order II and have to search for new ways of coping with it.

Put differently, in evolutionary development parameter values shift systematically according to some constant additive or subtractive pattern, whereas in breakpoint change parameter values pass beyond some threshold and shift exponentially. Evolutionary change, allowing as it does for adjustment to the shifting parametric values, does not substantially increase the complexity and dynamism of the system's variables. But when the parameters undergo a transformation that pushes their values beyond the breakpoint threshold, adjustment becomes difficult and the parameters become less effective as constraints. As a result, the members of the system, their relationships, and the interconnections of their institutions become more complex and more subject to variation as all concerned begin to acknowledge that Order II is vulnerable, that "things may no longer be that way." And as the structural complexities of the system deepen and the activities of its members fluctuate more widely, the hallmarks of turbulence begin to appear.

The three patterns that will be posited here as the primary parameters of postinternational politics—the readiness of publics to give or withhold support, of subordinates to defy or accede to authority, and of sovereignty-bound and sovereignty-free actors to engage in cooperation or conflict—all can undergo either evolutionary or breakpoint change. They continue to operate as limits for political systems as long as the analytic skills of people, the stability of authority relations, and the centralization of global structures are altered at an incremental pace. However, if the pace of such changes passes beyond a certain threshold, breakpoint transformations will ensue, and sharp conflicts will arise over what the parameter values should be. There is apt to be a lengthy period of turmoil before consensus on the parameter values emerges and the system moves on to a new equilibrium. That is, in the absence of clear-cut parameters during the period following breakpoint change, the complexity and dynamism of the system are likely to be exceedingly high, thus subjecting it to the conditions of a turbulent field.

What makes political systems cross over the threshold into parameter transformations? Some breakpoints occur when a technological development enables individuals to engage in previously unimagined activities and collectivities to pursue previously inconceivable policy goals. The jet airliner, the communications satellite, and the nuclear weapon are examples. Other thresholds are of the kind often referred to as the straw that broke the camel's back: a turning point that occurs when the resources or practices of a system can no longer cope with one more increment of change and its parameters give way under the cumulative load. The long attrition and eventual transformation of single-party regimes in Mexico, Chicago, and Jersey City exemplify such breakpoints at the level of national and local politics.

Still other thresholds fall between the abrupt shifts induced by technological innovation and the slow cumulation of marginal adjustments. These intermediate types of thresholds combine technological innovations with psychological dynamics in which shared perceptions and orientations accelerate the rate of change in parameter values. All three of the parameters viewed here as primary to the global system are of this kind. Doubtless, the expansion of the analytic skills of individuals has been continuous since the onset of industrialization in the eighteenth century, but it was not until the communications revolution enabled people to perceive that distant others were altering their circumstances through collective action that the world passed through a threshold and the decentralizing complexities and dynamism of empowered citizenries, authority crises, and a bifurcated global structure amounted to a thoroughgoing system transformation. Thus, to anticipate the analysis of the next chapter, the breakdown of superpower alliance systems, the breakup of the European empires, and the proliferation of states in the Third World in the 1950s provoked a breakpoint change that continues to find expression in post-Mao China, in Gorbachev's Soviet Union, in Western Europe, and in many other places where dissatisfied leaders are discerning virtue in decentralized structures and restless citizens are beginning to apply performance criteria of legitimacy.

This is another way of saying that thresholds are reached and crossed when people become aware that things are fundamentally different. During evolutionary change, few recognize that the incremental alterations may be moving in a particular direction; but when events culminate in a breakpoint, the movement becomes an issue in itself. Journalists, politicians, and academics begin to speak of the attenuation of old patterns and the emergence of new ones. As a consequence, the presence of a threshold becomes a matter of systemwide cognizance and the basis for new orientations at the micro level and new practices at the macro level. Sometimes, in fact, the breakpoint is so widely perceived that the changes wrought by it are explicitly defined as new continuities rather than merely as possible departures from past practices.[19]

A recent instance of evolutionary change being retrospectively recognized as culminating in breakpoint change is provided by the reactions of neoconservatives to developments in the Soviet Union, Eastern Europe, and China during the late 1980s. Having been skeptical that the incremental alterations of earlier years amounted to meaningful change, by the late 1980s, these analysts were ready to acknowledge that a threshold had been crossed, that "the flow of events over the

---

[19] A recent instance of this process at the national level occurred in Israel, when people openly came to acknowledge that the uprisings on the West Bank and Gaza Strip might continue indefinitely, that the system could no longer go back to the structures, relationships, and orientations that had prevailed eight months earlier. See Joel Brinkley, "For Israel, Uprising Is the Status Quo," *New York Times*, July 14, 1988, p. A3.

past decade or so . . . [made it] hard to avoid the feeling that something very fundamental has happened in history," that "there is some larger process at work, a process that gives coherence and order to the daily headlines." In contrast to the theory of change developed in the present work, the neoconservatives discern this "larger process" to involve the decline of communism as an ideology that shapes policy and impels behavior. For them the decline was so precipitous, so unequivocally a breakpoint, that, as one of them declared, "What we may be witnessing is not just the end of the Cold War, or the passing of a particular period of postwar history, but the end of history as such: that is, the end point of mankind's ideological evolution and the universalization of Western liberal democracy as the final form of human government."[20]

However the "larger process" presently at work in world politics may be interpreted, clearly breakpoint change is not the equivalent of instantaneous change. By definition, it involves abrupt ruptures in a pattern, but these need not occur in an hour, day, or week, Indeed, as will be seen in the next chapter, it may be years before a sharp turn in a pattern is properly viewed as a permanent change rather than a brief perturbation. What distinguishes a breakpoint change, in other words, is the sharpness of the break and not the time it takes to become manifest. For when turbulence overtakes a political system, its old parameters may not be quickly superseded by new, more appropriate ones. Given the complexity and dynamism inherent in turbulent transformations, the time it takes for new parameter values to emerge varies widely. As the old parametric arrangements become less and less constraining, there may be a long interregnum during which complexity and dynamism remain high and systemic rules and principles remain obscure.

This interregnum is the period of greatest turbulence for a political system. During this period, a form of uncertainty and unpredictability develops that is so unusual and extensive as to confound and impede the processes through which new parameter values emerge. Some uncertainty is always present in any social system, either (1) *pluralistic* uncertainty, in which the behavior of an actor cannot be predicted from the observation of other actors because the system's parameters permit, encourage, or even prescribe diversity among subgroups, or (2)

---

[20] Francis Fukuyama, "The End of History?" *National Interest*, no. 16 (Summer 1989); 3–18 (quotations on pp. 3 and 4). The same issue of this journal presents (pp. 19–35) comments on the Fukuyama article by Allan Bloom, Pierre Hassner, Gertrude Himmelfarb, Irving Kristol, Daniel Patrick Moynihan, and Stephen Sestanovich, all of whom accept his main thesis.

statistical uncertainty, in which outcomes depend on the confluence of too many variables to be predictable. But the uncertainty that accompanies turbulent conditions is different in that it arises out of the diversity inherent in the absence of constraining principles and practices. That is, lacking reasonably clear parametric values, what might be called *anomic* uncertainty sets in, as individuals and groups no longer feel obliged to perform the roles to which they have been assigned and in which they have hitherto been comfortable. Thus do organizations lose their cohesion, subgroups reject the preferences of higher authorities, and the normal constraints that govern the life of collectivities cease to be effective controls. In terms of postinternational politics, therefore, turbulence means that actors pay few if any costs for violating the conventions of international law or the established procedures of the state system. Thus are embassies ransacked, sovereign privileges ignored, commercial airliners shot down, arms offered for the return of hostages, light planes landed in Red Square, and so on through a long list of seemingly anomic events that presently occur in world politics with a fair degree of frequency.

Furthermore, the longer the interregnum lasts, the greater is the inclination to stray from whatever parametric rules and principles may be operative or emergent, with the result that turbulent conditions begin to feed on themselves. This is why the duration of turbulence can itself be a highly unpredictable dimension of postinternational politics.

The distinction between parametric transformations and variable fluctuations also anticipates the importance attached to micro-macro interactions in chapter 7. Obviously, breakpoint transformations are necessarily systemwide in their scope, which means that they must be perceived and accepted by the citizens who sustain the operation and structures of their macro collectivities and institutions. If the cultural norms, habits, and attitudes that operate at the micro level are inhospitable to change, so that the system's members are not ready to take advantage of the opportunities or bow to the limits that the changes portend, then significant systemwide transformations will not occur and the continuities will be maintained. An insight into these micro-macro interactions is provided by Gorbachev's inclusion of severe curbs (subsequently relaxed) on the sale of vodka among his efforts to redirect the Soviet system: if the initial policy had proved so unacceptable on a large scale as to detract from the energies and support required to bring about the desired economic reforms, then the macro transformations envisioned by the new program would have lagged.

In short, if only macro parameters are affected by change, without corresponding alterations at the micro level, the functioning of the system will not be deeply disturbed and the parameters will settle back into their previous patterns. Similarly, if change is confined to the micro level, the system's parameter values will remain intact, until such time as the stirrings at the micro level percolate to and find expression at the macro level.

The necessity of micro shifts explains why the parameters of political systems are so rarely caught up in turbulence and undergo transformation. The cultural norms and the habits of compliance of citizens are not easily redirected on a permanent basis. The tendency toward inertia and the preference for the known over the unknown are so great that only under extraordinary conditions are micro transformations initiated. The dramatic moments of history are those marked by turbulent change, but most of its moments, an overwhelming preponderance of them, are suffused by continuity, by systems moving through time very much as they have always done.

THREE GLOBAL PARAMETERS

The foregoing conception of the variabilities and constancies of political systems helps explain why, as our assumption (2) implies, fundamental transformations of world politics are the exception rather than the rule, and also why such changes, when they do occur, are likely to be turbulent rather than evolutionary. Because of its scope, the global system is governed by only a few parameters, thus affording ample room for fluctuations in its variables without their intruding upon or extending beyond its conventions and structures. That is, only a few parameters are both so primary and so extensive as to be major sources of Order II. There are, obviously, many technological boundaries that significantly affect the conduct of world affairs—the state of weapons development, the geological distribution of energy resources, and the capacity of computers to process information are perhaps the most salient in the present era—but there are only a handful of individual and organizational activities that are sufficiently pervasive to constrain and shape global life. National systems may have a number of parameters, but these are limited in scope, given the enormous variations that differentiate the histories and cultures of the world's regions and states. Similarly, some parameters may influence the politics of several national systems (e.g., the same secular norms are parametric for all the Western democracies); but, again, these are mere variables from a global perspective, since there are a number of countries responsive to other value systems (such as those of Islam or the Orient).

In short, the key parameters of the global system are those structural and normative constraints that are worldwide in scope and primary in effect. In the present work, one micro, one macro, and one mixed pattern are postulated as sufficiently broad and fundamental to be called parametric on a global scale. These three parameters, moreover, are so intimately interrelated that if any one of them is disturbed by the dynamics of change, the other two become vulnerable as well, thereby increasing the likelihood that turbulence will overtake world politics.

The micro parameter consists of those predispositions and practices by which people relate to higher authority, a cluster that includes their loyalties, legitimacy sentiments, compliance habits, analytic skills, and cathectic capacities. This cluster is a micro parameter because it refers to the orientations and behavior of individuals, and it is a global parameter inasmuch as people everywhere, notwithstanding their cultural differences, tend to allow their leaders to speak and act on their behalf in world politics. Historically, the orientations and behavior of citizens and subjects have accorded their leaders great leeway. Most people were socialized into the norms of their own systems, unexposed to the world beyond their local and national communities, and thus responsive to the demands of the other two parameters inherent in a state-centric world of industrialized communities and empires; hence, they tended to be minimally and simplistically oriented toward world affairs. Leaving aside elites and attentive publics, citizens in every part of the world related to political and organizational authorities with rudimentary analytic skills, with a disinclination to become emotionally involved in foreign situations or outcomes, with a readiness to accept as authoritative whatever the duly constituted leaders asserted as their policies, and thus with a predisposition to comply automatically with the initiatives or directives to which such policies gave rise.

The historical significance of this micro parameter has thus been that people were unwilling or unable to locate themselves in the complex processes of global affairs but were inclined instead to accord legitimacy to whatever was undertaken by the officials who made or enacted policies on behalf of their nation-state. If these policies were in conflict with those of other organizations or groups with which they were affiliated, or if the officials pursued policies that required mobilizing men for war, this micro parameter conferred the highest priority on national loyalties and led people to march proudly off to battle. In short, given an industrial order that fostered centralizing dynamics, self-interests readily became equated to national interests, good citizenship to unthinking loyalty and automatic compliance with established authority.

This micro parameter will be more fully discussed in chapters 9, 12, and 13, but it may be noted here that the turbulence accompanying the postindustrial order is seen as marked by decentralizing as well as centralizing dynamics, subjecting traditional authority relations to considerable stress. The argument will be advanced that such stresses are transforming the analytic skills, compliance habits, legitimacy sentiments, and cathectic capacities of individuals in every part of the world. Although it is multidimensional, this micro parameter will be treated as a single parameter, because the predispositions and capacities it encompasses are so closely linked to and shaped by each other. It will be referred to as the *orientational* or *skill* parameter.

The other two global parameters have some common elements, but they are differentiated enough not to treat them as a single cluster. The *structural* parameter consists of those rules of governance, informal regimes, formal alliances, legal conventions, and other arrangements through which the issues contested on the global stage are processed and managed by macro collectivities (states, subnational groups, or supranational organizations). These collectivities, in turn, are sustained by one or another form of hierarchical authority relations (e.g., pluralistic and class structures in national systems and balance-of-power and dependency patterns in international systems), which are here designated as the *relational* parameter.

The structural parameter is subjected to scrutiny in chapters 10 and 15, with alternative systems for maintaining global order considered in the context of the anarchy that has long characterized the state-centric world. Shifts in the other parameters, along with the tensions between the changes induced by growing global interdependence and those fostered by decentralizing dynamics, are believed to have initiated the transformation of the structural parameter. The conclusion is that Order II may involve a bifurcation of global life wherein the course of events unfolds in both a state-centric and a multi-centric world.

Starting with a focus on the techniques of control through which collectivities seek to manage their affairs, chapters 8 and 14 elaborate on the relational parameter. The emphasis is on how authority and hierarchy within and among collectivities are sustained. The advent of parametric turbulence is seen to occur when the authority relations of collectivities undergo crisis or redirection on a global scale. Partly in response to comparable tendencies at the micro level, and also as a consequence of the decentralizing dynamics inherent in the structural parameter and the fast-changing technologies of the postindustrial order, the relational parameter is conceived as being presently caught up in turbulent change, as the authority of diverse subgroups has been strengthened at the expense of both the collectivities and the Western state system of which they are a part.

Earlier, the strategy of simply comparing the global system at time *1* and time *2* was rejected on the ground that the concept of change needed to be more precisely specified. Now, having identified three primary parameters, and having stressed that a transformation in the global system involves changes in these parameters, we can turn to historical comparisons and examine the orientations and skills of citizens at the micro level, the authority relations that link individuals and groups to their collectivities at the macro level, and the structures through which political issues are processed in the global system for signs that turbulence (high complexity and dynamism) or even hyper-turbulence (unmanageable complexity and dynamism) has overtaken world affairs. To the extent that such turbulence can be depicted, the comparison between times *1* and *2* will then uncover the emergent nature of Order II.

Anticipating the thrust of the next chapter, time *1* is defined as the three centuries prior to the 1950s, and time *2* as the following decades. The 1950s are a purposefully broad dividing line. As will be seen, no particular date or event is posited as distinguishing time *1* from time *2*. Indeed, even fixing on a decade as the point of change may be unduly exact; the parametric transformations may still be under way.

CHAPTER 5

TRACING TURBULENCE
The History of Three Parameters

The merger of, among others, computers, microcomputers, te-
lephony, cable, fibre optics, videotape and communication satellites is creating a new world. . . . The ways in which citizens
perceive and respond to events, and therefore the interactions
between them and their governments, are bound to alter substantially. The structures and organization of private enterprises and governments will likewise undergo major changes.
Furthermore, the very process of acquiring facts and values
and the means through which people act will substantially alter
in both the private and public spheres. The ubiquitous tension
between centers and peripheries may assume entirely new
forms; class distinctions will be related to the use people make
of the new technologies; new technocratic elites will emerge;
the size and nature of communities within which individuals
and groups identify themselves will reflect the capabilities of
informatics or of telematics. All these and other developments
are certain to make for a different political process from that
known so far, both within and between states.

—John Meisel[1]

Turbulence provides a description of why choices today are
more difficult than fifty years ago, not a prediction of irreme-
diable chaos.

—Ernest B. Haas[2]

HAVING CONCEPTUALIZED the nature of fundamental change so
that its presence can be more precisely ascertained, we must now move
beyond the simple assertion that profound transformations are occur-

---

[1] "Communications in the Space Age: Some Canadian and International Implications," *International Political Science Review* 7 (April 1986): 300.

[2] *When Knowledge Is Power: Three Models of Change in International Organizations*
(Berkeley: University of California Press, 1989), p. 111.

ring in global life. Narrowing the search for systematic transformations to parameters undergoing turbulence is helpful, but clearly it is not enough. We need a conceptual map that allows us to trace the outlines of the "new world" to which Meisel refers and that Haas says has rendered decision making more challenging than was the case five decades ago. More specifically, we need to locate the bases for the observation that the present era is host to unprecedented change. The aim of this chapter is to describe how each of the three primary parameters has been swept up by the dynamics of change. The task of explaining these changes and assessing their implications for the future will be dealt with in subsequent chapters.

Two main kinds of supporting evidence are available for the conclusion that profound changes are underway. One is the almost daily appearance of anomalies that do not fit well into existing frameworks for understanding world politics. Another consists of statements by cautious observers who are so convinced that these anomalies are patterned that they have asserted that a new Order II is emerging.

The Ubiquitousness of Anomalies

Inasmuch as our views of change and continuity derive from our philosophical perspectives, we are likely to see the course of events as confirming the framework we employ to interpret them. Thus, our paradigms are perpetuated, and we find it difficult to remain open to altering or abandoning them even if the real world appears to be inconsistent with them. Anomalies are one form of evidence that can help us deal with this problem. Occasional exceptions can be easily accommodated or dismissed, but when they recur with some frequency we feel compelled to pause and wonder whether our paradigms are losing their explanatory power.

Such is the case in the social sciences today. As the epigraphs at the beginning of chapter 2 indicated, the dominant perspectives in the social sciences are being challenged as to whether their paradigms still fit the worlds they purport to describe and explain. In the field of world politics, the challenge appears especially serious. With individuals more self-conscious and competent, with subgroups coalescing and governments foundering, with multinational corporations collaborating in joint economic enterprises and multilateral alliances faltering over monetary and economic policies, with international regimes seeking to develop the global commons and national actors trying to extend and enclose their piece of the commons, and with technological changes leading to the social and political changes noted above by Meisel, the

fit between our paradigms and the structure of world politics has become incongruous. Compared to the past, the authority of actors in
world politics is less comprehensive and the boundaries between them
are less clear-cut. Gone is the relative tidiness provided by customary
jurisdictions and stable polities, by legal precedents and accepted procedures, by shared values and cultural continuities. Where the legitimacy of states was once taken for granted, today it is frayed or (as in
Poland and Lebanon) virtually nonexistent. Where rebel organizations
used to join together against a common enemy, today they oppose each
other (as among the Afghans) or even war on each other (as among
Shiite Muslims in Lebanon). Where geographic borders once delineated a people, today they surround partial and mixed populations and
the flow of refugees, immigrants, and illegal aliens swells in all parts of
the world. Where economies were once largely self-contained, today
they are permeated by goods, services, ownerships, and financing from
abroad and by underground markets and exchanges at home. Where
Europe once had hard-and-fast boundaries dividing its eastern and
western sectors, today its postwar arrangements are coming undone
and new, continent-wide institutions may be forming. Where the UN
Security Council once voted on resolutions, today it mostly holds debates.[3] Where embassies were once immune and inviolate, today they
are subject to violent intrusions and serve as targets for explosives.
Where the flights of commercial airliners once constituted a simple
transnational pattern, today they can be hijacked or shot down and
become the foci of superpower disputes.

In short, the frequency of anomalies seems too great to ignore or
rationalize. Each might be explicable by a particular set of historical
circumstances, but taken together as a series of exceptions, they culminate to a pattern that is not easily explained. In particular, neither
the dominant paradigm of the field, realism, nor its more recent variant, neorealism, any longer does well in accounting for them. Consider, for example, its core concept: that the course of events is explained mainly by the interaction of states acting to advance their own
interests, and that in this anarchic world no higher authority is able to
restrain them. The more the industrial era recedes into the past and the
more its postindustrial successor becomes the basis for organizing human affairs, the less does this *state-centric* principle describe world
politics. For every quintessential "realist" happening—such as the Soviet invasion of Afghanistan or the U.S. intervention in Central Amer-

[3] Bernard D. Nossiter, "Diplomats at U.N. Fear Council Is Losing Its Teeth," *New
York Times*, April 25, 1983, p. 2.

ica—innumerable events and developments occur for which realism has, at best, a strained and insufficient explanation. A private group, the Natural Resources Defense Council (NRDC), negotiates with the superpower governments to monitor nuclear test-ban agreements; a representative of the Church of England serves as a link between terrorists and governments in the Middle East; a variety of organizations make decisions to invest or disinvest in an effort to alter the social policies of the South African government; the IMF instructs national governments on their economic policies; the Nicaraguan chief of state campaigns for support on the streets of New York; the Israeli foreign minister conducts a telephone call-in news conference with callers from the Arab world; a news anchorman for the Columbia Broadcasting System presses a member of the Soviet Politburo on a nationally televised news program for information on what happened during a closed meeting of the Central Committee of the Communist Party of the Soviet Union; the Nobel Peace Prize Committee, an autonomous unit of the Norwegian parliament, enters into a fragile diplomatic situation in Central America by awarding the prize to one of the participants, President Oscar Arias of Costa Rica; a leader of the anti-apartheid movement in South Africa, Archbishop Desmond M. Tutu, is elected to the Board of Overseers of Harvard University; American scientists of the NRDC, climbing atop the launching tube of a Soviet nuclear-armed cruise missile, test its warhead with sophisticated measuring devices; a papier-mâché statue of the "Goddess of Liberty" is installed briefly in Beijing's Tiananmen Square; Poles in the United States are given the franchise in the 1989 Polish elections, and their ballots are believed to be decisive in one Warsaw district; officials of the U.S. National Security Council circumvent the Department of State in an attempt to alter international relationships in both the Middle East and Central America; a novel published in England leads to the withdrawal of ambassadors from Iran and to an assassination in Belgium; two poisoned grapes from Chile disrupt world markets, provoke actions by several governments, lead to labor tensions in the docks of Philadelphia, and foster disarray in Chile itself—to mention only some of the myriad of recent incidents that indicate the emergence of a new global order.

Nor are the anomalies confined to specific events. None of the conventional paradigms adequately account for the impact of global television on the conduct of world affairs; for the appearance on the global agenda of issues—such as currency crises, terrorism, trade imbalances, environmental pollution, AIDS, or the drug trade—growing out of the world's increasing interdependence; for the prominent public role played by private citizens such as Nicholas Daniloff, Terry Waite, Eugene Hasenfus, Andrei Sakharov, Salman Rushdie, Fang Lizhi, Samantha Smith, Armand Hammer, and Joseph Cicippio in international processes (not to mention the private roles played by public officials such as Oliver North and William Casey); for the failure of governments and states to control events in the Middle East and Central America; for the fact that public demand compelled the United States to withdraw from Vietnam but failed to prevent the placement of cruise missiles in West Germany; for the aggregation of national intelligence agencies into "one of the largest [transnational] bureaucracies in the world";[4] for the way in which subgroups such as refuseniks in the Soviet Union, Solidarity in Poland, and the Tamils in Sri Lanka become focal points of global contentiousness; or for the breakdown of treaties, such as that between Australia, New Zealand, and the United States, in the absence of alterations in the power balance.

Consider also the persistence of the classical economic model of international trade. The belief that a decline in the value of the dollar will reduce the U.S. trade deficit continues to organize the thinking of many analysts and politicians, despite such contrary evidence as a 40 percent drop in its value between 1985 and 1987 that was unaccompanied by a corresponding decline in the trade imbalance.[5] Many have preserved their faith in the model by attributing the imbalance to certain "unusual" conditions that would soon yield to the underlying tendency toward comparative advantage. At first, Japanese inroads into U.S. markets were said to result from their making cheap copies of American products. Even when the inroads extended to automobiles and consumer electronics, they were dismissed as resulting from effective imitation rather than from a creative and entrepreneurial culture, an explanation that in turn broke down when the United States also fell behind in semiconductors, robotics, and supercomputers. Even then, the compulsion to preserve the model led to the assertion that, because the United States was the financial center of the world, the trade deficit was bound to disappear once the dollar came down. Yet the Japanese now have eight of the ten largest financial institutions in the world, raising still another doubt about the key assumption in the

---

[4] Jeffrey T. Richelson and Desmond Ball, *The Ties That Bind: Intelligence Cooperation between the UKUSA Countries—The United Kingdom, the United States of America, Canada, Australia, and New Zealand* (London: Allen & Unwin, 1985).

[5] For a succinct account of how the classical economic model of free trade has survived in the face of contrary evidence, see Jeff Faux, "Here Lies Free Trade, R.I.P.," *New York Times*, August 31, 1987, p. A19.

classical model that free and competitive international markets are conductive to stability and the diminution of imbalances.[6]

Anomalies as Patterns

There is, of course, no magic formula to tell us when to stop treating events as anomalies and to treat them instead as newly emergent patterns. As indicated in the previous chapter, some analysts believe it is premature to do so now, claiming that the episodes recounted above are not sufficiently numerous or important to be regarded as patterned. One colleague, for instance, read an early draft of this chapter in 1987 and objected to the inclusion of downed commercial airliners among the anomalies on the ground that the shooting down of the Korean airliner was only one incident among tens of thousands of uneventful flights. Perhaps the downing of an Iranian airliner by a U.S. naval vessel in 1988 would lead him to pause and reflect on how many anomalies make a pattern, or perhaps he would simply say "two incidents" instead of "the incident," a plausible reaction that would highlight the essential point that drawing a line between continuity and change is difficult at best.

Nor is rejection on the ground of insufficient numbers the only basis for discounting anomalies. Some analysts reconcile their theories with the presence of change by making marginal adjustments to them. The concept of international regimes is an example: confronted with perplexing anomalies, some observers suggest that patterns of international cooperation have been maintained because such regimes have evolved to supplement states as managers of key issues on the global agenda. Others concede the presence of transforming dynamics but evade the task of theory-building by attributing them to the ever-greater interdependence of world affairs, as if that relieved them of the obligation to construct a coherent theory. Still others insist that all the changes do not offset the prime fact of global life, the continued hegemony of the United States, and that therefore new theory is needed to account only for marginal phenomena.[7]

In other words, it has proven to be much easier either to sweep the problem of new theory under the rug of "interdependence"—a word

[6] Faux, "Here Lies Free Trade," p. A19.
[7] For vigorous assertions of this last position, see Susan Strange, "The Persistent Myth of Lost Hegemony," *International Organization* 41 (Fall 1987): 551–74, and Susan Strange, "Toward a Theory of Transnational Empire," in E. O. Czempiel and J. N. Rosenau, eds., *Global Changes and Theoretical Challenges: Approaches to World Politics for the 1990s* (Lexington, Mass.: Lexington Books, 1989), pp. 161–76.

that implies that everything is connected to everything else, thus obscuring the need to discern underlying structures and processes—or to assert that nothing has changed because the anarchical arrangements which presently mark the conduct of world politics are much like those that prevailed during earlier eras. Yes, the power of states has eroded and yes, the world is smaller and more interdependent than ever, but the state is still the predominant actor in world politics and the state system is still the main foundation for the course of events. That has been the litany in the literature of the field for several decades.[8]

The ensuing analysis self-consciously breaks with this litany. It breaks with the "state-is-still-predominant" tendency by positing a *multi-centric* world as having evolved independently of the one in which states function, a world in which actions and reactions originate with a multiplicity of actors at diverse system levels, all of which are motivated—and many of which are able—to maintain the integrity of their subsystems and to resist absorption by the systems of which they are a part. It seeks to avoid the "interdependence-accounts-for-disarray" tendency by pointing to new organizing principles, structures, and processes in this multi-centric world that are no less patterned and effective than those of the state-centric world. It counters the "continued-U.S.-dominance" tendency by arguing that, while the structures of the state-centric world permit the emergence of hegemonic leadership, the multi-centric world is too decentralized to support the hierarchy through which hegemons predominate. And it resists the "nothing-has-changed" tendency on the ground that therein lies blindness to the subtleties of history, that only by theoretically allowing for, and empirically exploring, the possibility of underlying transformations can their occurrence be either recognized or legitimately dismissed.

Given a readiness to break away from the neorealist litany, four broad patterns emerge as salient outcomes of the dynamics of change that are at work in world politics. Each of these patterns represents a break with the past, and all of them taken together accommodate the anomalies cited above. The four patterns are:

1. The universe of global politics had come to consist of two interactive worlds with overlapping memberships: a multi-cen-

[8] To be sure, a few analysts do see the need for theorizing afresh. Broad approaches based on long cycles, world systems analysis, historical materialism, and critical theory are illustrative in this regard. More often than not, however, such approaches are offered as alternative explanations of the same state-dominated world for which realism purports to account and not as means of addressing the possible emergence of a new global order.

tric world of diverse, relatively equal actors, and a state-centric world in which national actors are still primary.

2. The norms governing the conduct of politics in the multi-centric world have evolved so as to diminish the utility of force, compelling most of its actors to confine the threat of actual use of force to those situations that arise in the state-centric world of international politics.

3. An autonomy dilemma serves as the driving force of the multi-centric world and a security dilemma constitutes a dominant concern in the state-centric world; at the same time, in the latter case, acquiring or preserving what is held to be a proper share of the world market has come to rival the acquisition or preservation of territory as a preoccupation of states.[9]

4. Changes at the level of macro structures and processes have served as both sources and products of corresponding micro-level shifts wherein individuals are becoming more analytically skillful and cathectically competent, thus fostering the replacement of traditional criteria of legitimacy and authority with performance criteria that, in turn, serve to intensify both the centralizing and the decentralizing tendencies at work within and among macro collectivities.

Setting forth these patterns does not imply that the current scene is exclusively one of profound change. What follows does presume that powerful and transforming dynamics are unfolding on a global scale, but, as emphasized in the previous chapter, these dynamics are conceived as existing in continuous tension with a wide array of static forces that press for continuity. The norms of culture, the imperatives of geographic circumstance, the limits of resource availability, the constraints of historical experience, the attachments to territory, the dictates of memory, and the inertia of organizations are still very much a part of the human condition, and they interact with change in such a way that outcomes vary across time and place, giving rise to an appearance of randomness and chaos as much as of causality and pattern.

But there need be no concern that in acknowledging the statics of continuity, one obscures the enormous changes under way in every corner and at every level of the global system. The conceptualization of a multi-centric world of diverse actors that coexists with the state-

[9] For an elaborate formulation of this change, see Richard Rosecrance, *The Rise of the Trading State: Commerce and Conquest in the Modern World* (New York: Basic Books, 1986).

centric world of national actors virtually assures consideration of the tensions between the statics of continuity and the dynamics of change. For, as will be seen, this nexus of the two worlds is a prime arena wherein clashes occur between the past and the present, between the tendencies toward decentralization and those toward centralization, between the diminished relevance of force and the growing stress on increased shares of the global market.

Lest the discussion so far be viewed as an exaggeration of the magnitude of change entailed by the shift from the industrial to the postindustrial order, consider the reactions of several thoughtful observers of the global scene. One, for example, has said that "the electronic revolution, followed by the microelectronically based, information-technology revolution, are propelling Western society into a new period of history, as different from the industrial period as that period differed from the Middle Ages."[10] The authors of an important book have declared that the change "now taking place in the contemporary world is of an order as great as that occurring when large-scale societies with written languages first arose on the basis of agricultural communities."[11] Still another observer has said that "the entire Industrial Revolution enhanced productivity by a factor of about a hundred, [but] the microelectronic revolution has already enhanced productivity in information-based technology by a factor of more than a million—and the end isn't in sight yet."[12] Similarly, noting that "the acceleration of change compels us to perceive life as motion, not as order," a distinguished historian is bold enough to assert that, although "humans have lived on earth for possibly 800 lifetimes . . . the last two lifetimes have seen more scientific and technological achievement than the first 798 put together."[13] A prominent economist perceives the end of centuries-long patterns and argues that "the world economy is not 'changing'; it has already changed—in its foundations and in its structure—and in all probability the change is irreversible," a conclusion which leads him to ask, "Have we come to the end of the 300-year-old attempt to regulate and stabilize money on which, after all, both the

[10] Tom Stonier, "The Microelectronic Revolution, Soviet Political Structure, and the Future of East-West Relations," *Political Quarterly* 54 (April–June 1983): 137.

[11] F. E. Emery and E. L. Trist, *Towards a Social Ecology* (New York: Plenum, 1975), p. 120.

[12] Carver Mead, quoted in Walter B. Wriston, "Technology and Sovereignty," *Foreign Affairs* 67 (Winter 1988/89): 63–64.

[13] Arthur M. Schlesinger, Jr., "The Challenge of Change," *New York Times Magazine*, July 27, 1986, pp. 20–21.

modern nation-state and the international system are largely based?"[14] A leading social theorist has made the even more sweeping statement that the "era of 'civilization' which, having lasted some 5,000 years, is beginning to give place to a new type of social order."[15]

THE TRANSFORMATION OF THE THREE PARAMETERS

Provoked by the appearance of numerous anomalies, and impressed by the observations of other analysts, one is moved to investigate the possibility that world politics has become a turbulent field, that the complexities and dynamism unleashed by postindustrial technologies are so extensive as to have shattered the primary parameters of the global system. Table 5.1 presents an overall conception of this process. It suggests that the complexity of each parameter and the dynamism of the variables it encompasses have substantially increased at the global, national, and subnational levels. The table also hints at the interconnectedness among both the parameters and the levels: by reading either across the rows or down the columns of the table, one can begin to discern how the changes of each parameter or at each level are linked, so much so that none is likely to have occurred without facilitating developments in the other parameters or at the other levels.

The greater complexity of the structural parameter has come about through the replacement of the state system with a dual system in which a multi-centric world coexists with the state-centric world. These two worlds embrace the same actors, but they have distinctive structures and processes that require the actors to employ very different decision rules as they move back and forth between them. As individuals are active in both their personal and professional worlds, so do states, corporations, ethnic groups, international organizations, churches, and many other collectives with transnational aspirations and responsibilities live in two worlds.[16] To be sure, these two worlds are interactive and overlapping, but each nevertheless retains its identity as a separate sphere of activity because of the different structures and processes through which its actors relate to each other. Thus, the

[14] Peter Drucker, "The Changed World Economy," *Foreign Affairs* 64 (Spring 1986): 768, 790–91.

[15] Kenneth Boulding, quoted in Emery and Trist, *Towards a Social Ecology*, p. 120.

[16] The units of states active in the multi-centric world are those bureaucratic ministries and agencies that are below the state's top leadership and thus do not need to be preoccupied with the responsibilities of sovereignty, a circumstance that renders them responsive to the decision rules of the multi-centric world, even if they have to reverse themselves on those occasions when they report to their superiors in the state-centric world.

TABLE 5.1. Changes from Pre–1950s to Post–1950s
in the Three Primary Parameters of Political Systems
at the Global, National, and Subnational Levels

	Structural Parameter	Relational Parameter	Orientational Parameter
Global Level			
Pre–1950s	Western state system	Power and predominance derived from military capabilities, fostering hierarchical relationships	Individuals mostly unskilled and inattentive
Post–1950s	Bifurcated system	Power and predominance derived from diverse human and nonhuman capabilities, fostering cross-cutting relationships	Individuals more skilled, more involved
National Level			
Pre–1950s	Centralized organizations run by narrowly based elites	Power and predominance derived mostly from wealth, fostering an elite-mass hierarchy	Loyalties and legitimacy sentiments habitually directed toward state authority
Post–1950s	Tendency toward decentralized, mass organizations with pluralistic leaderships	Power and predominance derived from numbers as well as wealth, fostering diffuse relationships	Loyalties and legitimacy sentiments diffused widely, contingent on performance
Subnational Level			
Pre–1950s	Units of structures hierarchically organized at national level; little local autonomy	Power and predominance dependent on arrangements at the national level	Loyalties and legitimacy sentiments habitually directed toward states; readiness to comply with directives from national level
Post–1950s	Relatively autonomous units in loosely organized hierarchies	Power and predominance accrues to numerous, well-organized, or wealthy groups, fostering diffuse relationships	Loyalties and legitimacy sentiments diffused widely, contingent on performance; readiness to defy or ignore directives from national level

organizing principle of realism—that states continuously confront a security dilemma in the form of threats from other states—is joined in competition with the driving force of the multi-centric world—that systems and subsystems at diverse macro levels continuously face an autonomy dilemma in the form of challenges to their identity and integrity.

Virtually by definition, the greater complexity inherent in the need to seek goals and be active in two different worlds suggests that actors, both collectivities and individuals, have to use a wider variety of means and engage in a wider variety of activities on behalf of a wider variety of goals than was the case when the Western state system predominated and set the terms for what actors sought and how they conducted themselves. A logical consequence of the structural parameter's greater complexity, in other words, is a correspondingly greater dynamism on the part of the actors that populate the two worlds of world politics.

Adding to the complexity and dynamism at the global level are structural changes at the national and subnational levels. As table 5.1 also suggests, at both of these levels decentralizing tendencies are conceived to have fragmented long-established hierarchies presided over by narrowly based elites, replacing them with a multiplicity of organizations that have more pluralistic leaderships. By its very nature, such a structural arrangement means that actors are more interdependent, that they have a need for and relations with a widening array of other actors, and that consequently the patterns of interaction that mark their daily lives encompass more extensive networks than was the case in the industrial or agrarian eras. In short, the structural arrangements of postinternational politics are marked by considerably greater density and interdependence than those they replaced, and these characteristics are among the hallmarks of turbulence.

Turning to the relational parameter, table 5.1 indicates that the decentralizing tendencies of the postindustrial era have fragmented the previous sources of power and authority. Where authority relations at the global level in the state system were to a considerable extent established on the basis of military capabilities, the sources of power in the current era are much more varied, and authority links are thus that much more complex. A host of new actors at all three levels now have the wherewithal to lay claim to their goals and to pursue them in diverse ways. Moreover, this fragmentation of the number and diversity of relationships has altered the nature of authority, making compliance more problematical and venturesomeness more likely. Again, signs of a turbulent field can be discerned.

Much the same kind of conclusion can be reached about the orientational parameter. In previous eras, citizenship skills were much more rudimentary than is presently the case. Today, individuals, both leaders and followers, are conceived to have greater analytic skills and cathectic capacities with which to relate themselves to world affairs than did their forebears. Consequently, it is easier for them to identify where they fit in the course of events, to aggregate their values through collective action, and thus to sustain their involvement as citizens across more issue areas and for longer stretches of time. Table 5.1 suggests that the enlarged capacities of individuals have also led to a diffusion and reorientation in the levels at which loyalties and legitimacy sentiments are focused, with the main tendency being toward subsystems and away from national entities. This is why, to anticipate a central theme of later chapters, it may well be that the greater complexity and dynamism of individuals constitute the single most important source of the turbulence that marks our time.

While this description is still fairly sketchy, a mere glimpse of vast and deep historical processes, an initial sense of its validity can be obtained by noting its fit to the anomalies recounted above. All of them fit well. That a group of concerned scientists negotiates with superpowers to monitor nuclear testing or that a church official undertakes to mediate with terrorists for the release of hostages is readily explained, for example, by the advent of a multi-centric world in which authority is so widely dispersed that governments must be ready to accept the involvement of private actors if they are to move toward their goals. This very same devolution of authority to nongovernmental subsystems also serves to account for the actions of chiefs of state and foreign ministers in taking their cases to the streets of New York and the airwaves of the Middle East, just as the greater analytic skills of citizens and the shift of their loyalties and legitimacy sentiments towards subgroups facilitated the success of Solidarity in Poland, the Tamils in Sri Lanka, the antiwar movement in the United States, and the disinvestment campaign directed at South Africa. Likewise, the fragmentation of authority and the complex interdependencies accompanying the bifurcation of the global system provide a basis for understanding such developments as the ability of an international organization, the IMF, to alter the policies of national governments, the impact of the Nobel Prize committee on a delicate diplomatic situation, and the ability of a bureaucratic agency in the White House to implement (at least for a time) policies outside the framework of its own governmental structure. Similarly, the need to avoid the tarnishing of images of competence that results from complex interdependence helps account for the interview of a Soviet politburo member on a U.S. newscast.

Although the emergence of multi-centric world accounts well for the events and developments that are anomalous from a state-centric perspective, what accounts for the emergence itself? Why now, late in the twentieth century, has turbulence overcome world politics, weakening national states to the point where they must share the political stage with private subgroups, transnational organizations, and their own bureaucratic agencies? A brief answer is that the world has moved into the postindustrial era of interdependence. But, of course, these words are just a condensed expression for the culmination of a complicated and lengthy history. Although such a history cries out to be written, that is not the goal here.[17] We are concerned, rather, with the implications of global turbulence for the conduct of politics. On the other hand, the portents of a turbulent world politics cannot be assessed without some notion of how and why the three primary parameters have been caught up in so high a degree of complexity and variability. Thus, the analysis of each parameter in subsequent chapters has been made with a concern for its historical development, while the remainder of this chapter is devoted to an overview of how the dynamics of postindustrialism have brought about a breakpoint in international history.

ORIGINS OF THE BREAKPOINT

Let us begin with the exogenous sources of global turbulence, the alterations of environmental limits and opportunities. Here the dynamics of technology have been decisive, for at the heart of the postindustrial era are developments in agriculture, genetics, transportation, communications, and information processing that have greatly narrowed geographic and social distances as well as altered the availability, processing, and distribution of natural resources. Each of these developments has made people increasingly interactive with and interdependent on each other. Whether it be in the flow of goods, money, people, or ideas, what happens in one part of the world now has repercussions for the course of events in many other places. Goods are produced in one country with components mined or manufactured in every corner of the world, and money circulates within seconds in a

[17] For good, if preliminary, efforts, see Daniel Bell, *The Coming of Post-Industrial Society: A Venture in Social Forecasting* (New York: Basic Books, 1973), and Roger Benjamin, *The Limits of Politics: Collective Goods and Political Change in Postindustrial Societies* (Chicago: University of Chicago Press, 1980).

global market.[18] The quadrennial Olympics are watched by millions of sports fans in every country. Television spectaculars on behalf of starving masses in Africa raise funds from a global audience, and radio talk shows have experts who receive and answer questions about AIDS from callers on every continent. An explosion shortly after the launch of a space shuttle killing the seven astronauts aboard, is an immediate and searing experience for television viewers everywhere.

This is not to imply that the transformation of Order II is to be welcomed and valued. Changes such as the foregoing may be for the better or for the worse, depending on how they are filtered through the political system into which they are introduced. Technological innovations can lead to both resource shortages and gluts, to both the construction and the destruction of decent communities, to both the evolution and the suppression of intelligence, to both the protection and the exploitation of the natural environment, to both the spread and the alleviation of disease,[19] to both the liberation and the oppression of the human spirit.[20] Likewise, interdependence among peoples, groups, and societies can give rise to either conflict or cooperation, depending on how it is managed by the relevant political systems. Increased interdependence can lead to the spread of misery or to the sharing of artistic experiences, to the intensification of prejudice or to the integration of perspectives.

Not all the exogenous stimulants of global turbulence, however, have been of a nonhuman kind. In addition to the impact of technology, dynamics located in nonpolitical areas of human experience have had an impact on the environment with which political systems must

[18] Joseph Grunwald and Kenneth Flamm, *The Global Factory: Foreign Assembly in International Trade* (Washington, D.C.: Brookings Institution, 1985); James Sterngold, "Redrawing the World's Financial Map, *New York Times*, April 1, 1986, p. D1.

[19] It took nearly two decades for the great cholera epidemics of previous centuries to move across Europe; AIDS, by contrast, spread to a hundred countries in half of one decade. On the other hand, an impressive stock of biological and epidemiological information about AIDS, including identification of the virus that causes it, was also gathered within the space of five years, whereas eighty years elapsed between the first cholera epidemic in the nineteenth century and the isolation of its causative agents. See Lincoln C. Chen, "The AIDS Pandemic: An Internationalist Approach to Disease Control," *Daedalus* 116 (Spring 1987): 186.

[20] For a discussion of how "home-made video tapes of demonstrations and audio recordings of wall posters barely begin to exhaust the possibilities of dissent raised by the new consumer technologies," see Jim Mann, "Tape Recording: The Modern Medium of Dissent," *Los Angeles Times*, January 11, 1987, sec. 5, p. 2. That the same technologies can also serve oppressive purposes is illustrated by the way in which the authorities in China selectively used television to reconstruct their massacre of students in Beijing in 1989.

cope. Rapid population growth has also raised the degree of complexity of all three parameters.[21] Doubtless, some of the organizational proliferation that marks the postindustrial era is due to the sheer numbers of people and the organizational need to subdivide and specialize in order to cope with swelling memberships and expanding demands. The changes brought by the postindustrial order to the workplace, the family, the school, and the other institutions that infuse structure into daily life are also sources of greater complexity and dynamism at all political levels.

No less relevant as sources of global turbulence are the endogenous dynamics that derive from the interaction of the three parameters. Each of these is so closely linked to the other two that even slight changes in one can produce or reinforce changes in the others. As people become more analytically skillful, for example, they begin to question the legitimacy of their national system and to redirect their loyalties toward the subsystem level, a process which has here been designed as "subgroupism" and which is central to the onset of political turbulence. In like manner, tendencies toward subgroupism have been accelerated by the quickening pace of bifurcation and the increasingly clear-cut structures of the multi-centric world. The turbulent flows of world politics, in short, sweep back over each other, heightening their complexities and intensifying their dynamism as they course through the communications channels and political arenas of the global system.

Another way to grasp the dynamics of global turbulence is to realize that the centralizing and decentralizing dynamics at work in the world are simultaneous and thus in a state of continual tension. The tendencies toward centralization arise out of the greater interdependencies of people, groups, economies, and countries that have created a set of new issues we shall refer to as *interdependence issues*. They are distinguished from conventional issues by the fact that they span national boundaries and thus cannot be addressed, much less resolved, through actions undertaken only at the national or local level. Among them are unbalanced rates of exchange, Third World debt, terrorism, atmospheric pollution, AIDS, and the drug trade. But even while such issues tend to promote transnational cooperation among governments and other political units, the decentralizing tendencies inherent in subgroupism, shifting loyalties, and deteriorating authority relations generate conflicts within both the state-centric and the multi-centric

[21] See Nazli Choucri, *Population Dynamics and International Violence* (Lexington, Mass.: Lexington Books, 1974).

worlds, and the ambiguities and tensions that result from the overlap and simultaneity of these contrary pressures add further to the complexities and dynamism that underlie present-day global life.

Embedded within the tendencies toward both centralization and decentralization, moreover, are many sources of resistance to change. Public officials seeking to shore up the tattered authority of the state, political parties trying to mobilize publics on behalf of traditional values, educators espousing the civic virtues of a dying order, ideologues straining to preserve the purity of their beliefs, aging elites clinging to the vestiges of legitimacy, bewildered clergy endeavoring to place God's will on the side of continuity—these are but a few of the ways in which the global environment is roiled further as the postindustrial order comes up against the habits, norms, and cultural impulses of a time when the parameters of world politics were reasonably simple and stable.

ORIGINS OF TURBULENCE

These dynamics of systemic transformation and their interactions with each other were summarized diagrammatically in figure 1.1. The time line along the top of the figure gives a rough indication of the time in which the bifurcation of the global system has occurred. It suggests that global turbulence is a recent phenomenon, with its genesis located in the 1950s and its full emergence occurring some time after the 1960s.[22] Of course, no particular event or date can be cited as the point at which the winds of change gathered momentum or the bifurcation of the global system reached fruition, but its origins can be discerned in the years following World War II with the breakup of the British and French empires and the acquisition of independence and statehood by a number of former colonies beginning with India in 1947. The unfolding of this process is further reflected in the growth of the UN from 51 members at its founding in 1945 to 163 members in 1988.

[22] Similarly, Bell, *The Coming of Post-Industrial Society*, p. 346, specifies the 1945–1950 period as "the birth years" of the postindustrial era. Lyotard, in a classic treatise on postmodernism, locates the "temporal disjunction" in the same time frame: "This transition has been under way since at least the end of the 1950s, which for Europe marks the completion of reconstruction." Jean-Francois Lyotard, *The Postmodern Condition: A Report on Knowledge* (Minneapolis: University of Minnesota Press, 1984), p. 3. That the changes continue to evolve in the present is indicated by Pope John Paul II's encyclical letter of 1988, *Sollicitudo Rei Socialis*, which opens with the statement (or understatement) that "the social context in which we live today cannot be said to be completely identical to that of 20 years ago." *New York Times*, February 20, 1988, p. 4.

The immediate antecedents of the turbulence are also suggested in figure 1.1. The state system came out of World War II, especially after the Berlin blockade of 1948, in a tight bipolar condition, with both superpowers exercising strict controls over their respective blocs and with their authority to do so not subjected to effective challenges. Then, late in the 1950s, China broke with the Soviet bloc, France distanced itself from the U.S. bloc, and the nations of the Third World, beginning to sense their potential as neutrals between the blocs, acquired a separate status of their own, all of which initiated a transition from the tight bipolar system through a loose bipolar system to a multipolar set of structural arrangements. The advent of a bifurcated world followed as the next stage, if not the culmination, of these decentralized tendencies. The structural transformations, moreover, were accompanied by corresponding changes in the political culture of world politics, changes in which the Western state system's conception of legitimacy and authority was expanded to encompass new norms and values appropriate to the bifurcated world of sovereignty-bound and sovereignty-free actors.[23]

But, it may be argued, surely the global system experienced great upheavals prior to the 1950s. With two world wars and a severe depression in the first half of the twentieth century, a flowering of industrialization in the nineteenth century, and two major revolutions toward the end of the eighteenth century, it may seem absurd to assert that turbulence is unique to the latter half of the present century. But it must be recalled that by turbulence we mean a noteworthy increase in the complexity and dynamism of the three global parameters. The argument here is that, while the domestic and international upheavals of the two centuries prior to the 1950s were powerful and had ripple effects that were global in scale, they all took place within the structures of an unchanging international system. As one analyst put it, "We are so used to observing all the things states do that constitute a defiance of other states that we do not stop to recognize how few these things are, rather than how many. We are so used to thinking of the interstate system as verging on anarchy that we fail to appreciate how rule-ridden it is."[24]

To be sure, during earlier centuries the geographic scope of the system expanded across the globe as new transportation technologies re-

---

[23] For incisive essays on the transformation of the state system's basic premises, see Hedley Bull and Adam Watson, eds., *The Expansion of International Society* (New York: Oxford University Press, 1985), esp. Part 4.

[24] Immanuel Wallerstein, *The Politics of the World-Economy: The States, the Movements, and the Civilizations* (Cambridge: Cambridge University Press, 1984), p. 33.

duced economic, social, and political distances. During this period, too, the parameters of societies that underwent industrialization were thoroughly and permanently altered, with new classes and new voting franchises transforming social structures and with the advent of the assembly line adding greatly to the division of labor, the specification of roles, and the complexity of social life. It is also true that the identity of hegemonic powers and the number of major powers in the international hierarchy were profoundly altered by the great wars. Yet none of these transformations overwhelmed the three primary global parameters. Structurally, the state system remained in place and, indeed, unchallenged; states retained their sovereignty and their virtually exclusive control over the means of coercion even as they became more complex. Authority relations, the idea of hierarchy, remained unchanged even as trade unions and other groups proliferated. And individuals remained essentially unskilled in their citizenship and largely unmindful of world affairs even as they acquired the franchise.

In that system, legitimate authority was concentrated in the policymaking institutions of states, which interacted with each other on the basis of equality and accepted principles of diplomacy and international law. Their embassies remained inviolable and so did their domestic affairs. Intrusion into such matters were met with protests of violated sovereignty and, not infrequently, with preparations for war. For all practical purposes, the line between domestic and foreign affairs was preserved and clearly understood by all. The norms of the Western state system lodged control over external ties in the state and these were rarely defied and even more rarely revised. Accordingly, despite the ever-expanding interconnectedness associated with industrialization, and despite severe economic dislocations, the values of the historic state system's structural parameter remained intact. Changes in the number of its major actors and the degree of its polarity occurred from time to time as wars and technology altered the prevailing balances, but there was no change in the core arrangements wherein the system was organized in terms of state actors and the polarities among them. The system neither fragmented into small-scale units nor consolidated into a single, unitary actor. As Wallerstein notes, "What distinguishes the modern interstate system is that it was the first interstate system not to have been transformed over time into a world empire."[25] Indeed, the system's structure so thoroughly accommodated the shifts in the identity and realignments of its major actors that for more than four hundred years, beginning late in the fifteenth century, it exhibited

[25] Wallerstein, *Politics of the World-Economy*, p. 50.

a roughly fifty-year cyclical link between the onset of wars and periods of economic prosperity. With World War II, however, the cycle broke down and has yet to resume[26]—a finding that lends considerable support to the thesis advanced here that the onset of systemwide turbulence did not occur until the 1950s.

Authority relations within subsystems paralleled those within states. Hierarchy, subordination, and habitual compliance with established authority were accorded higher priority than subgroup autonomy. Thus, to the extent that it existed, subgroupism mirrored rather than negated the hierarchical patterns, and new subgroups developed within rather than outside existing organizational structures. In the most industrialized countries, government agencies became giant bureaucracies, local businesses became giant corporations, unions became giant federations, small colleges became giant universities, local parishes became huge churches, and family farms became giant agribusinesses, and these centralizing tendencies, being consistent with (or at least not contradicting) the norms of the state system, were emulated by other countries as they moved along the path to industrialization. The relational parameter of the historic state system was thus reinforced by comparable developments at the national and local levels.

The centralizing tendencies were experienced at the micro level, too, as support for the habit of accepting the authority of leaders, for the readiness to comply with directives from organizational headquarters, and for quelling any predisposition to question, much less resist, the policies framed and adopted through legitimate procedures by those at the top. If multiorganizational memberships placed the individual in conflictful situations, the priorities of the orientational parameter were clear: loyalty to the nation-state came first, and individuals would march off to war if called upon to do so.

In the case of the relational and orientational parameters, some allowances must be made for slow, evolutionary change. Knowledge about the vulnerabilities and limits of authority structures doubtless grew as a consequence of the American, French, and Russian revolutions. It is also the case that ever since the Enlightenment, individuals have been expanding their competencies. If for no other reason, they acquired new skills and attained new educational heights as the requirements of new technologies and the industrialization process hastened the division of labor and the specialization of economic functions.

[26] Cf. Joshua S. Goldstein, *Long Cycles: Prosperity and War in the Modern Age* (New Haven: Yale University Press, 1988), chapters 8–15.

Nevertheless, while it may be feasible to view the 1950s as the period in which evolutionary changes culminated and then passed over the threshold of global turbulence, it is not the gradualness of the process that stands out so much as the chaotic dynamics that followed the breakpoint. The collapse of empires and the repeated challenges to authority, along with the heightened sensitivities of citizens in industrial societies and the growing demands of those in less developed societies, sustained a momentum that reached crisis proportions for some polities in the late 1960s and for the global economy in the early 1970s. The more global turbulence gathered strength, the more were the established parameter values swamped in its wake. With neither states nor the state system any longer the exclusive bases of global structures, turbulence spread rapidly in local and national systems and added to the tensions and the agenda of world politics. The repercussions of the collapse of the global parameters were perhaps most noticeable in the Third World, where the transformation of skills and orientations at the micro level was conspicuous even in the early postwar period. As one observer has noted, "The psychological and spiritual awakening of Asian and African, Caribbean and Pacific peoples, beginning among small groups of the Western-educated, later affecting masses of people, . . . led them to perceive the old order no longer as a fact of nature, but as something that could be changed, to recognize that by mobilizing themselves to this end they could indeed change it, to abandon a passive for a politically active role in world affairs."[27]

When considered in the context of exploding technologies, the contrast between the pre- and post-1950 eras can be drawn even more sharply. Under conditions in which it took hours or days to send messages, pictures, and money abroad and weeks or months to move people, soldiers, and goods from one part of the world to another, the governments of national and local systems were able to absorb and channel the complexity and dynamism introduced by the industrial era, thus enabling the parameter values of the global system to contain the subsystemic fluctuations within acceptable limits. Similarly, the mechanisms of international governance associated with the state system, while rudimentary and often temporary, were sufficient to manage change and complexity. But when the time required to transmit ideas and pictures was reduced to minutes and then to seconds, and the transportation of persons, goods, and explosives to days and hours (even to minutes in the case of explosives), interdependence became

[27] Hedley Bull, "The Revolt against the West," in Bull and Watson, *Expansion of International Society*, p. 224.

increasingly unmanageable, national governments increasingly ineffective, national boundaries increasingly permeable, and the durability of the global parameters of the past increasingly questionable. As one astute observer put it in 1975, "We happen to find ourselves in an era in which a great many past parameters are becoming variables."[28]

CONCLUSIONS

Needless to say, this interpretation is open to dispute, depending as it does on how one conceptualizes world politics and differentiates between change and continuity. Paul Kennedy, for example, proceeds from a conceptualization in which the prime global structures are determined by the formal loci of authority in the international hierarchy, and he concludes that the "broad trends of the past five centuries are likely to continue. The international system, whether it is dominated for a time by six Great Powers or only two, remains anarchical—that is, there is no greater authority than the sovereign, egoistical nation-state."[29] Tellingly, however, as soon as he articulates this position, he immediately backs away and acknowledges that what is here called turbulence may be ushering in a whole new set of arrangements to which the anarchy of the state system appears to have little relevance:

> In each particular period of time some of those states are growing or shrinking in their *relative* share of secular power. The world is no more likely to remain frozen in 1987 or 2000 than it was in 1870 or 1660. On the contrary, certain economists would argue that the very *structures* of international production and trade are changing faster than ever before: with agricultural and raw-materials products losing their relative value, with industrial "production" becoming uncoupled from industrial "employment," with knowledge-intensive goods becoming dominant in all advanced societies, and with world capital flows becoming increasingly detached from trade patterns. All this, and the many new developments in science, are bound to influence international affairs. In sum, without the intervention of an act of God, or a disastrous nuclear conflagration, there will continue to be a dynamic of world power, essentially driven by technological and economic change. If the rosy forecasts of the impact of computers,

[28] John Gerard Ruggie, "Complexity, Planning, and Public Order," in La Porte, *Organized Social Complexity*, p. 138.

[29] Paul Kennedy, *The Rise and Fall of Great Powers: Economic Change and Military Conflict from 1500 to 2000* (New York: Random House, 1987), pp. 439–40.

robotics, biotechnology, and so on are correct—and if, in addition, forecasts of the success of a "green revolution" in parts of
the Third World (with India and even China becoming regular net
exporters of grain) do turn out right—then the world *as a whole*
could be a lot richer by the early twenty-first century.[30]

Thus, even if one acknowledges all the indicators of change, one can
still fall back on long-standing presumptions as to what they portend.
Kennedy does this by equating the "dynamic of world power" with the
emergence of new Great Powers, rather than allowing for the possibility that the dynamic may be of a fragmenting kind that disperses rather
than concentrates power.

As indicated earlier, some might reject the thesis of a breakpoint beginning in the late 1950s on the grounds that it underestimates the
power of long-term continuities and fails to appreciate how quickly
the seemingly huge changes of today can become mere fluctuations.
Such a line of reasoning would emphasize that the old parameters have
been in place too long to be susceptible to major alterations, and that
macro structures are too ingrained in global life to undergo more than
a marginal expansion in their range of variation. That may be; conceivably, the indications of fundamental change have been exaggerated
here. Perhaps the processes of world politics are still similar to what
they have always been, sovereign egoistic nation-states are still the
prime reality of global life, many authority structures are in place and
not in crisis, numerous people are so driven by rote habits as to be
incapable of shedding old patterns and forming new ones, and the perception of a global system in transformation is only wishful thinking,
fed by an idealism that can be satisfied only if forces of change are seen
to be conducing to a better world.

Allowing for these possibilities, and acknowledging that systematic
data on the degree of global change are not yet adequate, it is nonetheless difficult to avoid the conviction that the final years of the twenti-
eth-century constitute a period of profound change in the nature and
conduct of world affairs. The evidence of this may be more anecdotal
than systematic, but a sense of its cumulation continues to grow and
becomes increasingly hard to ignore.

---

[30] Kennedy, *Rise and Fall of Great Powers*, p. 440 (italics in the original).

CHAPTER 6

ANALYZING ACTORS
Individuals and Collectivities

[My daily jog] brings me back to the reality that I'm just a
human body like everyone else.
—Nicholas S. Daniloff[1]

It appears to be the case that the presence, potency, and persistence of these relatively new and certainly more numerous substate and suprastate actors and processes account for much of
the complaint that we have lost our ability to conceptualize,
model, and systematically understand events in the world today.
—Frederic E. Wakeman, Jr.[2]

IF TURBULENCE in world politics is as extensive as the preceding
chapters indicate, we need to pause and clarify exactly who and what
it is that resists, accepts, or is otherwise beset by it. It is not enough
simply to assume that change ultimately occurs in people, that the basic unit undergoing change is a person, a concrete, observable entity
who, as "just a human body," yields to pressures, makes calculations,
formulates decisions, and undertakes actions. Even if we enlarge our
frame of reference to include not only single individuals but also small
groups such as cabinets and large collectivities such as governments, it
is unduly limiting to proceed as if the challenge is only to identify these
actors and explain their actions. We must also be concerned with the
analytic aspects of the actors—their orientations, structures, processes,

---

[1] As quoted in *New York Times*, October 2, 1986, p. A7. Daniloff, a U.S. journalist,
was commenting about his newly acquired celebrity status, a consequence of his being
imprisoned for twelve days in the Soviet Union and becoming a focus of superpower
conflict.

[2] Frederic E. Wakeman, Jr., "Transnational and Comparative Research," *Items* 42
(December 1988): 88.

and hierarchies.[3] These, however, cannot be observed directly. They must be inferred from empirical observations.

Furthermore, if the dynamics that link the micro and macro phenomena to each other are to be adequately explored, we need to be able to perceive the variety of dimensions through which the links are established. Such problems as war and poverty cannot be dealt with without inquiring into their analytic dimensions. Thus do the stability of structures, the limits of dominance, the breakdown of authority patterns, the coherence of subgroups, the processes of cascading interdependence, the adaptation of systems, and the dynamics of change—to mention some obvious dimensions—become central concerns, and all of them involve only parts of concrete actors, not their entire beings. Stated differently, while concrete actors may act to preserve or promote particular values, we must often look beyond actors and their capabilities and values to the consequences of their actions for consensus formation, systemic structure, and a host of other analytic implications that are far removed from those who undertook the actions.

In short, a broad perspective on the specification of actors is needed, one that allows for treating them as conceptual parts as well as empirical wholes. Such a perspective facilitates the employment of individual-as-actor and collectivity-as-actor models in which analytic dimensions also serve as foci of inquiry, as phenomena that, like individuals, groups, and societies, can be aggregated by leaders, can adapt to change, and can be engulfed by turbulence.[4]

The task of identifying the relevant analytic dimensions, however, presents several difficulties. Perhaps the most severe of these is the inclination to treat individuals at the micro level as composites of diverse parts that cannot be separately examined. Our values stress the dignity of the person, the inviolability of the human spirit, and normative responsibility for one's own actions, thus impelling us to move quickly

[3] For a discussion of the distinction between concrete and analytic units of analysis, see Marion J. Levy, Jr., *The Structure of Society* (Princeton: Princeton University Press, 1952), pp. 88–89.

[4] It might be wondered whether broadening the conception of analytic units in this way will make it impossible to identify and trace global patterns empirically. However, moving up the ladder of abstraction does not necessarily take analysis beyond the realm of the empirical. Studies of informal decision processes, international regimes, and many other "entities" whose existence is inferred from observed behaviors have long been conducted from rungs high on the ladder. To be sure, the empirical tasks may be more complex, because the techniques for measuring the abstract aspects of phenomena are more intricate than those used to measure concrete phenomena. But in principle, models founded on abstractions as units are no less productive than those that employ concrete actors as units.

beyond the parts and to concentrate upon the whole, as if it were some-how knowable without comprehension of its parts.

Perhaps this is why students of world politics seldom attempt to draw precise conceptual distinctions among micro phenomena. One does not find in the literature of the field, as one does in sociology, distinctions between "individual$_1$, individual$_2$, and individual$_3$," in terms of analytical and theoretical primacies.[5] Rather, analyses that focus on individuals as actors on the global scene tend to be ambigu-ous. Clear-cut specifications of the concept of a "person" rarely ac-company the pleas that the person be made more central to the study of international affairs. Neither those whose concern stems largely from value considerations,[6] nor those who proceed from the convic-tion that macro analyses must have roots in micro phenomena,[7] ex-press puzzlement over what is meant by the "individual." It is viewed as a concept whose specifications are taken for granted, as if everyone, being an individual, knows what the concept signifies.[8]

Such lapses in conceptual rigor are regrettable. If micro units are to be incorporated into macro theories, the need to be precise in formu-lating what is meant by the "person" is no less acute than is the case for models of the "state," the "regime," or any macro unit. It is not enough to subscribe to Daniloff's modest self-assessment, or to pre-sume a world populated by the "real individual, that awful and incon-sistent person who does not fit into any convenient analytic model."[9] Indeed, it is highly misleading to treat people as inconsistent and un-predictable, given the extent to which structure and continuity are in-troduced into their behavior by habit, role expectations, culture, socio-economic circumstances, and a host of other stabilizing factors. More exact understanding of what underlies the actions of individuals is

[5] Individual$_1$ is found in studies that accord the discrete person both analytical and theoretical primacy; individual$_3$, in those studies that give analytical and theoretical pri-macy to society; and individual$_2$, in those that give the person theoretical primacy and the society analytical primacy. See Reinhard Wippler and Siegwart Lindenberg, "Collec-tive Phenomena and Rational Choice," in Jeffrey C. Alexander et al., eds., *The Micro-Macro Link* (Berkeley: University of California Press, 1987), pp. 140–50.

[6] See, for example, John W. Burton, "The Individual As the Unit of Explanation in International Relations," *International Studies Newsletter* 10 (February 1983): 14–17.

[7] Robert C. North and Nazli Choucri, "Economic and Political Factors in Interna-tional Conflict and Integration," *International Studies Quarterly* 27 (December 1983): 444–47.

[8] For an exception in which such specifications are explored rather than assumed, see V. Spike Peterson, "Re-Constructing the 'Individual' in 'Human Rights' " (paper pre-sented at the annual meeting of the International Studies Association, Washington, April 1987).

[9] Burton, "Individual As the Unit of Explanation," p. 1.

needed if our efforts to trace macro-micro interactions are not to be thrown off course by our sentimental attachments to their worth and dignity.

Individuals need to be treated, then, as complexes of roles and statuses, as members of a set of systems that so fully account for the expectations to which they respond that there is little meaningful left over as the quintessentially unique person. Stated more bluntly, so as to call attention to the need for more precise conceptualization, there is no individual apart from the network of systems in which he or she is embedded.

This is not to argue for a mechanistic view of people or otherwise to dismiss the values associated with the human spirit, nor is it to deny that people experience their own selves and the feeling of being unique. Rather, conceiving of them as role composites provides an analytic context in which theories about turbulence in world politics can be built on micro units expressive of needs, wants, orientations, skills, and actions at the individual level. If it is important to retain the belief that some variance reflective of the human spirit is left over after the expectations attached to a person's role networks are taken into account, then a concession to that effect can readily be made without undermining the role-composite formulation.

Much the same can be said about the task of conceptualizing macro actors. Again, a tendency to avoid breaking them down into analytic parts can be noted. Consider, for example, the ambiguities and myths that attach to the concept of the state.[10] All too many studies posit the state as a symbol without content, as an actor whose nature, motives, and conduct are so self-evident as to obviate any need for precise conceptualizing. Often, in fact, the concept seems to be used as a residual category to explain that which is otherwise inexplicable in macro politics. Such a usage takes macro analysis back to unitary actors and reified collectivities, in which micro sources are treated as uniform and thus taken for granted. Formulated, in this way, the concept of "state" obscures, even ignores, the dynamics of decision making, bureaucratic politics, and aroused publics. It dismisses the problem of system-subsystem relations by collecting all authority under the rubric of sovereignty instead of focusing attention on the conditions whereby authority is created, legitimacy sustained, and compliance achieved. It prevents the discerning of unintended consequences and the tracing of

[10] For an incisive discussion of seven of these myths, see Inis L. Claude, "Myths about the State," *Review of International Studies* 12 (January 1986): 1–11.

manifest and latent functions. It encourages reliance on intuition rather than observation, on anthropomorphism in place of empiricism.

However, in order to trace the relevant analytic dimensions at both the macro and the micro levels, we must first achieve clarity as to who the concrete actors on the global stage are. That is the task of this chapter, while the analytic dimensions will be discussed in subsequent chapters.

MICRO-LEVEL ACTORS

Eight types of generic actors, three at the micro level and five at the macro level, seem especially relevant to the course of events. These are identified in table 6.1, which also anticipates the discussion of the way each type is likely to be affected by turbulence.

The first of the three micro-level actors is the individual who belongs to macro collectivities and who, in this capacity, is a *citizen* or organization *member* subject to aggregation, mobilization, and control. The second is the individual who leads macro collectivities—that is, the public *official* or organization *leader* who does the aggregating, mobilizing, and controlling of citizens or members. The third is the *private actor*, the individual who, quite apart from his or her membership in or leadership of collectivities, either is unintentionally drawn into the cascades of world politics (e.g., Daniloff) or who is able, by dint of special circumstances, to carry out independent actions in the global arena that may be consequential for the course of events (e.g., among the private actors who became central in the Reagan administration's attempt to win the release of U.S. hostages by selling arms to Iran were a Saudi Arabian billionaire with close ties to the royal family, an expatriate Iranian businessman who may have doubled as an Iranian intelligence officer, and several Canadian investors).

The three types of individuals have much in common. They are all products of a family life, an education, and experiences in the labor force. They all have values and goals which they strive to uphold and advance. And they share a propensity for maintaining cognitive balances, along with many other intellectual-emotional processes that are vulnerable to disruption in times of turbulence (see chapters 9, 12, and 13).

But there are also three important differences among them. First, the skills and orientations they employ in their respective roles vary considerably. The activities of the member and leader take place in an organizational context, whereas the private actor's conduct is not so immediately bound by the rules and requirements that collectivities

TABLE 6.1. Likely Directions of Change for Micro and Macro Actors When the Three Parameters of World Politics Are Engulfed by Turbulence

	Structural Parameter	Relational Parameter	Orientational Parameter
Micro actors			
Citizens, members	Greater opportunities for, and inducements to, action	Demands for compliance fewer and less intense	Skills improved, loyalties diffused
Officials, leaders	Capacity to mobilize constituents diminished	More consultative and mindful of constituencies	Skills improved, more sensitive to members
Private actors	More openings for, and inducements to, speak and act	Fewer constraints on, and sanctions against, action	Greater readiness to act
Macro actors			
States	More decentralized, less coherent and effective	Authority more diffuse, hierarchy weakened	Citizens more defiant, loyalties more tenuous
Subgroups	More numerous, centralized, coherent, and effective	Authority more concentrated, hierarchy strengthened	Members more compliant, committed, and loyal
Transnational organizations	More opportunities to form and prosper	More interactions, authority more concentrated but still fragile	Members more active and committed
Leaderless publics	Likely to have greater impact	Coalesce more often and more spontaneously	Private actors more ready to join
Movements	More mobilizable, active and salient	More articulate leadership without corresponding concentration of authority	Greater consciousness of membership, greater readiness to be active

demand of those who occupy roles in them. Hence, for example, private actors are likely to be much more venturesome and capable of engaging in greater variety of behaviors than are leaders and members. Similarly, macro leaders become skilled at balancing off the internal needs of their macro unit with the external demands upon it, skills which neither of the other two types of individuals is likely to develop.

Second, the three types of individuals differ in terms of where they fit in the interactive processes through which the micro and macro levels are linked. Leaders circulate in, and are responsive to, the macro world. They are, so to speak, the channels through which macro-level continuities and changes are initiated and sustained. Thus, one focuses on organizational, bargaining, and other macro-level dynamics to comprehend leaders, whereas comprehension of members is best achieved through analysis of the intellectual-emotional dynamics that shape their behavior. To understand the role of private actors, one has to look to both the macro and the micro levels, the former to understand how circumstances may provide opportunities for the initiatives of private actors and the latter to probe how and why some such actors seize the moment and exploit the opportunities.

Third, the importance of each type varies with the presence or absence of turbulence. In nonturbulent times, when collectivities are stable and members relatively task oriented and accepting of the prevailing circumstances, leaders have the global stage pretty much to themselves. But when turbulence sets in, leaders become much readier to heed the demands and follow the leads of their memberships and to interact with private actors.

One way to put micro actors in perspective is to ask how each type can affect the course of events. Can any private actor single-handedly alter systemic structures and processes? In what ways, if any, can a leader redirect the global system? Is it possible for a citizen to have, on his or her own, an impact on regional or intercontinental structures? Or are social and political systems so deeply rooted in the habits and institutions developed in prior decades and centuries that no individual can create more than a momentary ripple in the stream of history?

Following the hypotheses, suggested in table 6.1, subsequent chapters suggest a range of possible answers to these questions of where individuals, acting alone, fit in postinternational politics. Two recent events are illustrative of the extremes within which private actors can play a global role. At the high-impact extreme is the case of Armand Hammer, a U.S. citizen and a corporate executive with long-standing business interests in the U.S.S.R., who has for decades consciously sought to serve as a communications link between the Soviet Union and the United States. In 1986, Hammer apparently persuaded Gorbachev to accept U.S. medical personnel and expertise to help cope with the accident at the Chernobyl nuclear plant. Noting that "I am a private citizen" and that "I speak for no government," he nonetheless also used the occasion to press Gorbachev to meet with President Reagan "this year." Gorbachev agreed, with the condition that the United States indicate its willingness to hold such a meeting. Hammer tells of reporting this reaction to U.S. Secretary of State George Shultz, who concurred in the idea.[11] While doubtless there were also official contacts between the two governments about a meeting, the Hammer initiative may well have been an important part of the process. In any case, the summit meeting he proposed to the two governments did follow shortly thereafter.

At the other extreme is the case of Heinz Braun, an East German who escaped to the West and then sought to initiate a sequence of events designed, first, to mar East Germany's commemoration of the twenty-fifth anniversary of the Berlin Wall and, subsequently, to force its dismantling. Braun escaped from East Berlin through the wall in a car painted to look like a Soviet patrol car with him as driver and with mannequins dressed as Soviet officers propped up in the other seats. Afterwards, he appeared at a news conference with his patrol car and one of the uniformed mannequins to describe his feat. Not only did the East Germans then tighten their control over the escape routes, but the small group of activists who had spent years facilitating escapes became the targets of ridicule. As one of the activists put it, "I'm horrified when I see all the damage [the ruse] is doing. I've taken many people out, some in the trunks of cars, but how can I help anybody now?" In effect, Braun's effort to have an impact strengthened rather than altered the macro structures of Berlin.[12]

Between these two extremes, of course, are numerous private actors who work doggedly to advance their ideas and have an impact, most of whom leave few traces but some of whom do contribute to an alteration in systemic structures of processes. An example of the latter is Jess Gorkin, who has been credited with a crucial input into the sequence of events that culminated in the establishment of a direct tele-

[11] Armand Hammer, "Let Leaders Start toward a New Summit," *Los Angeles Times*, May 29, 1986, sec. 2, p. 7. For a related account, in which Hammer suggests that he played an important role in the Soviet withdrawal from Afghanistan by conveying messages among Gorbachev, Reagan, and the president of Pakistan, see Armand Hammer, "Behind the Soviet Pullout from Afghanistan," *New York Times*, June 4, 1988, p. 27.

[12] John Tagliabue, "Escape Was Hoax, Berlin Police Say," *New York Times*, August 7, 1986, p. A3.

phone link—the "hot line"—between the White House and the Kremlin. As the editor of a popular magazine, *Parade*, Gorkin published an open letter to U.S. President Eisenhower and the Soviet leader, Nikita Khrushchev, in 1960 that concluded, "Must a world be lost for want of a telephone call?" Encouraged by the flow of letters from enthusiastic readers, Gorkin badgered presidential candidates Kennedy and Nixon into considering the idea, as he had done with Khrushchev a year earlier at a reception during the latter's visit to the United States. But not until the Cuban missile crisis in 1962 did events provide an impetus for translating the idea into reality.[13]

In like manner, Andrei D. Sakharov spent years in the Soviet Union seeking to ameliorate the plight of dissidents. A physicist who won the Nobel Peace Prize in 1975 but who subsequently spent seven years in internal exile at the hands of the security services, Sakharov's voice was muffled until macro developments in the Soviet Union led to his release and, through publicity for his views, heightened his impact upon the course of events.[14]

Much the same can be said about individuals in leadership roles. At the low-impact extreme are the many leaders who either lack the ability to overcome the constraints and inertia of the governments or organizations they lead or find themselves caught up in systemic situations that offer little opportunity for exercising effective leadership. At the high-impact extreme are those rare occupants of high office who, like Winston Churchill or Vladimir Lenin, have the personal gifts needed to seize opportunities that are available at times when the circumstances of their macro systems are amenable to creative leadership. Between these extremes are the occasional leaders who make a modicum of difference through a combination of talent and circumstance.

COLLECTIVITIES AND SYSTEMS

Collectivities are actors in the sense that they have authority structures and other mechanisms for sustaining the coherence and coordination of their members and for maintaining the boundary distinction between themselves and their environments, which makes it possible for their leaders to undertake actions on behalf of their memberships. Strictly speaking, of course, collectivities do not "act"; only individuals

---

[13] An account of these events is in Webster Stone, "Moscow's Still Holding: Twenty-Five Years on the Hot Line," *New York Times Magazine*, September 18, 1988, pp. 60, 67.

[14] Felicity Barringer, "Sakharov, in Official Setting, Speaks Out," *New York Times*, June 4, 1988, p. 1.

act, speak, or otherwise engage in behavior. Nevertheless, it is reasonable to speak of the activities of collectivities in two senses. First, when leaders speak for and are seen to speak for their followers, their behavior is regarded as stemming from prior processes that entitle them to act in the name of their collectivities. Second, collectivities occasionally become "tangible" actors when their members engage in concerted public activities (e.g., protest marches). In short, the actions of collectivities, are those of identifiable people who make demands, have aspirations, live with limitations, and engage in other kinds of behavior that are susceptible to aggregation.

It should be noted that collectivities rather than systems are viewed as generic macro actors because the actions of collectivities can be traced back to their memberships, constitutions, and procedures, whereas the concept of systems refers not to concrete organizations but to observer-defined relationships singled out for analytic purposes, relationships that may or may not be actually experienced by the persons or collectivities conceived to comprise the system. Actions can be seen as emanating from systems, but systems do not themselves act, or at least it is awkward to conceive of them as doing so. By definition, in other words, systems are abstract units, constructed by an observer in the light of specific analytic concerns that may be far removed from the preoccupations of the "actual" actors.

It must be stressed, however, that the focus in this chapter on collectivities as generic macro actors is not meant to belittle the system concept as an analytic tool. Far from it: it is a concept that facilitates inquiry into the conflicts that divide collectivities and the efforts they make to bridge the issues that separate them, and in subsequent chapters we shall have occasion to use systems and subsystems as bases for assessing parameter change and tracing turbulence. But in using the system concept for those purposes, the concern is with the dynamics of structures and other analytic aspects of collectivities rather than with their concrete behavior. All collectivities can be conceived as systems, but not all systems are collectivities.

The distinction between collectivities as concrete actors and systems as analytic constructs also helps to probe the impact of actors under turbulent conditions. By drawing out the full implications of a world in which all the concrete actors are conceived as systems comprised of subsystems which, in turn, have subsystems of their own, and so on until we reach the level of the lowest macro organizations (such as local courts), where the consequences of action do not flow across national boundaries, it becomes possible to trace the cascades that are the hallmarks of turbulence.

To distinguish between systems and subsystems is to provide a methodology for unraveling complexity. By their very nature, complex situations encompass both wholes and parts. We can begin to understand them only if we employ a method that allows us to move our analytic eyes back and forth between systems and subsystems and thus between collectivities, their subgroups, and the individuals who comprise them. As one astute observer has put it, in the context of historical inquiry:

> What distinguishes any complexity is that it is both a whole with parts and part of a whole. As a whole, an event can be absolute; as a part, an event can be elementary; but complexity requires both wholeness and partness, ruling out absolutes and elements. Historical events are distinguished because they are simultaneously wholes and parts. . . . To distinguish an historical event is to draw together its sub-events, making them into a whole which itself stands in relation to other wholes. These sub-events are likewise wholes, with sub-sub-events of their own. In this approach, every event is complex, even the smallest event must have subevents, and so on, and even the largest event must itself be a subevent of a still larger event, and so on. If there are ultimate wholes or parts, they cannot be historical events; an event that is not a part, or that has no parts, is no event. The complexity of historical events is that they stand to one another both as parts and as wholes.[15]

Macro-Level Actors

The variety of types of macro-level actors on the global stage is greater than that of micro-level actors. Here we shall confine the inquiry to five broad clusters: three involve collectivities with hierarchies of authority, the fourth is distinguished precisely by its lack of such a hierarchy, and the fifth lies somewhere between the two, with some of its activities organized hierarchically and others not.

The three collectivities are *states, subgroups,* and *transnational organizations.* These are differentiated from each other by the nature of their authority: states are not subordinate to the authority of any other collectivity, subgroups are at least formally subject to the authority of states, and transnational organizations are neither over nor under the authority of states, but, instead, span state boundaries.

The fourth type of macro actor is an exception to the notion of the

[15] Adrian Kuzminski, "Archtypes and Paradigms: History, Politics, and Persons," *History and Theory* 25, no. 3 (1986): 225.

collectivity as a generic type. It is produced by the convergence of the actions or orientations of a large number of people in the absence of organized authority. Opinion polls and spontaneous riots are but the more obvious ways in which the orientations and actions of individuals are introduced into the flow of action prior to the mobilization efforts of leaders. In the decentralized, multi-centric world, such leaderless aggregations cannot be ignored by those who are leaders, since they are signs of underlying predispositions that are always susceptible to activation. Thus, crucial elements of the cascading processes of politics in this world are those wherein leaders perceive and react to the orientations and actions of citizens whose aggregation occurs through the reports of journalists, pollsters, and other observers and not through responsiveness to the behavior of system mobilizers.

These inchoate publics are actors in the processes even though their members are not organized and may be unaware of themselves as contributing to collective consequences. The unplanned uprising that resulted in the ouster of Ferdinand Marcos as president of the Philippines, and the frenzied fluctuations of markets that produced a worldwide collapse of stock prices in 1987, illustrate this type of macro actor. Another particularly vivid illustration of how micro actions lead swiftly to macro consequences is provided by the reactions of hundreds of thousands of Americans to hijackings and the accident at Chernobyl in the spring of 1986: they simultaneously made the same decision, to cancel their European travel plans, with effects on the tourist business of Europe and on the inclination of European governments to develop coordinated policies toward terrorists.

Perhaps the most apt designation for such uncoordinated macro-level phenomena is that of *leaderless public*. The label is appropriate because such entities are not collectivities. They emerge, rather, out of the separate but convergent actions of many individuals who do not share organizational membership. Thus, their duration is typically short, with their energies either dissipating as the immediate issue that provoked their formation subsides or being co-opted by an organization that provides structure, a measure of authority, and an opportunity for common membership.

The fifth type of macro actor exhibits some of the traits of collectivities (such as individuals' identifying themselves as members) but at the same time is marked by some of the characteristics of leaderless publics (such as the absence of explicit and coherent procedures for making policy or selecting leaders). This actor is known as a *movement* (such as the peace, ecology, feminist, labor, black, and student movements). It is a loosely knit aggregate of like-minded individuals and organizations who seek to have influence on one or more aspects of human affairs, usually one considered to be undervalued by the world's established collectivities. Movements may have informally recognized leaders or spokespersons, but their position is based not on organizationally conferred authority but on the "moral" importance of the movement's goals. The movement's followers tend to be a disparate band, deeply committed to advancing their "cause" and readily mobilized on those occasions when their leaders call on them for some activity, such as a rally, boycott, protest march, or letter writing campaign.[16]

Just as the leaders of movements acquire their positions through informal processes, so also do their members. Indeed, one joins a movement simply by considering oneself to have joined. Because of their openness to membership, movements draw their followers from every stratum of society and often from different parts of the world, which is one important reason why they tend not to coalesce into centralized and structured organizations. Indeed, with their shared aspirations focused around the upgrading of groups or the resolution of issues that are not confined to a specific society, movements tend to be transnational in their composition and scope. Under turbulent conditions, which tend to weaken the authority of states and create opportunities for transnational collaboration, a movement can play a crucial role in the framing and course of a global issue through both the activities of their followers and the transnational conferences of their leaders. Not infrequently, in fact, their activities result in actions established by international organizations, such as has been the case with the women's, ecological, and peace movements.

Movements and leaderless publics are sources as well as beneficiaries of the turbulence that presently marks world politics. That is, from the perspective of the three types of macro collectivities, the activities of movements and leaderless publics serve to intensify the complexity and dynamism of the political environment. No matter how coherent the authority structures of collectivities may be, and irrespective of how capable they may be in concerting the energies of their memberships, under conditions of turbulence all collectivities have to confront a restlessness and uncertainty in the unorganized part of their environments that add further to the adaptive challenges they confront.

---

[16] For extended inquiries into the nature and relevance of social movements, see Francesco Alberoni, *Movement and Institution* (New York: Columbia University Press, 1984), and Alain Touraine, *Return of the Actor: Social Theory in Postindustrial Society*, trans. Myrna Godzich (Minneapolis: University of Minnesota Press, 1988).

States

Since states have for centuries been the basis of Order II, they exhibit perhaps the most noticeable effects of the changes wrought by turbulence. It is at the level of national societies and economies that the changes accompanying the dynamics of postindustrialism first took hold. In addition, however far they may have travelled down the path to industrial or postindustrial development, all states have had to cope with the centralizing and decentralizing tendencies inherent in global interdependence. Not even the least developed has been able to avoid them.

Whichever conceptualization of the state is used,[17] and despite the centralizing tendencies which are in some ways enhancing the competence of states, postindustrial interdependence has narrowed their scope, reduced their autonomy, and constricted their capacity to adapt to change. Their scope has been narrowed by the increasing obscurity of the distinction between foreign and domestic affairs. Their autonomy has been reduced by the fact that domestic problems now have an inescapable international component, with the result that long-established norms, habits, and practices of political management are less sufficient as a basis on which governments can resolve such problems on their own. Their capacity for adapting to change has been constricted by the inadequacy of resources for accomplishing all they might want to and by an increasing dependence on favorable circumstances abroad and the cooperation of foreign actors. Their effectiveness has been further diminished by subgroups that are increasing in coherence and in their readiness to press their demands (see below), processes that tend to paralyze governments and to further constrain the norms, habits, and practices from which they derive their legitimacy.

Nor is that all. Because the scope, autonomy, and capacities of all states have been lessened, the complexity and dynamism of the environments of each are intensified, and the task each one has in finding support and cooperation abroad is made more difficult. Illustrative in this regard are the problems that have lately been encountered with

[17] For discussions of alternative conceptualizations, see two recent symposia on the state, one in *Comparative Political Studies* 21 (April 1988): 3–168, and the other in *American Political Science Review* 82 (September 1988): 853–904. For an incisive analysis of the ambiguities of the concept of state as it is applied in Third World countries, see Bahgat Korany, "Alien and Besieged Yet Here to Stay: The Contradictions of the Arab Territorial State," in G. Salame, ed., *The Foundations of the Arab State* (London: Croom Helm, 1987), 1:47–74. A useful discussion of the differences between Eastern and Western ideas of the state is Ralph Ketcham, *Individualism and Public Life: A Modern Dilemma* (Oxford: Basil Blackwell, 1987), 88–96.

respect to managing the global economy and the instability of the United States to retaliate against the "enemy" in Lebanon during the 1980s, because it did not know who the enemy was.

There is, moreover, a momentum built into the proliferation of the forces that immobilize states. Each new evidence of reduced scope, legitimacy, and effectiveness encourages subnational and transnational actors to ignore or challenge established lines of authority and put forth their own codes of conduct. The recent domestic histories of Haiti, Israel, Yugoslavia, Poland, the Philippines, Lebanon, and Argentina, and the recent international roles played by Libya and Iran, are examples of the breakdown of traditional norms and the authority crises into which states have entered.

Challenges to state authority are not the only way in which subnational and transnational actors reveal the constraints within which modern states must function. Ironically, sovereignty-free actors in the multi-centric world sometimes come to the rescue of sovereignty-bound actors in the state-centric world and help them get through crises or otherwise move toward their goals. The network of private sources developed by Lt. Col. Oliver North in 1985 and 1986 to funnel illegal supplies to the contras in Nicaragua is a case in point. So is the reversal in U.S. policy toward granting visas to Soviet Armenian refugees, which took place in 1988. The processing of visas had been suspended in July because the money needed to run the refugee program had been exhausted and there would be no other funds until the new fiscal year began on October 1st. Faced with embarrassing outcries from a variety of friendly quarters, the U.S. embassy in Moscow resumed the processing of visas a couple of weeks later, with the explanation that "private funds, including money available from the immigrant families themselves and relatives in the United States, would now be used to keep the program going."[18]

Notwithstanding all of the constraints on their freedom of action, states are of course far from impotent. Indeed, there are indications that in some important ways they are expanding their domestic activities. The dominance of the state in the economic life of collectivities, be they organized along socialist or capitalist lines, is particularly great. It has been contended that "the active penetration of society and economy by agents of the state is as extensive as at any previous period in the several-centuries history of the modern state, including the so-

[18] Tyler Marshall, "U.S. to Resume Visa Program for Armenians," *Los Angeles Times*, July 17, 1988, sec. 1, p. 1.

called 'age of absolutism.' This situation is widely recognized and is true of virtually all countries. 'Statism' is pervasive."[19]

So involved has the state become in the economic growth of capitalist societies that it now rivals the marketplace as a determinant of the course of the economy. Actions of the state shape saving, investment, and consumption patterns as well as the financing of new industrial sectors and the preserving of old sectors, in some cases to the point of assuming the role of owner.

Nor has the state's widening competence been confined to the economic realm. Modern technology has enlarged its capacity to maintain order, mobilize consent, control opposition, and otherwise shape the social and political lives of its members. Most notably perhaps, the microelectronic revolution has enhanced the capacity of states (and other collectivities) to keep tabs on their members via the computer and to influence their orientations through the television screen. In sum, while the year 1984 fell far short of George Orwell's dire prediction, there are substantial indications that the last years of the twentieth century are and will continue to be marked by the increasing ability and inclination of states to intrude into their domestic arenas. Yet these greater competencies of the state do not necessarily result in greater control and dominance. States may possess ever more elaborate techniques for repressing rebellions and containing crises, but the maintenance of public order is not the same as framing effective policies and creatively adapting to change. A declaration of martial law can keep people off the streets and out of meeting halls, but it cannot lower a trade deficit or raise agricultural production. Neither the concentration nor the expansion of the resources presently available to states enables them to end poverty, eradicate unemployment, eliminate pollution, or overcome the many other obstacles to a better quality of life within their jurisdictions. There is too much internal division and too much dynamism underlying these problems to allow states to exercise full control over the course of events. The notion that they have a free hand in the conduct of public affairs is sheer illusion.[20] Domestic tran-

[19] Raymond D. Duvall and John R. Freeman, "The State and Dependent Capitalism," *International Studies Quarterly* 25 (March 1981): 100.

[20] For a particularly cogent analysis along these lines, see Joel S. Migdal, *Strong Societies and Weak States: State-Society and State Capabilities in the Third World* (Princeton: Princeton University Press, 1988). A similar conclusion, specifically, concerning the interaction between states and multinational corporations, can be found in Thomas J. Biersteker, "The Illusion of State Power: Transnational Corporations and the Neutralization of Host-Country Legislation," *Journal of Peace Research* 17 (September 1980): 207–21.

quility can be enforced, but successful problem-solving cannot. Indeed, the enforcement of tranquility can actually diminish a state's capacity to cope with its internal and external challenges, as regimes in Poland, the Philippines, and Argentina recently discovered, and as the regime in China is likely to find in the years after its violent crackdowns in 1989 on the students in Beijing.

Among the domestic sources eroding the state's competence, two are particularly relevant to the onset of global turbulence: the proliferation of subgroups and the extension of the analytic skills of individual citizens (which has further added to the effectiveness of subgroups). The very facets of the microelectronic revolution that have strengthened the competence of states have also enlarged the competence of citizens to articulate their interests, press their demands, redirect their support, and otherwise participate in public affairs. Taken together, the combination of a more aggressive subgroupism and a more skillful citizenry has fragmented states and made them increasingly vulnerable to paralysis. Even military dictatorships have lately failed to withstand the withering of state competence and, equally noteworthy, the militaries in stalemated countries such as Argentina, Brazil, Peru, and Uruguay appear to have withdrawn from governance out of an appreciation of the intractability of domestic problems and an unwillingness to bear the onus of failing to solve them.

But, to repeat, the main inroads into the competence and legitimacy of the modern state come from the previously noted dynamics of interdependence that underlie the emergence of turbulence on a global scale. As one observer has put it: "The nation-state can make good on so few of its promises. What nation can defend its borders against disease, ballistic missiles, the drug trade, or the transmission of subversive images? What nation can hold harmless its air or its water against the acid rain drifting across Canada or the radioactive cloud blowing west from Chernobyl? What nation can protect its currency against predatory speculations on the world's money markets?"[21] There are, in other words, just too many ways in which the life of communities has become inextricably linked to external trends and institutions for the state to retain intact the norms, habits, and practices that underlie the resolution of its domestic problems.[22] Even if subgroupism were to

[21] Lewis H. Lapham, "Notebook: Leviathan in Trouble," *Harper's*, September 1988, p. 9.

[22] For a demonstration of how "external, international factors" limit the control states can exercise over their own economic growth rates, see David R. Cameron, "Distributional Coalitions and Other Sources of Economic Stagnation: On Olson's *Rise and Decline of Nations*," *International Organization* 42 (Autumn 1988): 561–605.

give way to broad and solid national consensuses, states would still not have access to all the levers necessary to shape desirable outcomes for their "internal" problems.

Paradoxically, the international interdependence that has diminished the state's scope and authority in domestic affairs has also been a source of its widening competence in such matters. The shrinking economic, social, and political distances that have transnationalized global affairs have greatly increased the vulnerability of domestic economies to external influences, so that domestic market forces are decreasingly capable of sustaining stability and progress. Consequently, states have developed institutions and adopted policies that increase their ability to intervene in the internal flow of goods, services, and money in order to cope minimally with the internationalization of the market and banking systems. Thus, for example, the widened competence of states manifested in the imposition of austerity measures and travel restrictions stem to a large degree from their lessened ability to withstand the encroachments of a shrinking world. And yet those very same institutions and policies have become dependent on the course of events abroad whose vagaries they were designed to manage.

In other words, a direct relationship between internal controls and external vulnerabilities has emerged as a prime condition of the modern state. Since the state's vulnerability to global events and processes seems likely to increase in the future, the controls exercised by the state at home appear destined to undergo a corresponding expansion. Attempts to diminish the state's role in the domestic marketplace, for example, can result in lowered tax rates and relaxed regulatory mechanisms, leading to the influx of foreign capital and the growth of trade deficits and thus to an eventual return to and perhaps an even greater reliance on domestic controls.[23]

The close and complex connection between the state's widening domestic competence and its lessening ability to remain in control of its own destiny is also evident in the transnational flow of people and knowledge that has accompanied the emergence of a global economy. As labor migrations from the Third to the First World swell, as technology transfers in the opposite direction expand, and as the gap between computer generations in the First and Second Worlds grows, the state has become increasingly attentive to its policies regarding immigration, industrial peace, and the maintenance of high-tech facilities.

[23] For a formal economic analysis suggestive of these relationships see Kerry Schott, *Policy, Power, and Order: The Persistence of Economic Problems in Capitalist States* (New Haven: Yale University Press, 1984).

Efforts to manage the movement of Colombian peasants into Venezuela, of Hispanics into the United States, and of Turks into West Germany are among the examples of states becoming more active in their efforts to control cross-boundary flows. In the case of Venezuela, the state has apparently lost control over the migratory processes: not only do Colombians outnumber Venezuelans by fifteen to one in some border areas, but neither the Venezuelan nor the Colombian government is able to exercise control over drug traffickers and guerrillas along wide stretches of their common border.[24]

In sum, the competence of states is both widening and withering, with each being a function of the other as the dynamics of global life intensify both the centralizing and the decentralizing tendencies already at work. The forecasts of those who see the state being eventually replaced by new forms of whole-system organization seem headed for negation, as do the predictions of those who anticipate that the state will become ever more dominant in the life of societies. Rather, given the continuing need for whole-system institutions that concentrate authority and facilitate collective action in a bifurcated world, the foreseeable future is likely to be one in which states survive, limping along, buffeted by internal and external forces that drive the norms, habits, and practices relevant to their capacities for cooperation to the brink of transformation, and yet managing to persist, sometimes resisting the tides of change and sometimes astride them, but with few exceptions retaining sufficient legitimacy to sustain their essential structures and undertake collective action. Put more succinctly, "The state has its difficulties, but clearly it has not yet gone, or begun to go, out of fashion."[25]

Subgroups

As collectivities located within states and at least technically subject to their authority, subgroups are distinguished from unorganized actors (e.g., crowds), objective categories (e.g., the aged or the middle class), one-time issue publics, and social movements by virtue of having enduring memberships and specifiable authority relationships in which their members and leaders are located in a hierarchy of roles. The hi-

---

[24] Alan Riding, "Colombian Drugs and Rebels Move In on Venezuela," *New York Times*, January 20, 1988, p. A9.

[25] Claude, "Myths about the State," p. 10. Similar lines of analysis are developed in Hedley Bull, "The State's Positive Role in World Affairs," *Daedalus* 108 (Fall 1979): 111–23, and Philippe C. Schmitter, "Neo-Corporatism and the State," in Wyn Grant, ed., *The Political Economy of Corporatism* (New York: St. Martin's, 1985), chapter 2.

erarchy is, in some respects, subject to the sovereignty, tolerance, and policies of the state, but on a day-to-day basis subgroup actors in most states are in charge of their own affairs and can act with considerable autonomy to preserve their integrity and move toward their goals.

While most subgroup actors are found in the economy and society, some are in the polity. Local governments and even bureaucratic agencies of national governments are structured along lines that are more characteristic of subgroups than of states. They have identifiable hierarchies of authority and specialized tasks that set them apart in terms of their aspirations and even their autonomy, although they too are formally subject to the authority of the state.

Like subgroups in the economy and society, those in the polity are also capable of influencing world politics by reaching out to and interacting with foreign counterparts. Indeed, one of the main characteristics of postinternational politics is the high degree to which subnational governments and bureaucratic agencies of national governments conduct their own relationships abroad. Ostensibly, they do so within the policy guidelines of their country's foreign offices, in the case of subnational governments, and of their cabinet ministers, in the case of bureaucratic agencies, but they nevertheless bargain in their own interests. In 1987, for example, 6 Canadian provinces maintained 46 permanent offices in 11 foreign countries, and 29 U.S. states had 55 permanent representatives in 17 foreign countries.[26]

A question may be raised as to the distinction between national states as macro actors and governmental bureaucracies as subgroup actors. Since bureaucratic agencies presumably act on behalf of states, it could well be argued that, for all practical purposes, they are part of the state. For analytical purposes, however, such an argument is misleading. Even if they may have once been unitary actors, states and governments no longer are. Or at least this is the case for those states that are founded on a minimally developed industrial base. Today, their leaders preside over a vast array of agencies which are able, as a result of the very complexity that accounts for their diversity and number, to give voice to contradictory goals and policies. Frequently, therefore, relations among bureaucratic agencies at the national level and governmental units at the local level are as likely to be marked by rivalry as by cooperation, with each interpreting the policies of state leaders in ways that preserve their own autonomy and serve their own

[26] Ivo D. Duchacek, *Toward a Typology of New Subnational Governmental Actors in International Relations* (Berkeley: Institute of Governmental Studies, University of California, 1987).

goals. Accordingly, it is imperative to treat states as governments that act and speak for the whole collectively—for the economy, society, and polity as a single entity—and to view the agencies and local governments below them in the polity as subgroup actors.

The trend for subgroups as macro actors is in some respects quite contrary to that for states. While the latter are being weakened by decentralizing tendencies, the former are the beneficiaries of decentralization. Obviously, they, too, are beset by the problems that accompany the transformation of systemic parameters, but their capacity to meet the challenges seems likely to expand. The dynamics of the bifurcated postinternational order are favorable to subgroups by virtue of the benefits of specialization. With like-minded people being drawn to each other by common needs and aspirations, the subgroup has begun to develop a more homogeneous and thus a more committed, compliant, and loyal membership. As a consequence, it seems likely to acquire more clear-cut lines of authority and a degree of centralization that will render it more coherent and, within the constraints of its resources, more effective.

These developments clearly owe something to the weakening of states, whose diminished capacities create, as it were, an authority vacuum into which subgroups have moved. More precisely, with the state performing less effectively, and with more and more diverse services needing to be performed, new tasks and increased responsibilities tend to be lodged in subgroups. The state may maintain legal jurisdiction and exercise supervision over its proliferating subgroups, but in important respects these arrangements may well become mere technicalities.

But it is not only the reduced authority of states that promotes the proliferation and growing importance of subgroups; these changes also stem from the very nature of global interdependence. Among other things, it requires new services to cope with the rising aspirations of people and their increasing need for information about the course of events in distant places. Public-relations firms that represent foreign governments and businesses, specialized trade papers and magazines, research institutes, and small professional firms are but a few of the new types of organizations spawned by an exploding technology that are not confined by national boundaries. Similarly, it is in the nature of postindustrialism to call attention to the plight of such newly salient groups as the poor, handicapped, children, refugees, minorities, and political prisoners, all of whose needs are then aggregated in organizations designed to improve their circumstances. One only need consider the seemingly endless growth in the number of appeals—from foreign as well as domestic organizations—that one receives in one's personal mail to appreciate the extent to which subgroups continue to proliferate.

Although subgroup actors are both sources and beneficiaries of decentralization, the same process can also undermine them. The dynamics that lead to the fragmentation of authority and the splitting off of subsystems from whole systems can also operate to break up a subgroup. More than a few cases can be cited wherein subgroups have fallen victim to subgroupism. It seems likely, moreover, that this process will continue, as authority crises and the need for ever greater degrees of specialization lead to the fracturing of subgroups into sub-subgroups.

Developments in the U.S.S.R. offer a vivid example of the tendency toward subgroupism. Private groups and organizations had been prohibited in the Soviet Union for decades, and yet Gorbachev's call for *glasnost* and a measure of democracy in Soviet life was promptly followed by the emergence of scores of unofficial groups representing a wide variety of political perspectives. As one news report put it, "The groups range from secretive, nationalistic organizations, through a variety of 'new left' Socialist clubs, to Western-oriented dissident groups. Some lobby for specific cases, such as halting the construction of a flood control dam in Leningrad or promoting a memorial honoring victims of the Stalin terror."[27]

It would seem, in short, that subgroupism is a phenomenon endemic to political systems caught up in the turbulent winds of change. It reflects a multiplicity of processes, some legal, some political, some perceptual, and some emotional, all of which contribute to a devolution and refocusing of activity to levels of organization less encompassing than the nation-state.[28]

[27] Bill Keller, "Soviet Youth Unit Seeks to Rein In Political Groups," *New York Times*, November 8, 1987, sec. 1, p. 1.

[28] Since the concept of subgroupism as an emotional-perceptual process is central to the ensuing analysis, the distinction between it and "nationalism" needs to be made clear. The latter term tends to be used in two different ways. In one usage, it refers to the emotional-perceptual orientations shared by a group of people toward their particular culture and history, while the other refers more broadly to orientations toward nation-states as whole systems. This distinction presents a terminological problem in that some subgroups, such as the Armenians, Kurds, and Tamils, are "nationalities" that coexist with other groups within nation-states. It is in order not to confound the demands of nationality groups for autonomy and recognition with the orientations focused on states as whole systems that the term "nationalism" has been eschewed here in favor of "subgroupism," while "nation-statism" is used to refer to those whole systems that are also nation-states. Thus, for example, the Armenian pressure for autonomy in the Soviet

Transnational Organizations

Although hardly new on the world scene, transnational organizations have become much more numerous and prominent as the interdependence of global life has increased and as technology has made it easier for people to convene and communicate across great distances. Similarly, greater interdependence has fostered the spread of transnational organizations needing to maintain their shares of the global market or to monitor the orientations and actions of competitors and adversaries.

The transnational proliferation of these various types of actors has occurred among both governmental and nongovernmental organizations. Along with the UN and its associated agencies, transnational governmental links have evolved in all the world's major geographic regions and with respect to many major recurring issues (see table 14.4). Private transnational associations have been established in all the professions and arts and in many areas of commerce. Some forty foreign corporations now have lobbying offices in Washington, and there are two Washington lobbies (the Association of Foreign Investors in America and the Association of Foreign Investors in Real Estate) that specialize in representing foreign financial interests in the U.S. political process.

Some idea of the pervasiveness of transnational actors in world politics can be gleaned from their role in two crises that broke out late in 1979, the Iranian seizure of the U.S. embassy in Teheran and the Soviet invasion of Afghanistan. No fewer than twenty-nine such actors, from the UN to the International Olympics Committee, from the Helsinki Watch Committee to such ethnic groups as the Baluchis, were deeply involved in one or both of the crises.[29] Given the bifurcation of global structures, moreover, it is hardly surprising that a complex set of relations has grown up between transnational organizations and national governments. Often these are marked by conflict, but on occasion they can be highly cooperative. In the late 1980s, for example, banks in the multi-centric world assisted states in preserving the fiscal integrity of their state-centric system.

Authority relationships and decision-making procedures in transnational organizations are less hierarchical than they are in subgroups

---

Union is viewed as a form of subgroupism, even though Armenian "nationalism" is the impetus behind the pressure.

[29] The twenty-nine transnational actors are identified in the account of the crises presented in Philip Taylor, *Nonstate Actors in International Politics: From Transregional to Substate Organizations* (Boulder, Colo.: Westview, 1984), pp. 6–17.

and states. Since their memberships are dispersed across national boundaries, so are the privileges, responsibilities, and opportunities involved in the conduct of their affairs. As a result of these decentralized structures, organizational headquarters of transnational actors normally encounter some difficulty in implementing their policies. They lack the authority needed to frame goals and commit resources, thus rendering them more reliant on discussion and voluntary compliance than are national and subnational collectivities.[30] Alliances such as the North Atlantic Treaty Organization (NATO) and nongovernmental associations such as the International Political Science Association are illustrative of the nonhierarchical structures that tend to characterize transnational actors. Neither of them can undertake important actions without the consent of its membership.

Finally, it is important to appreciate that, although transnational organizations come into being as responses to the centralizing dynamics of interdependence, they are also subject to the decentralizing forces of turbulence. They, too, experience the tensions that lead to subgroupism and fragmentation, as the recent history of the PLO and UNESCO shows.[31]

ACTORS AS ADAPTIVE LEARNERS

Although macro and micro actors have different characteristics (which will be examined more closely in subsequent chapters), there is one trait common to both types that is central to the dynamics of change and should thus be considered at this point. All macro and micro actors possess a capacity for learning. That is, they are capable of acquiring information and skills and retaining them for use at later times. Neither the individual nor the collectivity is simply a preprogrammed entity that always responds in the same way to the same stimuli. They may react in repetitive ways over a long period of time, resisting opportunities and temptations to shift the direction or intensity of their responses, but the potential for learning, for permanently altering response patterns, is always present, and once in a while it may break through the resistances. Such, at least, is a reasonable inference from

---

[30] For analyses of the diverse structures of transnational associations, see Peter Willetts, ed., *Pressure Groups in the Global System: The Transnational Relations of Issue-Oriented Non-Governmental Organizations* (London: Frances Pinter, 1982).

[31] Kemal Kirisci, *The PLO and World Politics: A Study of the Mobilization of Support for the Palestinian Cause* (London: Frances Pinter, 1986); Youssef M. Ibrahim. "UNESCO in 1988: A Forum Adrift in a Sea of Ideas," *New York Times*, July 6, 1988, p. A6.

the well-documented finding that "the entirely evolutionary record on our planet . . . illustrates a progressive tendency toward intelligence."[32]

Every situation, then, can be viewed as an occasion for learning by the individuals and collectivities that are party to it, even though many of them do not learn from it. Consider, for example, the extreme case of protests, riots, and other forms of mass behavior not accompanied by the deliberative reasoning normally associated with learning. Often such situations are seen as having no long-run consequences because the participants are impelled by momentary conditions. If riotous situations are interpreted in a learning context, however, their meaning and consequences become much more enduring: the rioters may learn about adversary relations, about opponents that stand in the way of realizing their goals, about alternative futures that can be achieved through collective action, about the relationship of means to ends, and about the substantive issues over which the rioting occurs. Viewed from a learning perspective, therefore, the phenomenon of increased rioting and protesting around the world can be seen not only as a re-flection of greater manipulatory skills on the part of leaders; the pat-tern may also reflect mass publics who possess greater analytic skills and more knowledge about the risks, potentials, and consequences that attach to collective action.

The capacity for learning, for abandoning old habits and adapting to new conditions, lies at the core of change and turbulence in world politics. Without it, many collectivities would decline and eventually cease to exist in the face of the dynamics inherent in the transforma-tions from agricultural to industrial to postindustrial conditions. Put even more forcefully, without a capacity for adaptation, collectivities could not withstand the onset of turbulence and world politics would collapse in sheer disarray.

But old habits do not give way readily. Quite the contrary: they are a continual source of tension for all types of actors. Furthermore, what is adaptive learning for one generation is often the habit of the next generation, for all habits were originally new learnings. Indeed, that is how collectivities persist across generations: by inculcating their goals, norms, loyalties, and practices as habits through processes of sociali-zation and periodic rituals, so that new members learn to act in ways that are appropriate to the maintenance of the collectivity.

A vast literature is available on the ability of individuals to learn and the obstacles that impede their learning. A great deal less is known

---

[32] Carl Sagan, *The Dragons of Eden: Speculations on the Evolution of Human Intel-ligence* (New York: Random House, 1977), p. 230.

about how collectivities learn and adapt. As they blunder their way through situations, sometimes grossly misperceiving the resources and motives of adversaries and committing grievous errors of judgment about themselves as well, it often seems they are in fact incapable of learning. Indeed, some analysts interpret the poor performance of collectivities as evidence of such an inability, of the fact that leaders and members are different individuals from their predecessors and are thus unable to benefit from their predecessors' experience.[33] That point of view is rejected here. Collectivities are conceived as having institutionalized ways of storing information and memories of historical turning points, of transmitting goals and values, and of maintaining procedures for adapting to new challenges. These institutionalized mechanisms can break down and lead to blunders that, in turn, could result in the demise of the collectivity. Normally, however, the learning mechanisms of collectivities enable them to recognize the difficulties in time to allow for appropriate adaptation to the emerging circumstances.[34]

The Stability of Actors

Although leaderless publics tend to come and go rather quickly, and social movements wax and wane erratically, other macro collectivities are highly persistent. Their hierarchies of authority and mechanisms for learning accord to them the leadership and the capacity for decisiveness that, under most conditions, enable them to adapt and remain viable. Indeed, both individuals as leaders and individuals as members are normally inclined to be conservative, to maintain the loyalties and undertake the actions that are necessary to preserve their collectivity's integrity and that avoid risking its coherence or autonomy. To a large extent, both types of individuals are driven by habits of acceptance and compliance that suffuse their collectivities with inertia and set them firmly onto historic paths from which there are few deviations.

Ordinarily, in short, most collectivities are stable. Both their micro and their macro components are able to cope with the challenges of a moderately changing world. This is so for all three types of collectivities; indeed, the stability of each type contributes to the stability of the other two, thus helping keep all of them on the paths they have long traversed.

[33] See Lloyd S. Etheredge, *Can Governments Learn? American Foreign Policy and Central American Revolutions* (New York: Pergamon, 1985).

[34] Cf. Donald A. Schon, "Organizational Learning," in Gareth Morgan, ed., *Beyond Method: Strategies for Social Research* (Beverly Hills, Calif.: Sage, 1983), pp. 114–28.

But the conditions of turbulence are very different from the ordinary ones. As emphasized in the previous chapter, the high complexity and dynamism that define such conditions introduce extensive fluctuations into all three of the basic parameters—the orientations that prevail at the micro level, the structures that operate at the macro level, and the authority relations that link the two levels. With these parameters in flux, the habits, structures, and stability of the various actors are undermined and their adaptive capacities severely tested. The centralizing and decentralizing tendencies precipitated by turbulence impose upon micro actors a need to redirect their orientations, and upon macro actors the task of adjusting their relationships and adapting their structures. Both micro and macro actors may move on to new equilibria once turbulence subsides, but none are likely to retain, unaltered, the orientations and capacities they possessed prior to its onset.

CHAPTER 7

MIXING MICRO-MACRO

The Aggregation of Parts and the
Disaggregation of Wholes

Every time a person sacrifices themself for a larger injustice, it aids in the cycle of change.
> —Amy Carter, daughter of former President Carter[1]

Without leaders, we're just bands of raiders. Leaders are what makes us an army. We have to follow their orders.
> —Marcos, a Nicaraguan Contra[2]

THE OBSERVATIONS of these two eighteen-year olds suggest some of the ways in which the expanded analytic skills and cathectic capacities of people have rendered micro-macro interactions ever more dynamic. Amy Carter, having seen the world from the White House, expresses these enlarged talents by asserting that the individual counts in world politics, and she then acts accordingly, thereby initiating micro-macro interactions from the micro side. On the other hand, Marcos, having seen the world from a tropical jungle, gives voice to the expansion of skills by grasping that his actions become meaningful only in an aggregated context, thereby sustaining micro-macro interactions initiated on the macro side.

While Amy sounds autonomous and Marcos subservient, their perspectives have common elements. Both of them display an awareness that individuals play a role in world politics, that what they do has

---

[1] As quoted in *New York Times*, April 14, 1987, p. A17. Amy was commenting on her trial growing out of a campus protest against the activities of the Central Intelligence Agency in Central America.

[2] As quoted in *New York Times*, April 1, 1988, p. A5. Marcos was responding to a question as to whether guerrillas operating in northern Nicaragua were ready to stop fighting and resume civilian life if their leaders directed them to do so.

larger consequences, that individual actions can cumulate into system-wide outcomes. Thus, both are profoundly expressive of the ways in which people are becoming ever more powerful as galvanizers of global change.

Many analysts would say that Amy is wrong, that her idealism and activism exceed her understanding of how things work—but in fact public protests over U.S. policies in Central America did contribute to restraining the Reagan administration from fully implementing its policies in Nicaragua. It may be that in a bifurcated, turbulent world her vision is closer to the nature of global life than is the conception held by many professional observers. Many would also say that Marcos is wrong, that soldiers obey orders because they do not have the choice to do otherwise—but in fact modern history contains enough instances of defections at the military grass roots to render the compliance of troops problematic and success in combat that much more delicate. Marcos may not be conscious of his organizational wisdom, but again it is a perspective that may be more reflective of the emergent role of people in world politics than is conventionally recognized.

Such observations are controversial, because the links between micro-level activities and orientations on the one hand and macro-level outcomes and patterns on the other constitute an unexplored area of inquiry. It is not that analysts have avoided making assumptions about the links; rather, they tend to posit the links either as theoretically untenable or as empirically irrelevant.

In the present work, the links between micro and macro occupy a central place. Having identified micro orientations and skills as one of the three parameters of world politics, and having postulated this parameter (like the others) as being engulfed by change and thus contributing to the turbulence of our time, here a continuous process of interaction between micro and macro phenomena is hypothesized, and the analysis seeks to explore its theoretical and empirical implications. After the nature of the interactive process has been examined under various conditions in this chapter, we shall turn, in chapters 9, 12, and 13, to take a closer look at the micro parameter itself, at the ways in which the skills and orientations of individuals are changing. In this chapter, in other words, we examine the extent to which Amy Carter and Marcos may be right, and in later chapters we will consider the question of the extent to which they are representative of the world's adults.

SIX APPROACHES TO THE MICRO-MACRO LINKAGE

As noted, the nature of the interaction between micro and macro phenomena has been the subject of controversy.[3] At stake are questions about the worth of the individual, the nature of societies, the rational bases of action, the potential of democratic forms of governance, the dynamics of leadership, the exercise of free will, and the imperatives of determinism. People argue about whether their voice counts, and scholars differ over the propriety of analyzing macro-level institutions and collectivities as if they had an existence and autonomy of their own. The methodological debates over the derivation of macro conclusions from micro observations can be as intense as the theoretical differences over the loci of causation.[4]

As a result, the study of the interaction between the two levels is often referred to as the micro-macro "problem," a characterization which emphasizes the difficulties in differentiating macro structures from their micro components and tracing how the former are related to the latter. Indeed, frequently the problem is posed in conflict terms—the individual *versus* society, or behavior *versus* structure—as if whatever happens at one level is necessarily detrimental to the other.[5]

Here, however, the "problem" is looked upon as an opportunity. The relationship between micro and macro is regarded as a juxtaposition involving "and" rather than "versus"—"people and their community" or "actions and their outcomes." Focusing on the interactions between the levels enables one to get to the core of global life, to the ways in which large, impersonal forces at work in the world *both* derive from *and* influence the actions of people in coping with challenges and conducting their affairs. The micro-macro opportunity amounts to nothing less than a means for treating world affairs as the affairs of

[3] For a historical account of the disputes over this question, see Jeffrey C. Alexander and Bernhard Giesen, "From Reduction to Linkage: The Long View of the Micro-Macro Link," in J. C. Alexander et al., eds., *The Micro-Macro Link* (Berkeley: University of California Press, 1987), pp. 1–42.

[4] For a succinct and detached effort to distinguish among the theoretical and methodological approaches to the links between micro and macro phenomena, see James A. Caporaso, "Microeconomics and International Political Economy: The Neoclassical Approach to Institutions," in E. O. Czempiel and J. N. Rosenau, eds., *Global Changes and Theoretical Challenges: Approaches to World Politics for the 1990s* (Lexington, Mass.: Lexington Books, 1989), pp. 135–39.

[5] As Alexander and Giesen put it, "The micro-macro distinction ranks with the core oppositions in Occidental thinking." "From Reduction to Linkage," p. 3.

people who aspire, fear, avoid, compete, and otherwise behave in the organizations that clash and converge on the global stage.

The conceptual and methodological consequences of the decision to treat micro and macro phenomena as interactive are not to be underestimated. Inquiry would certainly be much easier if one or the other level could be treated as a constant. If, for example, actors at the micro level could be assumed to be so totally a product of macro forces as to be undifferentiated from one another, a wide range of conceptual complications would be bypassed. Allowing for significant variability at this level, however, necessitates inquiry into the perceptions, cognitive balance, analytic skills, action scripts, and the many other psychological mechanisms through which individual orientations are translated into action or inaction. Likewise, to proceed from the premise of interactive variability at both levels is to require concern with leadership, followership, authority relations, aggregation, consensus formation, institution building, momentum, intergroup bargaining, and the many other sociopolitical mechanisms through which micro actions are converted into macro collectivities and policies. Clearly, one is not opting for simplicity when yielding to a theoretical preference for treating individuals as both sources and products of world politics.

The variety of approaches to the study of micro-macro interaction can be discerned from the kinds of responses that are likely to be evoked by this question: If the capacity of every adult in every country to think in multivariate terms were to improve by one JND in the next ten years, would the structures and processes of world politics then be different?[6] Five theoretical perspectives can be distinguished that would, for very different reasons, give a negative response.

Two of these, realism and Marxism, argue that individuals are a consequence and not a source of macro-level institutions and collectivities. Neither school denies the existence of micro-macro interactions; rather, both presume that all the interaction goes in one direction, from the macro to the micro level. Although there are differences among Marxists,[7] the preponderant perspective is one in which individuals are

[6] The importance of this question is suggested by the fact that, while our theories acknowledge that proliferation of nuclear weapons would lead to substantial alterations in the patterns of world politics, they say virtually nothing about what might be the systemic consequences of proliferation in the analytic skills of publics, which may well result from the microelectronic and information revolutions which mark the postindustrial era.

[7] Andrew Levine, Elliott Sober, and Erik Olin Wright, "Marxism and Methodological Individualism," *New Left Review*, no. 162 (March/April 1987): 67–84, and Pauline Vaillancourt, *When Marxists Do Research* (Westport, Conn.: Greenwood, 1986), pp. 26–31.

seen as so totally the product of class structures that their behavior derives entirely from their position in society and their relation to the institutions that determine ownership of the means of production.[8] Indeed, some Marxists are so adamant on this point that when the individual acts in ways that seem contrary to their "class interests," they attribute the anomalous behavior to the subtle ways in which institutions exercise their influence. Just as they tend to view religion as an opiate the ruling classes employ to exploit people, so they are likely to view increased analytic skills to be mechanisms for securing popular support under postindustrial conditions.

For political realists, the actions that matter in world politics are those undertaken by states, which act according to their national interests as calculated in terms of their geopolitical circumstances, a viewpoint that leaves no room for the effects of actions by citizens. They presume that it is in the nature of states to be able to mobilize people to provide the support necessary to carry out their policies; hence, micro phenomena are essentially irrelevant to the course of events. As long as nation-states centralize authority and exercise it through macro collectivities, behavior at the micro level is considered insufficient to overcome the authority and conditioning of states and thus has no significant macro consequences. For realists, therefore, it is fruitless, even misleading, to investigate how change in a micro parameter may serve as a source of global transformations. They regard such an inquiry as a form of reductionism, which is viewed as an especially grievous error in that it seeks complicated explanations where simple ones are available.

For both realists and Marxists, in short, micro phenomena, having been conditioned by the structures of which they are a part, are bound to conform to macro requirements. Neither type of theorist experiences puzzlement over the deeper foundations of macro processes, structures, and institutions. For both of them, it is self-evident that today's collectivities will be functioning tommorrow, and thus they treat shifts at the micro level as peripheral and confine their analyses to macro dynamics.

A third perspective in which micro phenomena are irrelevant is that held by those who might be called "hardened elitists." These are observers who do not subscribe to an overall philosophical perspective, preferring instead to view themselves as pragmatists. They proceed

---

[8] Interestingly, in his own early writings Marx articulated a contrary position, arguing against "the materialist doctrine that men are products of circumstances," stressing instead "that it is men who change circumstances." Quoted in Alexander and Giesen, "From Reduction to Linkage," p. 5.

from the premise that people everywhere are remote from and uninformed about world affairs.[9] As one elitist has put it:

> There is no mystery about why there is . . . a tendency for popular opinion to be wrong in judging war and peace. Strategic and diplomatic decisions call for a kind of knowledge—not to speak of an experience and a seasoned judgment—which cannot be had by glancing at newspapers, listening to snatches of radio comment, watching politicians perform on television, hearing occasional lectures, and reading a few books. It would not be enough to make a man competent to decide whether to amputate a leg, and it is not enough to qualify him to choose war or peace, to arm or not to arm, to intervene or to withdraw, to fight on or to negotiate.[10]

In addition to viewing people as too preoccupied with other concerns to develop expertise in foreign affairs, some hardened elitists proceed from a conception of citizens as simplistic, as incapable of improvement, as rabble, or as masses that are normally quiescent but that can be easily manipulated and aroused by demagogues. The scenes of screaming and chanting mobs in the streets of Teheran during the occupation of the U.S. embassy were dramatically illustrative for those who perceive publics as uneducated masses. Irving Kristol acerbically phrased this perspective with the comment, "I do indeed have faith in the common people—only I don't have very much faith in them."[11] George Kennan gave voice to a particularly harsh version of hardened elitism in 1959, when he observed that the American electorate resembled "one of those prehistoric monsters with a body as long as this room and the brain the size of a pin: He lies there in his comfortable primeval mud and pays little attention to his environment. He is slow to wrath—in fact you practically have to whack his tail off to make him aware that his interests are being disturbed; but, once he grasps this, he lays about him with such blind determination that he not only destroys his adversary but largely wrecks his native habitat."[12]

Not all hardened elitists share this negative conception of the con-

---

[9] For an analysis in which this remoteness is derived from the need of elites to maintain a "top-down vision of reality" that helps maintain their leadership, see Majid Rahnema, "Power and Regenerative Processes in Micro-Spaces," *International Social Science Journal* 117 (August 1988): 361–76.

[10] Walter Lippmann, *Essays in the Public Philosophy* (Boston: Little, Brown, 1955), pp. 24–25.

[11] Irving Kristol, "Republican Virtue," *Kettering Review*, Fall 1988, p. 8.

[12] Quoted in Norman J. Ornstein and Mark Schmitt, "Foreign Policy and the Election," *National Interest* 12 (Summer 1988): 5.

sequences of mass tendencies. A minority perceive the noninvolvement of citizens as so resolute as to render them oblivious to the manipulatory efforts of leaders and thus as a healthy and desirable feature of political systems. It is argued, for example, that the general public's "apathy, indifference, quiescence, and resistance to the consciousness industry is especially impressive in an age of widespread literacy and virtually universal access to the media. Indifference to the enthusiasms and alarms of political activists has very likely always been a paramount political force, though only partially effective and hard to recognize because it is a nonaction. Without it, the slaughter and repression of diverse groups in the name of nationalism, morality, or rationality would certainly be even more widespread than it has been."[13] In any event, whatever the virtues or defects they ascribe to mass publics, hardened elitists share a belief that macro-micro interactions flow in only one direction, not so much because macro collectivities are capable of dominating their micro components, but because the latter lack the wherewithal to have any effect on the former.

An exactly contrary line of reasoning constitutes a fourth basis for rejecting the salience of macro-micro interactions. Here the argument is essentially methodological. It is advanced by micro sociologists and structuration theorists. The former adhere to a version of their field known as ethnomethodology and argue that the world can be understood only at the level of micro units.[14] For ethnomethodologists, it is in the nature of human experience that micro-macro interactions flow only from the micro to the macro level. This perspective "claims nothing less than that macro-social phenomena are *unknown* and *unknowable* unless they can be based upon knowledge derived from the analysis of micro-social situations."[15] The structurationists offer a variant of this idea: while their analyses focus on the operation of macro structures, they regard such structures as existing only as "human agents" (i.e., individuals) absorb, reveal, and reproduce them. For structurationists, therefore, structures are not directly observable and thus macro-micro interactions cannot be empirically traced, but this does

[13] Murray Edelman, *Constructing the Political Spectacle* (Chicago: University of Chicago Press, 1988), pp. 7–8.

[14] Harold Garfinkel, *Studies in Ethnomethodology* (Englewood Cliffs, N.J.: Prentice-Hall, 1967).

[15] Karin D. Knorr-Cetina, "The Micro-Sociological Challenge of Macro-Sociology: Towards a Reconstruction of Social Theory and Methodology," in K. Knorr-Cetina and A. V. Cicourel, eds., *Advances in Social Theory and Methodology: Toward an Integration of Micro- and Macro-Sociologies* (Boston: Routledge & Kegan Paul, 1981), p. 8 (italics in original).

not prevent extensive structural analyses because the structures are presumed to be the product of the empirical agents who embody them.[16]

The fifth perspective that downplays the consequences of increases in the skills of micro actors locates all causation in the rational capacities of individuals and thereby, in effect, eliminates micro-macro interactions as a process relevant to the course of events. For rational-choice theorists, the individual counts for everything in world politics. What societies or states do, or whatever else may occur at the macro level, is built into the utility functions through which individuals as rational actors calculate their next move in an endless contest among the occupants of leadership roles in competing macro collectivities.[17] But these are not individuals in the ordinary sense of people who are motivated, cling to habit, experience ambivalence, engage in bureaucratic diversions, exaggerate power potentials, project their own fears on to adversaries, or, indeed, do anything other than engage in value-maximizing behavior. Viewed from this perspective, the individual's analytic skills cannot undergo improvement because they are presumed already to be operating at maximum potential. For all practical purposes, the rational-choice approach allows for neither micro nor macro inputs into the interactive process as these inputs and this process are conceived here.[18]

While none of the ways in which micro-macro interactions are discounted can be lightly dismissed, and while they collectively serve as a brake on excessive claims about the salience of individuals as nonrational actors, neither alone nor together do they compel abandonment of the thesis advanced in this chapter. Here the aggregation of micro parts is conceived to result in macro wholes that, by being accepted (or

[16] I am indebted to Geoff Martin (personal correspondence) for clarity on the assumptions of structurationist theory. For lengthy expositions of this theory, see Anthony Giddens, *Central Problems in Social Theory: Action, Structure, and Contradiction in Social Analysis* (Berkeley: University of California Press, 1979), and Anthony Giddens, *The Constitution of Society: Outline of the Theory of Structuration* (Berkeley: University of California Press, 1984). An application of structuration theory to the processes of world politics is in Alexander E. Wendt, "The Agent-Structure Problem in International Relations Theory," *International Organization* 41 (Summer 1987): 335–70. For a somewhat different formulation, see David Dessler, "What's at Stake in the Agent-Structure Debate?" *International Organization* 43 (Summer 1989): 441–73.

[17] A concise statement of how an expected-utility model of rational choice can be applied to issues of world politics can be found in Bruce bueno de Mesquita, David Newman, and Alvin Rabushka, *Forecasting Political Events: The Future of Hong Kong* (New Haven: Yale University Press, 1985).

[18] A more extended evaluation of the role of rationality in the processes of world politics is undertaken in chapters 9 and 12.

not accepted) at the micro level, have an existence of their own and interact with the micro units of which they are comprised. None of the foregoing perspectives is so persuasive as to justify rejection of the theoretical possibility that such interactions occur and that they flow in both directions. The shortcomings of all five—the failure of realists and Marxists to account for the blunders of states and the ineffectiveness of classes, the failure of hardened elitists to account for the impact of broad social movements, the failure of ethnomethodologists to account for the responsiveness of micro actors to the authority and directives they attribute to macro wholes, the failure of structurationists to posit macro structures that can be distinguished from micro actors, and the failure of rational-choice theorists to allow for nonrational bases of action—are sufficiently conspicuous to warrant consideration and elaboration of how micro-level phenomena may serve as sources of macro global change.

Furthermore, all five of these perspectives seem ill-suited to a world undergoing profound and rapid transformations. With many organized groups fragmenting into smaller entities while others are joining together in larger collectivities, and with still others caught up in authority crises that are weakening governments, one is compelled to wonder what is happening to individuals that their organizations are so marked by dynamism and change. Surely they are not mere bystanders as subgroupism cascades across the global landscape. Surely their orientations are affected by the vacillations of their governments, the demands of their leaders, and the restructurings of their organizations. And surely, too, their readiness to see themselves as agents of change increases the more they observe and experience the transformations that are going on around them. Approaches that do not allow for this potential dynamism, and for the ways in which it sends tremors through macro structures, cannot account for essential aspects of the changes in global life.

In the high dynamism and complexity of turbulence, it seems risky indeed to ignore or take for granted the presence of the nonrational individual in the configurations of global life. Ethnomethodologists and structurationists to the contrary notwithstanding, one must give due consideration to the macro structures, institutions, and collectivities of world politics while at the same time attending, unlike Marxists, realists, elitists, and rational-choice theorists, to the nonrational individuals—be they officials, producers, workers, or citizens—who are embedded in and linked to these macro phenomena. One can acknowledge that most citizens in most countries are entrenched in long-standing habits and that they are nevertheless manipulable while also affirming, unlike the hardened elitists, that such characteristics can change.[19]

Put in another way, the age-old debate over free will versus determinism takes on a special cast under conditions of turbulence. Whatever may be the merit of the deterministic perspectives of realists and Marxists, their presumptions that individuals lack free will and that individual action is determined by the macro dynamics of societal institutions, historical imperatives, and cultural precepts are plainly misleading in times of high complexity and dynamism. For it is exactly at such times, when the certainties of institutions, history, and culture are being subjected to intense challenge, that individuals are most free, if not compelled, to make choices that previously might have been made for them through their links to macro structures and processes.[20]

In sum, without denying the existence of the state, the state system, or any other macro phenomena, one ought not be content with them as sufficient explanations of change. International systems and their collectivities do have boundaries and parameters that limit the range of variation within which institutional, structural, and process variables stimulate demands, constrain action, encourage resistance, or otherwise operate. Even so, a collectivity's actions and reactions may be shaped by the individuals of whom it is comprised, and it is this possibility that should make us wary of metatheoretical premises that locate causation exclusively in either micro or macro sources.[21]

Underlying this reluctance to focus exclusively on phenomena at either level is the perplexing question of how it is that, more often than

[19] For a similar formulation, interpreting empirical data as demonstrating that "Americans have generally responded rationally to changing circumstances," that the public's "foreign policy preferences have in fact had considerable stability and, when they have changed, have done so in ways that can be judged as reasonable," see Robert Y. Shapiro and Benjamin I. Page, "Foreign Policy and the Rational Public," *Journal of Conflict Resolution* 32 (June 1988): 211–47.

[20] For a discussion of how the free will–determinism debate is altered by the advent of systemic transitions, see Immanuel Wallerstein, "World-Systems Analysis," in Anthony Giddens and Jonathan Turner, eds., *Social Theory Today* (Cambridge: Polity Press, 1987), esp. page 323.

[21] It would be highly misleading to imply that this inquiry is the first to seek an interactive synthesis of micro and macro phenomena; other analysts have also been resistant to an exclusively micro or macro perspective. For the outlines of a particular promising synthesis, called "methodological situationism," see Karin Knorr-Cetina, "The Micro-Social Order: Towards a Reconceptualization," in Nigel G. Fielding, ed., *Actions and Structure: Research Methods and Social Theory* (London: Sage, 1988), pp. 20–53. For an attempt to explore micro-macro links empirically in the context of cognitive theory, see John S. Dryzek, Margaret L. Clark, and Garry McKenzie, "Subject and System in International Interaction," *International Organization* 43 (Summer 1989): 475–503.

not, organized collectivities manage to cohere and persist. History is, after all, marked by enough instances of societal breakdown; recent developments in Beirut at the local level and Poland at the national level are among the reminders that large-scale coherence and persistence cannot be presumed as the underlying state of political nature. As a corollary, it seems unwarranted to assume that micro actors are constant with respect to the processes whereby authority is organized and centralized. These are not narrow processes confined to the macro level. They invoke, rather, relationships that extend throughout collectivities, which means that authority can be only as effective as the readiness to comply of those toward whom it is directed. While this readiness may normally mark the life of collectivities, it cannot be assumed to be permanent. Hence, if the successful exercise of even the most centralized authority is always problematic, one must seek to comprehend the micro foundations of the macro phenomena.

So we return again to the premise that, in Order II, postinternational politics is sustained by both macro and micro dynamics. It consists not of one or the other but of both and of the interaction between them. Whatever the nature and direction of this interaction, it is posited here as being capable of altering the parameters and extending the fluctuations of the variables through which global life unfolds from day to day and era to era.

It is important to note that this approach to world politics derives from empirical and not value considerations. Although the stress on interactive processes may seem to stem from an underlying commitment to the inherent worth of individuals and an aspiration to save them from the conceptual clutches of those who see people as merely responsive to the requirements of macro institutions, such is not the case. It stems, rather, from an understanding of how global life acquires form and is organized. Individuals must serve as conceptual foci for the same reason that states and other macro institutions must serve as conceptual foci: because the interactions among and between them can have relevant consequences.[22]

[22] That the presumption of macro-micro interaction is not a sly way of infiltrating individual dignity under the guise of an analytic requirement can be further demonstrated by pointing out that this theoretical position tends to ignore the whole person and to focus on only those of his or her aspects that are involved in specified interactive processes. It is not the worthiness of individuals that is of analytic concern but, rather, how their actions shape and are shaped by the cognitive maps, role expectations, and belief systems intrinsic to their macro circumstances. Indeed, in order to focus attention on the need for more precise conceptualization of the person as a political actor, I will argue (chapter 9) that analytically there are no individuals apart from the systems in

Levels of Aggregation

But how, through what sorts of processes, do the three types of micro actors interact with the five types of macro actors? Macro collectivities acquire structure and substance through the repeated actions and reactions of identifiable and observable people. Hence, to understand their coherence and persistence, as well as their potential for disarray and collapse, it is necessary to look closely at the processes through which micro and macro phenomena shape each other.

To trace these shaping processes, we must make use of a conception of the macro-micro distinction that is at variance with the conventional one. Where the usual approach is to differentiate between macro and micro *levels of analysis*, here the focus is on macro and micro *levels of aggregation*. The first of these approaches focuses on analysts and the intellectual processes whereby they structure world politics; the second calls attention to the world itself and the processes whereby its smaller units are aggregated into larger ones.

In the level-of-analysis approach to the macro-micro distinction, there is a tendency to equate the macro level with systemic phenomena and the micro level with subsystemic actors, processes, and structures. Such a formulation acknowledges that some phenomena encompass others—that governments and economies are subsumed by nation-states, and nation-states by international systems—but it does not require inquiry into the roles played by less comprehensive entities. The micro level is identified with nation-states as subsystems, and macro-micro interactions are studied in terms of how states shape and are shaped by the international systems of which they are a part.[23] Occasionally, interest groups and domestic publics may also be treated as micro-level subsystems,[24] but rarely does the level of analysis go lower than that. Aside from the fact that this approach disregards the possibility that individuals may be essential actors on the global stage, it also violates the commonsense notion that micro phenomena are small, even minute, in scope.

The level-of-aggregation approach, on the other hand, distinguishes between macro and micro levels by the form, structure, or scope of the aggregated entities: the least encompassing, and most concrete of them

---

which they are located. My theoretical premises simply do not take a value position on the "worthiness" of the individual in the global system.

[23] See, for example, Morton A. Kaplan, *Macropolitics: Essays on the Philosophy and Science of Politics* (Chicago: Aldine, 1969), pp. 30–31, and Kenneth N. Waltz, *Theory of International Politics* (Reading, Mass.: Addison-Wesley, 1979), pp. 91, 110.

[24] Robert O. Keohane, *After Hegemony: Cooperation and Discord in the World Political Economy* (Princeton: Princeton University Press, 1984).

are treated as micro phenomena, while others are placed at the macro level. In other words, the macro-micro distinction is a dichotomy between the smallest units out of which world politics can emanate and any larger units.[25] It distinguishes between individuals and face-to-face groups at the micro level and larger actors, processes, or structures in which the participants are unknown to each other at the macro level.[26] The inclusion of face-to-face groups in the micro level is based on reasoning not unlike that which leads to the inclusion of firms as key actors in microeconomics: namely, that face-to-face groups, like individuals, are able to set priorities, assess possibilities, bargain over costs, take decisive steps, and accept responsibility for their actions, behaviors that are characteristic of interpersonal settings and not operative in large, impersonal aggregations.

There are several reasons why the macro-micro distinction is best made in terms of levels of aggregation. Most notably, of course, virtually by definition it prevents one from ignoring the relevance of individuals to international processes.[27] Second, it focuses attention on the question of how the dynamics of aggregation enable macro entities to cohere and persist: since they are conceived as being collectivites or activities in which the participants are unknown to each other, one can

[25] It must be emphasized, however, that the dichotomy is not posited as a distinction between intrinsically micro and intrinsically macro phenomena. It is, rather, a matter of the analytic problem addressed and how the phenomena at the two levels are conceived to be related to each other. For a cogent discussion of this point, see Dean Gerstein, "To Unpack Micro and Macro: Link Small with Large and Part with Whole," in Alexander et al., *Micro-Macro Link*, chapter 3. For an analysis in which the micro and macro levels of aggregation are dichotomized in terms of small- and large-scale motives rather than small and large units of action, see William O. Chittick, "Macromotives and Microbehavior: A Prescriptive Analysis," in Gary K. Bertsch, ed., *Global Policy Studies* (Beverly Hills, Calif.: Sage, 1982), pp. 205–29.

[26] A similar formulation is in Hans Haferkamp, "Complexity and Behavior Structure, Planned Association and Creation of Structure," in Alexander et al., *Micro-Macro Link*, pp. 177–78. For a somewhat different categorization, distinguishing among micropolitics, group politics, macropolitics, and megapolitics, see Harry Eckstein, "Case Study and Theory in Political Science," in Fred I. Greenstein and Nelson W. Polsby, eds., *Handbook of Political Science*, vol. 7, *Strategies of Inquiry* (Reading, Mass.: Addison-Wesley, 1975), esp. p. 134. On the other hand, Jeffrey C. Alexander, "Action and Its Environments," in Alexander et al., *Micro-Macro Link*, p. 290, declares that any formulation equating the micro level with individual "is extremely misleading."

[27] For elaborations of this point, see Roger A. Coate, "Bridging the Micro-Macro Gap in Global Relations Theory" (paper presented at the annual meeting of the International Studies Association, Washington, March 1985), and Chadwick F. Alger, "Bridging the Micro and the Macro in International Relations Research," *Alternatives* 10 (Winter 1984–85): 319–44.

hardly avoid pondering the processes by which strangers manage to coordinate their actions over long periods of time.

Related to this is a third reason: dealing with levels of aggregation assures a preoccupation with the processes whereby micro parts are transformed into macro wholes. People do not concert their energies automatically. They have to be mobilized and then aggregated by leaders; and whether this occurs through evocative rhetoric, persuasive reasoning, or dire warnings, the leaders are dependent on the followers' recognizing that they have common concerns and that the joining of their concerns—that is, the creation of macro wholes through aggregative processes—can yield collective consequences.

A fourth advantage of the level-of-aggregation approach is that placing face-to-face groups at the micro level facilitates study of the interactions of those who speak and act on behalf of collectivities. Summit meetings, cabinet sessions, and a host of similar transactions can be probed for their micro dynamics, whereas under the level-of-analysis approach they tend to be viewed exclusively as macro phenomena, with the result that the impact of interpersonal interactions may not be given due consideration. Put in structurationist terms, the face-to-face interactions of macro leaders is the closest the analyst can get empirically to observing the ways in which people become the carriers of structure, so that the interplay among them can aid in comprehending the structural flexibilities and rigidities of a macro system.[28]

In other words, the inclusion of interpersonal exchanges at the micro level of aggregation enables us to cope better with the discrepancies between what we observe in world politics and how we articulate our observations. We observe identifiable, concrete persons engaging in identifiable, concrete actions; we see identifiable, concrete objects, such as weapons or statues, being used in identifiable, concrete ways. What we say or write about these observations as macro phenomena, however, is usually far removed from anything identifiable or concrete. Rather, we normally speak in vast abstractions, such as "states pursue their goals" (when what we observe are persons shouldering weapons) or "societies enshrining their symbols of unity" (when what we observe are persons laying wreaths at the base of statues).[29]

---

[28] For a systematic inquiry into how face-to-face micro interactions can shape macro dynamics, see Paul A. Anderson, "What Do Decision Makers Do When They Make a Foreign Policy Decision? Implications for the Comparative Study of Foreign Policy," in Charles F. Hermann, Charles W. Kegley, Jr., and James N. Rosenau, eds., *New Directions in the Study of Foreign Policy* (Boston: Allen & Unwin, 1987), pp. 285–308.

[29] For an analysis of how the size of social structures and the scope of social processes can have important methodological consequences, see Charles Tilly, *Big Structures,*

These disparities between observed realities and the rhetoric of observation arise out of leaps of faith that transform concrete micro phenomena into broad macro abstractions. We see or experience a minute, particular event, but we infer from it an indication of a larger pattern. Having made this inference, we then proceed to treat the larger pattern as if it is in fact an observed phenomenon. Thus, world politics is said to have a state system, hierarchical structures, a balance of power, allies and enemies, and a host of other features that have never actually been observed.

While there are many reasons to be wary of such inferential leaps, it would be virtually impossible to proceed without making them. They are essential to our ability to focus on the large problems—on those problems that are macro in their scope, content, and consequences. Without the inferences that lead to the description and assessment of abstract phenomena, we would be hopelessly mired in a profusion of details that would surely preclude any comprehension of global issues.

Even greater than the danger of excessive detail, on the other hand, is the danger of forgetting that we have made inferences, of taking the micro phenomena for granted and assuming that the macro wholes are accurate reflections of the micro parts. Most notably, there is an ever-present danger of presuming that the micro parts are homogeneous rather than differentially susceptible to various influences, a danger which can readily lead to erroneous attributions of intent to the macro wholes.

Finally, let us admit that, in addition to its several analytic advantages, the appeal of an interactive perspective also derives from a poetic wonderment, a sense of awe, over what the interactive processes produce. The formation of structured and purposeful collectivities is a process that is never automatic, sometimes circuitous, often obscure, and always awesome. It is awesome because most of the diverse individuals that comprise a modern collectivity do not know each other, much less interact directly with each other, and yet somehow they acquire coherence and structure as a collective actor which develops,

---

Large Processes, Huge Comparisons (New York: Russell Sage Foundation, 1984). Other cogent inquiries into micro-macro interactions can be found in Fielding, *Actions and Structure*; Randall Collins, "On the Microfoundations of Macrosociology," *American Journal of Sociology* 86 (March 1981): 984–1014, and "A Micro-Macro Theory of Intellectual Creativity: The Case of German Idealist Philosophy," *Sociological Theory* 5 (Spring 1987): 47–69; Alexander et al., *Micro-Macro Link*; Michael Hechter, ed., *The Microfoundations of Macrosociology* (Philadelphia: Temple University Press, 1983); Knorr-Cetina and Cicourel, *Advances in Social Theory and Methodology*; and Thomas C. Schelling, *Micromotives and Macrobehavior* (New York: W. W. Norton, 1978).

possesses, and uses resources on behalf of goals. That this occurs is self-evident, but to explain how it occurs is a stern challenge to our grasp of the human condition.

THE AGGREGATION OF MICRO PARTS

To discern how various aggregative processes underlie turbulent change, we need to start by pointing out that they all share a tendency toward a balance between their macro and micro components. The interactive conception which allows for transformations originating with micro actors disallows a lasting disjunction between the macro and micro levels: alterations at one level require some kind of adjustment at the other. Indeed, the balancing process is continuous: alterations in macro structures, processes, and collectivities affect the ways in which micro actors comply with the directives of macro institutions; in turn, these changes in the modes of compliance lead to further alterations in the macro phenomena.

Thus, over long periods of time—that is, until parametric changes set in—the macro and micro phenomena that make up any large-scale structure, process, institution, or collectivity are linked together in continuously reinforcing interactions. It is only for analytic purposes that we separate them out to trace and assess their consequences.[30]

A closer look at these balancing processes reveals the crucial role played by individuals. To speak of macro structures (such as the balance of power), macro processes (such as war), macro institutions (such as the UN), or macro collectivities (such as China) is to use shorthand labels for very elaborate interaction patterns among micro actors. As noted earlier, the labels obviate the need to describe all the concrete individuals, with their different goals and styles, whose interactions give rise to and make evident the macro phenomena. Over time, as the use of the labels becomes widespread, as a few persons (i.e., private leaders or public officials) are authorized to speak and act on behalf of the many, and as records (such as speeches, constitutions, and treaties) documenting the existence of the macro phenomena accumulate, the macro structures, processes, institutions, and collectivities come to be widely accepted as "real" entities that have acquired an existence of their own apart from the individuals they comprise.

[30] For some analysts, "the continued back-and-forth movement between [as Clifford Geertz puts it] 'the whole conceived through the parts that actualize it and the parts conceived through the whole that motivates them' is what is commonly referred to as the hermeneutic circle." Michael T. Gibbons, ed., *Interpreting Politics* (New York: New York University Press, 1987), p. 14.

Even when shared perceptions accord them a kind of autonomy, however, they remain crucially shaped by the values inherent in their micro origins. Collins succinctly summarizes this process with respect to the modern state: "In so far ... as people take the 'state' to be not an intermittent collection of actions by certain people, some of whom have weapons, but as an expression of the collective will of the people, or a manifestation of God, or simply as a self-subsistent entity, they bolster the power of those who enact the 'state.' "[31]

Of course, the more firmly macro entities are conceived to be in place, the more are they experienced as reinforcing the shared patterns of the micro actors who are embraced by them. This is why global structures and processes do not readily change. They may fluctuate in response to daily events, but usually within limits that are consistent with the range of tolerance inherent in the inertia of the underlying habits. Notwithstanding this tendency, however, macro-micro interactions cannot be taken for granted; the skills and orientations of people at the micro level are at least theoretically capable of undergoing enough change to have significant consequences for macro structures and processes.

If macro phenomena are aggregations of vast numbers of individual actions that form recognizable patterns for which leaders speak and act, thus making the wholes seem greater than the sums of their parts, a question arises as to the accuracy of these sums. Do the habits, qualities, motives, and actions add up to the macro patterns we say they add up to? During stable periods, macro events and interactions do indeed conform to the patterns we ascribe to them. We know this from historical records and present-day observations as well as from the relative paucity of disconfirming or contrary patterns. But from the same sources, we also know that if these interactive and summed micro components undergo major alteration, the autonomy ascribed to the macro phenomena is in jeopardy. Macro structures and collectivities may have a perceived existence of their own, but they draw their sustenance from their micro components, and, like any system, they eventually have to adapt to the sources of their support if they are to persist.

This adaptive requirement highlights again the impossibility of taking macro-micro interactions for granted when turbulence sets in. Since changes at one level are bound to induce shifts at the other, the failure of memories, beliefs, expectations, and networks to perpetuate themselves at the micro level can be viewed as related to the alteration

[31] Randall Collins, "Micro-Translation As a Theory-Building Strategy," in Knorr-Cetina and Cicourel, *Advances in Social Theory and Methodology*, p. 86.

of macro circumstances such that they no longer serve the needs on which those memories, beliefs, expectations, and networks rest. Thus, for instance, the rise of Solidarity in Poland and the uprising against Ferdinand Marcos in the Philippines can be seen as a shift in orientations occasioned by the failure of macro structures and institutions in those countries to meet certain needs and goals. To be sure, Solidarity came into existence through hard organizational work and mobilization that helped undermine old beliefs, memories, expectations, styles, and networks; but such macro activities could not have succeeded without corresponding changes at the micro level. The Philippine uprising dramatically demonstrated this link: it occurred with a minimum of organization and a maximum of spontaneity among hundreds of thousands of individuals, who seized an opportunity to break their habits, redefine their memories, alter their expectations, and redirect their networks.

TYPES OF AGGREGATIVE PROCESSES

The processes whereby the orientations and actions of individuals are transformed into collective orientations and behavior take many forms. They can involve the aggregation of citizens or leaders, basic attitudes or transitory opinions, supportive actions or protest behaviors, sustained commitments or impulsive outbursts. These micro units can be aggregated through education, bargaining, appeals to loyalty and shared interests, sanctions, and coercive action. The processes can be direct or circuitous, spontaneous or mobilized, brief or prolonged, intended or unintended, subsystemic or global. For officials, leaders, and spokespersons at the macro level, both within the aggregating system and in other systems, events at the micro level can be experienced as rewards or punishments, sensed as opportunities or threats, perceived as latent or manifest, interpreted as trends or exceptions, treated as habitual support or signs of opposition, inferred from isolated anecdotes or systematic evidence. The aggregative outcomes can consist of reinforced norms, collective behavior, public policies, declarations of intent, or demands for action that are enduring or transitional, generalized or specific, permissive or restrictive.

Perhaps the best way to sort out these various dimensions and types of aggregative processes is by finding answers to a series of questions about how, when, and why the summing occurs one way rather than another. Under what conditions is the interaction between micro and macro units susceptible to aggregation? At what points and through what mechanisms do the wholes become greater than the sum of their parts? When do the parts add up to *less* than the whole? Need the sums be founded on quantitative evidence, or can they be based on qualitative indicators? Who does the summing? How is the presence of the summed whole recognized and articulated? What political consequences follow from its articulation? Why are some sums accepted as valid while the accuracy of others is contested? When does a sum need to be recalculated and rearticulated for a collectivity to retain its vitality in global politics? Are the processes and politics of disaggregation or subgroupism, wherein wholes are reduced either into lesser sums or into parts no longer summable, comparable to those of aggregation?

Observed, Inferred, and Mixed Sums

The summing of micro parts into macro wholes is not inherent in political nature. The members of collectivities do not necessarily recognize that they have shared interests. To be sure, they are responsive to the dictates of culture and the lessons of history which lead them to engage in common behavior, but neither of these inexorably impels them to join together as parts of a whole. They could go their separate ways—and, indeed, the members of most collectivities do not know each other and do go their separate ways, even as their conduct is being pieced together into a larger context by public officials, opposition leaders, journalists, scholars, and others who may have reason to focus on macro phenomena.

The sums and the summing processes—their reliability, validity, flexibility, desirability, and implications—thus become a major preoccupation of those responsible for preserving and enhancing the welfare of collectivities. Any issue can be viewed as a contest over the meaning of sums, how they were calculated, what they portend, and how they can and should be altered.

Neither the sums nor the summing processes necessarily result from simple, mathematical constructions. In order to know where they stand either with their followers or with the environment they are trying to affect, macro leaders occasionally need to resort to precise quantitative assessments of their support or opposition, but many situations do not lend themselves to such calculations, and the leaders then have to depend on more impressionistic appraisals. Scholars may contend that "aggregation and disaggregation involve shifts in the locus of numerical certainty from the small to the large [through] the formation of sums, products, vectors, or parametric statistics,"[32] but politicians

[32] Gerstein, "To Unpack Micro and Macro," p. 97.

cannot easily avail themselves of such techniques and often have to rely on an intuition which may be a synthesis of qualitative and quantitative components.

Accordingly, the questions posed above can be addressed in the context of a continuum that locates at one extreme aggregations arrived at exclusively through direct observation and systematic counting of units of behavior and, at the other extreme, sums developed through the unsystematic juxtaposing of inferences from disparate actions and events. These will be called, respectively, *observed* and *inferred* sums or aggregative processes. The distinction between them is much the same as that between "hard" and "soft" data, between measured and estimated quantities, between quantitative and qualitative analysis, between tangible and intangible phenomena, between objective and intersubjective conditions, between additive totals and multiplicative composites. In practice, of course, most aggregations fall between the two poles and are reached partly through systematic observations and partly through unsystematic inferences, a result which can be called a *mixed* sum or process.

Observed sums are obviously the easiest to trace. People engage in similar actions—voters vote (or they abstain), volunteers give time or money (or they withhold contributions), protesters march (or they stay at home), boycotters refuse to buy (or they do buy), strikers stay away from work (or they cross the picket lines), traders trade (or they do not), citizens express opinions (or say they are unsure), draftees comply (or they defy); these actions are observed and counted by those concerned with the micro bases of macro phenomena, and the resulting totals are pondered, interpreted, rejected, or used in some other way. Assessments of a sum's reliability and meaning may vary considerably (those for whom a sum has negative implications usually have no trouble finding reasons for questioning it), but as a quantitative process it is essentially a simple construction. The numbers reveal a pattern of convergence around a common behavior, and if they have been similarly calculated at regular intervals in the past, they also tell a simple story of growth or decline in that behavior.[33]

[33] Indeed, the story may be too simple. For a convincing discussion of how and why macro entities compiled by quantifying micro parts oversimplify the dynamics of aggregation, see James S. Coleman, "Microfoundations and Macrosocial Behavior," in Alexander et al., *Micro-Macro Link*, pp. 153–57. Another interpretation of the problem of drawing conclusions from an additive process is that "many of the familiar deficiencies of individuals' opinions—weak informational bases, lack of structure, instability over time, and the like—are overcome in the aggregation process, so that collective opinion

Inferred sums, on the other hand, are anything but simple. They are constructed out of particular incidents, puzzling anomalies, presumed coalitions, leadership actions, shifts in tone, partial mobilizations, declarations of intent, pleas for cooperation, and many other forms of behavior whose significance is far from unequivocal, or they may reflect a tendency to treat a few cases, or even one, as symptomatic of an entire pattern. Consequently, they are much less direct, linear, and verifiable than those derived from the process of counting heads. Scholars may wince at the unsystematic bases for such aggregations, but in many respects it is precisely the capacity to infer accurate sums from such fragmentary data that distinguishes successful political leaders from those who lose out in the competition for influence.

As composites to which diverse meanings can be attached by the parties to a situation, inferred sums are crucial components of the dynamics whereby political issues are framed, contested, and resolved. Only rarely are political processes suspended in order to allow the meaning and reliability of alleged sums to be checked out systematically. Public officials and organizational leaders may prefer to proceed on the basis of clear-cut, quantitative evidence, but they cannot afford to refrain from acting in its absence. Often, reliable observed sums showing the distribution of support and the degree of aggregation are not available at the time when decisions have to be taken or challenges confronted. Yet leaders need to have some notion of how much support each of them can bring to bear on behalf of a given policy; otherwise, they run the risk of being unable to back up demands or ward off threats, or being bested in the contest over resources and influence. It follows that they are frequently compelled to rely on more or less impressionistic data—a change of emphasis in a speech ("If the foreign secretary said that, then we must now . . ."), a symbolic gesture, a press report, a surprising event, an official's resignation, an unexpectedly large turnout for a speech or a smaller-than-predicted observance of a strike, a faction's reluctance to press its demands, a conciliatory offer, and so on. As the interaction proceeds around such developments, and as journalists, bureaucrats, academics, and others interpret them, an intersubjective consensus may or may not evolve among the leaders of macro collectivities as to how micro support is distributed among them and whether the distribution is tending in one direction or another.

At any moment in time, a consensus around the meaning of soft indicators constitutes an aggregation no less politically relevant than

is highly stable, well structured, and responsive to the best available information." Shapiro and Page, "Foreign Policy and the Rational Public," p. 213.

one composed of hard data. For, while it consists of qualitative components, it is nonetheless the equivalent of a sum—a reasoned rather than a computed total, but a total nonetheless. Despite the absence of precision and persuasive evidence based on recurring patterns, the inferential process has yielded a perceived whole that consists of specifiable (albeit ambiguous) parts and is believed to represent the prevailing distribution of support. Seen in this way, inferred sums are an important part of the processes whereby micro orientations get transformed into macro outcomes.

Consider the role that inferred sums played in the efforts of U.S. citizens, in the mid-1980s, to weaken apartheid in South Africa by pressing disinvestment policies on corporations operating in that country. At one point, for example, with protest campaigns, resolutions by city councils, and boycotts devoted to the issue occurring with increasing frequency, the *New York Times* saw fit to infer the presence of an aggregation by commencing an editorial with the observation, "The urge to punish South Africa for apartheid is *now palpable* throughout the United States."[34]

However, most of the politically relevant sums consist of both inferences and observations, of diverse estimates, interpretations, declarations, denials, and hints of underlying support as well as of direct measurements. Few situations can be adequately described and assessed through quantified observations. The tolerance of citizens, the hidden agendas of leaders, and the coherence of collectivities are but a few of the innumerable factors that do not lend themselves to objective measurement.

Furthermore, no matter how reliable a quantitative sum may be, it cannot be free of controversy. Given different needs and motives among the participants in a situation, some will surely find that the data are skewed in their disfavor and will contend that fraud, error, or some other kind of bias was at work in their compilation. Others will doubtless declare, perhaps not without reason, that the observations are obsolete, that recent events have altered the circumstances that prevailed at the time the data were gathered. In short, some degree of inference is inherent in any aggregative process.

On the other hand, at least a minimum of quantitative observation is crucial to any summing process. There are time limits beyond which inferred sums do not retain their viability, so that on occasion they have to be supplemented by some degree of systematic observation. Thus, periodically, one or another party, and perhaps all of them, will

[34] June 9, 1985, sec. 4, p. 22 (italics added).

feel the need for more than crude inferences about the support they or their adversaries can command. Eventually, they will want solid information about the obstacles and opportunities that lie ahead, which means that sooner or later they will have to supplement inferred sums with objective data from opinion polls, elections, protest rallies, trade statistics, government commissions, or whatever sources may be available.

In short, aggregation in postinternational politics is a clumsy, ungainly process operating through a diversity of cues. The process is rendered further chaotic by the great speeds at which the microelectronic revolution has enabled information and pictures to circulate. Among the many consequences of these technological developments, people can now observe support or opposition gathering momentum as street rallies, the pronouncements of officials, the responses of adversaries, the comments of citizens, and a variety of other events are portrayed on television screens throughout the world, leading to swiftly fluctuating alterations in the breadth and strength of the consensus as to how much support exists and how solid it may be. Unlike earlier times, when communication was less instantaneous and consensuses were thus relatively slow to form and change, today the processes of aggregation are fast-moving cascades, a fragile set of competing estimates that can readily shift direction and that form a volatile environment that collectivities can ignore only at great peril.[35]

Unintentional and Participatory Aggregations

However aggregated sums may be calculated, one can begin to grasp the dynamics of micro-macro interactions by drawing a distinction between sums arising out of the uncoordinated, private acts of individuals and those that come about through the self-conscious participation of individuals in their formation and maintenance. We shall refer to the former of these two types as *unintentional* aggregations and to the latter as *participatory* aggregations. The distinction between them is the difference between unplanned consequences and calculated orga-

[35] It is noteworthy that some observers see a peril in the mixed process of aggregation itself. Consider, for example, the lament of one U.S. journalist concerned about the role of the press in the process: "We are in a loop without exit signs. We influence politicians. We are influenced by polls. The American people are polled. They provide answers based upon what they have read or seen or heard. Politicians set their agendas on the basis of what tracking polls tell them. It is conceivable that this loop is destructive to the continuation of a vibrant and free democracy." Marvin Kalb, quoted in *New York Times*, November 13, 1988, sec. 4, p. 3.

nization, between latent and manifest cumulation, between individual and collective action, between diffused and mobilized behavior.

A more concrete distinction between the two types concerns the identity of the micro actors who constitute their memberships. In the case of unintended aggregations, individuals contribute to the aggregated outcomes through their occupancy of a *social* role—consumer, producer, farmer, parent, churchgoer, and so on through all those spheres of life in which they may be involved and with respect to which their common behavior may become the focus of a public issue. In participatory aggregations, on the other hand, the contribution of micro actors is confined to the *political* roles they occupy—citizen, activist, bureaucrat, elected official, and other roles in the political arena.

Participatory aggregations consist of similar behaviors undertaken by citizens or organizational members on the basis of similar beliefs about the achievement of collective goals. These actors either participate directly in the aggregation by contributing their own actions to the sum or they do so indirectly by permitting the sum to be claimed on their behalf. Whether the desired effect occurs or not, aggregation ensues because those seeking to mobilize the citizens or organizational members are able to call attention to their shared purposes and thereby concert the supporting behavior and give direction to its cumulative impact. The efforts of a government to activate the citizenry for war or of opponents to generate public protests against military action are obvious examples of participatory aggregations. Indeed, many attempts to initiate the processes of participatory aggregation spring from a desire to offset or undo the consequences of unintended aggregation. Advocates of governmental policies to control rising birth rates, for instance, are seeking to reverse or moderate the course of an unintended aggregative process.

When participatory aggregations endure and expand their concerns beyond the issues that underlay their formation, they become the equivalent of a collectivity. That is, viewed from an aggregative perspective, a collectivity involves individuals who are seen, and who see themselves, as parts that sum to a whole which is differentiated from other wholes and exists as a reality in the minds of both those who occupy its roles and those external to it, in other collectivities, who must take its existence into account. The summing of its parts is carried out and proclaimed by those who seek to organize and mobilize them in a particular way for particular purposes. If the sum is found compelling by those who form its parts, it spreads and acquires legitimacy, thus providing the perceptual base through which the collectivity takes on an existence of its own. Subsequently, whatever its nature and goals—whether it is weak or strong, system or subsystem, government or transnational association, international regime or revolutionary movement—the collectivity persists only as long as its policies successfully reinforce the values, authority structures, and compliance patterns on which its existence rests. Normally, the longer it survives, the more it accumulates written records and unwritten traditions that become deeply ingrained cultural premises which, in turn, reinforce the expectations embedded in the collectivity's roles occupied by successive generations of individuals whose actions sustain the aggregative sequences.

However, not all aggregative processes culminate in collectivities or in support for their policies. Some give rise simply to aggregations— that is, to wholes that lack the organizational and purposeful characteristics of collectivities and that consequently are equal to, and neither more nor less than, the sum of their parts. These are unintended aggregations, which come into being when a multiplicity of individuals undertake similar but unrelated actions in pursuit of their own goals or to meet their own needs. These goals or needs may be diverse, but because the actions are similar, they are summable either through direct observation or by inference. If the similar actions are relevant to the concerns of those who are expected in their professional roles to be alert to change—such as journalists, scholars, bureaucrats, and politicians—then the patterns they form will eventually be recognized, summed, and publicized. Once note has thus been taken of the similar behaviors, they can be said to form a whole even though the parts may be neither interactive nor connected. Depending on how it is perceived and publicized, the unintended aggregation can thus become the target of public policies and an issue in global politics. Population explosions, resource shortages, or financial crises are cases in point. A family has a child, fills its car's fuel tank with gasoline, or purchases a television set made abroad, unconcerned that elsewhere millions of families are doing the same. When the cumulative implications of these private acts (crowded cities, energy shortages, trade imbalances) are discerned, evaluated, and proclaimed by observers or spokespersons for collectivities, the aggregated sum enters the public arena.

This is not to imply that unintended aggregations depend on consciousness-raising. The sums get calculated whether or not people are cognizant of the public consequences of their private actions; indeed, more often than not they are unaware of the summations to which they have contributed. As one observer puts it, "Many acts when aggregated do affect the social structure—choice of occupation, religious conversions, changing one's mix of purchases, joining a political movement, moving to a different region, giving to charity, and so on—but in only a few of our daily acts do we carry it out with the intention and goal of supporting or rejecting the existing social order."[36]

Not all unintended aggregations, however, are dependent on overt actions. They can also be based on common orientations that are uncovered through opinion polls and interpreted by journalists, scholars, bureaucrats, and politicians. As such, as survey samples that reveal new and pronounced trends, the unintended aggregation can seem either promising or ominous to one or another macro actor and thereby occupy a central role in the course of events.

There may be a considerable time lag between the cumulation of micro patterns and their public acknowledgment by leaders of macro collectivities. In effect, these lags describe the informal and latent structures of certain issues. Prior to the identification of an aggregation, or during subsequent periods when it is quiescent as a public issue, policymakers may unknowingly encounter the opportunities and limitations inherent in the aggregate patterns without realizing it. The aggregate consequences of population explosions or of widespread distrust of government, for example, surely affected policies long before they were explicitly recognized.

The time lag between the cumulation and the articulation of an unintended aggregation helps clarify how the whole can become different from the sum of its parts. During that period, word of the existence of the aggregation spreads—in academic circles, legislative corridors, and editorial boards as well as among interest groups, politicians, and public servants—and as the word spreads, the meaning, relevance, and future development of the aggregation becomes increasingly salient as a problem and a source of contention. At some point, one or another actor finds reason to proclaim its existence as a matter of public concern. If the surfacing of the pattern leads to further debate, the aggregation can be said to have become a political issue. However accurate the proclamation of a sum may be—and often the initial contention over the issue involves arguments over what the correct sum is—it serves as a basis for subsequent action in the public arena.

While unintended aggregations can give rise to macro consequences and can become issues on the global agenda, they are, so to speak, leaderless. They have neither designated spokespersons nor positions in which leaders could be placed. As in the example of population ex-

---

[36] William J. Goode, "Individual Choice and Social Order," in James F. Short, Jr., ed., *The Social Fabric: Dimensions and Issues* (Newbury Park, Calif.: Sage, 1986), p. 45.

plosions, these "hard realities" simply exist. They have no leaders who speak for them or who are otherwise authorized to act on their behalf.

Virtually by definition, on the other hand, participatory aggregations do have leadership positions and people who occupy them. Whether the participants are linked together in organizations (collectivities) or are mobilized to act even in the absence of common membership (transnational movements or international regimes), the resulting structures contain some roles whose occupants are responsible for advancing the general organizational goals and the specific purposes for which mobilization was initiated and who thus seek to promote or preserve values in the global system. Viewed in this context, much of world politics is a contest among leaders of participatory aggregations over the legitimacy of their claims to shares of global resources.

Participatory aggregations do not come into being, however, only through the mobilizing activities of their leaders. As previously noted, the interaction of leaders and followers is a two-way process: the participatory aggregation could not form without leaders leading, but neither could it take shape without followers ready to follow. Usually these interactive dynamics begin with an energetic leader, but on occasion they originate with a restless follower. The sudden willingness of hundreds of thousands of Chileans to defy the regime of Gen. Augusto Pinochet with protests in May 1983 is a case in point. Apparently, no one anticipated the protests, least of all the man who touched them off: a twenty-eight-year-old clerk in the state copper industry, Rodolfo Seguel, who had been elected to his first post in the copper union the previous December and became its president in February. One of his first acts was to call for a strike in May. This was eventually moderated to a call for a day of protest, but the intended aggregation brought into being that day was so large as to astonish Seguel along with everyone else. "I found I had said what everyone was thinking and no one dared to say," he was quoted as observing. "Suddenly people began to lose their fear."[37]

Collectivities can aggregate greater or lesser sums, according to the extent to which their resources and structures enable them to move toward their goals. Collectivities whose resources and coherence are insufficient to the realization of a particular set of goals sum to less than their parts. Their members do not contribute enough to allow their leaders to take effective action on their behalf. When resources

[37] I. Hilton, "Bankruptcy Goads Middle Classes to Challenge Pinochet," *Sunday Times* (London), August 7, 1983, p. 8.

support the collectivity's goals and policies, on the other hand, the leadership is able to press, bargain, or otherwise move toward the goals, in which case the collectivity can aggregate a sum that might even seem to be in excess of its parts.

Distinctions can be made among aggregations in terms of capability statements derived from the difference between a collectivity's performance and the claims made on its behalf. Political parties in open societies are illustrative of these statements and their implications. A party is seen to sum to less than its parts if the support it gets on election day falls short of either its totals in prior elections or of the votes its leaders claimed they could muster. Under these conditions, the influence of the party is diminished by its failure to make good on its claims. If, on the other hand, the vote exceeds the claimed support, the subsequent activities of the party's leadership will be believed to represent more than the sum of its parts. The retreating or advancing army, the faltering or expanding economy, and the unexpectedly small or large rally are other examples of aggregations that are, politically, less or more than their parts. As the case of the Chilean copper union suggests, moreover, abrupt alterations in the sums can lead to profound effects.

Periods of global turbulence are marked by a high degree of participatory aggregation and considerable fluctuation in the sums aggregated by collectivities. As the fragmenting of whole systems and the coherence of subsystems cascade across previously stable boundaries, leaders become more active in mobilizing the energies of their members and finding ways to demonstrate that the emergent sums are consistent with their claims. Then, as the turbulence peaks, both the sums and the claims made about them lurch erratically as the contrariety, simultaneity, and expansivity of tensions and changes flow swiftly within and among systems.

The evolution of the Polish trade union Solidarity offers an example. As its core expanded from a small nucleus of workers in Gdansk in 1980, the union became a political force in Poland far more powerful than the size of its formal membership indicated. As it expanded, the Polish government and Communist party became increasingly helpless, their fragmentation revealing them to be collectivities considerably less than the sum of their parts. At the same time, repercussions were felt in other Eastern European countries, with their governments fearing that the cascades might pour over them and reveal their own aggregations to be fragile and those of their subsystems to be increasing. Then, when martial law was imposed by the Polish government in 1981, the direction of the cascades was reversed and the relative sums

fluctuated through still another phase of uncertainty and reaggregation. Another reversal occurred in 1989, when the Polish government
and Communist party, finding themselves still without the legitimacy
needed to govern effectively, instituted constitutional reforms that allowed Solidarity to offer candidates in elections to the national legis-
lature, leading to sweeping victories by the union's candidates and revealing again that the sum of its support far exceeded its formal
membership.

TYPES OF PARTICIPATORY AGGREGATIONS

Participatory aggregations can vary along a number of dimensions.
One of these, the scope of the macro unit to which the micro parts sum,
seems so important as to warrant making further distinctions within
it. Three subtypes can be discerned: (1) aggregations that consist of
people with common membership in a collectivity, whether a whole
system or a subsystem; (2) aggregations that consist of people drawn
from different subsystems of the same whole systems; and (3) aggregations that consist of the memberships of two or more whole systems.
We shall refer to these three subtypes as, respectively, *within-system*
aggregations, *issue* aggregations, and *between-system* aggregations.

In the case of within-system aggregations, all the adult members of
the system or subsystem are relevant micro actors—even those who are
apathetic, inasmuch as their apathy contributes to, or detracts from,
the coherence of the collectivity and its effectiveness. A collectivity's
effectiveness is a long-term condition that is a function of the degree to
which its members are ready to support the actions undertaken by its
leaders. The aggregation of system support, involving as it does the
building of loyalties, respect for system authority, compliance habits,
and a readiness to sacrifice time and energy if circumstances call for it,
is a continuous process, one that is always moving toward the
strengthening, maintenance, or decline of support and thus toward
more or less effectiveness. Within-system aggregation builds on the
most basic political orientations to be found at the micro level.

Issue aggregations, on the other hand, are sustained by active citizens or organizational leaders who seek to mobilize transitory opinions or private actions around a systemic or subsystemic issue that
public officials either perceive or experience as requiring a policy response. These aggregations use whatever support has already been
fashioned as a base upon which more immediate appeals are made,
sanctions evoked, and bargains struck.

In between-system aggregations, system leaders reach across the divides that separate systems and act together with their counterparts in

other systems to build still more encompassing aggregations in order to address common conflicts and problems. Here, individuals are, in effect, representatives of collectivities whose within-system and issue aggregations serve as the basis for their transactions. These representatives negotiate within limits set by prior issue aggregations; hence, the role they play is more restricted and evokes a narrower set of skills than is the case for leaders in the other two subtypes. This is especially true of persons representing collectivities in the state-centric world. In this more formal, sovereignty-bound world, between-system relationships mainly involve individuals in the tasks of diplomacy, whereas in the less hierarchical, sovereignty-free multi-centric world, people may engage in a wider variety of aggregative processes and thus may be called upon to employ a wider variety of orientations and skills as they pursue their collectivity's goals.

The more interdependent the world becomes, the greater is the overlap among the three types of participatory aggregations. That is, the effectiveness of any one type is increasingly a function of the effectiveness of the other two types. A between-system aggregation, for example, is likely to cope with a challenge only to the extent that the within-system and issue aggregations of its participant macro actors are well crafted and enduring. Soviet-American arms control efforts, for example, are likely to be no more successful than is allowed by the coherence of the within-system and issue aggregations that each superpower brings to the negotiations. Viewed in this way, every citizen in both countries is, through the circuitous processes of micro-macro interactions that underlie the convergences of aggregations, a contributor to the prevailing state of the global arms race. The scenarios through which individuals understand these convergences constitute one aspect of their analytic skills that may be undergoing change today and thereby adding to the complexity and dynamism of our time.

Table 7.1 sets forth the main differences among the four types of aggregations. A comparison across the rows suggests that the conversion of micro parts into macro wholes is a highly variable process, while reading down the columns suggests that all aggregative processes are cooperative endeavors and are vulnerable to being stalled, diverted, terminated, or otherwise thwarted at many points.

At the same time, table 7.1 affords an insight into the relative difficulties of achieving effective aggregation. Other things being equal, for example, it is clearly easier to fashion an effective issue aggregation than any other type. Efforts toward that end can tap into and use transitory opinions and activist orientations, whereas the other types are more dependent on deep-seated loyalties and cultural predispositions.

TABLE 7.1. Characteristics of Four Types of Aggregations

| | Participatory Aggregations | | | Unintended Aggregations |
	Within-System	Issue	Between-System	
Micro actors	Mostly citizens	Citizens and officials	Mostly public officials	Consumers, workers, parents, etc.
Orientations, skills, and activities	Loyalties, legitimacy sentiments, cultural norms, habits of compliance	Opinions, activist habits, articulatory skills, self-interests, zero-sum demands	Sense of shared fate, nonzero-sum tendencies	Potentially all beliefs and behaviors
Aggregating agents	Schools, parents, churches, media, etc.	Journalists, politicians, bureaucrats, academics	Mostly public officials	Politicians, scholars, journalists
Main aggregative techniques	Socialization, education, ceremonies, opinion polls	Opinion polls, rallies, law, organizational mobilization	Diplomacy, bargaining	None
Time span	Long-term	Short-term	Variable	Variable
Determinants of effectiveness	Historical continuity, extent of value consensus, strength of compliance habits	Ability to extend scenarios, mobilizability of citizens, mobilizing capacities of leaders	Degree of interdependence	Not relevant
Connections between micro and macro levels	Shared values, norms, memories, socialization, mass media	Opinion polls, letter campaigns, protest marches, leader perceptions	Elite media, overlapping self-interests	Common orientations and behaviors
Main threats to effectiveness	Socioeconomic disparities, subgroupism	Apathy, dissent, subgroupism	Mutually exclusive goals, cultures, authority structures	Not relevant

Plainly, too, the role played by particular leaders in issue aggregations is much greater: where they can get results with short-term mobilizing techniques, leaders of the other participatory types must count on their predecessors and successors to help bridge the much longer stretches of time that are needed to develop the habits of compliance and degrees of consensus on which they depend.

By highlighting both the commitments and the vulnerabilities of citizens, the table also hints at why it is that their orientations and skills introduce a measure of stability into politics and why so much change can set in when turbulence overtakes the micro parameter. The deepseated micro orientations and skills on which macro collectivities are founded are likely to be so long in the making as to be conducive to the constancy which, by definition, underlies parameters. On the other hand, when these long-term loyalties, norms, practices, and habits get caught up in the tides of change, the uncertainties thereby unleashed are bound to be extensive, since the micro precedents that have sustained a collectivity or policy can no longer be taken for granted.

THE SPECIAL CASE OF BETWEEN-SYSTEM AGGREGATIONS

It may seem inappropriate to view as aggregative the processes whereby systems with separate and mutually exclusive memberships converge around common problems and policies. Normally, the relationships among systems are marked by conflict rather than cooperation, by bargaining rather than convergence, by accommodating parts to each other rather than fashioning a larger whole. Indeed, it could well be argued that the quintessential nature of politics is to be found in the competitive interaction of independent groups with their own authority structures and that therefore agreements among such groups are better regarded as temporary coalitions than as meaningful aggregations. Yet in a multi-centric world of shifting allegiances, multiplying interconnections, and groups forming and reforming at a rapid pace, there are advantages to placing the processes of conflict, bargaining, accommodation, and coalition formation in a larger context. Such a perspective highlights the possibility that the sovereignties, boundaries, and loyalties that separate mutually exclusive membership systems are susceptible to redirection and are capable of combining in new ways to create new collectivities and subgroups.

By positing between-system negotiations as an aggregative process, moreover, one insures a continuing focus on micro phenomena. In the absence of such a focus, there is a danger of concentrating so much on the bargaining as to lose sight of the ebb and flow of support from the individuals on whose behalf the bargaining is being done. As previously noted, bargains do not get struck, or at least they do not work, without the active or passive support of those who will be affected. To be sure, the details of the agreement, and the interactions among the negotiators, ought not be ignored, but these are only elements of a larger process wherein separate memberships aggregate their endeavors on matters involving shared or overlapping interests. Or, if their interests are so deeply in conflict that negotiations break down and between-system aggregation does not occur, such a focus insures that attention will be given to the biases and resistances of citizens as a factor in the breakdown.

To treat between-system processes as a special case of aggregation, however, is not to dismiss the legal and cultural boundaries that divide systems. These boundaries constitute enormous obstacles to the concerting of energies and the convergence of perspectives among diverse peoples and groups. They call our attention to the orientations and skills needed by public officials who want to be builders and users of bridges to other systems. The formation of between-system aggregations requires leaders to piece wholes together even as they represent and protect their memberships as component parts. When there is an absence of common membership rules, habits of compliance are of little help, and alternative bases for aggregation are not easily developed. Under these circumstances, a leader's talents in forging macro wholes are, as the history of international relations so poignantly demonstrates, subjected to particularly delicate challenges.

PROCESSES OF DISAGGREGATION

Not all micro-macro interactions, of course, culminate in new aggregations. In many instances, they result in no change, as the interactions unfold in such a way as to maintain the prevailing balance in systemic coherence and policies. In some instances, the interactive dynamics between the orientations of micro actors and the socializing and mobilizing efforts of macro collectivities culminate in disaggregated outcomes—in wholes judged to have undergone a diminution in their sums, perhaps even resulting in sums that are less than the total of their parts. Indeed, what makes politics so problematic is that the outcomes of micro-macro interactions often hang in the balance, teetering between aggregative and disaggregative results as various subgroups vie among themselves and with the systems of which they are a part for the micro support that will expand their coherence and viability. Put differently, the ever-present tendencies toward centralization and decentralization take concrete form in the clash between the impulses to form enlarged aggregations and those pressing for disaggregation.

There is no need to elaborate on the dynamics of disaggregation, inasmuch as they are the obverse of those of aggregation outlined above. Given the centrality of subgroups to the turbulence of world politics, however, note must be taken of one important aspect of disaggregative processes. Change in the direction of disaggregation is apt to take place at a faster pace than movement in the direction of aggregation or reaggregation. This is especially the case within systems, which are so dependent on long-standing habits and loyalties. Once habits of compliance attenuate at the micro level—i.e., once actors begin to move outside the framework of their habits and to see them as unduly binding—it is not easy to fall back into the old patterns. Habits of compliance are not easily broken, but once they do begin to give, the changes are likely to accelerate. The cycles of conflict that have marked Beirut in recent years, and especially the repeated failure of efforts to reverse the cycle back toward reaggregation, are poignantly illustrative of this point. In effect, the habits of compliance in that troubled city have been so fully replaced with habits of defiance that the aggregation of support now seems to be confined largely to the small, face-to-face subgroups that man the barriers to movement around the city.

AGGREGATIVE DYNAMICS IN THE POSTINDUSTRIAL ERA

It should be clear from the preceding analysis that both aggregation and disaggregation are continuously dynamic. Actors and situations evolve, new forms emerge from old patterns, feedback processes are such that circumstances prevailing at one time are altered by their own consequences. The rhetoric of aggregation reflects this movement: shifting tides of opinion, the buildup of opposition, bandwagon effects, the surfacing of support, a soaring or plunging market, an oscillating climate, a surge of sympathy, a restless mood, a collapsing consensus, an aroused electorate—these are the kinds of phrases that are used to connote the momentum of aggregations.[38] And the more such rhetoric becomes commonplace, the greater are the tendencies to act as if aggregative processes are moving at an ever greater pace, thus further heightening the sense of volatility.

This rhetoric has special relevance in the present period. With the

[38] For a full discussion of momentum and the terms associated with it, see Peter Adler, *Momentum: A Theory of Social Action* (Beverly Hills, Calif.: Sage, 1981).

technologies of the postindustrial era having greatly hastened the velocity of aggregative and disaggregative processes, there is an acute need for a vocabulary that expresses the dynamism of feedback loops, the swift movement of ideas, the repercussive impacts of historic events, the accelerated rates of change.[39] Here, we have sought to help meet that need with the term *cascade*. A cascade is the sequence through which developments pass in the multi-centric world. It encompasses not only the sequences of action and interaction among the micro and macro actors, but also the intervening perceptual steps in the interactions through which they assess how an action is likely to affect the orientations of the others and thus alter their own behavior accordingly. (This concept will be discussed further in chapter 11.)

Issue aggregations can involve especially swift-moving cascades. Sustained more by the leaders of collectivities than by their members, and organized around short-term goals rather than around the time-consuming processes of political socialization, issue aggregations allow their participants to move as quickly as their ideas can be communicated and their support summed and demonstrated. Such aggregations thus tend to build or founder through a spate of interpretations issued by those leaders who have a stake in the controversy, some making claims and others denying them, and still others offering assertions about how they think the issue aggregation has been affected by what one or another has said or done. At each point in this support-building process, all concerned participate on the basis of their notion of where and how the aggregation is likely to culminate and whether or when they should begin to accommodate to the emergent possibility that the proposal will be adopted or rejected.

The technologies of the postindustrial era have collapsed virtually to zero the time required for cascades to flow from one stage of aggregation to the next. As the world found out within months after Gorbachev's accession to leadership in the Soviet Union, as the Reagan White House discovered within days after the Iran-contra scandal first surfaced, and as President Marcos of the Philippines learned even more abruptly, the present systems for generating, communicating, and summing opinions, pictures, support, falsehoods, rumors, and all

---

[39] Journalists have been perhaps especially responsive to this need. In seeking to depict the shifting climate in Moscow, for example, one reporter wrote: "Sometimes it seems there is a *collective instinct* here that tells the unorthodox economists, the muckraking journalists, the anti-Stalinist writers and other warriors of glasnost when it is time to gather for another storming of the barricades. Now is such a time." Bill Keller, "Once More into the Literary Breach! Ink-Stained Warriors Rush the Citadel Anew," *New York Times*, January 28, 1988, p. A6 (italics added).

other bases for thought are making the dynamics of aggregation nearly instantaneous. Pictures of developments are transmitted "live," or at most "tape delayed," newspapers are distributed electronically for printing and delivery within hours to distant points, opinion polls are conducted by telephone. The sense of dizzying momentum is further intensified by the fact that all the participants in a situation are aware, or at least presume, that the evolving and shifting sums are being watched by all the other parties to it as well.

The statistics descriptive of the global system of communications in the postindustrial era are staggering. It has been estimated that the world now possesses 550 million telephones, some 600 million television sets, over 1.5 billion radios, several million communicating personal computers and facsimile and telex machines, millions of mobile radio units, over 100 civilian and military communications satellites, over 100 submarine cable links, thousands of microwave towers, and millions of miles of cable, and that every day, between five and ten billion telephone conversations flow through the global electronic network.[40] Moreover, those estimates were made in 1986, and they are probably already an understatement. The completion of the first fiber-optic telephone cable across the Atlantic in 1988, for example, means that 40,000 telephone calls can be carried simultaneously, compared to the 20,000 that could be carried by the three existing copper cables together with communications satellites.[41]

In the United States alone, not only are its myriad television sets on for an average of more than seven hours a day,[42] but it has been estimated that in 1984 its residents sent 976.4 billion messages: 600 billion phone calls, 250 billion internal business memos, 125 billion first-class letters, 1 billion telegram, telex, and facsimile messages, 125 million letters and packages sent via overnight couriers, and some 250 million messages sent between computers.[43] Another estimate is that, as a consequence of all this activity, the total number of words produced by the various media in the United States grew at an annual rate

[40] Richard R. Calino, "International Communications: Coping with Disasters and Crises in the Electronic Village" (remarks at the Annenberg Schools of Communications, Washington, October 1986), p. 1.

[41] A single optical fiber can transmit more than 8,000 conversations simultaneously, whereas the figure for a copper wire is 48. Calvin Sims, "New Atlantic Cable Makes More Calls Possible," *New York Times*, December 14, 1988, p. A1.

[42] Cf. Sally Bedell Smith, "New TV Technologies Alter Viewing Habits," *New York Times*, October 9, 1985, p. C22.

[43] William C. Rempel, "Electronic Mail: A Revolutionary Courier Aims to Become Routine," *Los Angeles Times*, February 24, 1985, sec. 6, p. 1.

of 8.9 percent between 1960 and 1977, more than double the annual 3.7 percent growth rate for the gross national product.[44]

We shall examine in chapter 13 how this burgeoning communications system is affecting the analytic skills and orientations of citizens, but the numbers themselves should make clear that the aggregations linking the micro and macro levels are susceptible to a volatility, a potential for sudden change, that has no parallel in earlier periods. Given the rapidity with which claims and counterclaims can flow through the communications channels of the postindustrial collectivity, one can almost literally see the summing of support and the forming or fragmenting of consensuses.

Looked at from a micro perspective, this openness, rapidity, and diversity of aggregative processes mean that individuals have available a great number of entry points at which their analytic skills and orientations can be brought to bear on collectivities and policies. The more salient of these entry points are examined in chapter 10, but the foregoing discussion suggests that an expansion and refinement by even one JND of analytic skills at the micro level can be a powerful force for parametric change. Amy Carter and Marcos, one could well conclude, may not be misguided in their understanding of politics.

[44] Herbert S. Dordick, "The Information Technology 'Revolution' and National Sovereignty" (paper presented at the Eleventh World Congress of Sociology, New Delhi, August 1986), p. 9.

PART THREE

PROBING
PARAMETERS

CHAPTER 8

REVIEWING RELATIONSHIPS

Authority and Its Alternatives

The army keeps trying to do various things against the people
. . . But none of these things are changing anybody's behavior.
It just causes grudges.

—Iman Shamrukh,
an 18-year-old resident of the Israeli-occupied West Bank[1]

When a bishop speaks, we don't goosestep.

—Father Anthony J. Helinski,
priest at St. Ignatius of Antioch in Detroit[2]

Diplomats said the streets of Rangoon remained quiet today,
although the armed forces resumed a heavy presence, with ar-
mored cars and truckloads of troops standing by. "They don't
look very threatening," a diplomat said. "It's sort of coexistence. People ignore them."

—News item[3]

OUR ANALYSIS of the three parameters begins with the relational
parameter because it lies between the other two, between the actors at
the micro level whose orientations and activities get aggregated and
the structures at the macro level where the aggregation culminates. Relational phenomena are not any more important than those expressive
of the other two parameters. Turbulence results from interactive
changes among all three, and in that sense each is a necessary, and

[1] Joel Brinkley, "Some Israelis Sense a Futility in Steps to Suppress Uprising," *New York Times*, October 12, 1988, p. A1.

[2] Isabel Wilkerson, "Detroit Catholics Vow to Fight Closings," *New York Times*, October 3, 1988, p. A1.

[3] Seth Mydans, "Burmese Reported to Rally in Peace," *New York Times*, August 18, 1988, p. 5.

none is a sufficient, source of postinternational politics. But by being, as it were, a transmission belt through which a preponderance of the interactions between individuals and their collectivities occurs, the relational parameter serves as a logical point of departure.

A second reason to start with the relational phenomena is that they are especially compelling. Pertaining as they do to what happens when one actor seeks to modify the behavior of another, such phenomena tend to provoke our curiosity much more than do orientational or structural phenomena. Orientations and structures tend to be highly patterned, while interpersonal relationships never seem quite so predictable. They are composed of many dimensions that can undergo wide and sudden fluctuations. The possibility of such swings renders relational phenomena especially problematic, and as puzzles in which outcomes can be difficult to anticipate, they are irresistible objects of attention.

The location of the relational parameter as a transmission belt between the other two was only hinted at in the analysis of aggregative processes presented in chapter 7. Indeed, in the case of unintended aggregations, there are no direct relationships between the micro and macro levels. Under such circumstances, developments at the micro level are perceived, counted, or otherwise combined at the macro level without the individuals being aggregated realizing it. Only as processes of aggregation enter consciousness at the micro level do relational phenomena begin to acquire form and substance. At that point, individuals at the micro level and leaders of macro collectivities begin to perceive each other as relevant to their respective goals, with the result that—even while the inferring, counting, and combining continues—actors at both levels begin to aspire to modifying or preserving each other's orientations and behavior. Inevitably, therefore, efforts to control and influence, to exercise power on behalf of goals, evolve in a relational context.

Possessional and Relational Phenomena

Some analysts tend to focus on the possessions—the power bases—that actors bring to bear in their relationships, as if these were the relationships themselves, or at least as if they explained most of what happens in relationships. There often is, indeed, a close correspondence between the power actors possess and the degree to which they move toward their goals: the strong tend to accomplish more than the weak, the well-organized more than the disorganized. But these tendencies do not always hold. As indicated by the quotes that open the chapter, sometimes those who seem weak prevail, and sometimes the disorganized best those who are more organized. Such unexpected outcomes are sometimes explained on the ground that the assessments of relative strength were inaccurate—that the seemingly weak were "really" the strong. Obviously, however, such retrospective explanations are easy; after the fact, one can always ascribe greater power to the actor that prevailed.

To anticipate outcomes that may deviate from the expectations based on power differentials, one has to appreciate that there is much more to political relationships than the actors' bases of power. Equally important are the ways in which the parties to a relationship perceive the intentions and power of the others and, accordingly, respond to each other. Subtle perceptual and psychological dynamics are involved. In any relationship there are at least twice as many relevant actors as there are concrete, empirical actors, because each of the latter also exists in the minds of the other parties to the relationship. In a dyadic situation, for example, actors A and B are joined by A's perception of B and B's perception of A. In short, dynamics operate in any relationship that are inherent in the interaction among the parties and not in the power each possesses.

The prime concept used here for describing and analyzing relational dynamics is *control*, which is inherently relational in the sense that it requires that there be one party doing the controlling and another being controlled. The exercise of control, in other words, implies attempts on the part of one actor to modify, preserve, or otherwise affect the orientations or actions of another. Thus, it is a concept rooted in interactions, and its existence can be determined empirically only by observing the degree of correspondence between what the controller does and how the object of control responds.[4]

Some would argue that power is also a relational concept, that to observe the exercise of power is to look at both the possessor and the target of the power with a view to grasping how the former affects the latter. The trouble with this formulation, however, is that power, un-

---

[4] The concept of control has much in common with that of influence, but the differences between them are sufficient to prevent using the terms interchangeably. Control is a less encompassing concept, inasmuch as it tends to refer to conscious efforts to modify the behavior of others, whereas influence can occur as a result of factors that lie either within or outside interactive relationships. Since the concern here is with the dynamics of the relational parameter, the ensuing analysis is organized around the processes of control. For an extended discussion of the two concepts, see James N. Rosenau, *Calculated Control As a Unifying Concept in the Study of International Politics and Foreign Policy*, Center for International Studies Research Monograph no. 15 (Princeton: Princeton University, 1963).

like control, cannot be used as a verb (without playing havoc with language), and one is thus forced to use the rhetoric of possessions, saying, in effect, "A *has* power and that is why B yielded."[5] But B may not always yield because of A's superior power. B may have a variety of reasons for resisting A, and A may have a variety of reasons for not employing all the power resources at its command, and thus one cannot begin to understand what may happen until one focuses on how A and B are likely to interact in a control situation. History is replete with episodes in which seemingly more powerful actors failed to overcome seemingly weaker ones.

Put somewhat differently, whether it is local, national, or international politics that are of interest, one tends to be less concerned with what actors possess than with how they do or do not respond to each other. It can even be argued that, with respect to any situation, issue, or problem, boredom is bound to set in if analysis does not turn soon from capabilities to relationships. To understand a superpower's hegemonic status by toting up its possessions, for example, is of little interest, even utterly dull, unless the results are used to assess the responses abroad.

This is not to downplay the importance of possessions. Plainly, the capabilities that political actors bring to situations significantly shape their actions and interactions, so that to ignore their resources would make it impossible to understand their relationships. Nevertheless, as noted, it is the relationships and their outcomes around which our questions revolve. For this reason, it is important to stress the dangers of being driven by syntax to focus on possessions whenever the concept of power is used. So as to insure that the analysis does not inadvertently slip back into an exclusive focus on what actors possess, henceforth the word "power" will be eschewed. Instead, the term *capabilities* will be used to refer to the possessional side of power, and *control* to the relational side.

CONTINUA OF CONTROL

If politics is conceived of as activities in which one actor—citizen, politician, terrorist, interest group, bureaucracy, government, state, transnational agency, or international organization—seeks to modify or preserve the behavior patterns of functionally distant others,[6] then it is

[5] For an elaboration of the linguistic constraints on power analysis, see Rosenau, *Calculated Control*, pp. 44–45.

[6] The others may be temporally or physically proximate, as when heads of state confer in summit meetings, but they are nevertheless functionally distant in the sense that they

important to probe the form such activities take and the kinds of responses they evoke. These interactions might be called the relations of control, and we need to consider the means or techniques through which control is sought and established.

A useful way to begin this inquiry is to posit a continuum of control techniques, ranging from the most violent at one end to the least violent at the other. Brute force and other forms of physical coercion are found at the former extreme, scientific proof and reason at the latter. In between these two extremes lie a number of techniques involving interactions that are more complex than both the control achieved through the use of coercion and the compliance that results from the presentation of irrefutable evidence. Appeals to shared values, trade-offs, bargaining, arm-twisting, and economic sanctions are among the nonextreme techniques.

At any level of politics, the techniques close to the scientific-proof end of the continuum are generally preferred, not so much because people are committed in principle to pursuing their goals through co-operative and peaceful means as because these techniques are likely to be the least costly. If the desired changes in the control targets can be accomplished through the provision of evidence justifying the changes, that is the course that will be followed, rather than expending political capital through hard bargaining or consuming material and manpower in the application of violence. When proof evokes compliance, more-over, those whose behavior has been modified are unlikely to carry resentments forward to the next situation, whereas those coerced into a desired response are likely to approach the next set of control relations with animosity and an inclination to resist.

Just as control is exercised through a range of techniques, so also the responses of those toward whom the techniques are directed can be usefully placed along a continuum. At one end is full agreement and compliance; at the other, disagreement and defiance. Between these two extremes lie such reactions as avoidance, disputation, conditional agreement, alternative interpretations, bargaining, delay, and counter-force. Somewhere in the middle of the continuum are the responses of disinterest and apathy.

From the perspective of controllers, of course, the ideal response is automatic compliance, acceptance that is unthinking and not condi-

---

occupy roles in distinctly different and competitive systems. For a discussion of this point and of the general notion of politics as activities designed to exercise control over a remote environment, see Rosenau, *Calculated Control*, pp. 8–19.

tional on any concessions.[7] The least desirable response, on the other hand, is a defiance that not only thwarts the immediate purposes of the control but also leaves residues that foster further defiance in the future.

The long-run patterns of compliance and defiance serve as the foundations of the relational parameter. The patterns form partly because the relative capabilities of the parties to relationships tend to be enduring and hence to produce recurring outcomes, and partly because compliance and defiance tend to be habitual and thus to become institutionalized. The most notable outcome of these enduring control relationships is hierarchy, that structure of control whereby actors in a system acquire superior, inferior, or equal status in relation to each other. Viewed from a control perspective, hierarchical structures refer to the norms, habits, and formal arrangements through which individuals, groups, and collectivities dominate, submit, or otherwise relate to others at the macro level.

RELATIONS OF AUTHORITY

Another enduring outcome of control relations is *authority*, that set of premises and habits on which macro leaders are entitled to rely to obtain automatic compliance from their followers. The processes whereby authority is created in a collectivity are the subject of a vast literature that need not detain us here. It is sufficient to recognize that no collectivity could persist for long without having authority as a legal basis for the conduct of its leaders and the maintenance of its hierarchical structures. It is through the exercise of authority that decisions are made and implemented and the coherence of collectivities thereby preserved. If a collectivity lacked authority relations, if its members felt entitled to do as they pleased, goals could not be framed and energies could not be concerted; there could be no collective action, and the collectivity would soon lose its identity as a social system distinct from its environment. Authority relationships, in other words, are those patterns of a collectivity wherein some of its members are accorded the right to make decisions, set rules, allocate resources, and formulate policies for the rest of the members, who, in turn, comply with the decisions, rules, and policies made by the authorities.[8]

[7] A discussion of how controllers "create compliance" through "strategic interaction" with the targets of their control is in Margaret Levi, *Of Rule and Revenue* (Berkeley: University of California Press, 1988), chapter 3.

[8] For extended discussions of authority relationships in and between collectivities, see James S. Coleman, "Authority Systems," *Public Opinion Quarterly* 44 (Summer 1980):

In many collectivities, authority relations are formally incorporated into their interaction patterns through constitutions, bylaws, statutes, and judicial decisions. Yet it would be erroneous to limit the concept of authority relations to formal structures in which the source of authority can be documented. The exercise of authority also occurs in informal settings, in decisions that evoke compliance even though the right to make them has not been stated in legal form. As one observer has said, "The smallest microunit of modern political action systems is authority to make a new decision in a manner that may become binding (at least through its consequences) on another."[9] Authority relations are thus to be found wherever people undertake collective tasks—in families, classrooms, religious groups, unions, athletic teams, business firms, revolutionary movements, terrorist organizations, and a host of other social formations beside governmental entities—and any such relationships that have consequences across national boundaries can be considered part of world politics. One way to appreciate the turbulence of postinternational politics is to recognize that its decentralizing tendencies lead to the proliferation of boundary-spanning relationships, thereby undermining the hierarchy and intensifying the volatility of global authority structures. To quote the same observer, "A political environment becomes most volatile when there are multiple decision makers of roughly equal power and when opportunities exist to form and reform factions or coalitions."[10]

There are various reasons why people accord legitimacy to the acts of authorities and comply with their directives. One is fear of the consequences of noncompliance; another is an understanding that collective coherence and action serves their needs and goals; a third is the expectation that others will also comply.[11] Mostly, however, compliance is a matter of habit; repeated instances of compliance become deeply ingrained as a response when certain procedures are followed and certain kinds of pronouncements are issued. The longer authority has been in place, the greater is the legitimacy that attaches to it, and thus the more deep-seated are the habits of compliance it evokes. Under these conditions—which is to say, under circumstances where the

---

143–63, and Oran R. Young, *Compliance and Public Authority: A Theory with International Applications* (Baltimore: The Johns Hopkins University Press, 1979).

[9] Dean R. Gerstein, "To Unpack Micro and Macro: Link Small with Large and Part with Whole," in J. C. Alexander et al., eds., *The Macro-Micro Link* (Berkeley: University of California Press, 1987), p. 103.

[10] Gerstein, "To Unpack Micro and Macro," p. 103.

[11] For a cogent discussion of this point, see Kenneth J. Arrow, *The Limits of Organization* (New York: W. W. Norton, 1974), chapter 4.

parameters of a system are stable and its dynamism confined to selective variables—actions and policies authorized at the macro level are simply accepted unquestioningly by those toward whom the actions and policies are directed. The compliance may be preceded by argument, bargaining, and delay, and the actions and policies may thus be moderated, but in the end the habit of compliance will normally prevail as the relational outcome.

For several centuries, the highest authority has been lodged in states. Their sovereignty, which accords them the final say in disputes among their members or in the conduct of relations with actors abroad, has entitled them to take authoritative actions which have not traditionally been challenged as being subordinate to some more encompassing authority. Both the citizens of a state and actors external to it have accepted its acts and policies as decisive; accordingly, its citizens have long been habituated to complying with them, and the citizens of other states have long acknowledged that they are not entitled to interfere in the processes whereby the acts and policies are framed and implemented.

However, while the sovereignty of states accords their officials an ultimate authority, most authority relationships are not of this character. What distinguishes authority relations is not the finality of the decisions rendered by those authorized to act on behalf of the collectivity, but rather the relationship between those who have the authority and those who comply with it. Thus, for example, parents have authority and children habitually comply with their decisions, yet there are a number of issues involving children wherein the authority of the parents is subordinate to that of others (e.g., teachers or public officials).

Is authority a "possession" that leaders bring to bear in their control relationships? Is it a capability, like weapons or mineral resources, on which they rely to obtain compliance? For two reasons, these questions seem best answered in the negative. First, unlike weapons and minerals, authority is not tangible or fixed in time and space. Often, to be sure, its nature and limits are spelled out in documents, and for some observers these pieces of paper are the authority itself. In practice, however, the exercise of authority depends on the intangible bases on which it is accepted by those toward whom it is directed. Written words that do not evoke widespread compliance are not authority, even if they have long served as authorizing instruments.

The second reason for a negative answer to those questions is that authority inheres in roles and not in people. Individuals do not bring authority to their high offices; rather, they acquire it when they occupy the offices, and what they acquire is not so much a fixed possession as it is a dynamic variable in their role relationships. Authority can be enlarged or diminished by statute or other legal means, but such changes take on meaning only as they evoke correspondingly different responses from those toward whom they are directed. That is, they add not to the possessions of the role but to its relationships. Roles may differ in the degree to which they permit their occupants to exercise authority, but authority is enhanced, dissipated, or otherwise altered only by virtue of variations in the responses of those whose compliance is sought.

Consider, for example, how inescapably relational is the authority that is enhanced by personal charisma. Charisma may seem to be a possession that enables some leaders to bring audiences to their feet or into the streets, but it is not a possession at all, because it cannot be observed and measured by examining the personal qualities or behavior of leaders. Leaders are not charismatic because their talents are somehow larger than those of other leaders, or their speeches delivered more evocatively. There can be no charismatic leaders without followers ready to be, so to speak, "charismaticized," and charisma is thus fundamentally relational. History is replete with leaders whose charisma has deserted them when circumstances change and their followers cease to comply.[12] Variations in the extent to which authority is effective, then, derive not from the way it is embedded in roles or from the characteristics of their occupants, but from the dynamics of control relations. As one astute observer has put it: "Authority is another name for the willingness and capacity of individuals to submit to the necessities of cooperative systems. Authority arises from the technological and social limitations of cooperative systems on the one hand, and of individuals on the other. Hence the status of authority in a society is the measure both of the development of individuals and of the technological and social conditions of the society."[13] It follows that

[12] President José Sarney of Brazil is a recent example. When the country's inflation reached 933 percent in 1988, whatever charisma he may have had dropped to the point where he was, according to one account, "unable to appear in public for fear of being heckled and treated with derision by newspapers. . . . Abandoned by political allies and widely blamed for an acute economic crisis, Mr. Sarney is today a lonely and discredited figure whose political influence is so eroded that, even with 14 months of his five-year term still to serve, his actions as well as his words are largely ignored." Alan Riding, "Lonely Leader in an Uncertain Brazil," *New York Times*, January 13, 1989, p. A3. For a more general analysis of the fragile nature of leadership, see Warren Bennis, *Why Leaders Can't Lead: The Unconscious Conspiracy Continues* (San Francisco: Jossey-Bass, 1989).

[13] Chester I. Barnard, *The Functions of the Executive* (Cambridge: Harvard University Press, 1938), p. 184.

substantial alterations in the analytic skills of individual followers are bound to have consequences for the nature of authority relations to which such followers contribute.

Although the rules and procedures for exercising control may be codified and cited as the "authority" for policies pursued, this is only a shorthand and legalistic way of referring to complex relational processes. Whatever the extent to which it is formalized in statutes and constitutions, authority is maintained only to the degree that the membership continues to treat the leadership as having the right to lead. When the acceptance of this right is automatic and unchallenged by the membership, the decisions, rules, and policies that flow from its exercise are said to possess legitimacy. Like authority, therefore, legitimacy is rooted in relational phenomena. The two are, so to speak, different sides of the same coin: authority attaches to the actions of leaders and legitimacy is the acceptance attached to the actions by the membership.

The willingness of a membership to accept and abide by the decisions of its leaders varies along two dimensions: the scope of the relationship and its degree of integration. The latter ranges from highly integrated relationships, in which the membership habitually and automatically complies with the leadership's decisions, to those in which the decisions are chronically resisted. Between these extremes, compliance may be subject to reflection over, skepticism toward, and anguish about the decisions.

It is in the deterioration of habit that authority crises originate: the more a membership moves away from automatic acceptance and toward outright rejection, the more is an authority relationship subjected to strain. Indeed, the beginnings of a crisis are signaled by a breakdown in the compliance habits of the members or of the units of a collectivity. As the habits wane, the crisis deepens, until either the habits are restored through effective bargaining or they collapse altogether and are redirected toward other collectivities.

The other variable dimension of authority relationships, their scope, refers to the number of issues across which the compliance of a membership is operative. Some relationships, especially those maintained by governments and certain religious movements, have a broad scope, in the sense that the habits of compliance can be evoked on a wide range of issues. Others, such as business firms and universities, embrace a limited number of matters with respect to which the leaders can rely on automatic compliance. Ordinarily, leaders prefer to protect their authority by not exceeding its scope, with the result that the fewer the issues it spans, the more likely an authority relationship is to be integrated and the less it is susceptible to crisis.

When authority relations are clear-cut and accepted, as is the case in stable collectivities, the habits of compliance are likely to remain intact. People can tolerate the uncertainty that accompanies external threats or internal divisiveness if they know that the collectivity's established procedures are firmly in place and not subject to rapid change. In democratic collectivities, for example, calling out the national guard is usually acceptable because all concerned are aware that the decision has been reached through legitimate means and that those implementing it will confine their activities within known limits. However, authority relations can undergo change if forces at work within or external to the collectivity erode the habits of compliance. Sometimes, the erosion reaches the point where leaders are inclined to resort to coercion to implement their policies. Such a shift in the nature of leadership is likely to erode the habits of compliance still further and bring on a full-blown crisis of authority.[14]

BARGAINING RELATIONS

If authority relations have entered a period of crisis, then both leaders and members will have to turn more frequently to other techniques of control to retain a collectivity's coherence and move toward its (and their) goals. For reasons indicated below, coercive techniques are likely to be less and less available in the absence of effective authority relations, and so persuasion, trade-offs, and other forms of bargaining become the main techniques by which control is sought.

In bargaining relations, compliance is induced by trading some benefit in exchange for it. In this situation, authority is absent from the relationship; compliance occurs not because those who accept a decision believe those who made it were entitled to do so, but because they are willing to comply in order to achieve the benefit that has been offered.

Authority and bargaining relationships are, obviously, quite differ-

[14] For revealing inquiries into the potential fragility of authority relations, see Richard E. Flathman, *The Practice of Political Authority: Authority and the Authoritative* (Chicago: University of Chicago Press, 1980); William A. Gamson, Bruce Fireman, and Steven Rytina, *Encounters with Unjust Authority* (Homewood, Ill.: Dorsey, 1982); Myron J. Aronoff, ed., *The Frailty of Authority* (New Brunswick, N. J.: Transaction Books, 1986); and Yale H. Ferguson and Richard W. Mansbach, "Beyond the Elusive Quest: A Search for Authority Patterns in History" (paper presented at the annual meeting of the International Studies Association, London, March 1989).

ently organized. The former tend to be essentially hierarchical and vertical, in the sense that the interaction begins with those who exercise authority and ends with those who accept it as legitimate. Bargaining relations, on the other hand, tend to be more equal and horizontal, in the sense that none of the parties lie in the others' spheres of authority and their interactions are shaped by offers and counteroffers, with no clear-cut beginning or end point.

This is not to imply, however, that bargaining and authority structures are necessarily independent of or antithetical to each other. Such may be the case when the terms of a bargain struck within a collectivity undermine the habits of compliance that sustain its leaders' authority, but often the contrary is true: the habits are reinforced and enlarged by a bargain that the leaders make on behalf of the collectivity's membership. Some bargained outcomes in the life of a collectivity promote discontent with its leaders, but others bring satisfaction and enhance their legitimacy.

However, enthusiastic support for leaders can never be a full and enduring substitute for habitual compliance. The test of viability of an authority relationship occurs not when things are going well, but when uncertainty marks the course of events and the impulse to accord leaders the right to make decisions becomes problematic. If at such times the collectivity's members do not fall back on long-standing habits of compliance, if systemic complexity and dynamism intensify to the point where the appeals of leaders are questioned or even defied, the relational parameter begins to undergo turbulence. As will be seen in chapter 14, these circumstances appear to be spreading throughout the world in the present period.

RELATIONS OF COERCION

To facilitate inquiry into the impact of postinternational politics on the world's authority relations, it is instructive to examine how the two extremes on the control continuum have been affected by turbulence. When scientific proof and coercion are effective in achieving compliance, it is not because either is a derivative of authority. Proof induces acceptance through evidence and logic, and coercion gets results either because people are unwilling to contest superior force or because they view it as legitimately linked to authority. When proof or coercion is successful as a control technique, in other words, it is in addition to, and not because of, any authority that may be operative. Hence, if there is validity in the contention set forth below that coercive techniques are becoming decreasingly effective and the criteria for proof increasingly rigorous, these two forms of control relations seem bound to become more tense and troubled. Stated differently, if authority cannot be backed up as easily with force or proof as may have been the case in the past, then presumably its effective exercise is more problematic and the likelihood of authority crises that much greater.

In the bifurcated global system, the use of coercive techniques is confined mostly to the state-centric world. It is not entirely absent from the multi-centric world, but relations of coercion are a particular province of nation-states. They use force against each other and against segments of their own society, and they also engage in or facilitate trade in the instruments of force so that their friends abroad can improve their own coercive capabilities. These long-standing patterns have been reinforced by the principles of sovereignty and the norms of the state-centric system (e.g., "to the victors go the spoils"), so that, until recently, there have been few inducements to avoid coercive techniques when superior force capabilities are judged to be available in support of threatened goals.

With relational phenomena being engulfed by turbulence, however, the significance attached to the use of coercion has begun to change. The advent of the multi-centric world and the concern of its actors for realizing autonomy through economic and social means has tended to direct attention away from military action and toward the complex choices that delineate the better from the worse courses to follow. Even the defense of borders is no longer an exclusively military task. The flow of electronic data across borders can present security problems no less challenging than the movement of troops.[15]

To be sure, territorial boundaries are still matters of dispute, sovereign rights are still used as justifications for the application of force, and reference to historic missions or grievances can still arouse a readiness for collective sacrifice; but in an era of postinternational politics, these traditional claims appear less commanding than they once were. They seem to evoke less sympathy abroad and to be asserted with less vigor at home, as if the preoccupations of the state-centric world are considered secondary under multi-centric circumstances. Thus it is that coercive actions like the shutting down of embassies and the shooting down of commercial aircraft, which would have once led to violent retaliation and perhaps war, are now merely the subject of pro-

[15] Cf. Clarence J. Brown, "The Globalization of Information Technologies," *Washington Quarterly* 11 (Winter 1988): 97–98; John Markoff, "Breach Reported in U.S. Computers," *New York Times*, April 18, 1988, p. 1; Nikki Finke, "Does Your Computer Have a Virus?" *Los Angeles Times*, January 31, 1988, p. D1; and Vin McLellan, "Computer Systems under Siege," *New York Times*, January 31, 1988, p. C1.

tests and the basis for severing diplomatic ties. And thus it is, too, that foreign expressions of concern for the treatment of minorities and external sanctions imposed in an effort to enhance human rights, which would have once provoked saber-rattling rhetoric about violations of sovereignty, are now met with denials, justifications, and occasionally even policy changes that implicitly acknowledge the criticisms.

Furthermore, the powerful moral stigma that attaches to the use of nuclear weapons has tended to tarnish the use of any weapons, thereby contributing to the ideas that the authority of the state is limited and that there are certain forms of action in which it ought not engage. Political authority, in other words, is changing because it is becoming increasingly difficult to support it by conventional military operations. For states to threaten or use organized force today runs the risk of an escalation that may involve the superpowers and raises the specter of nuclear war, results that can bring as much harm to those who employ coercive force as to their targets. Hence, threats of force by states command less support at home as well as abroad. Indeed, when they do resort to military action, states can no longer presume the domestic support necessary to carry out their goals in combat. Given the enormous power of modern weapons and the enormous complexity of the social systems toward which they might be directed, wars no longer seem as winnable as has been the case, and publics are not prepared to support them as unqualifiedly as they once did. The patriotic readiness to be conscripted or otherwise mobilized for war has been attenuated, if not superseded, by a skepticism as to whether policies leading to violent conflict are justifiable. As Michael Howard has put it, the consequence of these developments

> is that the State *apparat* is likely to become isolated from the rest of the body politic, a severed head conducting its intercourse with other severed heads according to its own laws. War, in short, has once more been *denationalized*. It has become, as it was in the eighteenth century, an affair of *states* and no longer of *peoples*. The identification of the community with the state, brought to its highest point in the era of the two World Wars, can no longer be assumed as natural or, militarily speaking, necessary. No Third World War is likely to be fought by armies embodying the manpower of the Nation while the rest of the population work to keep them armed and fed.[16]

[16] Michael Howard, "War and the Nation-State," *Daedalus* 108 (Fall 1979): 106 (italics in the original). See also chapter 15 of the present work. For a related argument, that "major war—war among developed countries—has gradually moved, like dueling and

This blunting of conventional military approaches has had a crucial, if subtle, impact on the nature of authority in world politics. It has tended to diminish the long-standing advantage of states in crises to resort to the ultimate sanction inherent in the call to do battle, to legitimately impose their will by coercive means. It may not be the case that the capabilities of actors in the state- and multi-centric systems are equal, but the declining effectiveness of coercion has surely narrowed the gap between them. Indeed, as will be seen, there are many ways in which those in the multi-centric world are able to exert control over state actors.

Moreover, as war has become less viable and credible as a policy option, the delicacy of the balance that allows those who have authority to exercise control and achieve compliance has been more clearly revealed. The degree to which compliance is not automatic has become evident, and, accordingly, so has the capacity of the subjects of authority to demand higher standards of performance on the part of the authorities as a condition of their compliance. In a curious way, the changes in postinternational politics at the coercive end of the control continuum have had consequences for the criteria of proof that are demanded and for other behaviors elsewhere along the continuum.

To note that authority has become harder to exercise and compliance more difficult to achieve, however, is not to say that coercive techniques are no longer among the means available to actors on the world stage. Obviously, there are still circumstances under which states go to war with each other and, indeed, as the governments of Burma and China so brutally reminded the world in 1988 and 1989, there are still occasions when they will make war on their own people. Perhaps less conspicuously, states continue to be vigorous in selling arms abroad, thereby making it possible for certain subgroups, particularly those organized around ethnic ties that isolate them within their states, to wage armed conflict in pursuit of their goals.[17]

---

slavery, toward terminal disrepute because of its perceived repulsiveness and futility," see John Mueller, "Retreat from Doomsday: The Obsolescence of Major War" (paper presented at the annual meeting of the American Political Science Association, Washington, September 1988), p. 1. A similar analysis can be found in James Lee Ray, "The Abolition of Slavery and the End of International War," *International Organization* 43 (Summer 1989): 405–39. The belief that the advantages of military superiority are still likely to incline states to make war on each other is expressed in George F. Will, "If War Is Out of Style, Why Do Soviets Furiously Rearm?" *Los Angeles Times*, December 7, 1988, sec. 2, p. 7.

[17] In addition, certain actors in the multi-centric world, especially those that engage in activities which tend to be universally regarded as illegal, have armed themselves for the purpose of protecting their operations from intrusions by actors in the state-centric

While these exceptions do not negate the underlying dynamics that are fostering a reduced reliance on violent techniques of control, neither can it be said that the world is headed for an era of unbroken peace. The trend is toward a diminished use of coercion, but there are good reasons to believe that the downward slope will level off. With the trade in arms continuing, and with the dangers of nuclear escalation restraining superpower involvement, local conflicts and violence are likely to persist, even intensify, since the dynamics of decentralization weaken the control that can be exerted over ethnic and other aggrieved groups. When the latter define their demands as irreconcilable with the prevailing arrangements, they may resort to force to achieve them, in the belief that external powers will not interfere. Such circumstances are perhaps especially likely to obtain in the Third World, where actors may feel that nuclear weapons are particularly unlikely to be used and where there may thus be fewer inhibitions on their readiness to engage in military operations on behalf of expanded influence (as Libya sought in Chad), public order (as India sought in Sri Lanka), or religious ideals (as Iran sought in Iraq).

The superpowers, moreover, are likely to continue to employ coercive methods against perceived threats from lesser states within their accepted spheres of influence. With the dangers of escalation minimized by the very acceptance of such spheres, they may still be willing to employ force when they believe their security is jeopardized, as the Soviet Union did in Afghanistan and as the United States did in Grenada and Nicaragua. Even here, however, change is at work. Retreat and withdrawal are strikingly characteristic of recent military actions by the superpowers: the Soviet Union eventually ended its military incursion into Afghanistan, just as the United States had earlier in Vietnam. Equally indicative, the Soviet Union has also moved to reduce its forces in Eastern Europe, just as the United States has done in Central America.[18]

---

world. In these cases, however, coercive techniques tend to be used more for defensive purposes than for controlling the evolution of new outcomes favorable to their interests. The Mafia and South American drug lords are examples. So is Akmadzhan Adilov, the director of a state cotton farm in Soviet Uzbekistan, who built a small empire on millions of rubles in stolen revenues and who, until his arrest in 1984, "maintained a small private army, a dozen vacation homes, an underground bunker with its own prison and a legion of cowering subordinates whom he sometimes tortured in public." Bill Keller, "Once More into the Literary Breach! Ink-Stained Warriors Rush the Citadel Anew," *New York Times*, January 28, 1988, p. A6. Similarly, but to a much lesser extent, a variety of other sovereignty-free actors, from multinational corporations to universities, maintain independent police forces to guard their facilities.

[18] For further discussions of the changing nature of coercion in the present era, see

What may become the typical mode of coercion, then, is low-intensity warfare. This has already acquired a strategic doctrine that is quite unlike any standard approach to conventional warfare.[19] In the United States, this doctrine was implemented in 1981 through the creation of "special operation forces" within the military establishment. As one student of warfare put it, "With continuous, sporadic armed conflict, blurred in time and space, waged on several levels by a large array of national and subnational forces, warfare in the last quarter of the twentieth century may well come to resemble warfare in the Italian renaissance or warfare in the early seventeenth century, before the emergence of national armies and more organized modern warfare."[20]

Viewed in this way, and given the evolution of limits on the use of conventional military techniques, along with a shift in global values that allows for the pursuit of goals through illicit channels, it is hardly surprising that postinternational politics has come to be marked by tendencies to resort to new forms of coercion as instruments of policy. Organized terrorism, both that of states and of subgroups, stands out in this respect. As a technique that can easily achieve worldwide publicity and precipitate global repercussions at little cost, terrorism is a relation of coercion that reveals the interdependence and vulnerabilities of postinternational politics. As a means of expressing alienation, calling attention to grievances, and disrupting unwanted circumstances, its use is likely to continue to be widespread even as military techniques become increasingly eschewed.[21]

However, even if the complexities of the postinternational era foster resort to the tactics of terrorism, this form of coercion can hardly be

---

Gordon A. Craig and Alexander George, *Force and Statecraft: Diplomatic Problems of Our Time* (New York: Oxford University Press, 1983), and Klaus Knorr, "On the International Uses of Military Force in the Contemporary World," *Orbis* 21 (Spring 1977): 5–27.

[19] "It draws on wide-ranging study of the different elements of conflict, few of which are strictly military. Researchers at think tanks and universities attempt to analyze and mimic the politico-military structures of revolutionary movements; others study the 'backwards' tactics of guerrilla warfare, which invert traditional military rules of engagement, or delve into anthropology and social psychology; others . . . dwell on the British and French colonial experiences." Sara Miles, "The Real War: Low-Intensity Conflict in Central America," *NACLA Report on the Americas* 20 (April/May 1986): 24.

[20] Brian Jenkins, *New Modes of Conflict* (Santa Monica: Rand Corporation, 1983), p. 17.

[21] It has been estimated that the overall growth rate in the volume of terrorist activity has been around 11 percent annually since 1970 and that between 800 and 900 incidents a year will occur by 1990 if the rate of increase continues. Brian Michael Jenkins, "The Future Course of International Terrorism," *Futurist* 21 (July–August 1987): 8–13.

viewed as an emergent form of authority. On the contrary: the activities of terrorists reflect not a close connection between authority and force but, rather, the bankruptcy of coercive instruments as the world becomes increasingly interdependent. Terrorists do induce fear, they do get wide publicity, and the repercussions of their actions can be extensive; on occasion, their bombings, assassinations, and hijackings may even bring compliance with their demands. Such accomplishments, however, are bound to be short-lived, because terroristic coercion is, virtually by definition, incapable of engendering the kinds of predispositions on which authority must rest if it is to remain effective when the threat of force is removed.

On balance, then, even if terrorism serves the expressive needs of the alienated—and occasionally the instrumental needs of those governments that resort to covert violence to remove perceived obstacles to their goals—it plays an essentially peripheral role in the functioning of the state-centric and multi-centric systems. To understand the core structures and processes of these systems, one has to focus on the nonviolent mechanisms by which actors mobilize others to accept their goals and allocate resources and energies to achieve them. One has to recognize, too, that the probabilities of effectively exercising authority and obtaining compliance are declining as the bifurcated world of global politics becomes simultaneously more decentralized and more interdependent. Indeed, it is that very decentralization and interdependence that enable actors to function and flourish in the multi-centric world despite the greater coherence and military capabilities of their counterparts in the state-centric world.

RELATIONS OF PROOF

The restraint in the use of military force that characterizes postinternational politics is dramatically illustrated by a recent incident that also shows the rising importance of proof on the world stage. The incident occurred in September 1983, when the navies of the two superpowers converged in the Sea of Japan. There was frantic activity, as U.S. and Soviet ships maneuvered for position and focused their most advanced technology on the target. The "battle" lasted several weeks, until both sides finally conceded defeat.

For all its military appearances, however, the battle was waged and defeat acknowledged without the loss of human life or even the firing of a single shell. Why? Because the "victory" being sought was to locate a small black box that lay at the bottom of the Sea of Japan. Both the United States and the Soviet Union wanted to recover the box because it contained a recording of the conversation among the pilots of a South Korean airliner moments before it was shot down by a Soviet fighter plane, and each hoped that the recording would prove its version of why the airliner was off course and over Soviet airspace.

This battle to recover a recording is but one instance of the extent to which issues in this era of postinternational politics have become suffused with technical and scientific content. In good part, this is due to the same technologies that have made relations within and between nations increasingly complex. They have given rise to what might be called a "technology of eavesdropping," to a host of electronic and robotic techniques for probing not only under the sea but also behind closed doors and in outer space, in search of information, evidence, and proof. Far more than in the past, controversial questions are now pervaded with elements that can be subjected to objective observation and measurement. The pressure to generate scientific proof and utilize it for control purposes—for getting people to cooperate, comply, desist, or otherwise to alter their behavior—has reached the point where its availability and adequacy can be a matter of keen dispute, setting off, for example, a feverish search of the sea bottom.

As the adequacy of information and the very nature of knowledge have emerged as central issues, what were once regarded as the petty quarrels of scholars over the adequacy of evidence and the metaphysics of proof have become prominent activities in international relations.[22] The arguments over whether Libya was building a chemical-weapons plant and was involved in the bombing of a Berlin discotheque, the difficulty in agreeing on methods for verifying compliance with arms-control agreements, the intense demand for data on what happened at Chernobyl in the Soviet Union, the debate over Nicaragua's role in providing aid to insurgencies in Central America, the controversy over Nicholas Daniloff's activities as a journalist in Moscow, and the questions of who planted the mines in the Persian Gulf and who supplied Iran with Silkworm missiles are among recent examples showing that issues of evidence and proof have become foci of global controversies. In most of these controversies, information acquired through new technologies in aerial photography, electronic spying, and atmospheric monitoring played a key role.

---

[22] Ironically, the political world's growing interest in evidence and proof has been accompanied by an increasing skepticism toward them on the part of some in the scholarly world—those who have become enamored of semiology, deconstructionism, and discourse analysis. See, for example, James Der Derian and Michael J. Shapiro, eds., *International/Intertextual Relations: Postmodern Readings of World Politics* (Lexington, Mass.: Lexington Books, 1989).

Indeed, with the advent of the Intermediate Nuclear Forces (INF) treaty and continuing momentum toward arms control, the question of proof seems destined to move to the top of the global agenda in the decades ahead. Whether missiles are in fact dismantled, rendered unreconstructable, or destroyed, and whether the data attesting to these steps are reliable, are bound to be urgent questions.

If the significance of proof as a technique of control is to be fully grasped, clear distinctions need to be drawn between *information*, *evidence*, and *proof*. In the value system that prevails in industrial societies, these forms of knowledge all involve description and imply a commitment to empirical observation instead of intuitive or emotional assertion, but they are also different in important respects. Information is neutral as to the portent of what it describes, while evidence and proof are forms of information that has been processed specifically to allow for inferences as to the meaning of what is described. Evidence is information that is deemed to shed light on the existence of that which is claimed to exist. Proof is evidence arranged so as to demonstrate that the claim is beyond question and, thus, "true." If by proof is meant that which scientific procedures affirm, as is usually the case in industrial societies, a proven claim is viewed as the derivative of a methodology that is independent of those who used it; it is "objectively" true. Whereas evidence is viewed as indicative, in other words, proof is seen as conclusive.

Unlike information, therefore, both evidence and proof imply a relationship between the generators and the consumers of knowledge claims. Information is gathered or is made available, but evidence is offered, and proof is used, for a particular purpose—namely, to convince their recipients of the nature, structure, and implications of the described phenomena. It follows that, while information can be controlling in the sense that its acquisition provides a basis for acting differently from what would otherwise be the case, evidence and proof, being inherently relational, are more active forms of control. Not only do they enhance capabilities, as information does; they also link their possessors to the audiences toward whom they are directed. Evidence and proof can facilitate the realization of goals because they are addressed to those who resist the goals and who might be persuaded that the evidence or proof justifies ending, or at least reducing, their resistance.

To observe that actors place more reliance on evidence as a means of getting others to modify their attitudes and behavior is not to say that such a technique is invariably successful, or even that its chances of producing effective control are greater than those that could be achieved by the use of coercive techniques. For, to repeat, proof is relational in character, and thus its success as a control instrument will depend on the criteria its recipients use to assess the evidence provided by controllers. But does scientific proof so transcend culture and politics that global norms governing its acceptance have begun to emerge? Or are the ideologies and passions that differentiate national publics and officials so great as to render even the most objective of proofs subject to varying and contradictory interpretations? Under what conditions can control over foreign publics and officials be exercised through the proffering of evidence and proof? And if assessments of evidence tend to be subordinated to political considerations, why is so much energy in world politics devoted to the generation and dissemination of proof? Put in concrete terms, if the flight recorder of the South Korean airliner had been found and had contained succinct and explicit comments by the pilot as to his reasons for being off course, would this evidence have been accepted by *both* superpowers?

Precise answers to these questions cannot be given. On the one hand, there plainly are severe limits on the extent to which proof can be effective as a control technique. Not only are the technical and social aspects of situations so complex that developing full information with respect to them is extremely difficult, but, equally important, evidence is rarely so airtight as to exclude all but one interpretation. Events are inevitably viewed through cultural and political lenses, which derive their strength from a basic human tendency to structure the perceived environment so that it is balanced and not marked by conspicuous discrepancies. Thus, a situation never impresses itself in the same "objective" way upon all those who interpret it. Inevitably, rather, the "truth" is teased out of situations by actors who bring their values, level of information, perceptual skills, and criteria of evidence to bear on their interpretations.

In short, there can be as many truths about any situation in world politics as there are observers with different perspectives. Furthermore, the role of truth varies with different viewpoints about where observable truths stand in relation to other values. Where political or religious passions run strong, for example, scientific evidence may be dismissed as either irrelevant or erroneous.

On the other hand, to stress that proof gets filtered through value- and skill-colored glasses should not lead us to exaggerate its subjective nature or to understate the degree to which it has a consensual foundation within certain value systems. There may not be an objective reality about a given situation that is clear to everyone, but there can be broad agreement within a community as to what constitute proper criteria of evidence. In the Middle East today, for example, relations of proof are such that any action of Israel is seen by many Arabs as an expression of hostile purposes, and any action of the PLO is seen by many Israelis as an expression of hostile purposes.

In still other parts of the world, passions and ideologies are subordinated as bases for evaluating evidence. Wherever the processes of industrialization have woven the scientific creed into the fabric of society, the criteria of proof generally require repeated empirical observations and evidence independent of the observer. In the Western democracies, such an ethic is manifest in the skepticism of publics and journalists and the caution of politicians. Publics insist on being shown a "smoking gun," journalists abide by rules that inhibit reporting events without corroboration of their occurrence from more than one source, and politicians feel impelled to back up their assertions by citing statistics or other authorities.

Accordingly, while there may not be a single basis for establishing the truth about international issues, neither are relations of proof totally unstructured. Consensuses about the nature of evidence do exist, and the politics of the communities encompassed by a consensus is crucially affected by the criteria of proof that prevail. This is a major reason why intraregional conflicts in international politics tend to be less complex than interregional conflicts. In the former, disputes can more easily move beyond differences over the meaning of facts, while in the latter, these differences can in themselves become the issue. Viewed in this way, it can be said that there is a consensus in the First World, and a consensus in the Third World, on the nature of proof and the proper criteria of evidence, even as the long-standing friction between them in UNESCO over information policy signifies sharp differences between these consensuses.

Although the boundaries that demarcate these proof consensuses help explain why people can be so surprised when an event whose meaning seems self-evident to them can be so differently interpreted by others, it also must be noted that the boundaries are not impervious. As industrialization and the microelectronic revolution gather strength in the less developed parts of the world, so are scientific criteria of proof likely to become increasingly salient, at least in the sense that they cannot be summarily dismissed and that some effort will be demanded to demonstrate the empirical bases of alternative proofs.

A good insight into the way in which proof can serve as a control technique is provided by the explosion in the nuclear reactor at Chernobyl. It showed that proof consensuses can override ideological and political commitments when the facts in question can be precisely and reliably measured. Too many recording instruments in too many countries yielded evidence of a dramatic rise in atmospheric radiation for the Soviet Union to deny what had happened. The Soviet government was not immediately forthcoming with information, and its responses were initially disappointing to many European countries, but it eventually yielded to the demands for detailed accounts of the disaster.[23] Subsequent developments in the environmental-protection arena of world politics, it can fairly be said, have been heavily influenced by the relations of proof initiated at Chernobyl.

In other words, while proof relations vary in different regions of the world, and while a universal consensus about the nature of proof may never emerge, some understanding of the criteria of evidence employed by others does now exist. As a result, the tendency to contest issues with alternative proofs seems likely to grow as a central feature of world politics.

A major reason for the persistence of competing criteria of evidence is that the processes of assessing proof are embedded deep in the underpinnings of culture. Whether the norms of science, the passions of politics, the dictates of ideology, or the fervor of religion guide the interpretation of evidence, proof assessment consists of unwritten rules and unspoken norms on which people rely to give meaning to the world around them, to make judgments about what is desirable and feasible, and to anticipate problems in the future. The more technical a proof is, the more cerebral are the operations performed to assess it; but the readiness to use such operations itself originates in cultural premises. Viewed in this way, the criteria of proof associated with the norms of science are both demanding and vulnerable to manipulation. They are demanding in that they do not automatically provide foregone conclusions. Political passions, ideological precepts, or religious fervor often require only the identity of the actors in a situation to determine the side on which "truth" lies, but scientific criteria require their user to suspend judgment while seeking further information and sifting through alternative explanations. At the same time, criteria of scientific proof are vulnerable in that other values and habits can undermine the willingness to suspend judgment and tear away at the inclination to apply objective criteria to the assessment of evidence.

Scientific assessments are also vulnerable to the extent that fallacious observations are supplied and alternative explanations implied

---

[23] For a lengthy analysis of both the explosion at Chernobyl and the political events that followed it, see Christopher Flavin, *Reassessing Nuclear Power: The Fallout from Chernobyl* (Washington: Worldwatch Institute, 1987).

through disinformation techniques. No amount of tampering with data is likely to undermine the reactions of those whose criteria of proof are founded on political passions, but at least in the short run those whose judgments depend on data are open to being misled by findings obtained with biased procedures or from questionable sources. (In the long run, of course, distorted data will be discredited as the scientific criteria of evidence are applied.)

It follows that using scientific proof as an instrument of control is no simple matter, even when the targets of control give top priority to systematic evidence. To be sure, their compliance can be expected if the evidence is convincing, but there is no automaticity in this process. They need to be persuaded that the proof is sufficient to justify their compliance, and the evidence must be so powerful that their scientific criteria overcome national loyalties, biases against adversaries, and distrust of modern technology.

Consider, for example, the evidence of Libyan involvement in the bombing of the Berlin discotheque. The Reagan administration claimed that there was "irrefutable" proof in the form of electronically intercepted messages from Tripoli to Libyan diplomatic posts in Europe. In Western Europe, however, where doubts about the utility of economic sanctions and fears of inciting more terrorist attacks were strong, the reactions to the information were less clear-cut. In West Germany, officials called it "circumstantial," although subordinates in the intelligence field accepted the evidence as valid. "Indications but no concrete proof," "the pattern of evidence clearly points to a Libyan hand," "strong but not conclusive evidence" were other reactions.[24] Similarly, to cite an example where divergent political commitments can compete with proof-assessment habits. U.S. senators showed quite different responses when Reagan officials showed them classified material purporting to prove that Nicaragua was active in supporting insurgencies throughout Central America: "There is, to me, clear and convincing evidence of Sandinista involvement in other countries," said one; "I am not convinced by the evidence I have seen," said another.[25]

Relations of proof in postinternational politics can be described as

[24] James M. Markham, "Germans Reported at Odds over Libyan Terrorist Ties," *New York Times*, April 11, 1986, p. A10; Bernard Weintraub, "Reagan, Weighing Retaliation against the Libyans, Keeps Carriers at Sea," *New York Times*, April 10, 1986, p. A8. For an account of differences over the evidence pertaining to whether Libya embarked on the construction of a chemical-weapons plant, see James M. Markham, "As Talks End, Skeptics Lower Tone," *New York Times*, Janaury 12, 1989, p. A4.

[25] "C.I.A. Aid to Rebels Reported," *New York Times*, April 14, 1986, p. A8.

beset with constant tension between a felt need to act and a felt need to legitimize the action with a compelling knowledge base. Indeed, so crucial has the adequacy of proof become that often the energies that governments extend to procure evidence seem out of proportion to the potential degree of control involved, as if the responsible officials define their problem less by its content than by the quality of proof associated with it. A good, if grisly, example of this can be seen in the U.S. government's effort to prove that the Soviet Union employed chemical warfare in Afghanistan by sending special missions to sites where such weapons were thought to have been used, with the charge to obtain blood and tissue samples from corpses. As one news report described the effort: "Afghan freedom fighters and others on the mission—presumably equipped with sensors and protective clothing that would permit them to move safely though contaminated areas—must bring back enough of the victim's body to make it credible under laboratory analysis. 'It has to be a sufficient portion so that it is clear the chemical agent entered the bloodstream and that the piece was not simply dipped in a chemical agent after death,' one source notes, adding that several samples that have already been obtained have met this tougher standard."[26]

Several factors help to explain the increasingly important role that scientific proof is playing in world politics. Perhaps most noteworthy is the growing competence of publics. For a variety of reasons (discussed in chapter 13), the analytic skills of citizens everywhere are being refined, so that their understanding of world politics is more elaborate and complex. These skills also enable them to evaluate more critically the explanations that governments offer for their actions. The considerable effort officials make to "cover their trail" in covert operations is testimony to their recognition of how skillful publics and journalists have become in uncovering such operations. As one observer has said: "Communication and media gullibility have changed substantially. Virtually nothing can be kept secret from the press. Thus an operationally successful covert action has a high chance of being revealed eventually."[27]

Second, and related, public trust in the integrity of governments appears to have declined. As governments are revealed to have lied in previous situations and to have resorted to issuing disinformation, citizens have tightened the standards they use to evaluate leaders and

[26] *Newsweek*, July 25, 1983, p. 17.

[27] Allan E. Goodman, "Covert Action Is Overdue for a Cost-Benefit Analysis," *Los Angeles Times*, October 21, 1986, p. B5.

206 | CHAPTER 8

their conduct. (See chapters 13 and 14 for further discussion of this point.) Third, the microelectronic revolution has given citizens the ability to "see" for themselves what international actors are doing, how they go about it, and the consequences that follow from their actions and interactions. The pictures relayed by satellites onto television screens may not be "firsthand" evidence (since they are selected by those who photograph, gather, and edit them), but they are live and not oral or printed reconstructions of what happened.

Fourth, the capabilities of producers of evidence have also been enlarged by technological developments. In the past, charges of bad faith and allegations of misconduct had to be founded on inferential data, but now a number of techniques—such as aerial photography, electronic eavesdropping, seismological monitoring, forensic instruments, and computer simulations—are available for reducing human error in the measuring process. Illustrative in this regard was the debate over responsibility for the downing of Iran Air flight 655 by the U.S. Navy cruiser Vincennes in 1988. Among the questions were whether the airliner was ascending or descending and whether its radio transponder was tuned to Mode II (used only by military aircraft) or Mode III (used by both military and civilian planes). In addition to the testimony of the crew on these matters, an electronic recording of the events was made by computerized equipment aboard the Vincennes, equipment so new that it provided the first electronic record ever made of a naval clash. This record, consisting of digital displays that could be played back in both real time and slow motion, yielded conclusions quite at variance with the recollections of the crew. Indeed, for at least some of the facts, the memory of *every* witness was negated by the data tapes. The report of the navy's investigation of the incident made this comparison between the testimony it received and (in italics) the data from the electronic record: "[One crewman] observed TN 4131 (the Iranian airliner) at 445 knots at an altitude of 7,800 feet and descending during engagement. He recalled it being a minute from [missile] launch. *USS Vincennes' system information showed TN 4131 at an altitude of 12,000 feet, ascending and at 380 knots.*" Similarly, while the crew differed on whether flight 655 was using Mode II, the nine consoles on the Vincennes that were monitoring the airliner all showed that it was using Mode III.[28]

Despite the increasing precision and versatility of the technology of

[28] This account of the equipment that "has revolutionized our ability to piece together what has happened" is drawn from Les Aspin, "Witness to Iran Flight 655," *New York Times*, November 11, 1988, p. A35.

measurement, however, relations of proof are likely to remain complex. Readings of needles on dials, of patterns on screens, and of graphics on printouts are subject to erroneous calculations and opposing interpretations. It is perhaps merely amusing to recall that the U.S. Department of State declared it had proof that Soviet forces were using chemical agents that resulted in "yellow rain" in Laos and Afghanistan—which a Harvard biochemist attributed to bee excrement. On the other hand, the crucial importance of a proof's reliability is discernible from the fact that when a panel of independent U.S. scientists challenged their government's operational procedures for estimating the yield of large Soviet nuclear tests, the CIA subsequently changed the procedures.[29] Here, nothing less than the question of whether the Soviet Union was in compliance with the 1974 Threshold Test Ban Treaty was at stake.

Of course, technological devices are not the only mechanisms for generating and presenting evidence in world politics. There remain numerous situations in which the crucial information has to be uncovered through traditional methods of observation. The question of how many pro-democracy demonstrators were killed in Beijing when Chinese soldiers opened fire on them in June 1989 is one recent instance. An accurate count of the dead was considered critical to whether China faced a long period of international isolation or one of gradual forgiveness. To achieve the latter outcome, the Chinese regime resorted to an extensive propaganda program to "prove" that the toll was at the most two hundred, much lower than the initial but undocumented reports of the Western news media, which ran as high as three thousand. Western analysts, on the other hand, were eager to establish a more reliable estimate so that the issue could be addressed on a realistic basis. Hence, "for days" subsequent to the crackdown, reporters, scholars, and others

> combed the streets, sidewalk cracks and cement crevices near Tian
> An Men Square and the scenes of other clashes in the city, searching for hard evidence of what had really happened. They collected hundreds of spent machine-gun cartridges and flattened bullet heads. They scanned bullet-pocked walls and scorched patches of concrete where, according to some reports, the soldiers had stacked and burned scores of bodies. And, ever since, they have

[29] Michael R. Gordon, "Scientists Challenge Method Used to Measure Size of Soviet Atomic Tests," *New York Times*, November 4, 1985, p. A13, and Michael R. Gordon, "C.I.A. Changes Way That It Measures Soviet Atom Tests," *New York Times*, April 2, 1986, p. 1.

been analyzing the few bits of physical evidence they have gleaned from a night that may have altered the course of the most populous nation on Earth.[30]

Nor is the compilation and publication of statistical patterns the only traditional method for enhancing relations of proof. Other techniques include the appointment of commissions of inquiry and committees of experts, the release of classified information by governments, the reports of nongovernmental organizations such as Amnesty International, the legislative testimony of masked witnesses who fear reprisals for publicizing their observations, the accounts of bystanders in conflict situations, and the stories and photographs of investigative journalists. Because they are more subjective in nature, these techniques yield evidence that is more open to diverse interpretations than that produced by technological devices. However, the statistical patterns published by a reputable source tend to carry more weight than the conclusions of a commission of inquiry, and the judgments of the latter are usually more influential than the account of a single observer. In relations of proof, in other words, the further the methods of generating evidence are removed from susceptibility to bias, the greater is the likelihood that control will be effectively exercised. Nevertheless, the pull of political prejudices and other distortive habits is such that no mechanism for presenting evidence can ever lift issues of proof above the realm of politics.[31]

Nor are relations of proof confined to the question of the credibility of the evidence. Often there is the further problem, at least for democratic systems, of whether evidence should even be made available, since the mechanisms for generating it might thereby be compromised. Ironically, much of the evidence gathered by electronic and aerial monitoring is classified as secret, because publication of the evidence would suggest the techniques that procured it, and once the techniques are known by adversaries they can be combated. Hence, increasingly politicians claim that they have evidence that supports their position on an issue but that they are not at liberty to provide the evidence "for security reasons." The Reagan administration's effort to show that the Soviet Union was supplying arms to Nicaragua is an example of this dilemma. As one report noted, after an account of a variety of ways in

[30] Mark Fineman, "China's Propaganda Tries to Sow Death Toll Doubts," *Los Angeles Times*, June 30, 1989, p. 1.

[31] For an indication of how proof-generating mechanisms can themselves become embroiled in political issues, see Katherine K. Wallman, "The Statistical System under Stress: Framing an Agenda for Success," *ICPSR Bulletin*, December 1988, pp. 1–3.

which Soviet supplies were said to be sent to Nicaragua, "The officials said they were unable to provide documenting evidence because of sensitivity over how the information was obtained."[32] In effect, they were asking for trust in themselves instead of in the processes of data generation, a request that seems unlikely to be granted at a time when publics are demanding more precise and elaborate forms of proof.

If in the end political considerations outweigh those that attach to scientific proof, why is so much energy invested in the development of evidence? Does it matter whether or not the habit of proof assessment is expanding and evolving into a "politics of proof"? The cynical response might be that respect for scientific proof can never replace a commitment to subjective values and goals. A more optimistic response would be that the demands for proof signify a welcome shift in the dialogues of world politics, in which the trend toward greater rigor will cast doubt on the subjective preferences of officials and publics.

In sum, as with coercion or any other control technique, there are limits beyond which proof is not effective as a means of generating compliance. There is nothing automatic about the effects of even unambiguous evidence on the behavior of others. On the other hand, there is a trend under way, albeit a gradual one; all the indicators point to an increasing reliance on relations of proof in world politics.

If relations of coercion are also undergoing alteration in response to postinternational politics, and if centralizing and decentralizing dynamics are introducing tension into the coherence and effectiveness of collectivities, it is clearly reasonable to anticipate that the world's authority relationships will undergo strain as conditions become more turbulent. Before inquiring into whether the strain is likely to undermine these relationships and produce a world authority crisis, it is important to examine the other two global parameters and to estimate the extent to which the habits of micro actors and the stability of macro structures are similarly vulnerable to transformation. This is a central task of the next five chapters.

[32] Gerald M. Boyd, "Reagan to Accuse Soviet of Sending Arms to Managua," *New York Times*, June 8, 1986, p. 1.

CHAPTER 9

INVESTIGATING
INDIVIDUALS

Roles, Scenarios, Habits, and Learning

I find that even though I am eating corn flakes every morning
for breakfast, deep inside of me is a sympathy toward an old
era.

—Michiko Hirai, a Japanese college student[1]

THIS COMMENT, made by a young woman as an era in her country
came to an end with the death of Emperor Hirohito, captures well a
central theme of this chapter. It reflects both the strengths and the limits of habit in human affairs. Ms. Hirai did break with the past, but she
did not do so with ease or without regret. The tension she felt between
old modes and new patterns is a reminder that social systems are
founded on the repetition of predictable behavior, that the micro parameter is not readily engulfed by turbulent change. It alerts us to the
necessity of demonstrating how, and under what circumstances, the
habits of people will give way to new mechanisms for handling challenges to their long-standing values and goals. To assert that people
are flexible and open to change is not enough. In fact, impelled by their
habits, they can be quite rigid and resistant to new patterns.[2]

The purpose of this chapter, then, is to examine the intellectual,
emotional, and habitual processes through which the several types of
individual actors identified in chapter 6 relate to public affairs and,

[1] Susan Chira, "On a Japanese Campus, a Time to Take Stock," *New York Times*,
January 10, 1989, p. A4.

[2] In the case of mass habits, for example, it has been estimated that "since about
1700 . . . from a global point of view, the time which a basic innovation requires to grow
from a market share of 10% to a market share of 90% is usually 50 years, regardless of
whether this innovation is margarine, a vacuum cleaner, or the theory of relativity."
Cesare Marchetti, quoted in Ortwin Renn, "High Technology and Social Change," *High
Tech Newsletter* 1 (1983): 15.

especially, to note the ways in which these processes are susceptible to influence and transformation. Then, in chapters 12 and 13, the extent to which they have actually undergone transformation will be assessed.

Table 9.1 lists the nine attributes of individuals that have the greatest potential for change in the context of micro-macro interactions. If it is the case, as presumed here, that people matter in world politics, and if it is unimaginable that their skills and orientations have not been substantially affected by the dynamics of the postindustrial era, then it is with respect to these nine attributes that turbulence is most likely to be felt. Table 9.1 also indicates the probable nature of the change in each attribute if and when turbulent change occurs.[3]

The dimensions which, taken together, comprise the entity we call a person include skills, attitudes, motives, perceptions, cognitive balances, roles, action scripts, loyalties, authority orientations, and legitimacy sentiments—to mention only the dimensions with special relevance for political behavior. As noted in chapter 6, comprehension of where individuals fit in world politics requires one to suspend the conception of each of them as a unique, coherent, and concrete whole and, instead, to treat them analytically as composites of diverse parts. As also indicated earlier, the concept of role provides a useful point of departure in this regard.

TABLE 9.1. Attributes of Individual Actors
Most Likely to Change in the Postindustrial Era

| Attribute | Nature of Change | |
	From	Toward
Learning	Habitual	Adaptive
Analytic skills	Rudimentary	Developed
Cognitive maps	Simplistic	Complex
Role scenarios	Truncated	Elaborate
Cathectic capacities	Dormant and crude	Active and refined
Compliance orientations	Unthinking	Questioning
Legitimacy sentiments	Traditional criteria	Performance criteria
Political loyalties	Focused on nation-state	Variable foci
Locus of control	Distant	Close

[3] It should be noted that these attributes of individuals are not the equivalent of their "political action repertory." The latter refers to modes of political participation, whereas the attributes discussed here are skills and orientations that precede and underlie the choice and use of modes in the action repertory. A thorough, data-based discussion of these modes, including unconventional as well as conventional forms of participation, is in Samuel H. Barnes, Max Kaase, et al., *Political Action: Mass Participation in Five Western Democracies* (Beverly Hills, Calif.: Sage, 1979).

ROLES AS ANALYTIC UNITS

The key to a role lies in the expectations that inhere in it as a consequence of its place in the systems of which it is a component. That is, a role is defined by the attitudinal and behavioral expectations that those who relate to its occupant have of the occupant and the expectations that the occupant has of himself or herself in the role. Some of the expectations are formally defined in the system's rules and laws, while others develop informally and operate as implicit norms and procedures. Roles vary in the extent to which they allow their occupants discretion in interpreting the expectations and in resolving the conflicts that stem from the occupancy of multiple roles. Other things being equal, the more authority and power resources that attach to a role, the more discretion is likely to be accorded to its occupants. Thus, assuming authority relations are not in flux, leaders are freer to exercise their idiosyncratic preferences than are the members of the organizations over which they preside.[4]

If only because they are members of families, all individuals occupy a multiplicity of roles through which they engage in the various relationships that comprise their lives. The more industrialized and complex the society to which they belong, the greater is the number of roles they occupy and, accordingly, the greater is the potential for conflicts and overlaps among their roles. Citizens in present-day societies, for instance, occupy roles in their national state and their local community merely by becoming adults, and through birth they also acquire a culture, an ethnic affiliation, a social class, a gender classification, a religious faith, and many other *ascribed* roles. In addition, they occupy *chosen* or *achieved* roles when, as adults, they join any of a variety of organizations at the global, national, and local levels.

Attached to all these ascribed and chosen memberships are expectations as to how and when their occupants should undertake initiatives and how and when they should engage in followership. While these expectations can often be met simultaneously, there are circum-

---

[4] For more elaborate conceptualizations of the role concept, see Bruce J. Biddle, "Recent Developments in Role Theory," *Annual Review of Sociology* 12 (1986): 67–92; Donald D. Searing, "Roles, Rules, and Reasons: A Little Political Behavior for the New Institutionalism" (paper presented at the annual meeting of the Midwest Political Science Association, Chicago, April 1988); and Stephen G. Walker, ed., *Role Theory and Foreign Policy Analysis* (Durham: Duke University Press, 1987). My own formulation of the concept can be found in James N. Rosenau, "Private Preferences and Political Responsibilities: The Relative Potency of Individual and Role Variables in the Behavior of U.S. Senators," in J. David Singer, ed., *Quantitative International Politics: Insights and Evidence* (New York: Free Press, 1968), pp. 17–50.

stances when performing appropriately in one role precludes successful performance in others. Good citizenship in the community and the
nation usually requires similar behavior, but on occasion loyalty to one
may require disloyalty to the other, compelling the role occupant to
make choices among alternative courses of action. As previously implied, such role conflicts are increasingly common in conditions of turbulence.

The role of citizen is characterized by those attitudes toward authority and legitimacy that are appropriate to the country's structure and
history. Accordingly, conceptions of sovereignty, loyalty, compliance,
defiance, and a wide array of other mechanisms through which followers respond to leaders are also to be found in the expectations that
define the citizen role. These mechanisms are crucial to the ensuing
analysis, because it is through them that the postindustrial era makes
its impact on global politics. The dynamics of subgroupism and the
lessening effectiveness of governments are closely linked to the ways in
which citizens are reorienting their loyalties, legitimacy sentiments,
and predispositions toward complying with authority.

Thus the dynamics of the postindustrial era have led to the reorientation of citizens and have catapulted them to the center of the global
stage. The confluence of conflicting role demands on their priorities
and commitments has brought them into an arena in which the cascading processes of turbulence flourish. In effect, individuals have become,
both as group members and as citizens, a major battleground on which
states, governments, subnational groups, international organizations,
regimes, and transnational associations compete for their support and
loyalties, thereby posing for them choices that cannot be easily ignored
and that serve as both a measure of global change and a challenge to
global stability.

Much the same can be said about the individuals who act on behalf
of collectivities and publics. Public officials and the heads of private
organizations also occupy a multiplicity of roles. In addition to those
they occupy as citizens, their official positions accord them responsibilities in a variety of systems and subsystems that can be both overlapping and mutually exclusive. Not only may ministers of foreign affairs be spouses, parents, cousins, churchgoers, and so on, but they
also occupy roles in their cabinets, governments, parties, and societies
as well as in the bilateral, regional, international, and global systems
in which their countries are active. These officials can be simultaneously subjected to all the conflicts that beset the systems in which
they are role occupants—the private systems in which they are or previously were members, the policy-making institutions in which their

policy-making position is located, the societal system for which they make policy, and the international systems in which their society is a subsystem. The interactions among these systems, in other words, converge on the individual policy maker, creating role conflicts that reflect the different values, capabilities, and histories of the various systems to which the policy-making position is linked.

In short, with systems viewed as role structures and with individuals conceived as composites of roles, the ground is laid for tracing micro-macro interactions in global politics. Systems require appropriate role performance on the part of citizens and officials, thereby shaping what happens at the micro level, just as the performance of individuals shapes what happens at the macro level.

It follows that global politics, national politics, bureaucratic politics, and local politics are separate enterprises only to the extent that the individuals involved can maintain a separation among their roles in the various systems and conduct themselves accordingly. To the extent that they cannot do so, to the extent that issues span the boundaries that divide systems, as is usual under the conditions of extensive interdependence that mark global turbulence, then to that extent micro-macro interactions are at the very core of world politics. Like the citizen, the official has become a battlefield on which the conflicts that constitute the global agenda at any moment in time are played out.

One example of this is President Reagan's retreat from long-standing personal commitments and campaign pledges that depicted the Soviet Union as an "evil empire" to which concessions ought not be made. Instead of attributing the shift in his behavior that resulted in summit meetings and an arms-control agreement to vague forces at work in global politics or to personal aspirations to a favored place in history, it can usefully be treated as the outcome of a competition between the expectations attached to his party role as a conservative "hawk" and those embedded in his role as the leader of a superpower in a system marked by crosspressures from economic exigencies, peace movements in Europe, dramatic changes in the Soviet Union, and aroused publics at home. Similarly, President Richard M. Nixon's trip to China in 1972 can be viewed as resulting not from an idiosyncratic trait or skill, but from the requirements of a superpower leader whose country needed more leverage in the increasingly significant Chinese-Soviet-U.S. triad.[5] Or, to use still another American example, it has

---

[5] For an insightful discussion of the powerful impact the presidential role can have on its occupants, see John S. D. Eisenhower, "The White House Mystique," *New York Times*, January 16, 1987, p. A31.

been said that John Foster Dulles's conduct as secretary of state can be appraised in terms of the strength of his roles in the policy-making process on the one hand and his devotion to the Presbyterian church on the other.

A number of additional advantages flow from conceptualizing roles as common denominators in the systems that comprise global politics. For one, it is responsive to the plea of those who want to resurrect the individual as the prime unit of analysis. To treat the individual as a composite of identifiable and competing roles does not, admittedly, fully meet the plea, for it divides people up into analytical parts rather than treating each person as an entity. Nevertheless, it does call attention to micro phenomena bounded by individuals as well as to the aggregative processes that produce and differentiate collectivities and global structures.

As the Dulles example suggests, moreover, granting a central place to role expectations facilitates clarification of a research issue that has troubled many analysts: where policy makers' idiosyncrasies fit in the dynamics of world politics. At stake here are questions about how much discretion individuals can exercise as officials and about the extent to which the policy-making process can be distorted, improved, or otherwise affected by the unique talents and beliefs that particular officials might bring to their responsibilities. Although systematic inquiries into the vagaries of their behavior are now available,[6] the predominant tendency has been to view officials as so capable of variability as to constitute a realm of global life in which inexplicable and unpredictable events originate. If the belief systems of officials are seen as reflective of role phenomena, however, the task of accounting for their impact on world politics is eased considerably.

Another virtue of conceiving of leaders as role occupants is that it facilitates analysis of the state. Instead of being treated as an abstract, vague, and undefined actor, the state can be seen as a precise and observable set of phenomena: the actions of those who are expected—and who expect of themselves—to act on behalf of the polity rather

---

[6] See, for example, Alexander L. George, "The Causal Nexus between Cognitive Beliefs and Decision-making Behavior: The 'Operational Code' Belief System," in L. S. Falkowski, ed., *Psychological Models of International Politics* (Boulder, Colo.: Westview, 1979), pp. 95–124; Margaret G. Hermann, "Personality and Foreign Policy Making: A Study of 53 Heads of Government," in D. A. Sylvan and S. Chan, eds., *Foreign Policy Decision Making: Perception, Cognition, and Artificial Intelligence* (New York: Praeger, 1984), pp. 53–80; D. Stuart and H. Starr, "The 'Inherent Bad Faith Model' Reconsidered: Dulles, Kennedy, and Kissinger," *Political Psychology* 3 (Fall/Winter 1981–1982): 1–33.

than any other social system or subsystem. That is, if the state has interests beyond government and party, as many analysts contend, surely the interests will be manifest in the recurrent activities of those in political and military organizations who are expected to articulate and serve them. Obviously, the servicing of these interests is not likely to be easily accomplished; those who occupy state roles are subject to numerous role conflicts arising from both domestic and international disputes.[7]

Finally, and perhaps most important, the role concept helps us to discern the micro dynamics of the cascading processes of turbulence. To the extent that citizens and officials occupy multiple roles in some systems dominated by integrative processes and in others marked by fragmenting processes—as do citizens in Poland and Lebanon, labor leaders in Detroit and Great Britain, and political leaders in Nicaragua and Israel—their role conflicts are precisely those that cascade change across systems. In such conflicts, individuals have to decide which roles in which systems have the greater legitimacy and which are linked to the highest authority, and the aggregate consequences of these choices then shape the flow of change throughout the global system.

ROLE SCENARIOS, OR ACTION SCRIPTS

But the foregoing understates the potential of the role concept. As a common denominator across system levels, the notion of roles as sets of formal and informal expectations experienced and held by their occupants tends to be static. These expectations specify the attitudes and actions a person is expected to maintain in order to perform effectively in the role, but it does not anticipate what the occupants will do when they find themselves in role conflicts. To fill this conceptual gap and infuse dynamism into role expectations, roles can be viewed as embedded in more encompassing schema, which we will refer to as *role scenarios* or *action scripts*. These locate the expectations of a role in those more elaborate and precise premises upon which its occupants are likely to draw in order to determine where they fit in relation to other role occupants in a system as they conflict, collaborate, or otherwise cope with the chores and challenges of its daily life.

The occupants of a role not only have an understanding of what is expected of them, but they also carry around a multitude of premises or assumptions about how others in relevant systems will conduct

[7] A cogent analysis along these lines is K. J. Holsti, "National Role Conceptions in the Study of Foreign Policy," *International Studies Quarterly* 14 (September 1970): 233–309.

themselves in relation both to them and to the problem at hand. From these premises, they derive scenarios as to how events are likely to develop as they and the others, all conforming to the expectations of their roles and exercising whatever flexibilities they may have in performing them, may react to each other.[8] As will be seen, the capacity to spell out such scenarios is a central analytic skill that is conceived to be undergoing change in the present era.[9]

To return to the example of President Reagan's role conflict in the field of arms control, the concept of action scripts enables us to understand his behavior as much more than simply a choice to favor his role as a superpower leader over his role as a party conservative. Presumably his decisions to retreat from campaign pledges and to make negotiating concessions also sprung from a choice among conflicting scenarios in which the foreign policy responses of the Soviet Union, the domestic changes initiated by Gorbachev, the demands of the peace movement in Western Europe, and the attitudes of publics in the United States would vary, depending on whether he acted out of his role as superpower leader or party leader.

As another example, consider how Prime Minister Margaret Thatcher of Great Britain moved in fifteen months from a tough to a weak stand in negotiations with the Chinese over Hong Kong—from

[8] For a thorough analysis in which emphasis is placed on the metaphoric foundations of scenarios, see Gareth Morgan, *Images of Organization* (Beverly Hills, Calif.: Sage, 1986).

[9] It is also a skill which has only just begun to come into focus empirically. Due to great strides in understanding the functioning of the brain, knowledge about scenario construction—what psychologists call "imaging" or "imagery"—is presently undergoing a veritable explosion. As one analyst puts it, "We truly have learned more about imagery in the past 15 years than in all the preceding centuries combined, and the end of progress is not yet in sight": Stephen M. Kosslyn, "Stalking the Mental Image," *Psychology Today*, May 1985, p. 28. For nontechnical, overall perspectives on this research, see Jon Franklin, *Molecules of the Mind: The Brave New Science of Molecular Psychology* (New York: Atheneum, 1987), and George Johnson, *Machinery of the Mind: Inside the New Science of Artificial Intelligence* (New York: Times Books, 1986). Examples of the research itself are John R. Anderson, *The Architecture of Cognition* (Cambridge: Harvard University Press, 1983); Howard Gardner, *The Mind's New Science: A History of the Cognitive Revolution* (New York: Basic Books, 1985); Stephen Michael Kosslyn, *Image and Mind* (Cambridge: Harvard University Press, 1980); and David E. Rumelhart, James L. McClelland, and the PDP Research Group, *Parallel Distributed Processing: Explorations in the Microstructure of Cognition*, volume 1, *Foundations*; volume 2, *Psychological and Biological Models* (Cambridge: MIT Press, 1986). For good surveys of the consequences of the revolution in the cognitive sciences for the study of politics, see Robert Axelrod, ed., *Structure of Decision* (Princeton: Princeton University Press, 1976), and Richard R. Lau and David O. Sears, eds., *Political Cognition* (Hillsdale, N.J.: Lawrence Erlbaum, 1986).

insisting in late 1982 that Britain retain administrative control over the territory for an indefinite period after 1997 to settling in early 1984 for a takeover by China that guaranteed the territory's autonomy. Her earlier position was taken in the context of a recent victory in the struggle with Argentina over the Falklands. Subsequently, however, she discovered that the expectations in the East Asian system are not the same as those of the South Atlantic system, and that the strategic and legal circumstances surrounding Hong Kong, as well as the differences between the Argentine and the Chinese armed forces, were such that the original scenario was not valid when she occupied the British-head-of-government role in the Pacific.

The importance of role scenarios is also evident in the interactions that occur within as well as between governments. In the United States, for example, the main role occupants in the policy-making process have notions about the goals, calculations, constraints, and conflicts that the others experience in their multiple roles. Thus, all of them can envision a variety of outcomes ensuing from their interactions over a foreign-policy issue—specifically, the various segments through which different scenarios will unfold as they resolve their role conflicts in one or another way. The Democratic Speaker of the House of Representatives knows that if he is responsive to the partisan requirements of his party role rather than the bipartisan expectations of his governmental role on, say, questions involving Central America, the Republican president's reactions are likely to differ accordingly, as will those of the secretary of state, the Senate minority leader, the pro- and anti-military factions in the House, and others with responsibilities on this issue.

Scenarios often become the focus of political controversy. Either in anticipating how current policies may turn out or in assessing how and why past ones went astray, officials may differ in their analyses of how one or more segments of a scenario lead to others. In Israel—to cite a vivid example of this phenomenon—a bitter quarrel erupted over the claim of Trade and Industry Minister Ariel Sharon that a terrorist attack against a synagogue in Turkey was a consequence of peace overtures by Prime Minister Shimon Peres. A cabinet crisis ensued and was resolved only when Sharon was unable to offer a convincing case of the intervening steps in the scenario and retracted the allegation of causality.[10]

In one important respect, the foregoing examples are misleading.

[10] "Peres Accepts Sharon's Letter of Retraction," *New York Times*, September 9, 1986, p. A4.

They imply that the relevance of role scenarios is confined to the analysis of governmental decision making. Certainly they are central to the ways in which politicians and bureaucracies frame and make their choices, but they are also the bases on which citizens participate in global life, with choices among various scenarios underlying the degree to which they are active and the direction which their collective actions take. Stated more emphatically, role scenarios are among the basic understandings that are transmitted through political socialization and that sustain collectivities across generations. As such, as culturally derived premises for relating to the political arena, they are also among the prime phenomena that are aggregated when the energies of a collectivity are mobilized around goals. Put in another way, the task of leadership is that of "selling" action scripts—of getting citizens to regard one set of scripts as more viable and valid than any other.

It follows that faltering and conflicting role scenarios are among the conditions conducive to global turbulence. Whether it be a small group, a city, a nation-state, or an international system, the bonds that keep collectivities cohesive and enable them to reproduce themselves include a set of shared action scripts that designate who has legitimacy and authority in a collectivity and describe how all concerned will and should respond when the authority is exercised. Such scripts are, in effect, theories of how collectivities resolve their problems; and, like scholars in relation to their theories of world politics, the leaders and members of collectivities tend to be prisoners of such theories. As discussed below, they can be so habituated to the scripts that their compliance with them is taken for granted and they may be unaware that they are performing their assigned roles. When legitimacy is called into question, however, action scripts rise into consciousness, and scenarios involving noncompliance and the redirection of legitimacy sentiments emerge. At that point, a collectivity can enter into crisis, because the very basis for organizing its efforts has been undermined, giving rise to tensions that intrude into the action scripts of other collectivities and then cascade widely through the global system.

An example of how the action scripts of citizens in issue aggregations can become channeled into turbulent processes is provided by the involvement of the United States in the Vietnam conflict during the later 1960s. Impelled by moral outrage as well as by role scenarios that were perceived as potentially disastrous, many citizens placed themselves and their organizations at the center of action scripts in which their protests would lead to an American withdrawal from Southeast Asia. These scripts, often measured, aggregated, and publicized by opinion surveys, became, in turn, components of the scenarios on which officials in Washington, Saigon, and Hanoi based their actions.

Whether applied to micro decision-making activities or macro collective actions, role scenarios may be at once issue-specific and generalized in their scope. That is, while they are framed in the context of particular issues, they are not transitory in the same way issues are. Issues come and go, but the scenarios anticipating their course are based on the more enduring understandings which the occupants of any role are likely to have of the opportunities, constraints, and conflicts built into the other roles comprising the system. In effect, the scenarios reflect the comprehension attached to any role of how the system functions—its goals, procedures, cultural premises, capabilities, and historical patterns, both in general and in relation to particular issues.

It is important to recognize that the scenarios are inherent in the role and not in its occupants. Different occupants may resolve a role's conflicts differently, but all the resolutions are likely to be founded on similar conceptions of the alternative scenarios. The scenarios are the action side of a role's expectations: in experiencing and learning the expectations, the role's occupants become knowledgeable about the dynamics of other roles in the system and the contingencies that underlie the interactions among them. They cannot learn about the opportunities and limitations built into their own roles without at least a minimal grasp of the requirements faced by the other role occupants with whom they must interact. Accordingly, there are no role expectations divorced from the systems in which the roles are lodged, and thus there can be no system without role scenarios among which its members choose as they sustain or change its patterns through time.

This is not to imply that role scenarios are clear-cut, orderly, logical, or in any other way standardized. They are akin, rather, to what has been called *working knowledge*—an "organized body of knowledge that administrators and policy-makers use spontaneously and routinely in the context of their work," including "the entire array of beliefs, assumptions, interests, and experiences that influence the behavior of individuals at work."[11] Role scenarios can be thought of as deploying these arrays of understanding onto diverse paths that stretch into and anticipate the future, with each path consisting of segments that are linked by and fan out from choice points and with movement along any segment being a consequence of the interactive expectations held and choices made by all the participants whose paths cross in a

---

[11] M. M. Kennedy, "Working Knowledge," *Knowledge* 5 (December 1983): 193–94.

situation. At each choice point in a scenario, moreover, new segments may be introduced as the prior interactions create new circumstances that tap working knowledge in different ways and divert the path onto a new course.[12]

Thus, beyond the framework of segmented paths to and from the decision points in a situation, action scripts are anything but uniform. Founded on a composite of beliefs, assumptions, interests, and experiences as well as observations and information, their segments may form paths that are long or short, straight or circuitous, clear or obscure, continuous or broken. And the more that turbulent processes are part of the situation, of course, the greater is the likelihood of extensive and rapid fluctuations along these and other dimensions. Role scenarios are as operative under turbulent conditions as under normal ones, but their length, direction, clarity, and continuity are likely to be highly volatile the more changes cascade upon each other.

Role scenarios are likely to be marked by a tension between their tendency toward complexity and the limits to which their complexity can be comprehended. The complexity derives from the fact that an action script can potentially embrace a great number and variety of segments, as many permutations and combinations as those occupying multiple roles are able to visualize in anticipating how the choices they make among competing role expectations will interact sequentially with the choices that others in the system may make.

One can begin to appreciate the complexity of interactive scenarios by thinking of them as maps of the system, with decision routes tracing how the choices made by the actors crisscross and diverge as each selects one scenario rather than another. Viewed from the perspective of an observer outside the system, the routes either move forward to the conclusion of an issue or are marked by circularity or vacillation as the choices made by the role occupants reinforce, offset, or negate each other. Viewed from the perspective of the role occupants, the maps lie at the core of their activities and either (for the pragmatist) serve to guide the pursuit of their goals in the light of what is feasible or (for the idealist) highlight the obstacles that hinder the realization of their values.[13]

---

[12] John Maynard Keynes once captured this aspect of scenarios when he observed, in the context of how markets function, "We have reached the third degree, where we devote our intelligence to anticipating what average opinion expects the average opinion to be. And there are some, I believe, who practice the fourth, the fifth, and higher degrees." Quoted in Karen Arenson, "The New Trading Game," *New York Times*, September 20, 1986, p. 28.

[13] In the case of policy makers, who may occupy a number of roles in private systems

But as scenarios tend toward increasing complexity, so do the constraints against playing out in the imagination all the segments they might encompass. There is, it seems reasonable to hypothesize, a high inverse correlation between the length and clarity of a scenario: other things being equal, the longer and more diffuse it is—i.e., the greater the number of choice points involved—the more obscure will be its temporally distant segments. Anticipating the path beyond a few segments involves managing a great deal of complex information and confronting a great number of hypothetical situations for which prior experience provides no guide, and this combination of complexity and uncertainty tends to curb the ability to be precise as scenarios stretch further into the future.[14]

Thus, citizens and officials alike either tend to rely on the early segments when making their choices, or they act on the unconfirmed belief (as the United States did in Vietnam and the Soviet Union did in Afghanistan) that somehow the path will ultimately lead them to the goal they are pursuing even though the intervening segments are shrouded in obscurity. Consider, for example, an actor in a conflict with two other actors, each of which might move in three different directions at each stage of the unfolding situation. By the fourth choice point, the situation would require the anticipation of dozens or scores of possible scenario segments. Even highly skilled role occupants would probably want to simplify matters either by treating some segments as "unrealistic" or by assuming that they comprehend the organizing principles which underlie interaction in the situation.[15]

On the other hand, the expectations attached to roles also operate as constraints that keep scenarios streamlined. A number of the possible segments that could fan out from future choice points are likely to

---

as well as their official positions, the scenarios are even more elaborate and complex, since the crisscrossing patterns also include the personal conflicts and consequences that may follow from the actions taken in their public roles. For a stimulating discussion of the tension between private and public roles, see R. Sennett, *The Fall of Public Man* (New York: Alfred A. Knopf, 1977).

[14] However, given the possibilities for storing and analyzing large and interactive files of information that the microelectronic revolution has brought, public officials may be able to work with ever more complex scenarios. This point will be further discussed in chapter 12.

[15] For a provocative discussion of how conceptions of scenarios and time are central to the conduct of public affairs, see Charles S. Maier, "The Politics of Time: Changing Paradigms of Collective Time and Private Time in the Modern Era," in C. S. Maier, ed., *Changing Boundaries of the Political: Essays on the Evolving Balance between the State and Society, Public and Private in Europe* (Cambridge: Cambridge University Press, 1987), pp. 151–75.

require action that exceeds the maximum leeway that a role permits its occupants to exercise. During the controversy over the deployment of new weaponry in Europe early in the 1980s, leaders of the peace movement excluded from their scenarios those segments that might have flowed from choices that allowed for missile deployment in exchange for future compromises in arms control negotiations, and the NATO governments simplified their action scripts by refusing to consider any postponement of deployment. Hence, by making an unwavering commitment to "stay the course," the tendency toward complexity can be limited and the anticipated paths into the future kept straighter and more continous than might otherwise be the case.

Or consider the complexity involved when citizens try to trace shifts in the global economy to their own financial situations. In the case of an American, for instance, one can appreciate how the impulse to streamline scenarios is intensified by the following reasoning:

> If we let the dollar fall, German and Japanese goods will become too expensive for Americans to buy, and American goods will become better bargains for the Japanese. This will stimulate American exports and bring trade into balance. Besides, it will cause German officials to get so worried about a decline in their economy that they will lower interest rates, which will stimulate borrowing, which will further increase German demand for American goods. But a fall in the dollar will also make Third World debtor nations worse off, and they may default, injuring our banks. Furthermore, the Japanese will be less interested in buying American government and private securities, so we'll have to raise interest rates to attract their capital. But higher interest rates will make it more costly for our industrialists to invest in modernization, so we'll become still less competitive. On the other hand, suppose we don't let the dollar fall . . . Maybe I'd better make that big purchase while I still have the money. Or perhaps I should have a drink.[16]

It also seems reasonable to hypothesize that the longer people occupy a role, the more elaborate will be their scenarios, and the more elaborate their scenarios become, the more they are thought to have political wisdom. If the term means anything as it is normally used, political wisdom refers to an astute knowledge of a system and an ability to anticipate how its key actors are likely to conduct themselves under varying circumstances—which is another way of saying that

[16] Harry C. Bredemeier (personal correspondence).

those who are politically wise are able to operate with a wider set of scenarios than most people. Their "horizons of observability"—to use an apt phrase employed by sociologists to describe the distance in a communications network beyond which people are unlikely to be aware of the role performance of others—stretch widely across the relevant systems.[17]

The more elaborate a role scenario is, of course, the more does it encompass all the varied sources out of which action flows. Skillful politicians develop their scenarios out of their knowledge of the other relevant roles and their information about the goals others may seek, the means they may consider, the capabilities they may have available, the cost-benefit calculations they may make, and the support they may mobilize—all of this taken together with shrewd anticipations of how their own choices might affect the choices and scenarios of the others.

While role scenarios may include calculations in terms of game theory as to how role occupants may bluff, threaten, or otherwise pursue desired outcomes through strategic posturing in their interactions with each other, it would be erroneous to conclude that the scenarios are themselves necessarily game theoretical. They consist of empirical premises held by role occupants and not of hypothetical constructs employed by rational actors. They serve as means for processing information no less than as plans for action.[18]

Being inherent in the dynamics of a system, in other words, role scenarios are inferrable. They can be discerned in the position papers prepared for decision makers, in the public accountings of their actions and of what they hope to achieve, and in the problems they encounter and the choices they make. Action scripts can also be traced in the claims and actions of citizens, in the enduring collaborative and conflicting patterns of collectivities, and in the interactions of international systems.[19] Game-theoretical analysis can be useful in assessing the op-

---

[17] N. E. Friedkin, "Horizons of Observability and Limits of Informal Control in Organizations," *Social Forces* 62 (September 1983): 54–77.

[18] Cf. R. P. Abelson, "The Structure of Belief Systems," in R. C. Shank and K. M. Colby, eds., *Computer Models of Thought and Language* (San Francisco: W. H. Freeman, 1973), pp. 287–339, and Robert Axelrod, "Schema Theory: An Information Processing Model of Perception and Cognition," *American Political Science Review* 67 (December 1973): 1248–66.

[19] For examples of methods for systematically and creatively tracing action scripts, see Brian Job, Douglas Johnson, and Eric Selbin, "A Multi-Agent, Script-Based Model of U.S. Foreign Policy towards Central America" (paper presented at the annual meeting of the American Political Science Association, Chicago, September 1987); Richard Herrmann, "The Empirical Revolution: A Strategy for Drawing Inferences about Perceptions," *International Studies Quarterly* 32 (June 1988): 175–203; and Philip Tetlock,

tions open to a role occupant, but it is quite secondary if the analyst's task is to estimate how and why the occupant did or might behave in a particular way or to comprehend how diverse role scenarios aggregate to one outcome rather than another.

Furthermore, as noted, action scripts derive from deeply ingrained, subconscious predispositions as well as from explicit analytic assessments. The decision routes of scenarios are as much products of unstated cultural premises (such as "challenges should be met," "friends should be rewarded," and "alternatives should be considered") and of historical memories ("dictators cannot be trusted," "organizations can be paralyzed by inertia," and "unruly mobs can foment change") as of current role requirements and situational imperatives. Beginning in early childhood, people learn the "givens" of social interaction, the inclinations, perceptions, and values which structure role expectations, and as these implicit orientations cumulate into working knowledge they increasingly serve as predictions of the behavior of others as well as sources of the role occupant's own conduct. The scenarios that Western officials and publics developed after a Soviet fighter shot down the Korean airliner consisted of decision points shaped not only by the ongoing arms control negotiations but also by the cultural premise that killing innocent civilians in peacetime is unacceptable and the historical memory that the Russians are obsessed with territorial security.[20]

That action scripts are compounded out of tacit premises as well as explicit role expectations also accounts for the capacity of individuals to draw on a multitude of scenarios as they respond to the issues that evoke their interest. Every culture has its own logic, its own values and symbols for interpreting and adapting to challenges, and thus those socialized into it never lack scenarios for coping with the situations that claim their attention. Individuals need not be well informed, and they may even be uninformed or misinformed, about a situation in order to respond to it. Nor do they need to have clear and detailed picures of future choice points and the scenarios that connect them. The values and presumptions of their culture will always enable them to develop scenarios in which they can fit themselves and others.

"Monitoring the Integrative Complexity of American and Soviet Policy Rhetoric: What Can Be Learned?" *Journal of Social Issues* 44 (Summer 1988): 101–31.

[20] One account even suggests that top American officials clung to the scenarios derived from these cultural premises despite an initial intelligence assessment that the Soviet attack was based on a succession of blunders, including a failure to identify the plane. See Seymour M. Hersh, *The Target Is Destroyed: What Really Happened to Flight 007 and What America Knew about It* (New York: Random House, 1986).

It follows that role scenarios are closely linked to the processes of within-system aggregation. When widely shared, they are the cohesive that holds collectivities together; when they are discrepant and competitive, they paralyze collectivities or tear them apart. During the 1980s in Poland, for example, some of Solidarity's calls to rally were successful because enough members perceived that the greater the number that marched, the greater would be the impact on the government and on the union's friends and adversaries abroad. Those calls to rally that failed can be partly attributed to the presence of alternative scenarios among the union's membership, in which the risk of arrest or violence was seen as too great relative to the possibility of such an impact.

Similarly, widespread and rapid shifts in the shared action scripts of a collectivity's members can be said to underlie the momentum and success of revolutionary movements. For example, in Iran, at some point, perhaps upon Ayatollah Ruhollah Khomeini's return from France, the scenario of a successful overthrow of the shah became viable as well as desirable for millions of Iranians, and their collective actions that followed proved this assessment to be sound. Indeed, the convergence of a society around new role scenarios quintessentially reveals the aggregative dynamics that underlie system transformations.[21]

HABIT AND ADAPTATION

But how do role occupants, be they leaders or followers, converge around common scenarios? Given the many stimuli designed to shape, mobilize, and sustain alternative commitments, how do citizens choose among the available scenarios? And how do officials, who are normally faced with an even greater variety of stimuli from sources both within and outside their collectivities, choose among the alternatives in such a way as to enhance the effectiveness of their policies and the support they receive from the citizenry?

That people are socialized to conform to the expectations of their roles is not an adequate response to these questions. No set of expectations is so precise as to leave the role occupant without any room for

[21] This also points up why revolutions occur so rarely: given the complexity of social processes, the likelihood of simultaneous convergence around new scenarios is extremely small. Furthermore, profound collective changes tend to occur only when all the actors learn the new scenario together. See M. Crozier and E. Friedberg, *Actors and Systems: The Politics of Collective Action* (Chicago: University of Chicago Press, 1980), pp. 223–24.

choice. Conformity to expectations can be realized through several scenarios and with greater or lesser alacrity, diligence, imagination, responsibility, and competence. Accordingly, role occupants either have to ponder how to conduct themselves or must evolve mechanisms for making the choices without prior thought, or they must fashion some combination of these two extremes. The first of these two ideal types is often referred to as the *rational actor*: the citizen or official who more or less consciously synthesizes values and goals with respect to the relevant considerations in a utility function and then proceeds to maximize interests by presuming that the function depicts the most rational course of action.[22] The ideal type at the other end of the continuum is the *habit-driven actor*, whose behavior derives from a habit function developed over time out of memories, traits, beliefs, expectations, scenarios, and prior experiences that lead them to make the same choices that they made previously in the same context.[23] Where rational actors consciously calculate their utility functions, habit-driven actors do no make estimates or otherwise engage in a calculative process; rather, they are used to acting in terms of their habit functions and do so in a rote-like fashion with whatever degree of thought and emotion their particular functions have always required.

Whatever theoretical utility the rational and habit-driven models may have for identifying possible lines of action and interaction, they are of little value for our purposes. The habit-driven model is helpful in suggesting that cultural norms and bureaucratic inertia are integral to behavior, but it surely falls short as an analytic instrument for a dynamic world in which educational institutions, technological innovations, and sophisticated mass communications are actively challenging habits as well as reinforcing them. Likewise, the rational-actor model is inadequate in that it conceives of utility functions as calculative and not also impulsive; intellectual and not also organizational; reflective and not also routinized; self-interested and not also altruistic.[24] Even in those models that posit rationality as subject to specified boundary constraints, interaction is seen as a bargaining process in

[22] For examples of a growing literature in which students of world politics, borrowing from microeconomics and game theory, have developed models of international actors who conduct themselves in terms of rationally calculated utility functions, see Kenneth A. Oye, ed., *Cooperation under Anarchy* (Princeton: Princeton University Press, 1986).

[23] James N. Rosenau, "Before Cooperation: Hegemons, Regimes, and Habit-Driven Actors in World Politics," *International Organization* 40 (Autumn 1986): 884–94.

[24] For an analysis in which the self-interested commitments of rational actors are conceived as predatory orientations in a "theory of predatory rule" that offers "a micro-foundation to macro-processes," see Margaret Levi, *Of Rule and Revenue* (Berkeley: University of California Press, 1988), chapter 2.

which ends and means are assessed through an exclusively intellectual process. Such models are hardly appropriate to a rapidly changing, ever more interdependent world in which the task of calculating a utility function has been rendered virtually impossible. Even for a rational actor, as one observer puts it, habits have "the effect . . . of diminishing the probability that the [individual] will be conscious of the multiplicity of paths that are open to him."[25]

Empirically, in short, the vast preponderance of officials and citizens are both rational and habitual, both intellectual and emotional, and our understanding of turbulence in world politics is thus more likely to be advanced if we employ a perspective that posits individuals as falling between the two ideal types.[26] What is needed is a model organized around a central premise in which the form and direction of micro action is conceived to spring from a combination of habits that perpetuate continuity and orientations that allow for thoughtful estimates and are open to change. It is the shifting balance between rote behavior and adaptive learning that forms the conditions of postinternational politics.[27] To reflect this model, it seems worthwhile to coin a new term that expresses the synthesis of habitual and adaptive responses. Henceforth, where appropriate, we shall refer to individuals as *habdaptive actors* and to their location on the continuum between rote behavior and adaptive learning as their *habdaptive function*.

The significance of this terminology can be highlighted by noting that it is the possibility of change on the part of the habdaptive actor which underlies a prime argument of this book: that turbulence has engulfed world politics partly, even largely, because citizens and officials have moved away from the habit end of the learning continuum and toward the adaptive end. The movement may be no more than minimal—on the order of one JND—for any individual, but the aggregative consequences of the movement are not minimal at all. On the contrary, the breakdown of habits is a major reason for the transformation of the state-centric system into a bifurcated one.

While particular habits vary widely from culture to culture and era

[25] Raymond Boudon, *The Logic of Social Action* (London: Routledge & Kegan Paul, 1981), p. 154. For a full, but fair, critique of the limits of rational models, see Fred Eidlin and Andreas Pickel, "A Structural-Individualist Critique of 'Rational Choice' Approaches to Social Science" (paper presented at the twelfth World Congress of Sociology, New Delhi, August 1986).

[26] For a rich formulation embodying such a perspective, see Edward Shils, *Tradition* (Chicago: University of Chicago Press, 1981).

[27] For a discussion of the relevance of habit and learning to the conduct of world affairs, see John D. Steinbruner, *The Cybernetic Theory of Decision: New Dimensions of Political Analysis* (Princeton: Princeton University Press, 1974), chapters 2–4.

to era, it seems reasonable to presume that all people have a tendency to respond to stimuli in habitual ways.[28] However, habitual behavior is conceived here as a composite that is fed by the diverse wellsprings of human experience—a habit pool, as it were. That is, people are seen as engaging in actions that stem from a *combination* of past experiences, memories, cognitive styles, beliefs, personality, normative prescriptions, cultural and subcultural pressures, role expectations, and action scripts to which they have long been accustomed, by which they manage to maintain continuity in their affairs, and through which they are linked to the macro systems relevant to their lives. Depending on their unique combination, habdaptive actors can be more or less flexible or rigid, innovative or conventional, power-oriented or self-sacrificing, calculative or impulsive—but whatever the quality and direction of their behavior, it springs in good part from a readiness to respond to situations in a characteristic and repetitive fashion. Thus, both the political activist and the apathetic citizen are considered to be habdaptive actors, even though the import of their behavior may differ greatly.

Lest the word "habit" be taken to suggest behavior so physiological as to be addictive or so routinized as to be free of norms, it must be added that nothing in this formulation is conceived to be comparable to phenomena such as alcoholism or getting out of bed on the same side every morning. To be sure, microsociologists and ethnomethodologists have found that "most people most of the time operate on the basis of an assumed normalcy which is not subject to conscious reflection,"[29] and experimental psychologists have "solidly" identified some three thousand regularities in individual behavior, evidence of where "the machinery of the mind . . . shows through."[30] But such findings do not preclude occasions of deliberate reflection. On the contrary,

[28] One stream of findings in experimental social psychology indicates that the more a person has engaged in behavior previously, the less important is intention in predicting future behavior and the more important is habit. See, for example, D. Landis, H. C. Triandis, and J. Adamopoulos, "Habit and Behavioral Intentions As Predictors of Social Behavior," *Journal of Social Psychology* 106 (December 1978): 227–37. For a contrary pattern, in which the intention model is found to be as important as, or more important than, the habit model, see D. Brinberg, "An Examination of the Determinants of Intention and Behavior: A Comparison of Two Models," *Journal of Applied Social Psychology* 9 (November/December 1979): 560–75.

[29] Randall Collins, "On the Microfoundations of Macrosociology," *American Journal of Sociology* 86 (March 1981): 991.

[30] Allen Newell, quoted in David L. Wheeler, "From Years of Work in Psychology and Computer Science, Scientists Build Theories of Thinking and Learning," *Chronicle of Higher Education*, March 9, 1988, p. A4.

they indicate that the normal reliance on tacit understandings frees individuals' cognitive capacities to "concentrate instead on the . . . unpredictable and irregular."[31]

There are officials or citizens whose customary behavior involves an assessment of goals, a framing of alternatives, a systematic gathering of information, a cost-benefit analysis, and a consideration of feedback from prior decisions. Conceptually, however, they are but a subspecies of the habdaptive actor, a variant that has become habituated to using various methods of offsetting the distortions of memory, the compulsions of personality, the biases of beliefs, the constraints of role expectations, and the inhibitions of cognitive style. The behavior of even the most rational of actors, in other words, is always habit-driven to some degree.

It is important to stress that habdaptive actors are not the same as nonrational actors. By definition, both fall short of perfect rationality, but the concept of a habdaptive actor is not merely a residual category for all behavior which is other than rational. Whereas nonrationality can involve impetuous, erratic, spontaneous, and inconsistent behavior, the habdaptive-actor concept assumes specific and consistent dynamics that are far from impetuous or random. For being purposive, having preferences, and relying on a coherent set of goals as guides to behavior can also become habitual. Indeed, people may be well served by their habits. These have normally helped them in the past and can be expected to enable them to meet challenges in the future. There are good reasons to be comfortable as a habdaptive actor and, as such, to eschew capricious behavior.

While different habits drive people to engage in different forms of behavior, in each case the action is a product of antecedents that render probable a high degree of correspondence with previous actions in the same context, whether these actions tend to maintain or, in the case of dissenters and rebels, to disrupt the equilibrium of the systems in which the actions have consequences. The U.S. trade deficit offers a cogent example of how habit-driven behavior at the micro level can have significant macro consequences. Two long-standing practices on the part of American corporate executives, those of using imported parts and materials to manufacture products in the United States and of filling foreign orders from overseas factories rather than with goods from American plants, are said to be among the major reasons for the persistence of the deficit. That these practices are habitual, rather than rational, behavior is evident from the fact that the costs of using im-

[31] Collins, "On the Microfoundations of Macrosociology," p. 992.

ports and of relying on foreign factories are *higher* than would be the case for their domestic alternatives.[32]

Ordinary individuals do not always display the self-interested rationality attributed to them in public-choice models of citizenship. There is impressive evidence that, at least in the United States, a sense of fairness is no less relevant to their response to public issues than are narrow calculations as to how their interests will be served. A review of fourteen empirical studies of whether citizens judged policies by their beneficial outcomes or their fairness yielded consistent results indicating that ethical and fairness-based concerns are as much a part of the habit pools of people as are self-serving impulses toward personal gain. "In fact, when the relative magnitude of independent effects is compared, fairness often emerges as a more important political influence than outcome concerns."[33]

In like manner, several practices in Japanese culture militate against accommodation by its business community to the requirements of a globalized economy. Informal agreements in Japan, for example, can be used instead of written contracts, since they are rooted in a cultural premise that they express good will and a conviction that showing kindness in this way obligates the other party to reciprocate. As a result of this and similar habit patterns, Japan's role in tariff negotiations has become the focus of considerable controversy and has raised questions abroad about its reliability as a trading partner, provoking calls for protectionist measures. The Japanese, on the other hand, tend to view such cultural characteristics as desirable and in any event too deep-seated to change.[34]

Collectivities can also be viewed as habdaptive actors. Indeed, in a world of habit-driven individuals, collectivities and their organizations can hardly avoid conducting their affairs through habitual processes. A central purpose of organizations, in fact, is precisely to concert efforts so that outputs are consistent (i.e., habitual). To be sure, organizations also design their decision-making activities with a view to allowing for innovation and adaptation to new challenges, but like

[32] Louis Uchitelle, "2 Hard-to-Quit Habits Sustain Trade Deficit," *New York Times*, January 14, 1988, p. D1.

[33] Tom R. Tyler, Kenneth A. Rasinski, and Eugene Griffin, "Alternative Images of the Citizen: Implications for Public Policy," *American Psychologist* 41 (September 1986): 970–78; quotation is on p. 975. See also James Q. Wilson and Edward C. Banfield, "Public-Regardingness As a Value Premise in Voting Behavior," *American Political Science Review* 58 (December 1964): 876–87.

[34] Insight into this clash between cultural habits is provided by a series of ten dialogues sponsored by Fujisankei Communications Group; see, for example, "Can We Speak the Same Language?" *New York Times*, June 26, 1987, p. A11.

individuals, they never have sufficient information and must perforce rely on habitual procedures to resolve their differences over goals and over the meaning of such information as is available. In short, the macro world is dominated by habit-driven collectivities, each of which is so locked into its own history, geography, and socioeconomic conditions that it responds in recurrent ways to events abroad.[35] Indeed, every sovereignty-bound actor maintains a policy-making organization that aggregates habits and seeks to insure that its actions abroad are consistent with desired goals while also adaptive to changing circumstances.

Within policy-making organizations, the reliance on customary procedures is in constant tension with the need for adaptive innovation. Often, and perhaps especially when a collectivity's leadership is weak or divided, the established routines prevail, giving rise to a bureaucratic inertia that slows the pace of organizational learning. In the aftermath of the Iran-contra scandal, for example, the diminished stature of U.S. leaders produced a situation in which foreign policy making was said to be running by "habit, rather than by inspiration."[36] More recently, in the search for an understanding of why the Chinese regime cracked down on student protestors in 1989 and then resorted to severe repression as a form of control when it probably could have accomplished its domestic goals and reduced its global costs with less harsh measures, one Western observer found that habitual orientations were at least part of the explanation: "For 40 years, the leadership had used more or less the same method of dealing with dissent and unrest. This time around, though much had changed both in China's relationship with the rest of the world and in the attitudes of its own people, the leaders simply did not know how to handle the challenge of the student-led protests in any other but the time-tested way."[37]

Habdaptive actors, whether individuals or collectivities, do not draw on the same characteristics to respond to all situations. There may be some tendencies that are common to all responses, but for the

[35] For a cogent example of how a state is driven by habits derived from its own history, see Pike's discussion of what he calls "the first construct" in Vietnam's political culture that "posits a dark-edged, pessimistic philosphic view, a world filled with the untrustworthy, the undependable, in which betrayal is the norm," and that underlies the reactions of Vietnamese officials to the actions of communist friends and capitalist foes alike: Douglas Pike, "Vietnam and Its Neighbors: Internal Influences on External Relations" (paper prepared for the Third U.S.-ASEAN Conference, Chiangmai, Thailand, January 1984).

[36] Steven V. Roberts, "The Months of Scandal: A Bureaucracy Moves But in Fits and Starts," *New York Times*, March 9, 198/, p. B14.

[37] Richard Bernstein, "Why a Crackdown?" *New York Times*, June 27, 1989, p. A4.

most part the wellsprings of habit are at least moderately differentiated, so that habits regarded appropriate to one set of circumstances
are not relevant to others. When confronting an adversary, for example, one relies on memories, traits, precedents, scenarios, expectations,
and beliefs that differ from those on which one relies when negotiating
with an ally. To some extent, in other words, habits are derivatives of
systems, and their repeated performance in a systemic context helps to
sustain that system. Indeed, as previously indicated, it is this continuous interaction between macro systems and micro habits that lies at
the core of world politics in periods when the global system is free of
turbulence.

To stress the continuities embedded in habit pools is to pose the
problem of how the model accounts for change. If macro and micro
actors are predisposed to repeat past patterns, how can turbulence ever
set in and fundamental transformations ever take place? The answer
to this question is that in the habdaptive model individuals and collectivities are conceived to be open to new stimuli and capable of
change even though the memories, traits, expectations, scenarios, and
beliefs that guide them are deeply rooted sources of their behavior. To
be sure, some actors are more open than others for a variety of reasons,
but none is so closed as to be unresponsive to internal or external
stimuli. As stressed in chapter 6, all actors are potentially adaptive
learners.[38] Most may be normally comfortable with their habit pools,
but few, if any, are so fully content as to reject all new inputs. Every
actor has on occasion had to adapt to changing circumstances and has
thus learned there can be advantages in altering long-standing response
patterns. Hence, although all actors may be prisoners of their habits,
among these habits is likely to be at least a rudimentary readiness to
learn from experience and to acquire new skills that may, in turn, facilitate further learning. This readiness may consist of no more than a
dormant trait pervious to arousal—a discrepant memory trace, an un-
resolved past experience, an unexplored flexibility in role expectations,
an untested action script, or a cultural ambiguity. Activation of this
readiness to learn may require an unusually powerful stimulus, on the

[38] In a different formulation, a distinction is made between adaptation and learning.
The former is defined as the ability to change one's behavior so as to meet challenges in
the form of new demands without having to reevaluate one's entire program and the
reasoning on which that program depends for its legitimacy, while "learning" is reserved
for situations in which an organization is induced to question the basic beliefs underlying
the selection of ends. See Ernst B. Haas, *When Knowledge Is Power: Three Models of
Change in International Organizations* (Berkeley: University of California Press, 1989),
p. 3.

scale of a Pearl Harbor or a crisis over missiles in Cuba, or it may require repeated encounters with the same unfamiliar challenge,[39] but at some point every actor is at least minimally open to reorientation.[40]

Developments in the Soviet Union under Gorbachev offer a current example of the tensions between learning and habit in world politics. The reactions of Western officials and citizenries, both those inclined to believe that a system distrusted for so long could not in fact reverse itself as quickly as its rhetoric suggested and those persuaded that the evidence of change could not be simply dismissed, are typical cases of habdaptive dynamics. Hardly a week has passed since 1985 without a pronouncement or an action by the Soviet Union that was quite contrary to its conduct only a few years earlier. Repeated manifestations of open criticism and free expression at home and frequent policy departures abroad—from agreeing to arms-control measures previously rejected to pressing for a more effective United Nations that was once scorned—have cumulated to the point where many in the West are struggling with their habitual bases for responding to Soviet behavior. Indeed, the question of the possibility of change in the USSR has itself become an intense political issue, as some closer to the habit-driven end of the continuum interpret each pronouncement and action as merely a propaganda ploy, a deceptive effort to disguise old goals in new clothes, while those toward the learning end argue that the changes are genuine and still others begin to move in the learning direction as the evidence mounts and undermines their habits.[41]

In sum, actors must be conceived as learners and not as constants on the world scene. Their learning, and the change that follows it, can occur in one or both of two ways: (1) when external stimuli are persistently and startlingly new; (2) when new skills and orientations develop within the actor. Externally induced habit change is exemplified by the adjustments that accompany the waging and termination of an international war, a fundamentalist revolution, or a sharp and endur-

[39] Experimental psychologists have posited a "power law of performance," which stipulates that "the time it takes a person to perform a mental task has a fixed relationship to the number of times the person has practiced the task." Wheeler, "From Years of Work in Psychology and Computer Science," p. A4.

[40] David O. Sears, "Attitude Objects and Political Socialization through the Life Cycle" (paper presented at the annual meeting of the American Political Science Association, Washington, August 1984), and Steven D. Miller and David O. Sears, "Stability and Change in Social Tolerance: A Test of the Persistence Hypothesis," *American Journal of Political Science* 30 (February 1986): 214–36.

[41] For a discussion of Soviet-American relations in a learning context, see James N. Rosenau, "Learning in East-West Relations: The Superpowers As Habit-Driven Actors," *Australian Outlook* 41 (December 1987): 141–50.

ing shift in the cost of energy. Internally induced habit change is illustrated by the effects of the microelectronic revolution on people's analytic capabilities. When basic change does occur, external and internal stimuli are usually interactive and reinforcing. Together, they produce new modes of behavior, which eventually become new habits.[42]

However, the learning curve of both people and collectivities is marked by a curious paradox: other things being equal, those who can most afford to break with old habits are those least likely to do so. Actors who are strong, who are secure about themselves and have a clear sense of their own destiny, may be much less troubled by unfamiliar external stimuli than those who are weak and thus inclined to search for new ways of coping with their situations. As will be seen, this interaction between the capabilities of actors and the pace at which they learn takes on critical importance as global turbulence undermines the coherence of collectivities and fosters a greater sense of competence on the part of citizenries. For this and other reasons, there is a close connection between the habit of learning and the other habits in the pool. When learning is effective, when it "takes," that which is learned becomes the basis for the attenuation of old habits and the evolution of new ones. The ultimate outcome of learning is a new habdaptive function.

It might seem that the notion of a habdaptive function serves no analytic purpose. Unlike a utility function, which posits the actor as making choices to maximize payoffs on the basis of a deductive logic and thus allows for prediction, a habdaptive function cannot be subjected to deductive analysis; or, if it can, it is only by the loosest of logics, as variable as the habits that underlie the behavior of actors. Accordingly, it would appear, a habdaptive function cannot be used as a predictive tool; it serves only to highlight retrospectively the bases of decisions. But, as conceived here, the habdaptive function is neither so nebulous nor exclusively postdictive. Its main underpinings—such as cultural definitions, memories of past crises, predispositions toward closure, or recollections of rewards from learning in prior situations—are as readily understood and estimated as are the value priorities that

---

[42] Long ago, George Herbert Mead stressed, in *The Philosophy of the Act*, that habit formation was just as important a source of learning as problem solving. As a summation of Mead's work notes, he considered it "the express function of problem solving not only to bring acts to completion, but to form habits. These habits, represented by memories of successful acts, can then serve to guide action in the future. In short, this is how humans learn and 'accumulate knowledge.'" M. Schwalke, *The Psychological Consequences of Natural and Alienated Labor* (SUNY Press, 1980), p. 38.

underlie the calculation of utility functions. In prisoner's-dilemma situations, for example, we can as easily anticipate the choice of persons who are quick to anger and prone to distrust partners in crime, and whose vindictiveness makes them more interested in having their former partners receive a long jail sentence than in getting off lightly themselves, as we can the actions of those who act on the logic of self-interest. In effect, the vindictive prisoner is as much a problem for the rational-actor model as for the habdaptive approach; but whereas the former bypasses the problem by assuming that vindictiveness is built into the payoff structure, the latter undertakes to estimate how the presence of such nonrational factors will affect outcomes.

It might also seem that the distinction between utility and habdaptive functions is overdrawn, that the unthinking habits of a person are a form of rationality insofar as his or her wants and needs are concerned. Vindictive prisoners who make choices that serve their distrusting natures may appear to be acting in appropriate ways from a goal-attainment perspective. This reasoning is rejected here on the ground that collapsing all the ways in which people respond to situations into a goal-serving calculus is to ignore the differences among the forms and consequences of diverse behaviors. Most notably perhaps, by obfuscating the distinction between unthinking and calculative actions, such a perspective abandons hope of tracing the dynamics of change in the context of micro-macro interactions.

AUTHORITY, LEGITIMACY, AND LOYALTY

Among the orientations that link people to the systems and subsystems of which they are members, three are especially important: the authority and legitimacy of leaders and the loyalty of members. Authority is the source of official action in collectivity that sets it apart from all other behavior and endows it with a status that makes it more than arbitrary and capricious. Authority is derived from such sources as cultural traditions, constitutional documents, and religious precepts, and the way in which leaders exercise authority and followers respond to it is central to the effectiveness of any collectivity and any aggregative process. Citizens' reactions to the authorities who act on behalf of collectivities is crucial to whether or not groups remain coherent and consensuses form around a set of policies; leaders' use of authority is crucial to whether collectivities persist and move toward goals or atrophy and fail to achieve their goals. A role scenario, therefore, is bound to encompass some basic premises as to how one undertakes or relates to authoritative actions.

An individual can either accept authority as appropriate and comply with its directives or question its legitimacy and resist its directives. The party loyalist is at one extreme and the anarchist is at the other, but again, most individuals in all countries are located somewhere between the automatic compliance and defiance extremes as their readiness to accede to authority varies from time to time and perhaps from issue to issue. The older a collectivity is, the more its authority has endured the tests of time and thus the closer its members are likely to be to the compliance pole. Under normal circumstances, and for most people, compliance with the authority of whole systems is a deeply ingrained habit, a set of predispositions that is evoked without thought or calculation. On the other hand, the authority of subsystems tends to be more problematic; new subgroups have yet to instill habits of compliance, and both new and old ones are subject to the authority of the whole systems in which they are located. As will be seen in chapter 14, however, under turbulent conditions these patterns undergo considerable stress and not infrequently habits of compliance are transferred from systems to subsystems.

Ordinarily, acts of authority are clothed in some degree of claimed *legitimacy*: the contention that the policies or actions are undertaken by appropriate officials and conform to recognized principles and accepted rules. If the claim is not accepted—i.e., if legitimacy does not attach to the acts of leaders—authority is unlikely to sustain habits of compliance for long. Without legitimacy, authority can evoke compliance only by the use of brute force.

While the sentiments people hold toward the legitimacy of authoritative actions can derive from a variety of sources—ranging from unspoken traditions to explicit criteria of performance—again habitual tendencies tend to be operative. In the postindustrial era, however, these habits have lost some of their force, and, as will be seen, there are reasons to believe that a prime micro source of macro global change lies in the growing inclination to ground legitimacy sentiments in performance rather than traditional criteria.

In addition to their habits of compliance and their legitimacy sentiments, individuals also habitually prioritize their *loyalties* or feelings of attachment to the various systems and subsystems of which they are members. Under stable conditions, most people have no difficulty knowing which collectivity—the nation-state, the local community, the ethnic group, the professional society, the labor union, the church, the political party, etc.—commands their highest loyalties and where the others fit in an order of priority when two or more pull in different directions. But when turbulence upsets global parameters, when habits of compliance begin to come undone and criteria of legitimacy begin to shift, loyalties, too, become vulnerable to change. Conversely, wherever subgroupism or supranationalism begins to challenge nationalism for emotional support at the micro level, the dynamics whereby loyalties get aggregated become a major source of turbulence in world politics.

Authority orientations, legitimacy sentiments, and loyalties occupy a central place in the habit pools and action scripts by which citizens and officials participate in micro-macro interactions. Not only are citizens linked to global life through these forms of compliance habits, but their role scenarios are also likely to include presumptions about how other actors are disposed to deal with questions of authority, legitimacy, and loyalty. Officials are likely to be especially sensitive to these aspects of their role scenarios. Because officials are aware that public support and their capacity to aggregate it depends crucially on their ability to maintain the authority, legitimacy sentiments, and loyalties that their collectivities exercise or receive, they are apt to be keenly attentive to such micro phenomena.

ANALYTIC SKILLS AND CATHECTIC CAPACITIES

Despite the fact that role expectations, culture, and socioeconomic circumstances give rise to many uniformities of behavior, people vary considerably in the skills they bring to their tasks as organizational members and leaders. Roles have certain criteria for adequate performance, but beyond adequate performance lies meaningful and creative occupancy, and for this a person's skills and orientations are determining factors.

While role expectations shape attitudes and behavior, they are not directly linked to the capabilities people bring to their tasks. The expectations may tap and nourish latent skills; they may even encourage effort to improve and refine active skills; and in some cases, particularly for those recruited into leadership roles, there is likely to be a degree of correspondence between the requirements of the roles and the skills of the occupants. Yet, for many reasons, people are nonetheless variable in both their latent and their developed talents. Individuals everywhere, for example, comprehend world politics in terms of scenarios, but some are capable of cognitive complexity and can spell out scenarios through several segments, while the educational and experiential backgrounds of others limits them to cognitive simplicity and truncated scenarios.[43] Likewise, the capacity to counter habitual impulses and consider adaptive alternatives is a variable skill that, as will be seen, is particularly susceptible to enhancement in the postindustrial era.

At the emotional level, too, skills are operative. *Cathexis*, the capacity to attach emotion to issues and to care about a preferred solution, has obvious relevance to the dynamics of loyalty, the processes of subgroupism, and the viability of states as macro actors. It, too, can be viewed as a skill that varies from person to person and that can expand as the opportunities afforded by microelectronic technologies allow for growth.

The orientations, attitudes, opinions, and other mental activities of people are often thought to be the only relevant aspects of their citizen roles and to be so fully under the control of macro structures that they display no meaningful variation. It is clear, however, that the skill levels of citizens do vary and that the variations are not readily controlled by macro actors. The printing press, telephone, radio, television, and personal computer have created conditions for skill development among citizenries that governments could not totally control and that have helped make citizenries more effective in relation to the centers of authority. One need only observe the efforts of the South African, Israeli, and Chinese governments to keep the violence of their public affairs off the TV screen to realize that micro units are not viewed as constants by macro leaders. Alter the skills of citizens, the repeated lesson of history seems to be, and changes in their orientations may well follow, changes that in turn can be aggregated in such a way as to cause havoc for macro leaders who wish to maintain the status quo.

By any standard, however, the skills of people everywhere are far from fully developed. Opinion polls that reveal high levels of ethnocentrism, misinformation, apathy, and ignorance; interviews with the man and woman in the street; raucous and successful appeals by demagogs; mob actions; volatile and contradictory shifts in the fortunes of political parties; low turnouts in free elections—these are all common features of the political landscape. To many observers, such phenomena are sufficient to dismiss ordinary people as irrelevant to politics, or as so unskillful as to make any attribution of patterned behavior to them impossible. For the cynics among us, indeed, the skills of citizens are so meager, so lacking in structure and coherence, that the masses

[43] For an analysis of how people differ in their capacity to think in "sequential," "linear," and "systematic" terms, see Shawn W. Rosenberg, "The Structure of Political Thinking," *American Journal of Political Science* 32 (August 1988): 539–66.

are forever at the mercy of the manipulations of leaders. For empiricists seeking to comprehend the role of publics in politics, the prospects are hardly more encouraging. Those who focus on foreign affairs tend to follow Almond's lead and conceive of the public as a pyramidal structure, with elites at the top, below them a small stratum of "attentive" citizens who serve as an audience for debates among the elites, and the rest—the great preponderance of the citizenry—neither interested nor informed and referred to collectively as the "mass public," occupying the broad base of the pyramid.[44] Estimates of the size of the attentive public vary, but none exceed 20 percent for the United States, and estimates for other industrialized societies are not much higher. Third World countries are usually believed to have even smaller proportions—often tiny fractions—of citizens who can fairly be regarded as having moved beyond membership in the mass public.

In short, there is plenty of room for the expansion of analytic skills among citizenries. In chapter 13 it will be argued that such an expansion is presently under way, but it surely is the case that the habdaptive actor can continue to become more of a learning and less of a habit-driven individual.

Locus of Control

Another attribute of individuals that is subject to change and that affects the nature and direction of micro-macro interactions is the *locus of control*. This is a person's perception of where control over the course of events lies, an orientation that some psychologists argue is central to behavior.[45] As one has said, "We have a deep need to feel competent, to be in control of our environment; it is one of the primary motives in behavior."[46] The data suggest that "the higher a person's desire for control, the more persistently he would tackle difficult challenges,"[47] a point with considerable import in a world of increasingly skillful citizens.

If people feel remote from the centers of power and thus unable to affect public decisions, or if they feel events have overtaken the collec-

[44] Gabriel A. Almond, *The American People and Foreign Policy* (New York: Harcourt, Brace, 1950).

[45] For useful summaries of the literature on locus of control, see H. M. Lefcourt, *Advances and Innovations in Locus of Control Research* (New York: Academic Press, 1980), and J. R. Weisz and D. J. Stipek, "Competence, Contingency, and the Development of Perceived Control," *Human Development* 25 (July/August 1982): 250–81.

[46] Jerry Burger, quoted in Daniel Goleman, "Feelings of Control Viewed as Central in Mental Health," *New York Times*, October 7, 1986, p. C1.

[47] Goleman, "Feelings of Control," p. C11.

tivity's ability to manage them, their locus of control is said to be distant. In contrast, the locus is said to be close for those who believe that events are controllable and that they can contribute to the exercise of control through participation in collective processes. Normally, the locus of control is highly stable, whether close (as it tends to be in representative systems) or distant (as in authoritarian regimes). When systemic parameters are overwhelmed by turbulence, however, this orientation, like others, is unsettled. People begin to see the locus of control as becoming increasingly remote or, possibly, becoming so amorphous as to be nonexistent—i.e., to believe that no one is capable of controlling events.

Variability in the locus of control is related to the capacity of people to elaborate role scenarios, attach legitimacy, or otherwise employ their analytic and cathectic skills. There are sound bases for hypothesizing that, as people begin to believe that systems are too complex to meet their needs and wants, their conception of where control is located changes. The conviction spreads that, by reorienting their legitimacy sentiments and their loyalties toward subgroups instead of whole systems, they can narrow the gap between themselves and the centers of control. Viewed in this way, subgroupism is both an expression of disillusionment and of optimism, both a response to a feeling of lost control and an attempt to recapture a sense that control can be exercised.

A Genuine Puzzle

If, as argued in later chapters, systems and subsystems in the late twentieth century are marked by simultaneous coherence and breakdown that can in large measure be attributed to macro sources—the demands of subsystems, the ineffectiveness of governments, the emergence of international regimes and transnational issues, and the adaptation of societies—a genuine puzzle is posed.[48] How can the macro institutions be moving in two different directions at the same time—toward coherence and toward breakdown? The quickened pace of communications fostered by the microelectronic revolution is part of the answer, but it does not explain why neither coherence nor breakdown has predominated nor why they have occurred simultaneously rather than sequentially. Neither singly nor interactively do macro factors adequately account for the frequency of crises of authority, for the patterning of

[48] For an elaboration of the nature of genuine puzzles, see James N. Rosenau, "Puzzlement in Foreign Policy," *Journal of International Relations* 1 (Summer 1976): 1–10.

turbulence, for the structure of a world undergoing bifurcation. One is thus led to hypothesize that another part of the explanation lies in the changing orientations of citizens and officials fostered by the changing skills they have acquired in the postindustrial era—that dynamism at the micro level is a source of the macro patterns.

To emphasize variability at the micro level, however, is not to back away from the conception of people as prone to habitual responses, as role occupants whose scenarios and actions stem mostly from cultural and systemic expectations. From the foregoing discussion, it should be clear that the nine attributes of micro actors identified in table 9.1 are subject to variation irrespective of the uniformities produced by macro structures. Hence, without abandoning the presumption that role scenarios shape attitudes, channel personalities, and direct behavior, and without negating the premise that socialization and training shape a person's habits of compliance, legitimacy sentiments, loyalties, and locus of control, it seems imperative to explore the types of change suggested in table 9.1 and to determine whether these attributes are susceptible to alteration despite the habits people develop as occupants of historically defined and culturally shaped roles.

More specifically, in order for a bifurcated world to develop in which centralizing and decentralizing tendencies are at work simultaneously, it is reasonable to anticipate traces of the following changes in the habit pools of citizens: (1) rote habits begin to attenuate and adaptive responses become more frequent; (2) the tendency to fix on scapegoats begins to yield to more practical assessments; (3) scenarios of the future begin to project across longer time spans; (4) alternative explanations and perspectives begin to be acknowledged and considered more frequently; and (5) the inclination to treat the policies of one's government as sound begins to yield to doubt and skepticism. If empirical indicators of change along these lines can be found, surely it behooves us to accord the micro parameter a central place in a model of world politics. Chapters 12 and 13 explore the extent of these anticipated changes, but to facilitate comprehension of their significance (as well as to insure that the analysis does not slip out of an interactive context and exaggerate the causal power of micro-level phenomena), the next two chapters probe the emergent macro structures and processes of postinternational politics with a view to identifying the degree to which they may be influenced by the increasing complexity and dynamism at the micro level.

CHAPTER 10

STUDYING STRUCTURES
The Two Worlds of World Politics

By sapping the authority of the centralized state, the new technologies have shifted the locus of decisive action to the more modest concentrations of intellect and will. These smaller organizations can be defined as the transnational corporation, as the merchant city-state (Singapore, Taiwan, Hong Kong), as militant causes (the PLO or the IRA), even as individuals as intransigent as Manuel Noriega or Muammar Qaddafi, Israeli tank commanders, Colombian drug dealers, African despots, Turkish assassins, and Lebanese terrorists. . . . As yet nobody has drawn a map that reflects the new order.
—Lewis H. Lapham[1]

Modern society has no single designer nor an overall, coherent design. There are multiple sources of organizing principles, rules and policies, many of which compete with and contradict one another. The pressures for change are many and varied. Diverse rule-making groups and institutions pursue their own particular interests, visions, and modes of knowledge development. Coordination and integration among different rule-making processes, and the agents involved, tends to be weak. We refer to this condition as "structural incoherence."
—Tom R. Burns and Helena Flam[2]

TOGETHER THESE TWO OBSERVATIONS, one an empirical description and the other an abstract formulation, foreshadow the central themes of this chapter. The aim is to sketch the map of the new order called for in the first observation and to do so along the lines suggested in the second observation. For the multi-centric world, while

[1] "Notebook: Leviathan in Trouble," *Harper's*, September 1988, pp. 8–9.

[2] "Political Transactions and Regime Structuring: The Perspective of Actor-Systems Dynamics" (manuscript prepared for the Workshop on Political Exchange: Between Governance and Ideology, Florence, December 1986), p. 209.

not a society, also lacks an overall design, derives from multiple sources, and is marked by high degrees of diversity, decentralization, and dynamism that render coordination difficult.

However, the label offered for this condition is misleading. It suggests that a system lacking coherence lacks structure as well. But structural incoherence lies at one extreme on a continuum, at that end beyond which randomness prevails and structure collapses into formlessness. Inchoate as it may be, structural incoherence is a form of structure. The various collectivities encompassed by it do persist and they interact in repeated, patterned ways. If they did not, if complexity and dynamism were to overwhelm all structure, actors would have difficulty adapting, and their activities would be at such cross-purposes that they could hardly be called a society or a world.

Given that it encompasses collectivities most of which do manage to adapt, the multi-centric world can be presumed to have an underlying structure accessible to study. To explore this structure, we have thus far relied only on a series of anomalies and examples as the basis for discerning the emergence of a new global structure for the first time since the advent of the Western state system. Obviously, however, anomalies and examples can be neither proof of change nor a guide to assessing its sources and dynamics. They do serve as indicators of greater complexity and dynamism, and they provoke a search for the appearance of new structural arrangements. Still, they present no clear picture of what the foundations of a bifurcated global order might be.

To support the conception of a bifurcated world, therefore, the anomalies need to be located in a theoretical perspective that is internally consistent and empirically compelling. Such is the task of this chapter: to set forth a basis for stepping outside the state-system paradigm and framing an alternative one through which to assess the early indicators of a new, if structurally incoherent, form of world order.

An Old Paradigm

Abandoning existing assumptions is no easy matter. As noted earlier, students of world politics, like politicians, are prisoners of their paradigms, unwilling or unable to escape the premise of state predominance and constantly tempted to cling to familiar assumptions about hierarchy, authority, and sovereignty.

Those who adhere to a realist perspective are illustrative of these difficulties. Forced to acknowledge that profound socioeconomic changes have marked the latter half of the twentieth century, many realists contend that these have nonetheless taken place in an unchanging political context, that the socioeconomic transformations have not had an appreciable impact on the long-established international system in which states predominate and seek to solve their security problems through the maximization of power. While conceding that transnational processes and actors other than states have become increasingly conspicuous in world politics, they preserve their paradigm by insisting that this conspicuousness acquires meaning only in the context of an international environment controlled by states.

The work of Kenneth Waltz exemplifies this position. He argues that while states "may choose to interfere little in the affairs of nonstate actors for long periods of time," they "nevertheless set the terms of the intercourse. . . . When the crunch comes, states remake the rules by which other actors operate." As Waltz sees it, this structural predominance of states is sufficient to obviate the need for theorizing afresh: "A theory that denies the central role of states will be needed only if nonstate actors develop to the point of rivaling or surpassing the great powers, not just a few of the minor ones. They show no sign of doing that." Similarly, transnational processes are posited as "among those that go on within" the state-centric structure. Waltz contends that "the 'state-centric' phrase suggests something about the system's structure," and to question its existence by citing nonstate actors and transnational movements "merely reflects the difficulty political scientists have in keeping the distinction between structures and processes clearly and constantly in mind."[3]

A variant of this response to the conditions of the postindustrial era involves locating the new actors and transnational processes in the context of "international regimes," which are conceived to be sets of norms, principles, rules, and procedures that operate in particular issue-areas to guide the interactions among all the actors who may have interests at stake.[4] An international regime thus brings states and transnational entities into the same analytic setting, where they are seen as bargaining and conflicting with each other through nonhierarchical processes. While the regime concept offers some valuable insights into world politics,[5] it does not confront directly the possibility that the state-centric system is being bounded within a more encom-

---

[3] Kenneth N. Waltz, *Theory of International Politics* (Reading, Mass.: Addison-Wesley, 1979), pp. 94, 95.

[4] Stephen D. Krasner, ed., *International Regimes* (Ithaca, N.Y.: Cornell University Press, 1983), esp. p. 2.

[5] These insights are elaborated in James N. Rosenau, "Before Cooperation: Hegemons, Regimes, and Habit-Driven Actors in World Politics," *International Organization* 40 (Autumn 1986): 879–84.

passing universe. Rather, it merely grafts additional institutions and processes onto the state system without allowing for the possibility of its diminution. As Waltz sees it, for example, the advent of international regimes merely illustrates that the state system is flexible enough to "passively [permit] informal rules to develop," a flexibility that also enables states to intervene "to change rules that no longer suit them."[6] In effect, the regime concept updates the realist paradigm without altering its fundamental premises, producing a synthesis of long-standing assumptions and modern realities that some call "neorealism."[7]

TOWARD A NEW PARADIGM

But there are limits beyond which a theory cannot be preserved by grafting and patching. As indicated by the myriad anomalies and the evidence of change in the micro and relational parameters, which have been previously noted, there are reasons to suspect that the structural parameter is evolving in ways that neither the regime concept nor neorealism adequately explains. If it is the case that the profound socioeconomic changes of the postindustrial era necessarily have comparable consequences for world politics, and if existing paradigms are insufficient to account for these dynamics, some new organizing principles for understanding the political bases of global life are needed.

We begin with the assumption that the dynamics of postindustrialism are simultaneously fostering centralizing and decentralizing tendencies in global life, some of which cancel each other out but many of which progressively circumscribe nation-states and the international system they have sustained for several centuries. From there, we proceed on the basis of the five guidelines for an escape from the realist jail that were set forth earlier (see chapter 2). It will be recalled that these guidelines focus on authority, hierarchy, issue agenda, and systems as they relate to the identity, conduct, and interaction of the actors who produce outcomes in global politics. They depart sufficiently from long-standing presumptions to permit the delineation of parametric changes in which a new multi-centric world is discerned as challenging, rivaling, ignoring, and otherwise coexisting alongside—neither superordinate nor subordinate to—the historic state-centric world. The result is a paradigm that neither circumvents nor negates the state-centric model, but preserves it in a larger context, one that

---

[6] Waltz, *Theory of International Politics*, p. 94.

[7] See, for example, Robert O. Keohane, "Realism, Neorealism, and the Study of World Politics," in R. O. Keohane, ed., *Neorealism and Its Critics* (New York: Columbia University Press, 1986), p. 15.

posits sovereignty-bound and sovereignty-free actors as inhabitants of separate worlds that interact in such a way as to make their coexistence possible.

It might be argued that the integrity of the new paradigm has already been compromised: that a potential for backtracking is created by the proposition that the multi-centric system has come to coexist with, rather than to replace, the state-centric system, that retention of the latter represents a failure to engineer a thoroughgoing jailbreak, or a means of keeping open an escape hatch through which to beat a hasty retreat back to the neorealist paradigm in the event the multi-centric world proves too chaotic for incisive theorizing. Either states dominate world affairs or they do not, such an argument would hold, so that positing them as dominant in one world and merely active in the other is yielding to old analytic habits and avoiding a full, unqualified break with realist premises.

There is much to be said for this charge of timidity and compromise. After all, if states are still powerful, why have they not done a better job in managing world affairs? Why do world politics so often seem out of control, propelling communities and continents in directions that nobody wants? Has not the combination of dynamic technologies and global decentralization overwhelmed the state system and made it subservient to the multi-centric world? If so, is it not a distortion to continue to give conceptual importance to the state-centric world? Indeed, might it not even be the case that the state system is already well along the road to decay, so that the coexistence of the two worlds of world politics may be merely a transitional phase in global development?

All of these doubts notwithstanding, it is difficult to ignore the present capacity of states to control the instruments of coercive force and the publics needed to support their use. The range of issues on which these instruments can be used effectively has narrowed considerably in recent decades, but not yet to the point where it is reasonable to presume that states and their world are dissolving into the multi-centric environment. Instead, states must be regarded as still capable of maintaining the norms and practices of their own international system, and consequently, the interaction between the state-centric and multi-centric worlds emerges as the focus of important theoretical questions.

This two-world conception of global politics runs counter to the prevailing analytic mode, which presumes that, over time, the state-centric system either subsumes alternatives to it or fragments and collapses as the rival alternatives come to prevail. That both the system and the alternatives can co-exist is thus not viewed as a meaningful possibility:

a momentary and transitional condition, to be sure, but highly improbable as an enduring form of world order.

Hedley Bull's work is illustrative of this tendency. In a lengthy analysis, he delineates four structural arrangements—a disarmed world, a UN-dominated world of states, a world of many nuclear powers, and a world marked by ideological homogeneity—that "would be radically different from what exists now," but, he adds, they "would represent a new phase of the states system, not its replacement by something different."[8] He also considers the possibility that international politics will move beyond the state system to one of four alternative arrangements: a number of states forming a system but not an international society, a situation in which there are states but no system, a world government, or a new "mediaeval system" of nonsovereign actors. Nowhere, however, does he envision the development of another world operating alongside the existing political universe rather than superseding it. At one point in identifying the prospects for "a new mediaevalism," he seems on the verge of positing a two-world universe, when he asserts that "it is not fanciful to imagine that there might develop a modern and secular counterpart of [the mediaeval model] that embodies its central characteristic: a system of overlapping authority and multiple loyalty." Indeed, his account of this alternative comes close to the conception of the multi-centric world to be developed below:

> It is familiar that sovereign states today share the stage of world politics with "other actors" just as in mediaeval times the state had to share the stage with "other associations" (to use the mediaevalists' phrase). If modern states were to come to share their authority over their citizens, and their ability to command their loyalties, on the one hand with regional and world authorities, and on the other hand, with sub-state or sub-national authorities, *to such an extent that the concept of sovereignty ceased to be applicable*, then a neo-mediaeval form of universal political order might be said to have emerged.[9]

The italicized phrase is crucial. It takes Bull's formulation well beyond the conception of a two-world universe. He allows for the emergence of a multi-centric world, but at the same time suggests that it will culminate in the irrelevance of state sovereignty. In what follows, on the

---

[8] Hedley Bull, *The Anarchical Society: A Study of Order in World Politics* (New York: Columbia University Press, 1977), p. 238.

[9] Bull, *Anarchical Society*, pp. 254–55 (italics added).

other hand, the world of sovereignty-free actors is viewed as coexisting with that of sovereignty-bound actors, sustained by circumstances in which the state has become *"both indispensable and inadequate."*[10]

THE TWO WORLDS OF WORLD POLITICS

The main features of the two worlds are contrasted in table 10.1. Here it can be seen that the state-centric world is much more coherent and structured than is its multi-centric counterpart. It is to some degree anarchic and decentralized, because of the lack of an overarching world government,[11] but that anarchy is minimal compared to the chaos that results from the much greater decentralization that marks the multi-centric system. Not only are there many fewer points at which action originates in the state-centric than in the multi-centric system, but action and interaction in the former is also considerably more subject to formal procedures and hierarchical precepts than in the latter. In the multi-centric world, relations among actors are on more equal footing, are more temporary and ad hoc, and more suscep-tible to change, but are less symmetrical and less constrained by power differentials, formal authority, and established institutions.

Given these features of the multi-centric world, especially the un-availability and the disutility of physical coercion as means of pursuing goals, the question is raised of how the multi-centric world can remain independent in the face of the greater coherence and capabilities of its state-centric counterpart.

One response to this question is that many actors of the multi-cen-tric world are able to ignore or evade the demands of the state system. To be sure, with few exceptions the actors of the multi-centric world are located within the jurisdiction of a counterpart in the state-centric world and, accordingly, must abide by its rules. But their adherence to these rules is often formalistic. In their scenarios, they are the subjects of action and states are merely objects; they may sometimes, even fre-quently, have to work through and with the rules of states, but they do so in order to procure the resources or the other forms of support needed to attain their goals.

For the sovereignty-free actors of the multi-centric world, in other

---

[10] Karl W. Deutsch, "Learning-State and the Self-Transformation of Politics," in Mir-iam Campanella, ed., *Between Rationality and Cognition: Policy-making under Condi-tions of Uncertainty, Complexity, and Turbulence* (Torino, Italy: Albert Meynier, 1988), p. 54 (italics in the original).

[11] On the conception of anarchy in international politics, see the essays in Kenneth A. Oye, ed., *Cooperation under Anarchy* (Princeton: Princeton University Press, 1986).

TABLE 10.1. Structure and Process in the Two Worlds of World Politics

	State-centric World	Multi-centric World
Number of essential actors	Fewer than 200	Hundreds of thousands
Prime dilemma of actors	Security	Autonomy
Principal goals of actors	Preservation of territorial integrity, and physical security	Increase in world market shares, maintenance of integration of subsystems
Ultimate resort for realizing goals	Armed force	Withholding of cooperation or compliance
Normative priorities	Processes, especially those that preserve sovereignty and the rule of law	Outcomes, especially those that expand human rights, justice, and wealth
Modes of collaboration	Formal alliances whenever possible	Temporary coalitions
Scope of agenda	Limited	Unlimited
Rules governing interactions among actors	Diplomatic practices	Ad hoc, situational
Distribution of power among actors	Hierarchical by amount of power	Relative equality as far as initiating action is concerned
Interaction patterns among actors	Symmetrical	Asymmetrical
Locus of leadership	Great powers	Innovative actors with extensive resources
Institutionalization	Well established	Emergent
Susceptibility to change	Relatively low	Relatively high
Control over outcomes	Concentrated	Diffused
Bases of decisional structures	Formal authority, law	Various types of authority, effective leadership

words, states are external and not constitutive—obstacles, nuisances, or opportunities to be surmounted, tolerated, or seized—as long as security and territorial issues do not draw them into the sovereignty networks of the state-centric world. Contrary to Waltz's view, the prevailing presumption in the multi-centric world is that its actors, and not their sovereignty-bound counterparts, establish the terms of intercourse in world politics. Its actors accept that states establish legal boundaries within which they must conduct their affairs, even that states can employ considerable resources to fix political limits within which they must operate, but they do not view the exercise of state prerogatives as amounting to a "crunch" (as Waltz puts it) requiring them to set aside their own goals.

Moreover, not all the actors in the multi-centric world are caught up in the authority networks of the state-centric world. Some have managed to obfuscate, even elude, the jurisdiction of a single state. As one observer has pointed out: "In high growth areas such as financial services, increasingly large segments of international markets are outside the legal boundaries of the major trading nations. This . . . trend is disturbing because it implies increasing lack of control by national or international agencies."[12] To cite a specific case, a recently established computer-chip manufacturer called European Silicon Structures, or ES2, was deliberately formed as a company without a country, in order to attract customers throughout Europe. It is incorporated in Luxembourg; its central offices are in West Germany, its factory in southern France, its research facilities in England; and the eight members of its board come from seven different countries.[13] Such a company is illustrative of the degree to which separation between the two worlds has evolved.

The emergence of the multi-centric world has not, of course, undermined the autonomy of the state-centric world. Sovereignty-bound actors retain the capacity to set the rules by which their systems and subsystems conduct themselves. In their scenarios, they are entitled and obliged to protect the integrity and welfare of the sovereignty-free actors within their jurisdiction, a viewpoint that leads them both to rely on the threat or use of force vis-à-vis other actors in the state-centric world and to enter the multi-centric world whenever activities there impinge on their goals. For states too, therefore, the actors in the multi-

---

[12] Clarence J. Brown, "The Globalization of Information Technologies," *Washington Quarterly* 11 (Winter 1988): 96–97.

[13] For an account of the origins, procedures, and activities of this company, see Steven Greenhouse, "Chip Maker without a Country," *New York Times*, August 1, 1988, p. D1.

centric world, even those over whom they exercise sovereignty, are external and not constitutive—constraints and opportunities to be managed and developed through proof, persuasion, bargaining, and the exercise of authority whenever possible, or through coercive means if necessary.

Needless to say, neither the multi-centric nor the state-centric world is marked by as much uniformity as this formulation implies. In the multi-centric world, the actors vary widely from culture to culture and in terms of their goals, orientations, capabilities, and modes of organization. In the state-centric world, there are such obvious distinctions as those between countries with democratic institutions and those with authoritarian regimes. Without minimizing the importance of such differences, however, here the emphasis is upon the uniformities induced by the dynamics of postindustrial interdependence. Business firms, political parties, ethnic groups, and the other types of sovereignty-free actors tend to share an aspiration to maintain their autonomy with respect to each other and to any states that may jeopardize their prerogatives. Authoritarian states may control their citizens more thoroughly than do their democratic counterparts, but even they have been compelled to acknowledge the advent of a multi-centric world of diverse—and effective—sovereignty-free actors. For authoritarian states, the relevant comparison is not with nonauthoritarian actors, but with their own situations in earlier eras.

In sum, it is in the sense that both sovereignty-bound and sovereignty-free actors have come to define themselves as the subjects of world politics, while viewing the other as its objects, that global life can be said to consist of two worlds. Or, if the word "worlds" connotes a completeness and orderliness not fully substantiated by everyday observation, they can be thought of as two "domains" (as empirical theorists might say), "texts" (as critical theorists might prefer), or "projects" (as postmodernists might put it). Whatever the labels, the point is to distinguish between two separate sets of complex actors that overlap and interact even as they also maintain a high degree of independence.

It might be argued that to speak of all sovereignty-free actors as belonging to a single multi-centric world is to exaggerate its coherence, that it would be more accurate to speak of a multiplicity of worlds, each marked by its own decision rules. However, that would belittle the central tendencies at work on the global scene. It would invite a view of world politics as patternless, lacking any underlying structures. By adopting a "two-world" perspective, we are predisposed to probe for structural elements that lie outside of and coexist with those of the state-centric system.

STRUCTURAL FOUNDATIONS OF THE MULTI-CENTRIC WORLD

If the multi-centric world is not patternless, its structure ought to emerge from an application of rule 2 of the guidelines for a conceptual jailbreak set forth in chapter 2, which asserts that the importance of actors is determined by their "authority to initiate and sustain actions," rather than by their legal status, capabilities, or sovereignty. Viewed in this way, a great many whole systems—including states, international organizations, ethnic groups, political parties, opposition movements, a few labor unions, some subnational governments,[14] and many other types of collectivities—function as actors in the multi-centric world. Some of these actors may be located in, formally accountable to, and constrained by other whole systems—as is the case, for example, for the Catholic church in Poland—but nevertheless their actions can have substantial consequences abroad. Similarly, the bureaucracies of national governments, multinational corporations, professional societies, and a host of other subsystems with limited agendas have authority structures that enable them to initiate and sustain actions that reverberate across two or more countries. The term "multicentric," in other words, suggests overlapping jurisdictions and diffuse and diverse structures of control. This vast array of systems and subsystems that compete, bargain, cooperate, conflict, or otherwise seek to maintain their coherence and realize their goals can be seen as manifesting, at the very least, the patterns that have been attributed to within-system, issue, and between-system aggregations (see table 7.1 above).

Stated differently, the multi-centric world reflects the underlying tendencies toward both centralization and decentralization in postindustrial dynamics. Environmental pollution, currency crises, terrorism, and the other new issues growing out of greater interdependence impel coordination among systems even as the information revolution, global television, the proliferation of service activities, continued elaboration of the division of labor, and other features of the post-industrial era decentralize the loci of action, enhance the influence of subsystems, and enlarge the role of citizens. Depending on the autonomy and coherence of the systems and subsystems involved in an issue, the

[14] For an excellent analysis of the role of subnational governments in world affairs, see Ivo D. Duchacek, *The Territorial Dimension of Politics: Within, Among, and Across Nations* (Boulder, Colo.: Westview, 1986).

tensions between the centralizing and decentralizing dynamics are sometimes resolved in favor of the whole system, sometimes of the subsystem, though often the balance between them remains unaltered. In any event, the activation of whole systems and subsystems results in a welter of activity that is far more turbulent than is the case when states and their interactions serve as the prime analytic foci.

The complexity and dynamism of the multi-centric world are increased by the norms, pointed out in table 10.1, whereby any system or subsystem may place any issue on its agenda, initiate whatever actions seem appropriate to its interests, cope with situations on an ad hoc basis without great concern for policy consistency, make and break temporary coalitions, withhold cooperation and compliance when it seems necessary, and accord higher priority to the substance of policies than to the legal processes whereby their pursuit is undertaken. At one and the same time, therefore, the multi-centric world is both an open, raucous world, comprising demanding publics, aggressive organizations, and clamoring subgroups, and a private, often secretive, world of church leaders, arms dealers, investment bankers, and many other individuals who travel widely, bargain endlessly, and in other ways seek to work around and through the decentralized complexity that inhibits the realization of goals.

Individuals and collectivities in the multi-centric world have much freedom of action in part because the degree to which authority has been decentralized is so great that no system or cluster of systems has control over outcomes. For all practical purposes, the systems and subsystems of the multi-centric world are imbued with a sense of quasi-sovereignty, not in a legal sense but in the sense that they are independent agents relatively free to act as they please, restrained only by the counteractions of other collectivities. Dock workers or airline pilots who refuse to perform their tasks under certain circumstances, business firms that transfer arms to or conduct other business with boycotted states, ethnic groups that demand political autonomy, intelligence and national-security agencies that sink the ships of peace groups or support insurgencies without getting prior approval from "higher" authority, student groups that take to the streets to prevent the retention of old institutions (as in South Korea and China) or the initiation of new educational policies (as in France), countries that withdraw from an international organization out of displeasure with its administration, scientists who offer to monitor nuclear test-ban agreements, a winner of the Nobel Peace Prize who publicly chastises the president of the United States to his face, an eleven-year-old girl who visits with the leadership of the Soviet Union to plead for peace, a U.S. presidential candidate who seeks to establish contact with terrorists in an effort to persuade them to release hostages, an American industrialist who succeeds in having the Kremlin bring in U.S. medical experts to help deal with the aftermath of the explosion at Chernobyl—these are but a few examples of some important initiatives in the multi-centric world undertaken by other than top governmental officials.

A particularly incisive indicator of the autonomy that has accrued to actors in the multi-centric world is the readiness of U.S. companies to abandon their national identity and proclaim themselves global enterprises whose well-being is no longer dependent on the American economy. If trade once followed the flag, it is now propelled by the lure of markets irrespective of the flag that may wave over the production, purchase, and sale of goods. "The United States does not have an automatic call on our resources," an executive of a company that sells more of its products outside than inside the United States has commented, adding, "There is no mindset that puts this country first."[15] Similarly, conceding that their global strategy takes precedence over their commitment to their American employees, many U.S. executives acknowledge that their policies are putting their company at odds with widely advocated national goals, especially those pertaining to the protection of American workers and markets from foreign competition. "We need our Far Eastern customers, and we cannot alienate the Malaysians," said an executive who heads an electronics firm that produces telephone pagers in Malaysia as well as in Florida, noting that "we must treat our employees all over the world equally."[16] To be sure, such global orientations, and the autonomy they reflect, have yet to be tested in a recession, when American companies would likely be confronted by public pressure to preserve as many jobs as possible in the United States; but there is no reason to believe that they will revert to national loyalties if they can avoid economic disaster by retaining their autonomy as global enterprises. What has been described as "a decoupling of the corporation from the country"[17] is very much a consequence of the autonomy that adheres in the bifurcation of world politics.

[15] The observation is that of Cyril Siewert, chief financial officer of the Colgate-Palmolive Company, as quoted in Louis Uchitelle, "Firms Loosen U.S. Ties in Global Market Quest," *International Herald Tribune*, May 22, 1989, p. 1.

[16] The comment is that of Robert H. Galvin, chairman of Motorola, Inc., as quoted in Uchitelle, "Firms Loosen U.S. Ties," p. 11.

[17] Gus Tyler, an official of the International Ladies Garment Workers Union, as quoted in Uchitelle, "Firms Loosen U.S. Ties," p. 11.

If decentralization provides sovereignty-free actors with the freedom to pursue their goals, the peripherality of armed force in their world has enabled them to do so with relative abandon. Besides the reasons already mentioned for the declining utility of force in relations among states (see chapter 8), several additional factors can be noted as to why coercive techniques are perhaps even less useful in the multi-centric world. An obvious one is that most sovereignty-free actors do not possess the instruments of coercion and have little need to acquire them. They have no territory to protect, for the boundaries that differentiate them from their environments are abstract, dependent on economic practices or the bonds of social cohesion rather than on land, and thus normally their goals are not of the kind that can be advanced by threats of force. Second, while the norms of the multi-centric system are still evolving, a preponderance of its members seem willing not to challenge the exclusive right of states to use armed force. Third, the complexities of the multi-centric system and the limited scope of authority that is accorded to its actors are such as to render the use of coercion against them problematic, if not utterly fruitless. If there is any single lesson that the United States learned in Vietnam and the Soviet Union learned in Afghanistan, surely it is that conventional military operations do not have the expected outcomes when directed at unconventional and de-centralized opponents. A poignant symbol of the futility of coercive weapons in the multi-centric world was the picture of large U.S. naval warships firing hundreds of shells into the hills around Beirut in 1982 in the vain hope of striking an invisible adversary.

These reasons for expecting that relations in the multi-centric world will not rely heavily upon coercive techniques of control are not self-evident. One can easily cite counterarguments: Global arms sales are booming precisely because ethnic groups and other sovereignty-free actors perceive ways in which they can advance or protect their interests with weapons; many such actors, even if not a plurality of them, reject the norms against the use of coercive techniques; Beirut does not demonstrate the futility of armed force so much as it reveals the limits on superpowers' attempts to control a radicalized environment through traditional military means. Thus, perhaps it is a mistake to treat the readiness to resort to violence as a dichotomous variable in which sovereignty-bound actors have a high predisposition in that direction and their sovereignty-free counterparts a low predisposition. Indeed, the case of Beirut, and of Lebanon as a whole, may indicate the extent to which members of the multi-centric world have become increasingly competent in their ability to utilize coercive techniques even in the face of opposition from the sovereignty-bound world.[18]

Furthermore, it was hardly more than a century ago when pirates and mercenaries engaged in violent combat and defied the claim of states to exclusive use of the instruments of coercion.[19] If states acquired this right during a long period of centralizing authority, a reverse process may now be at work as decentralization attains momentum. The capacity and will to employ coercive techniques may well have spread through the multi-centric world in much the same fashion as other features of societal life that were once the exclusive prerogative of actors in the sovereignty-bound world.

However, this line of reasoning mistakes historic patterns for the central tendencies at work in the multi-centric world. To be sure, it is misleading to see the use of force as a dichotomous matter, and certainly it is the case that some examples allow for contradictory interpretations. Doubtless, too, the norms against the use of force have evolved unevenly and are still rejected by many sovereignty-free actors. Nevertheless, when the extraordinary density and complexity of the multi-centric world are taken into account, the central tendencies appear clear: most sovereignty-free actors do not resort to force, and a preponderance of them have abandoned any prospect of realizing their goals through military action.

On balance, it appears that the likelihood of achieving control and realizing policies are, at best, so problematic in the decentralized world of multitudinous sovereignty-free actors that the incentives to use force are minimized. Terrorists may capture the headlines, but their organizations do not play more than a peripheral role in the multi-centric world. Movement toward their long-run goals has been inconspicuous. Governments very rarely accede to their demands, and the complexity of the multi-centric world is such that their impact on mass opinion and societal institutions has also been imperceptible.[20]

This is not to say that there are no restraints, or that capabilities are

[18] I am indebted to David Andrews (personal correspondence) for the reasoning underlying these counterarguments.

[19] Janice E. Thomson and Stephen D. Krasner, "Global Transactions and the Consolidation of Sovereignty," in E. O. Czempiel and J. N. Rosenau, eds., *Global Changes and Theoretical Challenges: Approaches to World Politics for the 1990s* (Lexington, Mass.: Lexington Books, 1989), pp. 195–220.

[20] Again it is possible to cite contrary examples. The terrorist organization known as the Shining Path in Peru is one; it directs its efforts against both the facilities and personnel of multinational corporations and the institutions of the Peruvian state, and its impact has been considerable.

irrelevant, in the multi-centric world. Obviously, the more resources that systems and subsystems possess, and the greater their coherence and the commitment and shared sense of identity among their members, the more likely they are to prevail in conflicts with other systems or subsystems. The capabilities that underlie success in inter- and intra-system bargaining will of course vary with the circumstances, with whole systems requiring greater and more diverse capabilities than any of their subsystems. Nevertheless, whatever may be the relative resources of collectivities in a situation, each is restrained by the capacities of the others either to take counteractions or to withhold their compliance. All the actors of the multi-centric world enjoy the freedom to undertake new initiatives, but this freedom is no guarantee that their policy goals can be realized. The obstacles to success under conditions of high complexity are considerable, no matter how extensive may be the advantages of any actor.

Given the permissiveness and flexibility of life in the multi-centric world, can it be said to have any structures and processes at all? Does not its very decentralization prevent their evolution? Is not its apparent disarray its permanent condition? The answers to these questions are founded on the answer to another: What motivates the actors in the multi-centric world?

A generalized answer is possible here: despite the diversity in their cultures, aspirations, sizes, resources, functions, and memberships, all systems and subsystems are driven by the same purposes: to maintain internal integration while simultaneously obtaining needed resources or support from other systems and subsystems. Much as the coherence of realist theories derives from the premise that all states are power-maximizers confronted by a relentless security dilemma, so does the conception of politics in a multi-centric world acquire unity through the presumption that all the actors in it are adaptive collectivities faced with a never-ending autonomy dilemma. This dilemma is universal and enduring, because all systems are continuously subjected to internal frictions and external challenges that can lessen their coherence and effectiveness, possibly leading to the defection of their parts and the undermining of their integrity.[21]

At least four basic modes of adaptation are available to a system for achieving a stable balance between itself and its environment.[22]

---

[21] For a discussion of the premise that social systems are always on the verge of collapsing into their environments, see Rosenau, "Before Cooperation," pp. 884–91.

[22] The four modes derive from the presumptions that the system or subsystem makes about its relationship to its environment. It can seek to adjust its present self to its present environment (*acquiescent adaptation*); it can try to shape its present environment to

Whichever one is chosen, the commonality of the autonomy dilemma provides a theoretical potential that is much richer than is the case with the realist premise of a security problem addressed through power maximization. To know that states seek to maximize their power is to have no clue as to how they might proceed, whereas to recognize that systems need to maintain some type of external-internal balance stimulates thought about where, when, and how they are likely to approach their problems.

It must be stressed that autonomy is the central problem even for those systems or subsystems embedded in more encompassing systems to which they are legally, historically, and culturally bound. "Autonomy" means more than mere survival. It refers, rather, to those conditions under which a system is able to shoulder responsibilities, to perform assigned tasks, and to strive for whatever goals may be inherent in its raison d'être. The autonomy dilemma of a bureaucratic subsystem is no less intense than that which challenges the national system of which it is a part and to which it owes its existence. Like their governments, bureaucratic agencies experience internal rivalries that can interfere with their performance and external threats to their continued well-being. Indeed, it could be argued that precisely because subsystems are responsible to higher authorities, their autonomy problems are more delicate and, in times of budgetary constraints and policy crises, more acute. The fact that a subsystem must conform to requirements imposed by the system of which it is a part means that it must be especially sensitive not to overstep the boundaries that distinguish it from its environment—as Solidarity discovered when the Polish government incarcerated its leaders and imposed martial law in 1981.

The autonomy dilemma is further complicated by the fact that a system's or subsystem's members also occupy roles in other systems or subsystems and that these roles may require commitments from them that detract from their support. Indeed, one way to conceive of divisiveness within a collectivity is to see it as a reflection of multiple-system memberships in which some members have put their memberships in other subsystems ahead of the one in question. The fact of multiple memberships, however, does not diminish the value attached to auton-

---

its present self (*intransigent adaptation*); it can attempt to create a new equilibrium between its present self and its present environment (*promotive adaptation*); or it can accept the existing equilibrium between its present self and its present environment (*preservative adaptation*). For a full discussion of the adaptation model and of how these modes operate in the state-centric world, see James N. Rosenau, *The Study of Political Adaptation* (London: Frances Pinter, 1981). For their operation in the multi-centric world, see table 10.2 below.

omy as a systemic goal. While the support accorded leaders to act on behalf of a collectivity's autonomy can fluctuate widely, the goal remains as long as the collectivity manages to adapt and persist. To be sure, if too many individuals withhold their support from a collectivity in favor of one of its subsystems, the coherence of the collectivity will be weakened and its autonomy dilemma will become that much more acute.

STRUCTURAL DIMENSIONS OF THE MULTI-CENTRIC WORLD

The proposition that collective actors in the multi-centric world are driven by the adaptive requirements of the autonomy dilemma is only the beginning of ascertaining their structures and processes. The next step is to assess the structures of that world apart from those that sustain the state-centric world. To use the structures of the state-centric world as the basis for delineating the structures of the multi-centric world would be to treat the latter as subordinate to the former, a serious error in view of the emergence of the bifurcated global system.

To establish a baseline for identifying the structural arrangements of the multi-centric world, it is useful to superimpose a micro-macro perspective on the notion of structure that Waltz developed for the international system. In Waltz's view, a system's structure is "defined by the arrangement of its parts," and this arrangement is seen as consisting of three dimensions: "first ... the principle according to which [the parts] are organized or ordered, second ... the differentiation of units and the specification of their functions, and third ... the distribution of capabilities across units."[23] To locate these three dimensions in a micro-macro context requires the derivation of the micro foundations of each one from the habits and practices through which people participate in patterns of interaction and then the determination of the ways in which these patterns are incorporated into macro structures by virtue of being recorded in constitutions, legislative acts, court decisions, treaties, and other formal pronouncements.

Given the decentralized and relatively recent origins of the multi-centric world, however, these macro structures are sparse. There are few written principles on which actors in this world base their conduct. Hence, in tracing the organization, differentiation, and capabilities of the parts that make up the multi-centric world, the observer has to rely mainly on inferring its structures from the recurrent patterns of inter-

[23] Waltz, *Theory of International Politics*, pp. 80, 88.

action among sovereignty-free actors. Such is the procedure used in the discussion that follows.

In the multi-centric world, the main principle of the first structural dimension specified by Waltz—how the parts are ordered—is a mutual acceptance of the legitimacy of sovereignty-free actors. Thus equality comes to mark the structure of this world in the sense that its actors perceive each other as engaged in legitimate pursuits when they strive to procure external resources, preserve internal integration, and thus maintain their autonomy. With sensitivity to and comprehension of the complexity of the postindustrial era ever greater at the micro level (see chapter 13), the leaders and members of the collectivities of the multi-centric world share an appreciation that others are faced with the same problems that preoccupy them. So the structural arrangement that accords all of them the right to exist and initiate self-serving policies enjoys a wide acceptance. An extreme instance of this acceptance can be discerned in the absence of a universal condemnation of terrorist organizations. Such organizations are denounced and declared illegitimate by numerous actors in both the multi- and the state-centric worlds, but there are parts of the former where their activities are tolerated as an expression of legitimate grievances and aspirations.

The implicit legitimacy and equality of actors in the multi-centric world are the functional equivalent of sovereignty in the state-centric world. The equality is not backed by law, and the legal standing of any system or subsystem may be limited to the states in which it conducts its affairs. Nevertheless, systemic equality has an unchallengeable political standing in the sense that the multi-centric world is widely recognized to be so arranged.

The principle of mutual acceptance is not necessarily accompanied by a mutual sense of trust, cordiality, and approval. Actors in the multi-centric world may not be inclined to wish their competitors well; doubtless, many would prefer that their opposition fail in the effort to maintain autonomy. Indeed, as local and national economies have become increasingly globalized, as new market forces have increased the vulnerability of producers and challenged their ingenuity, the pressure for more information, the introduction of new product strategies, and the trimming of organizational hierarchies at the expense of local subsidiaries have steadily intensified competition in the economic sectors of the multi-centric world, compelling corporate executives to see themselves as embarked on "a steep learning curve."[24] Even as they

[24] An awareness of the need for acquiring new understandings of the changing world economy was one of the major findings of an inquiry based on interviews with the chief

compete fiercely, however, those involved are not challenging the organizing principles of the multi-centric world but acknowledging that its structure serves to protect their own equality and enhance their chances for survival.

In some instances, the diffuseness of structure resulting from the equality principle leads to self-regulation within particular industries, professions, or classes. The mechanisms for accomplishing this end have been called "private interest governments" in the domestic context and "regimes" in the international context.[25] In other cases, attempts to construct such mechanisms founder, and the result is contradictory responses to the same external challenges. OPEC, the Organization of Petroleum Exporting Countries, offers a clear-cut example of failed efforts at self-regulation in the multi-centric world.[26] So do the attitudes of seven U.S. chemical producers of chlorofluorocarbons toward an international agreement to cut their production when the ozone hole was found to be a global threat in 1987: the du Pont and Pennwalt companies decided they would eventually end the production of ozone-destroying compounds altogether, the Great Lakes Chemical Corporation announced that it saw no reason to go beyond the international agreement, and the other four companies adopted various intermediate positions.[27]

Whatever may be the degree of ferocity of the competition for markets and autonomy in the multi-centric world, it hardly resembles the mutual suspicion, fear, and mistrust that is so common in the state-centric world. The fact that the stockpiling of weapons and the resort to armed coercion and conquest is neither physically nor normatively available as a technique of control for most actors in the multi-centric world means that suspicion, fear, and mistrust are much less virulent

---

executive officers of sixty large corporations in North America, Western Europe, and Asia. A summary of the findings is in Grady Means, "Globalization of World Markets: The CEO Response," *Washington Quarterly* 11 (Winter 1988): pp. 151–57. For a more extensive discussion of the strategic problems that business firms must face in coping with the globalization of the world economy, see Kenichi Ohmae, *Triad Power: The Coming Shape of Global Competition* (New York: Free Press, 1985).

[25] See, for example, Wolfgang Streeck and Philippe C. Schmitter, eds., *Private Interest Government: Beyond Market and State* (Beverly Hills, Calif.: Sage, 1985); Krasner, *International Regimes*.

[26] Theodore H. Moran, "Managing an Oligopoly of Would-Be Sovereigns: The Dynamics of Joint Control and Self-Control in the International Oil Industry Past, Present, and Future," *International Organization* 41 (Autumn 1987): 575–607, and Bahgat Korany and Selma Akbik, "Decision-Making in a Nonstate Actor: OPEC," in Baghat Korany, ed., *How Foreign Policy Decisions Are Made in the Third World* (Boulder, Colo.: Westview, 1986), pp. 138–65.

[27] "Plans Vary on Ozone," *New York Times*, April 11, 1988, p. 30.

and also are less relevant to the way in which its systems and subsystems relate to each other. Aside from terrorist organizations, actors in the multi-centric world behave in accordance with a norm whereby collective resistance is to be undertaken through noncooperation and noncompliance rather than through a resort to weaponry.

The mutual acceptance that marks the multi-centric world does not protect its actors from collapse and demise. Some systems and subsystems do not resolve their autonomy dilemmas. Leaders can make fatal judgments; subsystems can have irreconcilable differences that lead to a system's dissolution; external difficulties can overwhelm a system's adaptive capacities. Indeed, for a variety of reasons, the fatality rate of actors in the multi-centric world is much greater than in the state-centric world.[28] Most states manage to make it through crises, but the probabilities that sovereignty-free systems will do so are considerably less, because virtually all of them lack the authority to raise necessary revenues and the capability to use instruments of force in times of crisis. Some business firms fall into bankruptcy, some unions do not recover from failed strikes, some bureaucratic agencies cannot ward off reductions in force during administrative reorganizations, some human rights groups fail to overcome government opposition, some political parties lose their electoral viability, and so on. Whatever the failure rate, however, it does not contravene the principle of the multi-centric world that all its actors have the right to undertake policy initiatives.

It should be emphasized that the nonhierarchical ordering of the multi-centric world is more facilitative than constraining. The complexity that underlies the proliferation of its actors and the disutility of coercive instruments reduces the sense of immediate threat and highlights the possibility of realizing and preserving modest gains. As viewed by the actors in this world, the environment may seem confining, in the sense that their initiatives may not always be productive, but at the same time they can be confident that the implementation of their policies will not be prevented. Occasionally, moreover, the interdependence of the multi-centric world even facilitates initiatives that avert crises and prevent the demise of a collectivity. For example, when Polish authorities announced that they planned to close the Lenin shipyard in Gdansk, a large enterprise and the birthplace of Solidarity, a search for financial assistance by Solidarity's leader, Lech Walesa, led to a Polish-born American heiress in Princeton, New Jersey, who

[28] Waltz, *Theory of International Politics*, p. 95.

agreed to pump $100 million into a newly created company that would renovate and operate the shipyard.[29]

Of course, the absence of hierarchy in the multi-centric world gives an appearance of considerable disarray. If anarchy implies a disorder resulting from the absence of a higher-level government, the anarchical conditions of the state-centric world of fewer than two hundred essential actors amount to a model of orderliness when compared to what is evident in the multi-centric world of hundreds of thousands of actors with the authority to undertake initiatives and make demands. But the appearance is deceiving: underlying the disarray are discernible patterns, in which the very equality principle that makes the multi-centric world seem so disorderly also lends structure to the interactions among its actors.

The second structural dimension identified by Waltz involves the ways in which the units of a system are differentiated and their functions specified. Assessing the habits and practices that make up this dimension in the state-centric world is simple compared to performing the same task for the multi-centric world. All the units of the former have the same functions, whereas the functions of the latter's units vary as widely as the interests of people. Systems and subsystems with authority structures that authorize, or at least do not prevent, activities with consequences that extend across the boundaries of countries can be found in every walk of life, but the nature and form of both their authority structures and their activities are far from uniform. Corporations have centralized and nonparticipatory authority structures whose functions are to generate and distribute goods and services and to increase their market share. Ethnic associations allow for some form of membership participation in decisions intended to advance their interests and protect their rights, serving thereby the function of coalescing the shared feelings of people with a common heritage. Government bureaucracies have flexible authority structures that try to enhance life in particular areas and thereby serve a variety of functions associated with the provision and preservation of the public goods in their domain. Professional organizations have diffuse authority structures designed to facilitate communications among their members and serve the function of advancing or applying knowledge in a specialized area. Trade unions tend to have authority structures organized along national lines, though these serve their members decreasingly well as the business firms that employ them are increasingly organized on a trans-

[29] John Tagliabue, "U.S. Angel with $100 Million Comes to the Aid of Walesa," *New York Times*, June 11, 1989, sec. 1, p. 6.

national basis.[30] Depending on a variety of circumstances, the authority structures of political parties vary from hierarchical to amorphous, as they seek to mobilize support on behalf of the value systems they espouse.[31] Opposition movements tend to have loose and fragmented authority structures and serve the function of providing alternative programs and checking those in power. In the same way, churches, universities, and other collectivities have their own mechanisms for allocating authority.

How, then, can one generalize across this diversity and depict the structural differentiation and functionality of the collectivities that constitute the multi-centric world? The answer lies in the requirements that actors must meet if they are to adapt successfully to their environments. Despite their diversity, and whatever their mode of adaptation, the collectivities of the multi-centric world have in common the necessity of maintaining mechanisms that procure external resources, resolve internal conflicts, frame policies, and otherwise attend to the needs and wants of their members or clientele. The maintenance of these mechanisms gives rise to typical orientations and decision rules, which can be conceived of in terms of four sets, each one corresponding to the basic mode of adaptation employed by the collectivity to maintain its coherence and move toward its goals (see table 10.2).[32]

That actors in the multi-centric world can be viewed as adaptive entities again raises the question of rationality. Adaptation suggests a

[30] Howard M. Katchen, "Transnational Labor Relations," *Jerusalem Journal of International Relations* 7, no. 3 (1985): 109–34.

[31] See Ralph M. Goldman, ed., *Transnational Parties: Organizing the World's Precincts* (Lanham, Md.: University Press of America, 1983).

[32] For applications of the adaptation framework to more specific types of systems, see James N. Rosenau, "The Adaptation of Small States," in B. A. Ince et al., eds., *Issues in Caribbean International Relations* (Lanham, Md.: University Press of America, 1983), pp. 3–28; id., "National (and Factional) Adaptation in Central America," in R. E. Feinberg, ed., *Central America: International Dimensions of the Crisis* (New York: Holms and Meier, 1982), pp. 239–69; id., "Beyond Imagery: The Long-Run Adaptation of Two Chinas" (Institute for Transnational Studies, University of Southern California, 1985); id., "The State in an Era of Cascading Politics: Wavering Concept, Widening Competence, Withering Colossus, or Weathering Change," *Comparative Political Studies* 21 (April 1988): 13–44; and id., "Toward a Single-Country Theory: The U.S.S.R. As an Adaptive System," in R. Kolkowitz, ed., *The Roots of Soviet Power* (in press). For an extensive application of the adaptation model to acquiescent systems, see Hans Mouritzen, *Finlandization: Towards a General Theory of Adaptive Politics* (Aldershot, Eng.: Gower, 1988). For the argument of one observer who is doubtful about the ability of the adaptation model to "help significantly in understanding" how internal and external demands get synthesized, see Alexander Dallin, "The Domestic Sources of Soviet Foreign Policy," in S. Bialer, ed., *The Domestic Context of Soviet Foreign Policy* (Boulder, Colo.: Westview, 1981), p. 388.

TABLE 10.2. Orientations of Actors in the Multi-centric World, by Mode of Adaptation

	Mode of Adaptation			
	Acquiescent	*Intransigent*	*Promotive*	*Preservative*
Defining characteristics	Sensitivity to external demands, high; to internal demands, low	Sensitivity to external demands, low; to internal demands, high	Sensitivity to both external and internal demands, low	Sensitivity to both external and internal demands, high
Typical actors	Weak states contiguous to superpowers; refugee groups	Ethnic groups; fundamentalist religious groups; labor unions; pariah states	Peace groups; superpowers; ideological political parties; multinational corporations; professional societies; terrorist organizations	Bureaucratic agencies; international organizations; subnational governments; pragmatic political parties; most states
Scope of external concerns	Narrow	Selective	Global	Variable
Adoption of new policies toward other actors	Nonexistent	Periodic	Frequent	Infrequent
Formation of coalitions with other actors	Unchanging	Minimal	Maximal	Variable
Dominant images of change	Short-run, external	Long-run, external	Long-run, external and internal	Short-run, external and internal

	Suppression	Intolerance	Deprecation	Tolerance
Posture toward divisiveness among subsystems	Suppression	Intolerance	Deprecation	Tolerance
Posture toward norms and institutions of state-centric world	Subservience	Obstinacy	Manipulativeness	Accommodation
Dominant leadership attitudes toward multicentric world	Pragmatic; accepting of complexity	Ideological; adamant; denial of complexity	Normative; complexity seen as manageable	Conciliatory; businesslike; complexity affirmed
Posture toward other actors with superior capabilities	Deference	Defiance	Resistance	Accommodation
Posture toward other actors with inferior capabilities	Wariness	Aggressiveness	Insistence	Accommodation
Posture toward external challenges	Avoidance	Confrontation	Opportunism	Flexibility
Posture toward formal agreements with other actors	Accepting	Ambivalent	Hesitant	Favorable
Priority for allocation of resources	External demands	Internal demands	Frequently altered between external and internal demands	Equal for external and internal demands
Efforts to develop new external markets and allies	Virtually nil	Limited	Extensive	On basis of quid pro quo

TABLE 10.2 (cont.)

	Mode of Adaptation			
	Acquiescent	Intransigent	Promotive	Preservative
Readiness to sustain cascades[a] involving environmental disturbances	Only if directly affected	Only if directly affected	Extensive	Variable
trade and currency	Only if directly affected	Only if directly affected	Extensive for whole systems and relevant subsystems	Extensive but cautious participation by whole systems and relevant subsystems
Dominant attitude toward cascades involving terrorist activities	Avoid involvement	Uphold norms justifying retaliation	Depends on the identity of the terrorists	Join efforts to prevent terrorism
Preferred form of participation in cascades	Abide by formal rules	Retain freedom of action; maintain low profile	Retain freedom of action; act authoritatively	Abide by formal rules where possible; bargain

[a] For discussion of cascades, see chapter 11.

capacity for learning and an ability to overcome habit when circumstances change. Are collectivities in the multi-centric world located toward the rationality end of the learning continuum? Some, particularly the more hierarchically organized ones such as business firms, do come close to exhibiting the behavior depicted by rational choice models. On the other hand, those with diffuse authority structures and intensely held grievances about the degree of their autonomy, such as ethnic groups or opposition movements, may be more prone to yield to the dictates of passion and habit than to those of calculation and reason. Thus, as is the case at the micro level, the macro actors who populate the multi-centric world are best conceived of as being ranged along the entire length of the continuum.

The fact that different actors have different adaptive orientations adds, of course, to the complexity and dynamism of the multi-centric world. With some collectivities committed to resolving their autonomy problem through acquiescent adaptation, while others seek resolution through intransigent, promotive, or preservative adaptation, the multi-centric world is pervaded by discontinuities, contradictions, and intense competitions. When viewed as attempts to balance external challenges off against internal demands, however, the variety of activities undertaken by such a diverse array of actors can be seen as occurring in a patterned and structured context.

Turning to the third dimension of structure, it might be wondered how, in the absence of hierarchy, the distribution of capabilities among the units of the multi-centric world can serve as a structural foundation. In such a decentralized system of actors with very different kinds of capabilities, there can be no hegemons nor functional equivalents of great powers, middle powers, or any other capability-assessed actors. How, then, can the distribution of capabilities within this world be seen as structured? The answer is, at once, obvious and complex. It is obvious in the sense that within specific spheres of activity, such as the production and distribution of computers, or particular issue areas, such as arms control, habits and practices have evolved that accord influence to actors in terms of their reputations and resources. There are giant firms and small companies, high-powered scientific establishments and limited research organizations, multi-purpose ethnic groups and narrow cultural associations, and such differences do make for a degree of structure.

The answer is complex in the sense that the spheres of activity and issue-areas encompassed by the global agenda are innumerable, thus making it extremely difficult to develop a full picture of how the capabilities of the actors in the multi-centric world underlie its structure.

While the structure of the state-centric system can be efficiently portrayed in terms of superpowers, regional alliances, medium-sized states, and so on, a succinct structural account of the multi-centric world is virtually impossible. At best, structures can be described only within spheres of particular interest. If one is concerned about the computer industry, for example, particular Japanese firms, IBM and other U.S. corporations, some university research centers, and some governmental agencies, together with the "crazy quilt of alliances between American and Japanese companies,"[33] are central to the capability-based aspects of its structure. Similarly, the habits and practices of foreign offices, military advisers, scientific and technological experts, leaders of the peace movement, and a limited group of other actors can be identified as the basis of structural arrangements in the arms-control field.

The distinction between whole systems and subsystems is another structural characteristic of the multi-centric world that derives from the distribution of capabilities within it. Politics in this world is dominated by whole systems, except to the extent that the highly specialized aspects of issues tap the expertise and evoke the concerns of those subsystems whose distinctiveness is based on such matters. Whole systems, including not only states but also private collectivities with broad and open agendas, have substantially greater capabilities because they embrace a large number of specialized subsystems (which is why they have broad agendas), thus enabling them to call upon both more people and more diverse skills on behalf of their adaptive purposes and strategies. On the other hand, subsystems have the advantage of greater internal cohesion than is the case for most whole systems. Founded on a narrower range of interests and bases for membership, the unity of subsystems is not as vulnerable to divisiveness as are whole systems. At the same time, the capabilities of subsystems may lead to repercussions that are as extensive as those caused by whole systems. Where a subsystem's expertise is central to the resolution of an issue, for example, the course of events may well be crucially shaped by its activities. The role of the International Airline Pilots Association in terrorist hijackings is illustrative: it said that its members would not land on the airfields of countries that accommodated terrorists.[34]

---

[33] David E. Sanger, "For American Technology, It's a Job Just to Keep within Sight of the Japanese," *New York Times*, January 29, 1989, p. E3.

[34] Kenneth Freed, "Punishing of Nations Lax in Air Security Urged," *Los Angeles Times*, June 28, 1985, sec. 1, p. 13. Although not formally organized, an epistemic community—defined by Haas as "a group of professionals (usually recruited from several disciplines) who share a commitment to a common causal model and a common set of

Yet the collectivities of the multi-centric world cannot take their unity for granted. As systems composed of subsystems, they, too, are susceptible to internal redirection and reaggregation. In effect, they are coalitions, and as such they are always subject to stresses and strains that weaken the bases of their cohesion.

This structural arrangement is in sharp contrast to that which prevails in the state-centric world. States may be plagued by separatist movements and other kinds of oppositions, but legally—and in realist theory—they are conceived to be unitary actors whose internal composition and coherence are not relevant to the overall structure of the state-centric world.[35] The variability in the coherence of actors in the multi-centric world imparts a degree of volatility to its structure that is not to be found in the world of states.

OVERLAP BETWEEN THE TWO WORLDS

Thus far, the analysis has proceeded as if the two worlds of global politics exist apart from each other, that each conducts its affairs without intrusion from the other. Having achieved the conceptual freedom to see beyond the state-centric world to one in which other types of actors may be just as important as states, the premise of mutual isolation now needs to be relaxed. Clearly, it is an empirically false premise. The two worlds do have their own structures and processes, derived from different sources, but obviously they are not self-contained. The interdependence of postinternational politics does not permit isolation for any system, but especially not for those that engage in transnational activities. What transpires in the state-centric world can have significant consequences for the multi-centric world, and vice versa. Put more strongly, since whole systems and subsystems can be actors in both worlds—with states being drawn ever further into the multi-centric world by an intensified interest in expanding their share of world markets and with other actors being drawn into the state-centric world by virtue of their physical presence on the territories of states—

---

political values"—is another example of a collective actor whose expertise serves as the basis for developments in particular issue areas: Ernst B. Haas, *When Knowledge Is Power: Three Models of Change in International Organizations* (Berkeley: University of California Press, 1989), p. 41. For an elaborate analysis of how the expertise of one epistemic community contributed to a transnational coalition that managed to achieve the compliance of national governments, see Peter M. Haas, "Do Regimes Matter? Epistemic Communities and Mediterranean Pollution Control," *International Organization* 43 (Summer 1989): 377–403.

[35] Cf. Waltz, *Theory of International Politics*, pp. 95–97.

the overlap between the two worlds is inherent in the structure of the global system.

To be sure, events in the state-centric world may occasionally unfold through state-to-state interaction with little involvement on the part of the multi-centric world. Foreign ministers confer, chiefs of state visit each other, and allies consult and coordinate. But few situations today are marked by conditions that accord states the freedom of action posited by the realist paradigm. Normally, in one way or another they must accommodate to the complexities of the multi-centric world.

Likewise, the daily life of the multi-centric world does include interaction among sovereignty-free actors that takes place independently of the state-centric world. Exporters trade with importers, professional societies provide expertise to clients abroad, and universities have overseas programs for their students. But neither are the actors in this world normally so free that they can proceed without concern for what may be transpiring in the other world. If nothing else, a preponderance of them have their headquarters within the jurisdictions of states and therefore have to conduct their affairs in conjunction with, if not in accommodation to, the activities of states. Knowing that the consequences can be costly to those who misperceive the boundaries between the two worlds, most sovereignty-free actors have learned to locate themselves appropriately in one or the other worlds and to comply with its rules. They know where the opportunities for initiative lie and where states can impose obstacles. Equally important, as indicated in table 10.2 and elaborated by many of the examples set forth below, they have developed adaptive strategies that enable them to move both between as well as within the two worlds.

To understand how it is possible for the two worlds to persist on a separate and relatively equal basis, despite the military capabilities and formal sovereignty possessed by the actors of the state-centric world, it is helpful to reiterate the extent to which formal authority is limited. For authority to be operative under any circumstances, both those who wield it and those toward whom it is directed must accept its scope and legitimacy. If the subjects of authority give it no credence or simply ignore the directives issued by authorities, and if the latter understand that resort to coercion in order to enforce their authority is bound to be counterproductive, then plainly relations between the subjects and the wielders of authority must be founded on a convention by which each accepts the legitimacy of the other.

Both sovereignty-bound and sovereignty-free actors know that the complexities of postinternational politics are more than states can manage, even as both also accept the fact that history's legacy is a state system with deep roots and durable institutions. Hence, a mutual acceptance has developed between them, and, with it, institutions and procedures for conducting the interactions through which the acceptance is continuously reinforced. One observer, using relations between a superpower and multinational corporations as an example, suggests that this mutual acceptance is, in turn, founded on a tacit bargain: "The United States now stands in the same relation to its larger corporations as the United Nations stands in relation to the United States—i.e., that the smaller and more coherent power (I.B.M., say, or Mobil) consents to the fictional dominion of the nominally larger but more diffuse power (the United States) in return for the right to do as it damn well pleases."[36] In any event, whatever the source of mutual acceptance, it seems clear that states have learned to live with a rival world in which they are active but over which they exert limited control, much as they may sometimes attempt to assert their authority in it.

That sovereignty-free systems and subsystems can survive and function in the presence of, even surrounded by, states that possess both formal authority and the weaponry to overpower them with armed force is vividly illustrated by events in Poland during the mid-1980s, when, despite the repressiveness of the regime at that time, the Poles maintained a vigorous intellectual freedom, including a flourishing, though nominally illegal, press that poured out a great quantity of papers, books, tapes, and videocassettes, thereby creating an atmosphere in which "people live without fear." The result was a

gap between the rulers and the ruled [that] is immense and unbridged. The regime keeps trying one way and another to woo at least the toleration, if not active allegiance of its dispirited people so as to renew their energies. But most Poles simply go about their personal lives, scrabbling for necessities and what comforts they can find, and ignore . . . the people in power. They are evidently trying, as best they can, to act on the advice of writer Adam Michnik to "live as if we were free." His remarkable phrase sums up the situation. The Poles have simply taken for themselves certain liberties that the state will not grant and that they exercise in the interstices of the regime's diminished power. . . . The deadlock is profound and there is no visible way out. The regime has even come to speak of "the opposition" instead of the underground or

[36] Lapham, "Leviathan in Trouble," p. 8.

the enemy, but the only political truce is one of impotence, on both sides.[37]

Nor is Poland the only present-day country in which the sovereignty of the state is insufficient to prevent the persistence of a coexisting system over which it is unable to exert effective control. Much the same has been said about the southern region of Vietnam in relation to the national government. As one leading Vietnamese exile put it, "South Vietnam is in a state of moral secession," a condition that is said to be described by Vietnamese as "one thousand pounds hanging by a hair."[38] The authority of states in Africa is also limited by the presence of antithetical value systems with respect to which their sovereignty is ineffective, even irrelevant:

> Most educated Africans are citizens of two publics in the same society. On the one hand, they belong to a civic public from which they gain materially but to which they give only grudgingly. On the other hand, they belong to a primordial public from which they derive little or no material benefits but to which they are expected to give generously and do give materially. To make matters more complicated, their relationship to the primordial public is moral, while that to the civic public is amoral. . . . The unwritten law . . . is that it is legitimate to rob the civic public in order to strengthen the primordial public.[39]

The difficulties that sovereignty-bound actors encounter in dealing with hostage situations offer still another insight into the substantial accommodations they have to make in the multi-centric world. President Jimmy Carter considerably reduced his efforts in the 1980 election campaign because of the Americans who were being held hostage in the embassy in Teheran, and in 1985 and 1986 President Reagan tried to win the freedom of hostages being held in Lebanon in ways that greatly undermined his capacity for leadership during the last two years of his presidency. "It is extraordinary," one specialist on terrorism has observed, "that you have groups the size of gangs dealing with heads of powerful nations as if they were co-equal heads of respective Mafia families. But the reality is that in these episodes, if they are in the headlines, they're in the Oval Office, and there's just no way of

[37] Flora Lewis, " 'As If We Were Free,' " *New York Times*, December 2, 1986, p. A35.
[38] Quoted in Barbara Crosette, "For Hanoi Chiefs, a List of Problems," *New York Times*, December 23, 1986, p. A6.
[39] P. Ekeh, "Colonialism and the Two Publics in Africa," *Comparative Studies in Society and History* 17 (January 1975): 108, as quoted in Robert H. Jackson, "African States and International Theory" (paper presented at the annual meeting of the British International Studies Association, Reading, December 1986).

avoiding that. It becomes extremely difficult for the political leadership to remain invisible."[40]

The drug trade is yet another issue-area where national governments tend to be helpless in dealing with actors in the multi-centric world. For a host of reasons, they are apparently incapable of bringing about reductions in the production and global distribution of drugs. In Colombia, for example, despite widespread publicity, expanded policing, and the capture of key drug-traffickers, the flow of cocaine abroad reached new highs in 1987, and officials were reported to be at a loss over what to do about it.[41]

These are, of course, extreme examples of the inability of the formal authority and police powers of states to evoke the compliance necessary to make the systems function along the lines sought by their leaders. But the very extremity of these cases, and the hardships and anguish with which they are associated, emphasize all the more the extent to which the two worlds are coexistent. If both the Polish and the Vietnamese regimes are unable to exercise effective authority and have in effect accepted the presence of autonomous systems within their nations, and if superpowers are unable to control terrorists and drug barons, surely we must entertain the possibility that there is a decentralized, multi-centric world functioning interactively with but independently of the state system under conditions in which complexity further confounds the lines of authority and reduces the utility of employing armed force. A forceful articulation of this conclusion, one that posits the state-centric world as even subordinate to the demands and activities of the multi-centric world, has been made by Richard Ashley:

> The territorial state is in a weak bargaining position because non-state actors with greater mobility can exploit resources, markets, and coalition-building opportunities available on a global scale, effectively redirecting the movement of political resources in ways that might either support or undermine the local conditions of stable rule within territorial bounds. The boundaries of the state—the competencies it has, the resources it can command, the range of social conduct subsumable under its interests, and the limits on its authority—are thus seen to be dependent upon interactions with and among nonstate actors.[42]

[40] Brian Jenkins, quoted in David K. Shipler, "U.S. and Battle against Terrorism: Can a Superpower Be Held Hostage?" *New York Times*, January 27, 1987, p. A10.

[41] Alan Riding, "Colombia Effort against Drugs Hits Dead End," *New York Times*, August 16, 1988, p. 1.

[42] Richard K. Ashley, "Untying the Sovereign State: A Double Reading of the Anarchy

Some of the difficulties that states encounter in dealing with actors in the multi-centric world derive from the limitations imposed by their own sovereignty. An example of this is the relationship between China and South Korea. The two countries do not formally recognize each other. Indeed, Chinese diplomatic commitments to North Korea are of such depth and duration—even to the point where Chinese maps show only one Korea, with its capital in the north—that China is bound by its sovereign obligations to act as if ties to South Korea did not exist and to make gestures suggesting that it would not consider establishing them, refusing, among other things, to let South Korea open a trade office in Beijing. But the two economies have much to gain from each other, with the result that trade is booming—doubling in volume between 1987 and 1988—and investment is also rising sharply, though much of this growth is being managed out of unofficial offices behind unmarked doors in Beijing hotels.[43] Bound as they may be by their sovereignty, states contrive to look the other way when they stand to benefit from activities on the part of sovereignty-free actors that run counter to their policies.

This is not to suggest that national governments are destined to become so tolerant of the multi-centric world as to abandon attempts to make it conform to the rules of their world. Top officials and ruling elites are accustomed to getting their way and to using their police or military powers when necessary, and they still maintain bureaucracies designed to expel foreign workers, to ward off trade competition from abroad, and to provide well-equipped fighting forces ready to do battle. Furthermore, top officials may still have occasion to contemplate going to war, thereby reinforcing their commitments to the rules that govern the state-centric system. For sovereignty-bound actors frequently define their security dilemmas in terms of their autonomy as actors in the state-centric world. Indeed, as the signs of global turbulence have mounted, states have become increasingly occupied with such questions.[44]

Thus, not every interaction between the two worlds ends with sovereignty-bound actors losing out to collectivities in the multi-centric

---

Problematique," *Millennium* 17 (Summer 1988): 246. For an extensive analysis that leads to similar conclusions, see Joel S. Migdal, *Strong Societies and Weak States: State-Society Relations and State Capabilities in the Third World* (Princeton: Princeton University Press, 1988).

[43] Nicholas D. Kristof, "China and South Korea Build Trade but Keep It Unofficial," *New York Times*, November 25, 1988, p. 1.

[44] So, too, have students of politics, if the recent explosion in the literature on the autonomy of the state is any indication. See, for example, Peter B. Evans, Dietrich Rueschemeyer, and Theda Skocpol, eds., *Bringing the State Back In* (Cambridge: Cambridge University Press, 1985).

world. Often states do prevail, compelling sovereignty-free actors to make accommodations to them. Clashes between subsidiaries of multinational corporations and their host states, for example, have as often as not resulted either in standoff or in the corporation making most of the concessions. The outcome in particular situations seems to depend on what each type of actor has to offer to the other. As one observer puts it:

> As long as a foreign-owned goose can still lay golden eggs . . . the policy of most developing countries has been to squeeze the goose, not to destroy it or have it fly away. Accordingly, multinational enterprises that provide a unique function, such as to provide access to some difficult technology or some otherwise inaccessible foreign market, have generally been less vulnerable to government pressures while subsidiaries where withdrawal is thought to entail very little national loss have been more vulnerable.[45]

Sometimes, the outcome is less than satisfying for both parties. When the International Committee of the Red Cross voted to oust the South African delegation from its quadrennial meeting in 1986—the first such action in the organization's 123-year history—South Africa retaliated by ordering Red Cross workers to leave the country, depriving South Africa of a valuable asset for coping with emergencies and tarnishing the Red Cross's reputation for political neutrality.[46]

In the same way that states seek to maintain their autonomy and control through intelligence agencies, computers, and satellites that monitor developments in the multi-centric world, so have sovereignty-free actors begun to develop mechanisms for monitoring the actions of states deemed to be potential threats to their well-being. It is a measure of the evolution of the multi-centric world that such private organizations as the Natural Resources Defense Council (NRDC), the International Physicians for the Prevention of Nuclear War (IPPNW), and the Space Media Network (SMN) have lately entered into surveillance activities in the state-centric world. In 1986, some two years before the INF treaty was ratified, the NRDC proposed to Soviet authorities that its representatives be allowed to monitor underground nuclear explosions in the USSR. While the U.S. government remained uncommitted on the

---

[45] Raymond Vernon, *Storm over the Multinationals: The Real Issues* (Cambridge: Harvard University Press, 1977), pp. 171–72. For other important samples of the literature on the interaction between states and multinational enterprises, see Joseph M. Grieco, *Between Dependency and Autonomy: India's Experience with the International Computer Industry* (Berkeley: University of California Press, 1988), and Louis W. Goodman, *Small Nations, Giant Firms* (New York: Holmes and Meier, 1987).

[46] *New York Times*, October 26, 1986, sec. 1, p. 1, and October 27, 1986, p. A1.

issue and on the possibility of a reciprocal arrangement for monitoring U.S. tests, the Soviet authorities acceded and an agreement was subsequently signed between the NRDC and the Soviet Academy of Sciences.[47] Some months later, the same group was an important participant in the discussions that ended with Soviet consent for Western observers to inspect its disputed radar installation at Krasnoyarsk.[48] In 1988, the IPPNW formed a commission of doctors to study the relationship between radioactive releases at a nuclear-weapons manufacturing site and cancer rates and genetic defects among plant workers and local populations. It invited participation by environmental organizations from some sixty countries and wrote to governmental leaders requesting "the widest possible access to information."[49] The SMN, formed in 1985 by a group of Swedes to use new technologies for the purpose of overcoming governmental attempts at secrecy, have developed a civilian ability to monitor important military programs in the same manner as the superpowers survey each other. It was the SMN that provided the first pictures and details of the Chernobyl disaster in 1986, and since then its accomplishments include publicizing secret Soviet preparations for a space shuttle, powerful Soviet laser installations, a site for Chinese missiles in Saudi Arabia, a huge new cocaine-growing region in South America, giant forest fires in China, and a new chemical warfare facility in Libya.[50] An even wider range of issues has been listed as subject to monitoring, through traveling subcommittees, by an organization of Nobel Prize winners,[51] and the Conference of American Armies, a biannual gathering of senior army officers from fifteen Western Hemisphere countries, has announced plans to monitor the activity of left-wing groups, terrorists, and drug traders throughout Latin America.[52]

The overlap of the state-centric and multi-centric worlds ought not be conceived only in terms of antagonistic relationships. Some activities and situations impel actors in one of the worlds to cross over into the other for resources, support, or ideas, without questions of surveillance, compliance, or legitimacy arising. Increasingly, for example, ac-

[47] For accounts of the agreement and its implementation, see "Group Seeks $500,000 for A-Test Project," *New York Times*, June 4, 1986, p. A13, and Michael R. Gordon, "U.S. Group Can Study Soviet A-Test," *New York Times*, December 20, 1986, p. A8.

[48] William J. Broad, "Soviet Radar on Display," *New York Times*, September 9, 1987, p. 1.

[49] "Physicians to Assess Hazards," *New York Times*, December 7, 1988, p. A10.

[50] Flora Lewis, "Little Brother Watches," *New York Times*, October 5, 1988, p. A33.

[51] Stanley Meisler, "Nobel Winners Plan Watchdog Group," *Los Angeles Times*, January 22, 1988, sec. 1, p. 5.

[52] Alan Riding, "Latin Military Still Seems to Stress the Role of Fighting Communism," *New York Times*, October 3, 1988, p. A10.

tors in the state-centric world turn to collectivities in the multi-centric world for specific contributions to delicate diplomatic negotiations, for generalized support, for expertise in implementing a particular policy, for direct foreign investments, for advancing projects they themselves are barred from undertaking for legal or political reasons, and for assistance in generating policy reversals in hostile governments. Particular instances of each of these forms of dependence on the multi-centric world can be readily cited:

For *diplomatic negotiations*: Seeking to promote talks between the United States and the PLO, Swedish diplomats turned to three leaders of private Jewish organizations in the United States and asked them to meet with PLO leaders, first in secret and later in a highly publicized meeting, as a means of getting Yasir Arafat to utter the exact words that Washington had set as a precondition to holding a dialogue. All concerned subsequently agreed that the dialogue would not have begun had these actors from the multi-centric world not played a crucial role in the negotiations.[53]

For *generalized support*: Eager to generate more favorable policies on the part of Washington officials, the government of Angola sought to systematically increase its support among key constituencies within the United States.[54]

For *expertise*: In 1984, the People's Republic of China and Hofstra University in New York signed a contract under which the latter agreed to form a corporation, headed by an academic dean, with the mission of seeking American companies that wanted to enter into joint ventures in China.[55]

For *direct foreign investments*: Once in disrepute, many governments have increasingly turned to the multi-centric world for this form of assistance.[56]

For *advancing barred projects*: During the U.S. government's secret efforts to obtain the release of hostages held in Lebanon, it turned, through Lieutenant Colonel Oliver L. North, to a private citizen, billionaire H. Ross Perot, for funds to pay the ransoms. Similarly, the Reagan administration publicly blessed and covertly supported the efforts of private groups to assist the Contras in

[53] Elaine Sciolino, "The Secret Effort on Arafat: Go-betweens Seize the Moment," *New York Times*, December 16, 1988, p. 1.

[54] James Brooke, "Blacks in U.S. Wooed by Angolans," *New York Times*, October 3, 1988, p. A3.

[55] David E. Sanger, "China Engaging Hofstra to Find U.S. Companies," *New York Times*, December 3, 1984, p. B1.

[56] Nicholas D. Kristof, "Multinationals, Once Shunned, Now Welcomed," *New York Times*, May 11, 1985, p. 1.

Nicaragua, a policy that critics called "the privatization of American foreign policy." When critics in Congress undertook to exert influence on their own by meeting privately with top officials in Central America, they were accused by the administration of conducting their "own foreign policy."[57]

For policy reversals by hostile governments: In 1986, while Nicaragua and the United States were in a de facto state of war, the former's president, Daniel Ortega, came to the United States partly to conduct business at the UN and partly to campaign for support among Americans. His travels included a dinner party in New York attended by journalists, entertainers, and political figures, a question-and-answer session at the *New York Times*, shaking hands with strangers in a shopping mall, visiting the Statue of Liberty, and flying to Denver for meetings with the mayor and the editorial boards of two newspapers, and with members of the National Bar Association who were holding their annual convention there.[58]

Sometimes, perhaps more often than is publicly known, one national government will respond to stirrings in the multi-centric world by seeking another government's assistance as a means of reducing domestic discontent:

Assisting other governments: In January 1987, for example, the Canadian prime minister, Brian Mulroney, lashed out at the United States during a visit of then Vice President George Bush. The latter's trip to Canada had been hurriedly arranged at the request of the former, whose slippage in the polls was attributed to the acid-rain issue and who used the occasion of Bush's presence to offer an image of himself as capable of "talking tough" to the United States. Following Mulroney's scolding, Bush was reported to have "stepped to the microphone . . . with remarks that appeared to recognize the political implications of the meeting for the prime minister." In effect, due to public pressures in the multi-centric world, two state actors conspired to convey sensitivity to the demands from that world.[59]

---

[57] Bob Woodward, "North Enlisted Perot's Help," *Los Angeles Times*, December 2, 1986, p. 1; Wayne King, "Private Role Increasing in Foreign War Actions," *New York Times*, October 12, 1986, p. 6; Elaine Sciolino, "Shultz and Dodd in Sharp Exchange," *New York Times*, February 25, 1987, p. A3.

[58] Larry Rohter, "Ortega Has Learned to Press the Flesh," *New York Times*, August 3, 1986, p. D4.

[59] John F. Burns, "Bush, in Canada, Gets a Scolding about Trade Ties and Acid Rain," *New York Times*, January 21, 1987, p. 1.

Conversely, sovereignty-free actors frequently turn to foreign governments to obtain moral support, policy shifts, or financial assistance, to their own governments for help in a business venture, and to other sovereignty-free actors so as to contest their own governments more effectively or to bypass, anticipate, or otherwise influence trends in the state-centric world. Again particular illustrations of each of these forms of interaction can be readily cited:

Moral support: Early in 1987, a Chinese student, Yang Wei, who had spent two years studying in the United States, was arrested on his return home for "counterrevolutionary propaganda and incitement" on behalf of the Chinese Alliance for Democracy, a dissident organization founded in New York in 1982. The Alliance launched a sophisticated effort to bring U.S. pressure to bear on the Chinese government. News of Yang's arrest was supplied to U.S. newspapers, sympathetic senators were lobbied, and Congress passed a resolution calling for Yang's release. The pressure irritated the Chinese, but Yang received a sentence of only two years, the lightest sentence known to have been given to a Chinese convicted of counterrevolutionary activity.[60]

Policy shifts: The Kurds are but one of many ethnic groups abroad that have sought to promote new orientations toward their adversaries on the part of the United States government.[61]

Financial assistance: In 1985, the Nation of Islam, a U.S. organization headed by Louis Farrakhan, obtained a $5 million, interest-free loan from Col. Moammar al-Qaddafi, the Libyan chief of state, for the purpose of enabling his organization to launch new business ventures.[62]

Assistance from own government: In 1987, representatives of General Motors and General Electric appeared before a subcommittee of the U.S. House of Representatives to request permission to negotiate "treaties" with the Soviet Union that would allow their companies to put communications satellites on Soviet space vehicles. At the time, the United States could not provide a means of getting the satellites into space, leading the two corporations to seek to take advantage of a Soviet offer to provide launchings at a cost of $30 million. U.S. law, however, forbids the hiring of Soviet

[60] Andrew J. Nathan, "Flowering of China Spring Puts Beijing in a Dilemma," *Los Angeles Times*, March 22, 1988, p. B7.

[61] Elaine Sciolino, "Kurdish Chief Gains Support in U.S. Visit," *New York Times*, June 22, 1988, p. A3.

[62] Lee May, "Farrakhan Reports Loan from Kadafi," *Los Angeles Times*, May 4, 1985, sec. 1, p. 8.

space vehicles, so the corporations were making an appeal to Congress.[63]

Contest own government: Prior to its legitimation in Poland, the Independent Polish Agency and the Conference of Solidarity Support developed networks of couriers and drivers for shipping books, printing presses, ink, video equipment and casettes, photographic equipment, microfiches and microfiche readers, radio and electronic equipment, and transmitters and other broadcasting equipment to opposition groups in Poland. This clandestine activity resulted in the publication of some five hundred periodicals a year, estimated to have been read by three million of Poland's thirty-eight million people. While much of this activity was covertly funded by foreign governments, particularly the United States through the Central Intelligence Agency (CIA), some of it was publicly appropriated by the U.S. Congress.[64]

By-pass national governments: The leaders of subnational governments sometimes deliberately avoid coordination with their national counterparts in order not to draw "unnecessary or premature attention from central authorities to local solutions of some local problems by means of informal contacts and 'good neighborhood' networks. Often, it [is] not a deliberate deception, just an avoidance of unnecessary complications."[65]

Anticipate reactions in the state-centric world: In 1987, the International Business Machines Corporation (IBM) offered to transfer computer chip technologies to its archrival, the Digital Equipment Corporation (DEC), in order to prevent DEC from becoming increasingly dependent on Japanese sources. Among the reasons for this unusual action was IBM's fear that if U.S. companies became too dependent on Japan, they would become politically neutralized in disputes between the two countries.[66]

Sovereignty-free actors located in one country can also engage in actions designed to influence directly the politics of other countries—including the outcome of their elections, the choice of their policies, the revival of their economies, the amelioration of their internal con-

[63] Lapham, "Leviathan in Trouble," p. 8.

[64] Robert Pear, "U.S. Helping Polish Underground with Money and Communications," *New York Times*, July 10, 1988, p. A14.

[65] Ivo D. Duchacek, "The International Dimension of Subnational Government," *Publius* 14 (Fall 1984): 25.

[66] Andrew Pollack, "IBM Said to Offer Chip Data to Rival to Thwart Japanese," *New York Times*, March 26, 1988, p. 1.

flicts, or the resolution of their disputes with other governments. Examples abound:

Electoral politics: The National Democratic Institute for International Affairs, an arm of the U.S. Democratic Party, recruited a dozen political consultants from the U.S. and Canada to go to Chile and work with the political coalition that campaigned in 1988 to defeat General Pinochet's bid for re-election as president.[67]

Policy choices: In monitoring Israel's immigration policies, Jewish groups in the United States often seek to limit and shape any alterations that may be made in those policies.[68]

Revival of economies: In 1988, the Rockefeller Brothers Fund arranged with Polish authorities to establish a Foundation for the Development of Polish Agriculture, believed to be the first organization in an Eastern bloc country to use private start-up money from the West.[69]

Amelioration of conflicts: In 1984, the Center for the Study of Democratic Institutions at the University of California, Santa Barbara, arranged for a public debate on the prospects for peace in El Salvador between that country's top government officials and leaders of its leftist rebels.[70]

Resolution of disputes: Early in 1986, Mohammad Medhi, a U.S. citizen serving as a spokesperson for the U.S. Moslem community through his position as secretary-general of the National Council on Islamic Affairs visited Libya in defiance of a U.S. ban on such trips and returned with an "open letter to the American people" from Colonel Qaddafi, the Libyan chief of state.[71]

The expanding volume of interactions between the two worlds ought not be interpreted as indicating that the adjustment of states to the presence of the multi-centric world has been easy. On the contrary, some of the most intense and prolonged global crises, such as the taking of hostages in the Middle East and, earlier, the Vietnam War, have

[67] Barbara Gamarekian, "How U.S. Political Pros Get Out the Vote in Chile," *New York Times*, November 18, 1988, p. B6. This incident also indicates that epistemic communities can be transnational in their composition.

[68] Joel Brinkley, "Angry American Jews Press Shamir on 'Who Is a Jew' Law," *New York Times*, November 18, 1988, p. 1.

[69] Kathleen Teltsch, "Western Fund to Aid Polish Farmers," *New York Times*, February 21, 1988, p. 14.

[70] James LeMoyne, "Salvadoran Foes Plan to Debate in U.S.," *New York Times*, November 12, 1984, p. A7.

[71] *USA Today*, December 1, 1986, p. 2A.

involved attempts by states to apply the rules of their world to the multi-centric world. Such attempts often prove to be hazardous and counterproductive, sometimes compelling governmental agencies to adopt elaborate schemes to carry them out. Agents of the French government blew up a peace ship in a New Zealand harbor, and their counterparts in the United States funneled arms to Iran and Nicaragua through a complex network of private individuals and firms.[72] The cascades that resulted caused considerable discomfort when the customary governmental secrecy in such matters was surmounted by actors in the multi-centric world. Indeed, it seems likely that such secrecy will become increasingly difficult to maintain. The multi-centric world has deep roots in the domestic politics of all the nations of the state-centric world, so that the points at which trails of intrigue will be exposed have multiplied, virtually insuring that all but the most trivial of covert actions will be revealed and then politicized.[73]

Difficult as the adjustment to the multi-centric world has been, however, states have begun to make it. They have learned at least the rudimentary lessons of accommodation in a number of issue-areas, with the result that they are now overtly as well as covertly active in the multi-centric world and have come to live by its rules to a considerable degree. Sometimes reluctantly and usually with great caution, states have been progressively drawn in as participants in global efforts to, for example, prevent currency crises, manage trade flows, curb terrorism, hasten economic development in the Third World, cope with AIDS, control the drug trade, and reduce atmospheric pollution. At the regional and dyadic levels, they have participated on an equal footing with other actors in the battles of Beirut, the famines of sub-Saharan Africa, and the agitation of the Tamils in Sri Lanka. Even the superpowers are beginning to move toward interaction with previously forbidden areas of the multi-centric world. The efforts of U.S. Secretary of State Shultz to establish contacts with Palestinians—first in Israel, then with well-known Palestinians in the United States, and finally with the PLO itself—despite a long-standing commitment not to engage in such contacts is surely an indication of the extent to which actors in the state-centric world have become reliant on actors in the multi-centric world for support in pursuing their goals.

[72] For an account of the elaborate network of firms and individuals used by the CIA in the United States, see Clyde H. Farnsworth, " 'The Company' As Big Business," *New York Times*, January 4, 1987, p. C1.

[73] Gregory F. Treverton, "Covert Action: From 'Covert' to Overt," *Daedalus* 116 (Spring 1987): 95–124.

THE INCREASED IMPORTANCE OF PRIVATE ACTORS

With states seeking support in the multi-centric world, and with collectivities in this world eager to maintain their links to the state-centric world, the bifurcated structure of postinternational politics has brought prominence to individuals as private actors (not as leaders of collectivities) who can have an impact upon the course of events. In the past, prior to the onset of global turbulence, the state-centric world was not particularly vulnerable to the actions of individuals. Like farmers in relation to the wheat market, individuals could not act in such a way as to determine outcomes, much less to alter systemic structures or processes. The price of wheat is a collective outcome, and so were the patterns of the state-centric world. In the present era, however, the decentralizing tendencies in world politics have rendered systems, subsystems, and the global agenda more subject to inputs from individual sources. Today, the proper analogy is not that of the wheat market but closer to that of the automobile market, in which the price of cars can be changed by the action of a single producer.

This is not to suggest, of course, that any individual can alter the course of events at will. The circumstances must be appropriate, and the private actor must (normally) occupy a professional role that accords weight to his or her words and actions. If these conditions are met, however, it is a feature of postinternational politics that individuals can make discernible contributions to the shape and outcome of issues on the global agenda. There are a number of ways in which this can happen: individuals can distribute information illegally,[74] can call public attention to an aspect of world affairs that concerns them,[75] can

[74] The classic case is that of the individual who, for reasons of principle, pique, or profit, leaks classified information. For example, the leak of a U.S. disinformation plan to deceive Colonel Qaddafi into believing he faced serious threats from both U.S. and domestic sources resulted in the plan's abandonment. Philip Shenon, "Official Is Cited in Leaks Inquiry," *New York Times*, October 26, 1986, p. 3.

[75] The late Andrei D. Sakharov, the Soviet physicist who endured years of harassment and exile for his opposition to Soviet policies, came to occupy a unique position in postinternational politics, one that was independent of any organization and that enabled him to make pronouncements on arms control and human rights which governments, peace groups, and journalists gave serious attention to. After his return from exile in 1986, Sakharov demonstrated an ability to convene press conferences and get a global airing for his views. See Bill Keller, "Sakharov Sees Major Changes in Soviet," *New York Times*, December 25, 1987, p. A3. Indeed, in one noteworthy respect his status as a private actor came to rival that of public officials in the state-centric world: during his 1988 visit to the United States, he was accorded an honor normally reserved for heads of government, when audiences rose to their feet upon his entrance: A. M. Rosenthal, "Gifts from Sakharov," *New York Times*, November 15, 1988, p. A31.

participate—even if inadvertently—in the competitive politics of the state-centric world,[76] or can make their expertise available in conflict situations.[77] In other cases, former or aspiring high-level public officials can use their previous position as a basis for continuing to exercise influence in world affairs,[78] and a few entertainers have had sufficient status to make their voice heard on the global stage.[79]

Perhaps the greatest access afforded private actors by the structures

[76] When Nicholas Daniloff, a U.S. reporter said to be "retiring, almost shy," was arrested, imprisoned, and charged with spying by the Soviet Union in September 1986, he became an instant (though unwilling) actor on the world stage. A summit meeting was pending, but his incarceration (apparently in retaliation for the arrest by the United States of a Soviet physicist and UN employee) threatened to bring superpower relations to a halt. Partly to extradite himself from an unpleasant situation but also out of concern that he not be a catalyst for increased U.S.-Soviet tensions, Daniloff successfully negotiated with the Soviet security police for a diplomatic solution to the crisis. William J. Eaton, "Daniloff Asks 'Cooling Off Period,' Says KGB Agrees," Los Angeles Times, September 11, 1986, sec. 1, p. 1. During his twelve-day stay in jail, Daniloff received support from a host of mass-media associations, all of which telegraphed their objections to the Kremlin and several of which asked permission to come to Moscow to bargain on his behalf. Upon his return to the United States, he was greeted by "Free Nick Daniloff" T-shirts, book contracts, TV interviews, a White House reception, and many other indicators of his newly acquired role as an actor in world affairs. Philip Taubman, "Reporter in Limelight: Daniloff Is Adjusting," New York Times, October 2, 1986, p. A7. It is perhaps indicative of the ways in which postinternational politics differs from earlier systemic structures that it can accord celebrity status to its private actors in the same way that this occurs in the mass-media and entertainment worlds.

[77] Paul S. Reichler, a U.S. lawyer, became a legal counselor to the Nicaraguan government when the Sandinista regime came to power in 1979. As a result, he was one of four Sandinista delegates appointed by President Daniel Ortega to participate in the 1987–1988 truce negotiations intended to bring an end to the seven-year-old civil war with the U.S.-backed contras. Reichler described his role in these words: "Unlike the Nicaraguan members of our team, I have not been touched personally by the horrors of war. None of my family members or close friends have been killed. As a result, as much as I am opposed to the war, it is not an emotional issue with me as it is with them. Hopefully this gives me a perspective together with my capacity as a lawyer, to see the other side's point of view more clearly and to serve as a bridge." "American Sitting opposite U.S.-Backed Rebels," New York Times, February 19, 1988, p. 12.

[78] Former U.S. attorney general Ramsey Clark was among the private lawyers hired by the PLO to prevent the closing of its mission at the UN by the U.S. Philip Shenon, "P.L.O. May Delay U.S. Ban on Mission," New York Times, February 27, 1988, p. 3. Similarly, Jesse Jackson, a prominent civil-rights activist and a candidate for the Democratic party's presidential nomination in 1988, tried to negotiate the release of U.S. hostages in Lebanon. Likewise, many former high-level officials give voice to their perspectives through the Trilateral Commission.

[79] In 1985, several leading entertainers sponsored a rock concert designed to aid famine victims in Africa. The TV audience was estimated at 1.5 billion people in more than one hundred countries, and the concert raised about $50 million. "Concert Raises $50 million in Famine Aid," International Herald Tribune, July 15, 1985, p. 1.

of postinternational politics is that enjoyed by journalists. In a world that places a high premium on information, their position astride the channels of communication offers them a number of ways in which they can become significant actors in global politics. The more prominent among them can conduct televised interviews with heads of state and thereby help to define how issues are framed and how world leaders are perceived. To be sure, their role in these interviews is limited by their news organizations and by the fact that the interviewees can to some extent set the tone and define the scope of the discussions. But the best-known newspaper columnists or television anchorpersons have an independent status that extends well beyond both their organizational affiliation and the role of mere questioner in an interview.[80]

Nor is the journalist's role confined to public settings. Having access to high places and privileged information, they are in a unique position to move effectively through or to bypass the complexities of postinternational politics, leading governments or private groups to occasionally seek them out for confidential assignments when the normal channels of communications are believed to be inappropriate. Early in the Cuban missile crisis in 1962, television correspondent John Scali acted as a courier between the Kremlin and the White House.[81]

However, the norms and policies of the journalism profession place limits on personal involvement in a news story, requiring that its practitioners maximize the distance between themselves and the subjects of their stories. Television correspondent Barbara Walters was widely criticized by professional colleagues for passing messages to the White House from Manucher Ghorbanifar, a middleman in the Iranian arms deal. She did so because she thought the messages might ease the plight of the U.S. hostages in Lebanon, but her colleagues contended that the task of the journalist is to report events and not initiate or shape them and that the information involved did not constitute a sufficient threat to life or national security to warrant a violation of the journalistic norms.[82]

There are even rare occasions when a person with no professional affiliations or role prominence, but perhaps possessed of an imagina-

[80] This was shown when, in 1988, Tom Brokaw conducted an hour-long, widely viewed interview with General Secretary Gorbachev, in which it seemed clear that his status as the NBC anchorman contributed to his ability to ask probing rather than superficial questions.

[81] Robert F. Kennedy, *Thirteen Days: A Memoir of the Cuban Missile Crisis* (New York: W. W. Norton, 1971), pp. 68–69.

[82] Dennis McDougal, "Walters As Courier Criticized," *Los Angeles Times*, March 18, 1987, p. F1.

tive zeal and an unsocialized ego, can have a considerable impact. Two recent events are illustrative. One involves Mathias Rust, a nineteen-year-old West German with no organizational ties who decided to act "on behalf of world peace" by flying a light airplane into Moscow's Red Square, an action that landed him in a Soviet jail for four months but also led to the dismissal of the Soviet defense minister and to the exposure of a previously unrecognized weakness in the Soviet defense system. The other is that of Robert T. Morris, Jr., a young graduate student in computer science at Cornell University who introduced a "virus" into a computer network that infected some six thousand computer systems. Interestingly, Rust's exploits were recalled when news of Morris's feat became public: a fellow graduate student was quoted as observing, "It's as if Mathias Rust had not just flown into Red Square, but built himself a stealth bomber by hand and then flown into Red Square."[83]

In sum, interactions between the two worlds are hardly simple or straightforward. With lines of authority obscure, and with precedents still in the process of evolution, relations between them can be tenuous and convoluted, often defying the fundamentals of world politics that have been standard practice for centuries. Consider once more the Iran-contra episode. The blurred nature of the conventional boundaries was revealed when Iranian officials offered to have their government intercede on behalf of U.S. hostages in Lebanon and to attempt to persuade their captors to release the hostages in exchange for U.S. concessions with respect to Iranian assets that it held.[84] Were the captors agents of Iran? If not, could the Iranians make good on their offer? Such questions underscore the complexity of relations between the state-centric and multi-centric worlds, just as the fact that they no longer seem like startling or urgent questions points up the large extent to which the arrangements that underlie the coexistence of the two worlds has come to be accepted as the basis for global politics.

THE DECLINE OF HEGEMONS

Whatever one's position in the debate over whether the United States has declined as the state-centric world's hegemonic leader,[85] it is clear

---

[83] Philip Taubman, "Moscow Frees Young German Pilot," *New York Times*, August 4, 1988, p. A3; John Markoff, "Computer Invasion: 'Back Door' Ajar," *New York Times*, November 7, 1988, p. A12. For a report showing that national boundaries are no obstacle to unwanted intrusions into computer systems, see John Markoff, "Breach Reported in U.S. Computers," *New York Times*, April 17, 1988, p. 1.

[84] *New York Times*, December 26, 1986, p. A13.

[85] For highlights of the debate, see Samuel P. Huntington, "The U.S.—Decline or Re-

that the emergence of the multi-centric world has sharply reduced the possibility that any single collectivity can dominate global politics. Earlier decades and centuries may have been commanded by hegemons which set the rules whereby global resources and statuses were allocated, but today's bifurcated structure, and especially the high degree of interdependence between the state- and multi-centric worlds, is simply too decentralized to be ruled by a single actor. Japanese firms may reign over the electronics industry, Islamic fundamentalists may control the politics of particular regions, New York City may be preeminent in the financial world, the superpowers may exercise disproportionate influence because of their stocks of nuclear weapons, and the English-speaking world may have considerable leverage as a result of the fact that so much of humankind's accumulated knowledge is stored in its language; but all these command posts are limited in scope and are not subject to hegemonic transformation.[86] For better or worse, hegemons and the stability they have infused into world politics are increasingly likely to become relics of the past, artifacts of an international history that came to an end with the advent of global turbulence toward the end of the twentieth century.

It must be emphasized that the decline of hegemons is not only a matter of fundamental shifts in the global economy. In a decentralized structure, with publics more analytically skillful and more ready to question authority, hegemons have found it increasingly difficult to exercise political control, even within their own spheres of influence. In addition to their setbacks in Vietnam and Afghanistan, for example, both superpowers have been forced to retreat from, or have otherwise been thwarted in, Central America and the Middle East, and the

---

newal?" *Foreign Affairs* 67 (Winter 1988/89): 76–96; Robert O. Keohane, *After Hegemony: Cooperation and Discord in the World Political Economy* (Princeton: Princeton University Press, 1984); Bruce M. Russett, "The Mysterious Case of Vanishing Hegemony; or, Is Mark Twain Really Dead?" *International Organization* 39 (Spring 1985): 207–31; and Susan Strange, "Toward a Theory of Transnational Empire," in Czempiel and Rosenau, *Global Changes and Theoretical Challenges*, pp. 161–76.

[86] In the case of New York, in fact, a decline in its position appears to have set in. It has been the prime center for business and finance since World War II, but in recent times other cities around the world have been gaining international business at a faster rate than New York, and the expectation is widespread that global enterprise will "continue to decentralize, which would mean a shift away from Manhattan of business now centered here." The dynamics underlying this pattern are numerous, but at their core is the microelectronic revolution and the ways in which it has enabled enterprises to disperse their operations around the world. As one business executive put it, "The whole notion of dominant financial centers became antiquated with the telecommunications satellite." Thomas J. Lueck, "New York City Is Challenged As Giant of Global Economy," *New York Times*, June 27, 1988, p. 1.

United States has been defied by its allies in the ANZUS and NATO organizations in much the same manner as the Soviet Union has had to endure a steady weakening of its hold over the countries of Eastern Europe.

In short, the rise of the multi-centric world has brought major changes to the state-centric world. The prospect that any sovereignty-bound actor will be able to prevail over, or even to coordinate, the decentralizing dynamics that are at work among sovereignty-free actors is highly remote for the foreseeable future. Analysts may be relying on outmoded logic to presume that the relative "fall" of the United States and the Soviet Union must be followed by the relative "rise" of one or more other nations.[87] Such a logic has been compelling for historical epochs marked by centralizing forces, but global life has turned in decentralizing directions that may make the notion of hegemony in world politics obsolete.

Although some might argue that the decentralization of world politics derives from the declining ability of the superpowers to maintain control over the course of events,[88] it seems more accurate to view hegemonic decline as a consequence rather than as a cause of the decentralizing tendencies. Superpowers do not parade their vulnerabilities for subgroups to seize upon; rather, the vulnerabilities tend to be exposed by the new skills and the new criteria of performance operative within subgroups that, through aggregative processes, are led to arrogate authority to themselves or to demand more autonomy. The rise of Solidarity in Poland and the continuing powerlessness of that country's Communist regime to oppose it, and Gorbachev's subsequent statement indicating that the Soviet Union would not intervene in Polish affairs, are quintessential examples of how diminished state control has been fostered by the dynamics of global turbulence.

This is not to suggest, however, that former or would-be hegemons are utterly helpless. As one observer put it, "A nobody-in-charge world doesn't mean a leaderless world. It just means that the governments of leading nations have to exercise their leadership not by threatening or browbeating or invading or colonizing peoples that don't agree with them, but rather in ways that are more multilateral, more coherent, more consultative, and more consensual than ever."[89]

---

[87] China and Japan are currently favored for hegemonic status in the twenty-first century; see, for example, Paul Kennedy, *The Rise and Fall of the Great Powers: Economic Change and Military Conflict from 1500 to 2000* (New York: Random House, 1987).

[88] This argument is implicit in Keohane, *After Hegemony*.

[89] Harlan Cleveland, "The Future of International Governance: Managing a Nobody-in-Charge World," *Futurist*, May–June 1988, p. 12.

The Changing Nature of Treaties

It can also be said that international alliances seem increasingly anachronistic as well. Given the high degree of interdependence among societies, the lines dividing adversaries are murky, and the challenges and uncertainties that mark their external environments derive more from considerations of economic than of military security. Sovereignty-bound actors are concerned with markets and trading partners as much as with defenses and allies, and whatever need for physical security they may feel can be met by informal agreements and arms purchases without the encumbrances of treaty obligations.

Moreover, with global turbulence having diminished the authority and lessened the reliability of potential allies, there are fewer incentives for sovereignty-bound actors to enter into formal agreements that commit them to the military support of other countries. If the governments of future allies are undergoing decentralizing tendencies, not to say authority crises, the calculations of expediency and the foundations of trust on which alliances rest are not likely to seem compelling.

It is hardly surprising, therefore, that recent decades have not witnessed the creation of new military alliances. During the epoch of the state-centric world, states continually formed, broke, and shifted alliances, but today, sovereignty-bound actors tend to avoid formalizing commitments or giving legal standing to their temporary coalitions. Nor have alliances that were concluded prior to the onset of turbulence fared very well. All of them have encountered difficulties in maintaining their coherence and effectiveness, with many having been plagued by budgetary and force deficiencies while others have suffered outright defections and still others have become dormant if not abrogated.[90] The ANZUS alliance, formed in 1951 by Australia, New Zealand, and the United States, for all practical purposes came apart in 1985 when skillful and mobilized publics in New Zealand upheld their government's objections to port calls by U.S. ships that might have nuclear weapons aboard.[91]

Even as the transformation of global structures has lessened the importance of broad-gauged security alliances, however, it has heightened the attractiveness of narrow, issue-specific legal arrangements. In arms-control treaties and trade-negotiation rounds, in cultural protocols and scientific and technological agreements, states have prolifer-

[90] Charles W. Kegley, Jr., and Gregory A. Raymond, *When Trust Breaks Down: Alliance Norms and World Politics* (forthcoming), chapter 10 and epilogue.

[91] Bernard Gwertzman, "U.S. Moves to End Its Defense Pact with New Zealand," *New York Times*, April 29, 1986, p. 1.

ated their formal links to each other as a means of reducing the uncertainties of a turbulent world. In some important respects, therefore, the density and interdependence of actors infuses postinternational politics with formal public as well as informal private dimensions.

THE STABILITY OF A BIFURCATED WORLD

In the absence of stabilizing hegemons and effective military alliances, the question arises as to what the bifurcation of world politics portends for global stability.[92] To posit the state-centric and multi-centric worlds as coexistent and interactive is not to say that their mutual acceptance can endure indefinitely. Indeed, since the structures of postinternational politics are marked by a high degree of complexity and dynamism that is not likely to diminish to any appreciable degree, it could readily be argued that the bifurcated world is inherently unstable. Surely, the turbulence that has engulfed the main parameters has yet to subside and, given the explosiveness of modern technologies, it may even intensify. Moreover, if bifurcation proves to be transitional, eventually giving way to a more permanent form of world order (see chapter 16), the question of stability is still important, because the effort to answer it compels further clarification of the emergent arrangements.

Actually, the question can be broken down into three questions: (1) How stable is the multi-centric world? (2) Do the dynamics at work in the state-centric world incline it in stable directions? (3) Does the interaction between the multi-centric world and the state-centric world tend toward a stable or fragile balance between them?

As to the first of these, it should be said that the decentralizing tendencies in both worlds have led to an increase in the number of their actors and, other things being equal, the very fact of large numbers is conducive to greater stability. It makes it increasingly unlikely that any single actor, or even any group of actors, will seek control over either or both worlds and thereby foment the kind of conflict that would tear either or both apart. To be sure, those with the greatest capabilities in both worlds may be dominant in more issue areas, but that does not affect the balance inherent in the fact of many actors. There is, in other words, safety in numbers—if by safety is meant continuation of the status quo.

In addition, the interdependence of postinternational politics is an

---

[92] For a cogent explanation of why unstable conditions have not accompanied the decline of U.S. predominance in recent decades, see Keohane, *After Hegemony*.

incentive for joint action in the event one or a few of the actors in either world does attempt to overturn, subvert, or otherwise alter the structural arrangements. This is most clearly evident in the state-centric world: in recent years, the states most directly involved have put aside their conflicts and sought to cooperate when Iran threatened the stability of the Persian Gulf area, when some Third World countries seemed to be on the verge of defaulting on their international debts, when Libya proclaimed its intent to pursue terrorist policies, and when nuclear proliferation posed a threat to the very existence of the bifurcated world. As noted above, comparable tendencies could be discerned among actors in the multi-centric world when such things as the fall of the dollar, Chernobyl, and AIDS posed threats to its order.

To be sure, other things may not always be equal, and interdependence among a large number of actors may not always be sufficient to maintain stability. Most notably, the nuclear balance could be shattered by a major technological breakthrough, and the world economy could be upended by a global depression. Such developments might well encourage actors in both worlds to pursue narrower definitions of their self-interests and thus make it impossible for either world to manage its affairs in customary ways.

It is also the case that stable structures do not necessarily portend a happy world of effective collectivities and satisfied people. Stability does not preclude policy failures, deterioration of the quality of life, or the many kinds of discontent that lead to the formation of new collectivities.

Nevertheless, at present both the state-centric and multi-centric worlds seem sufficiently pluralistic to be stable. The incoherence of their structures is, ironically, well suited to turbulence and inhibits the evolution of crises out of the structures themselves.

There remains the question of whether the interaction between the two worlds is essentially stable. Even if each of them is separately inclined in that direction, it is possible that the interactions between them and the orientations each has toward the other could promote an overall instability. If the present order proves to be transitional and contains the seeds of its own supersession, can such a potential be discerned in the ways the actors of each world relate to their counterparts in the other?

Important as these problems are, the answers to them are far from clear. In part, the lack of clarity is due to the recency of the bifurcated arrangement. Central tendencies are not yet discernible. In addition, as the examples above indicate, the answers are obscured by the fact that both conflict and cooperation are at work when the actors of the two worlds interact.

Even if the actors in both worlds prefer a condition of stable coexistence, there are a number of inherent obstacles to achieving it. The most obvious of these, already identified, derives from the recurrent attempts of multinational corporations to expand their operations within national societies and the counterefforts of states to monitor, supervise, and control the operations, personnel, and profits of the corporations within their jurisdictions. The balance here is a delicate one. States seek to maintain control over the corporations for a host of reasons, but often doing so runs the risk that the corporations will cease operations or move their resources and expertise elsewhere. Negotiations therefore often lead to outcomes that are neither completely satisfactory nor intolerable from either perspective—uneasy truces, as it were, that allow for continued interaction between the two worlds. Occasionally, the negotiations fail. When the Coca-Cola Company refused to reveal the formula for producing its well-known soft drink, for example, India refused to allow the company to manufacture and distribute it. At the other extreme is the recent attitude of China, which has invited Western corporations to build manufacturing facilities on its territory.[93] It is perhaps indicative of the limits to cooperation between actors in the two worlds that these ventures have been marked by wariness and suspicion on both sides.

But such conflicts are by no means confined to the realm of business. It is notable that recent Olympic competitions have been politicized, with conflicts between states being played out through the athletes, many of whom profess a desire to compete even as they proclaim that their national loyalties and responsibilities prevent them from doing so. The overlap between the two worlds in the realm of sports has broadened considerably in the era of postinternational politics. Even efforts to cope with natural disasters have been subjected to politicization. The difficulties encountered by the Red Cross in South Africa, mentioned earlier, and the inability of charitable organizations to sustain a flow of relief supplies to starving populations in parts of Ethiopia,[94] indicate that even humanitarian activities can no longer stay

[93] It has been estimated that "there are now more than 6,000 foreign ventures in China, some in cooperation with Chinese partners, others wholly owned by foreign companies." Edward A. Gargan, "China Nods Sagely at Soviet Changes," *New York Times*, July 4, 1988, p. 3.

[94] Clifford D. May, "Relations Sour between Ethiopia and Western Food Donors," *New York Times*, February 18, 1985, p. A8.

aloof from the stresses and strains of interactions between the two worlds.

Similarly, in the realm of ideas and science, the needs of states in the Second and Third Worlds have led them to seek knowledge from the private sector of the First World, making for dramatic conflicts when the intellectuals and scientists declare that certain policies of the requesting states are so objectionable that they will not participate in such relationships unless the policies are reversed. Examples abound. U.S. scientific societies rejected cooperation with Soviet counterparts in order to register their protest against the incarceration of dissident scientists in the USSR.[95] When the International Political Science Association convened in Moscow in 1979, a dispute occurred over the Soviet reluctance to permit attendance by scholars from Israel.[96] Indeed, as illustrated by the instances of U.S. refusal to grant entry visas to poets and humanists who have been invited to participate in intellectual meetings but who have alleged or actual Communist affiliations, such conflicts also arise in those realms where cultural exchanges and not scientific expertise are involved.

On the other hand, conflicts such as the foregoing arise precisely because actors in both the state-centric and multi-centric worlds have a need to cooperate across national boundaries. The conflictful situations capture headlines and rupture relationships, but there are also myriad less publicized cases in which the actors resolve their differences, compete amicably, share their knowledge, and maintain more or less harmonious relations over long periods of time. Often, in fact, the conflictful tensions and the cooperative endeavors exist side by side, as actors in the two worlds agree not to permit their disagreements on some issues to undermine their cordial relations on other matters.

As has already been implied, moreover, actors in each world sometimes try to come to the rescue of troubled counterparts in the other. The effort of a representative of the Church of England to mediate disputes involving hostages held by terrorists, the attempt of central bankers in the West to shore up falling exchange rates, and the role of private and UN relief agencies in natural disasters are illustrative. Such examples suggest that, despite the fact that relations between actors in

[95] Linda L. Lubrano, "The Political Web of Scientific Cooperation between the U.S.A. and USSR," in Nish Jamgotch, Jr., ed., *Sectors of Mutual Benefit in U.S.-Soviet Relations* (Durham, N.C.: Duke University Press, 1985), chapter 4.

[96] Richard L. Merritt and Elizabeth C. Hanson, *Science, Politics, and International Conferences: A Functional Analysis of the Moscow Political Science Congress* (Boulder, Colo.: Lynne Rienner, 1989).

the two worlds can be mired in intense conflict, they do need each other. Their goals may differ, but the structures and dynamics of post-international politics are such that neither can sustain forward movement without some dependence on and cooperation with the other. It cannot be otherwise, given the limited resources available to sovereignty-free actors and the weaknesses of states in a time of increasing interdependence.

In sum, it is possible to view the two-world universe of postinternational politics as inherently stable, even though it is not difficult to point to dynamics that jeopardize that stability. Further insights into these opposing forces can be obtained from an exploration of the cascading processes through which sovereignty-free and sovereignty-bound actors relate to one another. That is, having delineated the main outlines of the multi-centric world's structural incoherence, we can look more closely now at the processes whereby goals are pursued, conflicts intensified, and accommodations made. Structure and process are the obverse of each other, each shaping the form that the other takes. In addition, structure gives expression to the static, fixed characteristics of enduring patterns, while process encompasses the dynamics of change and turbulence. The next chapter inquires into the interaction of structure and process in postinternational politics.

CHAPTER II

PONDERING PROCESSES
Centralizing and Decentralizing Dynamics

When my mother calls me up and tells me what's going on in the Tokyo market, I know something has changed.
— Richard Brody, stock trader[1]

The narcotics trade is completely international. Cocaine may be grown in Bolivia and Peru, refined in Colombia, shipped through Mexico and the Bahamas, sold and consumed in the United States, with the profits deposited in a Panamanian bank and then invested in Britain, while the mastermind of the whole scheme lives in Honduras.
— Charles S. Saphos, U.S. Justice Department official[2]

We expect terrorist organizations to each have a distinct ideology, structure and membership. However, evidence is mounting that the situation is more fluid, that there are trades of people and matériel, that different groups are capable of forming alliances even for the purpose of carrying out a single operation.
— Italian judicial official[3]

The diplomatic universe is like an echo chamber: the noises of men and events are amplified and reverberated to infinity. The disturbance occurring at one point of the planet communicates itself, step by step, to the opposite side of the globe.
— Raymond Aron[4]

[1] Quoted in "How Merrill Lynch Moves Its Stock Deals All Around the World," *Wall Street Journal*, November 9, 1987, p. 1.

[2] Quoted in Robert Pear, "Draft Treaty Seeks to Take the Profit out of Drugs," *New York Times*, October 2, 1988, p. 11.

[3] Quoted in Roberto Suro, "Hunt for Pan Am Bomber: New Shapes and Shadows," *New York Times*, January 8, 1989, p. 8.

[4] *Peace and War: A Theory of International Relations*, trans. Richard Howard and Annette Baker Fox (New York: Doubleday, 1966), p. 373.

ONE WAY to think about process in any social system is to ask what daily or weekly life is like in that system. The interactive routines that constitute the normal course of events are, in effect, the processes that sustain the system and its structures. Some interactions may be so situation-specific as to be isolated occurrences and not reflective of inherent systemic processes, and some can seem so anomalous as to suggest the possibility of emergent processes—a possibility that the individuals quoted above seem to appreciate. But when the interactions become routinized and repeatedly exhibit the same characteristics, they can confidently be taken as the system's processes.

In important respects, the analysis so far has already identified certain key processes at work in world politics. The tensions between centralizing and decentralizing dynamics arise from recurrent interaction patterns whereby the loci of authority shift back and forth between organizational centers and peripheries. The dynamics of aggregation and disaggregation constitute recurrent patterns whereby organizations and groups gain, maintain, or lose their coherence. The techniques and dynamics of control involve recurrent patterns whereby actors seek compliance and provide support.

Beyond these generic processes lie the more specific variants that mark postinternational politics, and it is to these that this chapter is devoted. But it might be wondered whether, given the decentralized nature of the multi-centric world, there are any generalizations about its interaction patterns that can usefully be made. Can the "rules" for the maintenance of autonomy in the multi-centric world be laid down in the same way as has been done for the maintenance of security in the state-centric world?[5] On a day-to-day or week-to-week basis, in other words, what is it like to be active in the bifurcated world of postinternational politics?[6]

CASCADES AS ANALYTIC UNITS

One pattern that can be discerned involves the cascading nature of the interactions that characterize politics in the multi-centric world. While

[5] See Morton A. Kaplan, *System and Process in International Politics* (New York: Wiley, 1957).

[6] Among the very few efforts to answer at least some aspects of this question are Marvin S. Soroos, *Beyond Sovereignty: The Challenge of Global Policy* (Columbia: University of South Carolina Press, 1986), chapter 3; Peter Willetts, ed., *Pressure Groups in the Global System: The Transnational Relations of Issue-Oriented Non-Governmental Organizations* (London: Frances Pinter, 1982); and Lennie Copeland and Lewis Griggs, *Going International: How to Deal Effectively in the Global Marketplace* (New York: New American Library, 1985).

the state-centric world's processes are largely founded on reciprocal interactions, with states reacting to the actions of other states directed at them—reciprocity is not central to the processes of the multi-centric world. Instead, in this world of complex issues, overlapping agendas, diffuse authority structures, and a shared right to initiate action, the actions of A directed at B as often produce reactions by C directed at D as they do reactions by B. Thus, developments in the multi-centric world move forward in an asymmetrical, crazy-quilt fashion, with the sequences of action being propelled from one system to another and from subsystems to other subsystems in the same and different whole systems.

These action sequences cannot readily be called "events." They are more like *cascades*, analogous to a flow of white water down a rocky river bed: just as the flow churns and shifts, sometimes moving sideways, sometimes diagonally, and sometimes even careening in the reverse direction, and leaving sprays, eddies, and whirlpools in its wake, so do action sequences in the multi-centric world gather momentum, stall, reverse course, and resume anew as their repercussions spread among whole systems and subsystems.

If one were to sit on a river bank for any stretch of time and observe the water rush past, however, it would soon be clear that its flow is patterned, despite the churning splashes and mist that accompany it. For both the slope that sustains the flow and the rocks that divert it from one channel to the next are more or less permanently in place, with the result that the water continues to hit each rock at the same pace from the same angle and then bounces on to the next one at the same angle and rate, thereby tracing a pattern in which the areas of clear and white water are observable at the same points and in the same designs. And if the repeated pounding of the current alters the faces of the rocks, the resulting changes will again be patterned, not random, as the new angles alter the water's flow in the same new directions. In effect, the churning flow is systematic in its unruliness.

Much the same can be said about the cascades of the multi-centric world. The place of most of its actors is relatively permanent in the sense that their conceptions of autonomy, their agendas, and their modes of adaptation tend to be fixed, with the result that their participation in the sequences of action sustain the cascades in patterned ways. If some actors undergo adaptive transformations as repeated exposure to certain cascades shifts their priorities,[7] their new forms of

---

[7] Each of the four modes of adaptation noted in table 10.2 is conceived as theoretically

participation will move the cascades along paths that will once again become recurrent, in accordance with the learning and changes that gave rise to the altered modes of adaptation.[8]

But if the cascade is to replace the event as the basic empirical unit of action, its nature must be elaborated in concrete rather than metaphorical terms. This means that a cascade must be identified in terms of the basic dimensions that differentiate the issues and the systems, subsystems, and leaderless publics that get caught up in it. Three such dimensions seem especially important: scope, intensity, and duration. The key distinction in the *scope* of cascades is between those that extend across a wide variety of systems, each with different "angles" that send the flow on in new directions and thereby sustain it for a prolonged period, and those that follow a limited path among a few systems and peter out relatively quickly as the controversies that precipitated them are resolved, superseded, or rendered dormant. The difference between cascades brought on by ethnic riots and those originating in developments in the natural environment is illustrative. Ethnic riots such as have broken out among the Tamils in Sri Lanka and the Pathans in Pakistan usually initiate limited cascades that do not extend beyond neighboring systems (although in the Tamil case, North American subsystems got involved when refugees fled to Canada).[9] On the other hand, environmental disturbances such as occurred at Chernobyl trigger actions that rapidly spread the cascade into the orientations of many leaderless publics and onto the agendas of many systems, both of which then "bounce" it on to a great number of subsystems. Consider, for example, this account of the cascade started by the fire at the Chernobyl nuclear-power plant in 1986:

> Until the accident, large sections of the East European public were unconcerned about environmental issues. A few environmental groups, like the Polish Ecology Club and the Hungarian Blues, were fighting battles which remained relatively unpublicized.

---

capable of undergoing transformation to any of the other three; see James N. Rosenau, *The Study of Political Adaptation* (London: Frances Pinter, 1981), pp. 80–88.

[8] Since the concept of a cascade may suggest a downward flow of causal dynamics, it should be stressed that here it refers to flows "down" through time and not down through hierarchically ordered systems. It is in the nature of cascading interdependence that the demands and issues that precipitate the flows of action can originate at any systemic or subsystemic level and can then move up and across as well as down systemic structures.

[9] Steven R. Weisman, "Pakistani Riots Are a Symptom of Many Ills," *New York Times*, December 21, 1986, sec. 4, p. 3, and Douglas Martin, "Sri Lankans Found Adrift Paid up to $5,000 to Reach Canada," *New York Times*, August 13, 1986, p. 1.

Chernobyl was the greening of Eastern Europe. Overnight, groups sprang up everywhere, some 200 in Poland alone. Even the Catholic Church organized its environmental group, the Society of St. Francis of Assisi. The anti-nuclear protest in Poland set back the development of nuclear power, while in Yugoslavia the movement turned into a virtual moral crusade against the Communist authorities. Starting with small dispersed youth groups, the movement swept across republican lines with the aid of a sympathetic press and caught up intellectuals and ordinary citizens along [with] the young. Nuclear protest swept also across Western Europe, forcing Sweden to vote to phase out its nuclear plants within a twenty-year time span, and crossed the Atlantic, where an informal moratorium on the further development of nuclear power dating from 1978 was reconfirmed and supported by the governors of the states of New York and Massachusetts.[10]

The *intensity* of cascades refers to the pace at which they move through systems and subsystems. High-intensity cascades are those in which the participants are committed, vigorous, and tenacious with respect to the outcomes they desire, whereas in low-intensity cascades the actors' commitments are more ambivalent or less fixed on particular outcomes. Intensity is closely related to the participants' modes of adaptation (see chapter 10). The premises of the intransigent and the promotive modes are in conflict, and situations in which both are present are thus conducive to high-intensity cascades. This is why the cascades involving South Africa, which has long been committed to intransigent adaptation, are marked by resolute demands, sudden reversals, and heated exchanges. The premises of the acquiescent and the preservative modes are more compatible, and so interactions between actors using them are apt to give rise to low-intensity cascades, marked by conciliatory gestures and predictable outcomes. Illustrative here are cascades involving East European peace groups and the Soviet Union.

As for the *duration* of cascades, several variables differentiate those that continue for years from those that last only weeks or months, including the number and nature of cascades already in motion, the ability of a government to terminate a cascade with an authoritative initiative, and the nature of the values at issue. Cascades that arouse the participation of human-rights organizations and of governments com-

---

[10] Barbara Jancar, "Chaos As an Explanation of the Role of Environmental Groups in East Europe Politics" (paper presented at the annual meeting of the International Studies Association, London, March 1989), p. 18.

mitted to intransigent adaptation, for example, seem to persist much longer than those launched by export firms and a preservatively oriented government intent upon shifting the direction of a trade pattern. Thus, to be more specific, the cascade that revolves around apartheid in South Africa reaches deep into the politics of many countries and international organizations, and no action of South Africa's intransigent regime can terminate it. On the other hand, the cascade precipitated in 1981 by the U. S. objections to an oil pipeline from the Soviet Union into Western Europe resulted in a negative and noncompliant flow of reactions and did not endure because the adaptive inclinations of the Reagan administration enabled it to reverse its policy.

The importance of distinguishing cascades in terms of their scope, intensity, and duration lies in the way issues are transformed as a cascade encounters collectivities in its flow. As a cascade gathers momentum and drags in wider circles of actors, the values it encompasses and the consequences it portends change, and each change adds further complexity and dynamism to the interdependent structures that link the actors. Like the so-called butterfly effect in meteorology, an event in one part of the world can ultimately have unexpected repercussions in remote places.[11] Cascades in postinternational politics, in other words, give rise to new circumstances by the very fact of having been initiated. Thus, for example, domestic programs designed to enliven the Soviet economy cascade into the politics of Southeast Asia through the conflict over Vietnam's role in Cambodia; a dictator's overthrow in the Philippines has effects on political processes in Pakistan and Mexico; and efforts to control drug usage in the United States expand into the politics of Panama and introduce a new dimension into U.S. relations with many other nations of the Americas.

Cascading processes, in other words, are not only outcomes of turbulent conditions; they can also contribute to these conditions. They are the turbulence, and they are also among its sources. Elaborating upon their scope, intensity, and duration serves to highlight the shift from a suggestive metaphor to a serious social-science concept and an incisive analytic tool. It allows us to focus on those empirical points at which the change inherent in interdependent structures takes place.[12]

[11] The butterfly effect refers to the fact that a slight change of weather in one part of the world can have major consequences for the weather over distant continents. "A butterfly stirring the air today in Peking can transform storm systems next month in New York." James Gleick, *Chaos: Making a New Science* (New York: Viking, 1987), p. 8; see also pp. 20–23.

[12] For an attempt to analyze and compare the scope, intensity, and duration of cascades in a specific empirical context, see Jancar, "Chaos As an Explanation," pp. 18–21.

The cascade concept has already been employed in other sciences. In physics, a cascade is defined as a method for "attaining successively lower temperatures by utilizing the cooling effect of the expansion of one gas in condensing another less easily liquefiable." In electrochemistry, it refers to a technique for placing "electrolytic cells so that the electrolyte falls from one cell to the next lower in the series" and, more generally, to any electrical circuit in which "the first member of the series supplies or amplifies the power of the second, and so on through the series."[13] In medicine, it has become commonplace to conceive of a cancer as developing in several steps and to refer to this sequence as a cascade.[14] In all these definitions, it will be noted, each step of a cascade is transformed by its predecessor even as it contributes to the transformation of its successor.

There is thus a close correspondence between the operational uses of the concept in the physical sciences and the notion advanced here that the processes of the multi-centric world derive from interlocking tensions that gain strength and direction from each other as they spread through the global system.[15] Viewed in this way, it is hardly surprising that the course of events in postinternational politics seems so chaotic: the events contain and sustain their own dynamism, producing change as a consequence of the very processes on which their routines are founded.

The availability of computer and television networks that speed the flow of information, values, and decisions from micro to macro levels adds to the dynamism of cascading processes. Where the sales of stock and the protests of citizens were once counted by hand and circulated by stage coach, today the aggregation and communication of such phenomena are virtually instantaneous. Where trade-union decisions were once dependent on the dissemination of information to members by print and the hand-tallying of votes to begin or end a strike, today these can be made instantaneously as members in widely scattered locals are brought together through satellite hookups connecting them to regional and national offices. Where word of distant riots and assassinations once consisted of delayed and truncated newspaper ac-

[13] *Webster's New International Dictionary*, 2nd ed., s.v. "cascade."

[14] H. M. Schmeck, Jr., "Cancer Gene Linked to Flaws in Growth of an Ordinary Cell," *New York Times*, February 10, 1984, p. 1.

[15] For a different conception, in which the interlocking processes are posited as circuit-breakers rather than as cascades, see Peter Katzenstein, "International Relations Theory and the Analysis of Change," in E. O. Czempiel and J. N. Rosenau, eds., *Global Changes and Theoretical Challenges: Approaches to World Politics for the 1990s* (Lexington, Mass.: Lexington Books, 1989), p. 301.

counts, now a quick and full picture can be conveyed through TV broadcasts and videotapes. It has been widely reported that the revolution that brought Khomeini to power in Iran and the upheaval that ousted Marcos in the Philippines were greatly facilitated by the prior clandestine circulation of audio tapes of Khomeini's speeches and by the smuggling into Manila of videotapes of Benigno Aquino's assassination.

As a consequence of the rapidity with which situations unfold, leaders today have less time for research and reflection before they must respond to challenges, and as cascades gather momentum their decision criteria may become increasingly discrepant with the actions and presumptions of both their followers and their adversaries. Moreover, the cascades are increasingly sustained through the uncoordinated cumulation of micro choices rather than through the coordinated actions of macro collectivities. This is what happened when the world's stock markets crashed on October 19, 1987: "program trading" based on the information-processing capacities of high-speed computers swept the markets into outcomes that none of the existing macro regulations had anticipated. This is also what happened recently in the Philippines, Soviet Armenia, South Korea, Panama, Burma, and the West Bank, when the cascades of protest reached a level of self-generated momentum for which the rules of conventional politics had made no allowance. Stated more generally, just as the behavior of the earth's atmosphere is the product of the interaction of a nearly infinite number of molecules, and just as large-scale movements in the financial markets arise from multitudinous individual decisions to buy and sell, so do the cascades of world politics derive from choices on the part of numerous citizens to comply and defy.

Indeed, given the extraordinary speeds with which ideas can now be communicated and actions aggregated, it can be hypothesized that the cascades of world politics will be increasingly marked by surprising outcomes. That is, if the cascades accelerate the interaction processes of global life faster than those who observe or participate in them can revise their understanding of what the early phases of scenarios signify, then the course of events may often move in unexpected directions. For example, the cease-fire agreement between the Nicaraguan government and the contras in March 1988 startled politicians and journalists alike. They were caught off guard—so much so that the Reagan White House was in the midst of efforts to mobilize additional support for the contras—because a swift cascade had recast the shifting coalitions of the U.S. Congress and the new priorities of Gorbachev's Politburo, both of which suddenly converged around the politics of Central America. Ironically, even as officials and citizens have become more skilled at elaborating scenarios, the cascades of world politics have begun to flow at a speed and by rules to which their scenarios have yet to become adjusted.

DECISION RULES IN CASCADES

It is one thing to note that actions in the multi-centric world move in cascades, but it is quite another to identify the specific variants of behavior involved. In the state-centric world, actors conclude alliances, threaten war, enter temporary coalitions, make accommodations, switch blocs, and in other ways seek to maximize their power and pursue their interests. What are the comparable strategies that underlie the processes of the multi-centric world?

Many of the decision rules that actors in cascades follow have already been identified in the previous chapter, especially in table 10.2, which indicated the strategies pursued by collectivities committed to each of the four types of adaptation. The table shows that the kinds of action undertaken in the multi-centric world are in part dependent on the priorities the actors attach to the internal and external demands made upon them. Absent from the table, however, are the decision rules to which actors in the two worlds are likely to adhere in relating to each other. If the interaction between sovereignty-bound and sovereignty-free actors is as extensive as suggested in chapter 10, then attention must be paid to the strategies and tactics that guide that interaction.

In the case of states, we need to uncover the rules that govern their entry into, or their avoidance of, the multi-centric world: when governments will coordinate with each other as a means of dealing with problems posed by the interdependence of their societies, when they will yield jurisdiction to sovereignty-free actors at home or abroad, when they will allow circumstances at home to involve them in issues of the multi-centric world abroad, and when they will resort to covert actions as a means of moving toward their goals. Table 11.1 is an attempt to set forth some of these rules. Although it is hardly an exhaustive listing, it is suggestive of the frequency with which governments are compelled to move out of their interstate orbits and interact with the sovereignty-free actors of the multi-centric world.

Most of the rules in table 11.1 are straightforward and readily linked to the principles of the state system. Rule 5a is especially interesting in that it highlights the way in which the expanding interdependence of world politics is eroding the sovereignty principle. It suggests

TABLE 11.1. Decision Rules Underlying the Conduct of Sovereignty-Bound Actors (SBAs) in the Multi-centric World

1. SBAs yield jurisdiction, fully or partially, to transnational sovereignty-free actors when
    a. governments are paralyzed by prior commitments and sovereignty-free actors may be able to break the stalemate;
    b. the initiatives of sovereignty-free actors do not intrude upon prior commitments and may yield desirable results;
    c. there are advantages in a new course of action, but a public commitment to it prior to a demonstration of its merit runs the risk of public opposition;
    d. an issue has acquired such momentum in a particular direction that to attempt to curb the involvement of sovereignty-free actors is to risk unacceptable consequences in other policy areas.

2. SBAs allow domestic demands to take precedence over external requirements when
    a. the domestic economy stagnates;
    b. a major subsystem becomes agitated;
    c. domestic opinion coalesces around a specific perspective;
    d. internal strife threatens governmental effectiveness.

3. SBAs respond to or seek out relations with sovereignty-free collectivities abroad when
    a. they seek to bring pressure on governments abroad and the collectivities are seen as having influence on them;
    b. they are under pressures to do so from domestic groups at home;
    c. they perceive the foreign actors as helpful in building a policy consensus at home;
    d. they seek to increase their share of a foreign market.

4. SBAs coordinate both with other states and with sovereignty-free actors abroad when
    a. sudden crises occur in the world economy, the physical environment, or the social world that bear immediately upon the welfare of private groups in several countries.

5. SBAs coordinate with other states as a means of moving more freely in the multi-centric world when
    a. their governments agree on a course to follow, but one or more are severely restrained by the opposition of domestic groups;
    b. transnational interactions among sovereignty-free actors begin to impinge upon the stability of two or more governments.

6. SBAs avoid contacts in the multi-centric world when
    a. their involvement would catch them up in cascades that run counter to their values and policies;
    b. to do so would be to set precedents for future contacts that are deemed risky.

7. SBAs initiate covert policies and actions when
    a. the desired outcomes of international situations cannot be achieved under the norms of the multi-centric system;
    b. sovereignty-free actors have goals or resources that cannot be mobilized through conventional diplomatic channels or by accepted practices in the multi-centric world.

that there may be a number of situations in which governments have to engage in collusion in order to cope with their domestic problems. One can easily imagine a wide range of scenarios in which heads of state ask each other to desist from certain actions, undertake certain commitments, or make certain statements that will facilitate adoption or implementation of policies they both wish to pursue. This is particularly the case when a government has a stake in the outcome of a succession process or a policy debate in another state and coordinates its actions with the leadership of that state in such a way as to enhance, or at least not to worsen, the prospects of attaining the desired outcome.

The memoirs of statesmen are not filled with episodes of this sort, but that may be because to acknowledge engaging in such a practice is to concede having engaged in collusion with a foreign government to influence domestic politics. The 1987 Gorbachev-Reagan summit meeting in Washington, for example, was pervaded with the coordinated efforts of the Soviet and U.S. governments to make sure that, even if large issues could not be resolved, they each would come away with accomplishments that could assist them domestically—the Reagan administration with a treaty ratification in the Senate and the Soviets with a warm reception that could support efforts at domestic economic reform. Even the willingness on both sides to discuss issues they considered none of the other's business, such as human rights, seemed to have occurred by virtue of an agreement that each needed to establish having raised the issues with the other. The agreement may have been tacit, but one suspects that in this era of postinternational politics such matters are no longer the subject of innuendo but instead are discussed bluntly by the leaders involved.[16]

Indeed, the cascades of a bifurcated world are leading officials to enter into relationships that range them against some of their own domestic adversaries. Plotting against common external enemies has always been a basis for interstate coordination, but scheming to outwit their own peoples is surely a mark of the extent to which the structures of world politics are changing.

Table 11.2 presents the converse of table 11.1: decision rules that guide the conduct of sovereignty-free actors in the state-centric world. Again the listing is only selective, but it does suggest the complexities

---

[16] Sometimes, the bluntness is conveyed in a request to avoid discussing delicate issues in public. During his trip to Poland in 1989, for example, President Bush made few references to President Gorbachev of the Soviet Union apparently because "both Solidarity and General Jaruzelski [the Polish leader] had told aides to Mr. Bush that he would do them no favor by disdaining or criticizing Mr. Gorbachev." R. W. Apple, Jr., "A Polish Journey," *New York Times*, July 12, 1989, p. A4.

TABLE 11.2. Decision Rules Underlying the Conduct of Sovereignty-Free
Actors (SFAs) in the State-centric World

1. SFAs seek to strengthen their relations with states by
    a. defending the legitimacy of their organizational status and the worthiness of their activities and values;
    b. avoiding a reputation as an ineffective or unreliable transnational actor;
    c. demonstrating as often as possible a capacity to act independently of the state in which their headquarters are located;
    d. expanding their membership as widely as possible among citizens and organizations abroad and establishing local affiliates through which those in other countries can work;
    e. intruding themselves into situations where their values and competence can affect the course of events;
    f. maintaining a multiplicity of ties to other transnational actors in their own and related fields.

2. SFAs seek to enhance their internal coherence by
    a. offering support, financial as well as moral where possible, to affiliates and counterparts abroad whenever the latter are embroiled in conflicts;
    b. avoiding situations that require their membership to attach a higher priority to their transnational than their national loyalties;
    c. stressing their transnational ties and the benefits derived from them;
    d. resisting efforts by governments to narrow the scope of their activities.

3. SFAs seek to strengthen their relations with the state in which they have their headquarters by
    a. establishing a multiplicity of links to states and counterparts abroad, thereby increasing the costs to the host state for any effort to curb their activities;
    b. publicizing the contributions their transnational activities make to the welfare of communities in the host state.

with which such actors have to contend in order to preserve their autonomy. Most notably, the table points up the delicate nature of the strategies available to sovereignty-free collectivities for moving effectively among states while still retaining the loyalty of their memberships. To be free of the responsibilities of sovereignty has many advantages, but it also presents leaders in the multi-centric world with a multiplicity of simultaneous challenges.

CENTRALIZING AND DECENTRALIZING PROCESSES

The tumultuous nature of cascades reflects the tensions between the centralizing and decentralizing dynamics at work in both the multi-

and state-centric worlds. On a daily or weekly basis, one observes cascades; but on the scale of years or decades one observes postinternational politics undergoing, simultaneously, tendencies toward integration and fragmentation, toward authority being centralized in fewer, more encompassing whole systems and decentralized in numerous subsystems. Brief references to these processes have been made in previous chapters, but they will now be considered at greater length.

Perhaps the most visible (and surely the most remarked upon) discrepancy between centralizing and decentralizing dynamics is that the world economy is becoming integrated into a single coherent whole while the world polity is being fragmented into ever more numerous and competitive units. In contrast to the proliferation of states, subgroups, and transnational organizations, the global economy appears to be subsuming, or at least affecting to an important degree, more and more of the activities of national and subnational economies. Finance, trade, agriculture, labor migrations, production of raw materials, assembling of finished products, and a host of other economic functions are increasingly performed in the context of global demands, needs, and criteria. Yet these centralizing processes continuously encounter the organizations through which political management is exercised moving in the opposite direction, an encounter that introduces contradictions into the global economy and strains in and among national polities. As the periodic currency crises of the 1980s have demonstrated, these encounters between global economies and national politics can initiate some of the more powerful cascades that flow through the structures of postinternational politics.

The contradictions between centralizing and decentralizing processes are also manifested in actions designed to enlarge the scope of either central or peripheral authorities in a collectivity. Tensions are often generated thereby because the actions are cast in zero-sum terms, either promising benefits for the central authorities at the expense of their subgroup counterparts or vice versa. Efforts to restructure UNESCO, to achieve autonomy for the Tamils or for Quebec, to reorganize the relationship between the Canadian affiliate of the United Auto Workers and the UAW's governing body, to bring Egypt back into the Arab League, to coordinate the interest rates of the industrialized nations—these are a few of the recent instances in which the tensions in world politics have been expressed in terms of greater or lesser centralization.

In recent years, the tendency toward decentralization in political systems has intensified with the emergence of neoconservatism as a political philosophy and force in the West and with the realization in the

Communist world that planned economies lack the flexibility to sustain economic growth. Such changes have led to the adoption of decentralized economic policies in the People's Republic of China and to efforts along the same line in the Soviet Union, and to programs in the Western democracies designed to reduce the scope of governmental regulation, give greater freedom to the operation of market mechanisms, and even sell government-owned facilities to private interests. Nor have these procedures been confined to Western governments committed to laissez-faire principles; shortly after winning a majority in 1981, the Socialists in France began "a process of governmental decentralization which [within a few years] resulted in no fewer than five hundred pages of legislation encompassing over 33 laws and 219 decrees."[17]

On the other hand, it is important not to overlook the centralizing tendencies that are also operative. Even aside from such border-spanning issues as environmental pollution, the depleted ozone layer, and the drug trade, the degree of global interdependence is now too great for individuals and collectivities not to be drawn together in complex and overlapping linkages. Their needs and wants may not always be driven by economic considerations, but they are nonetheless led to reach out beyond system boundaries for information, moral support, aesthetic satisfactions, and other nonmaterial resources. And this is no less the case for the same political entities that are undergoing fragmentation. Whether they be denationalized industries in France or newly created local centers of decision in the People's Republic of China, they are not cut off from the dynamics of global life. Their decentralization refers to their relations with higher authorities within their own system and not to their ties with counterparts in other systems elsewhere in the world.

Indeed, with the possible exception of many families and some courts (and even these are only possibilities), it is difficult to conceive of any collectivities that have not experienced the centralizing dynamics inherent in a shrinking world. From local governments to ethnic minorities, from religious factions to sports teams, from conservative leaders to art museums, from trade unions to the Arab League, from the female half of the human race to entertainment groups, from rebel movements to automobile manufacturers, from the Catholic church to music festivals[18]—to mention but a few examples that gained public

[17] Vivien A. Schmidt, "Decentralization: A Revolutionary Reform," in Patrick McCarthy, ed., *Socialism in Power* (Westport, Conn.: Greenwood, 1987), p. 83.

[18] Citations illustrative of these diverse dimensions of interdependence are, respectively, Alfonso A. Narvaez, "2 Cities and a County in New Jersey Are Declared Nuclear-

notice in one short period—every sphere of endeavor has become enmeshed in global interdependence. A single organization, the International Monetary Fund, has alone become involved in thousands of authority relationships in dozens of countries.[19]

In short, the cascades of postinternational politics are marked by both centralizing and decentralizing tendencies, and they unfold within the social and political realms as well as the domain of economic activity. Sometimes these tendencies cancel each other out and sometimes they reinforce each other, and the tensions among them give rise to many of the issues on the global agenda.

It should be stressed that interdependence is not merely another term for the complexities of postinternational politics. It consists of concrete processes that are self-generating as people experience what shrinking social and geographic distances are doing to their lives and work. The more such processes become evident, the more do people perceive their worlds to be changing, and the more do they begin to develop habits that are appropriate to the changes.[20] This is also the case for collectivity leaders, with the result that the self-generativity occurs at both the micro and macro levels and gives rise to snowballing processes that intensify the cascades and widen the interdependence.

In the previous chapter, it was concluded that the relationships between the state-centric and multi-centric worlds are presently stable but vulnerable to corrosion. Could the dynamism of cascading pro-

---

Free by Law," *New York Times*, December 30, 1985, p. B4; Steven R. Weisman, "Talks in India Explore Sri Lanka Pact," *New York Times*, June 3, 1985, p. A5; David B. Ottaway, "Fixing Responsibility in a Vacuum of Power," *Washington Post*, June 21, 1985, p. A30; Sally Bedell Smith, "U.S. and Soviet Plan World Games," *New York Times*, August 7, 1985, p. 1; "By Any Other Name, Conservative," *New York Times*, July 17, 1985, p. A8; John Russell, "Modern Art Museums: The Surprise Is Gone," *New York Times*, August 4, 1985, p. B1; R. W. Apple, Jr., "Steep Fall in Power and Influence Hampers Labor Unions in Europe," *New York Times*, January 20, 1985, p. 1; Judith Miller, "Arab Meeting Opens amid Deep Splits," *New York Times*, August 8, 1985, p. A11; Elaine Sciolini, "In Nairobi, Consensus," *New York Times*, July 29, 1985, p. A6; "Concert Raises $50 Million in Famine Aid," *International Herald Tribune*, July 15, 1985, p. 1; James LeMoyne, "Captured Salvadoran Rebel Papers List Training Given in East Bloc Nations," *New York Times*, May 21, 1985, p. 11; John Holusha, "The Disappearing 'U.S. Car,' " *New York Times*, August 10, 1985, p. A31; E. J. Dionne, "A Synod Balance Sheet," *New York Times*, December 9, 1985, p. 1; and Michael Billington, "Politics Embroil a Famous Festival," *New York Times*, August 11, 1985, p. B1.

[19] See, for example, Robert Johnston, "IMF, Argentina Agree on New Loan Program," *Los Angeles Times*, June 8, 1985, sec. 4, p. 1, and Judith Miller, "I.M.F. Warned Egypt about Mounting Debts," *New York Times*, August 3, 1985, sec. 1, p. 31.

[20] For an extensive analysis of these processes with respect to a particular issue, see Everett M. Rogers, *Diffusion of Innovations*, 3rd ed. (New York: Free Press, 1983).

cesses give further impetus to the corrosive forces and perhaps ultimately upset the prevailing equilibrium? Are decision rules that foster competition between the two worlds likely to prevail over those that encourage collaboration between them? Are the present arrangements merely a transitional phase, which will come to an end as the state-centric world learns how to control its multi-centric counterpart or as the complexities of the postinternational order expand and overwhelm states? Or is it possible that the delicate balance will persist for a relatively long period of time? Table 11.3 outlines three equally plausible futures. Which of them is more likely depends on the ways in which the parameters of global politics have been and will be altered by the advent of turbulent conditions. That is the focus of the next four chapters.

TABLE 11.3. The Multi-centric and State-centric Worlds under Centralizing and Decentralizing Conditions

	High Degree of Centralization	*High Degree of Decentralization*	*Even Balance between Centralization and Decentralization*
Condition of the multi-centric world	Subordinate	Predominant	Nonhierarchical bargaining, tensions, and accommodations
Condition of the state-centric world	Predominant	Subordinate	Nonhierarchical bargaining, tensions, and accommodations
Dominant global issues	Territorial and military issues	Economic and autonomy issues	Mix of military and economic issues

PART FOUR

TURBULENT TRANSFORMATIONS

CHAPTER 12

ENHANCED ELITES

Information, Wisdom, and Artificial Intelligence

I think that Gorbachev's personality has just speeded up events. Thanks to his personal qualities, his political acumen, his education and a surprising ability to understand the rhythm and demands of the time. The times have persistently demanded changes, knocked at the door, and he earlier than others understood that the door should be open.

—Aleksandr N. Yakovlev,
member of the Politburo of the Soviet Communist party[1]

A DESCRIPTION of the major components of the bifurcated system does not account for what drives it, for the forces that sustain or extend the structures and processes by which actors in the multi-centric and state-centric worlds retain their autonomy even as they become increasingly interdependent. The causal dynamics have been summarized diagramatically (see figure 1.1) and brief references have been made to them throughout the previous chapters: the exogenous forces released by explosive technologies, populations, and resources, and the endogenous stimuli provided by the changing skills and orientations of individuals at the micro level and by subgroupism and authority crises at the macro level. However, a systematic exploration of the ways in which the conditions of turbulence have transformed global parameters has yet to be undertaken.

Accordingly, we seek here and in the next chapter to explain how it is that citizens and officials have moved sufficiently along the learning continuum, away from the habit end and toward the adaptive end, to make it possible to speak meaningfully of the micro sources of macro global change. We aspire to an understanding of why the bifurcated

---

[1] Quoted in "Words of a Gorbachev Aide," *New York Times*, October 28, 1988, p. A10.

universe of postinternational politics could not have come into being without major transformations in the competencies and predispositions of individuals throughout the world. This chapter considers such transformations among elites (officials of governments and leaders of private organizations). The next chapter will investigate the changes among individuals in follower roles (citizens of the state and members of sovereignty-free collectivities).

OLD ORIENTATIONS AND NEW SKILLS

While it is clear that elites have been acquiring new analytic skills as a result of the microelectronic revolution, it does not follow that their orientations have changed correspondingly. On the contrary, there are grounds for believing that public officials and organizational heads are still inclined to accord the highest priority to the welfare of the collectivity and to press for its interests; to adjust their goals to the resources available and to work at maintaining the support of their members; and to conform to the short-term perspectives of their members even when their own assessments tell them that other perspectives are more suitable for the long term. Indeed, if members have become more analytically skillful and demanding (as will be argued in chapter 13), and if collectivities everywhere have thus entered into the throes of authority crises (as will be argued in chapter 14), leaders may be more likely than ever to adhere to these long-standing modes of leadership, to put caution ahead of risk and preservation ahead of innovation.

Old and established as such orientations may be, however, they are now embedded in a context of new skills and knowledge. The new skills include a greater capacity to generate and analyze information relevant to the policies of their collectivities, and the new knowledge includes a more reliable set of theories, findings, and insights concerning the nature of collectivities, the processes of decision making, and the circumstances in which challenges to their leadership may arise. In many parts of the world, public officials and private leaders now have access to computers—what a recent advertisement called "power tools for the thinking class"[2]—and this technology has the capacity to process, simulate, and assess quantities of information on a scale not pre-

[2] Placed by NEC Information Systems, the advertisement set forth the idea that "one way to get a little farther, a little faster, is to consider making the NEC PowerMate 386/20 and PowerMate 2 part of your corporate climb. Because both help you do a faster, more thorough job of working and thinking." *Wall Street Journal*, November 23, 1988, p. A16.

viously imaginable.[3] Equally important, as a result of great strides since the 1950s in organizational theory, cognitive psychology, conflict management, business administration, game theory, and other social-science fields, those who head collectivities can now draw upon epistemic communities of experts for every aspect of every issue on the global agenda.[4] Unlike their predecessors, they can now rely on advice and information derived from sophisticated and complex models rather than from intuitive and simplistic formulations.

Of course, neither the technical nor the social-science equipment necessarily leads to wise policy making or effective leadership. Today's leaders are still habdaptive actors, subject to habitual impulses and the rationalizations that make change appear as more of the same. Nevertheless, it also seems to be the case that in important respects the new equipment is encouraging them to move away from the habit and toward the adaptive end of the learning continuum. The newly available knowledge has enhanced their sensitivity to the underlying dynamics at work in a situation. The improved analytic techniques have provided them with a greater competence for assessing their situations than earlier generations had. As Yakovlev's remarks quoted above imply, leaders are now able to use their own talents more effectively—to "speed up events" and "understand the rhythms of the time"—and thus to function ever more skillfully as the prime channels through which stirrings at the micro level are converted into macro outcomes.

To be more specific (and to readily concede that there are surely many exceptions), leaders are now more likely to be deliberative, to be alert to feedback from their own actions, to appreciate that what may once have seemed simple can be profoundly complex, to recognize that unintended consequences can thwart their efforts, to be aware of historical analogies, to measure gains against losses, to discern that the effectiveness of their policies is in part a function of the structure of their organizations, to be wary of single-cause explanations, to under-

---

[3] Although admitting that "there is little empirical research to document" its impact, one analyst argues that the new technology is "altering the framework within which large political systems, such as nation-states or central and peripheral governments, interact," that "this enormous expansion in information power makes governments more aware of the actions of other governments and more likely to act in order to protect actual or anticipated challenges to their goals." James N. Danziger, "Computing and the Political World," *Computers and the Social Sciences* 2 (1986): 191.

[4] See Ernst B. Haas, *When Knowledge Is Power: Three Models of Change in International Organizations* (Berkeley: University of California Press, 1989), and Peter M. Haas, ed., *Epistemic Communities and International Policy Coordination* (forthcoming).

stand that their actions have to be partly a response to what their adversaries expect them to do, to grasp that situations have to play out in certain ways prior to the successful culmination of negotiations, and so on through a long list of concepts and understandings that mark recent advances in the social sciences. A few findings and examples suggestive of these enlarged skills can perhaps usefully be noted:

More deliberation: The heightened inclination to deliberate derives from the vast new data resources as well as the analytic skills made available by computer technologies. As one analyst has put it, "The enormous increase in the availability of information . . . has accentuated the practice of seeking knowledge before making decisions."[5]

More appreciation of complexity: In a 1988 interview, Rev. Gustavo Gutiérrez, a Peruvian priest widely viewed as the founder of liberation theology in the 1960s, acknowledged that, in the intervening decades, liberation theologists learned that social, cultural, and gender factors, as well as economics and politics, had to be taken into account: "Nothing has been more important for us in recent years than to recognize the full complexity of the world of the poor."[6]

Sensitivity to historical analogies: During the negotiations that ended with Ferdinand Marcos stepping down from the presidency of the Philippines, for example, American officials were anxious to extend every courtesy to a long-standing ally. "We were all thinking about the [Shah of Iran's] miseries," observed one participant in the discussions, "and agreed this would not happen to Marcos." On the other hand, Marcos was apparently moved by an analogy to a different American ally, Ngo Dinh Diem, the president of South Vietnam who was assassinated during a 1963 coup. "Marcos had Diem on his mind at all times," another official commented. "He was very concerned about how he would leave his palace. He wanted to make sure he did not leave with a bullet."[7]

Awareness of organizational structure affecting effectiveness: This was "perhaps the most important finding" uncovered by an

[5] Harriet Zuckerman, "Uses and Control of Knowledge: Implications for the Social Fabric," in James F. Short, Jr., ed., *The Social Fabric: Dimensions and Issues* (Newbury Park, Calif.: Sage, 1986), p. 341.

[6] Peter Steinfels, "New Liberation Faith: Social Conflict Is Muted," *New York Times*, July 27, 1988, p. A2.

[7] Bernard Gwertzman, "Reagan Sent Marcos Secret Message 12 Hours before White House's Plea," *New York Times*, February 28, 1986, p. A12.

interview survey of sixty chief executive officers of multinational corporations.[8]

Wariness of single-cause explanations: By applying an elaborate and systematic content analysis to the speeches of American and Soviet officials, Tetlock found circumstances under which foreign policy officials in these countries are capable of becoming more analytically sophisticated and coping with cognitive complexities.[9]

Expectations of adversaries as a source of action: The globalization of the world's financial markets has heightened sensitivity to founding behavior partly on the basis of what competitors are expected to do. To note again the insight of John Maynard Keynes, "We have reached the third degree, where we devote our intelligences to anticipating what average opinion expects the average opinion to be. And there are some, I believe, who practice the fourth, the fifth and higher degrees."[10]

Negotiations: As the Speaker of the Philippine House of Representatives, Ramon Mitra, commented during a suspension of negotiations over the future of U.S. bases in his country, "It is just part of the dance. I am still confident there will be an agreement."[11]

A further insight into the importance of such new tools of social scientific analysis can be developed from a comparison of the way in which foreign policies are made today with the classic case of the great war no one intended. The spiralling processes of misperception that resulted in World War I could conceivably occur again, but the knowledge that policymakers now have about the dangers of misperception and the advantages of accurate comprehension of a situation is so much greater than was the case in the summer of 1914 that the probabilities of another such unintended conflagration, or at least one involving nuclear weapons, seem very remote indeed.[12] Moreover, the

[8] Grady Means, "The Globalization of World Markets: The CEO Response," *Washington Quarterly* 11 (Winter 1988): 156.

[9] Philip E. Tetlock, "Monitoring the Integrative Complexity of American and Soviet Policy Rhetoric: What Can Be Learned?" *Journal of Social Issues* 44 (Summer 1988): 101–31.

[10] Quoted in Karen Arenson, "The New Trading Game," *New York Times*, September 20, 1986, p. 28.

[11] Quoted in Mark Fineman, "U.S., Manila Disagree on Impact of Snag on Bases," *Los Angeles Times*, July 27, 1988, p. 5.

[12] For a cogent analysis in which this is a prime theme, see McGeorge Bundy, *Danger*

familiarity of foreign offices today with the technology of rapid communication is so much greater than it was then that the following explanation of that colossal "failure of diplomacy" is surely no longer relevant:

> One of the causes of that failure was that diplomats could not cope with the volume and speed of electronic communication. Most of the aristocrats and gentlemen who made up the diplomatic corps in 1914 were of the old school in many respects, as wary of new technology as some generals were wary of newfangled weapons and strategies. And as the generals failed to appreciate the significance of long-range artillery and machine guns . . . the diplomats failed to understand the full impact of instantaneous communications without the ameliorating effect of delay. They still counted on the ultimate effectiveness of "spoken words of a decent man" in face-to-face encounters but were forced to negotiate many important issues over copper wire. The piles of futile telegrams (like the later rows of dead soldiers) were the tangible remains of their failure.[13]

Succinctly stated, while modern leaders may be threatened by problems of system overload, they are increasingly equipped to cope with the challenges that face them. Greater complexity, it seems clear, has begat greater knowledge about complexity. Figure 12.1 is an indication of this change; it shows the variety of skills that present-day leaders in the multi-centric world are apt to find helpful in the performance of their duties. The very fact that such a range of competencies is now declared to be valuable is a sign of the enhanced capacities of elites to cope with, if not to take advantage of, the complexity and dynamism they confront in a turbulent world.

The computer is, of course, central to the enhancement of elite competencies, but this new capacity is grounded in more than simply new equipment. Not only do computer technologies facilitate the analysis of huge amounts of information, but they also impel their users to become more skillful. The very fact of being confronted with so much information that may contain important guides to action induces leaders to probe more fully for obscure patterns, multiple causes, and alternative interpretations, which, in turn, enlarges their store of analytic skills. The more their skills are engaged by the new technologies, in

and Survival: Choices about the Bomb in the First Fifty Years (New York: Random House, 1988).

[13] Stephen Kern, The Culture of Time and Space, 1880–1918 (Cambridge; Harvard University Press, 1983), pp. 275–76.

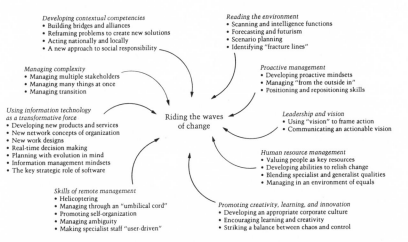

Developing contextual competencies
- Building bridges and alliances
- Reframing problems to create new solutions
- Acting nationally and locally
- A new approach to social responsibility

Reading the environment
- Scanning and intelligence functions
- Forecasting and futurism
- Scenario planning
- Identifying "fracture lines"

Managing complexity
- Managing multiple stakeholders
- Managing many things at once
- Managing transition

Proactive management
- Developing proactive mindsets
- Managing "from the outside in"
- Positioning and repositioning skills

Using information technology as a transformative force
- Developing new products and services
- New network concepts of organization
- New work designs
- Real-time decision making
- Planning with evolution in mind
- Information management mindsets
- The key strategic role of software

Riding the waves of change

Leadership and vision
- Using "vision" to frame action
- Communicating an actionable vision

Human resource management
- Valuing people as key resources
- Developing abilities to relish change
- Blending specialist and generalist qualities
- Managing in an environment of equals

Skills of remote management
- Helicoptering
- Managing through an "umbilical cord"
- Promoting self-organization
- Managing ambiguity
- Making specialist staff "user-driven"

Promoting creativity, learning, and innovation
- Developing an appropriate corporate culture
- Encouraging learning and creativity
- Striking a balance between chaos and control

FIGURE 12.1. An Overview of Some Emerging Managerial Competencies. SOURCE: Gareth Morgan, *Riding the Waves of Change: Developing Managerial Competencies for a Turbulent World* (San Francisco: Jossey-Bass, 1989), p. 3. © Jossey-Bass 1989; reprinted with permission of the publisher.

other words, the more do they learn about how to learn. The movement away from the habit end of the continuum thus tends to feed on itself and become self-sustaining.[14]

Admittedly, it has been argued that the improved analytic skills of elites can aggravate as well as alleviate problems. Some observers, for example, believe that part of the explanation for the crash of the world's stock markets in 1987 lay in the fact that, as the global network of buyers and sellers became increasingly interconnected and computerized, and as financial information thus flowed more efficiently and traders grew more sophisticated in responding to the flows, the markets became volatile to a degree never before experienced.[15] The aggregation of the very micro skills that made traders more competent, in other words, contributed to macro consequences that exceeded their ability to maintain orderly markets.

---

[14] For similar interpretations of the impact of computer technologies on those who occupy lower positions in organizational hierarchies, see James N. Danziger and Kenneth L. Kraemer, *People and Computers: The Impacts of Computing on End Users in Organizations* (New York: Columbia University Press, 1986), and Shoshana Zuboff, *In the Age of the Smart Machine: The Future of Work and Power* (New York: Basic Books, 1988).

[15] James Gleick, "When Chaos Rules the Market," *New York Times*, November 22, 1987, sec. 3, p. 1.

The fact that computers can readily display the consequences of interacting variables—with graphics, if desired—makes it easy for officials, or at least for their staffs, to appreciate how the choices made at one time relate to the alternatives available at a later time and thus how each stage of a situation is altered by the previous stage. Nor is it necessary that leaders be familiar with computer science in order to benefit from the new technologies. If they are clear about their goals and assumptions, and presuming they have the equipment and well-trained staffs, they need hardly do more than sit before their terminals and watch how their possible actions would play out in the context of various sets of premises.

In addition, leaders can turn to specialists in artificial intelligence (AI), expert systems, and political risk-analysis, who use forecasting models to assess the probable outcome of conflict situations. Most notably, "expected-utility decision" models have been employed with considerable success to anticipate the course of events in several complex and intense international conflicts. The fall of Italian governments, the Mexican response to IMF demands for austerity programs, strategic shifts in the Iran-Iraq war, uprisings in Iran, and the outcome of a successor crisis in the Soviet Union are among the situations which one such model is claimed to have accurately predicted.[16] To be sure, expected-utility models can also result in egregious errors, but they are due not so much to the forecasting methodologies as to the premises from which their users proceed. Improvement in the analytic skills of leaders does not guarantee a corresponding improvement in the quality of their decisions.

Computers can manage information on the scale of the *Encyclopedia Britannica* and can do so through structured networks of concepts.[17] It is estimated that the newest supercomputers are two hundred times faster than those of the previous generation and that those of the next generation may be another hundred times faster than the present machines. Computer memory devices will soon be operating on impulses of light rather than electronic signals and will be potentially capable of holding trillions of bits of informations in a space smaller than an ordinary home computer occupies.[18] If it is reasonable

[16] Bruce Bueno de Mesquita, David Newman, and Alvin Rabushka, *Forecasting Political Events: The Future of Hong Kong* (New Haven: Yale University Press, 1985), pp. 27–28.

[17] Douglas B. Lenat et al., "Knowsphere: Building Expert Systems with Encyclopedia Knowledge," in *Proceedings of the Eighth International Joint Conference on Artificial Intelligence* (Karlsruhe, West Germany, 1983), 1:167–69.

[18] New devices known as "heterojunctions" switch on and off in two picoseconds

to presume that solutions will be found to the problems associated with programming supercomputers to analyze vast amounts of data that depict micro-macro interactions across many levels of aggregation,[19] then it becomes possible to anticipate that postinternational politics will be conducted by officials who have extensive capacities for appraising their circumstances and framing a large number of alternatives from which they can choose courses of action.

Equally important, the information-processing techniques associated with the microelectronic revolution help develop analytic skills that can be used even in the absence of the electronic equipment that fostered them. Indeed, the impact of software programs on patterns of thought may well be the most significant consequence of the new technologies. There are lessons to be learned, for example, from the ease with which files can be merged, ideas inserted, sentences shifted, paragraphs replaced, and flow charts used to identify distant decision points, and these lessons can readily be assimilated into the processes whereby people think about problems, even when they are far removed from their computers.[20]

Again, this is not to suggest the coming of universal wisdom, or to claim that the world has witnessed the last foreign-policy blunder. Errors and misjudgments will continue to mar global politics, but their frequency and scope seem destined to diminish as the microelectronic technologies become standard equipment in foreign offices.

ALTERED METHODS OF DECISION MAKING

The microelectronic revolution should also lead to a reconsideration of the major premises that have long governed understanding of the limits on rational action in global politics. Some thirty years ago, Lindblom distinguished between the "rational-comprehensive," or "root," method of decision making and the "successive limited comparisons," or "branch," method. In the root method, the decision maker works from the ground up, carefully delineating and weighing goals, means, resources, and alternative courses of action before mak-

---

(trillionths of a second), compared with the several hundred picoseconds required for conventional silicon transistors. Andrew Pollock, "New Chips Offer the Promise of Much Speedier Computers," *New York Times*, January 4, 1989, p. A1.

[19] For an indication that the software problems can be resolved, see Frans N. Stokman, "Relational Databases, Network Analysis, and the Representation of Social Systems," *Connections* 11 (Fall 1988): 32–43.

[20] Sherry Turkle, *The Second Self: Computers and the Human Spirit* (New York: Simon & Schuster, 1984), and Zuboff, *In the Age of the Smart Machine*, especially chapter 5.

ing a choice. This method, Lindblom argued, was no longer a realistic option, given the limited time, information, intellect, and other resources available for coping with the myriad decisions that must be made in the complex press of daily events. Instead, policymakers were compelled to rely on the branch method, building out from the current situation step by step and in small increments, applying what has worked and is manageable while avoiding goals, policies, and means that are untried or that are based on long-term and thus uncertain perspectives. This has been the characteristic approach to policy-making; Lindblom called it "the science of muddling through."[21]

Cogent as this analysis may have been, however, it now needs to be reexamined in the context of the microelectronic revolution. It seems to be based on the following premises: (1) policymakers inevitably operate with insufficient information; (2) they cannot build nonquantitative considerations into their deliberations; (3) they cannot rank-order their preferences in enough specificity to be useful; (4) they cannot project the course of events beyond immediate circumstances; and (5) they do not have enough time to take into account all the factors that may be relevant to an issue. These premises may not have been fully negated by the microelectronic revolution, but they certainly have been called into question by it. The science of muddling through may well give way to the science of *modeling* through.

To recognize and accept that the root method of foreign policy making is not as impracticable as it once seemed, more is required than simply grasping what the new technologies can accomplish. One also needs to break free of a preoccupation with the limits of rational calculation. It is all too easy to dismiss the potentials of AI and the future generations of computers as exaggerated, because, after all, the human brain is too complex and the human capacity for nonrational action too great for any technology even to begin to emulate. One can also argue that world affairs are so overwhelmingly complex, affected by so many interacting variables, that no expert system can ever be developed that adequately reflects their dynamics. Such arguments, however, are blinding. They emphasize limits and not potentials. They preserve our self-esteem at the expense of our curiosity. They overlook the inclinations in our habit pools that are responsive to opportunities for learning. They inhibit us from asking questions that once seemed too absurd to consider, and thus they prevent us from probing for patterns and insights that were once consigned to the realm of the unknowable.

To be sure, the processes of both human thought and world politics

21 Charles E. Lindblom, "The Science of 'Muddling Through'," *Public Administration Review* 19 (Spring 1959): pp. 79–88.

are extraordinarly complex, and there probably are limits beyond which neither can be rendered machine-readable. And certainly it is also the case that a preponderance of our habits militate against rational action. Yet to dwell on these limitations is to risk foreclosing a recognition that greater degrees of rationality may yet come to mark the conduct of foreign policy.

Put more positively, skepticism needs to be balanced with playfulness, with a readiness to consider "as if" worlds as well as real worlds. Our commitment to focusing only on empirically verified or verifiable truths, though preferable to a devotion to ideological truths, can be unduly restraining if we do not also allow ourselves to treat imagined truths, even absurd possibilities, *as if* they prevailed, and then probe what follows from them. The capacity to play the game of "as if" more thoroughly is precisely one of the benefits of the microelectronic revolution.[22] Not only has the computer enhanced the ability of leaders to process information, but it also enables them to compare alternative strategies in more systematic ways. With new techniques for generating and probing imagined worlds having become available, policymakers might discern previously unsuspected courses of action that could move them more surely toward their goals than those they have been following.

Suppose public officials have instant access to all the information they may need to make decisions. If those responsible for the conduct of foreign policy need to know how armed forces are disposed in a situation, they can merely call up the appropriate file on their screens and study the charts, tables, and maps displayed before them. If they need to calculate the pressures and counterpressures in the multi-centric world that are salient for their policies, they can access the files on such variables as the identity of the sovereignty-free actors most likely to be supportive and the factions, enmities, legal procedures, and cultural premises that may constrain their freedom of action. If they need to assess the possible outcome of a crisis, they can call up information about the pressures that are likely to play on the parties involved and the ways in which they are likely to interact.

INFORMATION AND WISDOM

But is Lindblom still correct in his contention that rational decision making is inhibited by the inability of officials to project their estimates beyond the immediate circumstances into the medium and long term?

[22] For a discussion of the virtues of the game of "as if," see James N. Rosenau, *The Scientific Study of Foreign Policy*, rev. ed. (New York: Nichols, 1980), pp. 28–29.

Can computers, or even supercomputers, overcome that problem? Here again one can emphasize either the limits or the opportunities. Projections will be less reliable as the time span is greater, but the power of supercomputers certainly seems sufficient to begin to open windows on the medium term, if not on situations that consist of sequences of interaction going beyond that. Computers have been able to play games of chess encompassing fifty moves for each side;[23] surely, then, comparable scenarios in foreign affairs can now be analyzed. In particular, the technology of pattern recognition has great potential for making possible new insights into the regularities of behavior relevant to foreign policy. As one specialist has put it, the system-revealing capacities of the microelectronic revolution

> are likely to surprise even the most imaginative among us by the suddenness with which they will affect our lives. Procedures that effectively detect and expose lies, treachery, or deceit at high speed and with great reliability may soon be feasible. So are techniques for revealing to users of a system whether inputs are inconsistent. Newer methods of communications, such as computer conferencing, are opening up new modes somewhere between speech and writing that may amplify the parties' ability to debate in the sense of Anatol Rapoport, where each party understands the other. Systems to help people to realize that imprecise reasoning and communication is appropriate to some situations, and how to do it, are also new and promising possibilities. All these offer new tools, new options for controlling conflict or at least its study.[24]

Some qualifications are in order. The new technology does not have unlimited capacities. The previously unobtainable insight is not necessarily an accurate insight. Decision makers will always feel that more information is needed, and certainly foreign affairs do involve many more players and a much greater number of moves than chess games do. To repeat, however, an acknowledgment of limits does not amount to a dismissal of potentials. Just as a computer can be enabled to play a competent chess game by programming it for the *most likely* moves rather than for all those that are hypothetically possible, so can a for-

[23] It has been estimated that today's fastest computer would require close to a decade to process *all* the possible moves early in a game. Joel N. Shurkin, "Expert Systems: The Practical Face of Artificial Intelligence," *Technology Review* 86 (November–December 1983): 74.

[24] Manfred Kochen, "Can the Global System Learn to Control Conflict?" in Richard L. Merritt and Bruce M. Russett, eds., *From National Development to Global Community: Essays in Honor of Karl W. Deutsch* (London: George Allen & Unwin, 1981), p. 399.

eign-policy scenario be kept manageable by including only plausible events and choices. Such a procedure, of course, raises the problem of how "plausibility" is to be defined, but this problem can be at least partially addressed through the use of expert systems (see below).

Lindblom's analysis also presumed, as we have noted, that the root method does not allow policymakers to take advantage of nonquantitative considerations—the lessons of past experience, intuitive hunches, the creative insights. Raw information involves a concrete phenomenon, a single interaction sequence, an established finding, an observed event. It does not capture the more elaborate sequences of interaction and the motives, perceptions, and relationships that are at work in them. Impressive and powerful as the technology of pattern recognition has become, it can identify only those tendencies that are susceptible to quantification. It can display the disposition of forces around the world, for example, but comprehending the conditions under which actors would be willing to use the forces is more than a matter of technology. It requires a qualitative grasp of subtle dynamics that do not lend themselves to quantification.

It is here, in the area of nonquantifiable judgments, or wisdom, that AI becomes relevant. AI offers a means, known as *expert systems*, for including in the analysis of a problem the most up-to-date understandings of how and why its component phenomena function as they do. These understandings may be founded on scientific research, recent events, accumulated experience, logical inferences, rules of thumb, hunches, or any other bases. By systematizing these various sources, AI provides, through the supercomputer, a decision-making facility that humans could not begin to emulate. In such diverse fields as medicine, business management, geological exploration, telephone repair, and linguistic analysis, programs that incorporate human expertise into a computer's memory have been applied with reasonable success. In medicine, information about some five hundred diseases has been put into a program called Internist and made available to physicians who are remote from advanced medical centers. In a study of the program's utility, its assessments of nineteen actual cases involving forty-three different diagnoses were compared with those of the physicians who had tended the patients and the clinical experts who had studied them. The experts were right on 35 of their diagnoses, the physicians on 28, and Internist on 25, a finding that led one observer to conclude that "Internist did miss some diagnoses, but it generally did as well as most ordinary physicians."[25]

[25] Shurkin, "Expert Systems," p. 76, citing a report in the *New England Journal of Medicine*.

If such developments are occurring in so many diverse areas of knowledge, it is reasonable to suppose that AI may bring substantial advances in the analysis of foreign policy as well. At least, it seems feasible to build the wisdom of experts—experienced area specialists, theoretical modelers, foreign-service officers, journalists, and others with knowledge of particular issues, countries, or relationships—into programs that anticipate the actions that the parties to a situation might take under varying circumstances at each of the several choice points in the scenarios. It is at these points that the need is felt most acutely for historical analogies, long-term trend lines, cost-benefit analyses, accumulated experience, and other forms of expertise that AI can readily manage.[26]

Given the secrecy that generally surrounds foreign offices, it is difficult to estimate how many use or have experimented with AI and up-to-date computer technologies, but it is hard to imagine that at least the more developed countries have not sought to take advantage of such techniques—for example, to portray outcomes derived from competing schools of thought on the dynamics of Iran's revolution, the motivation of Iraq's President Saddam Hussein, the readiness of Saudi Arabia to become involved, and other components of the situation in the Persian Gulf area.

Some might argue that knowledge is too primitive in the field of foreign affairs to consider it as amenable to the work of experts and the construction of systems comparable to those used in, say, medicine. This field is founded on scientific experimentation, whereas foreign-affairs specialists have much less reliable materials to go on. Nevertheless, the use of expert systems does seem feasible if only to take advantage of the most reliable knowledge that is *currently available*. The fact that foreign-affairs knowledge is primitive relative to that in other fields does not exclude the possibility that some understandings are more sound than others.

Nor does the inchoate nature of foreign-affairs knowledge preclude differentiating among various degrees of expertise, between those who exhibit more of the attributes of experts and those who exhibit fewer. Seven such attributes can be cited—the ability to solve problems, explain results, learn from experience, restructure knowledge, break rules when necessary, determine relevance, and recognize the limits of understanding—and all of them are readily applicable to experts in the

---

[26] For a skeptical assessment of the utility of AI, see Hubert L. Dreyfus, *What Computers Can't Do: The Limits of Artificial Intelligence* (New York: Harper & Row, 1979).

foreign-policy field.[27] While computer-generated expert systems have so far assimilated only the first three of these attributes, they have nonetheless been put to valuable use in a variety of fields.

In short, the use of AI in a field is not dependent on the state of knowledge in it. AI is, after all, only a technique for analyzing problems and suggesting solutions. Its use is not as a substitute for humans but as a supplement to them. On the other hand, the problems to which such techniques can be addressed persist irrespective of the means adopted for comprehending and solving them, and conventional, nonmachine methods of assessing international situations have not proved so successful as to obviate the need to try out other methods.

Moreover, AI offers an opportunity to synthesize scientific and traditional approaches to world affairs. These two perspectives—one emphasizing rigorous inferences from recurring patterns and the other stressing experiential wisdom—have long been viewed as mutually exclusive,[28] but both can be incorporated with relative ease into an expert system. The process of transforming experiential wisdom into an expert system involves reducing it to a set of if-then rules. These rules, which may number in the hundreds, form a chain of reasoning in which the presence of condition X leads to conclusion Y, which in turn serves as a condition for reaching the next conclusion in the chain. A diplomat who has served in the Soviet Union for many years may be convinced that a time of leadership succession is a condition during which innovative policies are avoided. This conclusion may in turn be a condition influencing whether the Soviet government will be inclined to accept or reject an overture toward accommodation. If the diplomat believes, however, that a certain kind of overture overrides the connection, then this rule, too, is included in the expert system, with an appropriate weight. This process results in a complex web of weighted rules, known by AI specialists as an *inference engine*.[29] Thus, intuitive insights can be rendered systematic and, inasmuch as the work of scientists can also be translated into if-then webs of decision rules, the

[27] These attributes have been identified by Randall David, as cited in Shurkin, "Expert Systems," p. 75.

[28] See Charles A. McClelland, "International Relations: Wisdom or Science?" in James N. Rosenau, ed., *International Politics and Foreign Policy: A Reader in Research and Theory*, rev. ed. (New York: Free Press, 1969), pp. 3–5.

[29] For a cogent demonstration of how an inference engine can be developed out of empirical materials and historical analyses relevant to world affairs, see Dwain Mefford, "Formulating Foreign Policy on the Basis of Historical Analogues: an Application of Developments in Artificial Intelligence" (paper presented at the annual meeting of the International Studies Association, Atlanta, March 1984).

synthesis of the scientific, traditional, and other approaches to world politics becomes feasible through AI.

The inference engine also provides a means for preserving the expertise of practitioners who have left the foreign service, retired, or are otherwise no longer available. The cumulative wisdom of able cabinet officers who lose their positions in a change of administrations, as well as the insight of deceased officials and observers such as Dean Acheson, Walter Lippmann, and Raymond Aron, would not be lost to those active today if they had been interviewed earlier and their decision webs archived in expert systems. Even in the absence of such interviews, written accounts by and about previous officeholders can be used to build AI programs that model their thinking processes. For example, an experimental program called CYRUS, designed by Roger C. Shank, purports to make a computer act and think like Secretary of State Cyrus R. Vance by combining news stories about Vance with a generalized set of decision and action rules.[30]

BLUNDERS, SURPRISES, AND RATIONALITY

Again it seems necessary to emphasize the limits of AI. Lest the reader think that the foregoing analysis naively anticipates the disappearance of habit-driven actors, the end of blunders and surprises in foreign policy, and the unchallenged dominance of rationality in foreign affairs, it is important to reiterate that artificial intelligence can never transcend human intelligence (HI). Ironically, humans are not intelligent enough to understand their own intelligence sufficiently to construct AI programs that would encompass all seven of the attributes of experts. It is theoretically conceivable that the microelectronic revolution could lead to a technology that would allow for the storage and recall of all the if-then rules that underlie human ingenuity, but what does not seem possible is that a human being could ever frame these rules accurately enough to program for them in terms of the timing, flexibility, and diversity required in swiftly changing situations. Moreover, HI will always be distorted by the many perceptual and cognitive factors that impede rationality, and by the tendency of people to see what they want to see in order to maintain cognitive balance.[31] Not even in one's

[30] A brief account of CYRUS, drawn from Roger C. Shank and Peter G. Childers, *The Cognitive Computer: On Language, Learning, and Artificial Intelligence*, can be found in Judith Axler Turner, "An Enterprising 'Scruffy' Teaches Computers to Think . . . in English," *Chronicle of Higher Education*, April 17, 1985, pp. 5–6.

[31] For a discussion of these factors, see Jervis, *Perception and Misperception in International Politics*.

wildest imagination—perhaps excepting that distant time of the ninth or tenth generation of supercomputers—can one conceive of AI programs capable of knowing when and how to break out of paradigms and either restructuring knowledge under new criteria of relevance or backing away from conclusions because the circumstances are unfamiliar and the limits of understanding have been exceeded. But it is no more conceivable that most makers of foreign policy, locked into old habits and constrained by culture, will be able to achieve fully the freedom to acknowledge and act on conclusions that run counter to their prejudices. If an AI program confronted them with interpretations they found objectionable, policymakers would be as likely to find reasons to ignore as to accept the implications for their own future actions. Thus, the blunder and the surprise will continue to play a part in international politics.

Two events, the trip by President Anwar Sadat of Egypt in 1977 to Jerusalem and the dispatch of U.S. Marines to Lebanon in 1983, illustrate these generalizations. The first was a surprise, the second a blunder. Perhaps some day a computer may be able to store so many if-then rules as to include the conditions under which a future Sadat will break out of the prevailing diplomatic paradigm and lead a peace mission to Israel. There is, after all, no logical reason that the private calculations and personality drives of leaders cannot be transformed into webs of decision rules. The limit here is one of comprehension, not of the inherently indefinable nature of human beings. If enough had been understood about Sadat, an expert system could have "thought" its way through to anticipating his surprising move. Likewise, a tenth-generation supercomputer may have the capacity to manage all the if-then rules that would yield the scenario in which the United States felt obliged first to send the marines to Lebanon and then to withdraw them after a number were killed by a terrorist bomb. The limit in that situation was again one of grasp, not of complexity. If enough had been understood about the decision webs of the various Lebanese factions, an inference engine could have anticipated the outcome, and a blunder could have thereby been avoided.

In both instances, however, had the scenarios been accurately forecast by an expert system, the officials involved would probably have dismissed them as farfetched. Enmeshed in their assumptions about what was possible in world affairs, they would doubtless have been certain that Sadat would be restrained by the norms of international conduct and that the Lebanese factions would not contest the presence of the marines. Thus, AI does not threaten the extinction of HI. Even though the former can strengthen the reasoning power of the latter, HI cannot take full advantage of AI. The future of foreign-policy making is thus one of increased rationality in the continued presence of nonrational, habit-driven outcomes.

LEADERS AS MODELS

The preceding analysis has been marked by a tension between potentialities and limitations, between emphasizing the ways in which the microelectronic revolution has enhanced the skills of elites and recognizing the ways in which the policy-making process will remain unaffected by it. The greater emphasis here has been on the potentialities, because we are all too familiar with the limitations and all too inclined to interpret them as evidence that not much has changed. But the new technologies are changing the policy-making process, and that fact needs to be appreciated if the turbulence of postinternational politics is to be adequately comprehended.[32]

Whatever the degree to which the capacities of elites have been enhanced, perhaps the most noteworthy consequence of their greater competence is the learning opportunities they provide to their followers in the process of employing their analytic skills. Due to the advent of global television, most of these skills are now practiced in public. In interviews, press conferences, confrontations with opposition leaders, and other newsworthy situations, leaders are observed resisting single-cause explanations, acknowledging complexity, sorting through alternative scenarios, and guarding against unintended consequences. If, as is often alleged, publics in the past adopted their leaders' view of the enemy as nefarious and the cause of all problems, then presumably today they are exposed to a very different model, as officials acknowledge that world affairs are complex and not easily managed. As will be seen in the next chapter, there are reasons to conclude that these signals are being received, if not always emulated.

---

[32] For discussions of the potential for growth on the part of elites, see Gareth Morgan, *Riding the Waves of Change: Developing Managerial Competencies for a Turbulent World* (San Francisco: Jossey-Bass, 1989), and Danziger and Kraemer, *People and Computers.* For an analysis of some of the limits to that growth, see Warren Bennis, *Why Leaders Can't Lead: The Unconscious Conspiracy Continues* (San Francisco: Jossey-Bass, 1989).

CHAPTER 13

POWERFUL PEOPLE

The Expansion of Analytic Skills

The tin line had been done two weeks now. Mr. James [the manager] did not fill out the forms properly for to get the foreign exchange to buy the material. It comes from Canada. The IMF man control the thing now, you know, so things have to be just so. And we workers suffer 'cause production shut down 'cause we need those things. And Mr. James, he's a fool to play with it. We ask him where the material, and he say it's coming. We know he mess it up. Jamaica don't have the money no more. Each factory must wait a turn to get the money. I hear the tin is on the dock in Toronto, waiting to be shipped here.

—Unnamed Jamaican woman[1]

Why is it that in a socialist society prices are always going up? I tell you, people are fed up. People have no more spirit left. You work for years and years, and this is the result. People are losing interest in working. Before prices started rising, people were more honest. Society sure has gone to the dogs!

—Xu, a weaver in Beijing[2]

I was one of those people who never got involved and always voted for the PRI. [This is the first political demonstration I have attended in my life.] I feel moved to be here. We have to say what we feel, or else things will never change.

—Micaela Cuevas, a Mexican housewife[3]

Kids think we're not doing a good job. Kids think this government is not accurately representing people's opinions. My own kids call me a crony.

—South Korean assemblyman[4]

[1] Quoted in Chadwick F. Alger, "Perceiving, Analyzing, and Coping with the Local-Global Nexus," *International Social Science Journal* 117 (August 1988): 338.

[2] Quoted in *New York Times*, May 19, 1988, p. A4.

[3] Quoted in *New York Times*, July 11, 1988, p. A6.

[4] Quoted in *New York Times*, June 18, 1987, p. 1.

TO TAKE NOTE of the enhanced competence of leaders is not, of course, to account for the full impact of change at the micro level. Nor can this impact be satisfactorily explained by tracing how the several processes of aggregation identified in chapter 7 convert the activities of leaders and publics into macro outcomes. Rather a sound basis for the idea developed in chapter 5 that micro sources are driving global change and producing global turbulence requires a description of how followers at the micro level have undergone sufficient transformation—i.e., by at least one JND—to join with leaders in precipitating and steering the interactive aggregative processes by which macro changes occur. Clearly, micro-macro interactions are not so fine tuned as to be precipitated by leaders or by public opinion and transnational swings in issue salience. Leadership functions are as old as human organizations and fluctuations in public opinion have been commonplace for centuries without bringing about turbulent changes on a global scale.

Nor have changes on such a scale been precipitated by ordinary people being provoked by unwanted circumstances and launching mass uprisings and full-scale revolutions. These produced new regimes and orders in particular countries, and some of the upheavals even served as models for, and as stimuli to, developments in other countries;[5] but at no time in the past have dynamics at the micro level had macro consequences for political life in every region, community, and corner of the world.

The advent of postinternational politics derives, rather, from another micro dimension. If individuals were marked only by new attitudes and priorities, it is doubtful whether such a politics would have evolved. It has developed, instead, from fundamental and enduring changes in the analytic skills and cathectic capacities of people. It is not the attitudes of citizens toward politics that are transforming world politics, but their ability to employ, articulate, direct, and implement whatever their attitudes may be.

The world has always had a small stratum of active people who felt capable of affecting the course of events through aggregative dynamics. But until now it has not been populated by large numbers who, rightly or wrongly, believe they have the skills and orientations to participate in the processes of aggregation.[6] People may still be easily ma-

---

[5] For compelling analyses of the history of mass uprisings and revolutions, see Reinhard Bendix, *Kings or People: Power and the Mandate Rule* (Berkeley: University of California Press, 1978), and Theda Skocpol, *States and Social Revolution: A Comparative Analysis of France, Russia, and China* (Cambridge: Cambridge University Press, 1979).

[6] For data on the steady growth of the attentive public in the United States, as reflected

nipulated and may thus be led to support simplistic causes, but by at least one JND they are now a more dynamic factor in the micro-macro equation, a prime source of the bifurcated structure and the authority crises that mark postinternational politics.

EXPANDING SKILLS AND SHIFTING ORIENTATIONS

Perhaps it is ironic that in the last decades of the twentieth century, the abilities of individuals to connect to world politics and cope with its complexity have reached new heights while their sense of control over the complexity has fallen to new lows. Yet, to an increasing degree, world politics are being shaped by powerful and restless people who can discern their remoteness from the centers of decision, who have the skills with which to do something about their situation, who are questioning of authority, and who are willing to accept the fast-paced cascade of events that mark the decentralized structures of the postindustrial world.

The four quotations cited at the beginning of this chapter are illustrative of the newly acquired skills that have enabled people to be aware of their distant links to macro political structures. The unnamed Jamaican senses that the links are deficient; Xu sees them as deleterious; Cuevas seeks to enlarge them; the South Korean assemblyman's children are acting to sever them. In each case, the search is on for new loci of control and new sources of authority.

As indicated in chapter 9, the new capacities of people have grown out of shifts in nine basic attributes, five of which are skills and the other four, orientations. The shifts in the five skills involve movement away from habitual modes of learning and toward adaptive modes, away from rudimentary and toward developed analytic talents, away from simplistic and toward complex cognitive maps, away from truncated role scenarios and toward more elaborate ones, and away from dormant and crude and toward active and refined cathectic capacities. The main orientational changes, intensified by the interactive consequences of these enlarged skills and an acute sense of loss of control, involve movement away from unthinking and toward questioning compliance with authority, away from traditional and toward performance criteria of legitimacy, away from loyalties focused on nation-states and toward variable foci, and away from distant and toward close-at-hand loci of control.

---

in patterns of letter-writing to the White House and the *New York Times*, see James N. Rosenau, *Citizenship between Elections: An Inquiry into the Mobilizable American* (New York: Free Press, 1974), chapter 2.

To some degree, of course, these shifts are responses to developments at the macro level. All nine attributes are likely to be affected, for example, by government policies that persistently fail to prevent the cost of daily needs from constantly rising. However, the shifts are also partly a consequence of interaction among them. None of the changes has occurred autonomously; rather, the changes in each have accelerated the pace of change in the other.

In order to simplify matters, the analysis here will reduce the nine attributes to the two basic categories: skills, embracing capacities for adaptive learning, scenario construction, and cognitive mapping; and orientations, comprising perspectives on compliance, legitimacy, loyalty, and locus of control. Put in operational terms, skills involve the degree to which people can add segments of anticipated interaction to their role scenarios; they are seen as undergoing substantial expansion, perhaps even to the point of extending the scenarios by more than one time segment. Orientations concern the extent to which citizens recognize and resolve the conflicts among the values inherent in their scenarios; they, too, are hypothesized to be changing substantially, to the point where citizens can often discern the gain to systems at the expense of subsystems (and vice versa) and then identify clear-cut preferences between them.

It must be stressed that none of the changes examined in the ensuing analysis is conceived to be leading people in a particular value direction. There is no implication that a more analytically skillful person is likely to be more radical, more liberal, or more conservative, or that someone more cathectically capable is likely to rank conservation over consumption, slow growth over development, human rights over community order, or otherwise to attach priorities in specific ways. The skills and orientations, in other words, are politically neutral. They can promote a greater sense of self-interest as well as a keener appreciation of community service. The grasp of greater complexity can give rise to heightened activity directed at more precise targets, but it can also foster paralysis and discourage activity.

In short, whatever may be the values that move people, and whatever may be the dynamics whereby these change, citizens are likely to be increasingly aware of how their actions or inactions are or can be expressive of them. As such, as more self-conscious individuals who can better locate themselves in the causal sequences of world politics, they are likely to have a greater comprehension of how micro parts form macro wholes and thus to be more ready to be mobilized by organizations; but their reasons for supporting one organization rather than another will be linked to concerns that have little bearing on their improved ability to discern the potentials of collective action.

THE MACRO CONTEXT

In order to understand how the skills and orientations of individuals have operated as sources of turbulence, it is important to note the ways in which they have been linked to the macro-micro changes associated with the microelectronic revolution, the mushrooming of subgroups, the declining effectiveness of governments, the fragmentation of the state system, and the accompanying crises in authority structures within and among the world's collectivities. The proliferation of subgroups, for example, has resulted in the availability of a great many alternative collectivities toward which individuals can direct their loyalties and apply their criteria of legitimacy. Likewise, with a number of subgroups challenging the authority of larger collectivities, the ties of people to the latter are bound to be strained as they experience conflict between their system and subsystem memberships. The frequent inability of crisis-ridden collectivities to meet the subgroup challenges further undermines the loyalties and the legitimacy sentiments their memberships have previously accorded them out of sheer habit. Authority crises, in other words, afford citizens opportunities for learning and for applying new skills and orientations.

Even as orientations of people toward authority have been altered by the decentralizing tendencies underlying subgroupism, so have they been agitated by the centralizing tendencies inherent in the new interdependence issues that reach deep into the homes and pocketbooks of citizens everywhere. Currency crises, pollution disasters, terrorist attacks, ozone depletion, and a host of other problems that transcend national boundaries are recurrent reminders of the limits of effective action available to national governments. These virtually daily indicators that states have lost some of their competence have given citizens additional reasons to question the nature and scope of political authority. Even alienated or passive citizens are likely to find it increasingly difficult to close their eyes to the implications of distant events and the course of world affairs. In the words of one observer, "as the problems become more serious and obvious and the world becomes more interdependent, we have to work harder to deny the seriousness of the situation."[7]

[7] Norman V. Walback, "Speculations on Global Citizenship as a Problem for Personal Growth" (paper presented at the annual meeting of the International Studies Association, London, March–April 1989), p. 11.

In the analysis that follows, the process of micro change are examined in a context that emphasizes the ways in which the greater interdependence and the explosive technology of the postindustrial age have enlarged the skills by which individuals establish and maintain contact with world politics; and the analysis then explores how the individuals' orientations have undergone shifts that enable them to be both more effective and more affective with respect to the demands they make upon their collectivities. In effect, leaders of collectivities must now contend with citizens who, like themselves, are driven less by habit and more by a readiness to act on the basis of adaptive learning. More than ever, micro phenomena are caught up in circular processes whereby they are both products and sources of the proliferation of subgroups, the decline of stalemated governments, and the pervasiveness of authority crises that have come to mark and transform global politics.

Stated in more general terms, learning has been exponential at the micro level because there is so much macro change that needs to be accommodated. People in fast-changing, complex societies have little choice but to be more knowledgeable and skillful than their forefathers, who had fewer occasions for confronting new problems or adjusting to unfamiliar circumstances.

The Impact of Global Television

The new electronic technologies have led, in the words of one observer, to "the greatest bombardment of aural and visual materials that man has ever experienced in his history"; they have "brought the entire world to the instant attention of any listener."[8]

Live pictures of international events now appear on TV screens around the world. The electronic revolution has facilitated both the global coverage of news and, through lowered costs, the distribution of television sets to receive it. As can be seen in tables 13.1 and 13.2, between 1965 and 1985 the number of television transmitters at least doubled in every region of the world, and the number of receiving sets at least tripled; at the global level, the increase was sevenfold for transmitters and more than threefold for receivers. Equally noteworthy is the extent to which communications satellites have provided access to television signals to vast new areas.[9] Tables 13.3 and 13.4 provide data on

[8] Daniel Bell, *The Coming of Post-Industrial Society: A Venture in Social Forecasting* (New York: Basic Books, 1973), pp. 316, 317.

[9] During the 1970s "the Intelsat global satellite system expanded from a fledgling system to one that encompasses a majority of nations in the world. At the start of the decade, only 24 nations possessed earth stations and a few more had access to the system

TABLE 13.1. Number of Television Transmitters in Major World Areas, 1965–1985

	1965	1970	1975	1980	1985
World total	8,550	17,700	29,000	38,800	60,570
Africa	100	140	230	270	520
Americas	3,070	4,310	5,000	5,400	7,100
Asia	1,100	3,780	6,700	11,600	20,640
Europe (including USSR)	4,200	9,240	16,700	21,000	31,300
Oceania	80	230	370	500	1,010
Developed countries	8,100	16,900	27,580	36,800	49,920
Developing countries	450	800	1,420	2,000	10,650
Africa (excluding Arab states)	55	70	120	160	270
Asia (excluding Arab states)	1,070	3,730	6,630	11,100	20,340
Arab states	75	120	180	310	550
Northern America	2,820	3,850	4,360	4,700	5,560
Latin America and the Caribbean	250	460	640	700	1,540

SOURCE: UNESCO, *Statistical Yearbook* (Paris, 1987), p. 6.21. © UNESCO 1987. Reproduced by permission of UNESCO.
NOTE: Data prior to 1985 do not include China.

the increase in radio transmitters and receivers, and again they depict substantial growth on a worldwide scale.

Most notably, the worldwide audience for television in the last decade has been expanded enormously by the diffusion of transmitters and receiving sets in the Third World, especially in Mexico, Brazil, China, and India. A 1984 survey of the Beijing metropolitan area found that over 90 percent of the adults regularly watched television, and it is estimated that some 500 million Chinese, about half of that country's population, are in the television audience.[10] The data on India are also impressive. More than half of its 800 million people had access to television by 1986, more than double the proportion who had access only five years earlier (figure 13.1). The number of transmitters and receiving sets grew by three and four times, respectively, during the same period.[11]

through terrestrial connections with countries having earth stations. By the end of the decade, more than 135 nations were using Intelsat system services full time. Over the same period, the cost of television new transmission via satellite decreased dramatically." James F. Larson, *Television's Window on the World: International Affairs Coverage on the U.S. Networks* (Norwood, N.J.: Ablex, 1984), pp. 2–3.

[10] Everett M. Rogers, et al., "The Beijing Audience Survey," *Communication Research* 12 (April 1985): 179–208.

[11] Arvind Singhal et al., "The Diffusion of Television in India" (paper presented at the

TABLE 13.2. Number of Television Receivers, and Number of Receivers per 1,000 Inhabitants, in Major World Areas, 1965–1985

	Number of Receivers (millions)					Number of Receivers per 1,000 Inhabitants				
	1965	1970	1975	1980	1985	1965	1970	1975	1980	1985
World total	186	278	394	547	661	55	76	98	123	137
Africa	0.6	1.2	2.5	7.9	14	1.9	3.4	6.2	17	25
Americas	84	109	160	205	259	182	214	286	335	388
Asia	24	39	57	95	130	13	19	25	37	46
Europe (including USSR)	75	125	169	232	250	111	178	232	309	325
Oceania	2.4	3.5	5.5	6.6	8	137	184	262	275	333
Developed countries	175	255	353	471	531	171	237	315	403	447
Developing countries	11	23	41	76	130	4.7	9	14	23	36
Africa (excluding Arab states)	0.1	0.3	0.6	3.5	5	0.4	1.1	2	9.7	12
Asia (excluding Arab states)	24	38	56	89	123	13	18	25	37	45
Arab states	0.9	1.9	3.4	9.7	16	8.4	15	24	60	85
Northern America	76	92	133	166	203	355	407	564	660	769
Latin America and the Caribbean	8	17	27	39	56	32	60	84	108	138

SOURCE: UNESCO, *Statistical Yearbook* (Paris, 1987), p. 6.22. © UNESCO 1987. Reproduced by permission of UNESCO.
NOTE: Data prior to 1985 do not include China.

TABLE 13.3. Number of Radio Transmitters in Major World Areas,
1965–1985

	1965	1970	1975	1980	1985
World total	16,400	22,100	25,800	28,480	33,160
Africa	500	680	730	900	1,010
Americas	9,640	10,910	12,730	14,300	16,400
Asia	1,390	1,930	2,730	2,950	4,270
Europe (including USSR)	4,580	8,270	9,280	9,900	10,950
Oceania	290	310	330	430	530
Developed countries	11,670	16,200	19,100	21,000	21,800
Developing countries	4,730	5,900	6,700	7,480	11,360
Africa (excluding Arab states)	400	560	580	680	710
Asia (excluding Arab states)	1,330	1,830	2,630	2,810	4,070
Arab states	160	220	250	360	500
Northern America	6,170	6,770	8,530	9,700	10,200
Latin America and the Caribbean	3,470	4,140	4,200	4,600	6,200

SOURCE: UNESCO, *Statistical Yearbook* (Paris, 1987), p. 6.19. © UNESCO 1987. Reproduced by permission of UNESCO.
NOTE: Data prior to 1985 do not include China.

These data become all the more impressive when considered in qualitative terms. In Ocobamba, Peru, a Roman Catholic priest invites the Quechua Indians in this remote Andean village into his living room every day to watch the screen of a small television set connected to a parabolic dish antenna that he installed among the town's squat adobe houses. "Television is finally arriving in the backwaters of Latin America," a reporter commented, "reaching distant villages such as Ocobamba often before running water, telephones, regular mail service and—thanks to battery-powered sets—even before electricity. In many of the poorer homes, a TV set now ranks as the treasured next addition after the kerosene stove. For thousands of peasants, television is providing the first images of places beyond the primitive isolation of their own rugged existence."[12]

To be sure, data on the diffusion of television transmitters and receiving sets take no account of the content of the communication. The

annual meeting of the International Communication Association, New Orleans, May–June 1988).

[12] Bradley Graham, "Prime Time in the Andes," *Washington Post*, national weekly edition, March 21–27, 1988, p. 19. For an account of a similar impact in another remote corner of the world, see Christopher S. Wren, "TV (and with It the World) Comes to the Grasslands of Inner Mongolia," *New York Times*, November 14, 1984, p. A4.

TABLE 13.4. Number of Radio Receivers, and Number of Receivers per 1,000 Inhabitants, in Major World Areas, 1965–1985

	Number of Receivers (millions)					Number of Receivers per 1,000 Inhabitants				
	1965	1970	1975	1980	1985	1965	1970	1975	1980	1985
World total	535	684	961	1,233	1,698	159	186	238	277	330
Africa	10	16	28	49	77	32	45	69	103	139
Americas	285	357	505	571	655	617	701	903	930	981
Asia	53	70	138	245	408	28	30	60	95	145
Europe (including USSR)	184	233	277	349	434	272	331	380	466	564
Oceania	3	8	13	19	24	171	421	619	826	1,008
Developed countries	460	572	770	926	1,181	449	532	686	793	911
Developing countries	75	112	191	307	517	32	43	66	94	142
Africa (excluding Arab states)	6	8	17	31	48	26	30	56	86	113
Asia (excluding Arab states)	51	68	132	235	594	27	33	58	93	143
Arab states	6	10	17	28	43	56	81	121	172	229
Northern America	251	306	424	471	622	1,173	1,354	1,797	1,869	1,977
Latin America and the Caribbean	34	51	81	100	133	137	180	251	276	328

SOURCE: UNESCO, *Statistical Yearbook* (Paris, 1987), p. 6.20. © UNESCO 1987. Reproduced by permission of UNESCO.
NOTE: Data prior to 1985 do not include China.

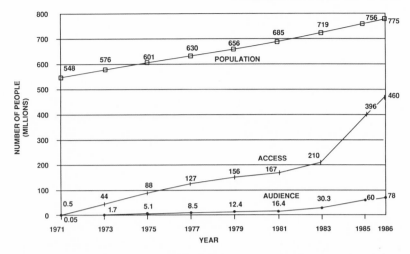

FIGURE 13.1. Population of India, Number of People Who Have Access to Television, and Number of People Who Watch Television, 1971–1986. SOURCE: Arvind Singhal and Everett M. Rogers, "Television Soap Operas for Development in India" (paper presented at the annual meeting of the International Communication Association, Montreal, May 1987), figure 2. Used with permission of the authors.

spread of television in the Third World occurred not because of a demand for programming on literacy, nutrition, birth control, economic productivity, and other public issues, but because of a demand for entertainment, typified by such U.S. shows as "I Love Lucy," "Kojak," and "Dallas." In Latin America, soap operas constitute the core of television programming,[13] and the surge of the TV audience during the 1980s in India coincided with the introduction of soap operas on national television in 1984.[14]

Nevertheless, access to television has become sufficiently global in scope that it must be regarded as a change of parametric proportions. Consider, for example, the implications of the fact that people everywhere are now frequently exposed to visual images of the two individuals who hold them hostage to nuclear destruction. They can see these two heads of state talking and acting in response to the crises of the moment. And, so, too, they have seen riots in Pretoria, a space shuttle explode after launch, a war being fought in Vietnam, ships probing the

[13] Everett M. Rogers and Livia Antola, "Telenovelas: A Latin American Success Story," *Journal of Communication* 35 (Autumn 1985): 24–35.

[14] Arvind Singhal and Everett M. Rogers, "Television Soap Operas for Development in India" (paper presented at the annual meeting of the International Communication Association, Montreal, May 1987), p. 3.

ocean's bottom for a downed airplane's black box, election fraud being perpetrated in Manila, an embassy surrounded in Teheran, and a hijacked airliner. Bitter adversaries confront each other on the TV screen,[15] and heads of state seek to mobilize support on TV talk shows.[16] Moreover, the contents of soap operas in the Third World have begun to include themes of family planning, equal status for women, and other developmental issues that contest traditional values.[17] For Shakespeare it was a metaphor, but for our generation it has become a reality: the world is now literally a stage, as its actors dance across the TV screen.

Furthermore, the TV screen offers opportunities to climb onto the stage and perform before the cameras. Not only are "ordinary" people often interviewed for their reactions, but in all parts of the world they are frequently asked to turn out for rallies or protests that are scheduled for live television coverage. Or, if they have spontaneously converged upon a site and formed a leaderless public, leaders are quick to seize the chance to get them on the global stage by calling the attention of the mass media to their presence, thereby transforming them into a participatory aggregation that can serve their shared purposes. Irrespective of the ways in which they may have been stage-managed, however, the participants are likely to experience such occasions as moments when they were actors on the global stage.[18]

Nor does such participation occur only in front of the television cameras. By bringing distant situations to the immediate attention of citizens, the television medium can indirectly evoke their participation in the course of events. Extensive TV coverage of a Kuwaiti airliner

[15] Using what was then the latest advance in television technology, for example, the ABC show "Nightline" brought on to the same (split) screen two leaders who had never communicated in person, South African foreign minister Roelof Botha in Capetown and Bishop Desmond Tutu at his church in Johannesburg, for an hour of heated interchange about South Africa's racial policies. As one reviewer noted, in placing Botha and Tutu side by side the program created "a striking picture by [giving] Tutu the parity on TV that he and his fellow blacks are denied in their South African homeland." Howard Rosenberg, "Getting South Africa Down in Black, White," *Los Angeles Times*, March 20, 1985, sec. 6, p. 1.

[16] James Reston, "The New TV Diplomacy," *New York Times*, February 26, 1986, p. 27.

[17] Singhal and Rogers, "Television Soap Operas," pp. 3–8.

[18] A good example of a situation that was both spontaneous and stage-managed is provided by this account of the 1989 student protests in Beijing. "Western newsmen, and particularly television cameramen, were sought out by demonstration leaders and parade marshals, eager to stage events for them, and even to hold up huge parades until the TV people could work out superior camera angles." Fred C. Shapiro, "Letter from Beijing," *New Yorker*, June 5, 1989, p. 75.

that was hijacked after it left Bangkok with many Kuwaitis aboard, for example, provided the Kuwaiti people with a vivid opportunity to experience their collective interests and to demonstrate their support for their government's resistance to the hijackers' demands that certain prisoners in Kuwaiti jails be released in exchange for hostages on the plane. One reporter said that "nothing in the short history of this country has so caught the attention of Kuwaitis as the hijacking, which galvanized a tiny nation of 1.8 million people into an impressive show of solidarity and pride."[19] In other words, television is not only a major source of information; it can also be a stimulus to action. More than that, since television brings words and pictures of crises abroad to the attention of people at virtually the same moment that top leaders learn about them, it serves to narrow the emotional and intellectual gap between citizens and officials, allowing the former to identify closely with the latter as they confront uncertainties and ponder the actions to be taken.[20]

Moreover, as previously implied in connection with the dynamics of aggregative processes (chapter 7), citizens are also indirectly present on the global stage through their role as viewers whose attentiveness to the TV screen can be of considerable significance. That is, officials are keenly aware that televised events are playing before huge and potentially critical audiences, and this knowledge can serve as a major influence on their conduct, as they imagine their viewers to be capable of undergoing transformation from an unintentional to a participatory aggregation. The live coverage of the new Congress of People's Deputies in the Soviet Union in 1989 was a vivid example of this process. The congress proved to be "the biggest television hit in Soviet history": with some 200 million viewers across twelve time zones, its audience was 25 percent higher than any previous televised event. As the nation's chief of broadcast news said, "Something is really turning over in our national consciousness. The deputies are realizing the people are

[19] Youssef M. Ibrahim, "All Hail the Sabahs for Their Gritty Hostage Stand," *New York Times*, April 16, 1988, p. 4.

[20] That the world presented in the mass media may not be substantially different from the world experienced by policy makers is a major finding of an elaborate inquiry in which the way a printed medium, the *Washington Post*, treated several major events was compared with the discussion of the same events in hearings of the U.S. Senate Armed Services Committee. This study discovered that there was "a quite remarkable homogeneity of communication in the public domain and the policy making domain." More precisely, "the upper limit on what can be learned from the media accounts of the events is isomorphic with the upper limit on what can be learned in the policy making domain." G. R. Boynton, "Communication and Cognition: News Accounts of International Affairs" (Iowa City, University of Iowa, 1988, photocopy).

watching them, the voters can see them live, and the level of discussion is rising. There's never been anything like this—people watching how the leadership is changing."[21]

However, though it may galvanize consensus and involvement in some instances and facilitate dissent and opposition in others, television overall is politically neutral, merely a channel through which the cascades of postinternational politics pulsate. The film director Federico Fellini has said that "television is like gravity. Gravity is not necessarily good or bad, it's just there."[22]

So commonplace has the presence of this channel become, and so routine is the presumption that officials and activists will seek to build images through it, that many analysts tend to dismiss it as simply one more development in the communications field. But considered from the perspective of how people learn, how the habitual foundations of their belief systems are reinforced, how they form new orientations and focus their emotional energies, the video dimension of the electronic revolution is more than merely a recent addition to the storehouse of manipulative techniques available to politicians. Image-building is not an aberration of political processes but an integral part of these processes, one of its aspects that helps people to evaluate performance and test reality, activities that are central to how they cope with the complexities of postinternational politics.

It is conceivable, moreover, that the impact of global television goes far beyond the intrusion of distant events into billions of homes. Besides offering vivid images of conflicts and providing occasions for participating in situations, television may also be reshaping the ways in which people think about world affairs. Living color, the split screen, the instant replay, and the zoom lens may, in subtle ways, affect the manner in which developments are understood. The split screen relentlessly insists that action derives from multiple sources and that connected events are happening simultaneously; the instant replay stresses that snap judgments can be erroneous and that events may have previously overlooked dimensions; and the zoom lens encourages viewers

[21] Francis X. Clines, "Soviet's Big TV Hit is Politics, Live and in the Raw," *International Herald Tribune*, June 1, 1989, p. 6.

[22] Quoted in Glenn Collins, "From a Vast Wasteland to a Brave New World," *New York Times*, March 20, 1988, p. A20. For a series of essays that take a contrary position, interpreting the spread of electronic media not as neutral but as either a sinister threat to traditional cultures or as a means through which the First World exercises control over the Third World, see Michael Traub, ed., *The Myth of the Information Revolution: Social and Ethical Implications of Communication Technology* (Newbury Park, Calif.: Sage, 1986).

to examine more intensely as new details are revealed from close up and then, as it moves back, are relocated in a larger context. Such techniques may seem routine as television fare, but as modes of thought they may replace the simplistic forms of evaluation that have hitherto been in the habit pools of citizens.[23]

Moreover, there are indications that people are developing a whole new approach to the video environment in what might be called, in the United States, "the screening of America." With computer screens being used widely in work situations; with video monitors displaying data in airports, schools, and home; with video conferencing being used in business and people shopping and banking by video; with educators combining video cameras, discs, and computers to create interactive lessons and training programs; and with cable television, videocassette recorders, and satellite dishes greatly expanding the choices open to the viewing public, a new way of life is emerging, one that enables people to become "video activists." Instead of sitting passively in front of their television sets, people today have the means to exercise control over the electronic environment; they can tape programs for viewing at their convenience, and they can easily change channels with remote-control devices. In the United States they can buy or rent shows from some 27,000 video stores, enabling them, in effect, to become their own television programmers and thus to refine further their analytic skills; indeed, video activism has advertisers concerned that their messages are not getting through as viewers "zap" them on live shows or "zip" through them during subsequent replays.[24]

Nor, of course, are the broadening techniques of television production and consumption the only source of expanded aptitudes on the part of citizens. As educational institutions enlarge their scope, as access to transistor radios, personal computers, telephones, and other products of the microelectronic revolution widens, as their slogans and traditional symbols fail to insulate people and their pocketbooks from the consequences of interdependence, and as political leaders acknowl-

[23] For an account of recent studies that have converged upon the finding that learning from television can begin at a very young age indeed, see Daniel Goleman, "Studies Reveal TV's Potential to Teach Infants," *New York Times*, November 22, 1988, p. C1.

[24] For elaborate portrayals of the video environment and its inducements to video activism, see Collins, "From a Vast Wasteland to a Brave New World," and Sally Bedell Smith, "New TV Technologies Are Starting to Change the Nation's Viewing Habits," *New York Times*, October 9, 1985, p. 19. For an analysis that highlights the way in which the video environment can be beneficial to children, see François Mariet, "*Laissez-regarder la télé: Le nouvel télévisual* (France: Calmann-Lévy, 1989).

edge the intractability of global problems, citizens everywhere are likely to experience additional pressure to refine their analytic skills and focus their cathectic orientations.

There are, of course, counterarguments. Television can suppress analysis and involvement, inasmuch as it does not actually require anything of the viewer other than passively sitting in its presence. Instead of encouraging thought, reflection, and cathexis, perhaps it simplifies, stultifies, and narcotizes, leaving viewers with blurred images rather than structured scenarios and giving them little incentive to ponder where they fit in the events unfolding before them.

A second criticism of the video medium is that it provides no moral guidance, no values by which to resolve the human conflicts and pathos that it depicts. Rather then pausing to consider the alternatives in situations, it is argued, TV news "simply shifts to the next story. The result is that the moral response provoked by pictures from a place like Gaza finds no outlet. We are left with our knowledge that the children of Gaza have been robbed of their childhood, and that someone must be responsible. But the pictures do not tell us who, and we begin to wonder if somehow the guilt is ours."[25] A third line of criticism holds that the ordinary person is uninterested in world politics, lethargic, and resistant to change. From this hardened-elitist perspective, the attribution of importance to the microelectronic revolution is viewed as a gross exaggeration. A related denial of television's relevance might be seen in the finding from microsociological research that "cognition is limited to a few relatively uncomplex operations [so that] people cannot follow a chain of thought very many steps, either forward to its consequence or back to its premises."[26]

Perhaps the most common counterargument weaves these perspectives together into the premise that television is omnipotent in its ability to manipulate the orientations of people and mobilize their support. In the hands of charismatic leaders, or merely of public-relations consultants and market researchers, television is viewed as a medium that can arouse involvement and sway voters in virtually any direction, without regard to issue content. Thirty-second spot advertisements and TV ministries banish the complexities of politics in favor of crude simplicities, deceiving large numbers of people into accepting distorted conceptions of public affairs.

But this picture of television as an omnipotent force has properly

[25] Jay Rosen, "Television's Image Problem Is That Its Images Move Us to Stand Still," *Los Angeles Times*, March 30, 1988, p. B7.
[26] Collins, "On the Microfoundations of Macrosociology," p. 992.

been called a myth, for it does not withstand close scrutiny.[27] To cite a specific case, Lieutenant Colonel North's handsome, rugged, and uniformed appearance and his strident nationalistic eloquence in the 1987 Iran-contra hearings did at first evoke a groundswell of support, but only a few months later a poll showed that 64 percent opposed a presidential pardon for him. More generally, interviews conducted before, during, and after political campaigns point clearly to the conclusion that people get their information from many sources and that as voters they cast their ballots on the basis of issues and events rather than on the bland messages of TV commercials.[28]

Furthermore, while much of television's fare may be truncated and passivity-inducing, its treatment of major world events is more vivid and less superficial than was the case before satellites allowed for live coverage. The scenes people witness on live television, rather than paralyzing their moral judgments, may tap deep into their own experiences or fears and thus stimulate thought about where blame ought to be placed and where right and wrong lie. People travel, affirm or question their own loyalties, suffer or worry about setbacks, know first- or second-hand about tragic accidents, and in other ways encounter situations that resemble those they see on the TV news. Hence, they can identify with one or another of the parties to a terrorist attack, articulate their reactions to an account of a KGB official's defection, understand the significance of a nuclear accident, and ascribe meaning and motivation to many other distant events for which their own lives have some parallel.

In short, while most of the world's people may be ignorant and apathetic, that does not mean they have been untouched by the communications revolution. Many of the cognitive skills required to construct chains of thought may still be in a rudimentary state of development, but this is not to say that they are as primitive as in past eras. With

[27] Douglas Davis, "Zapping the Myth of TV's Power," *New York Times*, May 20, 1988, p. A31.

[28] Davis, "Zapping the Myth of TV's Power." Interestingly, some argue that "this extraordinary mismatch . . . between our sophistication and the way our politicians and [TV] producers talk to us" is a prime source of low voter turnouts in the United States and of the pattern wherein people are turning away from network broadcasting and toward cable and public television. The politicians and producers, according to this interpretation, have not come to terms with "our increasing unpredictability, independence and intelligence (we are well-educated now compared with the voters and viewers of previous generations)" and thus "they haven't figured out that we have changed, that we want something better to see, hear, and do." Ibid. For the data on issue- and event-oriented bases of voting, see Thomas Patterson and Robert McClure, *The Unseeing Eye: The Myth of Television Power in National Politics* (New York: G. P. Putnam, 1976).

transistor radios, television sets, VCR's, tape decks, Walkmans, and other such gadgetry enabling people to locate themselves in larger settings and to experience acutely their feelings about their situations, it is difficult to conceive of them as immune to change and unable to tap those parts of their habit pool that involve a readiness to learn.

The potential for change inherent in electronic communication is perhaps best demonstrated by the lengths in which closed societies go to control their airwaves. In the long run, however, their efforts are unlikely to succeed. The cost of jamming foreign broadcasts is too great relative to the number and variety of sources from which these broadcasts emanate. Furthermore, jamming stimulates curiosity about what foreign sources are reporting. "It's amazing how many people listen to foreign radio stations now," a Soviet writer exiled in the West said after returning for a visit to Moscow eight years later. "It's not just a matter of where they get their information from. It's a psychological state of mind. Once you look for your information from somewhere else, it means you no longer accept the right of the state-run media to control your mind."[29] Lately, fax transmitters have been added to the array of techniques available to those who seek to get messages into closed societies. It was reported, for example, that during the 1989 students protests in China, "Chinese in Hong Kong, and Chinese students in American and European campuses, using fax transmitters wherever they could find them, fed Chinese business offices, universities and even state enterprises a steady flow of uncensored news about the tumult in Tiananmen Square and the world reactions to it." The potential for change in this form of communication is evident in the fact that "police and security officers [in China were] posted at all fax machines."[30]

Through audio- and videocassettes that can easily be slipped past border and police controls, closed societies are also vulnerable to outside information that is carried across borders and then electronically distributed. It may be more than mere coincidence that public unrest in Eastern Europe became increasingly manifest after 1981, when the first of some 700,000 VCR's were smuggled into or otherwise acquired in Poland and large numbers of sets also started coming into Hungary, Czechoslovakia, and Bulgaria; among other things, these sets allowed people to share and copy thousands of tapes.[31]

---

[29] Michell Dobbs, "For Communism, Another Acid Test," *International Herald Tribune*, May 22, 1989, p. 2.

[30] "China's Fax Invasion," *New York Times*, June 20, 1989, p. A22.

[31] Jackson Diehl, "East Europe on Cultural Fast Forward," *Washington Post*, national weekly edition, May 2–8, 1988, p. 10.

It is also important to note that the electronic revolution has diminished illiteracy as an obstacle to the expansion of analytic skills. Electronic voices and pictures may not be adequate substitutes for printed pages, but they do convey messages that were not previously received by the world's illiterates. The existence of a large amount of illiteracy in the Third World—and in some areas it may even be growing—does not necessarily negate the proposition that people are enlarging their capacity to comprehend and relate to distant events.

The same may be said about the supposed decline in the reading skills of the American public. Whether they read well or not, they are reading more—or at least they are buying twice as many books per capita than was the case prior to the advent of mass television in the 1950s[32]—and what is more to the point, an average of some fifty million Americans tune into national TV newscasts every evening, and the data indicate that by a wide margin the population regards television news as more reliable than that to be found in the print media.[33] Surveys have also revealed that the pictures on the nightly news accord television a credibility that exceeds not only that of the print media but that of public officials and private organizations as well.[34] Moreover, television news reaches many people who are not even seeking it. People do not unintentionally get exposed to world events in the newspapers; the average newspaper reader is neither attentive to foreign stories nor wants more coverage of them. "But the average television viewer, who spends one third of his day watching the screen 'by the hour instead of by program,' is exposed involuntarily to international news that he would not have chosen to learn. The members of this vast inadvertent audience, many of whom have little or no information on the world beyond our borders other than that conveyed to them by television, often find their attention unintentionally engaged by the picture unfolding before them, their interest aroused, their opinions formed, and their actions as voters and citizens motivated."[35]

One other way in which global television fosters turbulence is that it adds greatly to the porosity of political jurisdictions. Its messages

[32] Davis, "Zapping the Myth of TV's Power." See also Edward B. Fiske, "Americans in Electronic Era Are Reading as Much as Ever," *New York Times*, September 8, 1983, p. 1.

[33] Shanto Iyengar and Donald R. Kinder, *News That Matters: Television and American Opinion* (Chicago: University of Chicago Press, 1987), pp. 1, 126.

[34] Theodore C. Sorenson, "A Changing America," in Andrew J. Pierre, ed., *A Widening Atlantic? Domestic Change and Foreign Policy* (New York: Council on Foreign Relations, 1986), p. 92.

[35] Sorenson, "A Changing America," p. 93.

and pictures cannot be stopped for inspection by customs and immigration officials. The messages move through the upper atmosphere and outer space to distant audiences, sometimes reinforcing prejudices, sometimes undermining them, but in any event giving rise to what has come to be referred to as the problem of "transborder flows." Cultural and political leaders fear that the incoming flows may adversely affect the authority and legitimacy orientations of their citizens, and that fear is not unwarranted in view of the substantial evidence that cultures are vulnerable to transborder flows.[36] Thus, coverage of world events is not the only impact of television at the micro level. An equally important—and perhaps more enduring—impact occurs at the more subtle level of daily programming in those areas of the world where political boundaries are not coincident with the reach of broadcast transmitters.

The Impact of Computers

While the impact of television as a stimulus to learning is global in scope, another source of the movement away from the habitual and toward the adaptive end of the learning continuum can be seen in those parts of the world where the computer has become a part of daily routines. As noted in the previous chapter with respect to the enhancement of the competence of elites, there are a number of ways in which an individual's analytic skills might be extended by the personal computer. For those citizens who use this product of the microelectronic revolution, the notions of loading, saving, retrieving, reorganizing, and otherwise manipulating information with a word-processing program involve more than a set of mechanical tools for expressing ideas. Such functions can also become a basis for new modes of thinking.

But the impact of computers as stimuli to the expansion of analytic

[36] See, for example, John Meisel, "Communications in the Space Age: Some Canadian and International Implications," *International Political Science Review* 7 (April 1986): 299–331; George H. Quester, "Transboundary Television," *Problems of Communism* 33 (September–October 1984): 76–87; and Tapio Varis, "Trends in International Television Flow," *International Political Review* 7 (April 1986): 235–50. For more encompassing treatments of transborder communication flows, particularly those supported by computer networks, see Gerd Junne, "The Emerging Global Grid: The Political Dimension," in George Muskens and Cees Hamelink, eds., *Global Networks and European Communities: Applied Social and Comparative Approaches* (Tilburg, Netherlands: IVA, Institute for Social Research at Tilburg University, 1986), pp. 30–40; Hamid Mowlana, *Global Information and World Communication: New Frontiers in International Relations* (New York: Longman, 1986), chapter 5; and Brian M. Murphy, *The International Politics of New Information Technology* (New York: St. Martin's, 1986), Chapter 7.

skills is not confined to the writers and academics who most often work with word processors. It is perhaps even more pronounced in the working world where a vast array of jobs—in factories, mills, offices, travel centers, and in field situations—require people to spend much of their time in front of computer terminals and to use a wide array of analytic techniques to solve diverse production, supply, distribution, and consumption problems.[37] The transformation of the industrial order into its postindustrial successor, involves a transition from a reliance on *action-centered* skills, in which workers use their brains to coordinate their bodies, to a dependence on *intellective* skills, in which they use their brains to coordinate observations, concepts, and patterns.[38] Accordingly,

> as information technology restructures the work situation, it abstracts thought from action. Absorption, immediacy, and organic responsiveness are superseded by distance, coolness, and remoteness. Such distance brings an opportunity for reflection. . . . As [a] worker from [a pulp mill] summed it up, "Sitting in this room and just thinking has become part of my job. It's the technology that lets me do these things."
>
> The thinking this operator refers to is of a different quality from the thinking that attended the display of action-centered skills. It combines abstraction, explicit inference, and procedural reasoning.[39]

The study from which this quotation comes was organized around observations of pulp-mill operators, bankers, and clerical employees, all of whom were employed by firms in the process of computerizing their production operations and business routines. The patterns found were consistent across the different situations, they involved a transition frequently described "in the same words: 'It's a thinking job now'; 'You must use your brain, not your hands'; 'The job is more mental, it takes place in your head.' " In effect, "the terrain of effort has shifted, not from muscles to brain, but from the complete sensual involvement

---

[37] "The most important single fact to emerge" from a study of the "information workforce" is that some 80 percent of this new labor pool consists of people "who collect, arrange, coordinate, monitor and disseminate information about activities taking place within the economy." Anthony Smith, "Telecommunications and the Fading of the Industrial Age," *Political Quarterly* 54 (April–June 1983): 131.

[38] Shoshana Zuboff, *In the Age of Smart Machine: The Future of Work and Power* (New York: Basic Books, 1988), pp. 75–76.

[39] Zuboff, *In the Age of Smart Machine*, p. 75.

of the worker's physical presence to an involvement that depended more exclusively upon the worker's quality of mind."[40]

To the extent that today's citizens are thus ensconced in a world of the split screens, zoom lens, and instant replay of television and the graphics, spread sheets, data bases, and search-and-revise routines of computers, it is difficult to imagine that the capacities they bring to politics remain unaffected. If nothing else—and there is probably a great deal more—their ability to locate themselves in micro-macro interactions and to discern how they can contribute to collective action seems bound to be enhanced. Table 13.5 suggests the wide range of possible effects of computer technologies on individuals and collectivities.

The Impact of Education

The argument that people are increasingly skillful with respect to world affairs also rests on changes that have taken place in education. In all parts of the world, more and more people have entered upon one or another form of educational program, from the primary school to the university, and as a result have been exposed to the special kind of analysis that sets the classroom aside from other settings. To those who teach, it is not always clear that the analytic skills of students are capable of being enlarged, but the data are so consistent under so many different circumstances that it is difficult to reject the idea that education does indeed affect the skills and orientations of citizens.[41] Figure 13.2 shows that enrollments in higher education have been increasing since 1970 in every part of the world, and table 13.6 shows that, with few exceptions, the same has been true since 1960 in primary and secondary education as well, and for both males and females. Once again, it becomes unmistakably clear that our time is witness to the emergence of ever more analytically skillful and cathectically competent citizens.

[40] Zuboff, *In the Age of Smart Machine*, pp. 185, 188.

[41] For comparative date on citizenship skills, see Sidney Verba, Norman H. Nie, and Jae-on Kim, *Participation and Political Equality: A Seven-Nation Comparison* (New York: Cambridge University Press, 1978), p. 67. In those parts of the world that are organized along multi-ethnic lines, moreover, the classroom is also a setting where learning occurs through the convergence of cultures. In the City of New York, for example, it was reported that "one of every 20 students in the public schools has come from a foreign country . . . [and that] for 43 percent of students entering first grade, a language other than English is spoken at home." Neil A. Lewis, "Immigrant Achieves Top Rank in Class," *New York Times*, June 10, 1989, p. 29.

TABLE 13.5. Potential Social Impacts of Computing

Type of actor affected	Potential Impacts on			
	Orientations	Interactions	Capabilities	Value distribution
Individuals	Attitudes of self-worth, self-actualization Sense of competence in dealing with artifacts Feeling of control of environment Definition of personal values	Frequency, nature, and duration of interpersonal involvements at work Time spent in social interactions at home and leisure Extent of interpersonal contacts as a client	Productivity in workplace Information to support responsibilities in work and home life Capacity to complete work and home tasks	Influence in decisions of collectivities Privacy Material well-being
Collectivities	Importance of technical/instrumental/quantitative criteria for decision and action Emphasis on efficiency and rationality in operations Attitudes toward socio-technical (people-technology) interface	Relations with workers and unions Subunit autonomy Centralization of authority Superordinate-subordinate relationships Replacement of humans with machines Coordination among subunits Relations with clients	Capacity to achieve key goals Efficient use of available resources Access to relevant data Dependence on external skills Manipulation of symbols and data Mastery of environmental conditions Adaptation of resources to needs	Status of computer elite Power versus relevant other collectivities Expansion of domain Level of autonomy from public agencies Accumulation of material values National/international influence

SOURCE: Adapted from James N. Danziger, "Social Science and the Social Impacts of Computer Technology," *Social Science Quarterly* 66 (March 1985): 9.

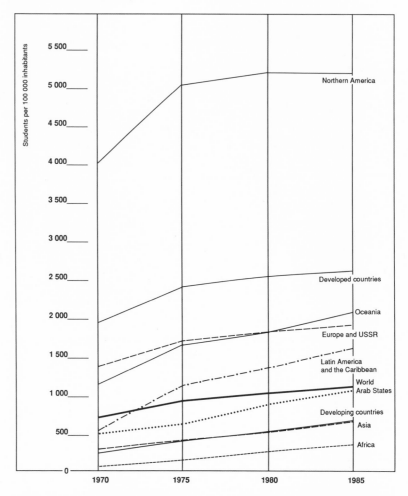

FIGURE 13.2. Number of Students in the Third Level of Education per 100,000 Inhabitants, 1970–1985. Note: Data do not include North Korea. SOURCE: UNESCO, *Statistical Yearbook*, p. 3.7. © UNESCO 1987. Reproduced by permission of UNESCO.

The Impact of Complexity

The microelectronic revolution and the educational explosion together do not fully explain the expanding competence of citizens. We must also take note of the fact that the greater complexity and interdependence of communities and countries are themselves compelling individuals to cope with a mounting volume of crosscutting messages and overlapping problems. The impulse to resort to head-in-the-sand solutions to the growing impingement of local, national, and international life may be as great as ever, but the ability of individuals to keep their heads covered with the sand seems likely to decline as the rising tide of global interdependence erodes the beaches.

Put less metaphorically, greater interdependence and faster communications have placed heavier emphasis on macro-micro interactions and made people more aware of themselves as participants in global scenarios. While the life of communities has always been founded on micro as well as macro processes, never before has the transformation of individual behaviors into collective problems seemed so poignantly evident. There are numerous occasions each day when citizens of the industrial nations are made conscious of themselves as links in casual chains. From the traffic jams in which they get caught to the boycotts they are asked to join, from the water shortages they are asked to alleviate to the tax revolts in which they can participate, from the workers' rallies in Poland to the urban mobs in Iran which they have seen on live television, today's citizens have had ample firsthand exposure to the links between individual and collective behavior. Similarly, when they start their automobiles, turn on their air conditioners, or buy their groceries, many may have a fleeting thought that those simple acts are among the worldwide processes that contribute to pollution, oil shortages, and famines.

For some people, of course, such causal chains will include multinational corporations or incompetent politicians as weak links, whereas others will develop scenarios in which their links involve hoarding or cheating on the grounds that elsewhere in the scenario everyone is doing it. Regardless of how accurate the scenarios are or how responsibly they are utilized, however, the point is that they are elaborate and they invoke familiar experiences for their users.

Likewise, in this era when national economies are so clearly and intricately woven into the global economy, people can hardly be oblivious to the once-remote sequences whereby global capital flows and banking practices culminate in threats to their savings, jobs, and ability to travel. Reports of volatile exchange rates among the world's currencies are constant reminders of the extent to which one's economic well-being depends on decisions made in distant places. Not long ago, a decline in the purchasing power of the Venezuelan bolivar made it difficult for the citizens of that country to go abroad, only a few years after they had become accustomed to moving easily around the world.[42] Indeed, a recent study has shown surprisingly few knowledge-

[42] James LeMoyne, "For Many Venezuelans, the Well Has Run Dry," *New York Times*, December 19, 1983, p. A2.

TABLE 13.6. Gross Enrollment Ratios by Level of Education, 1960–1985

		First Level			Second Level			Third Level			All Levels	
		Total	Male	Female	Total	Male	Female	Total	Male	Female	Total	Male	Female
World total	1960	80.7	91.1	69.9	27.5	31.2	23.6	5.2	6.9	3.4	43.8	49.8	37.6
	1965	85.0	95.3	74.3	32.1	36.9	27.1	7.4	9.5	5.3	48.3	54.8	41.6
	1970	83.8	90.9	76.3	35.2	39.6	30.7	8.8	10.8	6.7	48.1	53.0	43.0
	1975	94.7	102.7	86.4	43.1	48.3	37.7	10.3	12.0	8.5	54.1	59.3	48.6
	1980	94.4	102.3	86.2	45.1	50.6	39.5	11.2	12.6	9.7	54.7	60.0	49.3
	1985	98.8	106.3	90.9	46.3	51.5	40.9	11.8	13.4	10.2	55.5	60.5	50.2
Africa	1960	43.5	55.4	31.5	5.2	7.4	3.0	0.7	1.2	0.3	20.2	26.1	14.3
	1965	51.6	63.2	39.9	8.0	11.3	4.7	1.1	1.8	0.4	24.9	31.3	18.6
	1970	56.0	67.1	44.8	11.2	15.3	7.2	1.5	2.4	0.7	28.3	34.7	21.9
	1975	65.0	75.2	54.7	15.6	20.2	10.9	2.5	3.7	1.3	33.8	40.1	27.4
	1980	79.7	90.4	68.8	23.1	28.9	17.3	3.2	4.7	1.7	42.5	49.5	35.6
	1985	84.3	92.8	75.7	33.0	40.1	25.8	4.3	6.2	2.4	48.3	54.9	41.8
America	1960	81.4	82.9	79.9	50.6	50.7	50.4	13.4	17.0	9.8	57.3	59.0	55.6
	1965	86.4	87.7	85.1	57.0	57.3	56.7	17.5	21.4	13.4	61.9	63.6	60.1
	1970	90.5	91.5	89.6	58.6	58.9	58.3	23.1	27.3	18.8	64.7	66.4	63.0
	1975	98.0	99.2	96.8	60.5	60.8	60.2	29.0	32.0	25.9	68.8	70.3	67.3
	1980	104.0	105.2	102.7	59.1	58.5	59.7	29.6	29.7	29.4	70.0	70.5	69.6
	1985	106.4	108.0	104.8	65.2	64.2	66.3	31.6	31.9	31.3	73.5	74.0	73.0
Asia	1960	80.3	95.7	64.0	20.5	25.7	15.0	2.5	3.7	1.2	39.7	47.9	31.0
	1965	85.7	100.6	69.8	22.5	29.3	15.4	3.4	4.9	1.8	43.9	52.9	34.5
	1970	82.0	91.7	71.8	26.2	32.1	20.0	3.8	5.3	2.1	42.4	48.7	35.7
	1975	98.7	109.7	87.2	35.9	43.4	27.9	4.4	6.1	2.7	50.8	57.8	43.3
	1980	93.5	103.8	82.8	39.2	46.9	31.1	5.5	7.4	3.5	50.5	57.6	43.1
	1985	99.5	109.8	88.7	38.8	45.7	31.6	6.3	8.3	4.3	49.8	56.5	42.8
Europe (including USSR)	1960	106.3	107.1	105.6	51.3	53.0	49.5	10.2	12.9	7.6	61.0	62.8	59.2
	1965	104.7	105.3	104.0	64.8	66.5	63.1	16.0	19.2	12.7	67.4	69.1	65.6
	1970	105.1	105.6	104.6	70.8	72.0	69.6	17.4	19.6	15.1	68.1	69.3	66.7

	Year												
Oceania	1975	101.9	102.4	101.3	79.1	78.5	79.7	20.3	21.7	18.8	69.1	69.6	68.7
	1980	103.7	104.1	103.3	82.1	80.9	83.4	21.8	22.6	20.9	70.0	69.9	70.0
	1985	103.8	104.1	103.5	85.9	84.7	87.2	23.8	24.4	23.2	72.2	72.1	72.3
Developed countries	1960	101.6	102.1	101.1	53.1	54.4	51.8	9.9	14.0	5.6	62.9	64.5	61.3
	1965	102.4	104.2	100.4	61.6	63.1	59.9	11.4	15.4	7.2	64.6	66.8	62.2
	1970	103.5	105.5	101.3	68.1	69.8	66.4	13.9	17.8	9.7	67.1	69.5	64.5
	1975	98.0	100.2	95.7	72.3	72.7	71.9	19.7	23.2	15.9	67.2	69.3	65.1
	1980	99.4	101.1	97.6	70.3	69.8	70.9	20.6	22.5	18.7	66.5	67.4	65.4
	1985	97.2	99.0	95.3	74.5	74.0	75.0	22.9	24.2	21.5	67.4	68.3	66.5
Developing countries	1960	101.5	102.4	100.6	62.1	63.3	60.9	13.3	17.1	9.4	65.6	67.5	63.7
	1965	100.3	101.0	99.6	74.7	75.8	73.5	19.2	23.6	14.6	70.5	72.4	68.5
	1970	100.1	100.6	99.5	78.6	79.4	77.9	23.2	27.2	19.1	71.1	72.7	69.4
	1975	100.7	101.1	100.2	83.5	82.8	84.2	28.1	31.0	25.2	73.2	74.1	72.3
	1980	101.8	102.1	101.4	83.9	82.7	85.1	29.9	30.7	29.0	73.3	73.4	73.3
	1985	102.3	102.7	101.9	87.9	86.8	89.1	33.1	33.9	32.2	76.1	76.1	76.0
Africa (excluding Arab States)	1960	72.8	86.8	58.1	15.1	19.8	10.3	2.0	2.9	1.0	35.5	43.1	27.6
	1965	79.8	93.3	65.7	17.5	23.6	11.1	2.7	3.9	1.5	40.5	48.6	31.9
	1970	78.6	87.8	69.0	22.4	27.9	16.7	3.1	4.3	1.8	40.6	46.5	34.3
	1975	93.1	103.2	82.7	31.4	38.3	24.3	4.3	5.7	2.8	48.4	55.0	41.6
	1980	92.7	102.3	82.7	35.8	42.8	28.6	5.4	7.1	3.7	49.9	56.5	43.1
	1985	97.8	107.2	88.4	37.7	44.2	31.0	6.4	8.1	4.6	50.8	56.9	44.4
Asia (excluding Arab states)	1960	80.8	96.2	64.6	20.7	25.8	15.2	2.5	3.7	1.2	39.9	48.1	31.3
	1965	86.2	101.1	70.4	22.6	29.4	15.5	3.4	4.9	1.8	44.1	53.1	34.7
	1970	82.4	91.9	72.3	26.3	32.1	20.1	3.7	5.3	2.1	42.5	48.7	35.9

TABLE 13.6 (cont.)

		First Level			Second Level			Third Level			All Levels		
		Total	Male	Female	Total	Male	Female	Total	Male	Female	Total	Male	Female
Asia (excluding Arab states)	1975	99.1	110.0	87.8	36.0	43.5	28.0	4.4	6.0	2.6	50.9	57.8	43.5
	1980	93.6	103.9	82.9	39.1	46.8	31.0	5.4	7.3	3.4	50.4	57.4	43.1
	1985	99.6	109.9	88.9	38.5	45.4	31.3	6.2	8.2	4.2	49.6	56.2	42.6
Arab states	1960	50.0	65.0	34.4	10.3	15.2	5.3	2.0	3.2	0.7	24.6	32.9	16.1
	1965	60.9	76.8	44.1	16.1	23.1	8.7	3.3	5.2	1.3	31.9	41.8	21.7
	1970	63.7	79.2	47.4	21.1	28.8	12.9	4.3	6.5	2.0	35.3	45.2	24.9
	1975	73.6	89.4	57.0	28.3	36.3	19.8	6.9	9.6	4.0	42.0	51.9	31.5
	1980	81.9	94.7	68.5	37.0	45.2	28.3	8.4	11.2	5.4	47.8	56.4	38.7
	1985	86.4	97.2	75.2	47.4	55.0	39.5	9.8	12.5	6.9	53.9	61.4	45.9
Northern America	1960	91.3	92.2	90.4	105.1	104.3	106.0	27.9	34.8	20.8	80.1	82.0	78.1
	1965	92.7	93.5	91.8	113.5	112.7	114.4	34.0	41.2	26.8	83.0	85.1	80.9
	1970	89.3	89.9	88.7	112.1	111.2	113.1	44.5	51.7	37.1	82.8	84.8	80.6
	1975	98.0	98.6	97.5	104.6	103.4	105.8	52.3	56.8	47.7	85.8	87.2	84.4
	1980	100.1	100.5	99.7	93.2	92.0	94.4	53.7	51.3	56.0	82.7	81.9	83.6
	1985	102.9	103.6	102.2	99.7	98.5	101.0	62.6	60.6	64.6	88.9	88.3	89.5
Latin America and the Caribbean	1960	73.0	74.9	71.1	14.2	14.9	13.6	3.0	4.2	1.8	40.0	41.4	38.5
	1965	81.5	83.1	79.9	19.4	20.2	18.7	4.2	5.6	2.8	45.9	47.2	44.5
	1970	91.4	92.6	90.2	24.9	25.7	24.0	6.3	8.0	4.5	52.1	53.4	50.8
	1975	98.0	99.6	96.5	35.4	36.2	34.4	11.7	13.6	9.9	58.5	60.0	57.0
	1980	105.8	107.5	104.2	43.5	43.0	44.1	13.4	15.1	11.7	63.3	64.4	62.3
	1985	107.9	109.9	105.9	52.2	51.2	53.3	15.0	16.3	13.6	66.6	67.6	65.7

SOURCE: UNESCO, *Statistical Yearbook* (Paris, 1987), pp. 2.32–2.33. © UNESCO 1987. Reproduced by permission of UNESCO.
NOTE: The gross enrollment ratio for a given level of education is the ratio of the total enrollment at that level to the population of the age group that, according to national regulations, should be enrolled at that level. Ratios may be greater than 100 because of late entry, repetition, etc. Data do not include North Korea.

related differences between college students who have taken courses in economics and those who have not, suggesting that the economic events of everyday life can be sources of learning as powerful as the formal training provided in classrooms.[43]

Another noteworthy aspect of the complexity in which individuals find themselves today derives from the wide-ranging movement of people around the world as a consequence of expanded business and professional travel, tourism, programs for study abroad, and the flight of refugees. People today are participants in more extensive and numerous social networks than was the case for earlier generations. Many of them have become "boundary spanners," individuals who move freely around the world, interpreting its configurations and uncertainties for those who travel less than they do.[44] Recent figures on travel beyond contiguous countries are staggering: some 400 million people are estimated to have engaged in such travel in 1988 (thus leading tourism revenues in that year to rank third among all export industries and to represent 25 percent of international trade in services), and the number has been growing at an annual rate of 5 to 7 percent.[45] In the case of China, the annual rate of growth has been between 20 and 30 percent since 1978, when the People's Republic opened its doors to foreign tourists, and it is anticipated that by the year 2000 the number of visitors to China from abroad will exceed seven million a year.[46] Hardly less impressive is the growth rate for transatlantic travel: in 1987, there was an average of about 450 flights a day over the North Atlantic, carrying 25,841,000 passengers, or 23 percent more than in 1986.[47] These patterns were hardly altered even by the oil crisis in 1973. As can be seen in table 13.6, world tourism grew at a rate exceeding the growth rate of the gross national product of industrial countries both before and after the crisis.[48]

[43] James F. Voss et al., "Informal Reasoning and Subject Matter Knowledge in the Solving of Economics Problems by Native and Novice Individuals," *Cognition and Instruction* 3, no. 4 (1986): 269–302.

[44] Richard Leifer and George P. Huber, "Relations among Perceived Environmental Uncertainty, Organization Structure, and Boundary-Spanning Behavior," *Administrative Science Quarterly* 22 (June 1977): 235–47.

[45] Louis J. D'Amore, "Tourism: The World's Peace Industry," in L. J. D'Amore and J. Jafari, ed., *Tourism: A Vital Force for Peace* (Montreal: First Global Conference, 1988), p. 7; Louis J. D'Amore, "Tourism: A Vital Force for Peace," *Futurist* 22 (May–June 1988): 27.

[46] D'Amore, "Tourism: A Vital Force for Peace," p. 25. This estimate was made prior to the Chinese regime's crackdown on student protests in 1989.

[47] Steven Greenhouse, "Air Traffic '88: Vexing Summer over the Atlantic," *New York Times*, June 12, 1988, p. 1.

[48] Not all the patterns of widening movements of people, however, are likely to con-

TABLE 13.7. World Tourism Growth, 1960–1973 and 1973–1982

	Average Annual Growth Rate	
	1960–1973	1973–1982
GNP of industrial nations	5.0%	2.1%
World international tourism arrivals	7.8	4.3
World scheduled airline traffic (revenue passenger miles)	13.0	6.9

SOURCE: Child & Waters Inc., *Travel Industry World Yearbook* (New York, 1985), as reproduced in D'Amore, "Tourism: The World's Peace Industry," p. 7.

Bell has summarized the implications of such data in this way:

The most striking difference—and this is the real change of scale between 1798 and today—has to do with the number of persons each one of us *knows* and the number each of us *knows of*—in short, the way in which we *experience* the world. An individual today, on the job, in school, in the neighborhood, in a professional or social milieu, knows immediately hundreds of persons and, if one considers the extraordinary mobility of our lives—geographical, occupational, and social—during a lifetime one comes to know, as acquaintances or friends, several thousand. And through the windows of the mass media, and because of the enlargement of the political world and the multiplication of the dimensions of culture—the number of persons (and places) that one *knows of* accelerates at a steeply exponential rate.

What happens when the world's population begins to experience this leap—in social awareness, contact, and interaction?[49]

---

tinue. The flow of political refugees around the world—officially counted as twelve million people who have fled persecution or violence—has reached such large proportions as to foster a "compassion fatigue" that has inclined refugee-receiving countries to raise their immigration barriers. Henry Kamm, "In an Era of Mass Refugees, 'Compassion Fatigue,' " *International Herald Tribune*, March 28, 1989, p. 1. In addition, several of the refugee-receiving countries in Europe are becoming increasingly aware of the extent to which the flow of refugees is altering their social and political fabric, an awareness that is fostering resistance to further influx. In France, for example, "an estimated 700,000 Arabs will be eligible to vote in [upcoming] presidential elections, a number nearly twice as large as the margins that separated the candidates in the 1974 presidential election. [Similarly, it is estimated that] by 1995 every second child born in Brussels . . . will be Arab." Tyler Marshall, "Europe Busy Closing Door to Foreigners," *Los Angeles Times*, May 7, 1989, p. 1. For a discussion of the many facets of refugee flows, see Leon Gordenker, *Refugees in International Politics* (New York: Columbia University Press, 1987).

[49] Bell, *Coming of Post-Industrial Society*, pp. 171–72 (italics in the original).

While this last question can be answered in many ways, perhaps the most generic concerns not the substance of what people do in response to the "leap" in the complexity of their worlds, but the way in which they do it. Substance can change as agendas and issues change, but an enduring consequence of the greater interdependence is the competence people bring to bear upon it. What happens when the world's population expands its awareness, contacts, and interactions—to answer the question directly—is that its analytic skills undergo growth commensurate with the increased complexity. There are, to be sure, finite limits to any individual's capacity to absorb and process information. Overload can set in as more and more places, people, and organizations enter a person's perceptual and experiential space; but with the mass media, educational institutions, and organizational staffs providing means for interpreting new inputs, it seems doubtful that the point of overload has yet to be approached in a world that has only lately begun to come into focus for most people.

It seems likely, then, that people will come up with a classic adaptive solution to the problem of increasingly complex interdependence: they will become more able to learn and use the appropriate facts, procedures, methods, analogies, examples, and scenarios. The acquisition of computer skills is illustrative of this latest form of adaptation: while today's older generations are baffled by computers and tend not to use them or even to avoid learning about them, most members of the younger generations, being less habit-driven in their ways of processing information, pick up and apply the needed skills quickly and effectively.[50]

There are other, less constructive solutions to the challenge of complexity. Instead of engaging in adaptive learning, people can retreat to habitual and simplistic solutions. Low turnouts in elections, low levels of information, mob actions against minorities, and volatile and contradictory shifts in the fortunes of political parties, are some of the traces of these simplistic solutions still to be found on the political

[50] This example is especially relevant inasmuch as computers have contributed substantially to the growth of social networks as well as to the skills needed to function in the networks. As Gerstein notes with respect to the "nascent culture" that has evolved around the software of "operating system logics, programming languages, telecommunications, word processing, data bases, spread sheets, and graphic libraries," it is likely to grow into "a major source of cultural linkages between macro and micro, making possible the formation and integration of groups on the basis of images and information. The effectiveness and durability of such electronically mediated linkages may be a critical question of the age." Dean R. Gerstein, "To Unpack Micro and Macro: Link Small with Large and Part with Whole," in J. C. Alexander et al., eds., *The Macro-Micro Link* (Berkeley: University of California Press, 1987), p. 103.

landscape, and enticements to remain simplistic will remain as long as ideologues on the left and right extremes of the political spectrum play upon the ambiguities and uncertainties inherent in deepening degrees of interdependence as a means of mobilizing support for their panaceas. While such reactions marked the years before the onset of turbulence, especially in Europe prior to World War II and the United States during the early years of the cold war, they seem to have receded in frequency and force as the micro parameter of world politics has been changing. Admittedly, the extreme right has episodically captured attention in France, and formulations at the other extreme have enjoyed moments of support in parts of the Third World, but the tendency is in quite another direction—if not toward a nonideological center, then at least away from the extremes and toward a readiness to grasp and accommodate to the complexities inherent in change.

VARIABILITY IN THE EXPANSION OF ANALYTIC SKILLS

It would be an unwarranted inference to argue that the worldwide expansion of analytic and cathectic capacities has led to a diminution of the differences among individuals along these lines. The readiness to act analytically can, of course, vary considerably and may even be quite low in some instances.[51] For example, under conditions of urban poverty some people have difficulty grasping the basic causal relationships that would enable them to improve their lot.[52] To note a global expansion of skills is not to imply that those of the rural peasant have caught up with those of the urban sophisticate. The high-tech age of information has not resulted in an equal distribution of skills any more

[51] Barbara Geddes and John Zaller, "Sources of Popular Support for Authoritarian Regimes," *American Journal of Political Science* 33 (May 1989): 319–47; Milton Lodge and Ruth Hamill, "A Partisan Schema for Political Information Processing," *American Political Science Review* 80 (June 1986): 505–19, and Shawn W. Rosenberg, "The Structure of Political Thinking," *American Journal of Political Science* 32 (August 1988): 539–66.

[52] In the United States, a teenage girl in the ghetto "may study hard in school and have high intelligence, but she has almost no working understanding of the relationship of cause and effect in daily life. Her aspirations are vaulting—she wants to go to Harvard, wants to be a surgeon. But her understanding of what it takes to get from here to there is missing. She has very little sense of the standards that apply in the outside world; she does not understand that thoughts of Harvard are absurd if she has never read anything but comic books. She does not think in terms of a sequence of outcomes leading to a goal but of one great big outcome that will or won't occur. Most characteristically, she exhibits very little belief that she is to some extent in control of her destiny—that *her* decisions about *her* behavior will affect *her* future." Charles Murray, "No, Welfare Isn't Really the Problem," *Public Interest* 84 (Summer 1986): 96 (italics in original).

than the industrial era gave rise to an equality in the distribution of wealth. Indeed, the analytically and cathectically "wealthy" may be getting wealthier in their ability to elaborate and judge scenarios relative to those who have long been poor in this regard. In developed countries, 1 out of 3 persons receives a daily newspaper and 1 out of 12 has a TV set; the comparable figures for the developing countries are 1 out of 30 and 1 out of 500. In 1978, more than 80 percent of the world's books and more than 80 percent of the world's data processing equipment were produced in developed countries.[53]

On the other hand, the unequal distribution of analytic wealth is not evidence that the expansion of skills is less than global in scope. That some urban poor and some people in the Third World are less competent at constructing scenarios and focusing affect than are some affluent citizens in the West is not to say that they are incapable of raising their skill level. Cole and Bruner have put it well:

Those groups ordinarily diagnosed as culturally deprived have the same underlying competence as those in the mainstream of the dominant culture, *the difference in performance being accounted for by the situations and contexts in which the competence is expressed*. To put the matter most rigorously, one can find a corresponding situation in which the member of the "out culture," the victim of poverty, can perform on the basis of a given competence in a fashion equal to or superior to the standard achieved by a member of the dominant culture.[54]

They offer the following finding from another study as a "prosaic example" of the importance of cultural context. It involves the ability

to estimate the number of cups of rice in each of several bowls. Comparisons of "rice-estimate accuracy" were made among several groups of subjects, including nonliterate Kpelle rice farmers from North Central Liberia and Yale sophomores. The rice farmers manifested significantly greater accuracy than the Yale students, the difference increasing with the amount of rice presented for estimation.[55]

[53] J. F. Rada, "A Third World Perspective," in G. Friedrichs and A. Schaff, eds., *Micro-Electronics and Society: A Report to the Club of Rome* (New York: New American Library, 1983), pp. 204–5.

[54] Michael Cole and Jerome S. Bruner, "Cultural Differences and Inferences about Psychological Processes," *American Psychologist* 26 (October 1971): 870 (italics in the original).

[55] Cole and Bruner, "Cultural Differences," pp. 870–71, citing J. Gay and M. Cole,

In other words, it is a form of cultural arrogance on the part of educated analysts to interpret the "low scores" of less educated people on measures of skill as evidence of unchanging skills. The less educated may well be increasingly able to digest and interpret the course of events depicted on global television in ways that are appropriate to their needs and aspirations. Furthermore, psychologists have recently reported data indicating that for most people, the capacity to create problem-solving and logical images is "vastly underdeveloped."[56]

In short, despite continuing differences among groups, it is reasonable to presume that people everywhere are now better able to employ scenarios that are not obscure, truncated, or vacuous. The presumption is further supported by the "principle of social density," which holds that "the greater the diversity of communications one is involved in, the more one develops abstract, relativistic ideas and the habit of thinking in terms of long-range consequences."[57] Since it is precisely the nature of the postindustrial era that people have become enmeshed in diverse information networks, the logic of this principle argues that their analytic and cathectic skills have expanded accordingly. Indeed, recent research on the modernization process in six countries has led to the suggestion that "what is lacking in the traditional culture may be provided by the institutions of modern society—by the school, the factory, the newspaper, and the radio. These sources of influence evidently have an independent power to effect political socialization, training men to know more about polities, stimulating them to take an interest in political events and to participate in civic affairs, and fostering a shift in allegiance from tribal and local leaders to those representing a wider community of interest."[58]

The conclusion, then, is that citizens today are able to employ more elaborate scenarios than could their predecessors in earlier eras. The word "elaborate" is used quite deliberately. The contention is not that scenarios are now more "rational," "sophisticated," or "accurate."

The New Mathematics and an Old Culture (New York: Holt, Rinehart, & Winston, 1967).

[56] Daniel Goleman, "Mental Images: New Research Helps Clarify Their Role," *New York Times*, August 12, 1986, p. C1. For a thorough inquiry into the nature and limits of analytic skills, see Stephen Michael Kosslyn, *Image and Mind* (Cambridge: Harvard University Press, 1980).

[57] Randall Collins, "Micro-Translation As a Theory-Building Stategy," in K. Knorr-Cetina and A. V. Cicourel, eds., *Advances in Social Theory and Methodology: Toward an Integration of Micro- and Macro-Sociologies* (Boston: Routledge & Kegan Paul, 1981), p. 96.

[58] Alex Inkeles, *Exploring Individual Modernity* (New York: Columbia University Press, 1983), p. 256.

The new aptitude for thinking and feeling in dynamic rather than static, cross-sectional terms may not lead to sound conclusions or greater sophistication about world affairs. It may even, as Cox has cogently argued, underlie the recent resurgence of traditional religion on a global scale.[59] The scenarios of many citizens, moreover, may well be conspiratorial in tone and preoccupied with scapegoats. Yet, whatever their level of accuracy or logic, scenarios in the present era are likely to be more elaborate than ever before—that is, marked by longer causal chains and stronger feelings, by selective judgments, by connections between events, by feedback links, by the perception that action at one time and place will set limits to or create options for action at another time and place.

Among the many implications of the expansion of skills are those that pertain to the application of bargaining and game theory. While most people may not have heard of Pareto optimality, the Prisoners' Dilemma, Chicken, Stag Hunt, Tit-for-Tat, and the other generic situations involving interdependent perceptions, increasingly they may be able to fathom and employ the reasoning on which they are based. Moreover, unlike the hypothetical actors in game theory, citizens today are not lacking in information as to what the opposing parties may be thinking or doing. Electronic communication brings ample news about the interactive and iterative consequences of bargaining and about actors who conduct themselves in terms of what others may expect as well as in terms of their own goals. People have come to know, in their own terms, about public and private goods, free riders, saddle points, suboptimal alternatives, and other characteristics of the links between individual choices and collective outcomes. This understanding may not always be articulated; it may constitute, instead, what has been called "tacit knowledge."[60] As such, as understanding that is im-

---

[59] H. Cox, *Religion in the Secular City: Toward a Postmodern Theology* (New York: Simon & Schuster, 1984).

[60] Polanyi suggests that tacit knowledge serves to explain how it is that people know more than they can describe: "We know a person's face, and can recognize it among a thousand, indeed among a million. Yet we usually cannot tell how we recognize a face we know. So most of this knowledge cannot be put into words": Michael Polanyi, *The Tacit Dimension* (New York: Doubleday, 1967), p. 4. Similarly, Giddens, stressing that *"every social actor knows a great deal about the conditions of reproduction of the society of which he or she is a member,"* distinguishes between "practical consciousness, as tacit stocks of knowledge which actors draw upon in the constitution of social activity, and what I call 'discursive consciousness,' involving knowledge which actors are able to express on the level of discourse": Anthony Giddens, *Central Problems in Social Theory: Action, Structure, and Contradiction in Social Analysis* (Berkeley, University of California Press, 1979), p. 5 (italics in original). For another penetrating discussion of the dif-

plicit and not readily subject to inspection or revision, it might not often result in what could be called rational action, but neither can such an understanding be developed without a comprehension of the relationship between one's own behavior and the collective consequences of the actions of the other persons involved in the situation.

From frequent exposure to terrorist incidents on television, for example, ordinary citizens now know that the outcome of one such incident influences subsequent ones, that the values at stake in such situations can outweigh what might seem like the most efficient course of action, and that control over the outcome becomes increasingly difficult for the terrorist the longer the situation continues. Likewise, they have presumably learned that the powerful do not necessarily command situations, that bank loans involve politics as well as economics (as when Third World countries threaten default on their debts), that superpowers can feel compelled to cooperate even while they spy on each other, and so on through a host of game-theoretical situations that can readily be deconstructed into the personal perspectives of citizens.

The expanded ability to envision alternative scenarios and to discriminate among the roles played by various actors in the causal chains has, in turn, intensified people's cathectic capacities. Accurately or inaccurately, blame is fixed more readily, and approval is bestowed more confidently, as the sequence of events comes more clearly into focus. Thus it is, to cite still another example, that Athol Fugard, the author of several penetrating plays on apartheid, provides a measure of these changes when he explains the popular reception of his work as stemming from "an extraordinary degree of sensitivity. The degree of information an audience has is very different than it was 25 years ago. I'm very conscious of the degree to which the audience is now educated about the subtleties and complexities of the situation in South Africa."[61] For a variety of reasons, in short, the processes of micro-macro interaction and the consequences of collective action are probably much more central to the individual's scenarios today than has been the case in previous generations.

CATHEXIS AS A SUPPLEMENT TO ANALYSIS

Another significant element in postinternational politics is a marked increase in the number of spontaneous collective actions. In Taiwan,

---

ference between what people know and what they are able to articulate, see Zubuff, *In the Age of Smart Machine*, pp. 174–95.

[61] Leslie Bennetts, "Five Top Playwrights in a Dialogue," *New York Times*, June 18, 1988, p. A9.

during the first year following the end of martial law, thirty-eight years after it was first imposed, an "extraordinary upsurge of pluralistic activity" occurred, "including a total of more than 1,700 street demonstrations by official count."[62] Over the past ten years or so—in some instances within only a few weeks of each other—large crowds in Poland, Iran, the Philippines, South Africa, Tibet, the West Bank and the Gaza Strip, Soviet Armenia, Haiti, South Korea, Burma, China, and Panama have formed with such speed and coherence as to suggest that expanded analytic skills do not necessarily require the mobilizing efforts of leaders to be effectively applied. The Solidarity movement in Poland spread so swiftly during the summer of 1980 that even its leaders were caught by surprise:

> For a moment, they were not so much leaders as followers of a process of social combustion that raced forward spontaneously and uncontrollably: first came the mass movement; then came the demands and the negotiations. . . . Suddenly, there was a power in society where none was supposed to be. . . . Right in the heart of a totalitarian system, under which people are supposed to be at their most helpless, Solidarity gave the world one of the most startling demonstrations of the power of the people that it has ever seen.[63]

The uprising that toppled the Burmese government in August 1988 was similarly abrupt. Within a matter of weeks, the people of Rangoon "learned public defiance" and "tasted political power, through street demonstrations, for the first time since U Ne Win took power 26 years ago. . . . At first tentatively, then, flinging their masks away, more boldly, the people learned the satisfaction of voicing their grievances openly."[64] Indeed, this uprising has been called "one of the few examples of a pure popular revolution . . . There are no leaders, there is no organization and there is no international movement outside the country pushing the people one way or the other."[65] Accounts of the 1989 upheaval in China tell the same story of spontaneity and rapid coalescence:

> What we've been experiencing in China—mostly in Beijing—these past several weeks is unlike anything I've ever seen before. No

[62] David Holley, "New Openness Enlivens Taiwan Politics," *Los Angeles Times*, July 23, 1988, p. A4.

[63] "Notes and Comments," *New Yorker*, October 20, 1986, p. 35.

[64] Seth Mydans, "Brute Force in Burma," *New York Times*, September 23, 1988, p. A17.

[65] Robert Pear, "Burmese Revolt Seen as Spontaneous," *New York Times*, September 10, 1988, p. 3.

American student demonstration or mass civil-rights actions can begin to compare with it. . . . From one central square, Tiananmen, "People Power" (a slogan deliberately borrowed from the Philippine Revolution of 1986) has radiated out to control almost every Beijing intersection and, at last report, streets in forty other Chinese cities as well. This youth rebellion may not be able to hold out much longer, but . . . without weapons, without communications other than *xiaodao xiaoxi*, or grapevine, without transportation other than bicycles, and trucks borrowed from farmers and work units, without even any agreement on what they are demonstrating for—except for the right to demonstrate—the students and those protecting them are blocking a modern, well-equipped army. . . . The sight of [Tiananmen Square] covered by more than a million young people, most of them not angry but, rather, good-naturedly eager to match their collective strength against the limits of state power . . . is, quite simply, the most awesome thing I have ever seen.[66]

Much the same can be said about the seizure of the U.S. embassy in Teheran. In the context of newly acquired analytic skills, the daily scenes of Iranian mobs raging around the embassy can be seen as an instance not of unruly rabble, but of a highly elaborate scenario. The reports that the crowds were galvanized into action whenever the TV cameras were on and pointing in their direction suggest a keen understanding that pictures of outrage and protest relayed around the world would have consequences—i.e., would be links in scenarios—and that understanding may well have been the reason for milling around the embassy.[67] The scenes of citizens guarding ballot boxes in the 1986 Philippine election, and subsequently forming a vast human chain to protect the rebellious army command from attacks by Marcos's forces, were other instances of individual actions giving rise to global repercussions.

Such incidents pose challenging questions. How were these developments initiated and sustained? In the absence of detailed plans for

[66] Shapiro, "Letter from Beijing," p. 73.

[67] While there is some evidence that the mob actions outside the embassy were not entirely spontaneous, that they were in part responses to leadership cues as well as to the lights indicating that the television cameras were on, this does not negate the interpretation that the crowds operated with elaborate scenarios that linked their actions to worldwide repercussions. See Patricia A. Karl, "Media Diplomacy," in Gerald Benjamin, ed., *The Communications Revolution in Politics* (New York: Academy of Political Science, 1982), p. 142, and William C. Adams, ed., *Television Coverage of the Middle East* (Norwood, N.J.: Ablex, 1982).

action, how did the uprisings manage to be so focused? Why did they not result in sheer chaos, with different individuals and groups pursuing diverse and conflicting goals? How, in short, did so many micro parts spontaneously aggregate into a single, coherent macro whole?

The questions become even more intriguing when one recognizes that some of the instances of coherent collective action, especially those in Burma, the West Bank, and South Africa, persisted even after the governments involved clamped down on television coverage. Given the cognitive limits within which many people are confined in the absence of pictorial representation of events and their outcomes, how did the collective actions manage to endure and even gain momentum?

The answers may become apparent if we conceive of effective collective action as resulting from a two-stage process, in which the expansion of analytic skills is supplemented by a corresponding growth in cathectic abilities. First, through both direct observation and the mass media, people become aware of what those around them are doing. Perhaps aided by exhortations from their leaders, but also using their own analytic skills, they translate this awareness into scenarios that revolve around the instruments of change: the ballot box, the television station, the army base or the central square. Even with the availability of television broadcasts, however, cognitive appraisals of the situation are not easily made. In Manila, for example, so much was fluid and uncertain that it seems doubtful that people were moved by intellectualization alone to converge at the same locales. This is where the second aspect of this process can be discerned: analytic skills both respond to and are reinforced by cathectic capacities, which lead to common and seemingly spontaneous actions. Collins offers an account of how this form of cathexis contributes to such macro-micro interactions:

> The actual structures of the social world, especially as centered on the networks upholding property and authority, involve continuous monitoring by individuals of each other's group loyalties. Since the social world can involve quite a few lines of authority and sets of coalitions, the task of monitoring them can be extremely complex. How is this possible, given people's inherently limited cognitive capacities?
>
> The solution must be that negotiations are carried out implicitly, on a different level than the use of consciously manipulated verbal symbols. I propose that the mechanism is *emotional* rather than cognitive. Individuals monitor others' attitudes toward social coalitions, and hence toward the degree of support for rou-

tines, by feeling the amount of confidence and enthusiasm there is toward certain leaders and activities, or the amount of fear of being attacked by a strong coalition, or the amount of contempt for a weak one. These emotional energies are transmitted by contagion among members of a group, in flows which operate very much like the set of negotiations which produce prices within a market. In this sense ... the strengths of a market model for linking microinteractions into macrostructures can be salvaged without incorporating the weaknesses of traditional exchange theories.[68]

Insufficiencies of information and limits on cognition, in other words, do not necessarily inhibit the aggregation of micro actors. Through their cathectic capacities, people can sense the imminence of collective action and where and how they fit into it. To extend Collins's analogy, there is a marketplace for macro-oriented micro energies, and the trade-offs that occur in this market can follow patterns not unlike the transactions that take place in strict economic settings.

Indeed, this marketplace can even operate effectively at a time when collective goals are best served through restraint and inaction. Events involving Pope John Paul II, Bishop Desmond Tutu, and presidential candidate Corazon Aquino illustrate how people can employ their analytic and emotional skills to monitor and converge around the orientations of vast numbers of their fellow citizens gathered in a single place. Each of the three leaders presided over a huge rally—in Poland, South Africa, and the Philippines—convened to protest the policies of their states, and each was able to defuse the confrontation by persuading the restless crowds of the need for unified but nonviolent action. The analytic and cathectic skills of their audiences explain why such large crowds did not turn to violence even though they were acutely aware of their shared opposition to their respective regimes. If they had given free reign to their feelings of hostility, surely massive upheavals would have ensued in each case. But the elaborateness of their scenarios and their emotional monitoring of each other served to contain their anger and focus their action. Press accounts of the three situations make it clear that their scenarios included an appreciation of how large, orderly crowds, interacting supportively with John Paul, Tutu, and Aquino, and responding to their urgings that the gatherings be

---

[68] Collins, "On the Micro Foundations of Macrosociology," p. 944 (italics in original).

peaceful, could become a key link in causal chains that might force a modernization of the regime's policies.[69]

The enlarged analytic capacities of people are not confined to situations in which mass actions occur. They have also been detected by poll data. In 1983, a poll of the U.S. public's attitudes toward the conflicts in Central America aroused widespread attention because its results seemed so contradictory: a low level of information about U.S. policies in the region, on the one hand, and a high degree of skepticism toward any policies the United States might pursue there, on the other.[70] The discrepancy can be resolved, however, if the notion of "being informed" is expanded to encompass analytic and cathectic skills. If "being informed" refers only to levels of explicit factual knowledge, it is indeed perplexing that a low level of knowledge should be associated with skepticism rather than with disinterest. But if "being informed" also includes the elaborateness of the tacit scenarios people employ to react to world events, then the poll data make eminent sense. Americans may not have been acquainted with the facts about which factions the United States supported in El Salvador and Nicaragua, but at a higher level of abstraction they were apparently clear in their minds about how the scenarios might unfold if the United States stepped up its involvement in the region. Memories of the earlier involvement in Vietnam, along with the extended capacity to think analogically in terms of causal chains—the skill dimension—enabled those polled to assert positions on Central America even though they seemed "uninformed" as that term is conventionally used. A large amount of information, in other words, is not a prerequisite for expanded analytic skills.

MICRO CHANGE ON A GLOBAL SCALE

As already indicated, the expansion of analytic skills is conceived to be worldwide in scope. Not only for citizens in democratic and industrialized societies, but also for Afghan tribesmen and Argentine gauchos, for peasants in India and protesters in Chile, for guerrillas in Peru and students in the Philippines, for blacks in South Africa and Palestinians in Israel, the interdependence of global life and the consequences of collective action are daily experiences. The scenarios used in the Third World may not be so elaborate as those to be found in the First World,

[69] See the coverage of these events in *New York Times*, June 18, 1983, p. 1; February 17, 1986, p. 1; and February 19, 1986, p. A6.

[70] A. Clymer, "Poll Finds Americans Don't Know U.S. Position on Central America," *New York Times*, July 1, 1983, p. 1.

but they are far from crude or limited. As one investigator concluded after a lengthy analysis of data, "Mass publics in less developed countries have ... been strikingly responsive to changing international events."[71] Two sociologists who probed for indications of changing orientations in interviews with six thousand men from six developing countries concluded that their results provided "definitive evidence that ... essentially the same basic qualities which define a man as modern in one country and culture also delineate the modern man in other places," and they described those qualities as follows:

> He is an informed participant citizen; he has a marked sense of personal efficacy; he is highly independent and autonomous in his relations to traditional sources of influence, especially when he is making basic decisions about how to conduct his personal affairs; and he is ready for new experiences and ideas, that is, he is relatively open-minded and cognitively flexible.
>
> As an informed participant citizen, the modern man identifies with the newer, larger entities of region and state, takes an interest in public affairs, national and international as well as local, joins organizations, keeps himself informed about major events in the news, and votes or otherwise takes some part in the political process. The modern man's sense of efficacy is reflected in his belief that, either alone or in concert with others, he may take actions which can affect the course of his life and that of his community; in his active efforts to improve his own condition and that of his family; and in his rejection of passivity, resignation, and fatalism toward the course of life's events.[72]

Perhaps an even more telling—and certainly a more poignant—insight into the changing skills and orientations of people in the Third World is provided by this report of an astute journalist who was visited in her Paris office by a poor Iraqi exile:

> It made me impatient that he persisted in seeking a simple formula, that he was so totally concentrated on the pain and injustice in his own country, so unaware of other peoples' miseries, so confident that if the Americans and the French and others only knew

---

[71] J. I. Dominguez, "Public Opinion on International Affairs in Less Developed Countries," in Richard L. Merritt and Bruce M. Russett, eds., *From National Development to Global Community: Essays in Honor of Karl W. Deutsch* (London: George Allen & Unwin, 1981), p. 201.

[72] Alex Inkeles and David H. Smith, *Becoming Modern: Individual Change in Six Developing Countries* (Cambridge: Harvard University Press, 1974), pp. 290–91.

that things were bad in his homeland they would drop everything to fix them. I told him I had no more time.

But when he left, I kept thinking about him. He is a person from a long-darkened place who is coming to know what a human has a right to expect. He can no longer accept the old, dull submission. He had even managed to see that Iraqis were not alone, that their enemies, the Iranians, must be suffering horribly too.

His horizons have broadened. There must be quite a lot of people like him by now, emerging through education to question the definition of good and bad handed down by authority, noticing there may be other ways of seeing things, other people with real concerns and grievances.

The more I thought, the better I felt about him. He is part of change in the world.[73]

Well before Gorbachev introduced and encouraged the policies of *glasnost* and *perestroika* in the USSR, traces of new analytic and cathectic skills could be discerned in Soviet politics, too. Its closed system had not been able to shield Soviet citizens from the changes of the post-industrial era. Their expanded competence was quite noticeable, for example, in the extraordinary lengths to which the regime went to place the downing of the Korean airliner in 1983 in a favorable light. As one observer noted:

From childhood, Russians have been taught that they are surrounded by enemies, primarily the United States, and that sacrifices must be made to ward off attack.

Yet, in the view of Western diplomats, the plane incident raises troubling possibilities that the leadership cannot ignore. The average Soviet citizen is better educated than he was 20 years ago, and probably more inclined to make critical assessments.

In all of this, the diplomats believe, there is a potential difficulty for the authorities as ordinary people assess the incident and ask themselves whether it was handled responsibly.[74]

Since the Gorbachev reform, of course, these tendencies have become more obvious. A Soviet social scientist has said: "In comparison with the Khrushchev era, much has changed. There is no longer the dark masses which could be ruled easily, whose minds could be controlled.

[73] Flora Lewis, "Simple Questions," *New York Times*, March 15, 1984, p. A31.

[74] J. F. Burns, "Kremlin Hints at Concern over Domestic Reaction," *New York Times*, September 4, 1983, p. A18.

There are thinking people, who have been educated in how socialism ought to be, and they want it that way."[75]

Finally, lest there be any question about whether the analytic skills of citizens in the other superpower are changing as well, consider this comment about the challenge facing U.S. advertising agencies, those organizations that are allegedly masters at manipulating public perceptions:

> Many consumers appear frustrated with advertising's predigested and sugar-coated distortions of reality. Americans we have surveyed show a sensitivity to difficult matters such as Irangate, AIDS, and the plight of the homeless. . . . Fewer consumers are willing to swallow advertising's pat prescriptions that women must be youthful and thin to be desirable, that machismo and masculinity are synonymous, that various racial and ethnic groups have inherent, exaggerated mannerisms and behaviors. Consumers are turning away from ads that do not portray people truthfully and fairly, that do not allow people to "be themselves."[76]

A great many other illustrations of enlarged analytic skills and cathectic capacities could be cited, but obviously they do not constitute proof of the proposition that people everywhere are using increasingly elaborate role scenarios. To be sure, Inglehart has compiled persuasive systematic evidence that the political skills of Western publics have undergone changes that enable them to "intervene in the political process on a qualitatively different level," but these findings focus on modes of participation and only imply a shift in those analytic skills necessary to scenario construction.[77] Systematic data that allow for the comparison of scenario structures across eras have yet to be made; until they are, we can only stress that underlying the examples is a logic that argues in favor of the proposition.[78]

---

[75] Tatyana Zaslavskaya, quoted in Andrew Rosenthal, "Longtime Voice for Change Comes to Fore," *New York Times*, August 28, 1987, p. A6.

[76] Tom Pirko, "Advertising Has a Lot to Learn from New, Improved—and Smarter—Public," *Los Angeles Times*, February 21, 1988, sec. 4, p. 3.

[77] Ronald Inglehart, *The Silent Changing Values and Political Styles among Western Publics* (Princeton: Princeton University Press, 1977), p. 367. For comparable data through 1984, see Paul R. Abramson and Ronald Inglehart, "Generational Replacement and Value Change in Six Western European Societies," *American Journal of Political Science* 30 (February 1986): 1–25.

[78] There is a growing systematic literature on what is varyingly referred to as "cognitive complexity" or "political sophistication," but a careful examination of this literature over the past few decades as it pertains to the U.S. electorate has yielded contradictory conclusions. While most studies suggest the absence of a tendency toward greater

CONTROL LOST, CONTROL REGAINED

The expansion of analytic skills and cathectic capacities has been accomplished by a process, already noted in chapter 9, whereby people everywhere are sensing their control over their lives slipping away as public affairs become increasingly complex. The combined effect of these changes is to incline people to seek to regain control by selecting scenarios in which their needs and wants are met by collectivities that are relatively close in time, space, and function. When people discriminate among scenarios in terms of the effectiveness of subsystems, their actions seem very likely to be marked by new directions and greater intensities.

The evidence with respect to a diminished sense of control is, again, suggestive rather than clear-cut. Social psychologists have amassed data on locus of control, but these pertain to the sources of varying responses to close-at-hand situations rather than to distant events in large systems. Likewise, sociologists have developed both systematic findings and theoretical perspectives that bear upon such related processes as alienation, powerlessness, system blame, and norm emergence,[79] but again the results do not have immediate relevance for the new structures of postinternational politics other than to highlight the negative consequences of social, economic, and political complexity for the sense of control people have over their lives.

On the other hand, there are anecdotal indicators such as the anguish of the peace movement over the prospects of nuclear holocaust and the apathy of American students over U.S. actions in Grenada, Lebanon, and Central America. A feeling of powerlessness has been cited as the explanation for the difference between the tepid reactions of the campuses in the 1980s and the vigorous student protests in the late 1960s and early 1970s against the war in Vietnam. Poll data are consistent with this explanation; they "show that the number of people expressing at least a mild form of political alienation—'what I

---

sophistication, some inquiries indicate the contrary. Furthermore, none of the materials examined included longitudinal analyses of scenario structures. See Robert C. Luskin, "Measuring Political Sophistication," *American Journal of Political Science* 31 (November 1987): 856–99.

[79] Melvin Seeman, "Alienation Motifs in Contemporary Theorizing: The Hidden Continuity of the Classic Themes," *Social Psychology Quarterly* 46 (September 1983): 171–84; Charles Tilly, *From Mobilization to Revolution* (Reading, Mass.: Addison-Wesley, 1978); A. Portes, "On the Logic of Postfactum Explanations: The Hypothesis of Lower-Class Frustration As a Cause of Leftist Radicalism," *Social Forces* 50 (September 1971): 26–44; R. H. Turner and L. M. Killian, *Collective Behavior* (Englewood Cliffs, N.J.: Prentice-Hall, 1972).

think doesn't count,' 'those in power don't care what people like me think,' '*They* try to take advantage of people like me'—rose inexorably from one-third minorities in the nineteen-sixties to two-thirds majorities by the start of the nineteen-eighties."[80] A feeling of remoteness from the centers of decision making has been noted among citizens of affluent, culturally cohesive Japan as well,[81] and even among members of the Trilateral Commission, all of whom are recent occupants of leadership positions in industrial societies. An account of the commission's tenth-anniversary conference noted that a mood of despair marked the deliberations: "What comes through most clearly in these ostensibly inner circles of power is how little capacity these people feel they have to shape events. Far from flexing muscles to manipulate hidden levers of control . . . they are groping almost desperately for ways to bring back some order. If there is any conspiracy, it seems to be in the diffusion of power, of impersonal if not inhuman forces eluding and confusing the attempts to plan."[82] If the elite of the Western world are racked by such feelings, a fortiori the same can be said of those whose resources and influence are virtually nil.

This is the point at which interaction between subgroupism and the changing micro parameters becomes central: they feed on each other in the sense that the expanded analytic and cathectic skills facilitate close identification with subgroups even as the proliferation and successes of subgroups become increasingly relevant to the scenarios people construct about their future. Doubtless some part of the subgroup explosion has derived from the communications technology which enables groups in one part of the world to observe and model the activities of counterparts elsewhere. But the proliferation of subgroups stems from more than the diffusion of examples. There must, after all, be reasons to emulate others. There must be similar but unrelated circumstances at work throughout the world that account for the recognition of shared identity among the members of diverse subgroups in every corner of the globe. What are these circumstances? Why are people everywhere turning away from whole systems—the state, the society, the community—and turning to smaller collectivities?

Surely a major part of the answer is that people have come to believe that whole systems are too complex to meet their needs and serve their

[80] Daniel Yankelovich, *New Rules: Searching for Self-Fulfillment in a World Turned Upside Down* (New York: Random House, 1981), pp. 185–86.

[81] Susan Chira, "Rich Man, Poor Man in Japan: Not an Economic Party for All," *New York Times*, December 26, 1988, p. 1.

[82] Flora Lewis, "The Power to Propose," *New York Times*, April 22, 1983, p. A31.

wants.[83] And so they have sought to regain control by turning to subsystems, to the less remote and less complex groups to which they somehow feel related, in the hope that their interests can thereby be better served and a modicum of control exercised over the distant and impersonal forces that intrude upon their daily routines. The resurgence of the family and the church, and the emergence of long-dormant linguistic, nationality, and ethnic groups, are parts of this pattern,[84] just as "big is threatening," "small is beautiful," and "I count, too" have become recurrent themes of the postindustrial era.

It might be argued that people have been increasingly removed from the centers of decision ever since the onset of the industrial revolution and that it is another form of ahistoricism to treat the sense of diminished control as a recent development. This reasoning overlooks the interaction of expanded analytic skills and diminished feelings of control. While it is surely the case that the processes separating people from decisional centers have been intensifying since the eighteenth century, the argument here is that only in our time has this long-term trend reached the point where people have given up on the distant centers and turned to those closer at hand. Stated metaphorically, the trend has been a gentle slope rising towards skepticism and doubt, but the curve of the past few decades has been a steep climb, as the sense of lost control has risen exponentially. The newly acquired capacity to

[83] In addition, with corruption and deception on the part of top governmental leaders having become an ever more evident worldwide pattern, the level of trust accorded the elites of whole systems appears to have declined substantially. One U.S. observer recalled his confidence in public officials as having been high during the period which "brought us the civil-rights movement, the War against Poverty and the Great Society," and then went on, "Our innocence had not yet been taken away by the lies of Vietnam, the Watergate cover-up and the Iran-Contra Scandals. . . . Now I trust almost nobody in government. I have learned that many in positions of authority believe that it is part of their job to lie in the national interest. I suspect everything . . . I believe only what my own senses tell me, only what is demonstrably true, only what cannot be faked in sophisticated laboratories, only what was testified to by people with proven track records of credibility": Alan M. Dershowitz, "Trust Lost, New J.F.K. Probe Is Needed," *Los Angeles Times*, November 9, 1988, sec. 2, p. 7. For an analysis that distinguishes between the declining trust accorded elites and the continued legitimacy of whole systems, see Seymour Martin Lipset and William Schneider, *The Confidence Gap: Business, Labor, and Government in the Public Mind*, rev. ed. (Baltimore: The Johns Hopkins University Press, 1987), esp. chapter 12. For data indicating that the level of trust varies widely in different countries, see E. J. Dionne, Jr., "Government Trust: Less in West Europe Than the U.S.," *New York Times*, February 16, 1986, p. 6.

[84] For analyses that trace the "quest for community" back to subsystems, see William A. Schambra, "The Decline of National Community," *Kettering Review* (Spring 1986): 22–25, and David W. Brown, "Civic Virtue in America," *Kettering Review* (Spring 1986): 6–12.

elaborate lengthier scenarios, along with the access to world events provided by global television, has enabled people to discern more clearly the causal networks that distance them from whole systems and that put those systems beyond their control. Equally important, the new skills have heightened sensitivity to the risks inherent in complex systems—the risks of nuclear war, economic depression, political dominance, and social breakdown—and this new knowledge about the uncertainties of the postindustrial order "has led to increased concern and has reduced rather than increased a prevailing sense of power."[85]

Of course, the decline has not been a "free fall." Accounts of people like Samantha Smith who corresponded with Kremlin leaders and was welcomed by them to Moscow, and Mathias Rust, who landed his plane in Red Square, and other private actors whose actions have global consequences serve as reminders that the causal networks are not entirely impervious to individual effort. For some citizens, moreover, the symbols of whole systems—the flags, heroes, and historic monuments—still inspire hope and slow the decline in sense of control.

For most people, however, in the coming decades the whole-system symbols are likely to seem ever more vacuous and the symbols of subsystems are likely to become increasingly meaningful and compelling, leading to a sense of regained control and further strengthening the tendency toward subgroupism.[86]

It should be emphasized that subgroupism is an adaptive response to the problems of complexity, not an abandonment of responsibility. Subgroupism is not to be equated with indifference; turning one's vision to close-at-hand subsystems is not an expression of apathy or cynicism. Such reactions would involve the rejection of subsystems as well as whole systems, whereas subgroupism is a search for new outlets around which to organize scenarios in which the individual's micro actions can have macro consequences.

THE REDIRECTION OF LEGITIMACY SENTIMENTS

Another micro attribute that is undergoing change is people's legitimacy sentiments: those orientations whereby citizens do or do not ac-

[85] Harriet Zuckerman, "Uses and Control of Knowledge: Implications for the Social Fabric," in J. F. Short, Jr., ed., *The Social Fabric: Dimensions and Issues* (Newbury Park, Calif.: Sage, 1986), p. 341.

[86] This is not to imply that all systems and subsystems are involved in zero-sum relationships. There are nonzero-sum situations, too, wherein systems and subsystems interact harmoniously, reinforcing each other's structures and sharing the burdens and opportunities of common challenges.

cord legitimacy to the directives through which higher authorities seek their compliance.[87] The criteria for according legitimacy are becoming more exacting as people are better able to construct scenarios and fix responsibility for the course of events. Where legitimacy once derived from habitual and traditional norms perpetuated by macro structures and processes, today the enlarged analytic skills and cathectic capacities of citizens increasingly enable them to ascribe legitimacy on the basis of performance activities that they perceive as appropriate.[88]

Enormous macro consequences can follow from the replacement of traditional with performance criteria of legitimacy. If, as seems likely, "the macro-organization of politics hinges upon the micro-transmission of particularly dramatic events which are used as barometers of social confidence in the ability of public figures to muster support,"[89] a shift toward performance criteria is likely to strengthen the effectiveness of subgroups and weaken that of national governments. Indeed, it is precisely in these macro-micro interactions that the roots of a global authority crisis are to be found. If the loci of control and other micro dynamics are undergoing substantial change along the indicated lines, the structures of authority through which collectivities pursue goals, mobilize resources, and resolve conflicts are bound to be under siege. As people become more skilled at locating themselves in an ever more complex world, at seeing through the authorities who claim they have answers to the problems of complexity, and at identifying subgroups that seem to offer greater hope of satisfying their needs and wants, clearly they are less and less likely to accept as legitimate the directives issued by the leaders of whole systems.

Taken together, the subgroupism of citizens, their expanded analytic skills, their greater cathectic capacities, and their redirected legitimacy sentiments constitute a powerful drive for questioning, if not challenging, authority. And once authority is challenged, compliance is no longer assured; the authority relationship begins to lose its predictability and moves toward crisis.

A crisis of authority is not simply a replacement of compliance with defiance. Habitual compliance and outright defiance are two extremes, and direct movement from the former to the latter is an exceptional

---

[87] The concept of legitimacy sentiments is developed in Harry Eckstein, "Authority Patterns: A Structural Basis for Political Inquiry," *American Political Science Review* 67 (December 1973): 1142–61.

[88] For some data that support this proposition, see M. Stephen Weatherford, "How Does Government Performance Influence Political Support?" *Political Behavior* 9 (1987): 5–28.

[89] Collins, "Micro-Translation," p. 104.

development which occurs only in those rare circumstances when full-scale revolutions are underway. The more typical authority crisis involves a shift in which performance criteria come to be attached to the legitimacy of the authorities' actions. Historically, legitimacy has been accorded to authorities automatically, out of traditions and habits that become deeply ingrained norms of conduct. As these norms begin to give way to sensitivity to the contents of the actions treated as legitimate, criteria for assessing the legitimacy of performances begin to emerge and become increasingly stringent.

It is with respect to the replacement of traditional legitimacy that the impact of global television has particular relevance. Subgroupism and expanded analytic skills may dispose people to rethink what has long been taken for granted, but it is the wider availability of a medium with which to make firsthand assessments of the authorities that activates these dispositions. Public officials may be granted a presumption of legitimacy upon entering office, but the TV cameras then subject their performances to close scrutiny, and the officials soon know that they must offer appealing reasons and compelling explanations of their actions to the TV audience in order to retain their legitimacy and effectiveness. Knowing that the attitudes of citizens toward particular leaders can fluctuate suddenly and erratically, they must continuously maintain or improve their performance level, often to the point of accommodating their daily activities and agenda to the TV programming schedules. Furthermore, it has been demonstrated that television has not only facilitated the shift from traditional to performance criteria of legitimacy, but that it also has importantly shaped the performance criteria themselves through the authoritative way in which it presents the course of events.[90] Viewed in this context, it is little wonder that South African, Israeli, and Chinese authorities have prohibited international television coverage of riots in their countries. To do otherwise would have been to allow the brutality shown on the world's TV screens to weaken their legitimacy.

Since it involves the opening rather than the closing of communications channels, the recent history of the Soviet Union offers perhaps an even more clear-cut illustration of the relationship between a leadership's legitimacy and its performance. With the policies of *glasnost* and *perestroika* leading to strikes and ethnic protests, questions arose about the Communist party's ability to maintain power. General Secretary (and now President) Gorbachev understood that the answer lay in the party's performance: "The party cannot gain authority by de-

[90] Iyengar and Kinder, *News That Matters*, pp. 126–27.

cree. No mighty decree or decision can do this now. . . . Today authority can be won only by the decisive and consistent carrying out of the
policy of perestroika. There is not nor will there be any other way for
the party to win authority. If someone thinks otherwise this is unrealistic, comrades."[91]

THE SELF AS AUTHORITY

As suggested above, disappointment with whole systems can lead to a
withdrawal from politics altogether, a decision often seen as exiting
from the citizenship role instead of using it as a platform from which
to voice concerns, a turning away from public affairs in favor of focusing exclusively on private matters.[92] This distinction, however, draws
an unnecessarily rigid line between public and private. It leaves no conceptual room for orientations toward the public arena that are refo-
cused on subgroups. In effect, it posits subsystems in the multi-centric
world not as foci of identification and legitimacy in their own right,
but as mere way stations en route to complete alienation from the
state-centric world. While there can hardly be any doubt that some
people do express their distrust of and disappointment with public
bodies by a retreat to personal concerns—the decrease in voter turnout
in the United States has been interpreted as just such a retreat—the
proliferation and vigorous activities of subgroups (see chapter 14) suggest that between exit and voice lies what might be called *simultaneous
reentry*, a shift in locus of control rather than an abandonment of efforts at control. The potentiality of simultaneous reentry is a critical
feature of the dynamics on which turbulence in postinternational politics is deemed to rest (see chapter 16).

It might be argued that even simultaneous reentry is an overly optimistic interpretation of where the decline in compliance is leading. The
global authority crisis may be much deeper than a shift toward subgroup loyalties and away from whole-system concerns. Rather, it may
be a matter of people focusing on *themselves* as the ultimate authority,
turning away from subsystems as well as whole systems. Widespread
corruption among leaders and the presence of underground economies
throughout the world are sometimes considered indicators of such a

---

[91] From a transcription of a meeting of top leaders of the Communist party published
in *Pravda* and translated in *New York Times*, July 23, 1989, p. A6.

[92] Albert O. Hirschman, *Shifting Involvements: Private Interest and Public Action*
(Princeton: Princeton University Press, 1981). Hirschman, in an earlier work, *Exit,
Voice, and Loyalty* (Cambridge: Harvard University Press, 1970), had applied this dis-
tinction to the behavior of consumers.

development, since taking a bribe, not reporting income, or otherwise feathering one's nest involves arrogating authority to oneself and substituting one's own welfare for that of any collectivity. Similarly, the "me" generation, the preoccupation with private gain, and the recruiting success of terrorist organizations can be cited as illustrative of a transfer of authority not in the direction of subgroups, but toward individuals. Bell, for example, discerns "crises of belief" in many countries, a "major consequence" of which is "the loss of civitas, that spontaneous willingness to obey the law, to respect the rights of others, to forgo the temptations of private enrichment at the expense of the public weal—in short, to honor 'the city' of which one is a member. Instead, each man goes his own way, pursuing his private vices, which can be indulged only at the expense of public benefits."[93]

The argument is not without merit. Underground economies are thriving throughout the world, and governments are increasingly failing to collect the full amount of tax revenues due them.[94] More and more individuals appear moved to spy on their country for cash payments rather than for ideological reasons.[95] From the Philippines to Lebanon, from Haiti to the United States, incidents of vigilantism—of groups taking the law into their own hands—appear to be occurring with greater frequency. And corruption of the public trust seems to be reaching into higher echelons than ever before: the leader of Panama is indicted in a U.S. court for his activities in the drug trade, the brother of a South Korean president is found to have had his hand in the public till, the attorney general of the United States is shown to have misused his office, the son-in-law of a former general secretary of the Soviet Communist party is shown to have profited from his father-in-law's position, and the leadership of the Liberal Democratic party in Japan is decimated by a bribery scandal that forces the resignation of the prime minister and several of his cabinet ministers.[96]

[93] Daniel Bell, *The Cultural Contradictions of Capitalism* (New York: Basic Books, 1978), pp. 244–45. A similar perspective is presented in Steven Kelman, " 'Public Choice' and Public Spirit," *Public Interest* no. 87 (Spring 1987): 80–94.

[94] The underground economy in Taiwan is considered to be equal to about 30 percent of that country's gross national product of $120 billion. Coleen Geraghty, "Grey-Market Deals Flourish in Taiwan," *International Herald Tribune*, May 22, 1989, p. 9. In the United States, it was estimated that taxpayers in 1986 would fail to report some $90 billion in owed taxes, a figure triple the amount estimated for 1974. David Burnham, "IRS Stepping Up Pressure on Cheats," *New York Times*, September 19, 1985, p. D17.

[95] Joel Brinkley, "Method and Aims Point to a New Breed of Spy," *New York Times*, June 9, 1985, p. 1, and Stephen Engelberg, "Jury Hears Tale of Spy Who Did It out of Greed," *New York Times*, July 19, 1989, p. A8.

[96] Philip Shenon, "Noriega Indicted by U.S. for Links to Illegal Drugs," *New York*

It is thus possible that subgroups are headed for the same authority crises that have beset governments, states, and other whole systems. Perhaps expanded analytic and cathectic skills are leading individuals to a profound and generalized cynicism in which the only satisfactory scenarios are those that culminate in their own advancement, without regard to the well-being of any collectivity to which they may belong.[97]

On the other hand, if such tendencies are in fact underlying the dynamics of subgroupism and the global authority crisis, if subgroupism is merely a way station in a long-term decline toward the disorganized war of all against all that Hobbesians presume, the macro consequences would not be nearly so patterned as suggested by the two worlds of world politics outlined here. Rather, the breakdown of subsystems into ever smaller collectivities, with individuals always retaining the prerogative of further defection, would probably truncate all processes of aggregation and result in a disarray that makes the present Order II seem a model of tidiness and symmetry by comparison.[98]

Furthermore, without denying the potential for a Hobbesian outcome, there are also persuasive reasons to believe that the decentralizing micro dynamics are self-limiting. Indeed, as suggested in chapter 16, for reasons pertaining to the dynamics of centralization and the need for organization to cope with the ecological consequences of present-day technologies and a shrinking world, it is not inconceivable that cyclical processes may set in at the micro level that would bring about a turn back in the direction of whole systems.

Furthermore, not all the regressions to individual authority are self-

---

Times, February 6, 1988, p. 1; Susan Chira, "Brother of Seoul's Ex-Leader Is Found Guilty of Corruption," *New York Times*, September 6, 1988, p. A6; Warren Weaver, Jr., "Serious Ethics Breaches by Meese Are Found In Justice Dept. Study," *New York Times*, January 18, 1989, p. A12; Bill Keller, "Brezhnev Son-in-Law Gets 12-Year Term," *New York Times*, December 31, 1988, p. 4; and Steven R. Weisman, "Takeshita to Quit as Japan's Premier over Gift Scandal," *New York Times*, April 25, 1989, p. 1.

[97] For evidence along these lines, see Donald L. Kanter and Philip H. Mirvis, *The Cynical Americans: Living and Working in an Age of Discontent and Disillusion* (San Francisco: Jossey-Bass, 1989).

[98] There would appear to be no end to the disruptive tendencies that the new information technologies are deemed capable of fostering. One list of "keywords" along this line included "social isolation, impoverished emotionality, constriction of thinking, lingual devastation, loss of grasp of reality, loss of creativity, reinforcement of mechanical fantasy, social disintegration, data abuse, a danger for privacy, development of a two class society, total surveillance and control of citizens, destruction of family life and primary group affiliations, [and] alienation from personal experience." Ortwin Renn and Hans Peter Peters, "Micro- and Macrosociological Consequences of New Information Technologies" (paper presented at the Eleventh World Congress of Sociology, New Delhi, August 1986), pp. 14–15.

serving. For example, a captain in the Israeli reserve army, Meir Amor, chose to go to prison rather than serve in the occupied territories, because, he said, "I have to take responsibility for what I do, and I can't just say that I am there because of orders . . . The real question is: do we leave it all for the politicians to decide, or are we participating in this decision?"[99] Similarly, a U.S. army captain, Angelo Liteky, who had been awarded a Congressional Medal of Honor for bravery in Vietnam, subsequently renounced his medal and went on a hunger strike as a protest against U.S. policy in Nicaragua, declaring: "I am not a devotee of the Nicaraguan government. I don't have to be. I don't pay taxes in Nicaragua. I am, however, an advocate of the U.S. government. I am responsible for what it does in the name of America. If I am to be a true patriot—that is, a person who loves this country even when it's wrong—I must monitor and criticize its policies. It's my duty and my right."[100] Less dramatic but no less telling is the case of Henry S. Dakin, who converted some of the wealth from his business successes into a compound of five buildings that house twenty different organizations, all of them devoted in one way or another to assuring that information is conveyed between Moscow and San Francisco, in forms ranging from cassettes of Soviet television shows (captured by a satellite dish on the roof) for Soviet consulate members to computers carrying electronic mail from the Soviet Academy of Sciences, from photophone conversations between recovering alcoholics in the two countries to a nonprofit television company that broadcasts unrehearsed discussions between members of Congress and the Supreme Soviet.[101] Still another instance is provided by the many people who have been inspired by the success of Alcoholics Anonymous to engage in efforts to find solutions to their own problems, resulting in a "self-help [movement] that is surging in the United States and worldwide. The movement includes Parents Anonymous, Emphysema Anonymous, Overeaters Anonymous, Debtors Anonymous, Pill Addicts Anonymous, California Smokers Anonymous, Gamblers Anonymous, Depressives Anonymous, Prison Families Anonymous, Impotence Anonymous, Cocaine Anonymous, WWL2M (Women Who Love Too Much) and thousands of others."[102] The Hobbesian war of all against all is far from universal.

[99] "A Captain's Ideals Lead Him to Jail," *New York Times*, March 20, 1988, p. A14.

[100] Quoted in "Notes and Comments," *New Yorker*, October 13, 1986, p. 35.

[101] Kathleen Teltsch, "Fortune in Toys Helps to Put Americans and Russians in Touch," *New York Times*, November 16, 1988, p. A18.

[102] Patricia Leigh Brown, "Troubled Millions Heed Call of Self-Help Groups," *New York Times*, July 16, 1988, p. 1.

In sum, decentralizing processes are both a reflection and a source of transformation in the micro parameter. They are a reflection in the sense that people would still be clinging exclusively to nation-statism if their traditional habits of relating to higher authority had not been undermined by their newly acquired analytic skills. At the same time, the processes of decentralization have contributed to the refinement of these skills by offering incentives and opportunities for applying them. For decentralizing processes mean change in the loci of control, inviting fresh thought about where one fits in the emergent structures. Even to consider simultaneous reentry is to exercise skills that might otherwise go untapped.

Quite apart from the extreme and cataclysmic possibility of a "me only" world of self-designated and self-serving individual authorities, the analysis in this chapter raises some difficult questions about the nature of postinternational politics. If the transformation from traditional legitimacy to performance legitimacy has been rendered permanent by global television, are authority structures going to be subjected to repeated crises? Are governments destined to be weaker because the roots of many of their problems are located abroad, beyond their capacity to resolve, thus rendering their performances less and less satisfactory to ever more skillful and concerned publics? Is conflict among groups likely to become incessant because the legitimacy of leaderships is always being questioned? Are the very same dynamics underlying the fragmentation of whole systems likely to set in with respect to subgroups, thereby leading to further breakdowns in social cohesiveness?

These questions about the macro consequences of a transformed micro parameter will be considered in the next two chapters. Then, in the final chapter we shall return to the possible lines of development that lie ahead for postinternational politics.

CHAPTER 14

RELATIONSHIPS REVISED

Proliferating Subgroups, Weakened Governments, and Eroded Authority

The unthinking acceptance of authority based on echoes from religion and kingship is, I believe, gone. Even the acceptance of the popular will as reflected in majorities is weakened, as is shown by the widening acceptance of civil disobedience.

—Kenneth J. Arrow[1]

Israel is still the compelling part of Jewish identity, but it isn't automatic anymore. In the past there was less of a tendency to ask questions, just simply to pass along the check.

—Rabbi Eric Yoffie,
director of the Association of Reform Zionists of America[2]

So they did what a group of Soviet citizens outraged over a local issue would never have dreamed of doing before: they mobilized. A meeting was called, leaflets were distributed and in early June nearly 5,000 people gathered on the banks of the Volga River, demanding the recall of Mr. Loshchenkov.

A plenary meeting of the local party was called, secret ballots were taken and, by the will of the people of Yaroslavl, Mr. Loshchenkov was replaced by Yuri I. Novikov, director of the local medicine institute and chairman of the regional peace committee.

—News report[3]

[1] *The Limits of Organization* (New York: W. W. Norton, 1974), p. 79.

[2] Quoted in Celestine Bohlen, "U.J.A., at 50, Is Thriving but Also Being Challenged," *New York Times*, November 28, 1988, p. A21.

[3] Esther B. Fein, "In a City on the Volga, Tears, Anger and Delight," *New York Times*, July 2, 1988, p. A7.

> The mayor was attacked, the village solicitor was pummeled, the fire station's pool table collapsed, a Village Councilman was charged with assault and the Councilman's father was hospitalized with a heart attack. "I'm not used to having that kind of breakdown of authority," said the solicitor, Brad Hillyer, . . . [after the] the council meeting.
>
> —News report from Sherrodsville, Ohio[4]

As conceptualized in chapter 8, the relational parameter involves the boundaries set on relationships by the necessity of exercising control on behalf of goals. The techniques available to actors for achieving the compliance needed to promote their goals are varied, ranging from the gentle persuasion inherent in the provision of proof to the harsh commands that accompany the exercise of force. Whatever the techniques, the greater the legitimacy that attaches to the authority seeking to exercise control, the greater is the likelihood that compliance will be achieved and that the coherence and stability of the collectivity will be maintained.

Ordinarily, authority relations are clear, settled, and not subject to renegotiation. They tend to be rooted in deeply ingrained habits, in the presumption that leaders are entitled to act on behalf of the collectivity and to receive compliant support in exchange for their efforts. When turbulence sets in, however, the habits start to come undone. The premises of compliance become unclear, unsettled, and open to bargaining; leaders have to devote time to assuring their support, and members begin to consider redirecting their loyalties and legitimacy sentiments. The more such circumstances impinge on authority relations, the more it can be said that they are in crisis.

Crisis in an authority relationship is not necessarily the outgrowth of differences within a collectivity over policy issues. Members of a collectivity express differences and even make gestures of defiance of authority without necessarily being ready to abandon compliance. To be sure, widespread manifestations of defiance may be precursors of a breakdown in compliance habits, but it is only when the breakdown has occurred that an authority structure begins to lose its utility as a mechanism for resolving the collectivity's disputes and moving toward its goals. Authority relations in crisis are thus fragile and uncertain. They hint at change, collectivities in flux, and the regrouping of lines of authority.

---

[4] " 'Breakdown in Authority' Breaks Up Town Meeting," *New York Times*, February 20, 1985, p. 9.

Toward Global Authority Crises

As suggested by Arrow's general observation and the specific thoughts and activities of U.S. Jews, the people of Yaroslavl, and the citizens of Sherrodsville, it is a major characteristic of postinternational politics that authority relationships have become unsettled on a global scale. The change is not always marked by a hostile confrontation, a threat of force, or an outright revolution. Occasionally, authority relations do turn hostile and violent, but more often they enter into crisis through an anger or alienation that culminates in noncompliance at the micro level and an inability to undertake effective action at the macro level.

The distinction between these two types of authority crises is important. The revolutionary kind usually comes to a climax quickly; a victor emerges from the upheaval, and authority relations are soon restored (if the original leaders put down the rebellion and preserve their authority) or rebuilt (if the rebellion is successful and a new leadership takes over) so that effective actions can again be taken. In the nonviolent type, on the other hand, the authority crisis can persist as noncompliance becomes habitual, no new leadership acquires the legitimacy to act effectively on behalf of the collectivity, and stalemate sets in.

To speak of postinternational politics as marked by a global authority crisis, therefore, is not to imply a single pattern or set of relationships. It is to call attention, rather, to diverse processes unfolding among a broad array of micro and macro actors, most of which lack clear-cut authority relationships and a few of which are so rent by conflict as to undergo revolutionary upheaval. The global authority crisis, in other words, is a series of authority crises that appear in every region of the world.

However, while the many authority crises are not linked together into one worldwide crisis, neither are they isolated and independent of each other. The world is now so interdependent that "crisis networks" evolve, as information about a crisis in one collectivity flows to others, and as its consequences ramify. By virtue of the information flows and of the interaction engendered by refugees, traders, terrorists, and other boundary-spanning individuals and groups, authority crises overlap and cascade across collectivities, forming linkages among them on an issue or regional basis. Thus, an authority crisis in Iran creates the potential for comparable breakdowns in Kuwait, Saudi Arabia, and other Middle Eastern countries; *glasnost* in the Soviet Union generates questions about political legitimacy in the countries of Eastern Europe; an upheaval in the Philippines agitates the politics of South Korea and leaves traces of its effects in Pakistan; a weak currency, a budgetary stalemate, an interest-rate change, or a faltering economy in the United States has repercussions for authority relations in many other countries; boatloads of Tamils fleeing Sri Lanka provoke a constitutional issue in Canada; an authority crisis in Peru leads to nonpayments of foreign debts that other countries of Latin America consider emulating; and internal wars in Afghanistan, El Salvador, Vietnam, and Nicaragua reverberate throughout the world.

The notion of a global authority crisis thus calls attention not only to a spreading and intensification of violent conflict in world affairs, but also, and more importantly, to changes in the underlying and enduring relationships by which collectivities concert their energies on behalf of shared needs and goals. In this sense, authority crises reflect deeper dynamics than even outright war, because they involve the day-to-day patterns whereby collectivities cohere and perform their tasks. Violent conflicts terminate, but the habits of compliance and cooperation may not follow the cessation of hostilities. Prior to the advent of global turbulence in the 1950s, authority relations were established and stable (see chapter 5). Actions were initiated and sustained through deep-rooted and long-standing autonomous hierarchical relationships—autonomous in the sense that the causal links were contained within sovereign states, hierarchical in the sense that authority flowed downward from central governments to publics and collectivities at regional and local levels while compliance flowed upward through the same channels. Such patterns as existed at the global level were less coherent and more "lateral," being largely ad hoc foreign policies undertaken by actors who were in bargaining rather than authority relationships with each other.

Despite two world wars and many lesser conflicts, at no time during the first half of the twentieth century could the world be described as being in the throes of global authority crisis. Political structures in Russia and China did, to be sure, experience traumas, but these were neither precipitated nor accompanied by endogenous challenges to authority on a global scale. Virtually all the other state and subnational authority structures were in place and functioning before, during, and after the Russian and Chinese revolutions. World War II did involve challenges to authority, but these originated exogenously as the Fascist powers resorted to conquest to topple authority structures and they were subsequently met by the war efforts of the Allied powers, which deposed the authorities of Germany, Italy, and Japan. Thus, only the turbulence and cascading interdependence of recent decades transformed the relative symmetry of global authority relations into the asymmetries of a bifurcated world and recurrent breakdowns in the habits of compliance.

Put more specifically, relations between those who exercise authority and those who respond to it are undergoing transformation at every level, sometimes resulting in stalemate but always creating circumstances in which compliance can no longer be taken for granted. Countries withdraw from UNESCO and refuse to pay their dues to the UN. Embassies are seized. Governments unilaterally declare that they no longer consider binding certain features of international agreements or law. Fragile coalitions govern Israel, Sri Lanka, the Philippines, and Yugoslavia, and two rival governments compete for power in Lebanon while not long ago two men claimed the presidency of Panama. Archbishops defy the Roman Catholic pope.[5] Students at a university for the hearing-impaired demand a deaf president.[6] A coup in Haiti results in a fifty-year-old general and a twenty-seven-year-old sergeant sharing the same office in the presidential palace.[7] Class politics decline in England.[8] There is an "explosion of independent political activity" in Hungary and soon thereafter the Hungarian Communist party declares its own termination.[9] The Afghan rebels split into seven factions.[10] Left-wing trade unions in Nicaragua defy the Sandinistas.[11] Growing numbers of Soviet young people reject membership in the Komsomol, the youth arm of the Communist party, and organize their own forms of political activity.[12] The Sikhs in India demand auton-

[5] Steven Greenhouse, "Archbishop Defies Pope on Bishops," New York Times, July 1, 1988, p. 1; Alan Riding, "Theologians in Europe Challenge Pope's Conservative Leadership," New York Times, July 14, 1989, p. 1.

[6] B. Drummond Ayres, Jr., "Protest That Turned Campus for the Deaf Around," New York Times, March 15, 1988, p. A16.

[7] Joseph B. Treaster, "Many in Haiti Wonder Who Is Really in Charge," New York Times, September 25, 1988, p. A3, and Joseph B. Treaster, "The General and the Sergeant: Confreres in Haiti," New York Times, October 3, 1988, p. A8.

[8] Suzanne Berger, "Politics and Antipolitics in Western Europe in the Seventies," Daedalus 108 (Winter 1979): 42–44.

[9] John Tagliabue, "Independents a Problem for Budapest," New York Times, December 19, 1988, p. A3; Henry Kamm, "Hungary's Extraordinary Charge Draws Critics of Varying Ideologies," New York Times, October 9, 1989, p. A1.

[10] Steven R. Weisman, "Rebels' Split Is Hindering Afghan Talks," New York Times, March 1, 1988, p. 1.

[11] Stephen Kinzer, "Leftists Defy Sandinistas as Labor Strife Hits Peak," New York Times, April 14, 1988, p. 1.

[12] Among those resistant to joining the Komsomol is Dima Mironenko, the 14-year-old son of the national head of the organization. Dima's father was quoted as saying, "I tried to talk with him twice about this subject. He evades the answer. He says, 'I have to think about it.' " Bill Keller, "Soviet Youth League Falls on Difficult Times," New York Times, February 7, 1988, p. 1.

omy, even while they themselves are riven by factionalism.[13] Soviet Latvians demand home rule, and Estonians assert the right to reject Soviet laws.[14] Dissidents organize throughout Eastern Europe.[15] A write-in candidate for the Supreme Soviet in Armenia wins an election when 78 percent of the electorate write in his name and cross out that of the interior minister.[16] Disputes erupt among Mafia "families."[17] Voters in Great Britain send to the House of Commons "a national firebrand" who advocates that Scotland pull out of the 281-year-old pact that binds it to England as part of the United Kingdom.[18] In China, even before the students protests in 1989, the regions of the country were competing with each other and ignoring the commands from Beijing, so much so that the officially sponsored *China Economic News* warned that "China today is divided into more than 20 independent kingdoms and more than 2,000 fiefdoms."[19] The examples could be multiplied endlessly, but these should be sufficient to show that new foci of loyalty, born sometimes out of desperation and sometimes out of sophistication (see chapter 13), have emerged to compete for the commitments of individuals and the orientations of collectivities.

Perhaps the most telling signs of the pervasiveness of challenges to authority have been the numerous instances in recent years of leaders of opposition groups being unable to maintain effective control over members who undertake initiatives on their own. Sometimes the initiatives were spontaneous, as in the case of Palestinians on the West Bank, students in South Korea, strikers in Yugoslavia, and workers in Polish steel mills, and sometimes they were organized, as among the contras in Nicaragua and the rebels in Afghanistan. In either case, they show a widespread pattern of disaggregation even within groups that would

[13] "Discord among Sikhs Block Amity," *New York Times*, May 6, 1985, p. A3.

[14] Bill Keller, "Latvian Cultural Leaders Issue Call for a Form of Home Rule," *New York Times*, June 22, 1988, p. A12; Philip Taubman, "Estonia Asserts a Right of Veto on Soviet Laws," *New York Times*, November 17, 1988, p. 1.

[15] John Tagliabue, "Network of Dissenters Expanding in East Bloc," *New York Times*, March 22, 1988, p. 7.

[16] Bill Keller, "Armenians Astir: Write-In Candidate Wins 78%," *New York Times*, October 12, 1988, p. A3.

[17] Robert D. McFadden, "The Mafia of the 1980s: Divided and under Siege," *New York Times*, May 11, 1987, p. 1. One leader's secretly taped observation, quoted in this account, is revealing, "Things change now because there's too much conflict. People do whatever they feel like. . . . There's no more—there's no more respect. If you can't be sincere, you can't be honest with your friends—then forget about it. Ya got nothing."

[18] Dan Fisher, "Scottish Nationalism Threatens British Unity," *Los Angeles Times*, December 25, 1988, sec. 1, p. 26.

[19] Nicholas D. Kristof, "Beijing Authority Being Challenged by Local Powers," *New York Times*, December 11, 1988, p. 1.

seem to have every reason to maintain unity. It is a pattern that reflects the central tendency of authority crises, a continuous reversion to the close-at-hand groups as the locus of control and legitimacy. The ultimate outcome of this reversion pattern is poignantly captured in a comment of an Arab journalist: "After 14 years, violence has become a way of life, and we are disintegrating, fragmenting into civil wars within civil wars."[20]

To some extent, the fragmenting of opposition groups can be explained by generational factors. The Palestinians at the core of the uprising on the West Bank in 1987 were much younger than the PLO leaders in Tunisia,[21] the workers in Poland who struck against the steel mills in 1988 were much younger than the leaders of Solidarity,[22] and the students who rioted in South Korea in 1988 were not supported by their elders in the opposition parties.[23] Partly, too, the explanation for this fragmenting, and for the challenges to whole-system authorities as well, lies in the electronic revolution and its provision of information about what counterparts are doing elsewhere in the world. If television enables one to "see" other people taking matters into their own hands, one may well be encouraged to emulate such behavior, especially if enhanced analytic skills facilitate the development of scenarios in which the strategies of successful challenges to authority abroad are tailored to local circumstances.

Whatever may be its sources, the global crisis of authority must be viewed as being even more profound than a revolutionary upheaval. It is not just a case of the have-nots wanting to depose the haves. Rather, the habits of compliance are being questioned, replaced, and abandoned on a worldwide scale, among the haves as well as the have-nots, the mainstream as well as the marginal, the established as well as the aspiring. As one observer notes:

> Authorities are now being challenged in all areas of human life. Institutions are no longer respected just because they are institu-

[20] Quoted in John Kifner, "Lebanon's Multiplying Rivalries Move Nation Closer to Breakup," *New York Times*, January 20, 1988, p. 1.

[21] As one young Palestinian put it, "Now we are directing the leadership outside," a reference to "the P.L.O. officials in Tunis and Baghdad who have been scrambling to keep up with the events in the streets" of the West Bank and the Gaza Strip. John Kifner, "From Palestinian Rage, New Leadership Rises," *New York Times*, February 6, 1988, p. 1. See also Dan Fisher, "Palestinians Turn Backs on Old Leaders," *Los Angeles Times*, January 10, 1988, p. 1.

[22] John Tagliabue, "The Very Young Decide to Form a Cutting Edge," *New York Times*, June 1, 1988, p. A4.

[23] Clyde Haberman, "Crisis Deepens for South Korea's Riven Opposition," *New York Times*, February 4, 1988, p. 3.

tions. The church, the school, the family, the state—those traditional bastions of authority—have lost a large amount of the respect that was formerly automatically accorded to them. In almost every country of the world, the young question the views of their elders to a degree never done before.

More is at stake . . . than the mere revolt of dissidents. At issue is a change in our way of thinking about the basic nature and function of *authority itself*. We are now witnessing a challenge to the very *idea* of authority. The crisis of authority is more than a reconsideration of how authority should be expressed in society. It extends also to a reconsideration of the *meaning* of authority.

Many of the questions now being asked about the nature and function of authority are quite healthy ones, motivated not from rebellion and revolt, but from a sincere quest to discover the true nature and locus, or *loci*, of authority. What is happening . . . is the attempt to internalize authority, that is to shift the basis of its verification from external and public modes to internal and private ones.[24]

Whether one views the global authority crisis as rooted in attempts to internalize authority, or in efforts (by Islamic fundamentalists and other groups) to externalize authority, the essential point is the realignment of authority relations within and between systems and subsystems, the transfer of legitimacy sentiments and compliance habits away from one collectivity and toward another. If the transfer is from a whole system to its subsystem, as happens much more often than transfers among whole systems, then subgroups gain in coherence at the expense of the larger system's integrity. Given the turbulent changes at the micro level that have marked postinternational politics, this dynamism of the relational parameter has become that much more extensive.

As elaborated more fully in chapter 16, moreover, the dynamism of these relational phenomena may prove to be cyclical in nature. If the enlarged analytic skills of people enable them to recognize the drawbacks as well as the virtues of whole-system incoherence and subsystem unity, then each realignment may contain the seeds of the next realignment, as individuals redirect their legitimacy sentiments and compliance back and forth between whole systems and subsystems. That is, as subgroups gain coherence at the expense of whole-system integrity, their members begin to realize that weakening the system

---

[24] R. B. Harris, ed., *Authority: A Philosophical Analysis* (University, Ala.: University of Alabama, 1976), p. 1 (italics in original).

may prove costly to them and that these costs may not be offset by the gains in subsystemic effectiveness. It is noteworthy, for example, that West Germany's Social Democratic party reversed itself after its unsuccessful 1984 campaign against locating U.S. medium-range missiles in Europe and sought to establish itself as a supporter of NATO and an advocate of centrist positions on foreign policy.[25] In effect, the coherence it gained by opposing the missile deployment was subsequently recognized as too costly in terms of the advantages of more secure ties to the whole system.

There is nothing in the state of political nature, in short, that enables a system to serve well all the relevant needs and wants of its members. Whole systems and subsystems alike are limited in what they can accomplish. The former do poorly translating the psychological rewards derived from a shared identity into tangible payoffs; the latter are ill-equipped to solve the material problems associated with physical security and well-being. So tensions between them are bound to persist, and the advent of more analytically skillful publics has linked each cascade of tensions to those that follow.

This does not imply, however, that systems and their subsystems normally return to a preexisting and stable equilibrium.[26] Sometimes that does occur, but often it does not. Frequently the outcomes of a cascade move a system and its subsystem into new relational patterns founded on a new equilibrium.

The ebbs and flows of authority crises, in sum, are causally connected. What seems like chaos is, in reality, a set of orderly processes whereby the simultaneity, the contrariety, and the expansivity of centralizing and decentralizing tendencies form the patterned authority relations of the postinternational order.

UNIQUE SOURCES OF SUBGROUPISM

Challenges to authority and shifting legitimacy sentiments are not, of course, new in human history. As one observer has said, "Traditional authority structures . . . are collapsing all the time. They collapsed during the French revolution, during the industrial revolution, after the abolition of slavery, after World War I, and after World War II, with

[25] James M. Markham, "Bonn Socialists Flirting with NATO," *New York Times*, March 12, 1984, p. A3.

[26] For a cogent discussion of the equilibrium concept, see Michael Brecher and Patrick James, *Crisis and Change in World Politics* (Boulder, Colo.: Westview, 1986), pp. 13–19.

the fall of colonial empires, with the advent of the transistor radio."[27] Nor is complexity new. Ever since the Enlightenment, societies have become increasingly complicated, more prone to the formation of new groups, and thus more unwieldy as collectivities. What, then, is so unique to the present era that authority relations have become unsettled on a worldwide basis?

Some parts of the answer have already been noted. More analytically skillful people are demanding more of their leadership and making it that much more difficult for the latter to fashion compromises with adversaries. Global media of communication have provided images of authority being successfully challenged elsewhere in the world, thereby emboldening followers to attach legitimacy to leaders on the basis of their performances rather than on traditional and habitual grounds. New issues arising out of the world's greater interdependence have exceeded the competence of authorities to address and resolve them on their own, impelling followerships to begin to look elsewhere for effective leadership and for psychological, if not physical, security. Technological developments have come so swiftly that they have overwhelmed long-established institutions designed to manage the pace of change. All in all, the interdependence of today's collectivities has become so extensive that the level of their external dependencies has begun to approach the level of their internal dependencies, a condition that undermines the existing lines of authority.

Another reason why authority relations are unique in the era of postinternational politics has to do with the advent of nuclear weapons. Historically, the communal impulses of people have been directed toward the collectivity that they felt assured them peace within and protection from without. Thus, for several centuries prior to the nuclear age, people were inclined to attach legitimacy to, and to be compliant with, the directives of the nation-state. In the nuclear era, however, the nation-state cannot provide external protection.[28] The communal impulses of people have therefore been freed to move toward more close-at-hand collectivities, toward subgroups that at least offer a greater sense of internal harmony and support, even though they, too, are unable to protect against the external threat posed by nuclear weapons. With an authoritative and effective alternative to the nation-state seemingly unobtainable as a mechanism for managing a

[27] Brian M. Jenkins, "Future Trends in International Terrorism," Rand Paper Series P–7176 (Santa Monica, Calif.: Rand Corporation, 1985), p. 6.

[28] For a clarifying analysis of how nuclear weapons have altered the permeability of the territorial state, see John H. Herz, *International Politics in the Atomic Age* (New York: Columbia University Press, 1959).

nuclearized world, recent decades have witnessed orientations toward subgroups emerge first to supplement, and then to supplant, those toward the nation-state as a prime political predisposition of citizens in the postindustrial order.

THE NARROWING COMPETENCE OF GOVERNMENTS

In order to grasp how proliferating subgroups have contributed to global authority crises, it is useful to note how the prime political actor in the state-centric world, the national government, has declined in terms of its capacity to generate compliance. The assertion of such a decline poses problems of perspective and measurement. It might be argued that governments have never been very effective, that their legitimacy has always been subject to question, and that current trends are thus mere fluctuations in a long-standing pattern. Hence, the assertion that a decline in the effectiveness of governments is under way should be verified with systematic longitudinal data. What follows is admittedly not based on data of that kind; the relevant materials have not been compiled. Perhaps, then, the postulated trend of declining effectiveness is a distortion or an exaggeration. Nevertheless, the impression of diminished competence is not easily dispelled, and there are also good theoretical reasons to expect that "as societies become more complex, government's burden of maintaining its authority by securing the consent of the governed becomes increasingly difficult."[29] Some have called this situation a "crisis of governability."[30]

By "declining effectiveness" is meant a progressive inability on the part of governments to provide their clients (elites, citizenries, allies) with the conditions and services that reflect the goals they have set for themselves and that their clients expect of them. Effectiveness, then, is more than the maintenance of order. It involves the solving of problems and the resolving of issues, or at least preventing the worsening of problems and the intensifying of issues. It pertains to policy outputs, to tangible services such as highways and unemployment checks, and to such intangible conditions as a feeling of physical security and a sense of optimism about what the future holds. Compared to earlier periods of this century, when politicians were looked upon as heroes because they delivered on promises and thus held high office for relative long times, the effectiveness of modern governments—their per-

[29] Richard D. Schwartz, "The Limits and Possibilities of Government: A Perspective from the Sociology of Law," in James F. Short, Jr., ed., *The Social Fabric: Dimensions and Issues* (Newbury Park, Calif.: Sage, 1986), p. 189.

[30] Berger, "Politics and Antipolitics," pp. 34–36.

formance records—seems conspicuously meager. Whether they be democratic or authoritarian, Western or Eastern, the outcomes of their efforts seem increasingly to fall far short of their aspirations. As Shils puts it, the conditions under which the task of government can be performed efficaciously

> no longer obtain in any country, advanced and rich or backward and poor. Everywhere there are clamorous demands for a great variety of governmental actions reaching deeply into society and extending over its entire breadth, and everywhere governments have undertaken to attempt to satisfy these demands. It is a hopeless undertaking . . . it is difficult for any group to stay in power for long except through yielding to demands. . . . These are among the reasons why the rate of inflation is so high in so many countries and why the rate of growth of investment in the maintenance of physical capital lags behind the rate of growth of consumption.[31]

Walter Lippmann, concerned about the erosion of executive power in democratic societies during the first half of the twentieth century, expressed the same idea in even more dire terms:

> Where mass opinion dominates the government, there is a morbid derangement of the true functions of power. The derangement brings about the enfeeblement, verging on paralysis, of the capacity to govern. This breakdown in the constitutional order is the cause of the precipitate and catastrophic decline of Western society. It may, if it cannot be arrested and reversed, bring about the fall of the West.[32]

This is not, of course, to deny that governments still have the capacity to maintain order with coercive methods. Perhaps that capacity is even greater than ever, given the informational and other resources now available to officials. But the maintenance of order by the exercise of force is not a measure of effectiveness, of whether government is performing its expected tasks and getting its jobs done. And if the political skills of publics are becoming ever more extensive, as has been suggested here, even the maintenance of order may prove to be diffi-

---

[31] E. Shils, "The Political Class in the Age of Mass Society: Collectivistic Liberalism and Social Democracy," in M. M. Czudnowski, ed., *Does Who Governs Matter? Elite Circulation in Contemporary Societies* (DeKalb: Northern Illinois University Press, 1982), p. 25.

[32] Walter Lippmann, *Essays in the Public Philosophy* (Boston: Little, Brown, 1955), p. 15.

cult, as such diverse regimes as those in Chile, Yugoslavia, Burma, South Korea, Peru, Haiti, the Philippines, Poland, and China have recently discovered.

Effectiveness is not easily measured in terms of outputs. It should be sought in the compliance attitudes and behavior of those toward whom the outputs are directed, in the orientations and activities of elites and citizenries in the case of domestic policies and in the reactions of allies and adversaries in the case of foreign policies. Systematically observing and aggregating such phenomena obviously presents enormous difficulties and most analysts have instead employed crude measures—such as the length of time that governments hold a legislative majority[33]—that are hardly more satisfactory than the mere impression of ineffectiveness derived from such developments as the near-total breakdown of governmental authority in Poland, Lebanon, Burma, Haiti, and Northern Ireland, the complete failure of both local and national governments in sub-Saharan Africa,[34] the persistence of poverty in all parts of the world, the failure of agricultural policies in many countries, the existence of underground economies, the unyielding resistance of the Afghans to Soviet power, the inability of the United States to achieve desired solutions in Central America and the Middle East, and the outbreaks of riots directed against government policies in Yugoslavia, Soviet Armenia, South Korea, the Sudan, and Sri Lanka.[35]

[33] G. B. Powell, Jr., *Contemporary Democracies: Participation, Stability, and Violence* (Cambridge: Harvard University Press, 1982), pp. 18–19.

[34] "The cold, dreadful conclusion to be drawn from a generation of independence is that African governments are incapable of providing the framework and services that development requires. Traditional village society, which succeeded at least in providing subsistence, has largely broken down. Nothing adequate is replacing it": Flora Lewis, "A Risk for Africa," *New York Times*, March 18, 1985, p. A19. On the other hand, in the Arab world a contrary pattern is discernible, wherein nation-states have contributed to "a modernizing trend, undermining myths and increasing the capacity to deal with practical issues. They are not yet firmly established but they are creating possibilities": Flora Lewis, "Arabs: Nation or State?" *New York Times*, January 4, 1985, p. A27.

[35] For analyses that rest on assumptions or impressions that a decline is occurring in the effectiveness of governments, see D. Fromkin, *The Question of Government: An Inquiry into the Breakdown of Modern Political Systems* (New York: Charles Scribner's, 1975); Editorial Research Reports, *Political Instability Abroad* (Washington: Congressional Quarterly, 1976); W. J. Geekie, *Why Government Fails* (Roslyn Heights, N.Y.: Libra, 1976); J. J. Linz, *The Breakdown of Democratic Regimes: Crisis, Breakdown, and Reequilibration* (Baltimore: The Johns Hopkins University Press, 1978); A. J. Vidich and R. M. Glassman, eds., *Conflict and Control: Challenge to the Legitimacy of Modern Governments* (Beverly Hills, Calif.: Sage, 1979); H. M. Ingram and D. E. Mann, eds., *Why Policies Succeed or Fail* (Beverly Hills, Calif.: Sage, 1980); R. Rose ed., *Challenge to Governance: Studies in Overload Polities* (Beverly Hills, Sage, 1980);

To be sure, effectiveness is not the only criterion by which governments are to be evaluated. Stability and openness may be equally important criteria, and in some instances their records in this respect may be more impressive. From the perspective of governments constrained by subgroupism at home and authority crises abroad, however, the criterion of effectiveness is especially important. For the greater the decline in the capacities of governments to realize their goals, the greater is the likelihood of resistance to their policies and of the erosion of their legitimacy, consequences which, in turn, detract further from their effectiveness. As Inglehart has demonstrated, the more governments seek to alter their course so as to increase their effectiveness, the greater is the likelihood of active resistance to their efforts.[36] It is no mere coincidence, for example, that rioting in Yugoslavia and the Sudan followed governmental initiatives to cope with inflation or that mutinies in the PLO followed Arafat's movement toward accommodation with Lebanese authorities, and it is in this sense understandable that many analysts have reservations about the capacity of the Gorbachev regime to overcome the resistance to change and turn the Soviet economy around.

Whether the decline in governmental effectiveness is a cause or a consequence of the trend toward attaching authority and legitimacy to nongovernmental collectivities—and doubtless it is both a cause and a consequence—the result is the same: the leaders of national governments have limited room for innovation. Internally, they are restrained from undertaking new policies by the lack of a political consensus and by the demands of more coherent subgroups, while externally their initiatives are limited both by the similar circumstances of the governments with which they must negotiate and by the demands of transnational actors in the multi-centric world.

These are, in short, the conditions of stalemate. Postinternational politics have deprived governments of room for maneuver, and even well-established policies may prove increasingly difficult to maintain if the global crises of authority continue to intensify and cascade tensions along the many fault lines of cleavage. From this perspective, the trip

---

Shils, "Political Class," pp. 13–32; B. Barber, *The Logic and Limits of Trust* (New Brunswick, N.J.: Rutgers University Press, 1983); C. Campbell, *Governments under Stress: Political Executives and Key Bureaucrats in Washington, London, and Ottawa* (Toronto: University of Toronto Press, 1983); B. I. Page, *Who Gets What from Government* (Berkeley: University of California Press, 1983); and J. E. Chubb and P. E. Peterson, eds., *Can the Government Govern?* (Washington: Brookings Institution, 1989).

[36] R. Inglehart, *The Silent Revolution: Changing Values and Political Styles among Western Publics* (Princeton: Princeton University Press, 1977), pp. 14–15.

of Egyptian president Sadat to Jerusalem looms as an extraordinary event, one of those exceedingly rare instances when a national leader broke free of the confines of world politics. Much more indicative of the vise-like grip of stalemated authority is the way in which Polish officials have been hemmed in by the strength of Solidarity.

Much the same can be said about Western governments. The polarization and volatility of voters have led to minority cabinets, fragile coalitions, frequent turnovers, arms scandals, and stalemated policy-making processes. Recent research on the foreign-policy belief systems of American leaders clearly points to enduring cleavages and a lack of consensus in the United States that are bound to be conducive to vacillation rather than innovation in the policy-making process.[37] In the absence of any dramatic consensus-forming event—and the likelihood of such an occurrence seems very remote—future American policy makers will apparently have little control over what they can undertake, much less accomplish, in foreign affairs.

Not all, of course, is disarray. Governments are increasingly circumscribed by domestic and foreign constraints, but they also continue to be key actors on the global stage. Many still enjoy considerable authority and legitimacy. Their foreign policies are still conspicuous components of postinternational politics. In the swirls and counter-swirls of cascading processes, they are the focal points, the managers of change and the preservers of continuities, even if diminished in their capabilities. They are not so restrained by current conditions as to have utterly lost the ability to adapt to demands from at home and abroad. They still have command of many mechanisms for bargaining, synthesizing, and playing demands off against each other and maintaining their identity as collectivities. Although less effectively than in the past, they still exercise control, obtain compliance, and meet challenges.

All of these actions, however, are now played out in the context of authority relations that are more unsettled and tenuous than they were before the onset of global turbulence. As authoritative actors in an era

---

[37] The most thorough presentation of these findings is Ole R. Holsti and James N. Rosenau, *American Leadership in World Affairs: Vietnam and the Breakdown of Consensus* (Winchester, Mass.: Allen & Unwin, 1984). For additional interpretations and updates of the data, see James N. Rosenau and Ole R. Holsti, "American Leadership in a Shrinking World: The Breakdown of Consensus and the Emergence of Conflicting Belief Systems," *World Politics* 35 (April 1983): 368–92; Ole R. Holsti and James N. Rosenau, "A Leadership Divided: The Foreign Policy Beliefs of American Leaders, 1976–1984," in C. W. Kegley and E. R. Wittkopf, eds., *The Domestic Sources of American Foreign Policy: Insights and Evidence* (New York: St. Martin's, 1988), pp. 30–44; and Ole R. Holsti and James N. Rosenau, "Foreign and Domestic Policy Systems among American Leaders," *Journal of Conflict Resolution* 32 (June 1988): 248–94.

when authority is suspect and delicate, governments must move slowly and allow for stalemated institutions that, in effect, preserve the sources of their authority.

THE PROLIFERATION OF SUBGROUPS

The fragmentation of whole systems into subsystems occurs either because decentralization of the system is believed to allow it to move more effectively toward its goals or because its subsystems' members become increasingly sensitive to the differences among them. In the former case, decentralization advances through formal and legal processes that accord it official approval. In the latter case, it develops through informal and ad hoc procedures that may be neither planned nor sanctioned. In either case, whether such changes stem from systemic planning or subsystemic stirrings, they amount to movement in the direction of what has here been called "subgroupism," a direction contrary to that of "nation-statism." Whereas nation-statism suggests convergence around the values and institutions of whole systems, subgroupism implies convergence occurs around subsystems. Subgroupism is a generic concept for the splitting away of one or more components of any collectivity, be it a nation, community, political party, opposition movement, or international organization. Viewed in this way, conventional definitions of a nation—e.g., that it is a "terminal community," by which is meant "the largest community that, when the chips are down, effectively commands men's loyalty, overriding the claims both of the lesser communities within it and those that cut across it or potentially enfold it within a still greater society"[38]— can be readily recast to fit any subgroup and the basis of its persistence through any historical period.

Subgroupism resulting from formal procedures can be discerned in the outcomes of deregulation in the United States, in the consequences of the devolution of national authority in France, and in the anticipated results of the decentralization that is widely viewed as a necessary precondition to any enduring solution of the Soviet Union's eco-

[38] Rupert Emerson, *From Empire to Nation: The Rise to Self-Assertion of Asian and African Peoples* (Cambridge: Harvard University Press, 1960), pp. 95–96. For additional discussions of nations, nation-statism, and variants of nationalism, see Ernst B. Haas, "What Is Nationalism and Why Should We Study It?" *International Organization* 40 (Summer 1986): 707–44; Louis L. Synder, *Macro-Nationalisms: A History of the Pan-Movements* (Westport, Conn.: Greenwood, 1984); and Edward A. Tiryakian and Ronald Rogowski, eds., *New Nationalisms of the Developed West* (Boston: Allen & Unwin, 1985). Also see chapter 6, note 28.

nomic problems. Some long-term data on this form of subgroupism are presented in table 14.1, which suggests the tension between the centralizing and decentralizing tendencies of modern history. As the table shows, while the number of European states dwindled from about 500 in 1500 to 28 in 1890 and has remained relatively constant since then, the number of cities of 10,000 or more population increased from 154 in 1500 to about 5,000 in 1980, roughly tripling since 1890. Table 14.1 also indicates that as the number of states fell and the number of cities rose, states were expanding their geographic boundaries while the opposite pattern obtained for cities. That is, instead of consolidating with each other, cities were settling for smaller geographic jurisdictions as the processes of decentralization gathered momentum. In any event, the increase in the number of cities in Europe during recent decades represents a corresponding increase in the systemic complexity of the continent; each new administrative center constitutes another point from which dynamism can spring and from which challenges to authority can be mounted. When it is recalled that comparable leaps have taken place in other regions and in the numbers of collectivities other than cities, the degree of present-day complexity and dynamism takes on staggering proportions.[39] Furthermore, al-

TABLE 14.1. Number and Area of Cities and States in Europe, 1500–1980

	1500	1800	1848	1890	1919	1980
Number of cities with 10,000 or more inhabitants	154	364	878	1,709	3,000?	5,000?
Number of formally independent states	500?	150?	100	29	23	28
Mean "radius" of city regions (kilometers)[a]	101	67	44	31	24	18
Mean "radius" of states (kilometers)[a]	57	103	126	234	263	239

SOURCE: Adapted from Charles Tilly, "Space for Capital, Space for States," *Theory and Society* 15 (1986): 307. Reprinted by permission of Kluwer Academic Publishers.
NOTE: The author points out that "the early numbers for states are frank guesses based on atlases and a few peace settlements, and the later ones are subject to fierce debates over definitions" (p. 306).

[a] This "radius" is "the radius of an imaginary circle having the mean area per city or state." Tilly, "Space for Capital, Space for States," p. 306.

[39] For another dimension of this decentralizing process and how it has fostered "the

though the number of states has declined in Europe, on a global scale the number has increased, in large part because of the breakup of the colonial empires. Table 14.2 shows that the number of sovereign states grew tenfold between 1800 and 1985, with most of the growth occurring during the current, relatively brief period of turbulence in world politics.

The magnitude of subgroupism becomes even more striking when we turn our attention to the number and variety of subgroups to which the informal and ad hoc tendencies toward decentralization have given rise. Perhaps the most conspicuous of these tendencies stems from the demands of the disadvantaged for a redistribution of wealth. Both within and among nations, those with small shares of the global pie have become increasingly restless, and their restlessness has brought them together in numerous organizations. But subgroupism has also encompassed skilled professionals and blue-collar workers, university faculties and students, wealthy industrialists and unemployed laborers, mainstream citizens and ethnic minorities. It would seem, in short, that wherever common ties can be identified, they have been, leading to the articulation of the ties and of the demands growing out of them, the restructuring of loyalties and authority relationships, and the weakening of the larger system in which the subgroups shared membership.

TABLE 14.2. Number of Existing States Formed before 1800, during 1800–1945, and during 1945–1985

	Old Continuous States	1800–1945	1945–1985	Total
Americas	0[a]	22	12	34
Europe	9	18	5	31[b]
Middle East	1	5	15	21
Asia	5	1	20	26
Africa	1	2	40	43
Oceania	0	2	8	10
Total	16	50	100	165

SOURCE: Gunnar P. Nielsson, "On the Concepts of Ethnicity, Nation, and State" (paper presented at the Workshop on the Sociology of Nationalism, Second World Basque Conference, Vitoria-Gasteiz, Spain, September 1987).

[a] The United States is classified as having been formed after 1800.

[b] Germany is entered twice, in 1870 and in 1949.

new international roles of noncentral governments" and a web of interactions among "perforated sovereignties," see the thorough and imaginative inquiry by Ivo D. Duchacek, *The Territorial Dimension of Politics: Within, Among, and Across Nations* (Boulder, Colo.: Westview, 1986).

Events in Lebanon offer a quintessential example of subgroup proliferation. At one point in 1984, military units of at least ten factions
were joined in battle in Beirut—the Amal Shiites, the Islamic Amal, the
Iranian Revolutionary Guards, the Druse, the Sunni Muslims, the
Phalangists, three smaller Christian militias, and the Lebanese army—
along with Palestinian guerrillas and the Syrian, Israeli, French, British,
and U.S. armed forces. If anything, the years since 1984 have seen a
further proliferation of subgroups, with some regions of the city having reached the point where authority is exercised by whoever controls
the checkpoints at the intersections of major streets. One can hardly
imagine a more acute crisis of authority.

Ethnic identities are another source of subgroup tendencies. A recent
compilation of the "nation-groups" (roughly equivalent to ethnic
groups) presently identifiable in the world yielded 575 categories and
1,300 groups, distributed throughout the state-centric world. Data
were available for 547 of the groups, and of these, 404 were confined
to a single state but 143 were found in two or more states. Slightly
more than half of the 547 were classified as "mobilized nations" (i.e.,
self-conscious and active political collectivities), 21 percent as "mobilizing ethnic communities" (in the process of becoming self-conscious
and active as political actors), and 28 percent as "unmobilized ethnic
categories" (persons identified by analysts as having common objective
attributes but not sharing political consciousness).[40] The potential for
decentralization inherent in this situation is revealed by an analysis of
the composition of 161 states for which data were available in 1981.
In only 27 percent did one nation-group account for more than 95
percent of the state's population; in 38 percent, one nation-group accounted for between 60 and 95 percent of the population; in 10 percent, one nation-group accounted for 40 to 60 percent, with the remainder of the population divided among other nation-groups,
ranging in number from seven to twenty-five; in 13 percent, the two
largest nation-groups together accounted for 65 to 95 percent of the
states population; and in 12 percent, the three largest nation-groups
combined to account for 34 to 97 percent of the population, with the
remainder being distributed among five to nineteen minority nation-
groups.[41] That these distributions point up the virtues of viewing the
structure of world politics as bifurcated into state- and multi-centric

[40] Gunnar P. Nielsson, "From Ethnic Category to Nation: Patterns of Political Modernization" (paper presented at the annual meeting of the International Studies Association, St. Louis, March–April 1988), p. 12.

[41] Gunnar P. Nielsson, "States and 'Nation-Groups': A Global Taxonomy," in Tiryakian and Rogowski, *New Nationalisms of the Developed West*, pp. 30–32.

worlds is captured in the summarizing observation of the analyst who compiled them: the "taxonomy demonstrates very clearly that the conventional concept of the nation-state fits only one-fourth of the members of the global state system."[42]

In the sense of a diversity that adds to the world's potential for decentralizing subgroupism, much the same can be said about linguistic groups. While some of these are coterminous with, even defining of, ethnic differences, many are also competitive within nation-groups. Indeed, the distribution of languages can be viewed as a major foundation of global political structures. One analyst has said:

> World politics in a monolingual world would be quite different from the conduct of international affairs in a world of a few quasi-dominant languages or one in which many languages enjoy equal status. The world's linguistic structure—which languages play what roles—shapes the habits of and facilities for communication, the mobility of individual citizens and their ability to link themselves to a worldwide information system (hence the permeability of national boundaries), the function and training of diplomats, and the diversity of sociocultural patterns.[43]

It is estimated that the number of languages spoken in the world today falls—depending on the definition used—between 2,500 and 7,000. Leaving aside distinctions among dialects, in 1984 there were 82 languages spoken by a least five million people. Not only were 63 languages used officially in the central administration of at least one state, but two-thirds of all independent states included linguistic minorities constituting more than 10 percent of their population.[44]

At the same time, the pattern of change in linguistic use hints at a centralizing tendency. "The number of effective languages is diminishing,"[45] as one language, English, becomes increasingly dominant. The proportion of articles indexed in *Chemical Abstracts* (more than 400,000 per year) that were written in English rose from 61 percent in 1977 to 65 percent in 1980 and 69 percent in 1984.[46] We shall return

[42] Nielsson, "States and 'Nation-Groups,' " pp. 32–33.

[43] J. A. Laponce, "Language and Communication: The Rise of the Monolingual State," in Claudio Cioffi-Revilla, Richard L. Merritt, and Dina A. Zinnes, eds., *Communication and Interaction in Global Politics* (Newbury Park, Calif.: Sage, 1987), p. 183.

[44] Laponce, "Language and Communication," pp. 185, 186, 192, 193.

[45] Laponce, "Language and Communication," p. 186.

[46] Laponce, *Languages and Their Territories* (Toronto: University of Toronto Press, 1987), p. 72.

to the implications of this pattern in the next chapter, but it should be pointed out here that there were fifty-five other languages in which at least one article listed in the *Chemical Abstracts* was published during that same time span. The potential for subgroupism with respect to linguistic groups continues to be considerable.

Although reliable data on organizations that form around common interests other than those involving ethnic and linguistic identities are not readily available, the diversity of subgroups appears to be increasing wherever industrial and postindustrial dynamics have become central to daily routines. Indeed, it is precisely because the tendency toward a recurring division of labor for productive and leisurely purposes is so pervasive that subgroupism in nonethnic and nonlinguistic realms is so difficult to monitor. Such organizations form, reform, splinter, and expire at such a high rate that tabulating their existence and activities presents enormous problems. Still, what little systematic evidence there is can surely be treated as further indication of the high potential for subgroupism in the multi-centric world. For example, the number of organizations listed in the *Encyclopedia of Associations* was greater in 1986 than it was in 1987 for each of the encyclopedia's seventeen major categories; in the later year, more than nineteen thousand formally organized, private associations were classified, and doubtless many organizations were not tabulated.[47]

No less relevant, and perhaps more important as channels for the cascading processes of the multi-centric world, are the associations that span societies and national boundaries: international governmental organizations, or IGOs, and nongovernmental organizations, or INGOs. While the measurement problems are hardly less acute at the international level, the available data again portray a vast and growing network of subgroups. As can be seen in table 14.3, from 1909 through 1972 there was an increase in the number of IGOs and of each of twenty types of INGOs. Table 14.4 shows that for each of thirty-seven countries in five world regions, the number of international organizations in which they were represented rose substantially between

[47] The seventeen categories are: trade, business, and commercial organizations, agricultural organizations and commodity exchanges; legal, governmental, public administration, and military organizations; scientific, engineering, and technical organizations; educational organizations; cultural organizations; social welfare organizations; health and medical organizations; public affairs organizations; fraternal, foreign-interest, nationality, and ethnic organizations; religious organizations; veteran, hereditary, and patriotic organizations; hobby and avocational organizations; athletic and sports organizations; labor unions, associations, and federations; chambers of commerce; and Greek-letter and related organizations. The *Encyclopedia of Associations* is published by the Gale Research Company, Detroit, Mich.

TABLE 14.3. Number of International Organizations by Category, 1909–1972

International Nongovernmental Organizations (INGOs)

Year	International Governmental Organizations (IGOs)	Bibliography, Documentation, Press	Religion, Ethics	Social Sciences, Humanistic Studies	International Relations	Politics	Law, Administration	Social Welfare	Professors, Employers	Trade Unions	Economics, Finance	Commerce, Industry	Agriculture	Transport, Travel	Technology	Science	Health, Medicine	Education, Youth	Arts, Literature, Radio, Cinema, TV	Sport, Recreation	Total INGOs
1909	37	19	21	10	12	3	13	10	2	1	3	5	5	5	8	21	16	10	6	6	176
1954	118	29	79	38	83	12	31	52	56	49	14	116	32	28	34	81	101	54	41	67	997
1956	132	26	70	57	61	13	28	52	67	48	15	123	27	40	36	69	100	56	34	51	973
1958	149	33	79	55	71	14	30	53	67	49	16	134	34	43	50	77	104	62	34	55	1,060
1960	154	34	87	57	92	17	37	56	73	54	26	163	46	57	60	83	123	68	57	65	1,253
1962	163	41	86	57	99	15	42	64	76	54	30	160	55	57	63	92	133	71	57	72	1,324
1964	279	54	87	67	106	14	45	70	78	59	33	168	64	63	70	118	150	83	65	76	1,570
1966	199	58	93	80	111	15	48	76	93	63	35	211	76	72	83	137	173	91	70	90	1,675
1968	229	69	103	90	125	22	54	88	105	70	40	233	83	76	102	152	214	105	75	93	1,899
1970	242	63	109	95	127	22	54	95	112	70	45	239	83	82	113	174	225	106	80	99	1,993
1972	280	72	112	104	144	27	58	104	119	70	47	251	88	89	133	184	256	116	80	110	2,173

SOURCE: Adapted from Anthony Judge, "International Institutions: Diversity, Borderline Cases, Functional Substitutes, and Possible Alternatives," in P. Taylor and J. Groom, eds., *International Organization: A Conceptual Approach* (London: Frances Pinter, 1978), p. 81. Reprinted with permission of the editors and publisher.

TABLE 14.4. Number of International Organizations in Which Countries Were Represented, 1960 and 1976

Africa	1960	1976	Australasia/Pacific	1960	1976
South Africa	367	602	Australia	424	870
Egypt	288	463	New Zealand	285	590
Nigeria	84	426	Fiji		107
Morocco	187	347	Other	84	260
Tunisia	139	341	Total	793	1,827
Kenya	73	316			
Ghana	126	307	Europe	1960	1976
Other	1,003	5,239	France	976	1,574
Total	2,267	8,041	German Federal Republic	911	1,480
			United Kingdom	818	1,473
America	1960	1976	Belgium	913	1,428
United States	671	1,190	Italy	884	1,402
Canada	535	1,046	Netherlands	909	1,384
Argentina	430	815	Switzerland	796	1,317
Brazil	458	807	Sweden	705	1,228
Mexico	379	720	Denmark	672	1,179
Venezuela	277	590	Austria	708	1,142
Chile	337	567	Spain	593	1,136
Other	2,787	6,358	Norway	602	1,053
Total	5,874	12,091	Finland	548	1,017
			Other	4,384	8,771
Asia	1960	1976	Total	14,419	25,584
Japan	454	949			
India	432	801			
Israel	402	778	Total (all countries)	27,260	56,442
Philippines	220	454			
Iran	186	406			
South Korea	121	400			
Lebanon	187	399			
Other	1,905	4,712			
Total	3,907	8,899			

SOURCE: Anthony Judge, "International Institutions: Diversity, Borderline Cases, Functional Substitutes, and Possible Alternatives," in P. Taylor and J. Groom, eds., *International Organization: A Conceptual Approach* (London: Frances Pinter, 1978), p. 83. Reprinted with permission of the editors and publisher.

NOTE: Organizations include both governmental and nongovernmental.

1960 and 1976; in twelve of these countries, the figure more than doubled. Among other things, these data are a measure of the overlap between the state-centric and multi-centric world.

All the groups noted thus far are organized, in the sense that they have members and designated leaders who speak on their behalf. But postinternational politics are also distinguished by the emergence of mass movements that are not organizationally coherent but are nevertheless politically influential. Trade unions are a good illustration of the distinction between groups and movements; what was once a "labor movement," consisting of disorganized segments of the labor force pressing demands in an uncoordinated way, now consists almost entirely of organized unions. Examples of movements that still have uncoordinated segments as well as formal associations are the antiwar, disarmament, and peace movements, the movements for women's rights and liberation, the civil-rights movements for Jews, blacks, guest workers, and refugees, and the movements devoted to environmentalism, consumers, the homeless, youth, and the elderly, not to mention a wide range of intellectual movements. It might even be said that subgroupism is itself a movement that focuses on dissatisfactions with the policies and programs of whole systems.

Since most movements have evolved on a transnational basis, their relevance to the authority crises that beset the world of postinternational politics can hardly be exaggerated. As one observer puts it:

> By contrast with interest groups, movements flow beyond the channels of social and political representation that the modern age has imagined to mediate among institutions. . . . Interest groups are legalistic and institutionalized; they are pragmatic, bureaucratized, and routinized. . . . Movements are charismatic and informal; and they are idealistic, disorganized, and surprising. Accordingly they remain suspect but unregulated as the main mode of action in societies that need fundamental change. Interest groups lobby, bargain, and compromise; movements overwhelm, demand, and criticize. Interest groups alter policies; movements change cultures.[48]

As inchoate structures that cut across associational, class, and geographical boundaries and drain off support from established organizations, movements add substantially to the dynamics of subgroup-

[48] John S. Nelson, "Postmodern Meanings of Politics" (paper presented at the annual meeting of the American Political Science Association, Chicago, September 1987), p. 4.

ism.[49] In any locale, for example, it is always possible that those who belong to a global movement will undertake to transform their shared concerns into an organized group that will diminish the support available to the other organizations in their community. It might even be argued that as transnational issues rise to urgent status on the global agenda, they galvanize global movements, which, in turn, intensify organization at the local level.[50] This suggests that subgroupism is part of a cyclical or dialectic process wherein tendencies toward global centralization contain the bases for renewing decentralizing tendencies. We shall return in chapter 16 to the prospects for a global order in which such processes are predominant.

THE EROSION OF INTERNATIONAL AUTHORITIES

The governing mechanisms of international organizations have not been immune to the global tendencies toward decentralization. While IGOs have never been accorded the privileges of sovereignty by their members, they do have assigned missions, administrative responsibilities, investigative and reportorial tasks, and the staffs and budgets required to perform these functions. As turbulence has mounted in recent years, however, a variety of international organizations—from global ones like the UN and UNESCO to regional and issue-based ones like the Organization of American States (OAS), the European Community (EC), and the UN Food and Agricultural Organization (FAO)—have undergone the same splintering and decline in effectiveness experienced by their sovereignty-bound counterparts. Like national governments, IGOs have become, with increasing frequency, plagued by the budgetary shortfalls, inefficient leaderships, bureaucratic inertia, and differences among their members that lead to paralysis. Recently, for example, the secretary general of the OAS, acknowledging that "historically . . . the OAS had [always] had crisis moments and difficulties," asserted that the 1988 budget crisis was "so serious that the essence of

[49] For discussions of how social movements may be enlarging the processes of subgroupism, see Mats Friberg and Bjorn Hettne, "Local Mobilization and World System Politics," *International Social Science Journal* 117 (August 1988): 341–60, and Claus Offe, "Challenging the Boundaries of Institutional Politics: Social Movements since the 1960s," in C. S. Maier, ed., *Changing Boundaries of the Political: Essays on the Evolving Balance between the State and Society, Public and Private in Europe* (Cambridge: Cambridge University Press, 1987).

[50] Francesco Alberoni, *Movement and Institution* (New York: Columbia University Press, 1984), contends that this may be one reason why class consciousness has lately declined on a global scale: "The more . . . global integration increases, so that every threat becomes general, the less important the class basis becomes" (p. 225).

the organization is in danger."[51] Within the same week, the UN General Assembly's Third Special Session on Disarmament came to an end, after two weeks of preparatory talks and four weeks of negotiations, with so many irreconcilable divisions over so many issues that a joint declaration setting out new goals and priorities for disarmament could not be drafted or adopted.[52] As for the EC, the data clearly indicate that for thirty years a progressive decline in compliance with the directives of its commission and suborgans has been underway.[53]

Specific reasons for the growing ineffectiveness of each international organization can readily be cited. In some instances, the unwillingness of the United States—reflecting sentiments in both the executive and legislative branches of the federal government as well as in key segments of the public—to meet its financial obligations has been a prime factor. In other instances, most notably those of UNESCO and the FAO, the policies and administrative styles of the Third World have come into conflict with those of the First World. In still other situations, such as the disarmament proceedings, a multiplicity of overlapping and crosscutting local and regional cleavages has made it virtually impossible to reach any consensus.

Underlying the difficulties of all IGOs, however, are the decentralizing tendencies of postinternational politics, eating away at their fragile structures of authority. It is true that the OAS's budgetary shortfall was due primarily to the failure of the United States to meet its financial obligations—but it is also the case that Argentina and several countries in the Caribbean and Central America had fallen behind in their payments. Particular leaders of UNESCO and the FAO did adhere to administrative styles that ran counter to those practiced in industrial democracies—but the election of new leaders has yet to reverse tendencies toward ineffective governance. Directives issued by organs of the EC are subjected to extensive negotiations prior to their issuance, and yet the result is what has been referred to as "the Paradox of Non-Compliance," because the directives are not successfully implemented or enforced despite the prior consultation.[54] Delegates from all the coun-

[51] David Johnston, "O.A.S. Says Aid Programs Are Imperiled," New York Times, June 25, 1988, p. 3.

[52] Paul Lewis, "Disarmament Parley Ends in Discord," New York Times, June 27, 1988, p. A3.

[53] Samuel Krislov, Claus-Dieter Ehlermann, and Joseph Weiler, "The Political Organs and Decision-Making Process in the United States and the European Community," in Mauro Cappelletti, Monica Seccombe, and Joseph Weiler, eds., Integration through Law (New York: Walter de Gruyter, 1986), book 2, pp. 3–110.

[54] Krislov, Ehlermann, and Weilen, "Political Organs and Decision-Making Process," p. 61.

tries represented at the Third Disarmament session concurred in their disappointment that the conference had broken up in disagreement, but nonetheless it was disagreement that prevailed over any forces conducing to consensus.

In short, the sources of subgroupism at work within countries also operate to undermine the organizational relations between them. At the international level, the nation-state is a subsystem, and thus at this level subgroupism can include an emphasis on the interests of nation-states as well as those of their subsystems; but the consequences are the same, in the sense that organizations charged with governance undergo a loss of support, a diminution of authority, and a slippage in effectiveness.

THE DECAY OF IDEOLOGY

Consistent with the decentralizing tendencies that have disrupted authority relations at all levels is the diminishing hold that all-encompassing systems of thought exercise over their adherents. This decay can be discerned in the pockets of disaffection with the scientific rationalism of Western thought—with what is considered to be the end of "progress" as defined by the "modernity project"—represented by postmodernist formulations in architecture, literature, and law. Even more conspicuous is the fragmentation of communism as a worldview which many people in all parts of the globe have long shared. The program of *perestroika* in the Soviet Union and the opening up of the People's Republic of China to foreign investment may be among the immediate causes of the diminution of communism's influence as an ideology, but surely this diminution can also be interpreted as another form of subgroupism. A reporter recently concluded, after interviewing twenty men and women in ten Third World countries:

> All declared themselves to be Communists, but no single set of beliefs, no unifying standard and no transcendent vision of the future emerged from the interviews. . . . The people who spoke made it clear that it was a time of revision, reformation and counterreformation, a time of confusion over what it means to be a Communist—particularly among those who once thought that Marxist analysis, Leninist party organization and adherence to the Soviet example would inevitably bring about revolutionary transformations of backward economies and unjust social systems.

The reporter acknowledged that "tendencies [toward] national Communism are hardly new," but, he insisted, "third-world Communists are questioning old authorities and old assumptions more often and more deeply. . . . Cohesion and discipline in the party are lessening, and old internationalist slogans are fraying."[55] Interviews of twenty ideologues in Europe yielded much the same conclusion: "the scattered Communist faithful no longer share a single set of beliefs."[56] In a decentralized world, where subgroups are the central focus, overarching ideologies are out of place.

From a micro perspective, the macro-level trend toward subgroupism constitutes an opportunity, in the sense that it offers individuals a series of alternative collectivities to which they can attach their loyalties and apply their criteria of legitimacy. In so doing, of course, it also intensifies crises in relations of authority as citizens become both more flexible and more fickle with respect to the attachment of their loyalties. From the perspective of the structural parameter, on the other hand, the decentralizing patterns of authority relationships are less an opportunity than a major challenge: they increase the complexity and dynamism of global politics and make it more difficult for collectivities, singly or interactively, to manage their affairs. Yet, as we shall see in the next chapter, some of the management tasks may be eased by centralizing processes that are fostering the development of shared global norms and a greater legitimacy for transnational actors.

[55] Michael T. Kaufman, "In Third World, the Legacy of Marx Takes Many Shapes," *New York Times*, January 24, 1989, p. 1.

[56] James M. Markham, "Across a Divided Europe, An Ideology under Siege," *New York Times*, January 23, 1989, p. 1.

CHAPTER 15

NASCENT NORMS

Legitimacy, Patriotism, and Sovereignty

We no longer know who's a patriot and who's not. I grew up in Shatila and was told that Arafat is a hero and father of our nation. Now they tell me he betrayed the Palestinian cause.
—Basem al-Awa, a Palestinian teenager[1]

We remain directly affected in Alberta and in Canada by decisions that are made in Riyadh, Geneva, Tokyo, Beijing, Hong Kong, London, or you name it.
—Peter Lougheed, premier of Alberta[2]

The important thing is that they come in large numbers and that they be qualified observers [of elections]. We are not asking for foreigners who are militant supporters . . . We are asking for true observers, people willing to work according to international recognized practice for observers.
—Genero Arriagada, executive director of the coalition of sixteen Chilean parties that campaigned against the reelection of General Pinochet[3]

In what amounted to an undeclared cease-fire, Government troops and leftist rebels stopped fighting this morning to allow medical teams to vaccinate more than 250,000 Salvadoran children throughout the country against five major diseases.
—News item[4]

[1] Quoted in Ihsan A. Hijazi, "To P.L.O., Base Is Not Home for Long," *New York Times*, July 5, 1988, p. 3.

[2] Quoted in Ivo D. Duchacek, *Toward a Typology of New Subnational Governmental Actors in International Relations* (Berkeley: Institute of Governmental Studies, University of California, 1987), p. 3.

[3] Shirley Christian, "Foreigners to Observe the Plebiscite in Chile," *New York Times*, September 18, 1988, p. 6.

[4] James LeMoyne, "War Stops in Salvador for Vaccination Campaign," *New York Times*, April 22, 1985, p. A3.

FROM A MICRO-MACRO PERSPECTIVE, the structures that organize global politics are located in the habits and orientations of people and in the practices of collectivities. At any point in time, citizens and officials, as both nationals and foreigners, respond to their environments and cultural heritages in such a way as to be oriented to one kind of collectivity rather than another. In some periods of history, usually those in which agriculture was primary, communities at what we now call the local level served well the needs of people, and thus the village, the town, the city, and the province were the foci of their loyalties and orientations. These local collectivities, out of their particular historical experience, evolved traditions and written records that undergirded the practices of their officials and that constrained, reinforced, and guided the conduct of their citizens.

Today as well as earlier, practices of officialdom and the behavior of the citizenry constitute the structures of a collectivity. As a combined resultant of technological conditions, individual orientations, and historical experiences, structures seem to develop an existence of their own, in the sense that they come to be thought of as independent realities that operate across generations. The longer they persist, and the longer their founding documents and their institutions are associated with effective governance, the more deep-seated do the structures become in the practices of leaders and the orientations of members. Moreover, as the collectivity acquires an existence and reality at the macro level that is perceived as something apart from the micro level, its leadership becomes concerned with insuring its reproduction across time, thus transforming questions of socialization and citizen training into permanent public issues.

The perceived separation of the micro and the macro, however, is to some extent an illusion. The collectivity may appear to have an existence independent of individual actors, but from a micro-macro perspective it continues to be sustained by the willingness of its membership to undertake the tasks and comply with the directives that the leadership requests in its name. Indeed, often the illusion is cultivated by leaders who find that the idea of the collectivity—its shared needs, illustrious past, and current challenges—is a major instrument for maintaining control over its affairs. On the other hand, for those individuals and groups exploited or suppressed by the collectivity, its existence is no illusion. For them, it has a reality with respect to which they either succumb or protest. Thus, the history of collectivities is marked by conflicts, to which most manage to adapt even as some are unable to make the adjustments in orientations and practices which enable the collectivities to persist.

As technology moved the bases of life beyond the agrarian stage into forms of industrial order, people became more interdependent and their needs changed. No longer could the local community resolve their problems. Orientations and practices began to shift toward more encompassing collectivities, in particular the national state, and macro structures underwent corresponding changes that in turn, reinforced the emergent orientations and practices at the micro level. Bell sums up the new situation well: "The domestic problems we confront . . . arise out of . . . the fact that a multiplicity of problems—education, transportation, welfare, urban renewal, air and water pollution, medical care and the like—no longer are manageable on the state and local level but are now passed on to the national society for solution."[5] Thus did the state-centric era begin, supported by the belief that national states could resolve the problems that people and their nonpolitical collectivities faced.

But what happens when technology moves the organization of daily routines and work beyond the industrial stage? If the foregoing analysis is sound, the emergence of societies based more on services and information than on factory production and material goods is bound to affect the orientations of people, the practices of their leaders, and hence the bases on which macro structures are founded and reproduced. To extend Bell's formulation, a multiplicity of problems—not only air and water pollution but also currency fluctuations, global manufacturing processes, the drug trade, ocean resources, flows of refugees, AIDS, ozone depletion, and cultural intrusions through the airwaves, trade, and travel—are no longer manageable on the national level but must be passed on to supranational levels for consideration, if not for solution.

Chapter 10 presented the outlines of the bifurcated world which is seen as the emergent form of global politics in the postindustrial era. It highlighted the extent to which the illusion of states as omnicompetent collectivities has been revealed by technological developments that render people ever more interdependent and allow them to transcend national borders ever more easily. Chapters 13 and 14 explored the ways in which this revelation was furthered in the context of the orientational and relational parameters. What the earlier discussion did not do, however, was identify explicitly the normative premises on which the macro structures of postinternational politics rest. That is, even though the macro patterns of the bifurcated world can be documented

---

[5] Daniel Bell, *The Coming of Post-Industrial Society: A Venture in Social Forecasting* (New York: Basic Books, 1973), p. 320.

in organizational charters and be discerned from other evidence, some of the crucial norms from which they derive are subtle and still inchoate. As restraints on or facilitators of micro orientations and behavior of which people may not be fully aware, these norms foster new illusions that come to underlie the macro structures through which collectivities are adapting to the emergent order.

The task of this chapter, then, is to probe some of the fundamental value shifts that are facilitating the bifurcation of world politics and enabling the multi-centric and state-centric worlds to coexist. The purpose is not to describe them exhaustively, but rather to indicate, by examining a few of them, that new normative orientations necessary to the functioning of postinternational politics appear to be emerging and that the decentralizing tendencies identified in the previous chapter are not without competition from counter-dynamics fostering centralization around these nascent norms. As the Palestinian teenager, the premier of Alberta, the experts called in to observe foreign elections, and the children of El Salvador referred to at the outset of the chapter surely appreciate, the emergence of these shared norms is not a trivial development.

An Emergent Global Culture

Yet it is easy to exaggerate the degree to which unrecognized dynamics of global interdependence are operating to broaden the cultural foundations of world politics and to facilitate cooperation between and among sovereignty-bound and sovereignty-free actors. It is satisfying, for example, to suggest the presence of global norms in the fact that the war in El Salvador came to a halt while children on both sides of the conflict were vaccinated, but such incidents also need to be assessed in the context of the many times that supplies of food and medicine for the victims of wars in Ethiopia and the Sudan were intercepted and never reached their destinations.[6] Similarly, as indicated by the drug trade and crime syndicates, not all of the consequences of interdependence can be regarded as attractive bases of a global culture.[7] The ad-

---

[6] For one of these instances, see Sheila Rule, "Ethiopian Guerrillas Raid Food Convoy, Halting Drought Aid," *New York Times*, October 27, 1987, p. 1.

[7] See, for example, Elaine Sciolino, "U.S. Finds Output of Drugs in World Growing Sharply," *New York Times*, March 2, 1988, p. 1, and Francis X. Clines, "Moscow Finds Organized Crime Is Gaining a Hold," *New York Times*, June 14, 1989, p. A7. The former story stressed the international dimension of the drug trade by quoting a U.S. government report that noted "the stark fact that nations are outmanned, outgunned, and outspent by narcotics traffickers, [which continues] to undermine global efforts to

vances in international transportation and communications can also foster conflictful outcomes as they narrow the distances and intensify the interactions among peoples. Accordingly, however much subtle sources may be enlarging the realm of shared culture, to argue that a harmonious world community is in the process of replacing or absorbing national communities is to fly in the face of daily evidence that global tensions are pervasive, enduring, and deep-seated. It is to root reasoning in idealism rather than empirical prospects.

On the other hand, it must also be recognized that interdependence may be slowly and incrementally expanding the realm of globally shared norms. The commitments that underlie today's cascading conflicts may be too great to yield to redefinition in the near future, but they are not immune to change. The hypothesis of this chapter is thus that shifts are occurring in the underlying culture of world politics which may eventually lessen the intensity and reshape the nature of global conflicts and alter the ways in which they are managed.

The world today can be viewed as fragmented into a number of mutually exclusive cultures that tend to foster divergent interpretations of the meaning of events. The norms of each culture nourish varying conceptions of their interests, thus opening gulfs between them and making it difficult to see the world through the eyes of adversaries or, indeed, from the perspective of any culture other than one's own. A good example of how cultural variety can fragment what might otherwise seem like an obvious focus of shared global norms is the prolonged debate under UN auspices over the welfare of children. It took more than a decade for negotiators from some eighty countries to reach a tentative agreement on the draft of a "Convention on the Rights of the Child."[8]

While the habits and impulses of self-interest may deepen cultural commitments and strengthen their mutual exclusivity, they can also be affected by external influences, and this possibility creates the conditions for a *global culture*, a set of norms that are shared on a worldwide scale. As technology shrinks the world and as cultural value sys-

---

stop narcotics production and trafficking." The latter account quotes the Soviet government's explanation that its problems with organized crime were becoming more intractable in part "because easier travel abroad has encouraged Soviet gangs to seek international ties." Further insights into these less attractive dimensions of interdependence are available in Jennifer Parmelee, "Europe in 1992: Wide Open Market for Mafia Inc.," and David S. Broder, "With Drug Traffic Rising, Europeans Vow War on 'Crack,' " both in *International Herald Tribune*, May 20–21, 1989, p. 1.

[8] "Child-Rights Treaty Ready, But Debate over It Goes On," *New York Times*, December 11, 1988, p. A15.

tems are increasingly exposed to the dynamics of life in the postindustrial order, global culture seems likely to undergo transformation toward a broadened conception of self-interest and an acknowledgment of the legitimacy of interests pursued by others.[9] After all, despite the protracted arguments over the rights of the child, external influences did eventually lead to the drafting of a treaty for consideration by the UN and ratification by its members.

The evolution of the state system since the seventeenth century is instructive in this regard. As nations became more interdependent, their conflicts intensified, but they also began to converge around norms that facilitated their interaction. One such shared norm, for example, was that an embassy of a foreign nation came to be considered its sovereign territory regardless of any enmity felt by the host country toward the state that the embassy represented. Without norms of this sort, imposing limits on the degree to which states could act out their enmities, their interdependent activities could not have been sustained.[10]

Much the same process may be occurring today. While changes in communications, transportation, and computer technologies highlight the differences and thus deepen the cleavages that separate the First, Second, and Third Worlds, they may also foster movement toward the common values that are necessary to manage the cleavages. Just as the strategies and weapons of defense eventually catch up to those of the offense, so shared norms may eventually limit the breakdowns inherent in greater interdependence. Unable to forgo access to each others' markets, anxious to avoid nuclear resolutions of their conflicts, and incapable of eluding the rippling effects of currency crises, environmental pollution, terrorism, and the drug trade, the First, Second, and Third Worlds seem destined to converge around new norms appropriate to their greatly intensified interdependence.

Already it is possible to detect the development of institutional mechanisms—often called "regimes"—embracing actors in both the

[9] The nature and future of global culture are discussed in Adda Bozeman, "The International Order in a Multicultural World," and Ronald Dore, "Unity and Diversity in World Culture," both in Hedley Bull and Adam Watson, eds., *The Expansion of International Society* (New York: Oxford University Press, 1985), pp. 387–406 and 407–27. For a specific example of both the potentials and limits of the global development of one cultural dimension, consumer tastes, see Steven Greenhouse, "Building a Global Supermarket," *New York Times*, November 18, 1988, p. D1.

[10] For a succinct account of how these evolving norms supported the consolidation of the state system after the seventeenth century, see Hedley Bull, "The Emergence of a Universal International Society," in Bull and Watson, *Expansion of International Society*, pp. 117–26.

state- and multi-centric worlds, for coping with issues on the global agenda.[11] Some of these regimes consist of mostly informal and irregular consultations among the interested parties. Others are in the process of institutionalization, either within or outside a UN framework.[12] Still others have already assumed the shape of formal institutions with regularized procedures. One example is the European Parliament, which is directly elected by a constituency of 320 million Europeans in twelve countries, meets one week of every month, and is steadily expanding its role.[13]

But international institutional mechanisms are not necessarily a reflection of globally shared norms. They can also reflect self-interest on the part of actors who find they must engage in cooperation if they wish to come to terms with the challenges of the postindustrial order. If the underpinnings of a genuine global culture are to evolve, there must be a sharing of basic values pertaining to how the world is perceived and how conflicting loyalties are managed.

Traces of this more fundamental convergence were suggested in chapter 8, where it was noted that actors in both the state- and multi-centric worlds seem likely to rely ever more heavily on proof as a control technique. Presumably such a reliance is rooted in newly emerging norms relative to the nature of truth as a basis for addressing problems. It is the appearance of such norms that underlies the subsequent analysis in this chapter, in which four sociopolitical processes—a trend toward performance criteria of legitimacy, a decline in virulent patriotism, erosion of the principle of sovereignty, and a growing demand for proof—are identified as emergent practices which, in subtle ways, may be reducing the force of self-interest and enlarging the degree to which worldwide interdependence is founded on common values.

It must be emphasized that an expanded global culture is not necessarily the same as an increasingly cordial world community in which shared perspectives overwhelm and supersede conflict. But neither are an expansion of norms shared on a worldwide scale, and a contraction

[11] The mushrooming of international regimes has provoked a corresponding explosion in the literature on the subject. For a good sample of the varying emphases in this literature, see the thirteen essays in Stephen D. Krasner, ed., *International Regimes* (Ithaca, N.Y.: Cornell University Press, 1983).

[12] At this writing, for instance, a treaty that would dramatically increase international cooperation to curb narcotics trafficking has been signed by some one hundred countries. "A U.N. Accord on Drug Trafficking Is Signed," *New York Times*, December 21, 1988, p. A6.

[13] See William Tuohy, "Parliament of Europe Looks to Expand Role," *Los Angeles Times*, December 25, 1988, p. 1.

in habitual acts of self-interest, trivial developments. The implications of all these processes need to be pondered.

OBJECTIVE AND SUBJECTIVE INTERDEPENDENCE

Implicit in the search for signs of a global culture is a conception of interdependence that differentiates between the objective circumstances that render systems dependent on each other and the subjective interpretations of these circumstances. A preponderance of the interdependence literature focuses on the former, on the ways in which interdependent interactions are made necessary by the division of labor, resource distributions, trading patterns, wage rates, geographic distances, and a variety of other factors.[14] However, the consequences of the objective circumstances for the course of events are partly shaped by the norms through which leaders and publics interpret them and the emotional context in which they experience them. Leaders and publics may cause themselves great hardships by ignoring the objective circumstances, but they are surely free to do so and to be impelled by reactions that exact a high price for defining the objective circumstances in subjectively satisfying ways.[15] Cultural traditions, national pride, subgroup loyalties, and many other sociopsychological dynamics can lead to a discrepancy between the way interdependence is assessed by leaders and publics and the way in which its objective foundations are evaluated by detached observers. It is demonstrable, for example, that protectionist policies have high long-run costs, because they ignore the realities of comparative advantage, but this argument falls on deaf ears if leaders and publics emphasize instead the short-run benefits of high trade barriers.[16]

It is also true, of course, that many of the objective indicators of a

[14] Some of the most important contributions to the literature are those that employ quantitative indicators of such factors to trace the changing patterns of interdependence over time. See, for example, R. R. Kaufman, H. I. Chernotsky, and D. S. Geller, "A Preliminary Test of the Theory of Dependency," *Comparative Politics* 7 (April 1975): 303–30; Richard Rosecrance and Arthur Stein, "Interdependence: Myth and Reality," *World Politics* 26 (October 1973): 1–27; and Richard Rosecrance et al., "Whither Interdependence?" *International Organization* 31 (Summer 1977): 425–45.

[15] An excellent discussion of the interaction between objective circumstances and subjective interpretations of them is Harold Sprout and Margaret Sprout, "Environmental Factors in the Study of International Politics," in James N. Rosenau, ed., *International Politics and Foreign Policy: A Reader in Research and Theory*, rev. ed. (New York: Free Press, 1969), pp. 41–56.

[16] I. M. Destler and John S. Odell, *Anti-Protection: Changing Forces in United States Trade Politics* (Washington: Institute for International Economics, 1987).

shrinking world cannot be easily overlooked or subjected to gross distortion. Currency crises and the widening gap in the ozone layer have clear-cut repercussions that even the most self-interested citizens cannot readily ignore. Such developments cry out for recognition as expressions of the limits of sovereignty and the porosity of national boundaries. They call attention to the complexity of world affairs and the vulnerability of collectivities to processes and structures located abroad. Frequently, therefore, the circumstances of objective interdependence serve to heighten awareness of their existence and, in turn, these subjective sensitivities can foster actions that affect the objective circumstances. Both currency crises and the problem of the ozone gap are illustrative of this process in the sense that both have led macro actors into agreements designed to minimize their impact in the future. Perhaps especially conspicuous in this regard is the call for concerted action on environmental problems, as well as the reaffirmation of current policies on a variety of economic issues, that came out of the meeting of the leaders of the seven largest industrial democracies in 1989.[17] Innovative technologies may not catch on immediately, but once they do, their consequences increase at an exponential rate as the circumstances they create are reinforced and extended by the subjective reactions to them.

It bears repeating that the direction of these consequences can vary. The interaction of the objective and subjective dynamics of interdependence is itself a dynamic that can lead to diverse outcomes. Rapid advances in communications, transportation, and computer technologies have greatly intensified global interdependence, but how the world's leaderships and publics cope with these changes is far from certain. Their reactions can be accommodative and reinforcing or resistant and at cross-purposes, and which of these directions they take can have enormous consequences for the future of world politics.

Unfortunately, the literature on interdependence offers little guidance with respect to its subjective dimensions. The interpretations set forth here on emergent criteria of proof, legitimacy, patriotism, and sovereignty may turn out to be exaggerated, but they may be at least

[17] Art Pine, "Summit Stresses Ecological Threat," Los Angeles Times, July 17, 1989, p. 1. Interestingly, true to the tendencies toward subgroupism and performance legitimacy presently under way in the bifurcated world, the summit's formal communique was followed shortly after by an action in a California community, Irvine, which expressed impatience with the pace of international efforts to protect the earth's ozone layer and approved an ordinance designed to limit its further erosion. Robert Reinhold, "Frustrated by Global Ozone Fight, California City Offers Own Plan," New York Times, July 19, 1989, p. A1.

suggestive of the ways in which inquiries into interdependence can be broadened to include the modes of its subjective experience in different parts of the world.

CRITERIA OF PROOF AS GLOBAL NORMS

The analysis in chapter 8 shows how evidence and proof can be used as instruments of control. Here, it is suggested that they can also serve as indicators of the changing norms of postinternational politics. By systematically tracing across time the kinds of criteria employed to assess the validity of knowledge claims, we can observe the degree of movement toward a shared scientific culture. If the trend favors criteria that focus on the processes by which the evidence was developed, as distinguished from those that are linked to the identity, reliability, and orientations of the persons, organizations, or collectivities that offer the evidence, it would suggest a wider acceptance of the notion of objectivity in human affairs, of the belief that descriptions of phenomena can be developed that are free of bias.

This is another way of saying that controversies over evidence and proof in postinternational politics amount to nothing less than a concern with the nature of "truth" and with what constitutes adequate documentation of its existence, issues that are at the core of any value system. There is likely to be considerable conflict in a system that lacks consensus as to the criteria of evidence to be used in reaching conclusions about empirical matters. Three basic future trends can be hypothesized. In one, the culture of science would prevail over national, religious, ethnic, and similar kinds of norms. To the extent that agreement occurs more frequently among officials and publics around the world as to the meaning and significance of evidence on the sequence, structure, and motives of events, the foundations of shared global norms can be said to be deepening. In the second trend, the culture of science would make only slight inroads into other criteria of evidence, although insofar as the frequency of arguments over the nature and sufficiency of evidence increases, at least one globally shared norm— that evidence does matter—could be seen as emerging. In the third trend, the commitment to scientific evidence would fail to gain or might even lose out to more value-laden measures. To the extent that criteria of proof vary so much from culture to culture and from nation to nation that issues of evidence rarely appear on the global agenda, the emergence of global norms is unlikely, blocked by the need to adjust the perception of truth to the exigencies of national policies.

It is probably easiest to make a case for the third of these trends. The tendency for people to see what they want to see could well be called the First Law of Social Dynamics, a law repeatedly affirmed in history. Myriad are the occasions in the past when officials and publics willfully interpreted evidence in ways that were consistent with the policies they were pursuing. The predisposition in the Second and Third Worlds to blame objectionable developments on the CIA and the United States, and the inclination in the First World to fix responsibility for untoward events on the KGB and the Soviet Union, are contemporary examples of the subordination of scientific criteria of evidence to national and cultural interests and passions. Even in this era of dramatic scientific and technological advances, the number of instances in which evidence is brought into line with values, rather than vice versa, appears to be no smaller than ever. The degree of distrust in many international relationships is simply too great for credence to be attached to any evidence that adversaries may offer.

Persuasive as this line of reasoning may be, however, the case for the first of the trends cannot be lightly dismissed. One astute observer has said that "the language of science is becoming a world view that penetrates politics everywhere."[18] In the present era, when science is employing so many methods for the mastery of nature, virtually every nation and culture is under pressure to remain open to scientific evidence, even if it runs counter to commitments and aspirations. Eventually, for example, the Soviet Union had to bow to the measurements made in Sweden which showed that an accident at Chernobyl had polluted the atmosphere with radiation. To be sure, the Kremlin interpreted the evidence in as favorable a light as possible; nevertheless, Soviet leaders were unable to simply dismiss the evidence. In a quite different sphere, foreign observers are being called in with increasing frequency to witness the conduct of national elections, not only to discourage violence at polling places but also to testify to the fairness of the electoral process and the accuracy of the vote count.[19] This practice reflects a shared commitment to empirical evidence as well as a consensus about the nature of proper political procedures.

Admittedly, the number of instances in which scientific evidence is accepted by governments may be infinitesimal compared to the number in which they dismiss or reinterpret evidence that puts them in a

---

[18] Ernst B. Haas, *When Knowledge Is Power: Three Models of Change in International Organizations* (Berkeley: University of California Press, 1989), p. 46.

[19] In the Chilean case cited in one of the epigraphs of this chapter, some four hundred foreign observers were estimated to have been present, despite the objections of General Pinochet, at one or another of the twenty-two thousand polling places. Christian, "Foreigners to Observe the Plebiscite in Chile," p. 6.

negative light. But our concern is with trends, so the exceptions in which the culture of science prevails cannot be simply ignored. At least they suggest that differences in the means by which evidence is generated—e.g., by mechanized devices as distinguished from human observations—can lead to different degrees of acceptance. Indeed, as the means for collecting persuasive evidence become increasingly effective, governments may even make efforts to render their activities easily observable when they want their compliance with laws and treaties to be widely appreciated. In announcing their plan to destroy radars near Moscow and Gomel, for example, the Soviet government indicated the action would be "carried out in such a way that is easily observable by American spy satellites."[20]

Nor can the second trend be rejected out of hand. The energy that officials and publics devote to generating, evaluating, and contesting evidence in international disputes is a sign that the culture of science is acquiring salience and credibility. Doubtless there are diverse reasons why governments have become so preoccupied with questions of evidence—not the least being the need to legitimate their actions in the eyes of their own citizens—but such efforts would not be so extensive if the assertion of national aspirations could automatically override any contrary evidence. Yet such overrides seem to occur with decreasing frequency. The growing signs (noted in chapter 13) that individuals everywhere are more analytically skillful and more distrustful of central authority suggest that publics are more insistent that governmental policies be grounded in what are deemed to be objective circumstances. While systematic data on the emergence of this pattern are not presently available, one has the clear impression that issues of evidence and proof arise more frequently and last longer on the global agenda in the 1980s than was the case in earlier decades. The struggle to recover the downed Korean airliner's black box from the Sea of Japan, mentioned previously, was one of the most dramatic instances of a felt need to demonstrate the soundness or justify the morality of policies through the citation of solid evidence and proof.

It should be noted, moreover, that the pronounced trend toward a limited number of languages as the basis for scientific discourse, business dealings, and diplomatic exchanges is also favorable to shared criteria of evidence. About 95 percent of the world's production of chemical knowledge in 1980, for example, was recorded in only six languages, and two of these, English and Russian, accounted for more

[20] Michael R. Gordon, "Kremlin Says It Is Destroying 2 Radar Units Cited by U.S.," *New York Times*, December 14, 1988, p. 1.

than 82 percent.[21] As noted in the previous chapter, this trend has been under way for some time, with the proportion of scientific discourse that takes place in English mounting at a steady rate. Some might argue that this trend merely reflects the hegemonic dominance of the United States in recent decades and that eventually English will decline as the world's core language when a new hegemon with a different language emerges. However, the use of English has reached new heights during recent years, when the United States was said to be losing its hegemonic status. Decentralizing dynamics and an emergent global culture may have broken the centuries-long connection between hegemonic and linguistic dominance.

There is one development that offers an opportunity to assess the three hypothesized trends through more scientific procedures, and that is the appearance of a gap in the ozone layer of the earth's atmosphere. Since national boundaries, resources, and histories will be irrelevant if the depletion of stratospheric ozone raises the ultraviolet radiation reaching the earth's surface to levels that increase skin cancer and eye cataracts, suppress human and animal immune systems, and damage fish larvae, plants, paints, and plastics, the ozone issue approaches the model of a "crucial-case study" for testing an empirical theory of macropolitics.[22] Indeed, it has perhaps already acquired the character of a crucial case, because there has emerged "for the first time a broad scientific consensus that man-made chemicals are to blame" for much of the significant decline in atmospheric ozone.[23] But will the evidence be accepted by political communities? Will the scientific consensus be translated into political agreements, or will various global actors interpret it in self-serving ways that prevent the emergence of a political consensus? The scientific consensus focuses on the human responsibility for the loss, but it leaves uncertain the gravity of the threat and it offers no acceptable substitutes for the chlorofluorocarbons. So it is more than a remote possibility that the scientific consensus will never be transformed into the political will and organization necessary to reduce the dangers. On the other hand, the early signs point to the

---

[21] J. A. Laponce, "Language and Communication: The Rise of the Monolingual State," in Claudio Cioffi-Revilla, Richard L. Merritt, and Dina A. Zinnes, eds., *Communication and Interaction in Global Politics* (Newbury Park, Calif.: Sage, 1987), p. 198.

[22] Harry Eckstein, "Case Study and Theory in Political Science," in Fred I. Greenstein and Nelson W. Polsby, eds., *Handbook of Political Science*, vol. 7, *Strategies of Inquiry* (Reading, Mass.: Addison-Wesley, 1975), pp. 79–137.

[23] James K. Hammitt, *Timing Regulations to Prevent Stratospheric-Ozone Depletion*, quoted in *Rand Research Review* 12 (Spring 1988): 6.

second or third trend. In 1987, more than forty nations agreed on a treaty to protect the ozone layer; in 1988, some actors in the multicentric world did accept the scientific consensus,[24] and public officials, scientists, and environmentalists from forty-eight countries endorsed a series of proposals that called for immediate action to halt degradation of the earth's atmosphere;[25] and in 1989, as noted above, the issue expanded to encompass the top leadership of the industrial nations at the international level and cities like Irvine, California, at the local level. The crucial-case test, in short, is under way.

PERFORMANCE CRITERIA OF LEGITIMACY

Just as people are increasingly inclined to demand that the claims of collectivities be grounded in persuasive evidence and proof, so they are more and more likely to insist that the legitimacy of leaders and their policies be grounded in appropriate and successful performances. This shift away from traditional criteria of legitimacy and toward performance criteria has consequences for macro structures as well as for the orientations of citizens at the micro level. It suggests another realm in which a new, globally shared basis for the conduct of politics may be emerging. Indeed, since such manifestations of interdependence as currency crises, terrorism, and pollution are among the major sources of this emergent norm, publics in diverse cultural traditions are confronted with the same objective situations and thus may be induced to evolve the same conceptions of what are appropriate performances by their respective public officials. Judgments about how the governments of Western Europe dealt with the fallout from Chernobyl, for example, converged readily around criteria of speed, thoroughness, and caution with respect to the monitoring of contaminated lands, produce, and cattle.

Furthermore, the issues arising out of interdependence can contribute to the evolution of common legitimacy sentiments by virtue of occupying a high position on national agendas while at the same time not

[24] For example, "just 20 days after he had dismissed the concerns of the latest critics, Mr. [Richard E.] Heckert [chairman of the du Pont company], announced a dramatic turnaround. Du Pont, he said, would get out of the chlorofluorocarbon business entirely. . . . In interviews yesterday, Du Pont executives said the change of heart was not an outgrowth of all the years the company had battled environmentalists about the ozone layer. It was a result of pure, hard, cold science making its points." William Glaberson, "Behind Du Pont's Shift on Loss of Ozone Layer," *New York Times*, March 26, 1988, p. D1.

[25] Philip Shabecoff, "Parley Urges Quick Action to Protect Atmosphere," *New York Times*, July 1, 1988, p. 3.

being susceptible to resolution through the authority of national governments. Whereas the issues of earlier times were seen as either domestic or foreign in scope and thus as belonging to two different policy-making processes, many of today's problems straddle the boundary between domestic and foreign, thus making national officials responsible for coping with challenges that require international cooperation to manage. Partly for that reason, these problems are more difficult to resolve, and so they are likely to contribute to public skepticism about the performances of political leaders. Previously, the habit of according legitimacy to officials was rarely challenged; leaders had the authority to cope with the issues that arose under their jurisdiction. In the present era, however, the correspondence between the locus of authority and its scope has diminished, with the result that officials appear less and less able to exercise control over the matters for which they are held responsible.

It is useful to reiterate, moreover, that the emergence of centralizing norms that accord legitimacy to performances may well be accelerating as a consequence of the growing capacity of publics to observe their leaders in action. With live pictures of national and international events displayed on TV screens all over the world, it seems likely that citizens everywhere are increasingly inclined to break with the habit of unthinkingly presuming that their leaders are competent and are authorized to act as they deem appropriate. Able to watch domestic and world politics unfold before them, people seem likely to evolve conceptions of effective performance that are more discriminating.

If this is so, if people in different cultures are beginning to converge around new criteria of legitimacy that stress appropriate and effective performance, it is reasonable to hypothesize that they are likely to be increasingly capable of seeing the world through the eyes of persons whose cultures are founded on different values. The rise of human rights as a global issue, for example, may well have its roots in a widespread sharing of values as to what constitutes the legitimate sphere of official coercion: "Increasingly the legitimacy of political regimes (and hence their capacity to rule non-coercively) is judged externally and internally, less by the standards of divine mandate, revolutionary heritage, nationalism, or charismatic authority, and more by the performance criteria specified in internationally defined standards of human rights."[26]

---

[26] Richard Pierre Claude and David R. Davis, "Political Legitimacy at Risk: The Emergence of Human Rights in International Politics" (paper presented at the Fourteenth World Congress of the International Political Science Association, Washington, September 1988), p. 2. A similar position is taken in Leslie J. Macfarlane, "Human

DECLINE IN VIRULENT PATRIOTISM

Associated with the demand for solid evidence and performance in the conduct of world politics is a decline in virulent patriotism, the kind that sees the state as doing no wrong and that glorifies resort to violence on its behalf. It is difficult to muster an unqualified commitment to the national government while subjecting those who act in its name to increasingly rigorous criteria of performance, and such a commitment is also inhibited by the recognition that the national well-being is interdependent with the well-being of collectivities abroad. In addition, with the prospect of nuclear warfare having virtually eliminated the sense of glory that once attached to fighting for the country's honor, the avenues for expressing the most virulent form of patriotism have been closed to those for whom national pride is a powerful drive. The military hero, the historic battle, and the cry for vengeance against the country's enemies are on their way out as cultural values in most parts of the world.

To be sure, a Margaret Thatcher can still evoke patriotism on behalf of a war in the South Atlantic, a Ronald Reagan can still call on national pride to support an air strike on Libya or a landing in Grenada, an Ayatollah Khomeini can still arouse masses on behalf of Islam, and an extreme right-wing political party in France can exploit antiforeign sentiment to press for the adoption of laws that limit access to citizenship.[27] Similarly, to cite a poignant example of the undiminished patriotism of some individuals, an Admiral Zumwalt can still say, "Knowing what I know now, I still would have ordered the use of Agent Orange to defoliate [river banks in Vietnam] to achieve the objective . . . of reducing casualties [even though that decision also led to my son's death from cancer and his son's severe learning disability]."[28] But such recent episodes stand out precisely because they seem so incongruous, so much a throwback to traditional practices that bear little relevance to the complexity of current problems.

More revealing of the emergent forms of patriotism, perhaps, are the quiet sense of relief that accompanied the release of the embassy hostages in Iran,[29] the troubling question in the U.S. medical community

---

Rights As Global Rights" (paper presented at the Fourteenth World Congress of the International Political Science Association, Washington, September 1988).

[27] Richard Bernstein, "Chira Bill on Citizenship Raises Debate on How to Become French," *New York Times*, November 13, 1986, p. 8.

[28] Elmo Zumwalt, Jr., and Elmo Zumwalt 3rd, "Agent Orange and the Anguish of an American Family," *New York Times Magazine*, August 24, 1986, p. 40.

[29] Milton Viorst, "Welcome Home to Us All," *Los Angeles Times*, February 1, 1981, sec. 5, p. 5.

as to whether foreigners should be the beneficiaries of transplant operations when there are not enough kidneys and other organs to meet the needs of ailing Americans,[30] the survey in Poland that yielded the finding that 69 percent of those polled said they did not believe a desire to emigrate signified a lack of patriotism,[31] the observation made during the celebration of the two-hundredth anniversary of the French Revolution that "the French are not patriotically aroused by the bicentennial; at times, they seem almost bored by it,"[32] the resistance of many Austrians to a presidential candidate who evoked memories of a shameful past,[33] the similar reaction in West Germany and the United States to leaders who wanted to commemorate the fortieth anniversary of the end of World War II with a ceremony at a cemetery where Nazi officers were buried,[34] and dismissal of a minister of education in Japan who sought to revive memories of his country's earlier military triumphs in China and Korea.[35] One of the most remarked-upon instances of the decline in virulent patriotism was that U.S. soldiers returned from Vietnam not as heroes but as victims (if not villains).

Perhaps it is also indicative of the changing nature of patriotism that, as the global agenda has shifted from military to economic conflicts, some of the most animated expressions of nationalist fervor have centered around trade relations. In the 1988 Canadian elections, for example, the central issue was the proposed Canadian-U.S. free-trade agreement, with the opposition parties and newspapers organizing

[30] Lindsey Gruson, "Some Doctors Move to Bar Transplants to Foreign Patients," *New York Times*, August 10, 1985, p. 1.

[31] John Tagliabue, "Poland Is Worried over Emigrant Flow," *New York Times*, February 9, 1988, p. A18.

[32] James M. Markham, "A Calm, Ambivalent France Looks Back to 1789's Fervor," *New York Times*, July 9, 1989, p. A1.

[33] James M. Markham, "Austrians Seem to Cut Support for Waldheim," *New York Times*, May 17, 1987, p. 1.

[34] Bernard Weinraub, "Weisel Confronts Reagan on Trip," *New York Times*, April 20, 1985, p. 1, and Charles Krauthammer, "The Living Must Pay the Debt of the Dead," *Los Angeles Times*, May 5, 1985, sec. 4, p. 5. For a discussion of this episode that suggests the decline of virulent patriotism is, in part, a generational phenomenon, see James M. Markham, "Old Germans and Young: Split Is Deep," *New York Times*, May 8, 1985, p. 1.

[35] For cogent discussions of alternative forms of patriotism and citizenship, see George Armstrong Kelley, "Who Needs a Theory of Citizenship?" *Daedalus* 108 (Fall 1979): 21–36; Herbert C. Kelman, "Patterns of Personal Involvement in the National System: A Social-Psychological Analysis of Political Legitimacy," in Rosenau, *International Politics and Foreign Policy*, pp. 276–88; and Tom R. Tyler, Kenneth A. Rasinski, and Eugene Griffin, "Alternative Images of the Citizen: Implications for Public Policy," *American Psychologist* 41 (September 1986): 970–78.

their campaign around the theme that the agreement threatened Canada's sovereignty through "economic integration with our Southern neighbor." As a front-page editorial in the *Toronto Star* put it, "With our hearts and our votes Canadians will decide next Monday the very future of our country. Nothing less. For this is more than an election; it is a referendum on what Canada will be."[36] In South Korea, mass anti-American protests in the spring of 1988 were to a large extent fueled by resentment over policies that lowered duties on U.S. goods imported into that country. Similar, though somewhat less strident, stirrings over efforts to achieve reciprocity in trade relations were being observed in Australia, Japan, and the United States.

Nevertheless, economically based patriotism does not have the same kind of emotional intensity as that based on territorial and security concerns. Its vigor can diminish quickly with a new trade agreement, an economic upturn, or a promise of high profits,[37] whereas the traditional form of patriotism is not so easily mollified in the face of threats to sovereignty or insults to national symbols. Furthermore, the nationalist sentiments that have lately sprung up over trade and tariff issues seem relatively mild in comparison to those of the 1930s. The powerful domestic pressures that resulted in extensive protectionist legislation and trade wars during that earlier period simply do not exist today. To be sure, the present is not lacking in protectionist orientations, but these do not approach the unqualified, raucous demands of the past.[38] The reaction in Michigan, for example, to the competition from Japanese automobiles has been nowhere near as intense as the self-righteous protectionism that led to the Hawley-Smoot Tariff Act in 1930. With many automobile parts now being manufactured outside the country, the arguments favoring higher trade barriers have lost much

[36] Quoted in John F. Burns, "Canada's Biggest Paper Crusading to Defeat Trade Treaty with U.S.," *New York Times*, November 17, 1988, p. A18.

[37] A good insight into the nature of economically based patriotism is provided by the discrepancy between the attitudes and the behavior of Donald Trauscht, vice president for finance and strategy of the Borg Warner Corporation, a U.S. firm that once had manufacturing facilities in six continents. Acknowledging that he intended to sell parts of his company to overseas buyers, he also said, "As a citizen and a patriot, I'm concerned. I don't want this country to be owned by foreigners. . . . There's sadness in my heart. But I'm a realist. I know where we are at." Quoted in Robert Johnson, "More U.S. Companies Are Selling Operations to Foreign Concerns," *Wall Street Journal*, February 24, 1988, p. 1.

[38] For an analysis in which the "economic nationalism" theme of the 1988 Democratic presidential campaign is viewed as embracing "less hostile notions of 'fair' and 'managed trade,' " as espousing "true, vigorous competition, with better schools and smarter management," as well as "changes in trade laws," see Peter T. Kilborn, "Economic Nationalism Shapes Democratic Campaign Debate," *New York Times*, March 22, 1988, p. 1.

of their force.[39] In the 1988 Canadian elections referred to above, voters rejected the economic patriotism argument and returned the Conservatives to office, thus assuring adoption of the free-trade agreement.[40]

The sum of the foregoing examples do not amount to evidence that justifies a clear-cut statement about the decline of virulent patriotism; the impression to that effect is strong, but systematic data need to be gathered before such a conclusion can be advanced. There are few indications that territorially oriented patriotism still dominates the life of nations.[41] At least, they are sufficiently scarce to warrant hypothesizing about the ways in which greater interdependence and the technologies accompanying it are altering the relations among nations. Certainly, a decline in uncritical attachment to the state is consistent with growing demands for proof and effective performance in the conduct of public affairs. And presumably, the less people are inclined to venerate the state and rely on unqualified patriotism as solutions to their problems, the more will they favor bargaining and accommodation over shrill and nonnegotiable demands as ways of handling conflicts. The futility of patriotism, in short, may be emerging as a transnationally shared norm, as both a source and a feature of global culture that may serve to constrain the propensity toward war in the state-centric world.[42]

[39] For a careful and cogent analysis in which global production processes serve as a restraint on patriotic demands for protection, see Destler and Odell, *Anti-Protection.*

[40] One U.S. newspaper editorialized that the failure of "protectionist nationalism" in Canada and of U.S. presidential candidate Richard Gephardt (who based his campaign on similar themes) indicated that "voters seem to have a more secure sense of national identity, recognizing that the competitive vigor that flows from free trade will create a stronger nation." *Wall Street Journal,* November 23, 1988, p. A14.

[41] Some of those indications, moreover, are subject to alternative interpretations. The patriotism theme of the Reagan presidency was said to have led to record sales of American flags, but the argument was also made that the flag has become not a banner of war but a symbol "of something we are prepared to live for rather than die for." "Increasingly, Every Day Is Flag Day," *New York Times,* July 4, 1988, p. A7.

[42] Some of the old belligerence of virulent patriotism is perhaps being displaced onto sports competition. Individual tennis, golf, and track stars are often seen as representatives of their country, and national athletic teams have become the focus of mean-spirited fervor. Between March 1984 and June 1985, for example, nine major incidents of violence marked soccer matches in China, England, Belgium, France, and Mexico. The most tragic of these incidents was a riot at a Brussels soccer stadium in 1985, in which thirty-eight fans were killed and two hundred injured before a match between British and Italian teams. While acknowledging that high unemployment among working-class youth may be one source of such aggressive behavior, one specialist in sports violence, Jeffrey H. Goldstein, observed that "social class or economic considerations are not the main roots—it's nationalism pure and simple. In an era of instant communications, peo-

This is not to suggest that the dynamics of interdependence are fostering a decline in the sense of in-group feeling per se. The impulse to elevate "us" at the expense of "them" is probably as common as ever. However, as indicated in chapter 14, the focus of the impulse is undergoing change, in that states are giving way to subsystems as the entities that arouse strong loyalties and feelings of identification. National patriotism is being supplanted by subgroupism. In some cases, particularly those involving ancient ethnic groups, such as Armenians, Estonians, and Latvians in the Soviet Union and the Tamil in Sri Lanka, subgroupism can be as virulent as that associated with nations. But for most collectivities in the multi-centric world, especially those that are narrow in scope and have only recently benefited from the dynamics of decentralization, loyalty is not a matter of great concern. Occasionally, their leaders may try to stimulate the same kind of loyalty as that which has been accorded to nation-states, but there is little sign that their memberships are galvanized by such efforts.[43]

THE EROSION OF SOVEREIGNTY

The expansion of interdependence has substantial implications for the concept of sovereignty.[44] Unabashed assertions of sovereign rights will

ple increasingly are making nationalist issues of international sporting events, and the people are abetted by the actions of the press, sports officials, politicians and the athletes themselves. Rightly or wrongly, international sporting events have become tests of the rightness or wrongness of ideology and everyone seems to be contributing to the notion that 'it's us against them.' " Quoted in Richard D. Lyons, "Sports Riot: Aggression As a Spiral," *New York Times*, May 30, 1985, p. 6.

[43] In one recent incident, the president of NBC sought to use company loyalty as a basis for asking employees to contribute to a proposed political action committee. His argument closely paralleled the kind of appeal often made in the state-centric world on behalf of national governments: "Employees that earn their living and support their families from the profits of our business," he wrote in a memorandum, "must recognize a need to ensure that the company is well represented in Washington. . . . Employees who elect not to participate in a giving program of this type should question their own dedication to the company and their expectations." The memorandum evoked few favorable reactions and much criticism, suggesting the limits to which state-centric loyalty patterns can be emulated in the multi-centric world. See Peter J. Boyer, "NBC Head Proposes Staff Political Contributions," *New York Times*, December 9, 1986, p. 1.

[44] For explorations of the sovereignty concept in the context of changing global structures, see Robert H. Jackson, "Quasi-States, Dual Regimes, and Neoclassical Theory: International Jurisprudence and the Third World," *International Organization* 41 (Autumn 1987): 519–49; Alan James, *Sovereign Statehood: The Basis of International Society* (London: Allen & Unwin, 1986); Cynthia Weber, "The Effects of Political Intervention Practices on Collective Understandings of Sovereignty" (paper presented at the annual meeting of the International Studies Association, London, March–April 1989);

diminish in frequency and intensity as adequate proof and appropriate performance become increasingly salient as criteria of national conduct. Indeed, one cannot help but be struck by the extent to which claims of sovereignty have waned in the discourse of states. The peremptory declaration that "this is strictly an internal matter" no longer commands global assent. Officials of one country can openly talk of bringing about alterations in the regime of another, and the articulation of such aspirations no longer invariably provokes complaints about the violation of sovereignty.

It is almost as if interdependence has been institutionalized through a worldwide acceptance of the principle that the territorial boundaries of countries are no longer relevant in efforts to alter political arrangements. In earlier eras, conflicts such as those that have recently occurred in and around the Middle East, Grenada, and Libya might have been cast in the context of clashes over sovereignty, but this theme was conspicuous by its absence in all three cases. Where overt efforts such as those of the United States to facilitate the ouster of Marcos in the Philippines and Gen. Manuel Antonio Noriega in Panama might once have provoked cries of violated sovereignty, today such assertions are muted and seem anachronistic, and their more extreme versions gain little attention. The attempts by some U.S. officials to use foreign aid as a means of altering China's coercive abortion and sterilization programs were criticized for a variety of reasons, but the contention that the United States had no right to interfere in the domestic affairs of the People's Republic was rarely voiced.

Much the same can be said about the debate that has raged over apartheid in South Africa: none of the arguments for or against imposing economic sanctions on that country have turned on whether such a policy violates its sovereignty. On the contrary, at a crucial moment during the 1986 debate on sanctions in the U.S. Senate, the South African foreign minister, instead of proclaiming that his country would not tolerate invasions of its sovereignty, in effect acknowledged that his country's race relations were a global issue by telephoning members of the Senate from the Farm Belt and threatening to end grain purchases.[45]

---

and Walter B. Wriston, "Technology and Sovereignty," *Foreign Affairs* 67 (Winter 1988/89): 63–75.

[45] Nor, incidentally, did the calls bring cries of violated sovereignty on the part of the senators who were telephoned. The most angry response was that of Senator Richard G. Lugar of Indiana, who angrily asserted, "I find this entire action—by a Foreign Minister of a foreign country, calling Senators off the floor—to be despicable." Steven V. Roberts,

To be sure, a Liberian foreign minister can still complain that a U.S. effort to link military aid to the holding of new elections, the release of political prisoners, and more effective guarantees of due process is a threat to his country's sovereignty, asserting that "we are a sovereign state" and "no 51st state of America." But the shrillness of the complaint is like a voice from the past, and even then its tone was moderated when the foreign minister added, "For Congress to pass a resolution to cut aid would be unkind and uncomplimentary."[46] Similarly, when the prime minister of England warned against Europe turning into a "superstate" that "submerges our identity and snuffs out our sovereignty,"[47] she, too, sounded like a voice from the past, and a majority of British voters subsequently rejected her appeal in their choice of representatives to the European Parliament.[48] Although Latin America tends to be one region where politics is still marked by reliance on the rhetoric of sovereignty, it is surely indicative of the deepening complexity of interdependence that such rhetoric has been peripheral to the controversies over efforts by the United States to cope with the drug-trade problem at its sources through search-and-destroy missions in Bolivia, Colombia, Ecuador, and Peru.

Even the superpowers do not always erect the shield of their sovereignty as a way of insulating their domestic affairs from interference by others. Perhaps the most obvious example in this regard is the Soviet Union's willingness to engage in diplomatic discussions of the emigration of Soviet Jews. These discussions have not always resulted in exit visas on a scale sought by the West, but the issue is accepted as a legitimate subject of diplomatic exchanges rather than being dismissed as an invasion of sovereign rights. Similarly, when critics abroad call attention to the treatment of minorities in the United States, it does not retreat behind its sovereignty to fend them off.

Indeed, the emergence of human rights as a central issue of postinternational politics testifies eloquently to the erosion of national sovereignty as an organizing principle. Soviet leaders used to argue that insistence on compliance with the Helsinki accords on human rights constituted an intrusion into national sovereignty, but more recently

"Pretoria Official Warns Senators over Sanctions," *New York Times*, October 2, 1986, p. 1.

[46] Kendall J. Wills, "Liberian Rejects Link of Aid to Rights," *New York Times*, December 23, 1985, p. 8.

[47] William Pfaff, "Thatcher Seems to Imagine Sovereignty Is Threatened," *International Herald Tribune*, May 24, 1989, p. 7.

[48] "How They Voted" and "While Those Behind Cried Forward," *Economist*, June 24, 1989, pp. 46, 55–56.

they have instead responded in terms of examples of human-rights violations in the United States, a reaction that tacitly acknowledges the legitimacy of the issue as a subject of international discussion.[49] Politicians, cabinets, and parliaments in many countries call repeatedly for the release of jailed dissidents in countries other than their own, and if results are not immediately forthcoming, they threaten to withhold economic aid and diplomatic courtesies.[50] As the foreign minister of West Germany has observed, "The objection that the discussion of human rights problems . . . amounts to interference in those countries' internal affairs has become completely untenable."[51] Similarly, the minister of foreign affairs of Hungary, while conceding that the enforcement of human rights is a task for each state, stressed that this "does not mean it is an exclusively internal affair" and that "the international community has the right to monitor compliance."[52] The active and often successful role of Amnesty International as a transnational actor amply demonstrates that the erosion of the sovereignty principle is more than just a matter of diplomatic rhetoric.[53]

The integration of national economies into the world economy is an equally important source of the decline of the sovereignty principle. Historically, the principle was in part founded on the consolidation of political territory and economic control through the establishment of national currencies coined and managed by states. With the interdependence among national economies and the emergence of transnational bank-managed money in recent decades, however, the link between political and economic systems at the national level has been weakened, and with it the grounds for adhering to sovereignty as a core value of national life. The moves in Western Europe toward a tariff-free zone in 1992, and even toward continentwide perspectives

[49] See Anthony Lewis, "Profound Change of Policy," New York Times, June 2, 1988, p. A27, and Flora Lewis "It's Worth Haranguing," New York Times, November 17, 1988, p. A31.

[50] See, for example, Stephen Kinzer, "2 Freed Nicaraguans Credit World Pressure," New York Times, November 27, 1988, p. 17.

[51] Steven Greenhouse, "West Praises the East for Strides toward Freedom," New York Times, June 4, 1989, p. A19.

[52] Greenhouse, "West Praises the East for Strides toward Freedom."

[53] Edelgard Mahant, "Amnesty International and the International Human Rights Regime" (paper presented at the annual meeting of the International Studies Association, London, March 1989). A more generalized discussion of human rights as a focus of globally shared norms is Alison Dundes Renteln, "A Cross-Cultural Approach to Validating International Human Rights: The Case of Retribution Tied to Proportionality," in David Louis Cingrenelli, ed., Human Rights: Theory and Measurement (London: Macmillan, 1988), pp. 7–40.

that rival those of the separate nations, are illustrative. As one observer has put it, "the pious principles of national sovereignty . . . are eroding, not just because of greed and cynicism but because of hard facts of interdependence."[54]

Several practical consequences follow from the trends that have been identified here. One is that the work of governmental bureaucracies will become all the more crucial and burdensome. Generating proof and defending performance require extensive and painstaking inquiry and coordination. Thus, the more rigorous the criteria by which proof and legitimacy are judged, the greater will be the demands placed on foreign offices and intelligence services. Likewise, as patriotism becomes increasingly sophisticated and less tied to simplistic symbols, the more elaborate and cogent will the mobilizing efforts of political leaders have to be.

It may appear naive to discern the emergence of a global culture at a time when intense conflicts and tensions pervade world politics. If anything, some might argue, fragmentation and disarray, rather than the cohesion and order implied by shared norms, are the chief characteristics of present-day global life. Such a contention, however, is based on a misunderstanding of the nature of culture. It presumes that culture is inherently integrative and that therefore a fragmented world is essentially immune to even the most subtle processes whereby cultural norms spread and take hold. This presumption seems unduly narrow. The preceding discussion may be open to the charge of naiveté, but not because the concept of a global culture is equated with the decline of global tensions. Shared values are no guarantee of social harmony, as the history of virtually any domestic polity reveals.

The argument here is that dynamic technologies are fostering profound changes in global life and that in subtle ways these changes are creating common grounds for assessing the course of events. This is not to say that convergence is occurring with respect to the values underlying the assessments themselves. Shared bases for evaluating evidence, judging legitimacy, experiencing patriotism, and eschewing sovereignty claims may facilitate a narrowing of value differences, but to

---

[54] Flora Lewis, "Shifting Standards for Sovereignty," *New York Times*, June 26, 1988, p. D27. For a lengthy discussion in which transnational corporations in the multi-centric world are regretfully considered the prime beneficiaries of the erosion of national sovereignty, see Herbert J. Schiller, "The Erosion of National Sovereignty by the World Business System," in Michael Traber, ed., *The Myth of the Information Revolution: Social and Ethical Implications of Communication Technology* (London: Sage, 1986), pp. 21–34.

anticipate such a trend is not to be naive about the prospects for the future if one acknowledges that the actual narrowing of differences in an increasingly interdependent world depends on far more than the emergence of a common culture. Nevertheless, the tendencies toward new criteria of proof, legitimacy, patriotism, and sovereignty underscores the effects of turbulence on the normative underpinnings of the structural parameter. Equally important, the trend also suggests that the bases of cooperation may soon be no less prominent in global politics than are those of conflict.

PART FIVE

SEEKING SOLUTIONS

CHAPTER 16

BEYOND TURBULENCE

Four Scenarios and a Cyclical Process

> What we continue to experience, then, is not the shaping of any new larger coherences but a world continuing to break up into its bits and pieces, bursting like big and little stars from exploding galaxies. Each one spins off in its own centrifugal whirl, each one strains to hold its own small separate pieces from spinning off in turn. The larger ones have a gravitational pull still too weak to create or hold on to new universes of their own; the small ones are strong enough to keep from being drawn into larger orbits but much too weak to establish effective orbits of their own . . . The new shape of world politics is made out of the sums of all these evolving parts. The paradox rolls over itself, the fragmented pieces become all together the globalizing whole.
>
> —Harold R. Isaac[1]

HIGHLIGHTING AS IT DOES the underlying tensions of postinternational politics, the clashes between the centralizing tendencies inherent in global interdependence and the decentralizing tendencies inherent in subgroupism, this observation serves to focus the attempt in this concluding chapter to explore and evaluate what might lie ahead for world politics. Despite the extent of the transformations that are presently under way and the unabated dynamism that sustains them, it is far from clear whether global turbulence is a temporary or a permanent condition. Even murkier is the likely evolution of the bifurcated structures if in fact the present conditions are only a transitional phase to a more enduring set of arrangements.[2] Will the global struc-

---

[1] *Power and Identity: Tribalism in World Politics*, Headline Series no. 246 (New York: Foreign Policy Association, 1979), pp. 19, 49.

[2] Writing from the perspective of leftist politics, one observer sees the present scene as a transitional situation in which "we are still experiencing the decay of the older order and not yet the inauguration of a new." David M. Gordon, "The Global Economy: New Edifice or Crumbling Foundation?" *New Left Review*, no. 168 (March/April 1988): 25.

tures fostered by ozone depletion, currency crises, and other transnational issues become increasingly manifest and dominant, thereby moving the world beyond turbulence to some kind of unitary order? Or will historical and cultural diversities prove so powerful as to absorb such issues and give added appeal to the principles of international anarchy, thereby leading to a renewed predominance of the state system? Alternatively, will pluralistic dynamics prevail and fragment the transnational issues into questions of immediate self-interest, thereby resulting in a subordination of the state system to its multicentric counterpart?

FORECASTS VERSUS PREFERENCES

Questions such as the foregoing tempt one to replace analytic concerns with personal preferences. Indeed, for this reason—and in order to maintain alliterative consistency—an early draft of this concluding chapter was titled, "Terminating Turbulence." Such a heading, however, would have suggested that the complexity and dynamism of global turbulence are undesirable, that the human condition would be improved if new equilibria could be nursed into existence and the disarray of postinternational politics thus terminated. But such a conclusion cannot be derived from the preceding chapters. At no point in any of them has either a positive or a negative judgment been recorded on the consequences of the turbulent transformations that are altering the structures and processes of world politics.

To be sure, changes involving the coherence and authority of collectivities and the skills and orientations of individuals cry out for normative assessment. At stake are nothing less than the dignity of people and the viability of democracy, the future of global cooperation and the prospects of collective disaster, the capacity to confront problems and the just way to solve them. Thus far, however, judgments about such matters have been eschewed on the ground that they ought not be made until after the dynamics of global turbulence, and the extent and direction of the transformations it both fosters and reflects, have been depicted. To have pronounced judgment beforehand would have been to risk building an uncritical case for a particular interpretation of the opportunities or dangers of a bifurcated world and in so doing, losing sight of the prime purpose of the analysis, which has been to emphasize the need to think afresh about change and the macro consequences of altered skills at the micro level.

In any case, whether the onset and persistence of global turbulence are to be applauded or regretted is not self-evident. Both opportunities

and dangers command attention, and assessing their relative importance depends on the value perspectives brought to bear. If stress is
placed on the untoward consequences of authority crises and the
breakdown of public order, then the uncertainties and irregularities
associated with transformed parameters will arouse a sense of regret
and lead to a search for ways to terminate the turbulence. But if the
emphasis is on the enlarged skills of individuals and their growing demands for effective leadership, then the transformations can be applauded and an exploration undertaken of ways to sustain them.

On the other hand, if both a measure of public order and an expanded pluralism founded on more self-conscious citizenries are valued, which is the position taken here, then a normative evaluation
must be based on an attempt to trace the likely paths that global politics will follow as the clashes between the centralizing and decentralizing tendencies shape the course of world politics in the next millennium. Those are precisely the purposes of this chapter: first, to speculate
on the probable outcome of the clashes between integrative and disin-
tegrative dynamics, and then to ponder their normative implications.

Four Scenarios

In addressing the question of what kind of global order may follow the
present period of turbulence, it is important to be on guard against the
presumption that some global structure does indeed lie beyond turbulence, that the bifurcated world is only a transitional arrangement
which is bound to yield to a more enduring structure as new patterns
evolve and settle into habit-driven behavior. For it may well be that
people will become habituated to the coexistence of the state-centric
and multi-centric worlds and that this coexistence will thus prove to
be an enduring structure. Indeed, as noted below, this appears to be
the most likely of four scenarios that can reasonably be projected for
world politics in the twenty-first century.

To caution against assuming further structural evolution is not,
however, to imply that the dynamics of change will soon run out.
Surely there is no reason to anticipate an attenuation of the high degrees of complexity and dynamism fostered by the technologies of the
postindustrial order. If anything, the pace of technological innovation
seems likely to quicken—and with it the density, interdependence, and
variability of the individuals and collectivities active on the world
stage—as each technological breakthrough opens up avenues for further breakthroughs. Yet, while the dynamism that has brought about
the transformation of the three fundamental global parameters is not

likely to abate, it is possible that future generations will become accustomed to it and will evolve habits and practices that will manage the flow of changes in such a way as to lessen their uncertainties and limit their fluctuations. In effect, the interaction of macro and micro dynamics may become institutionalized as the global parameters settle anew into place. Put in another way, people and their collectivities may learn to live with a rapid pace of change in such a way that the pace itself will become a constant and orderly procedures for the conduct of world affairs will develop around it.

From our present vantage point amid the turbulence of shifting parameters, four scenarios depicting an emergent Order II seem plausible. Three of these posit the current bifurcated world as a transitional phase that will eventually give way to one or another resolution of the clash between the centralization and decentralization. The fourth anticipates that the clashes will continue and structural bifurcation will be perpetuated. The first three of these are labeled the *global-society*, the *restored state-system*, and the *pluralist* scenarios, and the fourth is termed the *enduring-bifurcation* scenario. Table 16.1 displays the main characteristics of each scenario as a basis for the discussion that follows.

The Global-Society Scenario

In the global-society scenario, the potential sources of interdependence noted in the previous chapter will progressively deepen and widen to the point where explicit ties develop that bind communities together, ties that derive from aspirations, procedural norms, and loyalties that are globally shared—what one analyst refers to as the " 'Common Marketization' of international relations."[3] These ties may not lead to global governmental institutions with effective authority that can evoke compliance from people in diverse cultures with diverse histories, but they would reflect norms and orientations that are sufficiently widespread and powerful to serve as the context within which actors in both the state-centric and the multi-centric worlds conduct their affairs. Furthermore, this scenario projects the possibility that eventually the values of the global society will become more than contextual, that they may predominate even if they do not find expression in specific policies designed to institutionalize them. As Bull has noted, order on

[3] Francis Fukuyama, "The End of History?" *National Interest*, no. 16 (Summer 1989): 18.

TABLE 16.1. Four Scenarios of Future Global Order

	Global Society	Restored State-System	Pluralist	Enduring Bifurcation
Structure of the bifurcated world	Decentralized within a centralized context	Highly centralized	Highly decentralized	Balance between centralization and decentralization
Status of the multicentric world	Autonomous	Subordinate	Predominant	Autonomous
Status of the state-centric world	Autonomous	Predominant	Subordinate	Autonomous
Development of norms that govern both worlds	Full array of norms evolves	None: sovereignty-bound actors retain and exercise the right not to comply	None: sovereignty-free actors retain and exercise the right not to comply	Substantial: both types of actors comply on some transnational issues
Character of orientations at the micro level	Enlarged skills of individuals lead to an increase in their readiness to share in universal norms	Enlarged skills of individuals are not sufficient to prevent manipulation by state leaders, and thus a restoration of the predominance of states is accepted	Enlarged skills of individuals lead them to resist state leaders and to pursue own interests through subgroups	Enlarged skills of individuals lead them to perceive virtues of both centralization and decentralization, leading to fluctuations between support for authority of states and autonomy of subgroups
Primary direction of micro-macro interactions	Macro to micro	Macro to micro	Micro to macro	Two-way flow
Perspective on the human condition	Liberal and optimistic	Conservative and pessimistic	Liberal and pessimistic	Pragmatic

a global scale can take many political forms, of which an effective world government is perhaps the least likely.[4]

In addition to the procedural norms attached to legitimacy, proof, loyalty, and sovereignty that were discussed in chapter 15, there are a number of indications that substantive values are coming to be shared on a worldwide scale. Those centering around the natural environment and the possibility of nuclear war are obvious examples. The dangers of severe environmental degradation and atomic holocaust are recognized as universal problems, threats to the whole of humankind as well as to particular states and regions.[5] Similarly, with the growing understanding of the plights and needs of the countries of the Third World, the values associated with an equitable distribution of wealth among all peoples have come to be widely accepted. Institutions and practices designed to achieve such a distribution may or may not evolve, but the emergence of these issues as crucial agenda items is new and signifies a universalization of norms.[6]

However, as noted in the previous chapter, perhaps the strongest support for the global-society scenario comes from the emergence of human rights as a priority item on the world's agenda. It is surely a measure of the development of a global conscience, if not a global society, that everywhere, and often contrary to the wishes and efforts of governments, the rights of people to speak, assemble, and travel freely have become legitimate issues. South Africa may have daily violated these norms for decades, Israel may have done the same for several years, and President Mikhail Gorbachev may have protested that President Reagan was intrusive when he met with dissidents and voiced human-rights values during the 1988 summit meeting, but in all such cases the defense of repressive practices is weak and is not cast in terms that deny the legitimacy of human rights as a global issue.

There are, of course, numerous historical factors underlying the rise of the human-rights issue. However, it is noteworthy—and perhaps more than coincidence—that the issue became important during pre-

[4] Hedley Bull, *The Anarchical Society: A Study of Order in World Politics* (New York: Columbia University Press, 1977), pp. 20–22 and chapters 10–13.

[5] For commentaries suggesting that environmental issues are becoming comparable to, even rivaling, those involving nuclear holocaust, see Willis W. Harman, "Colour the Future Green?" *Futures* 17 (August 1985): 318–30; Flora Lewis, "The Next Big Crisis," *New York Times*, July 27, 1988, p. A25; Flora Lewis, "Environment: A Security Issue for Our Politicians," *International Herald Tribune*, May 25, 1989, p. 3; and Tom Wicker, "A Priority for Bush," *New York Times*, November 28, 1988, p. A25.

[6] Cf. Richard D. Schwartz, "The Limits and Possibilities of Government: A Perspective from the Sociology of Law," in James F. Short, Jr., ed., *The Social Fabric: Dimensions and Issues* (Newbury Park, Calif.: Sage, 1986), p. 199.

cisely that period when turbulence engulfed the micro parameter and citizens throughout the world were acquiring more refined analytic and cathectic skills. These two developments may have occurred independently of each other, but one cannot help wondering whether the greater cathectic capacities have not led to enlarged empathic capacities and thus to a tendency for people in all countries to identify increasingly with the violated rights of people elsewhere.

In sum, the possibility of a global society cannot be dismissed as naive idealism. The signs of its development may be elusive, but they are discernible, and allowance for their further development must be made.[7] To be sure, the dynamics underlying authority crises, subgroupism, and other tendencies toward decentralization will hinder the evolution of a global society. And doubtless the continuing competition between the Western emphasis on individual liberties and the emphasis on collective welfare commonly found in the Third World will impede the universalizing process. Nevertheless, if issues such as environmental pollution, AIDS, and nuclear war perdure (as seems likely), and if the dynamics of interdependence continue to shrink social and political distances (as also seems probable), it is not beyond the realm of plausibility that actors in the state-centric and multi-centric worlds—or in whatever may be the political structures that follow the present bifurcation—will become increasingly responsive to worldwide norms even if they continue also to be guided by essential elements of their own cultures.

The Restored State-System Scenario

The restored state-system scenario envisions that the clash between centralizing and decentralizing tendencies will be resolved in favor of the former and that sovereignty-bound actors will be the beneficiary of the resolution. Confronted with the disorder triggered by rampant subgroupism and the other tendencies toward fragmentation, publics will be persuaded by their leaders that no political unit other than the nation-state is capable of maintaining order and mobilizing the resources necessary to meet the challenges posed by the microelectronic

---

[7] For serious inquiries into the idea of a world society, see John W. Burton, *World Society* (Cambridge: Cambridge University Press, 1972); Bull, *Anarchical Society*; Hedley Bull and Adam Watson, eds., *The Expansion of International Society* (Oxford: Oxford University Press, 1985); and Alex Inkeles, "The Emerging Social Structure of the World," *World Politics* 27 (July 1975): 467–95. Although much less elaborately formulated, Daniel Bell also discusses the bases for anticipating the possibility of a "single world society" in *The Coming of Post-Industrial Society*, p. 348.

revolution and the cascading politics of interdependence.[8] And just as leaders succeed in arguing that the nation-state is the only political unit capable of coping with the dislocations of decentralization, so will they persuade their citizenries that no unit is better suited to preventing the chaos they claim is inherent in excessive centralization. As Prime Minister Thatcher of Great Britain put it, "We have not successfully rolled back the frontiers of the state in Britain only to see them reimposed at a European level, with a European superstate exercising a new dominance from Brussels. . . . It is a matter of plain common sense that we cannot totally abolish frontier controls if we are also to protect our citizens from crime and stop the movement of drugs, of terrorists and of illegal immigrants."[9] As a result of such reasoning, and aided by the ability to employ instruments of force legitimately and by "a nationalist coalition" that "might come to dominate and might impose restrictions on communications and the mobility of nonstate actors,"[10] sovereignty-bound actors will recapture the authority that was lost during the early decades of turbulence. Then, having done so, they will exercise their authority on behalf of national values and resist the encroachment of contrary universal or subgroup norms, thereby restoring the predominance of the state system over the multi-centric system and trimming the global agenda back to a preoccupation with territorial and jurisdictional issues.

This scenario gains its plausibility from the fact that nation-states have proven viable for several centuries precisely because they are of a size, scope, and legitimacy sufficient to protect the security of their members and to address the full range of problems that beset them. If other forms of political organization were more suitable to these tasks, they surely would have emerged in the last three centuries with the capacity to act effectively on behalf of large and heterogeneous populations. That no such organizations did emerge is testimony to the efficacy of sovereignty-bound actors and suggests that the weaknesses and decline attributed to them in chapters 6 and 14 is overstated. It is conceivable, for example, that a number of national governments will

---

[8] Clifford Geertz, *The Interpretation of Cultures* (New York: Basic Books, 1973), p. 259, states this position succinctly: "All but the most enlightened members of [new states] are at least dimly aware—and their leaders are acutely aware—that the possibilities of social reform and material progress that they so intensely desire and are so determined to achieve rest with increasing weight on their being enclosed in a reasonably large, independent, powerful, well-ordered polity."

[9] Quoted in Craig R. Whitney, "Taking Stand for Europe, Thatcher Says," *New York Times*, September 22, 1988, p. A5.

[10] Richard K. Ashley, "Untying the Sovereign State: A Double Reading of the Anarchy Problematique," *Millenium* 17 (Summer 1988): 259.

maintain sufficient control over the media of communication to use them to manipulate their citizens into supporting policies that contain the tendencies toward subgroupism and interdependence.

On the other hand, this scenario suffers from the premise that state structures are somehow independent of the complexities of the societies in which they are located and can manage to overcome the attendant authority crises and subgroupism that fall within their jurisdictions. Actually, as a rule, the mechanisms of governance are more likely to reflect than to stand apart from the complexity and dynamism of global turbulence, and thus it is difficult to imagine processes whereby nation-states will fully regain the authority and controls lost with the advent of turbulence. Even more questionable, given the enlargement of analytic and cathectic skills at the micro level, is the prospect that individuals will be persuaded, manipulatively or otherwise, by public officials to abandon their subgroup proclivities and uncritically redirect their loyalties back to the national level. Fatigue with the disorder of a decentralized world may indeed exert pressure for the firm exercise of authority and discipline, but it is far from clear that such pressure will overcome the dynamics that brought about and sustained decentralization in the first place.

The Pluralist Scenario

The pluralist scenario anticipates that dynamics of decentralization will in fact come to predominate, intensifying the authority crises confronting governments, strengthening the hand of subgroups, and encouraging individuals to turn away from national communities as they further narrow their conceptions of their self-interests.[11] Such an expectation derives not only from a projection in which there is no letup in the technological dynamics that underlie decentralization, but also from the premise that the new skills and orientation of citizens will be enduring and will make them unwilling to abandon performance criteria of legitimacy and at the same time able to resist being manipulated by national leaders seeking to recapture their loyalties. Under

[11] For a cogent argument that the dynamics of the present era are inducing citizens of all societies—postindustrial, industrial, and industrializing—away from whole systems, see Ralph Ketcham, *Individualism and Public Life: A Modern Dilemma* (New York: Basil Blackwell, 1987). A similar line of reasoning applied specifically to Americans can be found in Robert N. Bellah et al., *Habits of the Heart: Individualism and Commitment in American Life* (Berkeley: University of California Press, 1985). For more comprehensive analyses of decentralizing tendencies, stressing the advantages of subgroups, see Edward A. Tiryakian and Ronald Rogowski, eds., *New Nationalisms of the Developed West* (Boston: Allen & Unwin, 1985).

these conditions, the leaders might attempt to recover the support of their publics by making commitments that progressively lessen their capacity to fashion national solutions for their fragmenting systems. As one observer put it, "It is easier to obtain votes for appropriations than it is for taxes, to facilitate consumption than to stimulate production, to protect a market than to open it, to inflate than to deflate, to borrow than to save, to demand than to compromise, to be intransigent than to negotiate, to threaten war than to prepare for it."[12]

In effect, therefore, the pluralist scenario posits the multi-centric world as dominant over its state-centric counterpart. It envisions a diminution of the executive function of national governments and an increase in the concern with autonomy and economic issues, leading to acceptance of low-intensity violent conflicts and high-intensity public disorders as normal routines of global and national life. These pluralistic dynamics, moreover, are likely to feed on themselves as the authority of governments wanes, rendering them still less able to resolve national and transnational problems. Put in an extreme micro-macro context, these dynamics could lead to endless uncertainty and disarray; in the words of one observer, "The cumulative impact of you or me being selfish is a terribly selfish society where we don't know what to expect from people any more."[13]

From a macro perspective, on the other hand, some aspects of the pluralist scenario may be played out for other than self-serving reasons. Decentralization can also lead to an adaptive response by leaders who, unable to manage the complexity and dynamism confronted by their systems, deliberately devolve authority and responsibility onto their subsystems. To some degree, in other words, decentralization can result from planned partitioning as well as from uncoordinated fragmentation. Such, at least, has been suggested as among the more likely macro responses to unmanageable challenges—that is, to those conditions designated as hyperturbulence.[14]

The difficulty with the pluralist scenario is its assumption that there is a bottomless reservoir of toleration for the disorder that it anticipates. If self-interests are being served by the structures of the multi-

[12] Walter Lippmann, *Essays in the Public Philosophy* (Boston: Little, Brown, 1955), p. 45.

[13] Michael Josephson, as quoted in Richard Bernstein, "Moyers Designs a Talk Show for Thinkers," *New York Times*, September 11, 1988, sec. H, p. 41.

[14] For an analysis of how partitioning policies under hyperturbulent conditions give rise to two very different kinds of subsystems, "social enclaves" and "social vortices," see Joseph E. McCann and John Selsky, "Hyperturbulence and the Emergence of Type 5 Environments," *Academy of Management Review* 9 (1984): 460–70.

centric world, the accompanying low-intensity conflicts and other forms of disarray will probably not undermine them. But if the lack of order and effective governance persists for long and begins to impose insurmountable obstacles to the realization of self-interests, then acceptance of the predominance of the multi-centric world seems likely to decline. The very same performance criteria that lessen the effectiveness of states can be just as easily applied to actors in the multi-centric world and thus they too are subject to a diminution of their control.

The Enduring-Bifurcation Scenario

The fourth plausible scenario rests on the presumption that the clashes between centralizing and decentralizing dynamics will not be resolved, with the result that neither the state-centric nor the multi-centric world loses its autonomy and becomes subordinate to the other. This enduring-bifurcation scenario anticipates no moderation of the technological dynamism that promotes authority crises, subgroupism, and the competence of citizens. On the contrary, it assumes that people will continue to sharpen their analytic and cathectic skills, thus reinforcing the performance criteria of legitimacy and adding to the weaknesses of governments and the frequency and duration of low-intensity conflicts.

Unlike the pluralist scenario, however, this one does not project a weakening of national collectivities to the point where sovereignty-bound actors and the state-centric system become subordinate to, much less absorbed by, the multi-centric world. Rather, the same developments at the micro level that have fostered tendencies toward decentralization are conceived to embody a pragmatic capacity for appreciating that the unrestrained pursuit of narrow self-interests is counterproductive and that there are benefits to be gained, in some situations, from the centralizing mechanisms of sovereignty-bound collectivities and from compliance with globally shared norms.

In short, the enduring-bifurcation scenario depicts a future in which the tensions between continuity and change persist. Both sovereignty-bound and sovereignty-free actors would be sufficiently powerful to resist the other and thus to preserve their own autonomy, but neither would be powerful enough to subordinate the other. Sovereignty-bound actors would be unable to achieve control over those issues where transnational links were especially complex, but none of the other actors would be capable of replacing national governments as mechanisms for resolving the territorial imperatives and security dilemmas of organized societies. So an uneasy tension between the two worlds would emerge as the fundamental condition of global politics.[15]

Like the other three scenarios, this one is not free of uncertainties. It could well be argued that systemic parameters cannot long endure in a state of flux, that eventually the tensions between continuity and change will have to be reduced so that movement toward goals can be resumed. Collectivities either settle their authority crises or they collapse; either public order is restored through the convergence of subgroups or it dissolves into separate "public orders" as each subgroup goes its own way. Advocates of the pluralist scenario would thus reject the enduring-bifurcation scenario on the ground that the decentralizing tendencies powered by insatiable self-interests cannot be reversed, while advocates of the restored state-system scenario would reject it on the ground that the combination of habits, authority, and armed force lodged with sovereignty-bound officials will prevent a further weakening of centralizing dynamics.

A Cyclical Process?

A plausible extrapolation of the micro and macro dynamics presented in the previous chapters leads to a cyclical theory of the two-world universe in which the pace of change is unrelenting even as both worlds persist intact. More precisely, neither world remains permanently superordinate or subordinate because the dynamics of change evolve into a patterned sequence in which the tendencies toward centralization and decentralization shift the balance between the state-centric and multi-centric worlds, with periods of whole-system dominance preceding and then following periods of subsystem dominance. Stated differently, shifts in the balance between change and continuity will occur along systematic and cyclical lines, as the centralizing tendencies of the state-centric world fluctuate inversely with the decentralizing forces of the multi-centric world.[16]

---

[15] For an argument along these lines, leading to the conclusion that "the present system is marked by a peculiar mix of *resiliency* and *fragility*," see Stanley Hoffmann, "The Future of the International Political System: A Sketch," in Samuel P. Huntington and Joseph S. Nye, Jr., *Global Dilemmas* (Lanham, Md.: University Press of America, 1985), pp. 280–307 (quotation on p. 285; italics in the original). For an analysis in which it is anticipated that states "will continue to exist for a long time, perhaps one to three centuries or more," see Karl W. Deutsch, "Learning-State and the Self-Transformation of Politics," in Miriam Campanella, ed., *Between Rationality and Cognition: Policy-making under Conditions of Uncertainty, Complexity, and Turbulence* (Torino, Italy: Albert Meynier, 1988), pp. 71–97 (quotation on p. 69).

[16] The nature of the balance between the state-centric and multi-centric worlds, be-

If micro orientations are a prime source of the decentralizing dynamics of the multi-centric world, how can it be reasonably hypothesized that centralizing tendencies are also operative, that sometimes they even predominate, and that the periods in which they predominate are cyclically linked to corresponding shifts in the decentralizing tendencies? What, in other words, underlies the systematic fluctuations in opposite directions? The answers lie at both the macro and the micro levels. At the former are the centralizing processes inherent in the complexity of transnational issues, which lead governments to cooperate in order to gain control over them. At the micro level are the skills by which citizens come to appreciate that there may be conditions wherein subsystems are ill-suited to achieve control over such issues. These skills lead people to recognize the limits of subgroupism, to reconsider their rejection of whole systems, and thus to expand their understanding to include conceptions of self-interest that allow them to direct their loyalties and energies toward the state-centric world when it seems appropriate. Then, after a period in which the coordinated efforts of states fall short of effective management over the complexities of the multi-centric world, disappointment sets in and the pendulum swings back again toward sovereignty-free collectivities.

The history of Poland in the 1980s dramatically illustrates how learning at the micro level sustains the swings of the pendulum. In 1980, subgroupism among workers at the shipyards in Gdansk resulted in the creation of a trade union, Solidarity, that served as the focus of their orientations and that was sanctioned by the Communist regime. In 1981, the government imposed martial law and declared Solidarity to be illegal. There followed a long period of quiescence, as a large proportion of the population held their subsystemic loyalties out of public view, until they surfaced again in widespread strikes in 1988, which crippled the already weakened Polish economy. Under these circumstances, the government gave assurances that it would restore Solidarity's legal status if the strikes ended. Persuaded that the subsystem's fate was dependent on an economic revival of the whole system and that Solidarity could contribute to that revival, the union's leader, Lech Walesa, campaigned across Poland to get the strikers to return to work. His plea to workers that they lift their sights from the

tween continuity and change, need not be precisely the same in each period, so that this cyclical scenario escapes the potential criticism that, as two noted analysts have put it, "it is not the practice of history to repeat itself." They add that "the effect of change is generally stronger than that of continuity." Gordon A. Craig and Alexander L. George, *Force and Statecraft: Diplomatic Problems of Our Time* (New York: Oxford University Press, 1983), p. 146.

subsystemic to the systemic level met with grumbling and resistance, but eventually the strikers did return to work, and shortly thereafter Solidarity was again accorded a legal status. In 1989, with a new constitution in place that permitted open elections for one house of the national parliament but guaranteed that the Communist party would organize the government, the subsystemic orientations that prevailed at the micro level resulted in a massive victory at the polls for Solidarity. The result seemed to be a stalemate, with Solidarity's elected officials able to prevent the installation of a Communist president and yet not able to organize a government of their own. In this situation, many Solidarity delegates, remembering how they had been outlawed, jailed, or otherwise silenced for most of the decade, gave precedence to their subsystemic orientations; but again, with Walesa stating that he would support any Communist candidate for president, an appreciation of the virutes of the whole system, or at least the understanding that the lot of the workers could not be improved without a functioning whole system, carried the debate, and the Solidarity delegates engaged in some parliamentary maneuvers that allowed a Communist president to be elected without their voting for him.[17] The tensions between the whole-system and subsystem levels are likely to continue in Poland, perhaps even intensify, but this history suggests that the analytic skills of the Polish people have been refined to the point where they grasp how the cyclical swings of the pendulum toward and away from centralized authority can serve their needs.

It is perhaps useful to note that orientations at the micro level have served as bases for other conceptions of pendulumlike swings in politics. Nearly seven decades ago, for example, Lord Bryce raised such a possibility: "If it be improbable, yet it is not unthinkable that, as in many countries impatience with tangible evils substituted democracy for monarchy or oligarchy, a like impatience might some day reverse the process."[18] Similarly, Hirschman has commented:

> When for one reason or another participation in the public arena proves disappointing, a retreat into purely private concerns seems an obvious response that hardly requires justification. Certainly one would not expect perfect symmetry in these matters. But if the

[17] John Tagliabue, "Workers in Poland Heed Walesa and Agree to End Last of Strikes," *New York Times*, September 4, 1988, p. 1; John Tagliabue, "Poland Announces Solidarity Sweep and Party Losses," *New York Times*, June 9, 1989, p. 1; Serge Schmemann, "Walesa to Back a Communist Chief," *New York Times*, July 15, 1989, p. 1; and John Tagliabue, "Jaruzelski Wins Polish Presidency by Minimum Votes," *New York Times*, July 20, 1989, p. 1.

[18] James Bryce, *Modern Democracies*, vol. 1 (New York: Macmillan, 1921), p. 42.

move from public to private seems so self-evident after the public sphere has given rise to disappointment, there is some reason to think that, in the opposite situation, the pendulum will swing the other way, though quite possibly with less force and certainty.[19]

Such cyclical theories are quite different from the one advanced here, however. They rest on the presumption that citizens are easily disillusioned and all too ready to either accept authoritarian rule or lapse into apathy. But the formulation developed here does not rest on such an evaluative premise. Rather, it assumes a continuing expansion of the analytic skills that clarify people's understanding of their self-interest, lessen their habit-driven responses, improve their ability to learn, and thus enable them to alter their priorities among whole systems and subsystems as they discover that the former cannot provide satisfying solutions to major problems and that the latter cannot contain low-intensity conflicts and maintain a satisfying degree of public order. Each cycle of altered priorities contains the seeds of its own supercession as the defects of one phase come to be recognized once its virtues have reversed the defects of the previous phase. If this is the case, it follows that the cycles are likely to follow more and more rapidly upon each other as the analytic skills of individuals become increasingly sophisticated.

This is not necessarily to imply, of course, that the cyclical patterns will be uniform in all respects and everywhere. It has been noted, for example, that "the world economy ticks to two clocks—the fast clock of recessions, recoveries and other features of the business cycle and the slow clock of changes in economic philosophy and management."[20] Furthermore, since each system and each subsystem has its own unique history and circumstances, some may be moving in a centralizing direction even as others are moving toward decentralized arrangements. For example, in a single recent year, trade unions in Great Britain were being fragmented while union leaders in Poland, as noted above, were fashioning coherence among their members;[21] party splits over foreign policy were fostering political paralysis in Israel while mo-

---

[19] Albert O. Hirschman, *Shifting Involvements: Private Interest and Public Action* (Princeton: Princeton University Press, 1981), p. 62. For still another formulation, which posits activism in politics as generating "its own countervailing forces . . . which favor a downswing in political participation," see Michel Crozier, Samuel P. Huntington, and Joji Watanuki, *The Crises of Democracy* (New York: New York University Press, 1975), pp. 84–85.

[20] Peter T. Kilborn, "Economic Scene," *New York Times*, May 15, 1985, p. 26.

[21] Craig Whitney, "Labor Movement in Britain Ousts a Major Union," *New York Times*, September 6, 1988, p. A3.

mentum toward renewed bipartisanship began to build in the United States;[22] OPEC struggled to lower the production of oil while independent producers sought to enlarge their outputs and markets;[23] French Catholic monks lessened their resistance to the pope while their counterparts in the Western Hemisphere reiterated their readiness to oppose the Vatican;[24] some countries were lowering tariff barriers while others sought to maintain their restrictions on free trade;[25] and pressures for reversing the trend toward deregulation were being felt in the United States while regional forces in China were challenging central authority.[26]

Yet, while many contrasts such as these can be cited, so that cyclical patterns may seem more idiosyncratic than systematic, there is reason to anticipate that the dynamics of interdependence are likely to introduce a measure of uniformity into the cycles of postinternational politics. Time and distance have shrunk too much for centralizing and decentralizing tendencies not to cascade in patterned ways across the foundations of cooperation and the fault lines of conflict that underlie the global system. It is hardly coincidental, for example, that a reduction in cold-war hostilities and increasing accommodations between the superpowers in the late 1980s were accompanied by a comparable turn in the conflicts involving Iran and Iraq, the two Koreas, the two Chinas, Angola, Cambodia, the Western Sahara, Afghanistan, Nicaragua, and the PLO. These events surely reflect a cyclical phenomenon that is global in scale, but it is premature to describe them as an enduring reversal.[27]

In any event, regardless of the extent to which systematic factors introduce uniformity into the cycles of postinternational politics, it may well be concluded that the present structures and processes of

[22] Joel Brinkley, "Labor Party Quits Talks with Likud on Broad Coalition," *New York Times*, December 1, 1988, p. 1; Fox Butterfield, "Kissinger and Vance Issue a Call for Consensus," *New York Times*, June 3, 1988, p. A5.

[23] Youssef M. Ibrahim, "New Role for OPEC: Small Fish in a Big Pond," *New York Times*, October 2, 1988, sec. 4, p. 1.

[24] Roberto Suro, "Many Lefebvre Priests Going Back to Vatican," *New York Times*, September 4, 1988, p. 9; Peter Steinfels, "New Liberation Faith: Social Conflict Is Muted," *New York Times*, July 27, 1988, p. A2.

[25] Paul Lewis, "New Support Is Offered for a Stronger GATT," *New York Times*, March 29, 1988, p. D7.

[26] News stories on these two events appeared side by side in the *New York Times*, December 11, 1988, p. 1.

[27] For further reflections on this phenomenon, see James N. Rosenau, "Interdependence and the Simultaneity Puzzle: Notes on the Outbreak of Peace," in Charles W. Kegley, Jr., ed., *The Long Postwar Peace: The Sources of Great Power Stability* (forthcoming), chapter 14.

global life are more likely to be permanent than transitional. Neither of the two worlds of world politics is likely to be overcome by the other; both will probably endure as features of the global scene even as each also tends to foster an ascendency on the part of the other as time passes. The turbulence of world politics may not only be patterned; it may also display rhythmic cycles.

EVALUATING THE SCENARIOS

Readers' reactions to the plausibility of the scenarios set forth above are likely to be partly rooted in their conceptions of macro-micro interactions and, more specifically, of the changes that may be transforming the micro parameter. As indicated in table 16.1, each scenario is founded on a different notion of how much, if at all, citizens have been affected by the microelectronic revolution and the shifting patterns of world politics. To readers who are skeptical or rejecting of the possibility that shifts in the capabilities of citizens are under way, the restored state-system scenario (or, perhaps better, an undiminished state-system scenario) will seem most compelling. They would emphasize the continuities of history, arguing that the main consequence of the microelectronic revolution is to enhance the ability of leaders to manipulate their followers and thus to retain or recapture their predominance, thereby continuing to dominate global affairs. Those with such a perspective might acknowledge that the skills of individuals have been enlarged and that people are now more critical and demanding of their leaders, but they would add that these changes have been more than offset by the comparable growth in the ability of leaders to engineer consent on the part of their followers. If their skepticism is accompanied by conservative orientations, they are likely to regard the continued predominance of leaders as desirable, since they would be fearful that analytically skillful citizenries might undo the order that keeps societies intact, stable, and effective.

For readers whose liberal values lead them to applaud rather than fear the trend toward greater skills at the micro level but who are at the same time pessimistic that the newly acquired skills will include a capacity to change orientations toward societal concerns, the pluralist scenario is likely to be deemed most accurate. They are likely to see the new skills only as a source of demands for the satisfaction of narrow self-interests and as leading merely to new habit-driven behavior rather than to an understanding of the need for an enlightened self-interest that allows for the pursuit of collective goals. Readers who are both liberal and optimistic about people's capacity to be flexible as they acquire new skills, on the other hand, are likely to anticipate that the capacity for enlightened self-interest and adaptive learning will become widespread at the micro level and will eventually lead to the global-society scenario.

A more cautious perspective, tempered by a recognition that the habits that value narrowly defined interests do not readily yield to change, will lead some readers to perceive change as proceeding in fits and starts and by marginal adjustments. Populations and memberships will continue to be divided between those who give high priority to collective goals and those who are more concerned with their own interests. This pragmatic position on the transformation of the micro parameters would probably lead to an evaluation of the enduring-bifurcation scenario and its cyclical fluctuations as most convincing.

This consideration of the plausibility of the several scenarios on the basis of broad orientations brings important normative issues to the fore. Most notably, it raises the question of whether the turbulence presently engulfing world politics is to be applauded and encouraged or regretted and resisted. The former would be the reaction of those who interpret authority crises as moments when hitherto apathetic and manipulated people begin to come into their own and acquire the skills, self-confidence, autonomy, and control to improve their lot and enhance their dignity. In this perspective, the price of such advances at the micro level may be a diminution of public order and a reduced capacity to take decisive collective action, but that price is seen as worth the gains in people's self-respect and in their ability to act effectively on their own behalf. Besides, the costs may dwindle as people become more skillful and contribute to the reestablishment of an authority that is effective but also more sensitive to humane values.

Those who believe that the costs of these micro-level developments are too high would react differently. They are primarily concerned with the danger in a further deterioration of the sense of large community that enables governments to cope with serious problems. While there may be merit in the spread of subjective political competence and a rising level of individual dignity, failure to resist the tide of micro demands risks the collapse of civil society and the advent of a Hobbesian world in which all are at war with all. As Walter Lippmann put it a few years after World War II, at a time when the main parameters of world politics were just entering the period of turbulence described in this book: "Where mass opinion dominates the government, there is a morbid derangement of the true functions of power. The derangement brings about the enfeeblement, verging on paralysis, of the capacity to govern. This breakdown in the constitutional order is the cause of the precipitate and catastrophic decline of Western society. It may, if it cannot be arrested and reversed, bring about the fall of the West."[28]

These are, however, extreme positions. Between them lies a position in which one acclaims those decentralizing forces that enhance the capabilities and dignity of people and, at the same time, condemns the excesses that inhibit those centralizing tendencies that facilitate collective capacities to manage interdependence and sustain whole systems that are dedicated to an orderly realization of humane values. From this perspective, the bifurcation of world politics appears to be a structural arrangement worth defending. It has the potential for a creative reconciliation of all the great antitheses of politics—the conflicts between order and freedom, between the will of majorities and the autonomy of minorities, between individual needs and collective welfare, between technological innovation and cultural integrity, between growth and stability, and between change and continuity.

[28] Lippmann, *Public Philosophy*, p. 15.

INDEX